THE APPRENTICESHIP WRITINGS
of
FRANK NORRIS

Volume One

THE APPRENTICESHIP WRITINGS
OF
FRANK NORRIS

1896—1898

Volume 1: 1896—1897

Edited by
Joseph R. McElrath, Jr.,
and
Douglas K. Burgess

THE AMERICAN PHILOSOPHICAL SOCIETY
Philadelphia
1996

Memoirs
of the
American Philosophical Society
Held at Philadelphia
for Promoting Useful Knowledge
Volume 219

ISBN:0-87169-219-8
US ISSN: 0065-9738

LC Catalog Card No: 96-83741

DEDICATED TO

JOEL MYERSON

Carolina Research Professor of American Literature
The University of South Carolina

ACKNOWLEDGMENTS

Over the past decade, assistance to this editorial project has been generously extended by numerous individuals and institutions. The Bancroft Library of the University of California, Berkeley, has repeatedly been our benefactor. Its Franklin Walker and Frank Norris Collections contain essential data available nowhere else; the late Director James D. Hart and Anthony Bliss, Curator of Books, were our constant friends in every respect. The California State Library in Sacramento was also especially cooperative; California Section Librarian Sibylle Zemitis performed favors for which we will forever be grateful. Grants from the American Philosophical Society, the Bibliographical Society of America, and the Florida State University Research Foundation made possible travel to these and other research collections. The National Endowment for the Humanities provided subvention for the publication of this edition. Individual scholars who made their contributions include: Jesse S. Crisler, Robert C. Leitz, III, Richard Allan Davison, James B. Stronks, Don L. Cook, Donald Pizer, Don Graham, Joel Myerson, Lawrence Berkove, Benjamin F. Fisher, IV, Gary Scharnhorst, Stanley Wertheim, David Bevington, David Teague, Craig Westman, Lucia Kinsaul, Gwendolyn Jones, Amy Johnson, Charles Duncan, Sheryl Nadler, Eugene Crook, and David Johnson. The late Sal Noto and the late Oscar Lewis unstintingly shared their knowledge of *fin de siècle* San Francisco with us. Earle Labor, I. Milo Shepard, and Jeanne C. Reesman fully merit our hearty thanks for good fellowship along the way. It was a pleasure to receive editorial direction and assistance from Carole Le Faivre-Rochester of The American Philosophical Society.

The frontispiece portraits of Norris were reproduced from Bailey Millard's "A Significant Literary Life," *Outwest*, 18 (January 1903): 49 (Volume 2) and 51 (Volume 1). Courtesy of the California State Library, Sacramento.

J. R. M.
D. K. B.

CONTENTS: VOLUME 1

Introduction: xv-xlii

CONTENTS

CONTENTS

INTRODUCTION

Volume One

INTRODUCTION

Frank Norris (1870-1902) has long been recognized by cultural historians as a "touchstone" figure, clearly signalling in 1899 the emergence of an American school of Literary Naturalism. *McTeague: A Story of San Francisco* secured this honor for him that year as it registered more fully than any previous American novel the Darwinian view of life that is the essential characteristic of all subsequent Naturalistic fictions. It thus marked as well the rejection of the Victorian Era's habitually idealistic representations of human nature and its basically religious world-view, offering instead a post-metaphysical portrait of the human condition that has remained popular in 20th-century literary and intellectual circles. Verging toward the Modern sensibility in his thought and art, then, Norris was a transitional figure like Henry Adams and Stephen Crane. His *McTeague* is now a familiar landmark in university courses, providing a still-sensational reading experience which gauges both the decline of the transcendental view of life that was Emerson's and Thoreau's and the rise of a perspective common to writers so diverse as F. Scott Fitzgerald, Edith Wharton, and John Steinbeck. In February, 1899, when it first appeared, however, the book reviewers hardly treated *McTeague* as a classic or appreciated the new way of seeing things that Norris had proffered.[1]

Despite the marked intellectual limitations with which its hero is born, *McTeague* pictures him in its first half as having confirmed by pluck and luck the American success myth, bringing to mind the familiar paradigm of Benjamin Franklin's *Autobiography*. In the second half, however, the "American dream" becomes a nightmare. There Norris describes in chilling detail Mac's degeneration and impending extirpation. While not denying human freedom, Norris negates Victorian platitudes about the all-sufficiency of free will and self-reliance in the face of the complexities and uncertainties of a biological order governed by evolutionary processes. That is, *McTeague* demonstrates unsqueamishly how Mac, though basically a good person, proves "unfit" in the struggle for existence; he falls prey to the destructive sway of "bad" heredity, the debilitating effects of a stressful environment, and the unpredictable developments in life that are ever-present in Darwin's portraits of natural-selection-at-work. Norris thus troubled his readers by showing that the cardinal virtue of Victorian culture, "earnestness" in applying oneself to the control of one's life, was of dubious value when conditions actually beyond the individual's control rendered free will and benign intentions largely irrelevant. "Was he to blame?" is the question posed at one point. Norris is nowhere more anti-Victorian than when he dramatizes

Mac's situation as an almost wholly deterministic one and necessitates the conclusion that this individual, unable to cope with the demands made upon him, is not responsible for the debacle that his life became.

Even more offensive to 1890s values was Norris's portrayal of the equally maladapted heroine's gruesome descent into dementia, seen especially in her increasingly erotic mania for hoarding money and the masochistic extremes that develop in her personality. Trina McTeague hardly proved the spiritually-elevating "angel in the house" female figure that Victorians preferred to meet in art.

McTeague was consequently, and correctly, perceived by outraged critics as manifesting the unsavory influence of the French "father of Naturalism," Emile Zola. The "dirty" novels of Norris's principal mentor, which began appearing in 1867, knew no polite limits when it came to treating the whole of human experience—including the taboo functions of excretion and procreation. Both writers offended because they were intent on debunking genteel culture's pious sentimentalizing of *la bête humaine*, male and female. For both it was time to tell the whole truth about nature and the "human animal"; it was time to write as Darwin did, naturalistically.

By 1903, Norris's reputation as the "American Zola" was widespread. His most massive novel, *The Octopus* (1901), was a muckraking study of the arena for ruthless competition that was the American economy at the turn of the century. As Zola did in *Germinal* (1885), Norris not only examined the dog-eat-dog values of *laissez-faire* capitalism within an evolutionary framework but traced the essential characteristics of the economic system to their roots in genetically-determined human nature. *The Pit* (1903), Norris's runaway best-seller, focused upon speculation at the Chicago Board of Trade, again describing the survival-of-the-fittest competition in which the naturally-ingrained acquisitive instinct in individuals loomed large as a force shaping the socio-economic system. Both works figure largely in the history of Social Darwinism at the turn of the century, though with an important difference. Neither novel pairs Norris with individuals such as Andrew Carnegie and John D. Rockefeller who justified economic exploitation of others on the grounds of natural and divine law; Norris describes the cause-effect relationships that give rise to economic predation but refrains from condoning what he viewed as inhumaneness in the sphere of commerce. Like Zola and, in the 1930s, Steinbeck, he tempered critical objectivity with sympathy for those who suffered as a result of the operations of both nature and the economy.

Norris's fourth major novel, *Vandover and the Brute*, was not published until 12 years after his death. Begun in the mid-1890s, *Vandover* self-evidently could not have been published until 1914 since it very directly dealt with the ultimate forbidden topic for Victorians: the sexual drive in humanity, which

Norris amorally describes as a natural behavioral determinant in the young "brute" who is his hero. Vandover, a proper young Victorian in his thought, is plagued by guilt and confusion when acting upon the promptings of his libido; Norris, on the other hand, strikes the modern note by making it clear that his suffering hero is the victim of a puritanical morality rather than his ineluctable identity as a creature born to experience carnal appetite. Indeed, *Vandover* questions not only contemporaneous moral values but, in chapter 9, the Christian conception of the deity from which they were derived. It is, perhaps, the fullest example of Darwinism's influence on American literature at the turn of the century. Three other novels are presently viewed as minor accomplishments, though *Moran of the "Lady Letty"* (1898), *Blix* (1899), and *A Man's Woman* (1900) enjoyed commercial success and now further enhance our understanding of Norris's progressive thought and experimental artistry in 1898-1902.

These seven, frequently republished novels have, for nearly a century, made immediately available the evidence of what kind of writer and thinker made his mark in history. And yet, they do not tell the whole story; indeed, what each indicates about Norris's world-view has for decades been the subject of controversy in the scholarly literature on his thought and art. For example, still unresolved is one of the most basic questions imaginable concerning a *fin de siècle* thinker. Was Norris the kind of positivist and moral pragmatist described above? Or was he instead, as has been energetically argued by some, an optimistic evolutionary idealist articulating the essentially Victorian values and teleological view of history of his one-time Berkeley professor, Joseph LeConte?[2] This debate over Norris's alleged discipleship to LeConte, centered mainly on the themes of *The Octopus*, now promises continued deadlock, though a possible means of resolution of this and other interpretive cruxes is obvious: the full contextualization of the novels via reference to Norris's comparatively neglected, non-novelistic writings. How do these clarify and complement, or correct, our present image of the novelist's personality?

Until now, it has been difficult to answer such a question due to the lack of a complete edition of Norris's works.[3] Markedly less accessible than the novels have been the journalistic writings, particularly those that comprise the belletristic environment from which his novelistic works began to emerge in 1898. It remains unclear how Norris arrived at the point in his life at which he was such an adept that, in only four years, he could offer the public so many novels, as well as 79 post-1898 short stories and articles written before his early death in 1902. That is, his publications produced during the apprenticeship he served in 1896-1898 have never been assembled *in toto* for the scrutiny of biographers, critics, literary historians, and students of

American culture as a whole.[4] In fact, the publication record for 1896-1898 has only recently been established in two studies that appeared in 1988 and 1992.[5] For 1898 readers, Norris-as-novelist suddenly appeared, *ex nihilo*, on the American stage, earning his place in the limelight as he fashioned his national identity in short order. Unfortunately, the vast majority of commentators have maintained that perspective on Norris. They have focused almost exclusively on the writer of 1898 and thereafter—in the way the vast majority of Norris's contemporaries had to since they knew virtually nothing of his apprentice works.[6]

There was, though, another, regional identity that Norris previously established in San Francisco, where he was less the Literary Naturalist and more obviously the neophyte learning his craft by imitation and experimentation. The purposes of these two volumes, accordingly, are: first, to introduce the modern reader in full to the wide range of precocious displays of talent by this multifaceted individual in 1896-1898, immediately prior to the novelistic phase of his career; and, second, to offer at the same time all of the extant evidence of the character of Norris's thought during his apprenticeship, not only for the sake of establishing a more complete record of his intellectual activity *per se* but to recreate the ideational background against which his novels may be more profitably read and analyzed.[7] Most of these writings merit attention because of their intrinsic worth; many mark, as will be seen, the initial uses of story materials and concepts later developed more fully in the novels; and, most importantly, they provide a new perspective on Frank Norris, whose post-apprenticeship works did not, of course, materialize in a vacuum but in the onrushing course of a vitally—sometimes frenetically— active literary career.

*   *   *

These two volumes include all of the known writings of Frank Norris published between 11 April 1896 and 24 September 1898—less 1898's thrice-serialized novel, *Moran of the "Lady Letty": A Story of Adventure Off the California Coast*, which finally appeared as a book in late September.[8] With that exception, one will find here in these critically edited short works the full representation of Norris's publishing activities during one of the most important phases of his career as a professional author.[9] For, during this period he subjected himself for the first time to the discipline of producing timely copy for a San Francisco weekly magazine edited by John O'Hara Cosgrave, *The Wave*. Further, it was in these short works that the essential qualities of his prose, seen in fuller form in his novels, were developed. By the time

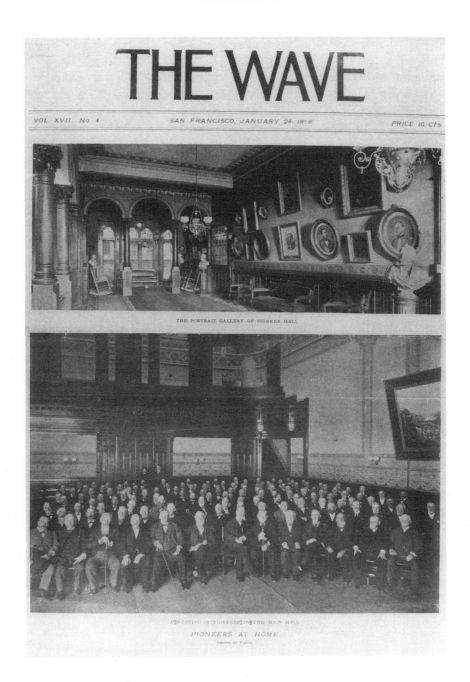

Courtesy of the Collection of Joseph R. McElrath, Jr.

that he left *The Wave* for employment in New York City with the S.S. Mc-Clure newspaper syndicate and *McClure's Magazine*—15 February 1898—the dominant patterns of thought and literary style had been largely fixed: the foundation for his major works was in place. Within the year, Doubleday & McClure Company began publishing the novels upon which his fame rests.

Prior to the spring of 1896, Norris's prospects were not so promising. He had been dilettantishly pursuing a belletristic course since 1889, when his first article, "Clothes of Steel," appeared in the *San Francisco Chronicle*. Not having to face the economic pressures known by contemporaries such as Stephen Crane and Theodore Dreiser, the well-to-do young man with literary aspirations luxuriated in his amateur status, occasionally publishing articles, poems, short stories, and a portion of a play he wrote while a student at the University of California in Berkeley (1890-1894). *Yvernelle: A Legend of Feudal France*, his first book, appeared in late 1891 when he was a sophomore. The richly illustrated, chivalric verse-romance marketed by J.B. Lippincott Co. for the Christmas book trade was the apotheosis of his early loyalty to and flair for the Romantic in art. To the end of his life, he championed Walter Scott and was enamored of Robert Louis Stevenson. Victor Hugo, too, he viewed with high regard. But this central piece of his juvenilia was soon accompanied in his growing canon by experiments in more modern modes of smart, snappy storytelling. Inspired by Kipling and Richard Harding Davis, he tried his hand as a popular, markedly less "literary" prose fictionalist in an 1894-1895 series of five short stories for the *Overland Monthly*, entitled "Outward and Visible Signs." Their success prompted him in the summer of 1895 to submit a collection of short stories to the prestigious firm that once rejected *Yvernelle*, Houghton, Mifflin and Company.[10] This volume, possibly including new work that Norris completed during his 1894-1895 sojourn as a "special student" at Harvard University, never materialized, however.[11] Returning to San Francisco without laurels, a *flâneur* yet to know the rigors of full-time employment, he turned from fiction to travel writing as a means of formally launching his career: in early 1896 a series of articles on life in South Africa as he found it there appeared in the *San Francisco Chronicle* and *Harper's Weekly*—but to little effect. He was still doing "occasional" writing rather than approaching his goal of national visibility as a professional.

By April of 1896, Norris appears to have concluded that the career he decided upon in the early 1890s required sharper definition. It was time, at 26 years of age, to apply himself in a more systematic manner. The portraits of the artist-heroes in two of his novels are autobiographically significant in this respect: *Blix* and *Vandover and the Brute* are *künstlerromana* reflecting

Frank Norris, circa *1891.*

Title page of Norris's first book, published in late 1891.

ᴛ̖ᴡᴏ ᴘᴀɪʀ.

A FARCE IN ONE ACT, BY FRANK NORRIS.

Presented by the Junior Class, December 10, 189⁊

SCENES IV–VII.

NOTE—The two pair in question in the following little farce are Mr. & Mrs. Fitzwoggins and Mr. & Mrs. Feversham, their guests. Each husband has become jealous of his wife, each wife of her husband. Mrs. Fitswoggins, suspecting thus the fidelity of Mr. Fitzwoggins, has resolved to test it by disguising herself and attempting to win his affections as another woman. On the other hand, Mr. Fitzwoggins, moved by a like anxiety as regards his wife, has done exactly the same thing. He decides to impersonate a bandit king, and to put his wife's affections for him to the proof by making love to her as such a character. The plan of each is of course unknown to the other. Unfortunately Mrs. Fitzwoggins selects for her disguise a bonnet and dress belonging to Mrs. Feversham.

SCENE.—The drawing-room of the country house belonging to the Fitzwoggins.

"BUT WE'RE NOT A BIT JEALOUS."
[*Exit* MR. *and* MRS. FEVERSHAM.]

MRS. FEVERSHAM. Where are you going, my love?

MR. FEVERSHAM. Why, my angel, I was thinking of taking a little airing in the garden.

MRS. FEVERSHAM (*aside*). And meet Anastasia Fitzwoggins. I think, heart of my hearts, I would like to go with you. (*Aside to the audience as she goes out*): But we're not jealous; O, no. [*Exit* MR. *and* MRS. FEVERSHAM.]

[*Enter* MR. FITZWOGGINS *carrying sombrero, cloak, etc.*]

MR. FITZWOGGINS (*in a mock stage whisper*). Fortune favors me designs; ha! ha! I feel like the bandit king or the dark and dreadful outlaw already. Stumbled across the very traps I was looking for in old Feversham's room. Now let's get into them. [*Exit* GILDERSAY FITZWOGGINS,—*re-enters as* HERNANI.] O, now how do I look. [*Looks in mirror.*] O, magnificent. If I didn't know I was myself I'd swear I was somebody else; ha! ha! What, h-ho, without there — hither minion! Holy mother of Moses, here comes my wife. [*Exit Hernani.*]

183

A portion of a play by Norris appeared in the Berkeley yearbook, Blue and Gold, *published by the Junior Class in 1893, pp. 183-192. Courtesy of the Moffett Library, University of California, Berkeley.*

his anxieties then about the hazards of being a dabbler who might squander his talents and drift into dissipation. In consequence, Norris repeatedly reveals in his 1896-1898 writings that his values are those of an achievement-oriented individual, the true-to-type son of a self-made, upper middle-class businessman who had hopefully named him, not Frank, but Benjamin Franklin Norris, Jr. *The Wave* was Frank's means of putting himself into harness for his own good and proving his mettle.

His high expectations for himself are especially inferable from his sports articles, wherein irritation with underachievers lacking the will to triumph is seen. Such impatience, that is, tells us as much about the author as about the athletes he evaluated. Literary essays such as "Zola as a Romantic Writer" and book reviews such as "A Summer in Arcady" make more explicit the criteria for literary performance that he was striving to meet in some of his own short stories, the then-in-process manuscripts of *McTeague* and *Vandover*, and the spin-offs from those manuscripts that appeared in *The Wave* (e.g., "Judy's Service of Gold Plate" and "*Fantaisie Printanière*"). Norris the local colorist is obviously the fictional recorder of life in San Francisco that he calls for—"*A qui le tour*, who shall be our Kipling?"—in "An Opening For Novelists." And in articles such as "A South-Sea Expedition" we find another measure of his willfulness, as self-consciously defined by his allegiance to contemporaneous racial theory: Anglo-Saxons, like himself, stood in his mind and should continue to behave as the accomplished, restless movers and shakers spearheading evolutionary progress. "Happiness by Conquest" contains, perhaps, the best measure of Norris's "type-A" personality in 1897: his fear of proving inadequate to the challenges of being a writer and his compulsion to excel in a survival-of-the-fittest world. His ideal is clear, and would later inform the Darwinian characterizations of his heroes in *A Man's Woman* and *The Pit*: "The feeblest of us feel a thrill for the successful hero. We like the vicious, wicked determination that suggests the thorough-bred bull dog, we cannot but applaud the fellow who . . . plans a certain action or course of life, and who grips his teeth together and clenches his fist till the knuckles whiten and says, 'By God, I'll put it through,' and *does* put it through *just* as he had planned it." As the self-recriminations of the writer-hero of *Blix* suggest, and as Norris's more insouciant, sometimes deliberately foppish compositions for *The Wave* indicate, his resolve was not always at such a white-heat. The lighthearted "Opinions of Leander" series provides a telling case in point. Still, the large number of works by Norris published during this period (along with an undetermined number of other *Wave* pieces not signed by him) measure the resolve of a writer approaching 30 who was determined to make a name for himself at last. One hundred fifty-nine short works, the serialized *Moran*, and *McTeague* (completed in manuscript in the autumn of 1897) were the tangible results of his decision to become serious about his work in 1896.

While Norris commented on the "grind" of producing copy for a weekly, Cosgrave hardly exploited him as a newspaper editor would have a cub reporter.[12] Indeed, writing for *The Wave* was in many ways a made-to-order situation for the realization of Norris's own goals, which had little to do with the churning-out of conventional news copy and much to do with more artful writing appreciated by the literary-minded Cosgrave. Cosgrave treasured style, doting in his own *Wave* essays on that of Lafcadio Hearn, and giving Stephen Crane's eccentricities considerable attention; his reviews of periodical and book-length fictions also make it clear that he was *au courant* concerning new tendencies in literature. He afforded Norris considerable latitude in his choice of topics: when not performing the routine work of an "associate editor," Norris-as-staff-writer appears to have been free to follow his bent in generating well-written accounts of city events, vibrant delineations of northern California life, interviews with various kinds of artists and entertainers, reviews of plays and books, translations of French fiction, essays on literary theory, sketches, dialogues, and short stories. One quickly receives the impression that Norris simply did what he liked, especially in his 1896 indulgences of his keen interest in sports. *The Wave* never printed so many articles of the kind before or after Norris's tenure. Volume 1 contains no fewer than 18 pieces dealing with football and other kinds of athletic competition—far more than the pieces concerning the visual arts that one might expect to see in greater number from a former student of world-class painter Guillaume Bouguereau at the Académie Julian in Paris (1887-1889).[13] In short, while Norris would become known by most late 20th-century commentators as having a single identity—that of a novelist who became "the American Zola"—what is remarkable about his apprentice work is the wide variety of *kinds* of writing that he did. When his third novel, *Blix*, appeared in late 1899, Norris's national reputation was primarily that of a fictionalist displaying startling versatility. Had the reviewers who described him thus traced the course of his career through the nearly two years in which he was employed by *The Wave*, though, they would not have been so surprised that Norris's hygienically idealistic paean to ideal womanhood was preceded the same year by such a "dirty" book as *McTeague*.

An even greater liberty granted Norris by Cosgrave was freedom from censorship of the kind that prevailed in high-toned publications of the day. Victorianism remained strong in the 1890s, and numerous *Wave* pieces defy the moral standards still in place in the realm of periodical publications today. *"Miracle Joyeux,"* for example, reveals Norris playing the part of a decadent artist, with full *fin de siècle* verve: where else but in *The Wave*

has been here her allotted time, the 'farewell to the pleasant friends with freight is all on board, and we must say whom we made the ascent.'

Mabel H. Closson.

THE BARRICADE ON THE GRAND PONT.

LAUTH.

I.

THE barricade upon the Grand Pont was very silent. On either side of the bridge as in a street stretched the houses and shops of the money-changers, which gave the bridge the name of Pont-au-Change in a later day. They stood there empty and full of dormant echoes; their windows shivered, their doors crushed in, leaving in their place yawning openings like eyes and mouths agape with wonder. Around the piles, which buttressed up their rearward projections, the yellow Seine licked incessantly, with a quickly stilled gurgle at long intervals.

The barricade was drawn across the bridge some eight feet back from the

VOL. xxi— 18.

keystone; directly in front of it at the extremity of the bridge squatted like a great toad, the massive, stunted structure of the Grand Châtelet. Its grate was down, its huge steel clamped gates were closed; it barred all advance into the Rue St. Dennis beyond. There, held the enemy, to wit, the Prevôt-des-Marchands, with the archers of the guard and eight hundred of the King's gens-d'armes. The two redoubts seemed to watch one another. Over the pavement, between the barricade and the Châtelet, all the fighting of the early morning had been done. It was now three o'clock in the afternoon. All the vicinity was very still; the street was empty, for by mutual agreement each party had removed

Norris drew illustrations for several of his works published before 1896. A gothic romance set in the Middle Ages and featuring the devolution of a man to a protoplasmic condition, "Lauth" appeared in Overland Monthly, *21 (March 1893), 241-260. Courtesy of the Strozier Library, Florida State University.*

MOST EXASPERATINGLY INDIFFERENT.

OUTWARD AND VISIBLE SIGNS.

V. THOROUGHBRED.

ONCE there were two men in love with the same girl and this is the story of how the one was taken and the other left.

The girl's name was Vance — Barry Vance of the Vances, who lived on Stockton street when Stockton street was the place to live and even afterward when it was not. In this story she shall be little more than a name. After all, a name (using the word largely) and a face are about all that men ask of a girl to-day. They are not so very far wrong. The best charactered girl is the girl with the least character ; that is — don't misunderstand — decided character. Just as the best tempered girl is the one with the least temper. So in this story Barry Vance shall be simply Barry Vance to the end, which was when she married one of the men and changed her name to his.

But the men were of temperaments sufficiently marked and were as widely different as one could well imagine. They were ex-

By 1895 Norris was writing and illustrating short stories with a more contemporary subject matter for Overland Monthly, 25 *(February 1895), 196-201. Courtesy of the Collection of Joseph R. McElrath, Jr.*

might Norris, in 1897, depict a disturbingly "human" Jesus who gives two scoundrels the horrific punishment for which Norris has made them so deserving? One is blinded by the Prince of Peace, while the miracle worked on the other effects the loss of sight in one eye. Further, the story adds to the New Testament, or its apocrypha, the sardonic "record" of the one instance in which Jesus was seen smiling—not compassionately, but immediately after giving the two rogues their rough come-uppance. Needless to say, perhaps, "*Miracle Joyeux*" was rewritten when it later appeared in another periodical then celebrated for its "progressive" outlook, *McClure's Magazine:* the offensive elements were excised in 1898; more than half of the tale was replaced by a well-executed though quite sentimental portrait of Jesus as he interacts with an unhappy young girl whose life is made joyous by Him.[14] What was passable in *The Wave* could not be tolerated elsewhere.

In other works as well, Norris made unbridled use of the opportunities afforded him by Cosgrave: "Little Dramas of the Curbstone" and "The Associated Un-Charities" disclose what may be termed a "dark side" of Norris's personality that it is difficult to imagine any magazine editor, then or now, countenancing: sociopathic rage is directed against a pathetic, deaf and blind "idiot" in the former; a cruel joke played upon three blind men is featured in the latter. Put another way, the extraordinary decision made by Doubleday and McClure Company to publish so offensive an *avant-garde* novel as *McTeague* was anticipated several times by John O'Hara Cosgrave. Given the new ground that Norris wanted to break as a post-Victorian author anticipating Nathanael West and Flannery O'Connor, his apprenticeship with *The Wave* was a serendipitous development of the first magnitude.

By the spring of 1897, though, it was time for Norris to move on. As he watched other young San Francisco artists, such as his friends Gelett Burgess, Ernest Peixotto, and Juliet Wilbor Tompkins, receive the call to the national centers of publishing in New York and Boston, he began to feel that his career had once again stalled. The proof of one's worth was such a summons from the East, not tenure on the staff of a regional weekly of relatively small circulation. Norris began to increase his production of short stories; and he finally effected his escape from *The Wave* with the *Moran* serialization that caught the attention of John S. Phillips of the McClure syndicate in early 1898. Norris was fully prepared for the next leg of his journey toward a permanent place in American literary history, but, one may reasonably argue, only because *The Wave* had provided the opportunity to develop himself as a professional, to trade his amateur and then apprentice status for that of an advanced journeyman.

* * *

Volume 1 finds Norris beginning his work for *The Wave* with a portfolio of sketches, drafts, and completed works following his travel-writing jaunt to South Africa. He had left San Francisco on 28 October 1895; by 25 February 1896, when his mother and he took rooms at the Hotel del Coronado near San Diego, he was back on the west coast, presumably enjoying the appearance of his illustrated articles in the *San Francisco Chronicle* and *Harper's Weekly*.[15] He had earlier written for *The Wave*; and these new publications undoubtedly cinched the matter when Cosgrave decided to hire a salaried staff-writer. Relevant also was the fact that he had become something of a local celebrity when the San Francisco press reported that he had mysteriously disappeared in South Africa at the time of the Jameson Raid presaging the Boer War.[16] "Rhodes and the Reporters," chronicling his return voyage, was his first contribution to *The Wave* in the 11 April 1896 issue. It was followed soon by other treatments of the South African experience: "Tales of the Day," "A Steamship Voyage with Cecil Rhodes" (in the *Chronicle*), and a portent of the flair for the outrageous that would manifest itself sporadically, the Kiplingesque short story "A Salvation Boom in Matabeleland." He would continue to exploit the subject, for example, his June 1896 account of dinner with one of the Jameson Raid conspirators in "Jack Hammond in Johannesburg and Pretoria." "The Strangest Thing" of July 1897, too, was South African in its setting; and, while its events occurred in California and Mexico, *Moran's* autobiographical roots were in his early 1896 adventure.[17]

In April, 1896, Norris's portfolio also contained the short story "Bandy Callaghan's Girl," dated 1894 but apparently seeing print in *The Wave* for the first time. With it, he staked out a territory previously identified by Stevenson and Kipling as literarily promising: colorful and, at times, lurid San Francisco.[18] Bandy, chasing a leprous Chinese-American into the recesses of exotic Chinatown, stumbles into an opium den, discovers a "white slave," and rescues her. It was the first of several excursions into this and other ethnic neighborhoods of the city that Norris would make for both factual and fictional purposes; it was also a "rattling good yarn" of the kind Cosgrave, a fan of Stevenson and Kipling, liked. Less sensationally, in May 1896, he established his stride as a local colorist with his series of sketches concerning types of Westerners to be seen in San Francisco, expanding that month his coverage of the Bay Area by focusing on Berkeley in "The Benefit Field Day for the California Eastern Team" and traveling down the peninsula for "Van Alstyn Sees Polo at Burlingame." And then Norris began adventuring beyond the immediate environs of San Francisco.

Norris would spend a good deal of time traveling to and from various regional events and colorful locales. June's "Man-Hunting" dealt with the coastal mountain range south of Monterey, but was based upon past experiences. "The Santa Cruz Venetian Carnival" and "A California Jubilee" were, however, most likely begun on the return trips from Santa Cruz and Monterey. "Italy in California," one feels, must have been initially drafted when, in October 1896, he was far to the north in the Sonoma Valley, enjoying the perfect meal he had at the Italian Swiss Colony in Asti. Through the end of Volume 1, and in Volume 2 as well, Norris is a peripatetic observer rendering his impressions of San Francisco's nooks and crannies, when not adventuring north, south, and east on ferries, trains, and horse-drawn conveyances.

How he rendered these "impressions"—an often-employed term indicating to his readers that he was not, strictly speaking, a reporter—reminds one of what his pieces concerning visual artists, such as "The Winter Exhibition" and "A California Artist," reflect: that Norris did receive formal instruction in drawing and painting through 1889 and continued his interest after he ceased illustrating his writings immediately prior to joining *The Wave*. He had a painterly eye that shows to advantage in his prose.

"The Sketch Club Exhibit" of 28 November 1896 squares with what one finds in his descriptive writing, for his familiarity with more traditional painters such as the *pompier* Bouguereau did not preclude his awareness of Impressionism as it was practiced both inside and outside of the Academic tradition by the 1890s. "Exhibit" discloses that Norris not only knew Impressionism but, it seems, Pointillism as well. How much a verbal Impressionist this writer—now known mainly for his Realism, Romanticism, and Naturalism—became is abundantly clear in the visual *tour de force* of "The Santa Cruz Venetian Carnival," and in other works such as the early "Steamship Voyage With Cecil Rhodes," the later "Tennis Tournament" of July, and the much later "How It Strikes an Observer" of December 1896. In the verbal medium, Norris was, of course, not restricted to visual effects. One finds in "Santa Cruz" and elsewhere that his Impressionism extends to the aural,[19] and the olfactory appeal of his self-consciously fashioned imagery is also strong, as in "The Bivalve at Home." Indeed, the rendering of olfactory stimuli became a distinguishing trait of his, made even more memorable by Zelda Sayre's letter to F. Scott Fitzgerald in which she expressed her hope that Scott would never "be a realist": "All authors who want to make things true to life make them smell bad—like McTeague's room—and that's my most sensitive sense."[20]

Norris's writings about literary creation, unfortunately, do not address this concern; he wrote as an Impressionist rather than addressed the style conceptually, just as he wrote popular-appeal love tales without ever feeling the need to produce a rationale for what one encounters in four of the five short stories in the "'Man Proposes'" series published between 23 May and 4 July 1896. "No. 2" in the series is the glaring exception since Norris did theorize about what one finds in this story so different from the others. This Naturalistic romance features a coal-heaver and a washing-woman, and it is a comic inversion of the other four tales featuring more conventional characters becoming engaged. The heroine is vulgar and the hero a randy brute bent upon marriage for the sake of satisfying his lust. Norris's account of male *and female* arousal is closely related to a similarly risible moment concerning Mac in chapter 2 of *McTeague* and to Trina's "surrender" to passion in chapter 5. The short story is the first overtly Naturalistic work of Norris's apprenticeship, as well as the initial prompting for consideration of the theory of progressive literary art that Norris was then developing and employing as he shaped his *McTeague* manuscript.

The focus on human sexuality in "No. 2" will, for those reading Volume 1's writings in chronological order, immediately recall the book review "Theory and Reality," which appeared four weeks earlier in May, 1896. Norris there concentrated on William Dean Howells' expert handling of the "'ultimate physical relation of man and woman,'" the quintessentially "delicate" topic of the 19th century. He celebrated Howells' tasteful daring in this respect in *A Parting and a Meeting*, drubbing at the same time Mrs. J.R. Jarboe for an impossibly moralistic novel, *Robert Atterbury*, that argued in behalf of celibacy and against the "legalized prostitution" that is conjugal love in marriage. Norris, however, does not treat sex in the manner of the Howellsian Realist in "No. 2"—nor anywhere else in his entire canon, including *Blix* whose sunshiny optimism may possibly bring Howells to mind. Characters like the frankly rendered, animalistic coal-heaver and washing-woman are never to be met in Howells' fictions or, for that matter, in the works of the Romantic author Norris so persistently admired, Walter Scott. In July, 1896, Norris made clear his predisposition to noncensorial honesty with the topic: in "A Summer in Arcady" he praised James Lane Allen for his Naturalistic representation of desire. The novel *Summer in Arcady*, he declared, bravely described the natural attraction between Hilary and Daphne; Norris was gladdened when finding these naturally good young people portrayed uncritically as what they actually are, "wholesome human brutes." "Brutes" is wholly positive in its denotation. It would, in consequence, be a mistake to read "No. 2" as a "cautionary tale" depicting two low-life, vile beasts in the throes of shameful passion. Norris *qua* Zolaesque Naturalist was well beyond such prudery, to the point that the rutting behaviors of the coal-heaver and his new fiancée are merely a part of the human comedy.

For a fuller understanding of Norris's nascent Zolaism, however, one turns to June 1896: to the book review "Zola's *Rome*," and the essay "Zola as a Romantic Writer." Whatever the degree Norris was original in his Naturalism, *Rome's* "gospel" concerning the deterministic situation in which humans find themselves and its typically emotive style of writing were major influences on Norris's later novels. *Rome*, wrote Norris, is "crammed with tremendous and terrible *pictures*, hurled off, as it were, upon the canvas, by giant hands wielding enormous brushes. . . . You lay the book down, breathless; for the moment all other books, even all other *things*, seem small and trivial." How Zola's style shaped Norris's in the Volume 1 writings will be immediately seen if one reads the extracts from *Rome* in Norris's review and then examines "Zola as a Romantic Writer." In the latter the prose is undeniably Zolaesque in its vigor, particularly in its second half. Descriptive articles such as "With the Peacemakers," "On a Battleship," "Moving a Fifty-Ton Gun," and "Fitting Cruisers for Service" also evince what Norris had learned from Zola: that the power of vividly imagistic, expansive language is to be derived from the writer's induction of imaginative excitation and willingness to engage in commensurate verbal exaggeration. The accuracy of the Realist, while desirable in itself, is not enough since these articles deal with what are, potentially, the dullest things imaginable. To bring empirical detail to life in art, the Realist must also exercise the inventiveness of the Romantic by elevating the commonplace to the status of material worthy of artistic, rather than reportorial, treatment. As Norris explains in "Zola," this is the stylistic essence of Naturalism—the synthesis of both the Realistic and the Romantic in one's writings. The Naturalist is simultaneously precise and dynamic.

Norris had begun imitating Zola's style before his apprenticeship started. "A California Vintage," published in *The Wave* in October 1895, treats winemaking in the Santa Clara Valley in the same big bow-wow manner seen in, for example, the extravagant sexual-initiation imagery used in "With the Peacemakers" to describe the firing of cannons. By the time he left *The Wave*, the resort to the gorgeously powerful in his prose style was a long-exercised, indelible trait. On the other hand, what is surprising in the writings of Volume 1 is how few overtly Zolaesque *fictions* beyond the comical "'Man Proposes': No. 2" Norris offered his readers. Zola's heavy, quite serious thematic emphasis on the governing power of heredity plays only a minor role in "His Sister": weakness of character is suggested by the mouth of the hero's sister-who-went-wrong, and there is a "reckless" appearance generated by her eyes and chin. Here Norris offers a minimal grounding of the young woman's wayward nature in her genetically-determined physical characteristics. The "Brute" section of "Suggestions" is more transparent in its Zolaism: it briefly sketches an even less mentally developed individual than the coal-heaver in the "'Man Proposes'" series; he is an especially important creation for those searching for Zolaesque themes since he is deftly described as molded by both heredity and environment. Still, the Zolaesque touch is light, and Norris closes the piece on a comic note. The allegory of the toys in "The Puppets and the Puppy," then, is the work in Volume 1 that most recalls Zola's perspective as a serious thinker: the brief fantasy focuses on the trinity of determinants that are heredity, environment, and chance; the grim scenario provides the earliest manifestation of the philosophical orientation that would inform Norris's major novels.

* * *

One closes Volume 1 noting, first, that the American author responsible in February 1899 for the initial, wholesale importation of the Zolaesque ideology and mode of storytelling into the American novelistic tradition did not, in this phase of his apprenticeship, actually publish much Naturalistic fiction. It appears that his *McTeague* and *Vandover* manuscripts were the principal repositories for themes, characterizations, and story-lines of the kind. One observes, second, that the more obvious consequences of Norris being inspired by the novels alluded to in "Zola as a Romantic Writer" are manifest instead in his local color articles: there he proved not only an Impressionist but a descriptive writer striving to achieve grand, sublime effects promised by his mentor's exaggerative methods. While Norris was hardly a Thoreauvian, the well-known statement of Thoreau's aesthetic in *Walden*— "I am convinced that I cannot exaggerate enough"—easily comes to mind when examining both Norris's and Zola's Baroque imagery and high-decibel, energy-suffused prose. Third, Norris emerges in this volume as more the theorist on Naturalism than its dedicated practitioner in his fictions. His writings *about* Naturalism are the earliest and fullest apologias for the sensibility in American literary history; contemporaries Hamlin Garland, Stephen Crane, and Theodore Dreiser, who might have written similarly, never did. By the summer of 1896, Norris was an ardent spokesman and proselytizer.

Another and perhaps surprising observation made possible by this volume concerns not only the dearth of Zolaesque tales but how few fictions of any sort Norris published during this phase of his apprenticeship. Again one imagines his energies being channeled into his novelistic manuscripts. Of the 95 titles in question, only 11 are strictly categorizable as short stories, if one treats the "1870" and "Brute" sections of "Suggestions" as discrete items, that is, as examples of "the 'very' short story" that Cosgrave identified as Norris's forte.[21] Three other works—"In the Heat of Battle," "The Puppets and the Puppy" and "Through a Glass Darkly"—are closet dramas, or dialogues. The remaining two sections of "Suggestions" are fictional sketches; and one may reach a count of 20 only by stretching the definition of fiction to include the four 1896 descriptions of "Types" of individuals living in the San Francisco area. On the other hand, Norris is so "literary" in his articles that the generic distinction made here may prove moot for many readers. "A Steamship Voyage" reads more like a short story than a news article; "Western City Types: The 'Fast' Girl" is so fictional in character that it was either extracted from or later added to the *Vandover and the Brute* manuscript. Norris's bibliographer was so impressed by the story-like qualities of "Miss Sabel's Husband" (in Volume 2) that he deliberately identified the interview as a short story.[22] Still, the fact remains that it was not until 26 June 1897 that Norris began publishing fiction with the frequency that one might expect: of the 64 pieces in Volume 2, one-half are short stories, dialogues, and fictional sketches.

Should one examine Volume 1 in terms of how it reveals Norris's progress as a fiction writer, the shortfall in evidence is complicated by another factor: the dating of the compositions. "In the Heat of Battle," for example, is a truly sophomoric piece that smacks of the early 1890s and Norris's fraternity-wit days at the University of California, where he wrote for amateur theatrical productions.[23] "Battle" may very well have been intended for performance as a play in 1893 or 1894 and resuscitated in late 1896 when a press deadline grew uncomfortably near. Indeed, "Battle" is so atypical of the pieces in this volume that, in all fairness, it should not be considered as evidence of either Norris's progress or regression—though it is telling that he would allow such an unflattering reflection of his abilities to appear in print. "Bandy Callaghan's Girl," as has been noted, was dated at the end of his senior year at Berkeley; and the similarly Romantic yarn, "The Heroism of Jonesee," may also date from that time or shortly thereafter. Its plumber-hero, then named Tug Wilson, appeared in one of the themes he submitted in the creative writing course in which he was enrolled at Harvard University in 1894-1895.[24] Like "Suggestions" which is strikingly similar to some of those Harvard themes, however, "Heroism" may as easily be contemporaneous with the 1896 "Man Proposes" series. A problem, then, is that some of the fictional pieces cannot be dated with certainty. What is less difficult to ascertain is that Zola's influence on Norris's fiction writing at this point was only one of many, including those of Richard Harding Davis, Rudyard Kipling, Stephen Crane, and Robert Louis Stevenson. Norris's dilemma was that of the writer-hero of "His Sister." Like Conrad Strelitz he had studied numerous models only to realize that what he had learned had already been "done." He had to add his own unique contributions to their formulas, and he did: South African conditions replaced Kipling's Indian specifics in "A

Salvation Boom"; Stevenson's lurid adventure-writing was transported to a modern urban setting in "Bandy Callaghan's Girl"; Conrad Strelitz's sister is made a denizen of the "tenderloin" world described by Stephen Crane while the main focus is on the problems encountered by writers like Norris who are striving for originality; and Davis's nice-boy-meets-even-nicer-girl short stories were given an uncharacteristic, sordid twist in the characterization of the crudely manipulative heroine of "'Man Proposes': No. 4." Originality, then and now, is difficult to attain, though "The Puppets and the Puppy" and "Through a Glass Darkly"—unalike as they are in spirit—do suggest that Norris was transcending his literary mentors. Reflecting quite different sides of the author's personality, both works are genuinely Norrisean.

The most remarkable instance of Norris transcending an influence in 1896-1897 is seen, however, in the absence of any overtly Howellsian writing in Volume 1, despite his celebration of the novelist in "Theory and Reality." There he lauded Howells' authorial detachment, ability to fashion credible characters and plots from which theme naturally emerged before the reader, and avoidance of message-driven fiction for the sake of picturing life-as-it-is. That Howells did not preach but allowed readers to draw their own conclusions from what they observed in his fiction did, in fact, eventually become one of Norris's own publicly proclaimed principles regarding the need for authorial self-effacement. "The Novel With a 'Purpose'" (1902), for example, reveals Norris much later articulating the values already attractive to him in 1896.

One finds at least a partial explanation for this absence of Howellsian stories in "Zola as a Romantic Writer," where Norris again praises Howells briefly but, while giving him his due, roughly uses him as the means of correcting the popular misconception that Zola is a radical Realist. To this end, Norris chides Howells for the imaginative limitations endemic to the school of Realism for which he was the chief spokesman; Howells is made to look petty, conventional, and dully *bourgeois* in his choices of subject matter, for the sake of limning the opposite, Romantic characteristics of Zola's personality. Norris was casting his lot in the Zola camp, of course. But, six months later, Howells was again the subject of an eulogy delivered by Norris, in "What Is Our Greatest Piece of Fiction?" His *A Modern Instance* (1882) struck Norris as the finest study of American life to date, and yet the praise is qualified. Here Zola is not cited as the preferred author; tellingly, Norris identifies another writer, romancer Lew Wallace, as the one who provides the superior reading experience. *Ben-Hur* (1880) simply engaged his imagination more forcefully than *A Modern Instance*. Howells did have a measurably immediate influence, but it was principally that of enabling Norris to clarify his desire to write fiction that was more Romantic than

Realistic. Becoming a Naturalist apparently meant not being able to do more than appreciate Howells in a limited way, though one wonders how Norris might have written about him once he had finished sowing his wild oats, and had he not died before he had the opportunity to enjoy his newly-won professional success into middle-age. Like "The Novel with a 'Purpose,'" the "Conclusion" of *The Pit* and the essay "Simplicity in Art" suggest that Norris was by 1902 becoming less conflicted in his attitude toward Howellsian literary values.

Two final observations are dictated by the writings of Volume 1. As a member of the *Wave* staff, Norris became an "insider" of the cultural establishment, and he seized the opportunity to construct two quite effective personas as intermediary between the producers and consumers of art. When interviewing performing artists at the San Francisco theaters, Norris projects the image of the likeable, inexperienced *naif* who amateurishly posed, or often failed to pose, the questions normally asked by other *Wave* interviewers —the queries which the interviewees themselves knew by heart from past experience. The strategy allowed for greater identification with Norris by his as-inexperienced readers; gave his more egotistical interviewees the opportunity to reveal themselves as such as they took control of the situations they were used to dominating; and allowed his less vain, more sympathetic subjects the opportunity to be themselves when relieved of the need to "perform" offstage for a seasoned interviewer. It was a promising strategy Norris adopted; and yet, one may be actually seeing in these interviews more of the private Frank Norris than in any of his other kinds of writing. The posthumous eulogies written by those who knew him intimately describe just such a man: kindly, considerate, possessed of a fine sense of humor, and never the egotist abusing the patience of others under the banner of "the eccentricities of genius." Although Franklin Walker egregiously overemphasized the point in his 1932 *Frank Norris: A Biography*, Norris perennially projected on the personal level a boyish charm.[25]

In his reviews of books and plays, however, this image of the approachable innocent was replaced by another reflecting a different Norris, a more sober one with a sharper edge to his personality. Here one sees the critical thinker and arbiter of taste who spoke authoritatively, and credibly so as he revealed the breadth of his literary experience and his grasp of the larger issues facing the writer and reader in the midst of a national debate over the relative merits of Realism and Romanticism—and the Zolaesque hybridization of the two that was Naturalism. Further, he is not reluctant to range beyond literary matters *per se* to larger cultural concerns. Volume 1, for example, concludes with a review of Lorrimer Stoddard's *The Question*, which chides the dramatist for some of the infelicities of its performance, but finally proves more an evaluation of its audience than of the play. Norris is hardly courting popularity when he chastises the theater-goers who did not share his appreciation of Stoddard's artful sophistication. Indeed, it is the acerbic indignation of Mark Twain that comes to mind as Norris explains the cause of the play's commercial failure. He archly observes that such a witty, cerebral drama "presupposes a rather unusual degree of intelligence on the part of its audience, an intelligence that can find more pleasure in an exchange of wit than in an exchange of blows, that rejoices in the thrust of keenly-pointed satire rather than in that of the assassin's knife. There are not many such people amongst San Francisco theater-goers. . . . They wanted blood and they got an epigram." Norris was not intolerant of diversity in point of view and taste. In "A Delayed Masterpiece," he reviewed Elizabeth Stuart Phelps' latest overtly Christian novel, *A Singular Life*, praising the skill with which she handled a subject matter about which he was not particularly keen; his tolerance did not, however, preclude his calling a spade a spade or using one to bury Arthur Morrison in "Fiction in Review." Like the San Francisco audience of *The Question*, the author of *Tales of Mean Streets* (1895) was capable of better behavior. His latest book, *Chronicles of Martin Hewlitt*, was nothing more than a plagiarism of Arthur Conan Doyle's Sherlock Holmes tales, inducing "a feeling of indignation."

In the interviews and reviews, then, one finds that Norris's personality as writer is multiplex. But, in the other kinds of writings as well this is also apparent, as a seemingly unwarranted exasperation in his sports articles counterpoints with an easy, droll acceptance of the human condition and unfeigned delight in the Dickensian quirks of the allegedly "rational animal." See, for example, "The Heroism of Jonesee." The ultimate measure of the instability of any monolithic definition of Norris, however, is that review of *The Question*, for Norris himself wrote and took obvious pleasure in "low" art that featured the thrust of the assassin's knife—as much as Zola himself did in the novel that Norris reviewed so ecstatically, *Rome*. Both writers were extraordinarily idiosyncratic in their tastes for the empirically true and the exotically imaginative; neither hesitated to blend the coarse with the refined.

Volume 1 features a writer who, on occasion, narrowly defines the essence of great art, only to defy such limitations for the sake of having a wider range of activity for himself. Volume 1 thus elucidates how Norris could puzzle later commentators by producing almost simultaneously *Moran* and *McTeague*, novels which are as different as night and day in their generic qualities and in what they suggest about divergent kinds of authorial personalities giving rise to them. This volume alone, then, solves one of the problems confronting those who have lacked a background against which to interpret the author who wrote those radically unalike works published a mere six months apart. Here we find that Norris is not a consistent partisan of one literary mode but an eclectic who could enjoy any kind of writing that provided an engaging reading experience, whether Romantic, Realistic, or—best—Naturalistic. He was a young writer willing to try anything that "worked," and, later, such a catholicity of taste modifying his primary loyalty to the Naturalistic would provide an explanation of the peculiarly rich mixture of ostensibly antithetical elements in his novels, for example, the Grannis-Baker subplot of *McTeague* that, since 1899, has struck so many readers as out of place, and the Gothic romance of the Vanamee subplot in *The Octopus* that brings Edgar Allan Poe to mind. As in *The Wave*, so in the novels: nothing was anathema to Norris, provided it promised the possibility of unique literary effects and the means of probing the truth of the human condition.

C. M. Davis Eng. Co.
FRANK NORRIS.

The Wave *author in his late twenties.*
Reproduced from The Land of Sunshine, *13 (June 1900), 18.*
Courtesy of the California State Library, Sacramento.

NOTES

[1]The majority of now-known reviews of *McTeague* and Norris's other books are included in *Frank Norris: The Critical Reception*, ed. Joseph R. McElrath, Jr., and Katherine Knight (New York: Burt Franklin, 1981).

[2]For the best and most influential interpretation of Norris as a LeContean evolutionary idealist, see Donald Pizer, *The Novels of Frank Norris* (Bloomington: Indiana University Press, 1966).

[3]Incomplete multi-volume collections of Norris's writings appeared in 1903, 1905, 1928, and 1983-1984; for descriptions of their contents, see Joseph R. McElrath, Jr., *Frank Norris: A Descriptive Bibliography* (Pittsburgh: University of Pittsburgh Press, 1992), pp. 187-196. One-volume collections including some of Norris's apprenticeship-period writings are *The Third Circle*, ed. Will Irwin (New York and London: John Lane, 1909); *Frank Norris of "The Wave,"* ed. Franklin Walker (San Francisco: Westgate Press, 1931); and two volumes edited by Donald Pizer: *The Literary Criticism of Frank Norris* (Austin: University of Texas Press, 1964), and *Frank Norris: Novels and Essays* (New York: Library of America, 1986). See *A Descriptive Bibliography* for their contents (pp. 164-168, 173-176, and 197).

[4]The present edition includes 64 apprenticeship-period publications by Norris never before reprinted in book form. One of them, "*Miracle Joyeux*," is closely related to the book publication *The Joyous Miracle* (see note 14), but the latter is actually a discrete work of art, radically different from the short story published in *The Wave*.

[5]All of Norris's apprenticeship writings for one magazine, *The Wave* (San Francisco)—signed, initialed, unsigned, and pseudonymously signed—are identified in Joseph R. McElrath, Jr., *Frank Norris and "The Wave": A Bibliography* (New York: Garland, 1988). The empirical and interpretive grounds for the attribution to Norris of unsigned and pseudonymously signed pieces are therein explained in full; works possibly by Norris and dubious attributions by previous bibliographers are also listed, and the specific grounds for not including them in the Norris canon are given in many cases. *Frank Norris: A Descriptive Bibliography* identifies Norris's publications *in toto*.

[6]An exemplary demonstration of how new insights are possible when a scholar interprets Norris's novels in the context of his earlier writing will be seen in Don Graham, *The Fiction of Frank Norris: The Aesthetic Context* (Columbia: University of Missouri Press, 1978).

[7]This is not to insist on gainsaying all previous commentators or to discount the continuing relevance of major studies such as Pizer's *The Novels of Frank Norris* and the following: Ernest Marchand, *Frank Norris: A Study* (Stanford: Stanford University Press, 1942); Warren French, *Frank Norris* (New York: Twayne, 1962); William B. Dillingham, *Frank Norris: Instinct and Art* (Lincoln: University of Nebraska Press, 1969); André Poncet, *Frank Norris (1870-1902)*,

2 volumes (Paris: Librairie Honoré Champion, 1977); and Barbara Hochman, *The Art of Frank Norris, Storyteller* (Columbia: University of Missouri Press, 1988).

[8]*Moran* was serialized in *The Wave*, 8 January-9 April 1898; the New York *Evening Sun*, 4-19 May 1898; and the Chicago *Inter Ocean*, 22 August-4 September 1898. For further publication specifics, see *Frank Norris: A Descriptive Bibliography*. Copyright deposit of the bowdlerized book version occurred on 19 September 1898, and it was first listed as available for sale in the 1 October issue of *Publishers' Weekly*. How *Moran* was bowdlerized is described by Joseph R. McElrath, Jr., "The Original Version of Norris' *Moran*," *Studies in American Fiction*, 11 (1983), 255-259.

[9]The character of these texts and how they were edited are explained in the "Textual Afterword" at the close of Volume 2.

[10]The Houghton, Mifflin letterbooks at the Houghton Library, Harvard University, do not include Norris's letters to that firm; but a letterpress copy of its rejection of his "little collection of sketches and tales," dated 21 June 1895, does survive. It refers to the collection as "much in advance of what we saw before from your hand," that is, *Yvernelle*. *Yvernelle* was rejected in a letter dated 30 December 1890.

[11]Why Norris's collection did not appear is not known. In early November, 1895, a writer signing himself "The Witness" announced that "a volume of his manuscripts has recently been accepted by Lovell, Coryell & Co." ("Personalities and Politics," *The Wave*, 14 [2 November 1895], 6).

[12]On 9 April 1900, Norris wrote to the editor of *The Land of Sunshine* in response to a request for biographical information. He described his *Wave* experience thus: "Returned to San Francisco '96 to take post associate editor S.F. Wave—wrote on an average of 30 000 words a week—including one short story —for this paper for two years, best and only literary training he ever had.—can think of nothing better for young man with 'literary aspirations' than grind of *this kind of paper (not* a daily but a weekly.)" (*Frank Norris: Collected Letters*, ed. Jesse S. Crisler [San Francisco: Book Club of California, 1986], pp. 108-109.) The "grind" dimensions of Norris's apprenticeship and their negative psychological effects in the spring of 1897 are examined in the introduction to Volume 2.

[13]During his apprenticeship, Norris wrote one short story set in the Académie Julian, "'This Animal of a Buldy Jones'" (in Volume 2). His description of his experience there was published much later, "Student Life in Paris," *Collier's Weekly*, 25 (12 May 1900), 33.

[14]The rewritten story is the work with which most students of Norris are familiar via *The Joyous Miracle* (New York: Doubleday, Page, and Co., 1906). Its source was the "Miracle Joyeux" published in *McClure's Magazine*, 12 (December 1898), 154-160.

[15]The date of Norris's departure was determined by Jesse S. Crisler in "Norris's Departure for Johannesburg," *Frank Norris Studies*, No. 3 (Spring 1987), 4-5. Crisler and Joseph R. McElrath, Jr., together discovered the indication of the date by which Norris had returned to California in the guest registers of the

Hotel del Coronado, now at the library of San Diego State University.

[16]See Jesse S. Crisler's history of the flurry of interest in Norris's disappearance in "Norris in South Africa," *Frank Norris Studies*, No. 7 (Spring 1989), 4-7. Frank's brother, novelist Charles G. Norris (1881-1945) provided another account. He approximated the sensation created in 1896 when he registered his recollection of Frank's flamboyant experience in his *Pig Iron* (New York: E.P. Dutton, 1926), p. 348. The character Vin Morrisey was assigned some of the details of Frank's adventure: "Vin had been having the most extraordinary experiences. He'd happened to be in Johannesburg at the time of Jameson's raid, had enlisted in the British army for the defense of the city, and upon the collapse of the column and the suppression of the insurrection, had been jailed by the Boers, and the State Department at Washington had had its hands full keeping him from being hanged. He had been finally released and ordered out of the country." Charles appears, however, to have had a exaggerated notion of what transpired: diplomatic dispatches of the State Department, now at the Library of Congress, focus on John Hays Hammond and several other Americans involved in the abortive coup; Norris, however, is not mentioned.

[17]Charles G. Norris, who virtually worshipped his brother, managed Frank's literary properties for his widow. As Richard Allan Davison has shown, it was he, with the aid of his wife Kathleen, who convinced the morally fastidious Gertrude Norris that *Vandover and the Brute* should be published in 1914, and that it would not tarnish the reputation of Gertrude's favorite son ("Charles G. Norris, Kathleen Norris and *Vandover and the Brute*: A New Letter," *Frank Norris Studies*, No. 3 [Spring 1987], 2-4). Charles ensured that his mother would not be troubled; he bowdlerized the now-lost manuscript. Six years later, he dramatized the fact that *Moran* was based upon Frank's apparent disappearance from the face of the earth during the trip to South Africa: the dust jacket of the 1920 printing of *Moran* by Doubleday, Page and Co. boldly declared "—'his First | published novel | Based on Fact.'" Charles was referring to the similar experience had by the hero of *Moran*.

[18]See "Among Cliff-Dwellers" in this volume.

[19]The conclusion of "The Santa Cruz Venetian Carnival" is typical of Norris's work in this regard. His keen sensitivity to sound, suggesting unusual sensory acuteness, is especially apparent in Volume 2's "Metropolitan Noises."

[20]*Correspondence of F. Scott Fitzgerald*, ed. Matthew J. Bruccoli (New York: Random House, 1979), p. 52.

[21]The editorial headnote to "In the Heat of Battle" reads: "Frank Norris, who has been a frequent contributor to 'The Wave' during the past year, is chiefly known as a writer of fiction that has appeared in Eastern and local publications. Mr. Norris's best work is in the 'very' short story, wherein a suggestive bit of action is condensed into the smallest possible space. During the winter of 1895-6 Mr. Norris was the correspondent for 'Harper's Weekly' and the San Francisco 'Chronicle' in the Transvaal, South Africa, at the time of the Uitlander insurrection and Jamieson's [sic] raid. Mr. Norris took an active part in the rising, and was expelled from the country on that account by the Johannisburg [sic] authorities after the Boer government had regained its supremacy."

[22]*Frank Norris: A Descriptive Bibliography*, p. 228.

[23]Norris wrote the 1893 Junior Farce, *Two Pair*, performed by his class of '94, scenes 4-7 of which were published with his illustrations in Berkeley's yearbook, *The Blue and Gold* (San Francisco: H.S. Crocker, 1893), pp. 183-192. He also provided the words and music for a collegiate fund-raiser staged on Thanksgiving Eve in 1893 (announced by The Witness, "Splashes," *The Wave*, 11 [11 November 1893], 2). A program for the event, citing Norris as the author, is in the Frank Norris Collection of the Bancroft Library, University of California, Berkeley. As the "leader" of a Phi Gamma Delta fraternity "entertainment" during his senior year, Norris undoubtedly had a hand in the writing of a musical parody of *Romeo and Juliet* presented (The Witness, "Splashes," *The Wave*, 12 [31 March 1894], 4). "The Isabella Regina" in Volume 2 also appears a product of Norris's university days.

[24]Forty-four of Norris's themes are collected in *A Novelist in the Making*, ed. James D. Hart (Cambridge, Mass.: The Belknap Press of Harvard University Press, 1970). See pp. 87-88 for the initial appearance of Norris's plumber-hero. One other theme was subsequently found by Jesse S. Crisler, and the holograph has been published in facsimile: *A Student Theme by Frank Norris*, introduced by James D. Hart (Berkeley, Calif.: The Frank Norris Society, 1987).

[25]*Frank Norris: A Biography* (Garden City, N. Y.: Doubleday, Doran and Co., 1932). For a collection of memoirs and eulogies concerning Norris, see Joseph R. McElrath, Jr., "Frank Norris: Early Posthumous Responses," *American Literary Realism*, 12 (Spring 1979), 1-76.

From the Christmas, 1894, issue of The Wave.
Courtesy of the California State Library, Sacramento.

THE APPRENTICESHIP WRITINGS
OF
FRANK NORRIS

1896—1897

Rhodes and the Reporters

The Wave, 15 (11 April 1896), 5.

I think all of us—that is to say, all of the fourteen first cabin passengers aboard the *Moor* on her homeward voyage—rose a bit in our own estimations when we found out that the Honorable Cecil Rhodes (the Colossus of Rhodes, as South Africa calls him) was to be our fellow passenger for the next two weeks. I am sure the other thirteen have gone their thirteen different ways and have told their thirteen different stories as to their intimacy with the great man during that long voyage. Somewhere upon the face of the globe you will find thirteen different versions of the matter. This is the fourteenth.

If you should ever meet with one of the *Moor's* passengers of that trip, and he should tell you that it was true he had made the voyage with the Honorable Cecil, and that he had become acquainted with him, and that they had talked together, don't believe him. It is not true that he talked with Mr. Rhodes, or did any more than look at him very humbly and at a respectful distance. Mr. Rhodes talked to the table steward when he ordered his meals, presumably he talked to his secretary, and once I heard him say "Good-morning" to the Captain of the ship. But I am sure that was all.

He boarded us after the *Moor* had left the docks at Cape Town and had anchored out in the stream, and he left us at Plymouth early in the morning in a very gay little steam-yacht, all white paint and nickel railings. Between the two ends of the voyage he walked up and down the decks, or leaned over the side, or read a very great deal in a red book called *The Sorrows of Satan*. But he kept his own counsel and never talked or laughed or descended to anything like familiarity.

Of course, the extraordinary news that he was on his way to England was wired all over the world, and when the ship called at Madeira the reporters and correspondents took us, as it were, by assault. They foregathered in the smoking-room and glowered at one another and began asking us all manner of questions. Most of them were English but one was an Anglicized

American, who said he represented a syndicate. We told this one that Mr. Rhodes was not to be approached and that he would not raise a line of "stuff" out of him. He wanted to bet us that he would, and offered great odds and talked very large. Of all the reporters who had stormed the ship, I suppose he was the most "enterprising." But afterward we were all sorry we had not taken him at his word and made a bet with him. I do not believe he even saw Cecil Rhodes. The great man took himself off to his stateroom at once and was either very sick or pretended that he was. None of us ever saw him after leaving Madeira and I am sure the reporters did not. They would congregate about the passageway that led to Mr. Rhodes' stateroom, peeping and peering, very alert and "enterprising," but they had their trouble for nothing. Rhodes did not even come out for his meals but had them brought to his room by the steward.

They would send their cards to him or notes or verbal messages, and for answer would be referred to the secretary, a fearful looking fellow who was monosyllabic and impolite and who swore at them like any troop-sergeant.

Finally, they gave it up, even the Anglicized American who was "enterprising," and who had talked so large. And then, by common consent, they fell upon Captain Thatcher.

Poor Thatcher! I can see him now, with his red face and awkward gestures, relating the story of the raid for the hundredth time, horribly bored, repeating the same expressions over and over again. He had been with Jameson from Pitsani to Krugersdorp, but he never knew his misfortune until the reporter fell foul of him. He had told his story some twenty or thirty times in Johannesburg, as often again in Cape Town, and fully twice as often aboard ship, always winding up with the same account of how he had besought Mr. Leonard of the Johannesburg Reform Committee for five hundred men to make a dash for Pretoria, and of how Mr. Leonard had replied that he could not give him fifty.

It was considered an amusement aboard ship to listen at the windows of the smoking-room while the miserable Thatcher was once more grinding out his tale. We would call one another to listen to him in his travail, and would hurry to the round ports of the smoking-room, on tiptoe, waiting patiently for the invariable climax which never failed of effect.

"And," Thatcher would say, "I said to Leonard—'for God's sake, give me five hundred men and *I'll* make a dash for Pretoria and give 'um what for!'

And he says to me—'My dear Thatcher' (here he would make the queerest, most awkward gestures with both arms, his fists closed tight), 'My dear Thatcher, I can't give you *fifty*.'"

This was funny. Somehow it always sent us into spasms of laughter, and we would tiptoe away, shaking our fists awkwardly, and exclaiming, "He says to me, 'My dear Thatcher, I can't give you *fifty*.'"

Bandy Callaghan's Girl

The Wave, 15 (18 April 1896), 4-5.

This story is about a certain street-car conductor named Bandy Callaghan. It all happened because of a Chinaman, who once rode on Bandy's car and in some way managed to cheat him out of five dollars. Bandy had to make good the amount at the "Old Man's" office, but he remembered that his Chinaman was marked with leprosy in a peculiar way, and so filled a piece of rubber hose with sand and hid it in the lamp-box against the possibility of meeting him again.

Some time after this Bandy got the receiver of his bell-punch plugged with punch-wads, and took it down to a gunsmith's on Kearny Street not far from the old Plaza to have it cleaned. As he could not call for it until he was off duty, about midnight, he arranged to have the gunsmith leave it at a neighboring saloon. When it was finished Bandy called for it there and started home, taking a short cut through Chinatown. According to his system of reckoning it was 12:27, for, if you will notice, a conductor always tells you the time with great exactness as to the minutes.

On the corner of Washington and Dupont, under a lamp-post, he caromed against a Chinese with traces of leprosy across his nose and eyes like a pair of spectacles. Bandy grabbed him at once by the slack of his blouse.

"Gi' me my five dollars," he said, breathing through his nose. "I knew I'd find you again some day."

The Chinaman wrenched back from him and his lip drew tight across his teeth.

"Wha's maär 'you?" he snarled. "I no sabe you. Wha's you want, you?"

"I want my five dollars," answered Bandy, taking a fresh hold, "an' I want it quick."

"Wha's maär 'you?" repeated the other angrily, "I no sabe you fi' dollar. Wha's maär 'you?" and he called Bandy a bad name which is the first English expression that a Chinaman learns. Bandy had his arm crooked to strike, when the coolie slipped away from him like a lizard and fled up Dupont Street toward Jackson; Bandy reached after him, missed him, and then gave chase.

Now, it is not good to try to run down a Chinaman in Chinatown at night, and none but a detective who has made the quarter a study would ever attempt it. In the first place you are not likely to catch your man, and in the second you are very likely to get into trouble. Bandy, because he did not know the rules of the game in Chinatown and because he was very close to the thief and because he was bent upon getting back his five dollars, closed in upon the coolie's tracks, followed around the corner of Jackson Street, and as he dodged down a miserable alley a few doors above Dupont, turned in after him, scarcely three yards behind.

Bandy's man dived into a door that looked like the entrance to a tan-room and slammed it behind him, but Bandy's foot was already between the door and the jamb, he flung the door open again and continued the pursuit down the corridor that ended at the head of a long flight of narrow stairs leading down into inky obscurity. It seemed like wilful self-destruction to go on now, but five dollars are five dollars when you get them by hourly instalments of twenty-two cents, and besides Bandy was so close to the fleeing coolie that he thought to overtake him at every step.

More stairways and galleries, passageways so low that Bandy had to bow his head to proceed, so narrow that at times he was obliged to advance sideways. Then he paused, panting for breath in the fetid reek of the underground atmosphere. He had lost his coolie, and now was lost himself.

Then all in a moment he grew thoroughly frightened and desperate; he plunged back through the maze of passages that were like tunnels in a mine, with his arms outstretched and with the readiness to fight a death-fight with any one who opposed him. In the darkness he stumbled down a pair of steps and fell against a green-painted door, with an iron-latticed hole near its top. The door was unfastened, and yielded as he struck it. He pitched forward into a very small and dimly lighted room, but sprang up in an instant looking about, his teeth and fists shut tight.

The room was a little larger than an ocean-liner's stateroom, and like a stateroom was surrounded on three sides by tiers of bunks. Besides these, there were two mattresses on the floor, and on a very low teak-wood table in the middle of the room were an American student's lamp, with a green shade, and a tray full of pipes. The whole place was full of a pungent blue haze of smoke. There were three Chinamen asleep in as many of the bunks, and on one of the mattresses a fourth was "coiled," half stupefied and lazily smoking. Bandy had stumbled into an opium den in full blast.

The sleepers awoke and bundled themselves out upon the floor, and he on the mattress reached out for the lamp. Bandy kicked his hand away and drew the lamp toward him. They all crowded together in one corner, blinking and chattering; one of them cried out to him and said: "You no take-um lock-up; find-um boss, take-um boss, we no sabe, you go find boss, all same take-um boss."

Bandy was puzzled; they evidently thought that this was a raid, and that he was a policeman, but why? Ah! exactly, he knew now; his conductor's uniform with its blue cloth and brass buttons; he was thinking very fast and felt that he must act on every thought; he could not afford to hesitate, letting them have time to discover their mistake, he was sure that he was master of the situation and his fear and excitement began to subside.

"Here you," he said, addressing the one who spoke, "I want *you*, come outside into the street with me, go on first and I'll follow you." He had thought by this means to regain the street without letting them know that he was lost and was about to follow the coolie, who had gone out before him, when he stopped short with an exclamation.

His first thought had been that it was another Chinaman, too far gone to wake up with the others. His next, (induced by the sight of a quantity of black hair tumbled about upon the pillow) was that a Chinese woman had found her way to the den and lay there on the mattress drugged and inert. But now the figure stirred, breathed heavily, and threw a bare arm free of the blankets. Bandy shrank back with an oath as he saw that the arm was

5

white.

The horror and cruelty of the thing for a moment turned him cold, and then all his excitement came over him again like a hot wave. He was persuaded the coolies were afraid of him. "Here's what I wanted," he cried; "come back here. This girl's got to go out with me."

They were silent for a moment and then they all rushed together, chattering angrily and stood between him and the door. Without knowing how it had been done, Bandy found that he had wrapped the girl in the blankets. Now he stood and faced them, with one arm supporting her as she leaned limply against him.

Bandy was a young man of limited education and highly colored imagination, apt to take things that happened to him as though they were the scenes of a drama in which he was at once the actor, the author, and the audience. Through all his hurry and excitement he found occasion to appreciate the drama of the present situation and felt heroic at once. It stood him in good stead. He was unwilling to back down now lest it should destroy the effect. With a quickness of eye that was born of the occasion he saw one of the coolies groping toward something on the ground near his feet. Looking down he saw that it was his nickel-plated bell-punch, fallen from his pocket during the moment he was upon the floor, at the same time he knew that the coolie had mistaken it for something else; he did not undeceive him but snatched it up and aimed it at them, shouting:

"It's a forty-eight and it's loaded to the muzzle, damn you all, stand out of the way." They fell back before him and he blundered out into the narrow passage carrying the girl with him.

Behind him he heard the sound of a shrill whistle, and shriller voices calling to each other up and down the tortuous stairways. He went on through the foul murk in a frenzy of excitement speaking all his thoughts aloud, as was his custom when aroused, ignorant of where he was going, and possessed of only one desire—to get above ground again and breathe the clear night air.

And then all his courage and resolution suddenly dwindled away and left him cold and shaking with fear. He knew that he was only a car conductor after all, and had neither the blind recklessness of the tough nor the reasoned obstinacy of the thoroughbred. With every minute of continued suspense he began to think less of the girl and more of himself. The idea of being set upon by Chinamen in that narrow tunnel, like a rat in its hole, filled him with terror, and he raised his voice in a quavering shout for help. He paused a moment and listened; a rising clamor in the gloom behind him prolonged the echo of his cry, while in front of him he heard the noise of feet descending a flight of invisible stairs. It seemed as though he were trapped. The strain of waiting there in the dark for the blow to fall was more than he was made to bear, so letting the girl slip from his grasp, he started forward with another shout and ran with outstretched arms against the blue-coated figure of a policeman upon the stairs in front of him.

At sight of the white face and at sound of the bass voice growling, "What was the matter down here *this* time?" Bandy's nerves snapped like a tense harp string, and he burst into weak tears, partly of pure nervousness, partly of joy at his release, partly of shame at his own cowardice, and partly because he had not been able to sustain the heroic role he had assumed.

Five minutes later he was much calmer, and in company with the girl, who was still unconscious, was being driven to the precinct station house in the patrol wagon.

*   *   *   *   *   *   *

Bandy had a "girl" whose name was Miss McCleaverty, and who ran the soda water fountain in a candy store on Polk Street. Miss McCleaverty wore very blonde hair, and imitation alligator skin belts. She exhaled alternate odors of sachet and chocolate caramels, and she knew how to play *My Lady's Bower* and *The Liberty Bell March* on the piano. Bandy thought her radiantly beautiful and divinely gifted.

The next time that Bandy went to see Miss McCleaverty, he told her all about it and was puzzled at her lack of enthusiasm and interest in the matter. She did not seem to care much about the thrilling details, and spoke carelessly of the girl as "this woman," which made him wince. But he finally got her promise to go with him and see the girl at the "Home."

At the "Home" it was quite different, however. As soon as she saw the forlorn little creature, Miss McCleaverty warmed toward her in a way that filled Bandy's simple heart with joy. She sat with her arm around her a long time, got her to talk a little, and left her with the assurance that she would come and see her again as soon as she could.

By the time Bandy saw Miss McCleaverty again she had been out to the "Home" twice, and had found out more about the Girl. "I guess she's Mexican-Spanish," she said to Bandy, "'n it ain't altogether her fault that she's what she is; of course she won't tell me everything, but she's got people in San Diego; 'n there was a fellow—I don't know—'n they ran away together, 'n he didn't do right by her. He left her after awhile, 'n then, well, she met a woman, 'n you know she's awfully young 'n ain't onto herself a little bit, 'n the woman did worse by her than the fellow, 'n she just went all to pieces. But you just bet I'm going to stand right by her 'n get her back to her folks, all right, all right."

"You didn't seem to be stuck on her much at first," observed Bandy.

"Well, I know," assented Miss McCleaverty, vaguely. "But she ain't got a friend in the whole city, 'n she ain't a bit bad, just kinda weak 'n inexperienced, you know. She's just awfully sorry about everything, 'n I mean to help her get set straight again. I tell you what," she went on, "that Home ain't a very nice place for her, b'cause she ain't one of that kind. My aunt was in the store yesterday, 'n I told her all about it, 'n she felt just as I did. She's going to let her come to stay with her until we get word from her folks. She lives way out on Geary Street, you know; she's all alone, 'n it's kinda lonesome like, anyhow."

"Well, say, that's pretty nice," said Bandy, "and it's just awfully good of you. Say, did she ever say anything about me?"

"No," answered Miss McCleaverty. "I guess she's got too many other things to think about."

"She's mighty pretty, don't you think?"

Miss McCleaverty shifted her gum to the other side of her mouth. "I wouldn't call her pretty at all," she responded.

Some time after this Bandy awoke to the fact that he had been visiting at the house on Geary Street as often as he could, and that after one of these visits he spent most of his time in looking forward to the next one. There was little enough that he had in common with the Girl, and heaven knows what they talked about. He thought that he had liked Miss McCleaverty more than any one else, but now he began to see that he had never known what it really meant to care for some one.

"This must be what it is," he said, "when people fall in love."

He felt mortified, too, over the fact that he was unfaithful to Miss

McCleaverty, who had been so kind to him.

"She ain't done anything," he observed, to himself, "but I just can't help it."

It came to be tacitly felt between himself and the Girl that Miss McCleaverty should know nothing of his visits, and this mutual understanding seemed in a way to draw them closer together. He began to perceive as well that the Girl was commencing to care for him, but this troubled him as much as it rejoiced him, for he felt that they were not fated for each other, and that no good could come of it all. Meanwhile Miss McCleaverty saw nothing, but continued to do all that she could for her. After a while she succeeded in getting her to tell her all about her parents and had written to them at San Diego; but Bandy could scarcely bear to look Miss McCleaverty in the face.

How the Girl had come into the opium den underneath the tan-shop in St. Louis Place Bandy never knew. It was more than likely she did not know herself, though he was sure she had not been there often. They never spoke of that night between themselves, and Bandy often wondered if she knew what part he had taken in the business.

The house, which was the Girl's temporary home, was far out on Geary Street, and close under Lone Mountain. Late one afternoon, when their acquaintance was three weeks old, Bandy went out there again as he had done so many times already. As he rang the bell, a woman in the adjoining house, who was watering some geraniums at her open window, called to him, saying:

"Mrs. Flint (this was Miss McCleaverty's aunt) told me as how I was to tell you if you called, that she had gone out and wouldn't be home till late this evening, but the young lady's at home; I guess you can walk right in."

The house was a small one and all on one floor, and Bandy shut the front door sharply behind him, so that the noise might announce his coming. He went into the little front sitting-room and moved about uncertainly, waiting till the Girl should come in. The house was so small that she could not help hearing him. He waited some few minutes, touching the keys of the cheap piano and whistling softly. Then, after a few moments' hesitation, he returned to the entry and called. There was no answer, and he turned back to the sitting-room, assured that she was not in the house. But the next moment he was persuaded of the improbability of this; she never went out under any circumstances, having an unreasonable dread of being seen a-broad. Yet in the bare possibility of her having stirred out of doors for once, he sat down and waited for upwards of half an hour.

At the end of this time he jumped up impatiently; it was growing dark, and he was positive she would not have stayed out so long, even if she had gone out at all.

"Can't be," he muttered; "she must be at home." For a second time he went out into the hall and called loud and long, with only latent echoes for response. Her room was at the end of the hall and he could see her door from where he stood. He went up to it and knocked, and then, receiving no answer, tried the knob. The door was locked. "This is getting queerer and queerer," he said, but he was uneasy as he spoke the words. As he turned away perplexed and hesitating, the noise of running water caught his ear; it came from within the room, and was as the noise of water running from the faucet of a stationary wash-stand. Not knowing what to think, he took a couple of turns up and down the hallway, his hands thrust deep in his pockets and his eyebrows knotted in a puzzled frown. The noise of the trickling stream followed him back and forth. It was the only sound throughout the house. "It sounds leery," he said to himself.

Returning to the door, he pulled out his bunch of keys from his pocket and tried one of them in the lock, and drew back in astonishment. The key was on the inside.

"This is funny, too," he muttered, more and more uneasy. "There's no other way out of the room, and how could any one go off and leave that water running, and lock the door from the inside?"

He started up suddenly and looked about him, bewildered and excited, drawing his breath quickly.

"Say, there's something wrong; I've got to get into that room."

He worried the key in the door loose with the butt of his pencil, and pushed it till it fell from the lock on the inside of the room. Before he tried again to fit one of his own keys to the lock, he bent down and peered through the keyhole. Then, as he did so, his heart jumped to his throat with a great bound, and stuck there quivering, and he sprang up, beating his hands together, crying out again and again. He had seen nothing in the room, but through the narrow vent of the keyhole was streaming a strangling odor of escaping gas.

For a moment in a frenzy of alarm and excitement he ran back in the front of the house, biting at the ends of his fingers and talking aloud to himself. A pair of disused Indian-clubs stood in one corner of the sitting-room. He caught up one of these and running back to the room splintered the door into long fragments in half a dozen blows.

Inside it was like breathing a vaporous brass, the poisoned air closed around him, and filled his lungs and breast and throat till it seemed as though he must suffocate before he could even reach the window on the other side of the room. It was partly open; he flung it higher still, and turned to the interior of the room. But though there was evidence that she had been there but recently, it was now empty.

He shut off the water and the escaping gas, and sat down on the window ledge, bewildered, and gasping for air. Where could the girl have gone? What was the meaning of it all? He glanced around the room for an explanation. His eyes rested on a little table at the bed-side and on it he saw something that explained it all: a little silver pipe and a half-empty package of unboiled opium. That was it, then: unwittingly, she had contracted the dreadful habit, had struggled against it, no doubt, since her rescue, and had succumbed to it at last, had turned on the gas, perhaps accidentally, in the course of her stupor, perhaps with design in a moment of remorse and grief and conscious helplessness, and then drugged by the poisonous fumes and equally poisonous smoke had wandered away into the night. How? Through the window. It was not four feet above the level of the ground; and swinging himself out Bandy saw the print of her feet in the soil.

And where now had she gone? What might not happen to her in her helpless condition?

Lone Mountain is one of the most conspicuous landmarks in the city, because it rises very abruptly and very steeply from the surrounding streets and because there are no other hills or tall buildings near by to obscure it. Being thus steep and abrupt there are no houses upon it and no streets, nothing but goat-paths and scrubby brushes, all covered with the red dust of the streets which the trade-winds blow there. There is a great wooden cross upon the top. It was a pretty idea to place it there, because you may see the mountain from almost anywhere in the city, and the cross upon it stands there in its simple isolation, sometimes clear-cut and black against the sun going redly down through the Golden Gate, sometimes blurred and indistinct in the rains and in the fogs, or sometimes silvery with great black shadows in the moon-light; but always there, looking far out over the city, its great arms stretched wide as though in protection and benison.

The house stood at the very foot of the mountain, and Bandy had not taken half a dozen steps into the night—for it was quite dark by this time—before he felt the slope rise under his feet.

By a sudden unreasoned instinct he knew where the Girl had gone, and ran scrambling and panting up the side and paused on the summit.

Below him, the city shrank away and spread out like an unrolled scroll, a blue-gray mass, pierced with many chimney-stacks, that were like the pipes of a great organ, on the unseen keys of which were forever sounded all the notes in the gamut of human happiness and human misery, that united in a single minor chord and rolled upward day and night toward the great and moveless cross with its outstretched arms.

The Girl was lying in the shadow of the cross, her hands reaching toward it and spread out before her, and her face bowed upon the ground. She must have died where she had fallen.

Bandy saw her as she lay thus, far above the turmoil and dirt of the city's streets and in a better air—one that was purer and calmer. She seemed, as she lay, to be quieter and more content than ever before. Above her towered the great cross with its outstretched arms of protection and benison.

Bandy told this story to me some time afterward, when its impressiveness had worn off and he could bear to talk about it. When he had finished telling it, he extended his remarks in comment:

"I don't know," he said, reflectively, "I thought a good deal of that girl at the time, and I guess I made an awful fool of myself over her. And when she died, oh, you don't know—it hurt. I tell you it hurt *bad*. I thought that I just naturally never *would* get over it. But I did get over it, you see. Oh yes, I got over it, but just the same there is always something—when I think of it, somehow it makes my throat ache. It's funny, ain't it?"

"But," said I, "where do *you* come in? What was there in it for *you*? What have *you* got left out of it?"

"Oh!" answered Bandy, "I got Miss McCleaverty."

SAN FRANCISCO, May 30, 1894.

12

Tales of the Day

The Wave, 15 (18 April 1896), 16, paragraph 5.

Speaking of South African affairs puts us in mind of a rather good story on Cecil Rhodes, the multi-millionaire and ex-Premier of the Colony. On his return journey to England recently, Mr. Rhodes was detained by the break down of his steamer, the *Moor*, which was obliged to put in to Dakar, on the Senegal coast. Mr. Rhodes went ashore with a boat load of passengers, and while strolling through the one street of the town was offered a beautiful rug—or it might have been a bed quilt—made of bird skins by a native who asked twelve shillings in return. Mr. Rhodes was delighted with the skins, but was unwilling to pay more than ten shillings. For fully ten minutes he chaffered and haggled over the matter, and finally went his way without making the purchase. He was many times a millionaire, and controlled the output of the De Beers diamond mine, but would not pay two shillings more than what he thought the rug to be worth.

A Steamship Voyage with Cecil Rhodes

Two Sides of the Cape Towner's Character——
Wonderful Skies and Seas in the Tropics

San Francisco Chronicle, 19 April 1896, 15

When the *Moor* left Cape Town with an empty hold and fourteen first-cabin passengers, she ran out say a quarter of a mile into Table bay and let go her anchor in the shadow of Table mountain. It was exasperating. There seemed no reason for delay, and yet for two, three, five hours she rolled and rolled in the long ground swell, while a cutting south wind, horribly out of place in an African harbor, made a long, unpleasant noise in the higher rigging. Then, at last, a little white steam packet of perhaps 200 tons made out toward her, and began to go around and around the ship, the whole fourteen of us following her course from one rail to another. There was a vague feeling among us that something unusual was going to happen, and the first officer stood by the charthouse in full dress and scowled at us in a very important and severe way. I cannot remember now how we first found out who was the great man who was coming out to us in the little white boat. But so it did come about that all of a sudden we were asking each other if it might be Cecil Rhodes, and if he was going back to England with us.

After that we all hung over the side of the rail and trained our glasses on the little white boat, and by and by the captain's "clark," who was not in full dress nor at all severe, and whom we afterward learned to call "The Scrub," exclaimed, "That's him," and shamelessly pointed out a huge red-faced man sitting in the stern with a hat in each hand and none on his head. That was Cecil Rhodes and I am sure we felt a thrill, or as Conan Doyle says, "pringly" at this first sight of the great statesman who had juggled with such vast fortunes, controlled such immense territories, who planned such great enterprises and who was responsible for so much disaster, so many ruined hopes and the lives of so many brave men whose bodies were not yet cold in the shallow trenches that furrowed the *kopses* and *kloofs* of Doornkop and Krugersdorp. We took him on board, this Caesar and his fortunes, and the *Moor* swung clear and headed to the north, plowing her way up the curve of the globe for twenty-one days.

When you hear people exclaim over the splendors of the tropic ocean or see them written about either in Robert Louis Stevenson's novels or in the guide books of the Peninsular and Oriental or Castle steamship companies, believe all that you hear and see and try to believe a great deal more. If you do this you will get an approximate idea of what can be done in the way of scenic effect south of the equator. But it is hard to imagine these waters without having passed through them.

You have heard of an ocean as smooth as glass, for instance, but have you any idea what such a sight really is? I remember having seen one thing that could approach it, and that was the floor of a certain basilica outside the walls of Rome (a certain San Paolo, if I remember right), a mosaic floor, polished and repolished till the great rose windows flashed from it as though from a mirror. We were given felt shoes that we might step out upon this floor, and we did so with trepidation and with reverence, while underneath us grew out myriads of very strange flowers, and arabesques and curious tracings that were as the weavings of many spiders. You must imagine a floor such as this stretching out from you on all sides forever and forever reflecting a sky filled at noon with the light of a vertical sun, and at morning and evening with all manner of red and pink and purple clouds. And very often the light of the sun in the sky and the flashing of his reflection in this wonderful sea would shimmer together at the star line and mingle and be as one, and the rim of the horizon would disappear and there would be no more sea nor any more sky, just a vast illimitable space, a vague, empty shimmer of light and air, a sort of glittering nirvana, through which you were floating, sustained by nothing and going nowhere. Everything else slipped from you. There was no longer sense of motion, or stability or anything that was of the earth. Nothing but yourself alone and looking out into this vast empty space full of light and air and glittering mist.

As we drew toward the equator the weather became warmer and the ship was covered with awnings from end to end. The officers wore white duck and the nine of us in the first cabin who were men took to tennis flannels and lemon squashes. At last sleeping below was out of the question. At night the cabin stewards would bring our beds upon the deck and make them up on the gratings of the hatchways, and here we would pass the nights, the long dark blue nights of the tropics, sometimes sleeping as the throbbing of the engines and the ripple of the water under the ship's fore-foot made us drowsy, but as often talking for hours over coffee and cigarettes until the sky began to whiten and the crew came to sluice down the decks, making it known that the day was breaking and that it was time for baths and breakfast.

These were days and nights to be remembered. It is just possible that I have exaggerated, or that I have remembered only their most perfect moments or that, just from Johannesburg stewing in the dust and smoke of abortive insurrection, ringing with the clamor of angry men, with memories of fever and bad food and drenching rains fresh in mind, they may have gained by contrast and appeared as it were in the glamour of a reflected light. At any rate they seemed very beautiful and it would be unfair to speak of them except from the point of view of a personal impression.

The Honorable Cecil kept much to himself, or rather to the party with which he was pleased to travel. This party was composed for the most part of Rhodes himself. The other members were a man named Beit—a multi-millionaire of Kimberley with abnormally short arms—his son, who played poker all day long, his secretary, two other featureless men and a young woman whom we outsiders called the "Startled Fawn" (why, I never found out), and who was too pretty to be really virtuous. The party did not count for much, as men and women go. Rhodes, I remember as a large red-faced man with a long thin nose and a short colorless mustache. Somehow I invariably recall him in the same position, leaning over the side, his arms folded and resting on the rail, looking vaguely out at the smooth, oily sea. He was always meanly dressed. All through the voyage he wore a pair of old leather slippers, a gray felt hat with no binding about the brim and a flannel shirt clumsily tied at the throat with a thin white necktie of pongee silk. On two different occasions during the voyage the character of the man revealed itself a little.

Almost mathematically on the equator the *Moor* broke down. I don't know what was the matter; passengers never do. Rhodes was in a hurry to reach England, and the company overdrove the ship under protest of the chief engineer. For eight days she made good time. About 10 o'clock on the morning of the 9th her engines stopped, and we lay inert for twenty-six hours. Then from most of the men passengers aboard a great cry went up, a cry of exasperation and complaint, each one declaring that he had most important business in England or Europe that would be jeopardized by this one day's delay. Little indignation meetings were held in the smoking-room or in the shadow of the wheelhouse, and very sarcastic remarks were made across the table at meals for the benefit of the miserable chief engineer who presided, and I believe they even went so far as to circulate a petition which was addressed to the captain with the sole intention of making him uncomfortable. The malcontents were chiefly diamond and gold brokers from Kimberley and Johannesburg, and it is just possible that the breaking down of the ship at that time would make them lose $50 or $100 apiece.

One should have seen the important airs they assumed and how they fumed and chafed and fretted. As for Rhodes, who probably had more at stake than any of us could imagine, and about whom the fortunes of an empire were centered, who had more to lose than the whole Union Steamship Company was worth, as for him he went a-fishing. The ship hadn't stopped for more than an hour before we saw the great dorsal fin of a shark riding slowly above the water near the ship and could make out the huge green and white body moving about close beneath the surface of the water. Ten minutes after that Cecil Rhodes had a shark hook out over the stern and was as intent upon the game as if there never had been any Reform Committee nor any insurrections or battles at Krugersdorp.

One should have seen him when the first shark struck and the barb went home, and the water under the stern of the ship was churned and lathered as though the screw had at length made up its mind to revolve. The honorable Cecil's hat was off, and his eyes were alight with the excitement of the thing, and the hands that guided empires were gripped over the taut, singing rope till the knuckles whitened, while his big, muscular body swayed and twitched and jerked with every struggle of the enormous maneater that fought him for the life he loved and measured his strength against that of the ex-Premier of South Africa.

It was a fine thing to see, and I would always like to remember Rhodes as he appeared at that time. Unfortunately I saw him in another scene a few days later, where another side of the man's character betrayed itself. The *Moor* broke down so often that our skipper was obliged to put in to the Senegal coast to a little port called Dakar. Of course, we all took this opportunity of going ashore, and Rhodes went along, too. Just as we were leaving the jetty to return to the ship, a native—a naked Senegali—came down to the boat offering for sale a sort of rug or counterpane made from the white breasts of some kind of crane or water fowl. It was a very lovely thing and the Senegali would have sold it for 12 shillings. I think the honorable Cecil really wanted the rug, or whatever it was, but he would only offer the Senegali 10 shillings. The great statesman and the naked savage chaffered and haggled over this through the interpreter for over ten minutes, while we sat back in the boat and waited to see what would come of the strange meeting.

What did happen struck us dumb with astonishment. Rhodes refused to come up to the Senegali's figure, and went away and left the rug for some other buyer. Think of the strangeness of that. Cecil Rhodes, two-thirds owner of the great De Beers diamond mine, practical controller of the gold output of the entire Rand, chief of the enormous Chartered Company and director of the vast tracts of Matabeleland, Mashonalands, six or seven times a millionaire, and yet refusing to pay that difference of 2 shillings! A strange man surely.

A Salvation Boom in Matabeleland

The Wave, 15 (25 April 1896), 5.

I think the story should be set down in this place because it is curious and worth its ink, and because it shows what strange manner of men are the Matabele—the music-mad, magnificent, brave, unspeakably cruel Matabele.

Ingodusi, who first told it, was an *induna* in Lobengula's pet regiment or *impi*, which afterward came to be the great *Imbezzu impi*. Since the tale is from such high authority, I think it must be true. Ingodusi is a ring-man and a head *induna*, and can have more than one wife, and can speak his thoughts aloud in the king's *indaba*.

It happened when Ingodusi was nineteen years old and was undergoing *Mahunda* with about a hundred other young Matabele, away up in the heart of Matabeleland, somewhere between Inyungo and the Umfuli River.

By some fearful mischance, at the very height of the *Mahunda indaba*, Otto Marks trekked full upon it. But the matter must be told from Otto's point of view.

Otto was a sergeant in the Salvation Army. He came from Toledo, Ohio, to Mafeking in Bechuanaland, which is as far north as the railroad goes. Otto used to play the little organ every evening at the gatherings in the Salvation barracks at Mafeking until his superior officer decided to boom salvation in that mysterious wilderness of South Africa known indiscriminately as "Up country," or Charter-land, or Rhodesia, or Matabeleland.

Otto Marks started up in April before the rains were done, with a transport-rider named West and a little nigger *voorlooper*, a ten-year old Zulu boy.

Eighteen bullocks were spanned to their wagon; but their load was made up chiefly of two Estey parlor organs from Boston that were to help out-fit the barracks in some up-country settlement.

That was a strange sight—the eighteen lean Basuto bullocks, very slow-paced, led by the little Zulu *voorlooper* and the big, strange Transvaal wagon loaded only with these two boxed-up organs, the name of the Boston firm stenciled on the outside of the boards.

For two months Otto trekked steadily northward, singing hymns upon occasion, and on Sundays spanning out all day long. At times he tried to revive the spirit of righteousness in his transport-rider, West, who blasphemed the bullocks hourly in more ways than you would believe possible, and at times he would try to convert the little *voorlooper*. The little Zulu was stunned and bewildered by Otto Marks' clamor, but Otto's swinging revival songs with their tambourine accompaniment sent him into a frenzy of delight, and he would invariably set to dancing, shaking his fists with vague and furious gestures.

After two months they were stopped by the Umnyati River, which was in flood, and were obliged to make a long cross-country detour, with the line of telegraph poles as their guide.

The huge wagon lurched down into the bed of the slue, ploughed across through the scattered boulders, and took the rising slope of the opposite bank with the heave and crash of a stranding galley. West lashed at the wheel bullocks with the *sjambok* of rhinoceros hide, and then swore in Bechuana at the little *voorlooper* because he was not prodding on the lead bullocks, but was standing motionless at the head of the span, his hands dangling at his sides, staring stupidly across the bush. He was dumb with terror. The wagon slipped backward into the bed of the slue, and the bullocks fell into confusion as the *voorlooper* came running back along the span, waving his arms wildly.

As was said before, Otto Marks had trekked full upon an *impi* of Matabele, doing *Mahunda*, and when that happens to a white man he were best to do himself to death as swiftly as he may. For a swift death, even if it be the kind that lies in the crook of one's forefinger, is better than the kind that comes slowly and in the midst of thick smoke, and screams and horrid twistings of the body. But Otto did not know this, and West, who should have known it, chose to think that they might even then escape. Otto climbed down from the wagon and he and West ran up the bank of the slue and looked out far across the bush and saw the Matabele coming down on them slowly, in two long lines. But West observed that they advanced with a regular cadenced movement and that many of them staggered in the ranks, sometimes reeling almost to the ground.

"Drunk!" he exclaimed. "Drunk with Cape-Smoke; blind drunk and dancing. I've seen these niggers before, we may get off, but oh, it's a *chance*. Pray your God for a miracle now, Otto Marks, for there's little short of it going to get us clear of here. Drunk and dancing," he repeated; "yes, it's our only chance. Quick now, off with the case of that melodeon."

Otto obeyed, at first stupidly and benumbed with fear, then, as West's crazy expedient flashed upon him, with an excess of frenzy tearing wildly at the stubborn boards, prying them up with his hunting-knife, wrenching them away with a strength that was born of the moment.

Meanwhile, West had started the bullocks again and the wagon was pulled up from the bed of the slue and rolled out through the bush, heading directly toward the line of dancing natives.

"They're close in," shouted West in a few moments. Otto raised his head from his work and saw that it was so. Then the last boards fell away and the little American organ stood out under the African sun, shining bravely with veneer and scroll-work and celluloid.

"Play," cried West again. "For God's sake, play, play *anything*. They'll dance so long as you can keep it up." And Otto Marks flung himself at the instrument and dashed his hands upon the keys just as the rush came, and the green bush was shut from view by the scores of crowding brown bodies, glistening with sweat and all a-jingle with beads and wire-work.

Otto was hiccoughing with terror but he stuck to his work, playing away at the only kind of music he knew, the Moody and Sankey Gospel hymns that he had learned in Toledo, Ohio, and that he had found effective in the Salvation Barracks at Cape Town, and at Mafeking.

Then that strange procession began. The eighteen bullocks, headed by the little *voorlooper*, gray with fear; West, his face set rigidly to the front, walking by the wheel-bullocks; the creaking wagon following, and upon it

Otto Marks toiling at the melodeon, playing Gospel hymns for the life he loved, while close pressed about them all, hemming them in on every side, the hundreds of naked Matabele, shaking their bull's hide shields and tossing their *assegais* and *kirris* high in the air.

Music-mad, as only the Zulu race can be, their minds all exalted and distorted by the self-imposed tortures of the *Mahunda* rites, dizzied and confused by the drunkenness of the Cape-Smoke, Otto's music caught them and held them and they danced and danced as though they would never tire, dazed and bewildered, working themselves into a fury, leaping and shouting aloud without knowing why.

Otto Marks struck into a fresh hymn with a veritable frenzy. The excitement and the strangeness of the thing was beginning to tell upon him as well. No barrack gathering had ever aroused such enthusiasm as this. By now he had come to

> Pull for the *shore*, sailor,
> *Pull* for the shore,
> *Heed* not the *raging* waves
> Though *loudly* they roar.

And after this without a moment's pause he dashed into

> I am so glad that Jesus loves me.

When that was done he dug his fingers into the celluloid keys again, kneading them with all the strength of his two arms, swaying from side to side, and while his feet threshed out the rhythm upon the pedals, played:

> Hallelujah 'tis done
> I believe in the Son.

Suddenly the Matabele began to sing, catching up the tunes with the quickness and facility of savages, singing to the airs of these Gospel hymns the words of the war-song of Moselekatse, the chant of the Black Bull:

> *Yaing-g'labi*
> *Leyo n'kunze*
> *Yai ukufa.*

Then at last the tension broke. The thing was more than Mr. Otto Marks of Toledo, Ohio, was made to bear. All at once his nerves crisped and recoiled like the broken ends of an over-strained harp-string, and he leaped into the air, suddenly seized with hysteria, shrieking and laughing and banging his fists upon the keys.

With the cessation of the music the spell was broken, the droning chant stopped in a medley of discords and the dancing feet grew still.

"Go on, go on," screamed West, "go on playing." But Otto neither heeded nor heard, for he was out of his head with terror and excitement and was dancing upon the wagon, shrieking out snatches of Gospel hymns. He was waving his fists above his head. His eyes were as the eyes of a fish and he was bleeding at the nose.

An *assegai* struck him all at once full on the face and he spun about twice gripping at the air and then went over side-ways upon the key-board of the organ, his blood splashing the dazzling white of the celluloid keys.

They ran in and overwhelmed the wagon like an ocean bursting a dyke, and the little *voorlooper* found his death amidst the panic-stricken oxen.

West tried to shoot himself underneath the wagon but was dragged out by one arm and a leg, with his chin shot away.

And what was done with Mr. West?

"*Maghwheena!*" exclaimed Ingodusi, as he finished the tale, "He was an *Umtagati*, a crawling snake. *Him* we crucified upon a telegraph pole—by the arms only."

Types of Western Men

I

The College Man

The Wave, 15 (25 April 1896), 6.

Well, to begin with, he is a good fellow, but by that I do not mean to say he is *good*. He is not good in that sense. In that sense I am very much afraid to say he is a sorry case. He loves his pipe and his glass and is given over to late hours and to riotous homecomings with a great noise of shouting, his pockets stuffed with spoons and beer glasses and individual salt-cellars and small tradesmen's signs which he hangs up in his room as souvenirs. One great difference between him and his Eastern brother is apparent here. The Eastern brother holds his diversions in his own rooms and calls them "smoke talks" or "low beers" or "punches" and gets his friends together and makes only so much noise as the Proctor of his hall will allow.

But the Western college man needs a larger horizon, a wider sphere of action, and goes out of the college precincts to seek it, from Broadway in Oakland to Kearny Street in San Francisco.

There are two varieties of the type, the variety that live at the college and the variety that live in the city and travel over the Bay daily to their lectures and recitations. You may see the latter variety on the ferryboats early in the morning and late in the afternoon, and you may recognize it at once by the small red satchel it invariably carries; as a rule—of course there are saving exceptions—but, as a rule, it wears a black, cutaway coat of diagonal cloth, and a white four-in-hand "necktie" of the kind that wash.

The other variety that live at the college differ from the traveling variety widely, one might almost say, in "language, institutions, and religion." If you belong to this variety you must wear either a cloth cap or a battered "plug," you must smoke a briar pipe, must own a dog, must carry a cane, and believe that the captain of the football team can do no wrong. If you wear moderately good clothes, "josh" about everything and everybody, never talk about yourself, and understand athletics, you are voted "on to yourself," and are popular and join a fraternity.

The Western college man differs from the Eastern brother in still another point. He never has very much money, and that's a good thing, too. The Eastern brother has the long green; the Western man the small brown, and sometimes, yes, sometimes, he hasn't even that. It is no rare thing for the Eastern brother to have a cellar and a suite of rooms. But the Western college man is a true bohemian, and smokes his chum's tobacco, and wears his chum's clothes, and borrows his chum's money—or tries to—without fear and without reproach.

There is still another variety. But this kind is not often seen in the streets of San Francisco. When it is seen, however, it is recognizable at once. It is generally large of build, and wears a brown Fedora hat with an enormous brim, and one of those negligé pink shirts with the very high turn-down collar. In the lapel of its coat is thrust a red flag-pin. This is the variety Stanford.

In his relations with the world of Society, the Western man differs still again from the Eastern brother. The Eastern brother gives "teas" to young lady friends in his "rooms," where his mother is the chaperon, and where his sisters serve the tea and help him receive, all very decorous and solemn. The Westerner orders the matter on a totally different plan; his fraternity is the center of his social life at college. He, with his fraters, keeps "open house" on public days (having made a carefully expurgated edition of his room beforehand) and fills the place with a lot of jolly people—girls from the city, and visiting cousins, and even "coeds," who eat salads and ice-cream in the smoking room, and play Virginia reels and popular songs on the rented piano in the back parlor, and who come out into the kitchen to help the Freshmen with the chocolate and ice-cream freezers. It's not a Society "function," and you don't have to wear a black coat if you don't want to. The girls have "the time of their life," and send over sofa cushions and lampshades the next week to show their appreciation.

In the matter of spending vacations, however, I am led to believe that the average Westerner and his average Eastern brother are very much alike.

Neither of them is in very great evidence at the fashionable summer-resorts. As soon as Commencement day is passed there is great talk of guns and maps, and the portage weight of cameras, and portable tents and salmon-flies. For the next two months the college man of the West and East alike is lost to view. Both of them like shooting better than dancing, prefer the climbing of mountains to the leading of germans, and would rather lie all night in the wet grass waiting to get a pot-shot at an elk than to pass an entire morning reclining in tennis flannels on the beach, talking to a girl, under a red parasol.

In the fall our Westerner comes back from the mountains, or, perhaps, from the desert, with his hair long and his chin rough with an incipient beard and the skin burnt off his nose, and tells of the fearful and wonderful times he has had. Then he settles to the grooves of his college life again, and after the pastime of camping is over, returns to the serious business of the fall term, which is coaching the football team.

And his work?

Oh, yes, his work; we had forgotten that.

Well, he graduates *somehow*.

A Delayed Masterpiece

———

An American Novel Which Has Achieved Great Success

———

The Wave, 15 (25 April 1896), 8.

———

In *A Singular Life* Mrs. Elizabeth Stuart Phelps has surprised both her public and her publishers. After an author has composed and given to the world fourteen successful novels, his or her relative rank in the realm of literature is usually clearly defined; one feels that one knows what to expect. The merit of the forthcoming product of his or her pen can be rather accurately foretold. Even the veteran author himself, after ten or twenty years of literary effort, has settled down to certain lines of thought, certain habits of style and of expression that can be broken with only by the greatest effort of the will. The author's *chef-d'oeuvre* is rarely made late in his literary career, certainly it is most extraordinary for it to appear at the end of a sequence of over a dozen strongly written tales. It is generally quite the other way. The *chef-d'oeuvre* is usually the author's first, or one of his very first, published books.

A Singular Life is, no doubt, Mrs. Phelps's greatest work. With it she has made a fresh start. The story has all the strength, the vigor, and the "go" of unexhausted, almost untried, powers.

The milieu is that of religion, the characters those of a town's parish, the hero, the new minister, and the motif of the story, a vigorous and telling onslaught upon theological bigots. All this material is not new, but its very conventionality is but one more factor in the surprising effect produced. You lay down the book with the impression of having lived in a new literary atmosphere, of having passed through fresh scenes, of having met new people. But this is not so. The material and the machinery are old, old as the days of George Eliot and Charlotte Brontë. It is, of course, the manner of treatment, the style, the point of view that is so new, so fresh, so original. In some subtle, delicate way of her own, the author lures the reader into seeing her story, her characters, and her incidents from her own standpoint.

For instance, what can be more hackneyed than the following contrivance? A drunken bully is beating a little child, the by-standers are helpless to interfere, the new minister, young and athletic, intervenes and knocks the bully down; the bully gets on his feet once more, surveys the stripling in some surprise, exclaims slowly "'Well I'll be d——d,'" and is forever afterward the young minister's very best friend. We have seen all this, under slightly varying circumstances, a score of times before, but as told by Mrs. Phelps and met with in its own place in the order of the story's events it comes back to us new, striking, even unusual. But not all the episodes of the story are of this character. Here is the conversion of the drunken bully:

> Suddenly Bayard (the new minister) dropped Job's hand and spoke in a ringing voice:
> "Job Slip, get down upon your knees—just where you stand!"
> Job hesitated.
> "Down!" cried Bayard.
> Job obeyed as if he had been a dog.

"Now, lift your hands—so—to the sky."
As if the minister had been a cut-throat, Job obeyed again.
"Now, pray!" commanded Bayard.

For some time Job demurs, then,

"*Pray!*" commanded Bayard.
"Oh—God!" gasped Job.
Bayard took off his hat. Job's arms fell; his face dropped into them; he shook from head to foot.
"There!" he cried; "I done it——I'll do it again. God! God! *God!*" . . . .
"Save him," cried Bayard. . . . "Save me this one man! I have tried and failed, and I am discouraged to the bottom of my heart. But I can't give him up. I will never give him up till he is dead or I am. If I cannot do any other thing in Windover, for Christ's sake, save me this one drunken man."
Bayard lifted his face in noble agony. Job hid his own before that Gethsemane. . . . The rain dashed on Bayard's white face. He rose from his knees.
"Job Slip," he said, "you have signed a contract which you can never break. Your vow lies between God and you. I am the witness. I have bound you over to a clean life. Go and sin no more —I'll risk you now," added Bayard, quietly. "I shall not even walk home with you. You have fifteen rum-shops to pass before you get back to your wife and child. . . . You will not enter one of them . . . and to-morrow you will send me a written testimony from your wife, Maria, that you came home sober. Now go, and God be with you."

* * * * * * * *

"This is to certify that my husband came home last nite sober and hain't ben on a Bat sence. God bless you ennyhow.

"MARIA SLIP."

This legend, written in laborious chirography on a leaf torn from a grocer's passbook was put into Bayard's hand at noon next day.

[*A Singular Life*, by Elizabeth Stuart Phelps. Houghton, Mifflin & Co., publishers.]

Types of Western Men

II

The Plumber's Apprentice

The Wave, 15 (2 May 1896), 6.

His name is "Jonesee," and he is a tinner and a gasfitter during six days of the week, or at least attempts to persuade his brother-in-law, into whose shop he has been received, that such is his serious occupation. Jonesee tried to impress the fiction upon himself during the first days of his apprentice-ship, but the strain of sustaining the character increased in proportion as the novelty of the work diminished, until he has come by gentle degrees to keep-ing up appearances only during the times when the boss is in, and they are literally "appearances" even then. He never works unless he is absolutely driven to it, and he probably never will as long as he can live at home and exploit his father—who is an annealer in the mint—for enough change to keep him in beer and "cigareets."

In the back room of the grimy tin-shop on Polk Street Jonesee languishes and chafes by turns. The only ornaments on the walls are a couple of pic-tures cut from bill posters of the "Danites," and a dirty map of San Fran-cisco, on which the location of the tin-shop is at once betrayed by a worn and soiled spot, the result of frequent contact with greasy finger-tips. Jonesee hates the place, and is much more content when he is sent out to do an odd job in the neighborhood.

At such times one sees him on the front platforms of cable cars, his hand-furnace for heating his soldering irons between his feet, together with his solder-sticks, pliers, clamping tools, etc., wrapped in their carpet case, his pockets loaded with brass faucets, short sections of lead pipe, and tweezers.

On these occasions he wears a suit that has once been black, but has now faded to a shade of green, except upon the trousers above the knee, where, by constant friction with lead and grease and dirt, they are thickly coated with a glazed and shining varnish of black. His battered derby hat is of a blackish green as well, and is marked with sweat stains around the band. He is always smoking the butt of a "cigareet," which sticks to his lower lip even when he opens his mouth to talk.

He is even more contented when he goes out to lunch at noon in the Polk-street restaurant, in the window of which one sees three china pigs and a plaster of Paris cow knee-deep in a thick layer of white beans. He likes to gabble and lounge at length among the postmen, car-conductors, and barbers who frequent the place, and hear the latest word on ward politics and prize-fights, or shake dice or match nickels for cigars.

Sunday, however, is Jonesee's great day. It is the one day of the seven when he is released from the work of seeming to work. He is not in evidence till the afternoon. Then sometimes he goes out to the Park or to the Cliff House, or sometimes, on rare occasions, rents a horse and buggy with a friend and *drives* there, sometimes he goes "across the Bay" on a public picnic, or sometimes "takes in" the races, or balloon jumps or high dives as opportunity affords.

But his favorite and characteristic occupation of a Sunday afternoon is general and promiscuous loafing, posing, trying to be tough, showing himself off in his cheap finery, for at such times he is dressed with scrupulous attention.

His soft felt hat is pushed back upon his head far enough to show his hair parted very much to one side, neatly oiled and plastered and brought down over his temple in a beautiful flat curve. He wears an inexpensive "Prince Albert" invariably unbuttoned to show the flowered design of his waistcoat. In the lapel of this coat he wears a tuberose. His stand-up collar is very low and overlaps in front, while around this collar and often getting above it is a crocheted four-in-hand "necktie" of salmon pink silk, tied very tightly and transfixed with a scarfpin representing a palette and brushes, with four colors in variously tinted Rhinestones. He fastens this necktie to the side of his shirt so that it traverses *diagonally* the whole of the triangular expanse left by the vest. His trousers fit him very tightly and are of light brown cloth with broad chocolate colored stripes. The cuffs around his thick red wrists are frayed and in one of his freckled fists he carries a cane, a slender wisp of ebony with a gold head, won at the Tinners' and Gasfitters' Prize Masquerade Ball.

Thus arrayed, and attended by odors of tobacco, beer, hair oil, and German cologne, he lounges with three or four others of his stripe about the entrances of corner groceries, where a Milwaukee beer sign decorates the salient corner and where you may see displayed advertisements for cheap butter, eggs, and tea, painted in green marking ink upon wrapping paper. Here, together with his friends, he will while the time away, talking loud, swearing, spitting, scuffling, and joshing the girls that pass in twos and threes. Now and then he and his friends will go into the bar behind the store and have a "steam" or sometimes himself and a comrade will take off their coats, go into the middle of the street and with frequent cries of "all de way now" pitch curves at one another with an adamantine ball. Toward the close of the afternoon he will sometimes go with them to Golden Gate Avenue and watch the "turn-outs" coming home from the park, commenting upon the horses, and joshing the girl bicyclists. In the evening he goes to a cheap theater, and occasionally closes the day's enjoyment by becoming drunk and disorderly.

Theory and Reality

An Old Author and a New Writer
Consider the Same Problem

The Wave, 15 (2 May 1896), 8.

There have recently appeared two books, both dealing with the same very delicate sex problem, a problem so delicate in fact that it is almost impossible to consider the books critically. One of these books is by Mr. W.D. Howells and is called *A Parting and a Meeting*. The other is by Mrs. J.R. Jarboe of this city and is called *Robert Atterbury*. Each book has to do with the "ultimate physical relation of man and woman." A dangerous subject truly.

Mr. Howells touches it lightly, delicately, handling it with the greatest subtlety and finesse. Mrs. Jarboe rushes in where Mr. Howells fears to tread, grapples the subject by the throat, sledge-hammers at it, tears the veil from it boldly, uncompromisingly.

Mr. Howells tells a story; Mrs. Jarboe develops a theory. The *Parting and Meeting* is a little tale of how a certain young man of some seventy years ago attempted to prevail upon his sweetheart to join the Shakers with him and to live out the remainder of their lives keeping the relations of brother and sister. In a scene of exquisite delicacy and sympathetic insight, the girl refuses. The man joins the Shakers and the girl marries elsewhere. Sixty years afterward they meet, and though Roger is so old as to be almost in his dotage, he recovers intelligence enough to say, "'I'm not so sure but I'd have done about as well to have gone with *you*, Chloe.'" That is all; this is the whole story, a touch, a suggestion, a hint.

According to Mrs. Jarboe's theory "there is no love which can justify marriage as it is at present understood. There is no law, no blessing of priest or church, which can render it anything but legalized prostitution. It is a crime against nature, against the race, against God." The author proposes as a remedy the Malthusian theory of restraint, a theory, beautiful upon paper but which practise and good political economists have long since demonstrated beyond question to be as delusive and impossible as the Ptolemaic system of astronomy. That the increase of the family after marriage should be restrained and limited is a fine and admirable ideal, but the idealists will close their eyes to the fact that men *and women* are after all only human. Even this word "human" is misleading. Is it not even truer that so-called humanity still is, and for countless generations will be, three-quarters animal, living and dying, eating and sleeping, mating and reproducing even as the animals; passing the half of each day's life in the performance of purely animal functions? This is lamentable, no doubt, but the grandest theory ever conceived by the mind of the most prodigious thinker is powerless to better the condition of the race, in this respect, as far as immediate results are concerned. There is no prospect for betterment except in the gradual evolution of the type through infinitely vast periods of time.

Mrs. Jarboe, however, does not apply her theory to her hero and heroine

—Atterbury and Sara—even after all its elaborate development throughout the first part of the story. In their case the two young people made a virtue of necessity, since one was a consumptive and the other under the shadow of hereditary insanity.

In the case of two healthy, natural young people in real life, or in a good realistic novel, Mrs. Jarboe's fine-spun web of logic would have been rent at the first breath. The greater author of the *Parting and Meeting* knew his real life better. Chloe even refused to consider a union of her life with that of her lover's, conceived upon any such morbid, Utopian principles, and even Roger acknowledges its futility in admitting that, after all, he would have done wiser to have gone back with Chloe.

Mrs. Jarboe presents her subject unskilfully. However admirable her theory—*as* theory—may be, it is not clearly and convincingly expressed in the pages of *Robert Atterbury*. No matter what its purpose or how great a lesson it purposes to teach, the novel should *be* a novel; first and foremost, it should tell a real story, of real people and of real places.

In Mr. Howells's story, even the old chaise horse becomes a character, "making snatches at the foliage and from time to time champing thoughtfully on his bit as if he fancied he might have caught a leaf in his mouth," and Chloe and Roger are flesh and blood characters from first to last. It is what *they* do and what *they* say that interest the reader. In *Robert Atterbury*, however, the people are little more than names and stand for nothing but the various mouthpieces for the author's theory. Chloe and Roger live and act by themselves, while Mrs. Jarboe shifts about the characters like a showman pulling the strings of his puppets. We forget Howells at once in the fortunes of his *dramatis personae*. We cannot lose sight of the author of *Robert Atterbury* for a single instant.

Western City Types

The "Fast" Girl

The Wave, 15 (9 May 1896), 5.

She dresses in a black, close-fitting bolero jacket of imitation astrachan with enormous leg-of-mutton sleeves of black velvet, a striped silk skirt, and a very broad hat, tilted to one side. Her hair is very blonde, though, somehow, coarse and dry, and a little flat curl of it lies low over her forehead. She is marvelously pretty.

She belongs to a certain class of young girl that is very common in the city. She is what men, amongst each other, call "gay," though that is the worst that can be said of her. She is virtuous, but the very fact that it is necessary to say so is enough to cause the statement to be doubted.

When she was younger and a pupil at the Girls' High School, she had known, and had even been the companion of, girls of good family, but since that time these girls have come to ignore her. Now almost all of her acquaintances are men, and to most of these she has never been introduced. They have managed to get acquainted with her on Kearny Street, at the theaters, at the Mechanics' Fair, and at baseball games. She tells these men that her name is "Ida." She loves to have a "gay time" with them, which, for her, means to drink California champagne, to smoke cigarettes, and to kick at the chandelier. Understand distinctly, however, that she is not "bad," that there is nothing vicious about her. Ida is too clever to be "bad," and is as morbidly careful of appearances and as jealous of her reputation as only fast girls can be.

She lives with her people on Golden Gate Avenue. Her father has a three-fourths interest in a carpet-cleaning "establishment" in the Mission, and her mother gives lessons in hand-painting on china and on velvet.

In the evening, especially if it be a Saturday evening, Ida invents all sorts of excuses to go "down town." You see her then on Kearny or Market Streets about the time the theaters open, arm in arm with one or perhaps two other girls who are precisely like her. At this time she is not in the least "loud," either in dress or in conversation, but somehow when she is in the street she cannot raise a finger or open her mouth without attracting attention.

Like "Jonesee," Sunday is her great day. Ida usually spends it "Across the Bay" somewhere. A party is gotten up and there is no "chaperon." Two or three of the men with whom she and her friends have become acquainted during the week arrange the "date." The day's amusement is made to include a lunch at one of the suburban hotels and a long drive in a hired "rig." The party returns home on one of the ferry boats late in the afternoon. By that time they are quite talked out, their good spirits are gone, and they sit in a row, side by side, exchanging monosyllables. Ida's face is red, her hair is loose, and the little blonde curl has lost its crispness. She has taken off her gloves by this time. In one of her bare hands she carries her escort's cane, and in the other a bunch of wilted wild flowers. Sometimes, however, the party returns to the city in a later boat, one that makes the trip after dark. Then everything is changed. The party "pairs off" at once. You will see Ida and her "fellar" sitting in one of the dark corners of the deck. The fellar sits as close as the length of his acquaintance with Ida will justify. He rests his elbow on the rail back of her and, by and by, carelessly lets his forearm drop at full length.

When the Mechanics' Fair opens Ida rarely misses an evening. I remember that I once saw her and the fellar in the art gallery upstairs. Ida's mother, "who gives lessons in hand painting," had an exhibit there which they were interested to find: a bunch of yellow poppies painted on black velvet and framed in gilt. When they had found it they stood before it some little time hazarding their opinions and then moved on from one picture to another, Ida had the fellar buy a catalogue and made it a duty to find the title of every picture, for she professes to be very fond of hand painting. She had "taken it up" at one time and abandoned it only because the oil or the turpentine or something had been unhealthy for her.

On this occasion she looked at each picture carefully, her head on one side. "Of course," she explained to the fellar, "I'm no critic, I only know what I like. I like those 'heads,' those ideal heads like that one," and she pointed with her arm outstretched to a picture of the head of a young girl with disheveled brown hair and upturned eyes. The title of the picture was

Faith.

"Yes," said Ida, reflectively, "I like that kind."

The Benefit Field Day for the California Eastern Team

The Wave, 15 (9 May 1896), 6.

Last Saturday was a Berkeley day beyond any doubt. The much-heralded, much-advertised championship games were held for the benefit of the Eastern Track Team of the California University, and, judging from the attendance, the team must have benefited largely.

Over a dozen different athletic organizations entered men in the events, the Berkeley contingent being, naturally, the largest; Stanford wisely held aloof; a week previous the tie, which seems to be the invariable outcome whenever the two Universities meet, had again been the result of the intercollegiate Field Day, and the athletic powers of the Cardinal College had apparently decided to let well enough alone. And, after all, Stanford did do well enough to tie the team that had tied Pennsylvania and beaten Princeton.

But the boys from Berkeley struggled hard to wipe the stain of practical defeat from their record, and took advantage of the championship games to prove that they, and not their red rivals, were the representative Western college athletes, and had the right and power to challenge Yale, Harvard, and Princeton to trials of strength on the cinder path and in the field.

Of all the contests of speed, the prettiest, to my taste, is the bicycle race, for you receive a very distinct impression of velocity minus the disagreeable sight of the foam and lather and bloody flanks of a horse race or the wavering gait, the distorted face, and the laboring muscles at the finish of a fiercely fought foot race. Of course, the effort is all there in a wheel race, but it is not nearly so apparent.

Nothing could have been prettier than the races last Saturday; run as they were upon a board track so steeply inclined at the turns that the whole thing looked less like a bicycle track than an enormous oval platter. It was impossible to resist a thrill when the racers turned into the straight just before the beginning of the last lap. It was the beginning of the end then. By that time the pace that kills had strung the riders out into a line, and only those who were well up to the front could hope to win. At "the turn into the straight"—that final fatal place where so many hopes have died—the leaders begin to ride in deadly earnest and the battle commences that is to be fought out all the way around the track. If you watch them close you will observe the leaders holding back, eyeing each other, each waiting for the other to begin the spurt, each maneuvering for that place which expert riders tell you is the best in a race—just at your opponent's rear wheel. Then the spurt comes all of a sudden, and a new life runs through the race like fire, the crowd shouts now one name, now another, the bell rings furiously for the last lap, and the glint of wheels comes spinning down upon you, the hollow boards of the track roaring under the flying tires, the race goes by with a flash and a rolling noise as of distant thunder, and the next instant you see it careening around the turn, the wheels canted over to the incline of the track like ships in a gale; the race flashes along the opposite side, strikes the turn again, the last turn, grows small and fore-shortened as it wheels into the home stretch and finishes close under you with a fleeting glimpse of whirling tires, gleaming colors and a momentary flash of the broken tape.

Yet for all this there was not very much enthusiasm at the meet, none of that infectious spontaneous thrill that runs from end to end of a crowd, and that drags you up to your feet, shouting and throwing things into the air. Only once was there a suggestion of this. It was when the man who did the announcing through an enormous extinguisher told the Berkeley element in the audience about the baseball game played that same afternoon on the Palo Alto Campus between the California and Stanford Nines. "Stanford—U. C. baseball game," thundered the extinguisher; "U. C. wins —score 13 to 3." These were winged words. For the second time in history California had beaten out Stanford on the diamond. Even the bicycle races were forgotten for the moment while the bleachers roared to the California slogan, and the air grew gray with the tossing arms, and hats, and canes.

California needed this victory, especially after the tied games of the week previous. It was vitally necessary that the College, and the outside world as well, should have ocular physical proof of the fact that a California team *could* win when matched with a strong rival.

What is the matter with the University across the Bay? Somewhere deep down in her complicated athletic machinery a little screw is loose. Even in the benefit field day California did not show as strong as was expected; three first places went to Stanford; Torrey was beaten out in the hurdles—though perhaps intentionally—but all through the events there was a noticeable lack of spirit. There can be no doubt that as far as material goes California has put into the field team after team equal to any college team in the United States. This may seem a large order, but it is, we believe, absolutely true. Of course it is not demanded that these teams win from Yale or Harvard, but it is not unreasonable to expect something more than a long series of tied scores in California's meets with Stanford.

It is quite possible that there is too much coddling of the California teams by the undergraduates; that the college at large is more responsible than the athletes themselves. It is the wrong spirit that pats the men on the back, that says, "You are doing well; you are a fine fellow; you are going to win hands down." A better spirit would be that which shuts its hands and teeth, and exclaims: "D——n you, win the game."

Hinckey, the Captain of the Yale Eleven, kicks Beard, his own right guard, before a crowded grand-stand for some delinquency in his play, and the college supports the Captain.

The spirit may not be a gentlemanly spirit, we admit—it's not the spirit that the player relishes, but it's the spirit that wins intercollegiate games.

The Heroism of Jonesee

The Wave, 15 (16 May 1896), 6.

For a moment be pleased to consider the moral quality of courage. There are three kinds of it. There is the courage that loves danger, and there is the courage that despises it; then there is a third kind—a kind that is born of more complicated motives, not a heroic kind of courage, but one that is oftenest met with. It is that peculiar, desperate sort of courage that comes of fear, and that makes a man courageous because he is afraid to *seem* afraid.

It was this last kind of courage that inspired Jonesee to do what he did on that particular Sacramento-street car. He was brave upon that occasion because he was scared to death. The thing he did was afterward told up and down the length of Polk Street; but Jonesee caused it to be believed that his courage was the kind that loved danger, or the kind that despised it—the heroic kind. Jonesee said things that were not so, because if you remember anything about Jonesee at all, you will remember that there was nothing heroic about him. He is a plumber's apprentice on Polk Street—you may recall the fact—and you would not expect heroic, noble things from him. He is common.

On a certain Sunday evening, Jonesee, with some friends, had a dinner, that consisted chiefly of things to drink, at a fearful place called The Rathskeller, and had gone to the Bella Union afterward. He drank a good deal more beer between the acts at the Bella Union, and about midnight was just sober enough to remember that he must take the last boat across the bay. Why he had to do so has nothing to do with this story. He boarded a Sacramento-street car about midnight. He was the only passenger.

Jonesee stood on the back platform and labored to convince the conductor that Billy McGovern was a light heavyweight and not a heavy lightweight. The conductor was filling out his time-forms for the trip, and his attention was so equally divided between elementary mathematics and Jonesee's pugilism, that he very nearly overlooked two fares that signalled to him at the corner of Sansome Street. Jonesee called them to his notice in time, and when the car stopped a fellar and a girl came out of the surrounding gloom into the circle of light thrown by the car lamps, and got aboard. The fellar pushed the girl into the car ahead of him. As he followed, Jonesee saw him give the conductor two dollars and heard him say in a low voice, "You can keep the change." Here was a mystery!

Jonesee affected not to hear, but began to pay close attention to what was going forward. Pretty soon the fellar leaned forward and called out to the conductor:

"Say, are we going to get that last boat?"

"No," answered the conductor.

When the girl heard this she suddenly began to cry violently. Then Jonesee knew. The conductor had lied—that was certain. Jonesee was not so drunk but that he knew the car would connect with the last boat; that in fact, it was run for that very purpose.

"It's a job to do the girl dirt," he reflected. Then he lit a cigareet.

"'f you wanta smoke, you'll have to go forward," observed the conductor.

As Jonesee went through the car, he took in the couple at a glance. The girl was not in the least pretty; her eyes were close together and her chin was large. Over her shoulders she wore a cape of flimsy red cloth with accordion plaits; her hands were bare, and her shoes were unkempt and showed blue at the toes and sides. Her crying did not become her; there were red spots over the bridge of her nose and about her eyelids, and her large chin quivered like a jelly. She was cheap and she was vulgar, but Jonesee told himself that she was no chippy.

The fellar, Jonesee recognized in an instant, with a simultaneous qualm. His professional name was The Spider, and one of the proudest moments in Jonesee's life had been when he had given a knee to the bantam-weight champion of Contra Costa County in his eight-rounds-with-a-decision go with French Frank at West Berkeley, the March previous. Jonesee gloried in the acquaintance he had with the prize-fighter, and often bullied his companions with the fact, lying about its different phases with brilliant audacity. The Spider did not recognize him now, or did not choose to, and Jonesee went out onto the front platform of the car, and slid the door to behind him.

Seated on the dasher, he watched what was taking place inside of the car. The Spider was talking earnestly to the girl, who was still crying. Jonesee could guess that he was trying to persuade her to get off the car, it being useless to remain on it now until it reached the ferry. He was confirmed in this by seeing him signal to the conductor to stop at the next crossing. His companion seemed to have yielded. "What could the poor girl do?" quoted Jonesee to himself.

Between Montgomery Street and the ferry landings, Sacramento Street runs fairly level. This neighborhood is taken up for the most part with wholesale houses, fruit-packers, commission merchants, broom manufacturers. After dark it is a solitude.

As the car trundled its way on with a grinding of wheels and a strident whirring of jostled glass, Jonesee could see the four squares of light thrown from the car windows running over the somber fronts of the closed buildings. Their doors and windows were covered with green-painted iron shutters; empty crates and flat blue boxes for shipping butter were piled at intervals along the sidewalk. At the crossings, vistas of sparsely lighted streets opened on either hand. No one was in sight, not a cat moved.

Jonesee was a coward. For all his posing and bullying when with his friends or when backed by a gang of his ward, he was horribly afraid of getting into a street fight, unless it was a sure thing. But what would have induced him to cross The Spider, the man with the scientific left, the hardest man in Contra Costa County—the man who had put out French Frank in eighteen minutes, whose friendship raised Jonesee to a glorious and envious eminence throughout all Polk Street? Was it for him—Jonesee—to call The Spider to account in a lonely part of the town, at midnight, with never a policeman within shouting distance? No, he would not interfere.

The car was within twenty yards of the next street when The Spider got up and Jonesee saw the conductor reach for the bell rope. Then, all at once, without knowing why, Jonesee put up his hand into the bell above his head between the hammer and the curve of the metal. As the conductor pulled the rope the hammer struck against his fingers, and made no sound. The car kept on its way. Then Jonesee realized the enormity of what he had done. He knew that The Spider would jump him now, and he shook again at the thought. Not only this, but he had forever sacrificed the precious acquaintance with the Contra Costa champion; never more would he be able to nod to him at local bars or "sporting resorts" with his invariable "Well, Spider, what's the good word to-day?"; never more would he be able to lie about what happened between "me 'n The Spider." Yet the next thing he did was to cut off as much of the bell rope as he could, and with it to lash the handle of the car door to the iron rods which guarded the front windows. He thought if he could keep the car going he might succeed in what he had undertaken. As long as the gripman received no sign from the conductor he would keep on. They were within three blocks of the ferry now, and if things could remain as they were but five minutes more all would be well. So thought Jonesee; he was too drunk to understand how impractical was his idea.

The conductor pulled the bell-rope again viciously, and Jonesee saw the severed end above his head disappear with a fillip through the hole and drop limply on the floor inside the car.

The conductor came forward through the car and looked out at Jonesee on the platform; he pulled and jerked at the door in vain, and then shouted at him to open it. He expressed an opinion as to the legitimacy of Jonesee's immediate ancestors and proffered doubts as to his future salvation. Jonesee returned appropriate blasphemies, and kept his eye on The Spider. All this time the car was lessening the distance that yet lay between them and the ferry; safety was but two blocks away. The conductor turned to The Spider.

"There's a drunk out here has cut the bell-rope and tied up the door; can't stop the car unless the gripman hears the bell."

"To hell with him," cried The Spider, getting to his feet in a fury. "Smash the glass an' *I'll* get holt of him."

"Yes," returned the conductor, with irony, "and me be stuck for the glass, huh? I guess not."

The Spider now approached and delivered himself of a long snarl of oaths and threats. Jonesee listened to the car-wheels telling off the rails, and, in a tremulous voice, said to himself over and over again, "You'se think you're hell, don't you? You'se think you're hell." The next moment the crisis of the matter had arrived.

Jonesee thought that The Spider had given up the affair and had jumped off the car, leaving himself and the girl to their own devices. Suddenly he found himself face to face with him. The Spider *had* got off the car, but instead of leaving it, had run forward, and now, with one hand on the rail of the front dasher, was preparing to jump on. From where he was he might easily have called to the gripman, but he was too excited, too angry, too bent upon having it out with Jonesee to think of this.

For an instant, as The Spider ran along parallel to the car, Jonesee saw his face a little lower than his own and saw it set with an expression of mean, vicious rage, bullying, aggressive; Jonesee remembered it had looked like this when the prize-fighter came from his corner for the last round with French Frank.

During the instant that immediately succeeded the sight of The Spider's face so close to his own, Jonesee observed several things. He saw that The Spider intended to jump him; but he saw, too, that he had not recognized him and was sizing him up, waiting for a chance. Jonesee saw that the instant he assumed the defensive, The Spider would swing himself to the platform and run in upon him; that the moment he showed fear it would be all over for him. He saw, too, with startling vividness, that if he was to stand any chance of escaping a terrible fight, he must take advantage of this one instant of indecision. On such occasions as these a man can think pretty fast. Jonesee reflected rapidly upon the different ways of injuring the vicious, cruel face that now looked into his out of the darkness. He might with whitened knuckles strike it heavily upon its salient chin; or he might, with the switch-iron hastily grabbed from the dasher, beat it in with two or three swift underhand strokes. It could be cut and slashed, too, to some advantage if he had time to get to his knife, or it could be shot into if one were handy with a revolver—and had one. All these things Jonesee realized could be done, but what he finally *did* do was none of them. What he finally did was to kick with the suddenness of a relaxed spring and with all the combined energy of hip and body. He felt his boot strike into the soft part of the throat; recovering himself as quickly as he could, he kicked again and again, felt his foot reach home; but the third time he only struck the empty air—the face was gone.

The Spider must have cried out or shouted as he went over backward into the street. Jonesee himself did not remember hearing any sound, but indeed all that happened in the next few minutes was ever afterward a matter of uncertainty to him; he could only suppose that The Spider had shouted, for the gripman, suddenly realizing what was doing behind him, let go the rope and stopped the car.

"Go on. Go on," screamed Jonesee. "It ain't anything. Just keep a going."

The gripman got off the dummy and hit him twice on the back of the head. Jonesee was accustomed to say afterward that the conductor attacked him, too, and cut his forehead with his bell punch. It is impossible to say whether he did or no, for Jonesee himself, after the gripman had finished with him, was too dazed to have a clear and connected recollection of anything. He could recall the rest of the evening by fragments only.

Somehow he found himself with the girl, too frightened now to cry, in the midst of a crowd, and there she suddenly recognized a man whom she called Dick, crying out, "Oh, there's Dick and Ma now." It afterwards turned out that she and The Spider were to have met this party on the last boat. Jonesee remembered that she told him this, but just where or when he could not say, the gripman having temporarily spoiled his process of reasoning.

After the girl had been taken off by her mother and her brother, Jonesee remembers of the crowd still remaining in a close circle about him, looking at him. He remembers, too, of the conductor holding him up by the arm, giving his number and that of the gripman to the policeman, who took them down in his note-book. Jonesee staggered when he tried to walk, and could not remember his name. Soon after he heard a sound which smote him with terror. It was the clanging bell of the approaching hurry-up wagon and the gallop of the horses over the cobbles.

When they tried to put him in the wagon, he pulled back stupidly with wide-opened eyes and seized hold of the brass railing of the wagon to brace himself against their efforts. He remembers how the policeman caught his thumbs and bent them back till they were nearly sprung from their sockets. He had to let go. Somebody put his hat on for him, tilted over one eye, and they took him to the station house. Once there he was entered on the books as drunk and disorderly.

* * * * * * * * *

But you must not think from this that Jonesee went unrewarded for his part in that night's affair. The opinion of the world notwithstanding, virtue *does* sometimes get its requital as well in real life as it does between paper covers or behind the footlights. It is true that Jonesee lost the honor that accrued to him from his acquaintance with The Spider. But this was as nothing when compared to the glory which he acquired when it became known that he was the man who could claim the proud distinction of having kicked the Contra Costa bantam into insensibility. Jonesee is the cock of Polk Street now, and, even beyond it, is occasionally spoken of as being "hard."

Van Alstyn Sees Polo at Burlingame

The Wave, 15 (16 May 1896), 7.

Dear Old Chap:—I tell you it's *man's* sport, this polo—a gentleman's sport it is; and when I use the word "gentleman" in such connection, I mean it in its best and broadest sense. It's not a game for the masses, but for the classes, like tennis and golf, like the running of tourneys used to be. Only it's better than tennis or golf, because it's more dangerous—a young girl can play these games. But to play polo—think of it! Think of all the things that a man must know and do to play polo. And, by Jove, Old Chap, he must know and do them *well*, if he loves his fair young life, and would come out of the game all in one piece. Did you ever see the game, Old Chap? Of course, you have; but do you remember your first impression of it? That first impression wears off, you say? Well, it never wears off with me, Old Chap. The wonder—the absolute marvel of the thing was just as fresh for me last Saturday as it was five years ago, when I saw the first game. Such riding, *such* riding! Positive centaurs, you know. It's football on horseback, and that's saying an awful thing, as you may well suppose. I am, as you know, a "rank outsider" on the subject of polo, and I went down to Burlingame last Saturday rather indifferent, if I must confess it, a bit sluggish in my nerves, a bit "off," as I might say. This was because I had forgotten.

Well, you missed it.

One thing that makes polo so fascinating is the background. The thing works itself out in the midst of a charming *mise en scène*. There was not much of a crowd at Burlingame; but it would have done your worldly, fashion-loving eyes good to have beheld what there was of it. Seen from the far side of the field, the grand-stand (it's not a very *grand* stand) had the air of a cluster of blazing flowers set in the dark green of the landscape. There was the gleaming and swaying of brilliant parasols, and the flash of silks and gay bonnets. There was the glitter of harness and clinking polo-chains; there was the satin sheen of perfectly groomed hides, and the dull glowing of the flanks of the lacquered tally-hos. To see all these colors moving and twinkling and shimmering in and out under a California sun, in the out-of-doors of a perfect California day, was in itself alone worth the trip. And the pretty girls, Old Chap—no, you can't match them anywhere else. It's the beauty of the Viennese, the chic of the Parisienne combined with her own good, splendid American dash and strength, the fine, hard, new strain in her blood, that makes the California girl what she is. Let the disaffected rail as they will against the "smart" set, I tell you, Old Chap, there is nothing in the world so fine, so beautiful, as a well-dressed, thoroughbred American girl.

But the game.

Poor Riversides. They made a gallant, uphill fight and they scored two hardly earned goals. But there was nothing on the field that day that could withstand the rush of the Burlingames. There was a furious recklessness about them, an absolute disregard of life and limb that could not be gainsaid. They would win if they broke their necks for it, and when men go into a contest with such determination as that, the other side may as well draw out from the start. The game in detail I shall not describe to you, Old Chap, you have no doubt had that already through the daily papers; suffice it to say that Burlingame started in slowly at first, not overconfident at the start. Then suddenly warmed to their work, struck a pace, a tremendous pace, held it—and won twelve goals. Toward the end they had Riverside "on the run." The instant the ball was tossed out, they rushed it. They were off as though from a starter's flag in a race, the hoofs rolled and rippled over the hollow ground, there was a cloud of gray dust shot through with brilliant flashes of color—a spot of red, or white, or more often the yellow of Hobart's cap, brilliant as a golden *casque*. Here and there the ponies' heads rose and fell, shadowy and phantom-like through the dust, then the scrimmage broke up. You heard the sharp "tock-tock" as the ball was struck out, and saw it spinning—a little white, bounding shape—down the field like a flying rabbit. The leaders go down the field after it, each riding *at* it like mad, the long polo sticks swing in the air like the swinging of slender spears, the grandstand rises to its feet, there is a craning of necks, then a cheer, and the scorer hangs up another goal to the credit of Burlingame.

Where is the man who says the young man of the latter day is degenerating through cigarettes and whiskey cocktails, or that the American race is enfeebled through dyspepsia and ice-water? Where is he who says that polo is a "dude's game"? I tell you, Old Chap, that man should have seen the game of last Saturday. He should have seen Walter Hobart win five out of Burlingame's twelve goals, win by some of the most magnificent as well as the most daring and reckless riding I have ever witnessed.

It's a good thing; it is as it should be. Sport such as this is the best thing a man can do in a recreative way, just because it *is* so difficult, so dangerous. It's better, Old Chap, than dancing, better than the cock-tail route, or the leather chairs of the club all an afternoon. By Jove, it's virile, it's manly. It's good for the race and I hope these masculine, dangerous sports like football and boxing and polo, the sports that *hurt*, will never lapse from among us Americans. It's good for the race, and it builds up a sturdy hard-muscled type, the type we had in '75. We may have need of that type again some day, may be in a short time. Who knows, Old Chap, perhaps many a future battle has been already won on our football gridirons and our polo fields.

Western Types

An Art Student

The Wave, 15 (16 May 1896), 10.

He is in evidence to the world outside, at the opening days of spring exhibits, and in and about the art gallery in the Mechanics' Fair. Sometimes you see him coming back to the city on one of the ferry boats late Wednesday and Saturday afternoons. He has been sketching over in Alameda or among the Berkeley hills. He carries his stretchers, camp-stool, umbrella, and paint-box in a clumsy shawl-strapped bundle, and his empty lunch-basket is full of faded eschscholtzias and wild flowers.

On week days he works—and he works hard—at the School of Design—the Art Institute. For the past five years he has been working away here desperately, painting carrots, dead fish, bunches of onions, and, above all, stone jugs. He toils at these jugs with infinite pains. If he can manage to reproduce truthfully the little film of dust that gathers upon them, he is happy. A dusty stone jug is his ideal in life.

He thinks he is an artist and he is quite conscientious about it, and thoroughly believes himself capable of passing opinions upon any picture painted. He expresses these opinions in a loud voice before the picture in question, looking at it with half-shut eyes, making vague gestures at it with his closed fist, moving the thumb as though it were a brush.

Once in a while you see his pictures—still life "studies" of stone jugs and bunches of onions—in the exhibits. Occasionally these are noticed in the local papers. He cuts out these notices and carefully pastes them in his scrap-book, which he leaves about in conspicuous places in his studio.

And his studio. His studio is his room at home (he lives with his people). He tries to hide the stationary wash-stand behind screens and hangings, and he softens the rigidity of the white marble mantel-piece by hanging a yellow "drape" upon one corner. The room is dirty and cluttered; studies of dusty stone jugs are pinned or tacked upon the walls; flattened paint tubes lie

about the window-sills, and there is a strangling odor of turpentine and fix-
ative in the air that mingles with the smell of tobacco and the odor of cooking food from the kitchen down-stairs.

Art with him is *paint*. He condescends to no other medium than oil and
colored earths. Bouguereau is his enthusiasm; he can rise no higher than
that, and he looks down with an amused smile upon the illustrators, the pen-
and-ink men, Gibson, Smedley, Remington, and the rest. "Good in their
way, oh, yes, but Gibson is very superficial, you know." He is given to astonishing you in this way. Pictures that you admire he damns with a phrase;
those you believe to be execrable, he enthuses over.

He believes himself to be Bohemian, but by Bohemianism he understands
merely the wearing of large soft felt hats and large bow scarfs and the drinking of beer in German "resorts." His Bohemianism is not dangerous.

What becomes of the "Art" student I have often wondered. He starts
early at his work. Even at the High School he covers the flyleaves of all his
books with pictures, and carves the head of the principal in chalk. At home
he has made fearful copies of the sentimental pictures in the *Home Book of
Art*. His parents are astonished, become vaguely ambitious and send him to
the Art School before he has hardly begun his education. Here, as I have
told you, he toils away the best years of his life over "still life" studies, enthusiastic over little things, very ambitious in small ways. A year passes, two
years, then five, six and ten, he is still working as hard as ever, and he is
nearly a middle aged man now. You meet him on his way home in the
evening and he takes you to supper and shows you his latest "piece." It is
a study of turnips and onions, grouped about a dusty, stone jug.

He never sells a picture. He has given his life to his work. He grows
older; he tries to make his "art" pay. He drifts into decorative art; is
employed perhaps as a clerk in an art store. If he's lucky he is taken on a
newspaper and does the pen-and-ink work that he once affected to despise.
He's over thirty by this time, and is what he will be for the rest of his life.
All his ambitions are vanished, his enthusiasm's dead, but little by little he
comes to be quite contented.

"Man Proposes": No. 1

———

The Wave, 15 (23 May 1896), 6.

———

It was at the seaside toward the end of the season. A cruiser had anchored just opposite the hotel, and there had been a ball on board. She and her mother had left early, and, of course, there was nothing left for him to do but to come home with them.

"If you want to very much," said her mother, as they reached the hotel veranda, "you can go back in the next launch, and come home later with your aunt, but I wouldn't stay much after eleven."

However, they didn't do this.

"I say," he exclaimed, as soon as they were alone, "you don't want to go back there, do you?—nothing but a lot of kid ensigns."

"Oh, I don't know," she replied, indecisively, looking vaguely toward the cruiser's lights.

"Well, what's the matter with sitting out here on the porch a little while?" he went on. "I don't think it will be cold, and there's a moon in about ten minutes."

They sat down together and talked in low tones about the "master of ceremonies of the hotel," who it was said had once been a monk in Lapland. Then the moon shrugged a red shoulder over the inky black line of the bath-houses.

"It *is* a little cold," she said. "Suppose we walk?"

There was a long board walk along the beach. It was here they found themselves in a few minutes. They walked slowly, he, bending a little forward, his hands thrust into his pockets, she, hatless, her hair a bit out of curl, her bare arms folded under her cape.

Rarely had he seen her in better spirits. They talked and laughed incessantly, and found huge amusement in trifles. For himself he was delightedly content. It was his hour, and he had her all to himself. There were no hectoring chaperones, no jingling pianos, no Other Fellows, no constrained and prolonged silences to mar his pleasure.

"It's a good thing I thought to wear my thick-soled shoes to-night," she ex-claimed, suddenly. "I shall catch it if they find out I didn't go back to the cruiser, but *I* don't care," she laughed. "But isn't this all so pretty?—the moon and the water and all—and so still. The noise of the breakers is just like part of the stillness, isn't it?—and, oh, *do* look back and see how pretty the ship looks from here."

It was pretty. The cruiser built itself up from the water as a huge, flat shadow, indistinct and strange against the gray blur of the sea and sky, look-ing now less like a ship of war than like an island-built fortress, turreted and curious. The lights from her ports glowed like a row of tiny footlights, while the faint clamor of the marine band, playing a Sousa quickstep, came to their ears across the water, small and delicately distinct, as if heard through a telephone.

All about them, seemingly coming from all quarters of the horizon at once, glowed the blue-white moonlight.

"Looks like a nickel-plated landscape," he remarked, looking towards the distant hills and promontories.

"Say *silver, do*," she answered, then suddenly interrupted herself, exclaim-ing, "Oh, I want to walk on the railroad track." They had come to that point where a disused siding of the railroad began to run parallel with the board walk. She stepped upon a rail and began to walk forward, swaying and bal-ancing. All at once, and without knowing why, he put his arm around her waist, as if to steady her.

Then he choked down a gasp at his own temerity. It was astonishing to him how simply and naturally he had done the thing. It was as though he had done it in a dance. He had not premeditated it for a single instant, had not planned for it, had felt no hesitancy, no deliberation. Before he knew it, his arm was where it was, and the world and all things visible had turned a somersault.

In making the motion he had somehow thought to slide his arm beneath her cape, and the sensation of his hand and forearm against her firm, well-laced waist was, he thought, the most delightful thing he had ever experi-enced. He believed that this was the best moment of his life.

The question now was, would she let his arm remain where it was, or would she be angry and hurt? Had he gone too far, or did she care enough for him to allow such a liberty? Everything was happening in an instant of time. For a fraction of that instant he waited in a tremor of suspense. He felt that the next thing she should do or say would decide whether or no she was ever to care for him. One of two things, he told himself, must surely happen. Either she would resent what he had done, or plainly let him know that it was permissible.

It was a crisis.

But instead of acting as he expected, she suddenly seemed to concentrate all her thoughts on keeping her balance upon the rail. She did not pay the slightest attention to what he had done, but walked on, swaying and laughing as before. For a moment he was perplexed; then he saw his answer in her very silence. He instantly fell in with her mood, joyfully affecting ignorance of anything unusual. For a moment he debated the question of attempting to kiss her, but soon told himself that he had too much delicacy for that. This one great favor was enough at first.

"Really, we ought to be going home," she said, at length. "Just suppose *and* suppose if my aunt should come back from the cruiser, and mamma should find out I wasn't with her. I'd *more* than catch it."

They turned back and started home, but he kept his arm where it was, both of them still pretending to think of other things. Part of the way she walked on the rail again, and at one moment, losing her balance altogether, swayed toward him, and throwing out her hand instinctively, seized his shoulder furthest from her. On the instant he caught her wrist with his free hand and held her arm in place where it was.

At this she could no longer affect not to notice. She stopped suddenly and tried to pull away from him. Now it was *his* turn to assume a blissful ignorance; he looked at her, surprised.

"Come along," he exclaimed. "I thought you said it was late; look there, the cruiser's lights are out."

"Oh, but suppose somebody should *see* us," she gasped.

They did not talk much on the way back.

It was about quarter after twelve when they reached the hotel. The elevator had stopped running, the night clerk had just come on duty, and a porter was piling the office chairs together, making ready to sweep. She drank a glass of water at the ice cooler in the corner of the office, and said she was going to bed. He went with her down the hall to her room, talking about a riding party the next day.

"I think I'll just see if Howard is in bed," she said, as she stopped before the door of the room that opened from her mother's and in which her little brother slept.

He followed her a couple of steps inside the room. Howard was there in bed, very warm and red, and sleeping audibly.

As she bent over the bed and smoothed out the pillows for her little brother, the sense of her beauty and her charm came over him again as keenly and vividly as when he had first met her. The hall was deserted, the hotel very quiet. He took a sudden resolution. He partially closed the door with his heel, and as she straightened up he put his arm about her neck and drew her head toward him. She turned to him then very sweetly, yielding with an infinite charm, and he kissed her twice.

Then he went out, softly closing the door behind him.

This was how he proposed to her. Not a word of what was greatest in their minds passed between them. But for all that they were no less sure of each other.

She rather preferred it that way.

"Man Proposes": No. 2

The Wave, 15 (30 May 1896), 7.

He was a coal-heaver, and all that day he had been toiling at the dockyards with his fellows, carrying sacks of coal into a steamer's hold. The fatigue of work had been fearful; for full eight hours he had labored, wrestling with the inert, crushing weight of the sacks, fighting with the immense, stolid blocks of coal, smashing them with sledge-hammers, sweating at his work, grimed like a Negro with the coal-dust.

It was after six now, and he was on his way home. A fine, cold rain was falling, and over his head and shoulders he had thrown an empty coal sack, havelock-fashion.

He was an enormous man, strong as a dray-horse, big-boned, heavily muscled, slow in his movements. His feet and hands were huge and knotted and twisted, and misshapen by hard usage. Through the grime of the coal-dust one could but indistinctly make out his face. The eyes were small, the nose flat, and the lower jaw immense, protruding like the jaws of the carni-vora, and thrusting the thick lower lip out beyond the upper. His father had been a coal-heaver before him, and had worked at that trade until he had been killed in a strike. His mother had drunk herself into an asylum, and had died long ago.

He went on homeward through the fine drizzle. He thrust his hands into his trousers' pockets, gripping his sides with his elbows, drawing his shoulders together, shrinking into a small compass in order to be warm. His head was empty of all thought; his only idea was to get home and to be warm—to be fed, and then to sleep. At length he reached the house.

He pushed open the door of the kitchen, then paused on the threshold exclaiming, "What *you* doing here?"

She straightened up from the wash-tub and pushed the hair out of her eyes with the back of one smoking hand. "Yi sister's sick again, so I come in to bear a hand with the wash," she explained. "Yonder's your supper," and she jerked a bare elbow at the table with its linoleum cover. He did not answer, but went straight to his food, eating slowly with the delicious pleasure of a glutton, his huge jaws working deliberately, incessantly. She returned to the tubs, her shoulders rising and falling over the scrubbing-board with a continuous rhythmical movement. There was no conversation.

He finished his supper and sat back in his chair with a long breath of satisfaction and content, and slowly wiped his lips with the side of his hand. Then he turned his huge body clumsily about and looked at her. Her back was toward him, but he could catch occasional indistinct glimpses of her face in the steam-blurred mirror that hung on the wall just above the tub.

She was not very young, and she was rather fat; her lips were thick and very red and her eyes were small, her neck was large and thick and very white, and on the nape the hair grew low and curling.

Still watching her, he straightened out a leg, and thrusting his hand deep into his trousers' pocket drew out his broken-stemmed clay pipe.

The tips of her bare elbows were red, and he noted with interest how this little red flush came and went as her arms bent and straightened.

In the other pocket he found his plug of tobacco and his huge horn-handled clasp knife. He settled his pipe comfortably in the corner of his mouth and began to cut off strips of tobacco from the plug with great deliberation.

As her body rose and fell, he watched curiously the wrinkles and folds forming and reforming about her thick corsetless waist.

He shut his knife with a snap and slipped it back into his pocket and began to grind the strips of tobacco between his palms, his eyes still fixed upon her.

Little beads of perspiration stood on her forehead and glistened in the hair on the nape of her neck. She breathed rapidly, and he remarked how her big white throat alternately swelled and contracted.

He took his pipe from his lips and filled it, stoppering it with his thumb, put it back unlit between his teeth and dusted his leathery palms together slowly. Then he let his huge hands fall upon his knees, palms upward. He sat motionless, watching her fixedly. He was warm now, crammed with food, stupid, content, inert, and the animal within him purred and stretched itself. There was a long silence.

"Say," he exclaimed at length, with the brutal abruptness of crude, simple natures, "listen here. I like you better'n any one else. What's the matter with us two gett'n married, huh?"

She straightened up quickly and faced him, putting back her hair from her face with the same gesture of her soapy hand, drawing back from him frightened and bewildered.

"Say, will you?" he repeated. "Say, huh, will you? come on, let's."

"No, no!" she exclaimed, instinctively, refusing without knowing why, suddenly seized with the fear of him, the intuitive feminine fear of the male.

He could only say: "Ah, come on; ah, come on," repeating the same thing over and over again.

She, more and more frightened at his enormous hands, his huge square-cut head and his enormous brute strength, cried out "No, no!" shaking her head violently, holding out her hands and shrinking from him.

He laid his unlit pipe on the table and got up and came near to her, his immense feet dragging and grinding on the bare floor.

"Ah, come on," he repeated; "what's the matter with us two gett'n married? Come on; why not?"

She retreated from him and stood on the other side of the tub.

"Why not," he persisted; "don't you like me well enough?"

"Yes."

"Then why not?"

"Because——"

"Ah, come on," he repeated. There was a silence, the hundred tiny bubbles in the suds of the wash-tub were settling and bursting with a prolonged and tiny crackling sound. He came around to where she stood, penning her into the corner of the room. "Huh, why not?" he asked. She was warm from her exertions at the tub and as he stood over her she seemed to him to exhale a delicious feminine odor, that appeared to come alike from her hair, her mouth, the nape of her neck. Suddenly he took her in his enormous arms, crushing down her struggle with his immense brute strength. Then she gave up all at once, glad to yield to him and to his superior force, willing to be conquered. She turned her head to him and they kissed each other full on the mouth, brutally, grossly.

Miss Papinta

The New Dancer Tells How She Commenced Dancing

The Wave, 15 (30 May 1896), 12.

The real true poet sings because he loves to sing and so we must believe that Papinta is the real true dancer because—so she says—she dances because she loves to dance. Personally, even when off the stage, and dressed in a tailor-made skirt and shirt-waist, she suggests the dancer. Even when on the ground the observer can feel that a bird has wings,—so it is with Papinta. Just the way she walks suggests the fact that she can dance. Being interested in dancing, and perhaps, a little in dancers also, I had called to ask Miss Papinta about herself. She is a temporary sojourner at an up-town hotel and I was ushered into a comfortable room fitted with a variety of lounges and wardrobes, and hung with innumerable photographs. She is a slim, brown-faced little woman, with blue eyes, and any color of hair that you like, but very graceful, in a charming, stiff, willowy sort of way, like a particularly tall reed is graceful. I sat down opposite her and we talked. Miss Papinta is very pleasant of manner, and quite unaffected. She tells you about herself with great naïveté and interest. "How about the training of a professional dancer, Miss Papinta?" I asked her first of all. "I believe it is the popular idea that it is rather severe."

"*Training*," she exclaimed; "*I* never had any training. I just *danced*. It's the *toe-dancers* that have to undergo training, and I'm no toe-dancer, you know. *They* must have an apprenticeship of ten years sometimes ere they are fit to appear before an audience, and then must wait a long time before they can become a *feature*. Now, I have always been a feature, never appeared where I was not the main attraction."

"Do you remember," I asked, "your first night?"

"Of course," she answered, beginning to laugh. "It was at Chicago during the World's Fair, and at a place called the Trocadero. How did I come to dance? To tell you truly, I haven't the faintest idea. I was taken with the fetching movement of some of the new waltz songs, and did my little steps before the glass—no teacher, mind you—and then went right bang-away on the stage as a 'feature.' Maybe I wasn't nervous. Frightened to death is no name for it."

"But your nervousness, didn't it affect your dancing?"

"Let me tell you something," she replied instantly. "It's when I'm the most nervous that I do my best. My first nights anywhere are the best for that reason, because I'm always nervous. Just fancy, I've been dancing for four years now almost incessantly, and yet I was just as wrought up and excited at my first night at the Orpheum as I was at my very first appearance at the Chicago Trocadero. I felt that I was out of form, that everything was going wrong, and yet when I came off the stage after the last dance, my manager shook hands with me and told me I had seldom done better."

"And how do you like dancing?" she was asked. "I suppose now——"

"Like it, of course I like it!" interrupted Papinta. "If I didn't like my dancing I couldn't make other people like it, could I?"

Now here is an idea as old as the days of Aristotle. It is the secret of the highest art, and behold it coming to the surface again in this *fin de siècle* dancing girl. Papinta must have the right idea about dancing as an art. Presumably she ·has not read Aristotle.

"Of course it's fascinating to dance," she continued, "and all that, but you have no idea of the amount of work that is behind it all; real, hard, disagreeable, serious work. Practically, you see, I am my own stage manager. You have to know so much about the work, especially in the *fire dance* of mine. Why just the effects that electric lights will produce on spangles sewn upon a black velvet skirt is a study by itself, and then all the details of stands, and glasses, and lights; I see to every bit of that myself; supervise everything before I go on every night, and all this besides the dance itself."

I asked her how she went about creating a new dance.

"It's very hard to say just *how* I do evolve a new dance," she answered. "I get an air,—a popular, lively air, you know—in my head, and get so I feel the movement and *swing* of it, and then the dance part comes almost instinctively. I place myself before a mirror and hum the air and dance to it—any old way—just so that it's a dance. When I get poses and combinations of steps that suit me, I try and remember them, and do them over and over again till I can do them spontaneously and naturally and as though I weren't trying. It goes of itself when you start right. That's much the best way, I'm sure, though I wouldn't advise an amateur to try it unless she was a born dancer. But if you are a born dancer and do a dance that you have worked out all by yourself, then you've got something new and original, and perhaps it will catch on. That's how I did with my *fire dance*—studied it out piece by piece, one thing suggesting another until I got at something that was entirely new, and my! how it *did* catch on.

"But it's not all fun, you know, that *fire dance*," she continued. "The heat from the lights is something terrific. Sometimes it is just as though I were really dancing in the fire. The big light is ten feet below me in that dance —full strength, right off the main, you know, and far up above it as I am, I can put my hand out over it and feel the heat just as if at the mouth of a furnace, and that isn't counting the other lights either.

"You know it takes six men and six thousand pounds of machinery, glasses, and so forth, besides myself, to furnish that fire dance. Yes, I thought

I'd surprise you, six thousand pounds. That's quite true, and I have to have my own light men. The ordinary theater supes wouldn't do at all."

I suggested tentatively that the fire dance must be one of extraordinary difficulty.

"It's more difficult than most dances," she admitted, "because you know I dance on glass, yes on *glass* that's as smooth and slippery as so much ice, and I can use only the ordinary dance slipper with 'Louis' heels. Think of going through that dance on glass. I've never fallen yet, only slipped once. One time though, the glass trap broke under me and I thought that Papinta had danced her last dance."

"But you saved yourself," I interrupted.

"It looks like it," she laughed, glancing over her sturdy, complacent figure. "But talking about myself," she continued, "let me tell you one thing, the next time you see me—(I know you've seen me once—but you'll go again, people always do)—the next time, don't sit so far front or too much to the side because the Orpheum stage is just a little too small for my mirrors. They have to be placed at such sharp angles that if you are at the side of the house you *can't see around the corners*. And now," she concluded, as I rose to say farewell, "now I am going out for a bike ride, but *hot*, my goodness, that forty ampere light in the fire dance isn't a circumstance to this weather."

Zola's *Rome*

Modern Papacy as Seen by the Man of the Iron Pen

The Wave, 15 (6 June 1896), 8.

M. Zola has just completed and published the second instalment of his great Trilogy, *Les Trois Villes*. The first was *Lourdes*, the one which is now in the hands of the reading public the world over—published simultaneously in four different languages—is *Rome*. *Paris* is the next to follow.

The main plot of *Rome* involves the doings of a French priest who visits the Eternal City and obtains an interview with the Pope in order to defend his book, *New Rome*, a work of radical and socialistic tendencies, which is about to be condemned by the Index. But, overwhelmed by the vast and changeless machinery of the Vatican policy, and disheartened by the blind adherence to dogma he is surprised to find in Leo XIII., he, of himself, repudiates his work, altogether disheartened. He is discouraged and can see no hope for the accomplishment of his purposes, when, on the point of leaving Rome, he picks up by chance a school book manual, a humble little work "containing little beyond the first elements of the sciences; still, all the sciences were represented in it, and it gave a fair summary of the present state of human knowledge." It dawns upon the young priest for the first time that here is the germ of the new power that is to revolutionize the world, and overturn and recreate all the great fabric of a purblind and tottering religion. Upon this slender framework M. Zola has constructed a vast panoramic picture of modern ecclesiastical Rome. While, of necessity, lacking in the magnificent action of some of the *Rougon-Macquart* series, *Rome* is, nevertheless, crammed with tremendous and terrible *pictures*, hurled off, as it were, upon the canvas, by giant hands wielding enormous brushes. As is the rule with this author's works, *Rome* leaves one with an impression of immensity, of vast, illimitable forces, of a breadth of view and an enormity of imagination almost too great to be realized. You lay the book down, breathless; for the moment all other books, even all other *things*, seem small and trivial.

It is almost impossible to criticize such a literary achievement. A few passages only can give one some idea of its character. Before actually beginning the story Zola poses his scenery, the background against which the drama is to be wrought out.

> Rome! Rome! the City of the Caesars, the city of the Popes, the Eternal City which has twice conquered the world, the predestined city of the glowing dream in which he had indulged for months! At last it was before him, at last his eyes beheld it! During the previous days some rain-storms had abated the intense August heat, and on that lovely September morning the air had freshened under the pale blue of the spotless far-spreading heavens. And the Rome that Pierre beheld was a Rome steeped in mildness, a visionary

Rome which seemed to evaporate in the clear sunshine. A fine bluey haze, scarcely perceptible, as delicate as gauze, hovered over the roofs of the low-lying districts; whilst the vast Campagna, the distant hills, died away in a pale pink flush. At first Pierre distinguished nothing, sought no particular edifice or spot, but gave sight and soul alike to the whole of Rome, to the living colossus spread out below him, on a soil compounded of the dust of generations. Each century had renewed the city's glory as with the sap of immortal youth. And that which struck Pierre, that which made his heart leap within him, was that he found Rome such as he had desired to find her, fresh and youthful, with a volatile, almost incorporeal, gayety of aspect, smiling as at the hope of a new life in the pure dawn of a lovely day.

In picturing the complicated machinery of the Vatican administration, the intrigue and red tape necessary to so much as even speak with the Pope, Zola doubtless has his own fruitless endeavors in mind. He observes, that to Pierre

The Vatican appeared like some enchanted castle, guarded by jealous and treacherous dragons—a castle where one must not take a step, pass through a doorway, risk a limb, without having carefully assured oneself that one would not leave one's whole body to be devoured.

And again in the same strain.

In the mournful silence which fell around, Pierre lingered for yet another moment in the deep embrasure of the window. Ah! what anxiety consumed his poor, tender, enthusiastic heart! On leaving Paris things had seemed so simple, so natural to him! He was unjustly accused, and he started off to defend himself, arrived, and flung himself at the feet of the Holy Father, who listened to him indulgently. Did not the Pope personify living religion, intelligence to understand, justice based upon truth? And was he not, before aught else, the Father, the delegate of divine forgiveness and mercy, with arms outstretched toward all the children of the Church, even the guilty ones? Was it not meet, then, that he should leave his door wide open so that the humblest of his sons might freely enter to relate their troubles, confess their transgressions, explain their conduct, imbibe comfort from the source of eternal, loving kindness? And yet on the very first day of his, Pierre's arrival, the doors closed upon him with a bang. He felt himself sinking into a hostile sphere, full of traps and pitfalls. One and all cried out to him "Beware!" as if he were incurring the greatest dangers in setting one foot before the other. His desire to see the Pope became an extraordinary pretension, so difficult of achievement that it set the interests, and passions, and influences of the whole Vatican agog.

Strongly materialistic, Zola never wearies of describing the exterior aspects of Rome. The old huge buildings of the classic Rome, as well as the Medieval and Renaissance city. What a splendid picture is this of the Colosseum. How much stronger and truer than Byron's melodramatic hysterics.

> But the horizon expanded toward the southeast, and beyond the Arches of Titus and Constantine he perceived the Colosseum. Ah! that colossus, only one-half or so of which has been destroyed by time, as with the stroke of a mighty scythe it rises in its enormity and majesty, like a stone lacework, with hundreds of empty bays agape against the blue of the heaven. There is a world of halls, stairs, landings, and passages; a world where one loses oneself amidst deathlike silence and solitude. The furrowed tiers of seats, eaten into by the atmosphere, are like shapeless steps leading down into some old extinct crater; some natural circus excavated by the force of the elements in indestructible rock. The hot suns of eighteen hundred years have baked and scorched this ruin, which has reverted to a state of nature, bare and golden brown like a mountainside, since it has been stripped of vegetation, the flora which once made it like a virgin forest. And what an evocation when the mind sets flesh and blood, and life again on all that dead osseous framework, fills the circus with the ninety thousand spectators which it could hold, marshals the games and combats of the arena, gathers a whole civilization together, from the emperor and the dignitaries to the surging plebeian sea, all aglow with the agitation and brilliancy of an impassioned people, assembled under the ruddy reflection of the giant purple *velum*.

Zola sees Rome through the eyes of his character Pierre, and he sees it in its entirety. When the great naturalist has done with a description, one may be sure that the last word has been said. The subjoined description of St. Peter's is absolutely complete. Every intelligent visitor must have been impressed by it precisely as was Pierre.

> On entering the basilica, Pierre had fancied that it was quite

empty and lifeless. There were, however, some people there, but so few and far between that their presence was not noticed. A few tourists wandered about wearily, guide-book in hand. In the grand nave a painter with his easel was taking a view, as in a public gallery. Then a French seminary went by, conducted by a prelate who named and explained the tombs. But in all that space these fifty or a hundred people looked merely like a few black ants who had lost themselves and were vainly seeking their way. And Pierre pictured himself in some gigantic gala hall or tremendous vestibule in an immeasurable palace of reception. The broad sheets of sunlight streaming through the lofty square windows of plain white glass illumined the church with blending radiance. There was not a single stool or chair; nothing but the superb, bare pavement, such as you might find in a museum, shining mirror-like under the dancing shower of sunrays. Nor was there a single corner for solitary reflection, a nook of gloom or mystery, where one might kneel and pray. In lieu thereof the sumptuous, sovereign dazzlement of broad daylight prevailed upon every side. And, on thus suddenly finding himself in this deserted opera-house, all aglow with flaring gold and purple, Pierre could but remember the quivering gloom of the Gothic cathedrals of France, where dim crowds sob and supplicate amidst a forest of pillars. In presence of all this ceremonial majesty—this huge, empty pomp, which was all Body—he recalled with a pang the emaciate architecture and statuary of the middle ages, which were all Soul. He vainly sought for some poor, kneeling woman, some creature swayed by faith or suffering, yielding in a modest half-light to thoughts of the unknown, and with closed lips holding communion with the invisible. These he found not; there was but the weary wandering of the tourists, and the bustle of the prelates conducting the young priests to the obligatory stations; while the vesper service continued in the left-hand chapel, naught of it reaching the ears of the visitors save, perhaps, a confused vibration, as of the peal of a bell penetrating from outside through the vaults above.

But *Rome* is not all mere description and ecclesiastical intrigue. A red thread of passion runs through the story. The critics who can see no romance in Naturalism may reflect upon this story of Benedetta and Dario. It involves a thwarted love affair, a stabbing at night in the shadow of a doorway, and culminates in the poisoning of Dario by his rival Prada, and Benedetta's death upon the dead body of her lover, the whole affair taking place in and about an old Italian palace. Certainly all this is romance enough. It is only in the details of some of the scenes and in the manner of their treatment that the naturalism is strong, as, for instance, the scene of the lovers' death. Especially faithful to the Gospel of Naturalism is the sudden return of the hereditary instincts in Benedetta, the fierce passion of the race blazing out at the supreme moment.

"Here I am, my Dario, here I am!" Then came the apogee. Amidst glowing exaltation, buoyed up by a blaze of love, careless of glances, candid like a lily, she divested herself of her garments and stood forth so white, that neither marble statue, nor dove, nor snow itself was ever whiter. "Here I am, my Dario, here I am!"

Recoiling almost to the ground as at sight of an apparition, the glorious flash of a holy vision, Pierre and Victorine gazed at her with dazzled eyes. The servant had not stirred to prevent this extraordinary action, seized as she was with that shrinking, reverential terror which comes upon one in presence of the wild, mad deeds of faith and passion. And the priest, whose limbs were paralyzed, felt that something so sublime was passing, that he could only quiver in distraction. And no thought of impurity came to him on beholding that lily, snowy whiteness. All candor and all nobility as she was, that virgin shocked him no more than some sculptured masterpiece of genius.

"Here I am, my Dario, here I am!"

She had lain herself down beside the spouse whom she had chosen; she had clasped the dying man whose arms only had strength left to fold themselves around her. Death was stealing him from her, but she would go with him; and again she murmured "My Dario, here I am."

And at that moment, against the wall at the head of the bed, Pierre perceived the escutcheon of the Boccaneros embroidered in gold and colored silks on a groundwork of violet velvet. There was the winged dragon belching flames, there was the fierce and glowing motto, "*Boccanera Alma rossa*" (black mouth, red soul), the mouth darkened by a roar, the soul flaming like a brazier of faith and love. And, behold! all that old race of passion and violence, with its tragic legends had reappeared, its blood bubbling up afresh to urge that last and adorable daughter of the line to those testifying and prodigious nuptials in death. And to Pierre that escutcheon recalled another memory, that of the portrait of Cassia Boccanera, the amorosa and avengeress, who had flung herself into the Tiber with her brother Ercole, and the corpse of her lover, Flavio. Was there not here, even with Benedetta, the same despairing clasp seeking to vanquish death, the same savagery in hurling oneself into the abyss with the corpse of the one's only love? Benedetta and Cassia were as sisters; Cassia, who lived anew in the old painting in the salon overhead, Benedetta, who was dying of her lover's death, as though she were but the other's spirit. Both had the same delicate childish features, the same mouth of passion, the same large, dreamy eyes, set in the same round, practical, and stubborn head.

"My Dario, here I am!"

For a second, which seemed an eternity, they clasped one another, she neither repelled nor terrified by the disorder which made him so unrecognizable, but displaying a delirious passion, a holy frenzy, as if to pass beyond life, to penetrate with him into the black Unknown. And beneath the shock of the felicity at last offered to him he expired, with his arms yet convulsively wound around her, as though indeed to carry her off. Then, whether from grief or from bliss amidst that embrace of death, there came such a rush of blood to her heart that the organ burst; she died on her lover's neck, both tightly and forever clasped in one another's arms.

But the crowning effort of *Rome* is the picture of the Pope. It is like a portrait by Velázquez, so well done that one feels assured that it is a good likeness. Faithful, rigidly so, it portrays carefully all the little weaknesses, the little, trifling defects, as well as the grander, nobler, imperial characteristics. It is human. Again Zola sees with the eyes of Pierre.

Pierre was in His Holiness's bedroom. He had feared one of those overwhelming attacks of emotion which madden or paralyze one. He had been told of women reaching the Pope's presence in a fainting condition, staggering as if intoxicated, while others came with a rush, as though upheld and borne along by invisible pinions. And suddenly the anguish of his own spell of waiting, his intense feverishness, ceased in a sort of astonishment, a reaction which rendered him very calm, and so restored his clearness of vision that he could see everything. As he entered, he distinctly realized the decisive importance of such an audience, he, a mere petty priest, in presence of the Supreme Pontiff, the Head of the Church. All his religious and moral life would depend on it; and possibly it was this sudden thought that thus chilled him on the threshold of the redoubtable sanctuary, which he had approached with such quivering steps, and which he would not have thought to enter otherwise than with distracted heart and loss of senses, unable to do more than stammer the simple prayers of childhood.

Later on, when he sought to classify his recollections, he remembered that his eyes had first lighted on Leo XIII., not, however, to the exclusion of his surroundings, but in conjunction with them, that spacious room hung with yellow damask, whose alcove, adorned with fluted marble columns, was so deep that the bed was quite hidden away in it, as well as other articles of furniture, a couch, a wardrobe, and some trunks, those famous trunks in which the treasure of the Peter's Pence was said to be securely locked. A sort of Louis XIV. writing desk, with ornaments of engraved brass, stood face to face with a large gilded Louis XV. pier table, on which a lamp was burning beside a lofty crucifix. The room was virtually bare, only three arm-chairs and four or five other chairs, upholstered in light silk, being disposed here and there over a well-worn carpet. And on one of the arm-chairs sat Leo XIII., near a small table on which another lamp with a shade had been placed. Three newspapers, moreover, lay there, two of them French and one Italian, and the last was half unfolded, as if the Pope had momentarily turned from it to stir a glass of syrup, standing beside him, with a long silver-gilt spoon.

In the same way as Pierre saw the Pope's room, he saw his costume, his cassock of white cloth and white buttons, his skull-cap, his white cape, and his white sash fringed with gold and broidered at either ends with golden keys. What surprised the young priest, however, was His Holiness's face and figure, which now seemed so sunken that he scarcely recognized them. This was his fourth meeting with the Pope. He had seen him walking in the Vatican gardens, enthroned in the Hall of Beatification, and pontifying at St. Peter's, and now he beheld him on that arm-chair, in privacy, and looking so slight and fragile that he could not restrain a feeling of anxiety. Leo's neck was particularly remarkable, slender beyond belief, suggesting the neck of some little, aged white bird. And his face, of the pallor of alabaster, was characteristically transparent, to such a degree, indeed, that one could see the lamplight through his large, commanding nose, as if the blood had entirely withdrawn from the organ. A mouth of great length, with white, bloodless lips, streaked the lower part of the papal countenance, and the eyes alone had remained young and handsome. Superb eyes they were, brilliant like black diamonds, endowed with sufficient penetration and strength to lay souls open, and force them to confess the truth aloud. Some scanty white curls emerged from under the white skull-cap, thus whitely crowning the thin, white face, whose ugliness was softened by all this whiteness, this spiritual whiteness in which Leo XIII.'s flesh seemed, as it were, but pure lily-white florescence.

At the first glance, however, Pierre noticed that if Signor Squadra had kept him waiting, it had been in order to compel the Holy Father to don a clean cassock, for the one he was wearing was badly soiled by snuff. A number of brown stains had trickled down the front of the garment beside the buttons, and just like any good bourgeois, His Holiness had a handkerchief on his knees to wipe himself. Apart from all this, he seemed in good health, having recovered from his recent indisposition as easily as he usually recovered from such passive illness, sober, prudent old man that he was, quite free from organic disease and simply declining by reason of progressive natural exhaustion.

Immediately on entering, Pierre had felt that the Pope's sparkling eyes—those two black diamonds—were fixed upon him. The silence was profound and the lamps burned with motionless, pallid flames. He had to approach, and after making the three genuflections prescribed by etiquette, he stood over one of the Pope's feet resting on a cushion in order to kiss the red velvet slipper. And on the Pope's side there was not a word, not a gesture, not a movement. When the young man drew himself up again, he found the two black diamonds, those two eyes which were all brightness and intelligence, still riveted on him.

At last, Leo XIII., who had been unwilling to spare the young priest the humble duty of kissing his foot, and who now left him standing, began to speak.

"My son," he said, "you greatly desired to see me, and I afforded you that satisfaction."

He spoke in French, somewhat uncertain French, and so slowly did he articulate each sentence, that one could have written it down like so much dictation. And his voice, as Pierre had previously noted, was strong and nasal—one of those full voices which people are surprised to hear coming from debile and apparently bloodless and breathless frames.

In denouncing Pierre's book, Leo XIII. breaks forth into a royal rage.

And from that puny old man before him with the slender, scraggy neck of an aged bird, Pierre had suddenly seen such a wrathful, formidable master arise that he trembled. How could he have allowed himself to be deceived by appearances on entering? How could he have imagined that he was simply in presence of a poor old man, worn out by age, desirous of peace, and ready for every concession? A blast had swept through that sleepy chamber and all his doubts and his anguish awoke once more. . . .

* * * * * * * *

Ah! that Pope! How thoroughly he answered to all the accounts that he (Pierre) had heard, but had refused to believe; so many people had told him in Rome that he would find Leo XIII. a man of intellect rather than of sentiment, a man of the most unbounded pride, who from his very youth had nourished the supreme ambition to such a point, indeed, that he had promised eventual triumph to his relatives in order that they might make the necessary sacrifices for him; while, since he had occupied the Pontifical throne, his one will and determination had been to reign, to reign in spite of all, to be the sole, absolute, and omnipotent master of the world. And now, here was reality arising with irresistible force and confirming everything.

With the Peacemakers

Lives of the Great Guns

The Wave, 15 (13 June 1896), 4.

They have been practising these days with the great guns out at the Presidio and at the military stations near by, with the fifteen-inch smooth bores and the twelve-inch breech-loading mortars.

The fifteen-inch smooth bore is the old style of cannon, such as was used in the war, and I was surprised to find that it is not so obsolete after all; that under certain circumstances and at short range it can hold its own with the more modern weapons, with the twelve-inch rifled cannon, for instance, that has been mounted but not yet tested. You are told that the old smooth bore is sometimes superior as far as casting goes. It is made of cast iron, which is cooled simultaneously from the outside and inside, whereas the rifled cannon is made up in a more complicated fashion of three jackets of steel, and that often there is not the proper homogeneousness throughout the three layers of metal, that sometimes the gun bursts. The more the old-fashioned is used, the sounder does it become, but this is not always the case with the rifled gun.

The twelve-inch breech-loading mortars are the kind that strike the observer with the most admiration. There are 16 of them at the Presidio, and there will soon be 154. They are fixed at an angle of 45° and throw an 800-pound shell from three to five miles. The man-of-war is not yet built that can withstand the shock of such a projectile. In falling it would crash through everything, would perforate the ship from deck to keelson. The aiming of these mortars is a study in itself, involving delicate calculations with transit, azimuth, and base line, observations to determine the vessel's rate of speed, and to predict her location on the chart; for it must be remembered that a whole minute elapses between the firing of the mortar and the striking of the shell—time enough for an eighteen-knot ship to steam far out of harm's way.

The fifteen-inch cannon throws a spherical shell weighing 450 pounds, and at short range may be as effective as the twelve-inch rifled gun with its 1000-pound conical shell and its 450 pounds of powder. The reason for this is that the conical shell is designed for penetrating armor; fired at such tremendous velocity it will make a comparatively small hole right through the ship. The area of destruction is small, and, unless a vital part is touched, the ship is not disabled. On the contrary, the spherical ball of the fifteen-inch cannon, while it will not penetrate armor, has nevertheless a tremendous force of impact; its effect is distributed broadly; the area of destruction is large; technically speaking, it will "rack" a ship from end to end, loosening beams and supports, starting bolts, wrenching and jarring everything. In the Civil War the rebel ironclad, *Atlanta*, was disabled and placed *hors de combat* after being struck by only three of these shells, none of which penetrated her armor. It would seem that the same principle applies in the fighting of ships as in the hunting of big game. The foe in either case must be *stopped* before coming to close quarters. The killing of the tiger or the sinking of the battleship is not the first thing to be considered. First of all, they must be "stopped," wounded, disabled. The killing or the sinking comes afterwards at one's leisure.

Such is the theory that obtains among many gunners of experience. One is rather glad of it. It is comforting to think that the old guns, the old iron war-dogs, have not outlived their usefulness after all.

The gunners at the Fort have an admirable expression, they speak of the "Life of a gun." Now this is fine and suggestive. It implies a certain individuality, a certain human or inhuman character to the guns that appeals to one. The "Life of a gun." You can fancy its birth in the forge in the midst of fire and molten ore; then its first shot and the certain grim quiver of joy running through its brazen loins with the recoil, when the savage, huge life is unleashed in a roar and a red flame.

I never tire of looking at such a monster. You see it in the bastion, gripped solidly upon the stone work, its chin salient and resting upon the parapet, silent, very watchful; its muzzle is, as it were, its only feature, combining alike the expression of an eye and a mouth. The gun is some enormous animal, sphinx-like, nursing mysterious thoughts, fed with powder, speaking one terrible word.

What is it in metal that endows these guns with a separate individual existence? Two guns cast at the same time, in the same forge, after the same pattern, twin brothers apparently, are as different as possible from each other. One may be docile, obedient, easy to manage, active, resistless, and the other may be perverse, obstinate, restive as a vicious horse, sulky and sluggish. They have their moods, these great soulless iron cyclops of a single feature. Of a time the best gun in the line may tire, refuse to do its allotted task, throwing its shell far short of its possible range, while the other gun, the perverse and sulky brute, may develop a sudden access of splendid fury, spitting its missile far beyond expectation, full of rage and strength.

And their length of life is as uncertain as human existence. The gun may last for years, solid and sound, and meet an honorable and glorious death in the midst of a battle. Or it may, without a moment's warning, develop a hidden and unguessed flaw, an organic weakness, and explode, collapsing all in an instant.

Or else an organic defect becomes suddenly apparent and the great gun is "condemned." What a degradation! How much better to explode in a red blaze of glory or to be destroyed in honorable war, annihilated on the battlefield. The "condemned" cannon is unlimbered and laid out by others of its "condemned" fellows, leprous with rust in the long grass. Then a dishonorable senile decay begins, the gun rots, and in its dissolution, rust, the gray hair of things metal, grows upon it. It crumbles in the grass, the sport of children that was once the fear of nations; perhaps it is melted up for other cannon and a second "life" begins for it, a sort of transmigration of the life of one gun into another. At least this is better than rusting to red dust. I hope it often happens.

Man-Hunting

The Coast Range as a Refuge for Bandits

The Wave, 15 (13 June 1896), 8.

There are probably few stretches of country throughout civilized nations the world over where stranger conditions exist than right here on the western slope of the California coast mountains. Think of it! To-day you are here in the midst of a great city, one of the world-cities; civilization is in great evidence, electric cars trundle past your door, and electric lights make a mockery of night. There is the drama, the opera, the great daily newspaper, all the outward conventionalities of progress and refinement. Really, for all practical purposes, it might as well be New York or London or Paris. Your dinner is laid for you on the table at home; it is a crime to go armed; you are *blasé*; you are over-civilized; you are effete even.

But go upon a three hours' journey to the southeast, into San Benito, Merced, or Fresno Counties, and you will find yourself in the heart of a country that has been, and that is even now, a very paradise for outlaws, bandits, and fugitive criminals. The same state of affairs can be found to-day throughout the Coast Range as existed there in the wild days before the fifties, the same romantic, melodramatic, absurd, over-wrought situations that sound so impossible in the dime novel and the penny dreadful.

A murder is committed, a stage robbed, a train held up in or near any of the Coast Range towns, in San Francisco, in San José, in Visalia, or in Fresno. The murderer, or robber, or bandit "takes to the hills." The countryside is aroused, proclamations are issued, rewards offered, descriptions of the man are distributed, posses are formed, the spirit of the man-hunt flares up, blood-hounds are put on the trail, the fugitive's track is struck, perhaps held; there is an encounter; a man or two is shot, perhaps the criminal is brought in, or perhaps he escapes, and public interest dies down and the affair is forgotten.

The ultimate result of the man-hunt is, however, not nearly so interesting as the curiously picturesque elements in the hunt itself, especially when one remembers how close it takes place to a great center of civilization. Imagine the flight of Dunham or the Evans-Sontag affair taking place in the vicinity of New York; yet who shall say that New York is more civilized than San Francisco?

It is the surrounding, outlying country, the Coast Range itself, that makes the thing possible. Yet the Coast Range is not the country that the majority of people, especially city-bred people, imagine it to be. The range of mountains that runs through the central and southern part of the State of California is not a vast, intricate, inhospitable reach of wilderness, uninhabited, savage, primeval. Speaking very roughly, this is the general lay of the land: there is the river in the midst of the valley, lined with towns and villages; between this and the foothills is a broad and uninhabited strip; then come the foothills themselves covered with ranches, ranges, and farm lands, and dotted over with villages; and after this the rise of the mountains through which the outlaw finds his way.

If he knows the country (and it is not a difficult country to know) traveling is comparatively easy. From the newspaper accounts of the criminal's flight, you imagine him crashing through breast-high chaparral, swimming breast-deep mountain torrents, scrambling over boulders, or wandering in the dizzying mazes of tangled forests. He is spent, he is exhausted, he is without food, without water, without shelter, the rain beats on his devoted head, and his feet are bloody; he sees by night the watch fires gleam, and he hears the distant baying of the blood-hounds—those much maligned, gentle little dogs, more like pointers than like the man-eating beasts of the *Uncle Tom's Cabin* drama, which are not blood-hounds at all, but Great Danes.

But if the fugitive—Mr. Dunham—for example, could be found (we must assume that the reader's imagination can stretch even to this extent), he would, in all probability, be seen to be in good physical condition. Through the daytime he has slept in one of the many ranch houses, cabins, or *jacals* that may be found almost anywhere throughout the mountains; he has refreshed himself at any quantity of springs and creeks in the cañon, he is well fed on the provisions he has found in the *jacals*, or that have been sold or given to him at the ranch houses. He may even be traveling on horseback, changing his beast whenever it shows signs of fatigue, stealing a fresh mount on any one of the numerous mountain ranges. For weeks he can follow easy, well-defined trails and paths; in certain portions of the mountains he can even keep to good roads perfectly practicable for buggy driving.

The rules of the game are simple. A man whose wits are sharpened by the stimulus of pursuit with intent to kill, easily evolves them of himself. He must travel at night, laying up in the daytime in any one of the admirable hiding-places with which the Coast Range abounds. When he does move he must keep to the ridges; this course has a double advantage: it is easier traveling, while at the same time the elevated situation often commands a view of the entire country for miles around; he must go to the south and east; any other direction will inevitably lead him into the noose; but let him once get into the Kern River country and "The devil himself" (so says Harry Morse, who surely ought to know) "will not get him out." There he can lie *perdu* for three, five, or ten years, until his affair is forgotten, then gently work down to the coast and ship for Australia or South America.

The Coast Range of California is made to order for outlaws—we again quote Mr. Morse. It would seem that in these mountains, and the country immediately surrounding them, can be found just the conditions necessary for profitable "operations"—precisely the right mean between civilization and barbarism. The fastnesses are finely proximate to the centers of the particular traffic or travel which is to be plundered. The lines of retreat lead directly and easily from the towns and villages which have been the scenes of the murders.

In almost every case the fugitive follows the same trails, heads for the same objective point, and is seen, or reported as seen, at the same places. During the flight of Dunham, readers of the daily newspapers have become familiar with the names of Panoche Cañon, Pacheco Pass, Tres Pinos, and Los Banos Creek. They are old battle grounds—old as the days of such "famous bandits" as Jesus Tejada, Tiburcio Vasquez, Chaves, and Juan Soto.

Tejada and two other Mexicans, in 1869, raided a store on the

Mokelumne road, near Stockton, killed the Italian storekeeper, his clerk, two Mexicans, and an Indian. The murderers "took to the hills," where they lay hidden for over a year, until Harry Morse, at that time sheriff, discovered their camp near Los Banos Creek in Merced County. Morse and a deputy, disguised as cattlemen looking for new pastures, started at once upon the hunt. They came upon the band—by that time a score in number—quite unexpectedly. Tejada was with this band, and though Morse suspected it, his description of the outlaw was so defective that he did not feel sure of his man. The sheriff allowed the gang to ride off, but obtained a closer description of its chief, located his next camp—again near Los Banos—drove one hundred and five miles in twenty-four hours, and made the capture.

If Mr. Dunham, as we have been led to believe, has chosen the Panoche mountains and the Pacheco Pass as temporary hiding-places, it would go far to prove that his plans were well laid and that he was thoroughly familiar with the country. In such case he would be but following in the trail of Juan Soto—Juan Soto, murderer of Otto Ludovici in Sunol in 1871; Juan Soto whose record of thefts, "hold ups," and highway robberies has never been surpassed in California.

The story of Soto's death at the hands of Harry Morse would be quite impossible in the most guarded and conservative fiction. It is one of those real-life stories that are too romantic, too improbable, to be put into a novel.

Immediately after the murder of Ludovici, Morse and a posse of some five or six took Soto's trail. On the third day out, in the neighborhood of Pacheco Pass, a sheep herder was captured, who conducted Morse's party to Sausalito Valley, where Soto was in hiding. Looking down into the Valley from the summit of the last ridge the party made out two or three adobe huts, which, it was learned, were only the outposts of the outlaw's camp. Morse sent the larger part of his posse up the cañon to make a descent on Soto's main stronghold, while he himself with Deputy Winchell proposed to secure the sentries of the outposts before they could alarm the chief.

Morse and Winchell rushed to the hut, flung open the door, and found themselves in the presence of Juan Soto himself surrounded by some dozen powerful Mexicans.

Morse did not hesitate, and so was saved. He covered Soto, who was sitting at a table, with his revolver and ordered "hands up," while, at the same time, he drew a pair of handcuffs from his pocket and passed them to Winchell, telling him to put them on the outlaw. Winchell dropped the handcuffs and fled. A huge Mexican woman caught Morse's pistol arm, one of the desperadoes jumped upon him from behind, and Soto sprang to his feet drawing his weapons. Here was a situation.

Morse managed to break away, and sprang backward into the open ground of the corral about the hut, Soto following. Both were firing continually. In his account of the affair, Sheriff Harris says: "The shots were fired in quick succession, Soto advancing upon Morse, every time he fired, with a leap or bound, with pistol held above his head, and, as he landed erect on his feet, bringing his weapon to a level with Morse's breast and then firing. After firing he never moved until he had recocked his pistol, when, tiger-like, he advanced on Morse again."

Finally one of Morse's bullets struck Soto's pistol, jamming the cylinder. Soto rushed back to the hut, forced one of his men to put on his long blue coat as a blind, and secured three more revolvers. Morse meanwhile had run back to where his horse was picketed and got hold of his Henry rifle. Just as Soto emerged a second time from the hut, making a dash for the hillside, Morse shouted:

"Throw down your pistols, Juan, there's been enough shooting."

Soto ran on without replying, when at a distance of 150 yards Morse shot him through the shoulder. Then, the outlaw badly wounded, giving up all hope of escape, turned back, drawing his revolvers, bent on killing the Sheriff.

One can imagine the looks of the man as he came running down the side of the cañon, a pistol in each hand, his hair in the wind, holding his fire till he should get within such distance that killing would be a certainty. He forgot that the Sheriff could adopt the same tactics. Morse did not fire until Soto was close upon him, then killed him with a single shot through his brain.

Nothing could be more dramatic than such an encounter. The rest of the posse were far distant; Winchell had fled, so Morse was left to face the outlaw and his men absolutely single-handed. That it was a victory for the Sheriff is almost beyond belief. It was a chance in a thousand. Even the author of *Nick Carter*, or *Old Sleuth*, might shrink from inventing so wonderful a situation.

"Man Proposes": No. 3

The Wave, 15 (13 June 1896), 9.

They had been out to the theater together and there was no chaperon. They knew each other well enough for that. On the front steps of her house she gave him her latch-key and he opened the front door for her. "You had better come in," she said, "and we'll find something to eat."

Every Monday evening they went to the theater and afterward had blue ribbon beer and *pâté* sandwiches in the kitchen of her house. It was a time-worn and time-honored custom of three months' standing, like his Thursday evening call and his meeting with her at the eleven o'clock service each Sunday.

She turned on the current in the hall and in the parlor, and went into the latter room and took off her things. He followed her about from place to place, and listened attentively to her chaffing him because he had passed her on the street car the day before and had not seen her. He protested his innocence of any premeditated slight, and they went out into the kitchen, both talking at the same time. It was all very gay and they felt that they sufficed to themselves.

The Chinaman had set out the beer and sandwiches on the top of the ice-chest in the laundry. She lit every gasburner in sight and fetched the tray into the kitchen and got down the plates, while he opened the beer and filled the two glasses.

"There's *pâté* sandwiches," she said, punching each little pile with the tip of her finger as she spoke, "and sardine sandwiches and lettuce-an'-mayonnaise sandwiches, and don't say 'and the sand-which-is on the floor,' because you say it every time, and it's become an old joke that was funny once but isn't funny any more at all. Here, don't talk so much, but drink your beer. Here's success to you." They drank to each other, she sitting on the deal table, clicking her heels together; he, with his chair tilted back against the sink, grinning at her over the top of his glass.

"Huh!" he exclaimed all of a sudden, as he set down his glass and glanced about him, "four burners going full head in the kitchen at this hour. I won't let you do that when we're married, young woman, I can't afford it."

"When we're——" she shouted, adding furiously "well, I *do* like *that*."

"Yes, I thought you would," he replied, calmly.

"You thought—you thought," she gasped, getting to her feet and gazing at him wide eyed and breathless, "you were—you are—we are——"

"I am, thou art, he is," he interrupted, beginning to laugh, "which means that 'I am' quite determined to marry you, and 'thou art' to be my wedded wife, and 'he is,' that is to say your father is to give us his consent and his blessing. I've been thinking it all over and I've made up my mind that it will be for next Thursday at twenty minutes after three."

"Oh, you have, have you?" she cried, breathing hard through her nose. "You might have asked *me* something about it."

"Oh, I didn't need to ask," he answered; "you see I'm pretty sure already."

"Pretty sure," she retorted. "Oh, this is fine. Oh, *isn't* this splendid! I just hate and loathe and detest and abhor and abominate you."

"Yes, yes, I know," he answered, putting up his hand. "Does Thursday suit?"

"No, it *don't* suit," she flashed back at him. "It will be when I say and choose; I mean—I mean——"

He shouted with laughter and her face blazed.

"I mean it won't *ever* be. Oh, I could—I could *bite* you."

"I think it will be Thursday," he said, reflectively. "I'll call for you here in a carriage at twenty minutes after three, and in the meantime I'll see your father and fix things."

She sank into a chair and let her hands drop into her lap palms upward, and drew a long breath or two, gazing at him helplessly and shaking her head.

"Well, of all the cool——"

"You see that will give us time enough for supper, and then we can take the eight fifty-five——"

"What are you talking about?" she inquired, deliberately. He went on unheeding:

"I got the tickets this afternoon."

"Tickets," she faltered.

"Um-hum," he answered, absently feeling in his inside pocket. "Here they are; see, this is the railroad ticket, and here's the Pullman ticket. Lower 10."

"Lower 10! It will be the *whole section*. I—I mean, of course—I—you. *Oh—h*, how I hate you!"

"That will give us two days in New York. I wired for a stateroom day before yesterday. It's the *St. Paul*. She sails on the twenty-third. Do you like the boat?"

"Oh, go right on, go right on!" she cried, waving her hands at him. "Don't mind *me*."

"Well, that's as far ahead as I've planned now. I don't think we would want to stay over on the other side more than four months. Then, you know, there's the expense."

She was about to answer, when they both heard the front door close. "That's Dave," she exclaimed. Her brother came out into the kitchen in evening dress.

"Hello, hello," he said. "Beer and skittles, domestic enough; can I belong? Beer's flat, of course, but I'll have a skittle, if you don't mind," and he began to eat a sandwich, telling them the whiles where he had been and what he had been doing.

He and the brother fell a-talking. She sat silent, very thoughtful, looking at him from time to time.

"Well," said he, at last, "I must be going," adding, as he turned to her, "I've a deal to do in the next few days." She made a little gasp, and got up and went with him into the front hall, leaving the brother to grumble over the flatness of the beer. She helped him on with his overcoat. There was a silence. He stood with his hand on the knob of the door. "Good night," she said, adding, as she always did, "when am I to see you again?"

"Well," he answered, suddenly grave, very much in earnest, "when *are* you to see me again? It's up to you, little girl; what's your answer? Now, when shall I come?"

She didn't answer at once. In the stillness they heard the humming of the cable in the street outside. Then there was an opening and closing of doors as the brother came out of the kitchen.

"Quick," he said, putting a hand on her shoulder, "he'll be here in a minute; when am I to see you again?"

Then she turned to him:

"Oh, I suppose Thursday, at twenty minutes after three."

Jack Hammond in Johannesburg and Pretoria

The American Leader of the Uitlander Insurrection

The Wave, 15 (20 June 1896), 5.

As far back as last January, the name of John Hays Hammond began to be heard in connection with South African affairs; a few weeks later he was spoken of around the world, and to-day you will see the same familiar name printed in the large type of the newspaper's scare heads. Mr. Hammond has become, as one might say, a maker of history. Occupying the prominent position he did in the Transvaal, it was but natural that the great political movement of the winter of 1895-96 should, little by little, settle about him as one of its centers.

Even in the face of imprisonment and sickness, I doubt if Mr. Hammond regrets the part he took in the Uitlander rising of the first day of the year of 1896. The insurrection has developed into an historical event, like John Brown's raid; the names of the men who were involved in it have become part of the chronicle of the world's doings.

In private life the American mining engineer is as entertaining and approachable as, in public affairs, he has shown himself to be keen, vigorous, and well able to grasp and to control a vast and complicated situation. It was my very good fortune to meet and to become acquainted with Mr.

Hammond in Johannesburg, at what was probably the most exciting and interesting moment of his career. He has his office in Simmonds Street, in what is one of the only brick buildings in the town. It is called the Gold Fields Building, and is a sort of center for the mining interests of the Rand.

The Consolidated Gold Fields of South Africa is probably one of the largest *concerns* in existence, aiming as it does to control the output of the whole Witwatersrand. Mr. Hammond's role is that of consulting engineer for this concern, and in return for his counsel and advice the Gold Fields pays him a magnificent salary.

But for all this the American engineer lives quietly enough. That his home is without the town does not imply any undue desire for magnificence or luxuriousness. No moderately well-to-do man would for a moment think of living in Johannesburg itself. The house is in the suburbs, at New Doornfontein, on the other side of Hospital Hill—the hill from which we were told the Boers were to shell the town. It, and Mr. Tilghman's place, out at the New Primrose Deep, were the only really habitable homes I saw in all the Transvaal. From Johannesburg it is precisely twelve minutes' easy drive.

This was on Christmas Day, and some half dozen of Mr. Hammond's friends were had out to dinner. The house, if I remember, is brick-built, of one story, very broad, low, and surrounded by an immense veranda. It is set in a garden of tropical plants. Taking it altogether, the place is suggestive at once of an American country-house and an Indian bungalow.

I have had occasion, later, to wonder at Mr. Hammond's self-possession during that Christmas dinner. In the Pretoria trials it was brought out that at that very moment our host was in the very thick of the tremendous movement which culminated in the Uitlander rising a few days later. Yet he presided in a delightful manner, talking and chatting with his guests as if the only care upon his mind was that the dinner should be successful and his friends entertained. It must be a man of considerable strength of character who can descend to the light commonplaces of dinner-table talk, and make himself agreeable to his company and at the same time keep his grip upon the vast and complicated forces of a great political uprising that is to disorganize the machinery of an entire empire.

Think of it, while Mr. Hammond sat there at the head of his dining-table chatting easily over his black coffee and cigarettes, Jameson and his six hundred with their Maxims and Lee-Metfords were straining at the leash, away

Mr. Hammond a Prisoner in His Own House.

Hammond's Residence at New Doornfontein, with Guards Posted.

Mr. Hammond Taking an Outing During His Imprisonment at Pretoria.

Hammond's Office, December 31, 1895.

up there at Pitsani on the Bechuanaland border, waiting and listening for the word from him to precipitate an insurrection, a crisis whose shock would be felt around the world.

A week later I saw our host in far different circumstances. War had practically been declared, the insurrection was an avowed and indisputable fact, the streets of the town were packed with excited men and with moving bodies of the irregular Uitlander troops. The American engineer's office was like the headquarters of a general of division. Mounted despatch riders came and went, armed guards were on the stair landings and before the doors, the hall below was filled with cases of ammunition, stacks of rifles, boxes of canned provisions, army blankets and all the *impedimenta* of a campaign, while, singular as it may appear, the flag of the Transvaal—as can be seen in the illustration—was flying over Mr. Hammond's office.

That Hammond's motives have been misinterpreted by many of his own countrymen is no doubt largely due to the feeling against England that sprang up during the winter. England came off second best in the Transvaal affair, and for that reason Oom Paul was hailed as the statesman of the hour, the man for the occasion. By implication Oom Paul's opponents, Rhodes, Jameson, and Hammond, were discountenanced. It became the thing to assert that Hammond would have received only his deserts had he been hanged.

But even admitting that the charges brought against the American were true, one cannot but admire the courage of the man who would confess himself as guilty of a capital crime in order to give his fellow accused the chance to plead guilty to a less serious offense which did not demand the penalty of death.

The Stage and California Girls

————

Society Plays, Their Element

————

The Wave, 15 (20 June 1896), 8.

————

Probably no State in the Union has furnished a larger number of successful actresses than has California. It is rather curious that this should be so. The circumstance occurs so frequently and with such unvarying regularity that there should not be wanting some good and sufficient reason to account for it. One thing, however, should be noted. Among all the throng of actresses that California has produced there is not one who has attained any noticeable success in tragic roles. Few have even attempted "the legitimate." California seems especially adapted to the growth and development of young girls who are strong in "drawing-room" parts.

It would seem that there are several reasons for this. Mr. Frawley of the Columbia Stock Company, who surely ought to know, does not think that the *desire* for dramatic success is any stronger among the California girls than among the girls of any other part of the country. Generally speaking, all young girls pass through a period of "stage madness," and generally speaking they get over it or make egregious failures before the disease has fully developed.

"There is more ambition among the girls of our State," Mr. Frawley observed, "more energy, more determination to succeed. Then, for one thing, our girls are usually very pretty, pretty and stylish, they have dash, they have manner—they are in a word 'fetching.' Then, again, the California girl is usually more refined. She comes of good stock; her home surroundings, as a rule, leave nothing to be desired. There, you see, is one reason why she is good in 'drawing-room' plays."

"How about native genius, inborn talent, and that sort of thing?" I asked.

"The California girl has not so much genius as she has capability of receiving instruction. She is, perhaps, pliable. It is the different social conditions which obtain with us that are responsible for this 'pliability.' In

Eastern communities girls are brought up more conventionally; they grow up along certain hard and fast lines, they are 'set in their ways.'"

Certainly this is not the case with the typical California girl, and I said as much to Mr. Frawley, who concurred, and added:

"Our girls are more romantic as well, and there must be lots of romance in the make-up of a good actress; a certain ideality that raises them above their work. California girls have plenty of this: they are natural, spontaneous, vigorous, pretty women, have more vitality and magnetism than any other class of girls I know of."

Some day, perhaps, we shall see this vigor and beauty and magnetism that Mr. Frawley speaks of devoted to graver, more serious—shall one say?—more intellectual, ends; and then California, and by implication, America, will produce a great tragedienne, a Bernhardt, possibly, or a Rachel, or, better still, a really great comedienne.

"It's the old question of supply and demand, in *my* opinion," observed Mr. Stockwell; "that and the stock companies. The facts of the case prove there is a larger percentage of theater-going people in San Francisco than in any city in the Union. People here go in large numbers, and they go regularly. I'll tell you why. In the East, summer is the dead season with the theaters. The hot weather comes on, and people don't want to be in a close theater in the evening when the thermometer is up in the nineties; they want to be out of doors. But with us in San Francisco the season is practically the whole year round; it is seldom too warm to be in a theater in the evening. People go winter and summer; the idea of dramatic entertainment is continually in their minds. For this reason, probably, our girls get more easily stage-struck than girls of other communities."

"And the psychology of the thing," said I, "should you say that our girls had a finer development of the peculiar temperament that makes good actresses?" Mr. Stockwell thought a moment and shook his head.

"No, I don't think so; I can see no reason why it should be so. I cannot say that the California girl is different from, say, the New Yorker, in that respect—she is prettier, though," Mr. Stockwell added quickly. "Of course, that counts, but it's the demand that creates the supply—that's the secret of it I'm sure. All girls, everywhere, are more or less stage-struck. Our girls have a better chance, that's the difference."

Zola as a Romantic Writer

The Wave, 15 (27 June 1896), 3.

It is curious to notice how persistently M. Zola is misunderstood. How strangely he is misinterpreted even by those who conscientiously admire the novels of the "man of the iron pen." For most people Naturalism has a vague meaning. It is a sort of inner circle of realism—a kind of diametric opposite of romanticism, a theory of fiction wherein things are represented "as they really are," inexorably, with the truthfulness of a camera. This idea can be shown to be far from right, that Naturalism, as understood by Zola, is but a form of romanticism after all.

Observe the methods employed by the novelists who profess and call themselves "realists"—Mr. Howells, for instance. Howells's characters live across the street from us, they are "on our block." We know all about them, about their affairs, and the story of their lives. One can go even further. We ourselves are Mr. Howells's characters, so long as we are well behaved and ordinary and *bourgeois*, so long as we are not adventurous or not rich or not unconventional. If we are otherwise, if things commence to happen to us, if we kill a man or two, or get mixed up in a tragic affair, or do something on a large scale, such as the amassing of enormous wealth or power or fame, Mr. Howells cuts our acquaintance at once. He will none of us if we are out of the usual.

This is the real Realism. It is the smaller details of every-day life, things that are likely to happen between lunch and supper, small passions, restricted emotions, dramas of the reception-room, tragedies of an afternoon call, crises involving cups of tea. Every one will admit there is no romance here. The novel is interesting—which is after all the main point—but it is the commonplace tale of commonplace people made into a novel of far more than commonplace charm. Mr. Howells is not uninteresting; he is simply not romantic. But that Zola should be quoted as a realist, and as a realist of realists, is a strange perversion.

Reflect a moment upon his choice of subject and character and episode.

The *Rougon-Macquart* live in a world of their own; they are not of our lives any more than are the Don Juans, the Jean Valjeans, the Gil Blases, the Marmions, or the Ivanhoes. We, the *bourgeois*, the commonplace, the ordinary, have no part nor lot in the *Rougon-Macquart*, in *Lourdes*, or in *Rome*; it is not our world, not because our social position is different, but because we are *ordinary*. To be noted of M. Zola we must leave the rank and file, either run to the forefront of the marching world, or fall by the roadway; we must separate ourselves; we must become individual, unique. The naturalist takes no note of common people, common in so far as their interests, their lives, and the things that occur in them are common, are ordinary. Terrible things must happen to the characters of the naturalistic tale. They must be twisted from the ordinary, wrenched out from the quiet, uneventful round of every-day life, and flung into the throes of a vast and terrible drama that works itself out in unleashed passions, in blood, and in sudden death. The world of M. Zola is a world of big things; the enormous, the formidable, the terrible, is what counts; no teacup tragedies here. Here Nana holds her monstrous orgies, and dies horribly, her face distorted to a frightful mask; Etienne Lantier, carried away by the strike of coal miners of Le Voreux, (the strike that is almost war), is involved in the vast and fearful catastrophe that comes as a climax of the great drama; Claude Lantier, disappointed, disillusioned, acknowledging the futility of his art after a life of effort, hangs himself to his huge easel; Jacques Lantier, haunted by an hereditary insanity, all his natural desires hideously distorted, cuts the throat of the girl he loves, and is ground to pieces under the wheels of his own locomotive; Jean Macquart, soldier and tiller of the fields, is drawn into the war of 1870, passes through the terrible scenes of Sedan and the Siege of Paris only to bayonet to death his truest friend and sworn brother-at-arms in the streets of the burning capitol.

Everything is extraordinary, imaginative, grotesque even, with a vague note of terror quivering throughout like the vibration of an ominous and low-pitched diapason. It is all romantic, at times unmistakably so, as in *Le Rêve* or *Rome*, closely resembling the work of the greatest of all modern romanticists, Hugo. We have the same huge dramas, the same enormous scenic effects, the same love of the extraordinary, the vast, the monstrous, and the tragic.

Naturalism is a form of romanticism, not an inner circle of realism.

Where is the realism in the *Rougon-Macquart?* Are such things likely to happen between lunch and supper? That Zola's work is not purely romantic as was Hugo's, lies chiefly in the choice of Milieu. These great, terrible dramas no longer happen among the personnel of a feudal and Renaissance nobility, those who are in the fore-front of the marching world, but among the lower—almost the lowest—classes; those who have been thrust or wrenched from the ranks who are falling by the roadway. This is not romanticism—this drama of the people, working itself out in blood and ordure. It is not realism. It is a school by itself, unique, somber, powerful beyond words. It is naturalism.

The Santa Cruz Venetian Carnival

Three Days and Nights of Fiesta and Fireworks

The Wave, 15 (27 June 1896), 8.

You got off the train feeling vaguely intrusive. The ride from the city had, of course, been long and hot and very dusty. Perhaps you had been asleep for the last third of the way, and had awakened too suddenly to the consciousness of an indefinable sensation of grit and fine cinders, and the suspicion that your collar was limp and dirty. Then, before you were prepared for it, you were hustled from the train and out upon the platform of the station.

There was a glare of sunshine, and the air had a different taste that suggested the sea immediately. The platform was crowded, mostly with people from the hotels, come down to meet the train, girls in cool, white skirts and straw sailors, and young men in ducks and flannels, some of them carrying tennis rackets. It was quite a different world at once, and you felt as if things had been happening in it, and certain phases of life lived out, in which you had neither part nor lot. You in your overcoat and gritty business suit and black hat, were out of your element; as yet you were not of that world where so many people knew each other and dressed in white clothes, and you bundled yourself hurriedly into the corner of the hotel 'bus before you should see anybody you knew.

It was a town of white and yellow. You did not need to be told that these were the carnival colors. They were everywhere. Sometimes they were in huge paper festoons along the main street of the town, sometimes in long strips of cambric wound about the wheels of the hacks and express wagons, sometimes in bows of satin ribbon on the whips of the private drags and breaks. The two invariable color notes sounded, as it were, the same pleasing monotone on every hand. It was Thursday, June 18th. By then the carnival was well under way. Already the Queen had been crowned and the four days' and nights' reign of pleasure inaugurated amidst the moving of processions, the clanging of brass bands, and the hissing of rockets. Nothing could have been gayer than the sights and the sounds of the town of Santa Cruz, as that hot afternoon drew toward evening. The main street seen in perspective was as a weaver's loom, the warp white and yellow, the woof all manner of slow moving colors—a web of them, a maze of them, intricate, changeful, very delicate. Overhead, from side to side, from balcony to balcony, and from housetop to housetop, stretched arches and festoons and garlands all of white and of yellow, one behind another, reaching further and further into the vista like the reflections of many mirrors, bewildering, almost dazzling. Below them, up and down through the streets, came and went and came again a vast throng of people weaving their way in two directions, detaching against the background of the carnival colors a dancing, irregular mass of tints and shades. Here and there was the momentary flash of a white skirt, again the lacquered flanks of a smart trap turned gleaming to the sun like a bit of metal, a feather of bright green shrubbery overhanging a gate stirred for a moment in the breeze very brave and gay, or a brilliant red parasol suddenly flashed into view, a violent, emphatic spot of color, disappearing again amidst the crowd like the quick extinguishing of a live coal.

And from this scene, from all this gaiety of shifting colors, rose a confused sound, a vast murmur of innumerable voices blending overhead into a strange hum, that certain unintelligible chord, prolonged, sustained, which is always thrown off from a concourse of people. It is the voice of an entire city speaking as something individual, having a life by itself, vast, vague, and not to be interpreted; while over this mysterious diapason, this bourdon of an unseen organ, played and rippled an infinite multitude of tiny staccato notes, every one joyous, the gay treble of a whole community amusing itself. Now it was a strain of laughter, hushed as soon as heard, or the rattle of stiffly starched skirts, or bits of conversation, an unfinished sentence, a detached word, a shrilly called name, the momentary jangling of a brass band at a street corner, or the rhythmic snarling of snare drums, as a troop of militia or of marines passed down the street with the creaking of leather belts and the cadenced shuffle of many feet.

And then little by little the heat of the afternoon mingled into the cool of the evening, and the blue shadows grew long and the maze of colors in the street was overcast by the red glow of the sunset, harmonizing them all at last, turning white to pink and blue to purple, and making of the predominant carnival colors a lovely intermingling of rose and ruddy gold. Then far down at the end of the street a single electric light flashed whitely out, intense, very piercing; then another and then another. Then as rapidly as the day darkened the little city set its constellation. Whole groups and clusters and fine nebulae of tiny electric bulbs suddenly bloomed out like the miraculous blossoming of a Lilliputian garden of stars. The city outlined itself, its streets, its squares, its larger buildings in rows, and chains and garlands of electricity, throwing off into the dark blue of the night a fine silver haze. Then all at once from the direction of the lagoon the first rocket hissed and rose, a quickly lengthening stem of gold, suddenly bursting into a many-colored flower. A dozen more followed upon the moment; where one was twenty others followed; a rain of colored flames and sparks streamed down, there was no pause; again and again the rockets hissed and leaped and fell. The lagoon glowed like a brazier; the delicate silver electric mist that hung over the town was in that place rudely rent apart by the red haze of flame that hung there, fan-shaped, blood-red, distinct.

* * * * * * * * * * * * * * * * * * *

Later that same evening, about ten o'clock, Queen Josephine made her entry into the huge pavilion and gave the signal for the opening of the ball.

The procession moved up the floor of the pavilion toward the throne (which looked less like a throne than like a photographer's settee). It advanced slowly, headed by a very little girl in a red dress, resolutely holding a tiny dummy trumpet of pasteboard to her lips. Then in two files came the ushers, Louis Quatorze style. They were all in white—white lace, white silk, white cotton stockings—and they moved deliberately over the white canvas that covered the floor against the background of white hangings with which the hall was decorated. However, their shoes were black—violently so; and nothing could have been more amusing than these scores of inky black objects moving back and forth amidst all this shimmer of white. The shoes seemed enormous, distorted, grotesque. They attracted and fascinated the eye, and suggested the appearance of a migratory tribe of Brobdingnag black beetles crawling methodically over a wilderness of white sand. Close upon the ushers came the Queen, giving her hand to her prime minister, her long ermine-laced train carried by little pages. Pretty she certainly was. Tall she was not, nor imposing, nor majestic, even with her hair dressed high, but very charming and gracious nevertheless, impressing one with a sense of gaiety and gladness—a Queen *opéra comique*, a Queen suited to the occasion. The Prime Minister handed her down the hall. He wore an incongruous costume, a compound of the dress of various centuries—boots of one period, surcoat of another, a sword of the seventeenth century, and a hat of the early nineteenth; while his very *fin de siècle* E. & W. white collar showed starched and stiff at the throat of his surcoat. He was a prime minister *à travers les Ages*.

When Her Majesty was at length seated, the dancers formed a march and, led by Lieutenant-Governor Jeter, defiled before the Queen, making their reverences. Directly in front of the throne each couple bowed, some with exaggerated reverence coming to a halt, facing entirely around, the gentleman placing his hand upon his heart, the lady sinking to a deep curtsy, both very grave, and a little embarrassed; others more occupied in getting a near sight of the Queen merely slacked their pace a bit, bending their bodies forward, but awkwardly keeping their heads in the air; others nodded familiarly as if old acquaintances, smiling into Josephine's face as though in acknowledgment of their mutual participation in a huge joke; and still others bowed carelessly, abstractedly, interrupting their conversation an instant and going quickly on, after the fashion of a preoccupied priest passing hurriedly in front of the altar of his church. The music was bad; there were enough square dances to give the ball something of a provincial tone, and the waltz time was too slow; yet the carnival spirit—which is, after all, the main thing —prevailed and brought about a sense of gaiety and unrestraint that made one forget all the little inconsistencies.

Friday afternoon brought out the floral pageant on the river. What with the sunshine and the blue water and bright colors of the floats and what with Roncovieri's band banging out Sousa's marches, it was all very gay, but nevertheless one felt a little disappointed. Something surely was lacking, it was hard to say exactly what. The tinsel on the boats *was* tinsel, defiantly, brutally so, and the cambric refused to parade as silk, and the tall lanterns in the Queen's barge wobbled. The program—that wonderful effort of rhetoric wherein the adjective "grand" occurs twenty-two times in four pages —announced a Battle, a "grand" Battle of Flowers, but no battle was in evidence. True, I saw a little white boy with powdered hair, on the Holy Cross float, gravely throw a handful of withered corn-flowers at an elderly lady in a pink waist, in a rowboat maneuvered by a man in his shirt sleeves, and I saw the elderly lady try to throw them back with her left hand while she held her parasol with her right. The corn-flowers fell short, being too light to throw against the wind; they dropped into the water, and the elderly lady and the little white boy seriously watched them as they floated down stream. Neither of them smiled.

* * * * * * * * * * * * * * * * * * *

At about half-past eight Friday evening the rockets began to roar again from the direction of the lagoon. The evening fête was commencing.

On one side of the river were the Tribunes, two wings of them stretching out, half-moon fashion, from either side of the Governor's pavilion, banked high with row upon row of watching faces. Directly opposite was the Queen's pavilion, an immense canopy-like structure, flimsy enough, but brave and gay with tinsel and paint and bunting. Between the two pavilions was the waterway where the boats maneuvered. The *Bucentaur*, the Queen's barge, came up the river slowly, gleaming with lanterns, a multitude of floats and barges and gondolas following. It drew up to the pavilion—the Queen's pavilion—and Josephine disembarked.

It was quite dark by now, and you began to feel the charm of the whole affair. Little by little the number of boats increased. Hundreds and hundreds of swinging lanterns wove a slow moving maze of trailing sparks and reflected themselves in the black water in long stilettoes with wavering golden blades; the rockets and roman candles hissed and roared without intermission; the enormous shafts of the searchlights, like sticks of gigantic fans, moved here and there, describing cartwheels of white light; the orchestra was playing again, not too loud. And then at last here under the night the carnival was in its proper element. The incongruities, the little, cheap makeshifts, so bare and bald in an afternoon's sun, disappeared, or took on a new significance; the tinsel was not tinsel any longer; the cambric and paper and paint grew rich and real; the Queen's canopy, the necklaces of electric bulbs, the thousands of heaving lights, the slow-moving *Bucentaur* all seemed part of a beautiful, illusive picture, impossible, fanciful, very charming, like a painting of Watteau, the *Pèlerinage à Cythère*, seen by night. More lights and lanterns came crowding in, a wheel of red fireworks covered the surface of the water with a myriad of red, writhing snakes. The illusion became perfect, the sense of reality, of solidity, dwindled. The black water, the black land, and the black sky merged into one vast, intangible shadow, hollow, infinitely deep. There was no longer the water there, nor the banks beyond, nor even the reach of sky, but you looked out into an infinite, empty space, sown with thousands of trembling lights, across which moved dim, beautiful shapes, shallops and curved prows and gondolas, and in the midst of which floated a fairy palace, glittering, fragile, airy, a thing of crystal and of gold, created miraculously, like the passing whim of some compelling genie.

While the impression lasted it was not to be resisted; it was charming, seductive—but it did not last. At one o'clock the fête was over, the last rocket fired, the last colored light burnt out in a puff of pungent smoke, the last reveler gone. From the hill above the lagoon on your way home you turned and looked back and down. It was very late. The streets were deserted, the city was asleep. There was nothing left but the immensity of the night, and the low, red moon canted over like a sinking galleon. The shams, the paper lanterns, and the winking tinsel were all gone, and you remembered the stars again.

And then, in that immense silence, when all the shrill, staccato, trivial noises of the day were dumb, you heard again the prolonged low hum that rose from the city, even in its sleep, the voice of something individual, living a huge, strange life apart, raising a virile diapason of protest against shams and tinsels and things transient in that other strange carnival, that revel of masks and painted faces, the huge grim joke that runs its fourscore years and ten. But that was not all.

There was another voice, that of the sea; mysterious, insistent, and there through the night, under the low, red moon, the two voices of the sea and of the city talked to each other in that unknown language of their own; and the two voices mingling together filled all the night with an immense and prolonged wave of sound, the bourdon of an unseen organ—the vast and minor note of Life.

"Man Proposes": No. 4

The Wave, 15 (27 June 1896), 9.

"Going away!" she echoed, suddenly facing him and looking at him with wide eyes.

"That's right," he admitted.

They were sitting on the green bench, all carved and whittled, that stood at the end of the pier. Behind them, on the shore, the lights of the huge hotel were winking out one by one. It was rather late.

"Yes," he went on, looking vaguely about on the floor of the pier. "The governor wired me two or three days ago, but I didn't want to say anything about it and spoil our fun. You see the governor is starting a branch agency in Liverpool and he wants me to go over there and take charge. I suppose I shall have to—well, have to locate there—live there—permanently. The governor knows a lot of people there. Then there's the business. You see I've been in the firm now for nearly ten years—ever since I graduated—and

I know the details pretty well—better than a new man—and the governor's business methods. That new lamp for the submarine torpedo boats is a pet hobby of his. I improved a self-adjuster to regulate the pressure that tickled him almost to death. He thinks I can get the contract for lighting all the new torpedo boats that the——"

"Oh, what do I care about all that?" she burst out, suddenly. "How about *me?*"

"How about you?" he repeated, pretending not to understand. "How—what do you mean about you?"

There was a silence. Then:

"Haven't you got anything more than that to say to me?" she asked, bravely, sitting up very straight and trying to catch his eye.

"Well, what can I say?" he answered, smiling at her. "We've had an awfully good time here, little girl, and I shall never forget you. You don't know how sorry I am to leave you. You must promise to write to me, won't you? Just 'care of the office' you know."

"But you—you don't seem to understand," she began.

"Send me a letter on board ship," he went on, quickly. "She sails a week from Saturday, just to wish me *bon voyage*. It's mighty good, you know, to get a letter when you are leaving for a long voyage like that. Oh, I say, little girl, don't do that. Look here; for heaven's sake don't take it to heart like that. Look here, look at me. I didn't know that you—that you really cared."

"Of course you know," she cried, looking at him from over her crumpled handkerchief. "How could you have thought anything else? I *told* you, didn't I? I made it plain enough, and you told me that you cared," she flashed out, "again and again—you know what you made me think—what you gave me to understand, and I—and—oh, what is going to become of me now?"

Suddenly she slid both her arms around his neck and turned her face close to his, as loving, as yielding, and yet as absolutely irresistible as when he had first known her. She was wonderfully pretty. He felt that he was weakening. There was something in him, some sensual second-self, that the girl evoked at moments such as this; something that was of the animal and would not be gainsaid. He saw her in a false light, knowing that it was a false light, yet willing to be deceived, finding a certain abnormal pleasure in the trickery. The odor of the cheap little sachets and toilet water that she used, mingled with the delicate feminine smell of her hair and neck, was delicious to him.

"Well, now, that will be all right, little girl," he said, taking her face in both his hands.

"How do you mean all right?" she demanded. "You *told* me that you loved me."

"Well, I *do* love you."

"As much as ever?"

He hesitated.

"Yes; as much as ever."

"Say it after me, then." She was so pretty and so pitiful as she looked at him through her tears, and he was so sorry for her, so loath to hurt her, that he said, half meaning, the words:

"I love you."

"More than any one else?"

"More than any one else."

"Say it all together," she insisted.

"Well, then, I love you more than any one else."

"And so—" she prompted.

"And so what?" he answered, fencing.

"And so you will—will. Oh, don't make me do it *all*. When two people love each other more than any one else, then what?"

He hesitated again. After all, she was very pretty, and she loved him, and he loved her—that is, he—but he had gone too far now. And, after all, why not?

"Little girl," he said, suddenly, "I think you'll have to marry me."

"Do you mean it—*really?*" she demanded.

He laughed a note, willing even then to draw back.

"Guess I do or I wouldn't say it."

"You wouldn't dare say that to my mother."

"I'm afraid I wouldn't take that dare."

"Well, then," she said, suddenly, rising to her feet. "I *dare* you to say so right now. We'll go up to the hotel right away."

He was in for it now, and so rose with her, saying:

"Come along, then."

They went up to the hotel and found her mother and father sitting on the porch in front of their rooms.

"Come inside, ma," she said, as they came up; "I want to speak to you."

He followed the girl and her mother into the little parlor of their suite. She turned to him:

"Now," she said, "say it now, just what you said to me." He smiled a bit, embarrassed. The girl stood to one side, glancing from one to the other. Then he spoke:

"This little girl says she loves—me—and I—and, well—we think—we want—we want to be married."

"Well, dear—me—suz," exclaimed her mother, and sat down with a gasp. She got up again immediately, calling: "Popper, for the land's sakes just come in here and listen all to this." Her father entered in his shirt sleeves. "If these two children haven't gone an' got engaged," continued her mother. "Now, what have you got to say to that?"

"I got no kick comin'," admitted the old man; "guess we know the young fellar well enough."

"Kick! no, of course, we've got no kick," answered his wife.

"But we don't want any five-year-engagement business about it; sooner the better. Guess that'll suit you," she added, turning to him.

"The sooner the better," he admitted, with a smile.

"Well, now, look here," said her mother. "My mouth is just as dry as a pocket; you go down to the bar and have 'em send up a couple of quart bottles of beer, and come up here and we'll talk this thing over."

He went out, and started down the porch in the direction of the bar. On the steps that led down into the garden, he paused and looked at his watch, wondering if the bar-room would be open as late as this.

Inside the case of his watch was pasted the photograph of the head of a girl. It was not the picture of the girl he had just left. Holding the watch in his hand, turned to the moonlight, he looked at it a long time, very thoughtful.

"I wonder—" he muttered to himself at length. Then he shut the watch with a snap: "What kind of a mess have I got into now?" he said.

"Man Proposes": No. 5

———

The Wave, 15 (4 July 1896), 12.

———

Immediately after the collision that night the stranger had backed off and by the time that the party on board the yacht had pulled themselves together and had begun to look about them after the first blind rush of terror, her lights had disappeared. It was not possible that the steamer which had run them down had sunk. She was no doubt a tramp cattle-boat, steel built, huge, well able to take care of herself. She had struck Trefethan's little thousand-ton yacht a glancing blow under the bilge, and then sheered off into the night as silently and as mysteriously as she had come up. What made matters worse was that the great hawk-beaked clipper bow of the tramp had smashed in the *Viking's* only seaworthy boat. All this had happened some eighteen hours since. During that time the party aboard the *Viking* had regarded their situation from three distinct and different points of view. First had come the panic, that blind, deaf fear of something terrible and unknown. Then as the day whitened and drew towards noon, and that menacing list to port grew no worse, a feeling of relief and ultimate safety began to spread among them, and Trefethan's skipper, who had been down in the hold with the carpenter all the morning, came on deck at last and smiled at them and shook hands with Trefethan.

And then after luncheon, with the wind shifting and coming in vast puffs out of the west and north, and the sea building up higher and higher over the port rail, the vague trouble and the sense of disaster returned and persisted, and they began to remember the smashed boat. This time, however, there was no panic. But there was something in the air, something in the very look of the yacht, and the feel of the rolling deck, and the queer laboring of the bows as she strained to right herself after each roll to port, that did not seem to need explanation. Then came the slow, cold clutch at the heart that tightened and persisted in spite of all effort at deception, first bewilderment, then an instant's return of the unreasoning terror of the previous night, a moment's hysterical protest against the inevitable, and last of all a certain grim calmness, an abandoning of all hope. The men and women aboard that pleasure yacht sinking in midocean turned about and faced, as best they might, the Death that reached upward toward them from the crest of every on-coming wave. The skipper had told them at last that it was but a matter of hours. If the sea went down with the sun, they might keep up until the next morning.

They two were under the lee of the wheelhouse. Some of the women were below in the cabin where Mrs. Trefethan was trying to read the services. Trefethan himself and the skipper were forward setting out rockets and roman candles against the coming of the night. She held on to the nickel handrail of the house and looked vaguely out across the empty waste of tumbling green water, her hair whipping across her face. He stood close to her, sometimes watching her, and sometimes fixing his eyes upon the distress signal, with its ominous reversed flag that was flying from the peak. For a long time neither had spoken. Then at last:

"I suppose—this is the end," she said.

"I suppose so," he answered.

"What *should* one do?" she went on, looking at him. "There is a best way to meet it but I *can't* think. It's all so confused. Death—this kind is—is so huge and so very terrible that *anything*—yes, anything—one poor human being can do or say seems so pitiful, so inadequate. The last thing one does in life should be—at least, one wants it to be—a thing that is good or noble or kind. It may be a false idea, but one has that feeling just the same, and instead of being noble or kind I can only feel bewildered and stunned and confused."

He was looking at her but he was hardly listening.

"It *is* the end of everything," he said. "That is why I want you to try and listen to what I am going to say. I know I could not choose a worse opportunity, but the power of choosing is beyond us now. Please listen. Nothing matters now, but, do I really need to tell you? Haven't you understood? Haven't you seen all the time how it was with me? How much I loved you? Do you know—it seems a poor, cheap thing to say—but if I thought that you cared—that you cared for me—in that way, I wouldn't mind about this business, if we were together and cared? What did I come with Trefethan for? You know it was just to be with you. I love you. Yes, I know it all sounds lame and poor, but I love you, and if things—if this had not happened, I would have asked you to be my wife. Of course, nothing matters now, but when I saw that there was no chance for the yacht I felt that I must let you know. No, not that either, for I am sure you know already, but I felt that I must be sure of you, must know your answer. Tell me. Suppose all had gone well, that we had got in safe, and I had asked you. You can tell me now. What difference does anything make now? What would you have said?"

While he spoke, she had been trying to think rapidly. She knew what he was going to say, had been long expecting it. Even before she had sailed, Jack had joked her about this man, declaring that he was "The Other Fellow." Jack had even wished their engagement should be announced before she had left him for that long summer's cruise. But she had told him—what he knew already—that he was sure of her, that it could be easily put off until she got back. To reassure him, she had even promised that she would marry him within a month of her return. Dear old Jack, he had not been out of her thoughts once during all the dreadful tension of those last eighteen hours.

But now this man, this "Other Fellow," who waited there for her answer upon this doomed wreck. What was she to say to him? She liked him, there was no doubt of that. After Jack there was no one else she cared for more. Two days ago she could have had the heart to tell him the bitter truth, almost as hard for her to utter as for him to hear. She had resolutely made up her mind to tell him that she did not care for him as soon as he should speak. There was a long silence.

"I know," he said, at length, "that I take an unfair advantage of you at such a moment as this. But it is quite impossible for me to tell you how much it would mean for me even in the short time that is left."

Never in all her life had she felt more pity and sorrow than she did for him at this moment. He was so fine and strong and virile, and she liked him so much in every other way. For her it was veritable anguish to hurt him in this the last moment of his life. In any other circumstances it would have been different.

At once an idea occurred to her. In the confused, distorted condition of her mind it seemed as if she had arrived at a solution. Why not tell him that which he wanted to hear, even if she did not mean it? What difference would it make if they were all to die within the next few hours? Would not this be the kind, noble deed that she had spoken about? Why not, if it would make him happier? Did anything matter now? There was little time to reflect.

"Tell me," he insisted, "do you care? Would you have been my wife?" She did not answer at once but put out her hand and laid it upon his as it was gripped whitely over the nickel handrail of the house, he caught it up suddenly in both his own.

"And you mean———," he exclaimed.

"If it would make you any happier to know," she answered, "yes, I *do* care."

He put his arm about her neck and she let him kiss her on the cheek, all wet and cold with the flying spray.

Trefethan and the skipper came running down the deck together with one of the sailors.

The sailor swung himself to the shrouds and ran aloft. Then he paused, sweeping the horizon with a telescope.

"What do you make her out?" shouted the skipper.

"She's truck down yet, sir," answered the sailor, "but I think she's a French liner. She's heading towards us by the way the smoke builds."

The Tennis Tournament

How Hardy Won the Championship at San Rafael

The Wave, 15 (11 July 1896), 4.

The tennis tournament developed quite a little scurry of gaiety and wild excitement all of a sudden over at San Rafael last week, which has relapsed as suddenly since. The great throng of pleasure seekers that stormed the Hotel Rafael on Friday and held possession over the Fourth melted quickly away during Sunday, and the place looks quite deserted by comparison; can there be anything more depressing than a deserted-looking summer hotel?

But it was all fine while it lasted. Everywhere one looked the same charming picture repeated itself under an infinite variety of forms: the deep green of palms and grass; the gleaming pink and blue sun-shades; the froth-like whiteness of the girls' dresses; the momentary flash of a gay-colored hat, and the white, white sun-light flowing around everywhere and quivering in heat waves from off the soft asphalt of the tennis courts like some sort of transparent, iridescent sea of light. The deep porches of the hotel were crowded and echoing with an incessant chatter of conversation. Smart traps and brakes came and went with a rhythmic clap-clapping of trotting hoofs. Somewhere, not too near, an orchestra was playing, while now and then a bunch of crackers went off with a great noise of sputtering and snapping. Everywhere a sense of gaiety and good spirits that was not to be resisted.

Somehow the tennis tournament seemed to be an incident only, a mere episode in the course of the day's round of enjoyment, like an afternoon's drive or a luncheon at the "Villa." Beyond a few of the more enthusiastic there appeared to be little speculation as to whether or no Mr. Driscoll would get in for the finals, or Mr. Whitney show good form against Mr. Hardy. I wonder if tennis is as popular as it was, say five years ago, and if it will have its day, as croquet has had, or archery, before that.

Of course one went to the courts in the afternoon to watch the final match, and the grand stand assumed a kaleidoscopic appearance, as the summer girls crowded into it: white everywhere as a background to a hundred varied and changing notes of color, pink and mauve and lavender and heliotrope, and delicious changing and uncertain shades that might have been any color, seen vaguely through the crystal heat-shimmer of the hot afternoon's sun.

The playing impressed one as being very good, good enough, at least, to have deserved better attention. There is a delicacy about tennis when it is played well—played as Mr. Hardy plays it, for instance—a certain finesse and admirable precision, which combines with good masculine strength and sand and endurance that make the game very fascinating to watch, even for an outsider, for whom it can be nothing more than the knocking of rubber balls to and fro over a strip of netting.

In the game, the final game that was to decide things, Mr. Whitney made a poor showing. He was "out of his class," as I believe a sporting editor should say. Mr. Hardy placed his balls here and there, wherever and however he wished, driving in like a catapult just at the time when Whitney least expected it, or dropping easily just over the net when his opponent was at the very bottom of the court. Hardy never seemed to tire for an instant; he was constantly on the alert, covering his courts as though he were half a dozen men instead of one. To watch him it hardly seemed possible the game was fatiguing, but he tired his adversary quickly enough. Whitney's drives and volleys lost their steam and precision, and for a time he seemed altogether unable to meet or return Hardy's hurricane attacks. But he rallied finely at the very last, and all of a sudden, smashing in again and again as though as fresh as at the very start; it was a spurt and a good one. The grand stand saw and appreciated it, and responded with the only genuine applause of the afternoon. It seemed as if Mr. Whitney had struck a winning gait. For about five minutes the pace was of the kind that kills, but in his case it killed Mr. Whitney. It was "4 love" against Mr. Hardy before that gentleman was aware that Whitney was away, but he held him there. Whitney tired himself out, and then Hardy went at him hammer and tongs, lightning quick, almost driving him out of the court, winning the game and the tournament and the championship simultaneously.

In the evening there came a dance, one of those very successful, brilliant, riotous hotel dances where the orchestra outnumbers the dancers and the chaperones gather in the back chairs and try to look interested in the three couples on the floor. It was too fine a night to be indoors. You suddenly remembered that it was Fourth of July, and you and your "crowd" elected to go outside and let off crackers on the horse-block rather than to remain inside and dance on the sticky floor of the dining-room to the music of an orchestra that played too slow.

There is a time for dancing, and that time is not a midsummer evening, when the Japanese lanterns are lighted in the trees outside and it's warm enough to go about without a hat.

A Californian Jubilee

Raising Sloat's Flag on the Monterey Customs House

The Wave, 15 (11 July 1896), 7.

Tuesday was the bright particular day of the Monterey celebration; the ceremonies appropriate to the occasion were performed under a cloudless sky and in the midst of enormous crowds. It would have been impossible to have recognized the old town of Monterey during the days of the celebration. Its sidewalks were jammed with a slow moving throng, its houses were festooned, its streets garlanded. At every turning and in every direction the eye was almost dazzled by the stretch of blinding tricolor that wound spirally around everything that could be called a pole. The main street of the town suggested the Midway Plaisance; every shop seemed a bazaar, while on either edge of the sidewalk sprang up a magic mushroom growth of booths and tents; peanut men, popcorn men, tamale and fruit men, chanted a minor chorus without a moment's interruption. There were public phonographs, merry-go-rounds, tintype photographers, nickel-in-the-slot machines by the scores. Even the calling-card writer with his famous bird of paradise drawn in lovely curves and sweeps was on hand and found occasion to turn the nimble penny. All sorts and conditions of men paraded the streets, Mexican War veterans, Grand Army men, militia, marines, cowboys, men in flannels and ducks from Del Monte, Mexicans and Spaniards in sugar-loafed sombreros, and touring Englishmen in tweeds and pith-helmets, very puzzled to know what was going forward.

On Tuesday morning occurred the laying of the foundation stone of the Sloat monument. It was deadly hot. Up the hill from all sides, across the potato and cabbage patches, over the slippery dry and yellow grass trudged and scrambled the assembling crowd. Many of them had come in dusty, rattling buggies from the surrounding country. The old rattle-traps stood about by the dozen, the aged horse, unhaltered, tossing at his nose-bag, the lunch under the back seat covered with a plaid shawl or a red table cloth, the old setter-dog asleep in the shadow of the lowered top.

The crowd was densely packed around the crane that held the corner stone. It was of country folk for the most part, to whom that day was a veritable event, something to be taken very seriously and to be talked about for the next five days. There, under the broiling sun, they stood, wedged-in, perspiring, very grave. A cordon of the Masons of the town made room about the unfinished monument. They wore white cotton gloves that showed the wrist below the cuff, red, fat and beaded with perspiration. In their left hands they carried long wands with all the gravity of lictors, while about their stomachs were absurdly tied their masonic aprons like flabby mail pouches, lamentably incongruous with their frock coats and carefully polished silk hats. The orations began. There were references to "Old Glory," "gratitude of the American people," "fitting tributes." The crowd listened with attention, carefully applauded the most distant allusion to freedom. Then, at last, with a great rattle of chains and a groaning of strained timbers, the huge stone was lowered into place. The crowd broke up, the women gathering up the hot and fretting bundles of infancy, the men tramping back to the buggies stolidly, thrusting out their chins in approbation. They had the air of men who have accomplished a duty, and they put on their coats again complacently.

That afternoon the Flag was raised. You had an undoubted thrill at the precise moment of the raising when the vast flag flew into the air like the slow flight of some immense, beautiful bird, and the salutes began to speak from the *Philadelphia* and *Monadnock*. It was fine and exhilarating, and worth while, and it made one forget for a moment some few of the drawbacks of the business—such, for instance, as the splendid new coat of whitewash that in honor of the occasion had been applied to the old Custom House.

Towards 2 o'clock the cortege arrived in front of this ancient building, preceded by a train of artillery and escorted by the *Philadelphia* marines. The main features of the procession were the two floats, one carrying the big blonde girl who represented the Goddess of Liberty, and the other the allegorical group of California made up of three very pretty girls in smart white frocks. Following these were the 200 Mexican War veterans, very old fellows, walking uncertainly, dazed for the most part, looking bewilderedly about them with wide eyes, and, after these, the little red-white-and-blue girls who sat in the grand stand in appropriate rows and made the "Living Flag." They were excited and chattering, and suggested a troupe of little trained animals on exhibition. Then, after the members of the procession had been disposed about the grand stand, more speeches were delivered, by the Mayor of Monterey, by Congressman McLachlan, the President of the day; then came a prayer by a naval chaplain, a reading of Sloat's proclamation by his grandson, a "vocal selection" and a chorus by the little red-white-and-blue girls and finally the reading of an address by E.A. Sherman, the Commander of the day.

Ah, that Commander of the day, what a figure he was with his bristling gray beard, his huge campaign hat and his fearful array of medals. Never was there a man so weighted down with the responsibility of his position. He directed, he organized, he presided, he exhorted and commanded, he shouted and roared like an unleashed lion, the fate of nations rested upon his shoulders, the destinies of a whole race trembled upon the utterance of his tongue. From dawn to dewy eve Mister Sherman played a part, a heroic, gold-laced part, and he played it well. He was a procession, a whole brigade, all in himself; he assumed commanding attitudes—Grant reviewing his army, Washington delivering his inaugural address, Wellington at Waterloo. He posed for the gallery. He was a series of living pictures all the more delightful because he succeeded in deceiving even himself.

Then at last out of all this fanfaronade, with the suddenness and unexpectedness of a rising rocket came the great flag, raised there by the same hands that raised it on that same staff, over that same old building so many years ago. There was a great cheer, genuine, true, with the right ring in it. And you were not ashamed to cheer yourself, and as the marines and officers saluted and as the great guns aboard the two war ships crashed and shouted, you felt a touch of the real thing itself, a touch of that fine enthusiasm which Sloat and his men must have felt when that flag strained at its halyards there on that desolate shore a whole half-century ago, when, for once at least, an English scheme of land-grabbing was balked and a strip of country far larger than the whole kingdom of Great Britain added to the Union.

It was fine and strong. Why not be glad in the great barred banner?—patriotism was, after all, something better than rhetoric and firecrackers. You felt glad that you were there, that, for all its failings, the ceremony of the Flag Raising stood for something that was good. It was worth while after all.

Fiction in Review

Chronicles of Martin Hewitt, His Honour and a Lady, etc.

The Wave, 15 (18 July 1896), 12.

Three new novels come to hand: *In a Dike Shanty*, by Maria Louise Pool (Stone & Kimball), *His Honour and a Lady* (Appleton & Co.), by Sarah Jeanette Duncan, and *Chronicles of Martin Hewitt* (Appleton & Co.), by Arthur Morrison.

Mr. Morrison's collection surprises me. That the man who wrote *Tales of Mean Streets* could descend to such crude, unoriginal, really amateurish compositions as these *Chronicles* is not to be explained. Of course it is just possible that the tales may have been written prior to Mr. Doyle's "Sherlock Holmes" stories, and, for Mr. Morrison's sake, I hope they were. However, I am afraid it is quite the other way about. You lay down the *Chronicles* with a feeling of indignation. The idea of the series is palpably, openly cribbed from Doyle. They are detective stories, bad detective stories at that. Martin Hewitt is but a copy of Holmes and Brett a feeble reproduction of his friend who accompanies him on all his adventures and relates them afterward. There is nothing new or original in any of the tales. If you have not read of Sherlock Holmes' adventures you may be interested in Martin Hewitt; but if you are familiar with the doings of that famous amateur you will not find these chronicles worth their ink.

Mrs. Coates' *His Honour and a Lady* is something better. It is a tale of modern city life in India, most of the characters being the officers and employees of the civil service and their wives and daughters. It is a bit dreary, I find, in spite of all its intrigue. Mrs. Coates is too literary in fact. One feels that there has been a polishing and a repolishing of the whole matter, a refining and filing down as it were, to twelve places of decimals until the verve and spontaneity, the life of the thing, in a word, has been quite covered up and lost under an exquisite cold veneer. It is impossible not to compare this elaborate study of Indian society with the rapid *ébauches* of Mr. Kipling flung off at white heat, crammed with living, breathing things, with no execrable "literary finish" to hide the true, honest grain of human life underneath. Mrs. Coates' novel makes fair reading, however, if one can be satisfied with its literature, or can forget it.

In a Dike Shanty, by Maria Louise Pool, is a novel—no, not a novel, nor yet a tale, nor collection of tales, but rather a picture of life, precisely the reverse of Mrs. Coates' production. *His Honour and a Lady* is essentially a work of the closet. The author sitting apart at her desk watching the world go by through her windows. But, it's a hundred dollars to a paper dime that the author of *Dike Shanty* actually lived the life she writes about. I honestly believe she and Caroline Branson did buy a tract of Dike. I believe in Orlando the terrier, in Mar Baker's "idjit," and in Rodge Peake's wife's niece. I believe in the tract of Dike and the flat grass land and the wind and the shanty and the hayricks. It's fine, and if there is little composition in it, little arrangement, or the pulling of concealed strings, there is at least the breath of real life. *In a Dike Shanty* is just what it pretends to be—a picture of open-air life on the New England coast, or rather a series of pictures, one for each short chapter, loosely held together by the little love affair of Leife and "Miss" Vance.

A romance may, of course, have excitement and brilliancy and any number of attractive things, but there is one quality it absolutely must have—that which prevents you from putting it down when you have once begun it. In this Elizabeth Knight Tompkins has succeeded very pleasantly in her new novel, *The Broken Ring.* (G.P. Putnam's.) The danger is nowhere uncomfortably thrilling, nor the mystery bewilderingly dark, but there is just enough of both to keep one well-absorbed until it all comes out right in the last chapter. There are some very pretty love scenes towards the end, notably the one in the park, where the broken ring and what the parrot said figure. The book is essentially a light one, more appropriate to a lazy afternoon than a serious morning, and must be taken as literary lemonade rather than beef tea or absinthe—pleasant and refreshing, with no lasting effects.

A Summer in Arcady

The Wave, 15 (25 July 1896), 9.

Startling enough surely is James Lane Allen's *Summer in Arcady*. It is quite a new note in American fiction. In the portrayal of the loves of Hilary and Daphne Mr. Allen is vitally, one may say, relentlessly true, he is loath to interpose any screen between the reader and the very essence of that bit of human life he is studying. He gets down very close at times, as for instance, in the scene where Hilary and Daphne are together in the meadow and Daphne hides in the grass at the approach of her father.

> He turned softly toward her. She was lying on her side, with her burning cheek in one hand. The other hand rested high on the curve of her hip. Her braids had fallen forward, and lay in a heavy loop about her lovely shoulders. Her eyes were closed, her scarlet lips parted in a smile. The edges of her snow-white petticoats showed beneath her blue dress, and beyond these one of her feet and ankles. Nothing more fragrant with innocence ever lay on the grass.
> "Is it time to get up now?"
> "Not yet," and he sat bending over her.
> "Now?"
> "Not yet," he repeated more softly.
> "Now, then?"
> "Not for a long time."
> His voice thrilled her, and she glanced up at him. His laughing eyes were glowing down upon her under his heavy mat of hair. She sat up and looked toward the wagon crawling away in the distance: her father was no longer in sight.

There is but little story to the book. No attempt at "plot," that miserable bugbear of authors which has been the ruin of uncounted numbers of good novels. *Arcady* is not a story, it is a picture, a picture of two young people, a whole definite piece cut from the canvas and set down in print. Daphne and Hilary meet, fall in love with each other, go through a short courtship and are finally married clandestinely. This is absolutely all, but the manner of treatment, the naturalistic point of view assumed by Mr. Allen makes the book one of the kind that will last. It is intensely original, as can be seen from a few extracts.

> The young trust themselves alone with Nature, who cares only for life and nothing for the higher things that make life worth the living. To them who understand her deadly approaches she can come least near with the power to harm. When her low storm threatens, they can rise to higher strongholds, perhaps to the great calm crags of spiritual retreat, and look down with pity upon her havoc in the plain. But the young, who have not learned and do not suspect, these from the creation of the world she has been engulfing as those who once walked between the walls of water.

*   *   *   *   *   *   *

> In a moment he was on his knees before her and had imprisoned her hand with the book in it. With the other he drew the book out and put it in his pocket. Then all at once the same unforeseen desire that had thrilled him that day in the meadow—the same unforeseen desire that had come over him as he braided the ring on her hand the day before—now rose in him with overmastering strength, and he held her hand.
>
> "Don't, Hilary!" she said sweetly, with a little wince of pain. "Let me go. You hurt me!"
>
> He caught her other hand.
>
> "Hilary!" she cried again, with a deeper rebuke in her voice, falling backward against the tree and struggling to release her hands.
>
> He tried to draw her to him with a low caressing laugh.
>
> "Hilary! Hilary!" she cried, resisting him with a sudden terror of his advances, his rough tenderness, the torrent of his feelings. Then with one awful thought, and the strength it gave her, she struggled out of his arms to her feet, and stood supporting herself with one hand against the tree. He rose, and they confronted each other. The great solemn voices were sounding now; the divine bell was tolling now. Her face seemed cut from marble, and her eyes were

full of fright and distress.

He looked at her, pale, without a word.

In this as in many other of the passages Mr. Allen strikes the keynote of the book, Daphne and Hilary are little better than natural, wholesome human brutes, drawn to each other by the force of Nature (Mr. Allen spells it with a big N) irresistible—blindly, moved only by an unreasoned animal instinct. In less skillful hands the thing might become revolting, with Mr. Allen it is little short of a charming idyll. The passage that follows is admirably handled. We have next a strange, intense love scene ending in an impulsive half-terrified elopement. The two are married by a county squire, the landlord of a county hotel acting as one of the witnesses. After the ceremony they return to the hotel. It is long since I have come across a stronger, truer, more pitiful picture than this, the closing scene of the book. It is late at night. Turning to the newly married pair the landlord says:

"You'll find your room at the head of the stairs, when you get ready to go up. . . . Take this lamp with you. Good-night."
He went out, but came back and thrust in his head.
"You can lock the front door," he said to Hilary, significantly.

* * * * * * *

It was all over now—the life of peril and unrest from which they had barely escaped—with its tossing nights, its wistful, heartsore days, its ungovernable yearnings. An awkward, embarrassed silence fell upon them the moment they were left alone. Daphne turned to a picture of the squire, that hung over the mantlepiece. From that she passed to a window, opening upon the rear of the yard, and stood for a little while, looking out tremblingly at the grass and the trees, silvered with moonlight. Then she sank upon a small, stiff chair, and dropping her eyes on her lap, began passing her fingers slowly, mechanically, around her handkerchief, going from corner to corner, corner to corner. Across the room Hilary had sat down by the table. His hand was shaking, his face was flushed and his tongue was palsied. The hour had come to him when, of all that can ever come to man, he feels that he must begin a new life and when he would like to begin it as one newly born; when his old past rises against him; when, if there is anything decent and manly surviving in him still, he is overwhelmed with some sense of the awful gift that love has brought into his unworthy life—a pure woman.

The great heights were never to be for Hilary. His ancestors, his companions, Nature, his own temperament and limitations, had appointed him his poor rough place far lower down; but if there ever descended upon him any rays of that divine light of the spirit which also rests upon such a union; if there ever reached him any fresh vision of the real manliness of what is right; these intimations from the wisdom of everlasting law, from the perpetuity of the species, and from the growing, triumphing movement of the world, conquered him and crushed him now.

*   *   *   *   *   *   *

The album slipped from his hands to the table. He started, and stole a look at her.

The moonlight, streaming through the window, rested upon her bare, lovely head, and upon one side of her face. He could see how white it was, how frightened, how appealing in its loneliness; a child —his wife—awaiting his will—submissive.

A new feeling of protective tenderness rose in him for her; and with a quick, deep breath he started up and went over, and took her hands softly in his and stood before her, looking reverently down at her.

"Will you go up now, Daphne?" he said, in a low tone. "It is so late, and you must sleep."

Her head dropped forward a little lower.

"Go, dearest," and his hands gathered themselves about hers with the strong, true pressure of a promise.

She lifted her face to him.

"You go with me," she whispered. "I'm afraid."

He turned to the lamp solemnly, and led the way. When he reached the door, he glanced back. She sat still in the chair.

"Come on," he said, with something in his voice that drew her irresistibly to him.

She rose and began to follow. But when she reached the foot of the stair, she stopped, faint and trembling, and watched him as he went slowly up. How heavy his tread was, how large his limbs were, how broad his back looked with the lamplight close in front of it! There was a pitiful fear of him in her eyes, and her bosom rose and fell with her quivering breath.

But at last she was happy and at peace: he was hers. The old, troublesome, uncertain life with him in the meadows, now so far away, at the picnic, in the pasture, was at an end. Girlhood, too, was at an end now; and with a certain new pity of herself she recalled the day when, careless and free, she had walked home across the fields in the warmth of early June, and had paused to hear him singing in the corn.

He reached the top of the stairs and, turning, raised the lamp above his head. But when he looked down and saw her at the bottom, he came down the stairs and put his arm closely around her, and they went up together.

The Bivalve at Home

A Visit to the Oyster Beds of San Francisco Bay

The Wave, 15 (3 October 1896), 5.

Did you ever visit an oyster bed? I never did until the other day. How many people have ever seen an oyster camp in full operation?—probably not one in a hundred. You see your oysters on your plate or on the shell in the windows of restaurants, where they are weighted down by a cube of ice with a bouquet inside of it, and that's about as far as your acquaintance goes. Just where they come from, how they are cultured, raised and brought to market and all that sort of thing you know nothing about.

And amongst other things of which you will know nothing until the day you pay your first visit to an oyster camp is the experience of eating an oyster alive just as he comes from the bottom of the sea with the fresh, clean savor of the salt sea in him and the weeds and barnacles sticking to his shell.

An oyster eaten in this fashion, sitting on the stringpiece of the wharf, you understand, with the wind in your face, and prying the wet shell open with your knife, is quite a different oyster from the one you eat, let us say, in a restaurant after the theater in a hot, gas-heated room (let us not say a private room), with all the delicate flavor blunted by highly seasoned sauces. And then how do you know what kind of oyster you are getting? If the *restaurateur* chooses, you may be getting a Texas oyster a week or so out of its

112

native water and that looks like the transplanted article, but that is shipped across the scorching Arizona desert.

It's worth the trip to an oyster camp—one of the Morgan oyster camps, off Belmont, for instance—just to eat an absolutely fresh oyster.

An oyster camp is a thing unique. It has its own particular local features, distinct and individual, just as a sardine village has, or a mining camp.

You go down a sandy road across the flats (fine, breezy flats they are, where all distant objects look half-buried in the ground), to where a very self-important little gasoline launch is snubbed up to the bank of a salt water creek, an inlet from the bay. You might be in Holland or in a New England "dyke." Everything is green and flat. The ground—some two feet above the water's level—is covered with reeds that go billowing and rippling seaward under the wind, wave-like, as if in anticipation of the ocean. There is a big desolateness about the whole thing that is almost inspiring. Somehow you walk with a larger stride and take deeper breaths and swing your arms, feeling very free and as restive of all control as the wind about you. No wonder the Hollanders fought for their liberty, if they lived in this sort of a land.

The gasoline launch takes possession of you, and you begin winding in and out in the most bewildering fashion. You are told that your objective point is a group of white buildings miles away beyond the flats, buildings that somehow look like a stranded excursion steamer. You spend most of the time in apparently going away from this stranded steamer. Sometimes it is on your right, sometimes on your left, oftenest it is dead astern. Then it disappears entirely, only to come in sight again, all of a sudden, ahead this time and close at hand.

The "camp" is some half dozen white buildings, built, so it would seem, on piles and surrounded by a broad wharf. The moment you arrive you recognize a familiar smell. Where have you met with that smell before? It suggests sanded floors and damp, thick table cloths and Gorham ware and other things. Then you remember it all at once. It's the smell of raw oysters. But hereafter whenever I meet with that smell I shall see those white buildings that look like a stranded excursion steamer and the blue-white sky and the pale green water and the distant rim of the low flats.

Seaward (of course it's the bay, not the sea, but then it looks like the sea), seaward the view is cut in two by an infinite line of bare, straight twigs growing out of the water, and marching along in single file away and away till they resolve themselves into a fine thin line. It makes one think of the pine swamps of Louisiana. These twigs are the stakes that bound the oyster beds; miles and miles and miles of them, and they are driven there to keep out the "stingerees" that will break you an oyster shell and grind it to fragments as handily as any vice. The "stingeree" is the sworn and natural enemy of the transplanted oyster, and to keep him off, the Morgan company must go to the expense of—well, four miles of stakes at 10 cents a stake—you may figure it out for yourself. And that's only in one camp.

Oyster culture in California is a far different affair from what it is in the East. Off New York the oysters lie in from two to ten fathoms of water, and must be dredged up, whereas the Belmont beds are nowhere more than fourteen feet below the surface, and may be gathered by the hand "tongs." The Eastern beds are naturally conducive to the growth and breeding of oysters. With us the beds must be prepared; and carefully, for your oyster is a delicate, sensitive little *mollusca*, and will none of mud and slime. Then again, as you remember, no one eats oysters in the East during the summer season, whereas for the more favored Californian every month of the year contains an R.

But the spawn of the Eastern oyster, the transplanted kind, will not thrive in California waters, will not live at all, for the matter of that. So twice a year, once in the spring and once in the fall, carloads of tiny oysters must be shipped from the Atlantic beds, brought across the continent in refrigerator cars and planted up at the company's camp at Dunbarton. Here they remain for a year or so, when they are once more "tonged up" and brought down to the lower camps. For another year they are allowed to grow, are again "tonged," "broken up" and replanted. A year later, when the oyster is three years old—it's at its prime then—it is marketed.

The "breaking apart" would appear to be quite a feature in oyster culture. Oysters are gregarious; they want the companionship of their fellows; they grow, often-times, in bunches and clusters, and have a way of attaching themselves to any object on the bottom, a boat, a bit of iron, an old shovel or tin can. Every now and then they are "tonged" up on to the barges, broken apart with sharp-pointed hammers, and thrown back.

One thing that surprises you at the oyster camp is the huge size that the oysters attain. Some shells I saw were nearly a foot in length (though these longer ones were, to be sure, rather thin, "pinched" is the technical word).

Others, when left to themselves, grow in thickness rather than in length, taking on layer after layer of shell, just as a tree takes on bark. An oyster will live for eighteen or twenty years, and the shell grow to tremendous size, though the oyster itself will be but little larger. He gets tough, however, and loses his flavor. Half the oysters that taste bad and seem to be spoiled are merely old.

The principal cause of the impossibility of raising the spawn of the transplanted oyster is a little shell insect called a "drill." The "drill" is the worst kind of pest. He thrives in precisely the same conditions as do the oysters, only in countless numbers. There is absolutely no means of getting rid of him. He's a tiny little beast, and can work between the most closely planted stakes. He fastens to the young oyster, whose shell is not hard enough to resist, and in a few minutes has drilled a pin hole into his very vitals, and of course the oyster dies at once.

In the morning I saw the men at work replanting and "tonging." A barge load of oysters that had been broken apart was poled out to a certain spot in the beds, where their particular variety was sown, and shoveled back into the water, so many shovelfuls to so many square feet of bed. It's surprising to see what rough handling the shells can stand, when you consider how delicate after all is the "bill" of the oyster (that part of the shell at which it is opened). But the barge was laden down with oysters as though with so much coal, and the men with the shovels attacked the pile with as little compunction as coal heavers. Throwing them back into the bed, however, is quite a knack, for one oyster must not lie above another. The men swing the shovels in a most peculiar fashion, turning them flat down just at the end of the throw; the oysters scatter like so much shot, one shovelful dropping over nearly ten feet of the surface of the water.

"Tonging" is the act of bringing up the oysters from the beds. Some half dozen scows go out every morning, two men to each scow. The "tongs" are for all the world like two garden rakes joined scissor-fashion very near the "tong" end. You plunge these to the bottom wide open, and gather anywhere from twenty to fifty oysters at a single scoop.

Oysters are best just after a rain—why it is not exactly known—a little fresh water fattening them and improving their taste.

Whenever you see a transplanted oyster of very unusual size you are at liberty to entertain suspicions. Either he is old and therefore tasteless or has been doctored and again therefore tasteless. You may fatten a turkey by blowing him up with a quill, and you may fatten an oyster by chopping off the end of his bill and forcing him to drink fresh water for an hour or so.

Popular prejudice to the contrary notwithstanding, an oyster must not be large, the larger he is the older he is, and the older he is the tougher he becomes and the more he loses his flavor. At three years old he is in his prime, he's fat then, and about as large as a silver dollar, and if he is a point—an oyster fit for the table of a gourmet—he is tipped with black about the edges.

These are the kind that grow rather close to the shore, where they obtain a richer and more generous nourishment. Be assured that more labor has been expended upon that oyster to bring him to this condition than you can have any idea of. Think of his long westward journey in refrigerator cars, think of the three years of constant planting and replanting and the army of abominable little drills that have been kept away from him, and the miles and miles of stakes—at 10 cents a stake—and the "breaking up" and the "tonging" and all that. Once I read about a Roman emperor warring in Palestine, who had oysters brought him fresh from Ostia, near Rome, by relays of runners. Surely an equal amount of labor has been spent over that oyster you will eat to-night after the theater (not in a private room), an equal amount of labor, surely, only, to really enjoy him, you should eat him sitting on the stringpiece of the wharf at the Belmont camp, prying open the wet shell with your penknife, the wind in your face and the smell of salt in your nostrils.

Trilby and Princess Flavia

An Interviewer, Two Actresses, and Several Confidences

The Wave, 15 (10 October 1896), 8.

It has been my very good fortune this week to enjoy a half hour's chat with two most delightful women, Edith Crane and Isabel Irving.

For two actresses who are so thoroughly alike in the art of pleasing Miss Crane and Miss Irving are surprisingly dissimilar.

Miss Crane is very tall and fair, Miss Irving rather small and dark; Miss Crane wore a wonderful pink gown, a "creation," of what a female novelist would call "some soft, clinging stuff." Miss Irving was dressed in the most unassuming black. The actress who impersonates Trilby, the poor little *grisette* of the "Quarter," had encircled her fingers with the most exquisite rings; she who interprets Flavia, the princess of a royal house, wore absolutely no jewelry at all.

While you are talking with Miss Crane you feel that at no instant does she forget herself and the fact that she is a brilliant and successful actress, assured of her position, conscious of her power. Whereas in five minutes Miss Irving has made you forget that she was ever on the stage at all, and you see only a very charming and gracious woman, without the slightest tinge of professionalism about her, straightforward, unaffected, sincere, altogether delightful.

I saw Miss Crane at her rooms in the Baldwin about three o'clock in the afternoon. She is very tall, indeed—that is your very first impression—tall enough to look most men straight in the eyes, her glance on a level with theirs, as tall, in fact, as Mr. Du Maurier intended Trilby should be, as tall as Miss Rehan, he says—just the right height.

I sat down on the sofa opposite Miss Crane, and we began to talk of things theatrical. I believe I commenced by remarking—interrogatively—as to the difficulty of preparing such a role as that of Trilby.

"You can have no idea," said Miss Crane, "how difficult it really was."

"Difficult in just what way?" said I.

"Difficult on account of its extreme simplicity."

I confess this had not occurred to me before.

"It's all very well," continued Miss Crane, "when you are preparing a strongly marked emotional part, where you can forget yourself and let yourself go," and she emphasized the last word with such a look and gesture that I know now just exactly how Miss Crane would let herself "go."

"You mean that you must keep yourself in restraint?"

"At every moment, and yet you must be strong and effective. And then the part is difficult in other ways."

"As, for instance?"

"To make Trilby unconstrained and free-mannered yet not hoydenish and vulgar. Trilby is not in the least vulgar, nor is she, on the other hand, in the remotest way conventional. You can have no idea how difficult it was for me to hit upon precisely the right balance between the two extremes."

"And having once hit upon it, to maintain it?" I inquired. Miss Crane did not seem to think this was so hard.

"That all comes with repetition and practice."

"And further. Tell me something else about your preparations and studies for the role—the details, you know."

"Ah, the details, those are the things that count, but as often as not the audience is not appreciative of them—it misses them."

"But if one slurred them over—"

"They would notice the slur at once and condemn you accordingly."

"Can you mention a particular case?"

"Well, Trilby's laugh, for instance. That was the most difficult of all. There is no mirth in that laugh. I found to arrive at that effect the laugh should come from the chest. I practiced that laugh and practiced it until my body was sore, but I finally got it."

We talked of Australia a few moments after that, and of Honolulu and the enthusiasm of *Trilby's* reception there, and then the conversation came back to the stage again.

I asked Miss Crane about first nights and nervousness and stage frights.

"Oh, I'm always nervous," she answered, "when I'm on the stage. I'm strung so tense at such times that the least little thing, a little noise in the wings or from the front jars inexpressibly. I get angry over trifles, I'm irritable and impatient. Oh," she continued smiling, "I'm quite a different sort of person when I'm on the stage."

"How about the appreciation of an audience," I asked, "and its effect upon your acting?"

"Well, it's not always mere noise that stimulates one to do one's best, not the mere hand clapping and bravos."

"That comes after the effort, of course," I suggested.

"Precisely; I can tell when an audience is sympathetic and appreciative long before they are ready to applaud."

"For instance?"

"In the death scene in *Trilby*. It's the silence in the house that counts then. If I feel that the audience is all tense and breathless with interest I can throw myself into the spirit of the lines with ten times the fervor and effect that I can when I hear those little jarring noises I spoke of. The dropping of a fan, the rustling of a program, or the sound of whispering. I know their attention is away then and my own interest wanes. I don't care to please them as soon as they don't care to be pleased."

A little after this, when we were talking of distinctions between tragedy and comedy, Miss Crane observed: "I'm one of those, you know, who believe that comedy is not only a higher form of dramatic art than tragedy, but also more difficult. In tragedy your emotions are strongly marked, sharply defined; you can scarcely go wrong. You require no effort to hold yourself in check; there is little repression. But in comedy, there are the little gradations of emotion, the delicate shades of sentiment, the fine play of light and shadow, all of which must run with the greatest vivacity and rapidity, must appear to be absolutely spontaneous. Oh, yes, comedy is the more difficult of the two."

I have never heard this distinction made before. It strikes me as very true, however.

I saw Isabel Irving in the parlor of her hotel just after she had come in from an afternoon's excursion. As I said before, she is a little woman, who dresses in black and with the least possible ostentation—from her appearance, one of the last women in the world you would take for an actress.

But not only do her appearance and mode of dress contribute to this impression. Miss Irving's conversation is not that of the professional actress. There is not the least pose about Miss Irving in her private life. Her acting ceases the moment she leaves the stage. Once outside the theater she does not seem to care to impress you with the fact that she is a renowned comedienne. In other words, she does not act the role of a celebrity—she prefers, which is far more pleasing, to be herself simply, frankly, without the slightest affectation. At once she evaded the subject of her profession.

"Please don't ask me to talk about that," she said. "One cannot help seeming egotistical when one talks in that strain. It would be I—I—I, to the end of the chapter. I would make myself and my work seem of too great importance."

"And yet I don't doubt," I hazarded, "that you take your chosen profession seriously."

Miss Irving sat up with sudden energy.

"Believe me," she said earnestly, "it is the only way to get on in any profession. The instant you make light of your work you lose your touch. Why, I have been nine years upon the stage, and it seems to me I have but crossed the threshold."

"And after nine more years?" said I.

"There will still be rooms beyond," she answered, smiling. "The further one goes, the further one sees."

For the moment I began to think that Miss Irving cared for little beyond her acting—that her whole life and energy were bound up in her profession. Perhaps I hinted at the possibility.

"No," she answered promptly, "I am very fond of my books, and of outdoor exercise. Don't ask me about bicycling—that's one of the stock questions of the interviewers."

I deprecated bicycles upon the instant.

"I prefer a horse myself," said Miss Irving. "I am fond of books and reading, and nothing pleases me better than to spend an afternoon in an old book store, picking."

Of the typical note-book reporter Miss Irving has a horror that is almost religious. It is amusing enough to hear her describe her experiences:

"They come to me," she said, "with their pencil and open book, and sit up there and bombard me with questions and—"

"What are some of the questions?" I interrupted, anxious to know what to avoid.

"Well, for instance, they begin this way: 'What are your fads, Miss Irving?'

(and I loathe fads), and again: 'Miss Irving, have you got any pets?' 'What do you think of the new woman?' 'Are you for gold or silver?' I just answer them in monosyllables."

"And that discomfits them?"

"Oh, no, indeed; not in the least," she answered.

I found it very hard to interview Miss Irving in the strict sense of the word. In spite of my best resolves our conversation wandered from theatrical matters, and before I knew it we were discussing the *Rubáiyát of Omar Khayyám*, and from that went on—I forget how the transition was made—to Justin McCarthy and the simplicity and unaffectedness of great men. Now this was not as it should be, for it was my bounden duty to ascertain Miss Irving's views as to what new plays she had in prospect, and what were her favorite roles, etc. Yet I enjoyed this sort of talk much better than the conversation I had anticipated, and after all it was characteristic, and so not out of place.

I think the most lasting impression that one carries away from a meeting with Isabel Irving is her absolute sincerity and conviction, her seriousness and her fine disregard for the smaller things of life. One especially noteworthy point of difference between Miss Irving and Miss Crane is the different standpoints from which each regards the play in which she is now starring.

"When I first played Trilby," Miss Crane had said, "I was delighted with the part. I have been acting it steadily now for nearly five months, and now I loathe it." Doubtless, however, Miss Crane exaggerated her ennui. Miss Irving, on the other hand, is still enthusiastic over *Zenda*.

"It seems to me I could never tire of it," she exclaimed. "The more I see of it, the more I am impressed."

You come away from a talk with Edith Crane with the impression that a brilliant and gracious actress has been good enough to grant you a half hour's interview. Isabel Irving makes you feel that you have paid an afternoon call upon some very charming woman of your acquaintance.

Football in Town

The First Match of the Season at Central Park

The Wave, 15 (10 October 1896), 9.

The California football season of '96 was opened last Saturday by a match game between Reliance and California. The line-up was as follows: Reliance——Burnette, center; Wells, right guard; Oliver, left guard; Sexton, left tackle; Middlemas, right tackle; Langan, left end; Racine, right end; Nahl, quarterback; Walton (captain), right halfback; Carter, left halfback; Arlett, fullback. California——Birdsall, center; Griesberg, right guard; Ludlow, left guard; Julian, left tackle; Castlehun, right tackle; Craig, left end; Hopper, right end; Kennedy, quarterback; Hall, right halfback; Whipple, left halfback; Ransome (captain), fullback.

Frankenheimer, umpire. Natt, referee.

It is too early in the season to criticise the work of either team except in the most general terms. Reliance had the heavier eleven, and chose to adopt a system of line bucking and mass plays that in the end netted two touchdowns. By the end of the first half Walton had about sized up the California eleven, and finding the weak points in its line between Ludlow and Julian and between Griesberg and Castlehun, sent his halves against them all through the second half. It was the weakness of California rather than the strength of Reliance that was responsible for the gains of the last named eleven. Walton and Carter should easily have been stopped in their attacks upon the California line. The ball was snapped and passed slowly, and as often as not the runner was far ahead of his interference by the time he struck the line. The insistent hammering at guard and tackle by the Reliance halves made the game a dull one. On the side of the Athletic Club but few end plays were attempted. Hopper gave good account of himself in his position on California's right end, and like Ransome or Kennedy stopped the runner when the play was around the left. On the defensive the Reliance was weak. Neither their ends nor backs could stop Ransome short of a ten or fifteen yard gain; nor could their line hold well against the rare wedge plays of the California team. If the collegians had chosen to play a running instead of a kicking game they would undoubtedly have scored during the first half.

Ransome played his team considerably in accordance with the new rules, which tend to bar mass plays. All through the first half California played a kicking game—often kicking upon the first down—and played it admirably, though Ransome had the wind directly against him. His center and guards were hardly able to hold the Reliance line long enough for a good punt, but his ends, Hopper and Craig, supported him well, Hopper getting down the field almost as rapidly as the ball. During the game on several occasions Ransome punted from a kick-off in a new and peculiar fashion, sending the ball along the ground instead of over the heads of the opposing team. This is a very clever tactic, as an oblong ball rolling along the surface of the ground is far more difficult to catch than the same ball when falling through the air. Besides this a ball kicked in this fashion is very apt to touch a player on the other side, after which the runners of the kicking side are at liberty to fall on it or even—if possible—to pick it up and run with it.

It would not be surprising to see this method of punting from a kick-off —first introduced by the Harvard team of '94—very largely adopted during the coming season. When successful it offers the advantage of a long gain acquired by little effort, while at the same time allowing the kicking side to retain possession of the ball. Even if it fails—that is, if the ends do not succeed in dropping on the ball—there is no more loss than that sustained by an overhead punt.

Ransome is far from 'varsity form as yet. In fact, the California fullback rarely is at his best until toward the close of the season. In Saturday's game his overhead punting—even making allowance for the weakness of the forwards—was unsatisfactory, and at the end of the first half he missed a very easy try for a field goal, and that at a moment when he was allowed plenty of time. In his running with the ball, especially in the round-the-end plays, it is apparent, even from Saturday's game, that he has improved. He is probably one of the hardest runners in the West, and one of the most difficult men to tackle, using, as he does, the straight-arm guard with more effect than any other runner yet seen on the coast.

Hopper (R.E.) is a promising end, getting into every play and rarely failing to break through the interference when the play is around his end. His best characteristic is the quickness with which he gets away after the ball is snapped. Under Butterworth's coaching he should make the 'varsity team this year.

For Reliance, Walton, Racine and Carter played the best game. Oliver, at left guard, was something of a disappointment. He seems to have gone back from his form of two years ago, and Ludlow of California had little difficulty in holding him. Speaking generally, the game was hardly more than a trying out; neither eleven put their best men into the field. California played but three of her 'varsity men, and in the second half the whole eleven were green hands.

California showed to far better advantage in the practice with the Olympic team on Monday. Sherman, Kennedy and Ransome went in at end, quarter and fullback, while Selfridge was moved out to tackle to make room for Birdsall at center. Selfridge can do himself better justice nearer the center of the line. At tackle he is slow.

Another point that California should and doubtless will improve is the slowness of putting the ball into play. The signal should be given to the team before the lineup, as soon as the scrimmage begins to break up. The other side should not be allowed an instant in which to guess at the next play. This improvement, no doubt, will come in time, however. The next Reliance game will doubtless show some sharp and aggressive work on the part of the Blue and Gold eleven.

Frank Butterworth, the California's coach, arrived from the East two days before the Reliance game. Butterworth is a graduate of Yale, class of '95. He made the 'varsity team in his first year at college, an achievement rarely attained by a Freshman. Though not especially athletic in appearance, Butterworth is accounted the greatest fullback who ever played upon a college team. He was one of the members of Caspar Whitney's all-America team. His tackling and running are beyond criticism, though it is to his method of punting that Mr. Butterworth owes most of his success upon the gridiron.

On a Battleship

Impressions of a Great War Engine
—A Near View of the *Oregon*

The Wave, 15 (17 October 1896), 7.

It seems to me that it is a willful misunderstanding of the nature of things to use the feminine pronoun in speaking of a battleship, or to suggest that the fighting machine in any way belongs to the class of things feminine. When you have visited the *Oregon* and seen the great ship inside and out, and have felt the vast, colossal forces that are leashed in there between the armored flanks and the protected deck and keelson you come away with an impression as of some tremendous brute, a thing without sex—like a monster of a legend—living a life apart, lonesome, formidable and, if needs be, very terrible.

You crawl about upon the thing like some insignificant parasite upon the back of a mastodon. You descend into the vitals of the monster, down there in the stifling lower levels, where the huge, hot heart beats, and you see and hear the little sights and sounds the great ship makes in its living—even while motionless—the slow inhalation and discharge of its breath of steam, and the persistent mutter of its furnace mouths—ever agape—devouring ton after ton of coal, always gorged yet always unappeased, the hunger of a glutton who is never satisfied.

Or else you climb to the airy fighting tops, with the cold, clean wind shrilling in your ears (so different from the atmosphere of the engine rooms, hot, thick and still), and look from above at the monster settling down below you, comfortably, vastly, wallowing its prodigious flanks into the muddy, lapping water around it. Just underneath you are the monster's eyes, the two search lights that can stab the darkest night with a long lance of silver light and discover at nearly a mile's distance the approach of the torpedo boats —the one thing of which the big ship is afraid. Or you may go forward, beneath the decks, beneath the water line, even, forward to where the bow narrows and the vessel's sides draw sharply to a point. You are behind the ram now. The brute's most formidable weapon—barring the greater guns, perhaps—the massive prong of steel that projects unicorn-like from the monster's front, the horn that gives the *coup de grâce* to the enemy, goring him to death as the ship rushes on at full speed. What a blow! backed up as it is by all the mighty weight behind, those tons and tons and tons of steel, rushing on there through the water, the engines working under forced draft, the tremendous mass tearing through the waves fast as any railroad train. What Harveyized plate could withstand a charge like that? The vessel is not yet made that could resist the impact of the *Oregon's* ram. The ordinary cruiser would be cut in two. The heaviest ironed first-class line-of-battle ship that ever flew the Union Jack would be hideously rent open, disemboweled in an instant, sent to the bottom handily with all her guns and men and armament. But that is not all. Just behind the ram, the *Oregon* has, concealed in a tiny, carefully protected chamber, a more deadly weapon still, more deadly, perhaps, than the vast thirteen-inch rifles in the turrets of the primary battery. This is the torpedo. Just at the moment of the charge, a few seconds before the ram strikes home, the port in the prow opens like a mouth, and the great ship spits its torpedo as a reptile spits its venom. If the delivery of the torpedo is successful there is little need of the ram. This handful of gun cotton at the torpedo's tip will do the work of all the guns aboard, will cause the ram to become a superfluity. When it is discharged at the right time and place the commander may give the order to cease firing. There is nothing left to be done then, but to lower the boats to pick up the wounded.

But—(there is always the element of uncertainty in the movement of such a vast and complicated machinery as that of the *Oregon*)—suppose the torpedo's engine is out of order—once shot from the *Oregon's* bow it moves rather slowly—suppose the tiny triple expansion engine that the torpedo carries stops, and the great ship coming on behind rides it down, or what if the torpedo should for some reason refuse to leave the tube? It is all charged and primed, a shock will explode it. The signal is given, the *Oregon* "stands by to ram," down she comes through the water, the ram crashes into the enemy's broadside, and the shock of the impact fires her own torpedo still left in her bow.

Beyond all doubt bow torpedoes are dangerous little things as well for your own ship as for that of your enemy. But there is nothing of this in the great thirteen-inch rifles of the deck, no possibility of treachery with them, no dishonesty, no fractious rebellion at the crisis when they are most needed. They are huge, honest beasts of simple, candid character, docile under management, so thoroughly under control that a woman could raise or lower them, but so terrible, so resistless, that steel armor a foot in thickness is perforated by the shell they throw as if it were so much paper.

They live in the revolving turrets—the barbettes, I think, is the technical name—at either end of the ship, and night and day they crane their long gray necks from the ports of these barbettes out over the ship and over the water, on watch always, occasionally moving from side to side with very slow, majestic motions, just as some enormous snake might stretch his neck and balance his head when aroused and ready to strike.

They live in pairs, two to each barbette, grim companions, brothers born in the forge, living their lives together fighting side by side, impassive and silent save at long intervals, when—their flanks all quivering—they speak one savage, terrible word.

Maud Odell and *Zenda*

The Carolina Girl's Interpretation of Antoinette de Mauban

The Wave, 15 (17 October 1896), 8.

Miss Odell had just come from the Sutro Baths, so, instead of talking about plays and first nights and experiences and such like, we started in on big baths and the possibility of their being filled with really fresh water. "Let me tell you," said Miss Odell, "I was standing on the float there waiting to go in, and I noticed a man who kept coming up every now and then, and clambering onto the float and diving down again in the greatest hurry. After a while I cried to him, 'For goodness' sake what are you after? you'll get my hair wet,' and what do you suppose he told me?" said Miss Odell. "This: 'There's a man lost three front teeth in here, and I am trying to get 'em out.'"

"Did he get them?" I thought to ask.

"I didn't wait to see," answered Miss Odell. "I went away. I thought I didn't care much about swimming that day."

Miss Odell is Southern, a Carolinian. She's an admirable type of the girl of the South; just the kind of girl the novelists have led you to expect to see when you visit the plantations—(the kind you so rarely do see, by the way). She is very tall and very dark, and her hair is dark brown, and her eyes are black, black as bitumen is black—an artist will understand what I mean at once—I mean black, with a suggestion of brown in certain lights. Also, she strikes one as possessed of tremendous vitality; she grips your hand almost like a man, and she tells you that she can ride her bicycle up the hill that leads to the Cliff House, and I'm free to confess that I can't do that. Like Miss Irving, there is no pose to Miss Odell when off the stage. In her rooms she is frank and unaffected and natural. You do not feel that you are an audience to be played to. Deliver me from these actors and these actresses who act even in their private life—even to the inadequate interviewer—who strive to impress him, to astonish him, and by making him—poor devil— seem small, to imagine themselves great.

I believe I spoke of the melodrama of the last two acts of *Zenda*.

"Oh, it's melodramatic enough," admitted Miss Odell, "only—"

"Only what?"

"It's good melodrama, don't you think? I know it's battle and murder and sudden death, and it's so hard not to overdo and yet do for all it's worth, and perhaps it is overstrained on that account, but just the same, there is a fine high-keyed spirit and dash to it all that's very exhilarating. But don't I have a hard time of it in those last two acts?"

I thought this a rather charming admission.

"They are a bit ungentlemanly to you," I concurred.

"It's a disagreeable part, of course," said Miss Odell.

"But then one condones Antoinette's—ah—her—"

"Oh, yes, she's not altogether bad, you know. When we were rehearsing for the piece I suggested to Mr. Frohman that Antoinette might commit suicide at the end of that act. Her death would cover all her failings, you know. But Mr. Frohman said: 'Now, Miss Odell, don't you think we are lurid enough as we are without that suicide? And then that "unhandsome corpse"—what could we do with it during the love scene between Flavia and Rudolf?'

"My first appearance? It was in a play called *Nerves*. I was in a school of dramatic art (you are only supposed to get in if you can pass an examination of 60 per cent, but then everybody gets 60 per cent), and I took the part of a society lady who comes into a candy store and says, 'I'll take a pound of that, please.'"

"Yes, and then what?"

"Nothing; that was all. 'I'll take a pound of that, please.' I was the most stage-struck girl you ever saw in your life. How I went over that line, trying the accent on every different word. 'I'LL take a pound of that, please,' 'I'll take a POUND of that, please,' 'I'll take a pound of THAT, please,' and so on. I never missed a rehearsal, and was as prompt as the clock, though I didn't come on till the second act."

"Nervous?"

"Actresses are always nervous."

I shall never ask that question again. They all say the same thing.

"I was supposed to come into the candy store from the matinée. I made it a point to carry an opera glass case, with the glasses inside. I would have sinned against dramatic art if I had left those glasses out. Wasn't I conscientious?"

"After that what happened?"

"Then *The Wife* happened, with Miss Odell in the title role, and then the *Amazons* and then all of Georgie Cayvan's roles, and then Antoinette de Mauban."

"And the one you like best?"

Miss Odell thought. "I believe it's Antoinette," she answered. "I've had a fine success with her. Don't you think now, I've had a pretty good success?" she said, leaning forward with her elbow on her knee, and nodding her head at me, "and I've only acted for four seasons."

It is fine, when you think of it. I told Miss Odell as much.

It occurred to me to ask her about interviewers—as I had already asked Miss Irving. I took an impersonal point of view.

"What do I think of interviewers generally?" said Miss Odell, gaily. "That depends upon the kind of notice they give me next morning!"

At this I came away.

The Evolution of a Nurse

A Brief Statement of Process, Conditions and Results

The Wave, 15 (17 October 1896), 8.

We will suppose—it is the average case—that she comes in the first place from an English, an American or a Canadian family, and that she is obliged —or, perhaps, prefers—to earn her living, but does not wish to do so either by teaching school or by typewriting or even by writing for the papers.

The profession of the trained nurse occurs to her, and if she is sound physically and has a fairly good education she can qualify. However, no domestics need apply. It does seem a little hard, but then a field is open to them from which the trained nurse is barred, by the nature of things. She is not called upon to undergo any preliminary examination other than that necessary to determine her fitness from a physical point of view—a mere assurance as to her nerves, her powers of endurance, etc.—such as a physician could ascertain at a glance. Of course a woman with nerves is out of the question. It not infrequently happens that the nurse is called upon to serve in a family who can afford a night nurse. Then, if the case becomes bad, she may have to be on duty in the daytime as well—when she should be asleep.

The first thing that occurs after she is adjudged fit is her entrance into a hospital ward. She is what is called a junior nurse now. For two months she is on probation as the assistant of the senior nurse. She helps to change and to make the dressings and bandages; she bathes the patients and makes herself generally useful. Most important of all, perhaps, she accustoms herself to operations; she gets used to the sight of blood and the sounds of suffering. In one way she may be said to harden herself.

It seems rather strange that a girl should be called upon to do this in any profession. Yet think for a moment how her pity and commiseration and tears and all that would interfere with her work, how in the end it would do the patient positive harm. The less she is affected by the sight of pain the better nurse is she adjudged. It would seem that she should regard the patient just as a joiner would regard a broken chair he was given to mend.

She has two months of this. You are told that the first feminine, inevitable shrinking wears away with marvelous rapidity. At the end of sixty days the girl who began by turning faint at the sight of a lanced finger will hold and steady an arm or a leg while the surgeon is at work at its amputation with never the quiver of an eyelash.

Meanwhile she has been attending lectures on physiology and hygiene by the visiting physicians, lectures at which she is obliged to take notes, and has joined a class of instruction that meets twice a week, and that is conducted by the superintendent nurse.

At the end of these two probationary months she is told by those in authority whether or no she is suited to become a trained nurse. If she is satisfactory—and nine out of ten usually are—she takes an examination on the lectures and classes she has attended. Every two months these examinations are held. At the end of a year comes a final examination, which, if she passes, entitles her to the distinction of senior nurse. She has a ward of her own then with assistants—the junior nurses—under her, where she takes over the entire responsibility of the care of a certain number of cases, or else she is given a private patient in a separate room of the hospital.

It is in her second year as a senior nurse that she makes the acquaintance of the contagious wards. You ask at this point if she ever flinches before her first experiences with diphtheritic and small pox and cholera cases, and are told—with a little accent of surprise at even the possibility of such a thing—that it never happens. This is even better than the joiner and his broken chair. It's not impassive indifference, after all.

At the end of her second year's hospital work she has become that indispensable ministrant of every sick room, deft of hand, light of touch, of boundless patience and of enduring faithfulness, an admirable product of

131

special education—a trained nurse.

Then she goes to live at the Directory. Some nineteen others are there with her. Their expenses are shared amongst themselves. Her name is entered on a list, and she takes her turn with her companions in answering calls. When she knows her name is next upon the list she gathers the necessaries of her profession together and holds herself—like a doctor—in instant readiness to respond to a call from whatever direction and of whatever nature. She leaves the Directory to answer it. She may return in two hours—or two years.

However, she does not always have to wait her turn. Perhaps she excels in her chosen work, is defter of hand, lighter of touch, more patient, more faithful than the others. In that case special calls are sent in for her every week, every day; she is known alike of physicians and patients. She is on the road to prosperity, and traveling faster—a great deal faster—than either the school teacher or the female journalist or the typewriter.

Following is the list of graduates who were awarded diplomas at the Occidental Hotel on Friday, October 9th:

Eleanor Williams, Elizabeth Woods, Nancy Place, Edna Shuey, Alice Burrell, Sarah E. Gray, Florence M. Pinninger, May Laughlin, Beatrice Noble, Maud Burnham, Octavine Briggs, Elizabeth Cole, Emma Bennett, Georgiana Flagg, Emily Norris, Helen E. Baker, Eleanor Holden, Eleanor Briggs.

The Week's Football

The Stanford-Reliance Game—A Third Rate Contest

The Wave, 15 (17 October 1896), 11.

The Stanford and Reliance elevens lined up against each other last Saturday for the second game of the season.

The game was third rate from the kick off till the call of time; a snappy High School eleven would have stood a good chance of scoring against such teams and such playing. Of course the old cry of "early in the season" might again be raised to justify such listless work, but no one who saw the playing of the California and Olympic teams on the preceding Saturday—ragged as that playing was—would for a moment doubt that the wearers of the red and white or the blue and gold were a far better trained and more aggressive lot of men than were their rivals of the cardinal and maroon and white.

A football game has degenerated pretty far when a center rush can repeatedly down an end-runner, or a guard tackle, from behind, a right half going around the left end, supposedly with interference. Yet both of these occurrences were to be seen in last Saturday's game.

The playing was of the crudest type, such as used to be seen some five or six years ago when Pacific Coast football was in its infancy. Not more than half a dozen end plays were attempted by either team throughout the entire game, though the Olympic eleven with its fairly good interference and with such a running-half as Stickney should have gained at will around the Stanford flanks. There was an utter lack of cohesion on both sides. Each man played his own game to suit himself, and there was that talking and squabbling in the lines that infallibly betrays the want of discipline and organization. The only men that Captain Smith of the club team could depend upon were Stickney (R.H.) and Robert Porter (L.T.). What gains the red and white made were largely due to the efforts of these two men, though as often as not they cut out their own work, totally independent of any assistance from the quarter or backs. When the run was around the flank,

133

Morse and Harrelson occasionally managed to put the opposing end out of the play, Stickney getting off with a really marvelous rapidity at times. If Stickney's signal for this play had been given oftener, especially toward the middle of the second half, the Olympic team would have scored.

Stanford should have put up a better game, with such men as Fickert, Thomas, Cotton, Dole and Soper on their team. But as in the case of their opponents there was no team-work to second their efforts. McIntosh at quarter was far too slow in getting the ball into play, and in passing it from the center to the runner. Time and again he was responsible for a fumble in delivering the ball to the half—though from the grand stand it always seems as though it is the fault of the half.

The delivery of the ball to the runner is perhaps one of the most difficult things to be learned upon the football field. The ball must not be thrown, even to the fullback for a punt, but must be passed easily and swiftly, and with the greatest accuracy. More than once during last Saturday's game the Stanford quarter flung the ball back in such a fashion that it struck the shoulder or breast of the man who was to receive it, and bounding off was secured by one of the Olympics' guards or tackles. Not infrequently a watchful and active end can secure the ball on such a fumble.

But the most inexcusable failing of both teams—failing for which the quarterbacks were alone responsible—was the slowness of getting the ball into play. Never was the signal given until after the teams were comfortably into line, sometimes even the quarters first made sure of the correct positions of the men before signing to the center to snap the ball. Such sluggishness is absolutely incompatible with good football. A sharp and aggressive rush line can divine the play to be made with the greatest of ease, and nine times out of ten can down the runner almost in his tracks.

Another point which cannot be too severely criticized is the long and intentional wait between the plays to allow the men to rest and breathe. The captains are directly to blame for this. It is a well-known maneuver of the game to "fake time" by a pretense of injury to a player, and while he is being patched up to afford the balance of the eleven a few moments to recuperate. The thing is not only unworthy of gentlemen players, but is a clumsy and shortsighted device as well, since it gives the other side precisely the same advantage.

The game this afternoon between California and the Olympic Club should by all signs go to the college eleven. Ransome should be able to hold the Red and White to at most a single touchdown, while I look to see the Blue and Gold players—that is, if 'Varsity men are played—hammer at least twelve points out of the athletic club's line.

The Olympic halves should not be able to make ground around either of California's ends, while Simpson and Ludlow ought to be able to make it exceedingly interesting for Stickney and Porter when the play is against the line.

Making of a Half-Back

The Evolution of a Football Player by Coaching and Training

The Wave, 15 (24 October 1896), 5.

'Varsity halfbacks are born and then made. For not only must the successful half fulfill certain rather rigid physical requirements, but he must also undergo a long and most difficult course of training and practice before he can be said to understand even the most rudimentary elements of the position he will be called upon to fill.

If he is born with unlimited "sand," with a heavy frame, long muscles that lay close to the bone and that act quickly, and a faculty of rapid and accurate judgment, he can be called good "material."

After this he is "made," made to use his weight and natural agility in the most effective manner, made to exercise his judgment, to use his eyes and hands and wits, made to concentrate every energy of mind and body at a given instant on a given point.

We will take a concrete example.

He is a Sophomore, let us say. He weighs anywhere between a hundred and fifty and a hundred and sixty-five pounds, has no physical defects, and isn't afraid of getting hurt. As a Freshman he saw the 'varsity game of the preceding year, and has become fired with an ambition to "make the team."

One day in the early part of the first term of his Sophomore year he sees a notice on the football bulletin board that candidates for the team of '96 will hand in their names to the captain without delay. He does so, and very shortly afterward receives word to call at the office of the gymnasium. Here he finds some thirty or forty of his fellows waiting their turn to be examined. When his turn arrives he is stripped, weighed and measured, his heart and lungs are sounded, his capacity of wind is tested, and all the results are carefully noted down against his name. He qualifies satisfactorily, and is told to apply to the manager for a suit.

Then comes the first day of practice. On the campus three elevens, roughly speaking, are being worked under the guidance of the coaches, the first eleven consisting of the veteran players, and the best substitutes, who take the places left vacant by the graduations of the previous summer, the second eleven, made up of substitutes largely and of new players—Freshmen for the most part—who have gained reputations on their school elevens, and last of all the "third eleven," who stand along the side lines in their suits, unknown aspirants, waiting for a chance to play.

The days pass. Our Sophomore "shows up" every afternoon, but as yet he is unnoticed. As often as possible one of the coaches gets this third eleven into line and drills them in falling on the ball, in passing and tackling. But the opportunity for which they are longing, the chance of "lining up" against a team, is as yet denied them. It's a trying thing for the Sophomore to stand there on the side lines and watch opportunities given to other players to distinguish themselves, when he knows he can do better.

At length his chance comes. Perhaps the head coach comes down the line one afternoon, calls out his name and adds: "Get the signals from So-and-So (the captain of the second eleven) and go in at right half." The Sophomore does as he is bid, and that afternoon plays on the third eleven in a practice game against the second.

His signal is given for a run. Maybe he fails at first, fumbles the ball, gets into the wrong hole, or runs back and is downed by the opposite ends. But he "stays with it," and is given another chance. This time he keeps his head and feet. He gets by the ends, his interferers block off for him. He makes a run, perhaps even a touchdown. The next day he distinguishes himself again, and the next, and the next also. The following week finds him on the second eleven and playing against the first. Then his troubles begin. He knows what it means to be tackled by a 'varsity end, to be caught between knee and waist when at top speed, jerked off his feet and slammed down upon the ground like a bundle of rags. He finds out what it is to try and stop a 'varsity tackle coming through the line, using his head like a battering ram, and running him down like a locomotive or a charging bull. He is bruised from head to foot, his ankle is twisted, his thumb sprained, his shoulder is lame. Every day the coach abuses him, urges him to harder and more accurate play. Seemingly the coach is never satisfied. The Sophomore is very discouraged, but his good work has made an impression at last, and one day he finds himself scheduled to play in a match, a real game before an audience and against some minor college or athletic club.

In this game he surprises himself, surprises everybody, his real ability becomes suddenly apparent. All those long days of practice have told. In that match game he "shows form," runs low and hard, tackles low, gets into the plays, keeps his head, breaks up interference, in a word, fulfills all the requirements of a good halfback.

At the end of the game, battered and sore and gasping for breath, streaked with dirt and perhaps with blood, the coach himself, the great man, compliments him, tells him he is doing good work. The Sophomore is happy. This is worth all the labor and disappointments of the last six weeks.

Meanwhile he has gone into training, he practices signals and plays, he diets, he rises early and gets to bed by ten, he runs on the cinder path to improve his speed, and does "chest weight" exercises to keep himself in condition, all under the supervision of the coaches.

A little later he has become a fixture on the substitute team. Sometimes he even plays upon the first eleven, and there, behind the superior interference (his efforts, seconded by trained "team work"), distinguishes himself more than ever. Upon the bleachers he begins to be spoken of as likely to make the team.

But he has his competitors. Some three or four others are trying for the coveted position of right half, and perhaps at the middle of the season an old player, a veteran half of a dozen match games, puts in a tardy appearance and plays in his old position for which the Sophomore is striving. These are hard odds against which to contend.

Then, some six weeks before the great game with the rival college, the training quarters are established, where the candidates for the team—sifted down to some sixteen or eighteen by now—live, eat and sleep together. The Sophomore is admitted to the number. This is a great step in advance. He is a 'varsity substitute now, and an injury to that veteran player will surely place him on the team.

Now he is in constant training. Every moment that can be spared from his college work is devoted to football. Light practice at signals, at punting and passing in the morning, practice games on the campus in the afternoon, with the bleachers roaring applause, lectures by the coach with blackboard diagrams in the evening and to bed and asleep by half-past ten at the latest. The great day, the day of "The Game," approaches. The practice becomes lighter and lighter. If the coaches can keep him in his present form it will be all they ask. Then in one of the last practice games, the veteran half, for whom the Sophomore is a "sub," is hurt a little. That same bad knee of his is lamed. A thrill of apprehension goes through the college. Everyone asks, "Will Jones be able to play 'in the big game'?" Perhaps. At any rate Smith, the Sophomore, is almost as good.

Then comes the great day. The sloping bleachers banked with tier after tier of watching faces, the air rent with the slogans of the rival colleges, the flutter of the rival colors everywhere, a whirlwind of excitement centering about the struggling teams out there on the gridiron.

Smith, the substitute Sophomore, at the side lines gnaws his nails in a fury of restrained impatience. He would play the whole game himself. If he could only have his chance now!

There is a pause in the play.

"Some one hurt?"

"It's Jones—the old knee again."

Jones can't go on with the game. They help him off. The grimed and gasping captain runs to the side lines, and the coach calls to the Sophomore.

"Go in at half, Smith."

In a twinkling Smith sheds his sweater. He rushes out on the field, his chance has come.

"What's the matter with Smith?" shout the bleachers.

Italy in California

_____

The Vineyards of the Italian-Swiss Colony at Asti

_____

The Wave, 15 (24 October 1896), 9.

_____

Last Friday I went to Italy. I went, I saw, I returned in one day. It cost me three dollars.

Italy in California means Asti, the Italian-Swiss colony at the head of Russian River Valley, not much of a town, as far as one could see, but acres and acres and acres—miles, for all I know—of grape vines inundating low, rolling hills and the lower slopes of little mountains, with here and there a white painted house far away, just a dot, rising out of the rolling sea of green something like a ship under all sail, or clumps of trees, bunched closely together, that can look for all the world like islands, if you put your imagination to it.

The transition from sand-dunes about San Francisco to hillsides in the neighborhood of Sienna is almost too brusque. Two or three hours of the jar and dust of the railroad come between, and then, long before you are prepared for it, a bit of landscape and environment of the Old World is under your eyes, real and vivid and unexpected. It is almost flippant, this rapid change of scene. It is a *coup de théâtre*, a shifting of flats and flies in a comic opera. You miss the stage carpenter's whistle.

This Italian colony planted here in Western America, working at its native industry, with native laborers and native habits, and customs and manners is curious enough. Probably in no other country than the United States could such a thing be witnessed. The best of it is that the colony is not on exhibition. Asti is not acting a part, for the instruction or amusement of the seer of sights, like the traveling colonies—Japanese and otherwise—that one visits at times. There is nothing Midway-Plaisance about Asti. That's what makes it so interesting. There is no artificiality about it, no pose. The colonists do not care whether you are interested and amused or not. There's no effort at imitation. It's the true thing, it's real life, it's business and bread and butter and all that. It's a little piece of Italy, with live Italians on it, cut out of the map, as it were, and taken up and transplanted to a congenial soil.

This sense of reality is keenest when you sit down to dinner for the first time at the colony—lamentable admission, that your most vivid impression should come by means of your stomach. But the "Italian dinner" you will eat at Asti is not that of the Italian restaurants, not even that of Martinelli's or Campi's. Such soup, such *bouillabaisse*, such macaroni, such salad, all with just a little—oh, a very little—suggestion of garlic. Each dish a course by itself, with the real sour European bread "on the side," and ripe olives and fresh butter. And remember that you do not eat all this delightful stuff in a hot and crowded restaurant, amid the clatter of dishes and the jangle of knives, but out of doors—think of that—on a stone floor, surrounded by a high trellis, where the cats come and rub against your legs and the giant Saint Bernard—straight from Switzerland—too self-respecting to beg, sits at a distance and watches you with grave attention. You weaken your table wine with plenty of water—not seltzer, thank goodness—and you eat bread by the pound, and you finish with cigarettes and bitter black coffee with cognac, and you go back five or ten years, as the case may be, to that never to be forgotten time when you were a *rapin* in Paris or in Turin or in Rome, or when you were even a simple tourist, inspired of Heaven to live the life of the Frenchman or Italian.

And the wine. (For Asti's *raison d'être* is its wine.)   I belong to that miserable army of laics whose motto is "I am no critic, but I know what I like." I know that I like the Asti wine, I mean, its clarets. The wine of Asti is the real California wine; not the kind that is crammed down the mouth of the public almost as soon as it is vatted, not the *vin ordinaire* of the "cheap restaurants"—the *vin très ordinaire*—but the proven stuff, guarded and tended three, five and seven years before it is marketed, rich and full of body, and mellow. What a difference between it and that other kind, thin and acrid and vinegared, fuming with alcohol.

At the time of my visit Asti was crushing its second crop of grapes. (I know little about vintages and such like, but it strikes me as extraordinary that there should be a second crop at all.)   The atmosphere inside the winery at the time of crushing is heavy with the smell of the crushed grapes. There is something very suggestive about this odor—an odor most like that of the core of an apple just as it begins to turn brown—only intensified a thousand times. It is overpowering, penetrating; it is the reek of the earth's blood squeezed from the harvest, as it is massacred and tortured here in the tremendous hydraulic presses.

About all vineyards, and especially about Asti, there clings a sense of vast richness and vitality—a luxuriousness and bountifulness almost beyond words, a vitality, a feeling of boundless teeming life that can hardly be conveyed through any media other than that of one's own five senses.

You stand in the winery of the Italian-Swiss colony and smell the reek of all this mashed pulp, and hear the dripping juice and the ripple and flow of the streams of fresh vinted new wine in the little sluices, and the squelching of the hydraulic crushers—you see the rows and rows of gigantic casks, high almost as the roof, full to their very heads, drawn up in ranks in the half-light of the cellars like vast pot-bellied gluttons, and you see the tons and tons of "must" simmering and fermenting in the vats, boiling with a hot, fierce energy of its own. Outside there, over those miles of low-rolling hills, stretch the vines themselves, sweltering under the sun, teeming with warm red liquor, loaded with heavy fat bunches, two crops every year, a vast, rich life, renewed with every season, inexhaustible, sucking up the red life-blood of the earth and pouring it out in rivers and rivers of wine.

And this goes on year after year, indefinitely. Think of the amount of wine that will have poured from Asti in twenty years from now! Wine enough to deluge an entire county, to carry away villages, to undermine and wreck churches, a veritable tidal wave. And yet it is consumed little by little the world over, drunk from little glasses, delicately, fastidiously. The torrent that you see at its fountain-head at the Italian colony in the Sonoma Valley, branches and branches, and is sub-divided and ramified to infinity, till at length the same wine that taxed the capacity of a vat as high as the roof beams of the Asti cellar is emptied by thimblefuls in glasses that you hold between thumb and finger.

The Week's Football

Pertinent Comment on the California-Olympic Game

The Wave, 15 (24 October 1896), 13.

What a difference in a game of football is made by just moderately good interference, fairly quick passing, and a couple of guards who have been coached to simply play their positions, was seen last Saturday by those who watched the game played by California against the Olympic Athletic Club.

The eulogiums of the enthusiasts to the contrary, there was nothing extraordinary about the college team's playing when judged by 'varsity standards. There was no great brilliancy, no especial dash, or verve—none of that lightning rapidity of attack and machine-like accuracy of manoeuvre (so completely demoralizing to ill-trained opponents) that characterizes a 'varsity eleven when brought to its highest pitch of perfection.

California merely played a somewhat unusually steady, rapid game, and played it as a team, not as eleven different men. That California scored so high is due to the fact that the Olympics were totally unprepared for even this moderately good condition on the part of the collegians, and that their own team showed, not so much a lack of practice and training, as it did a woful lack of sound physical condition.

California is far from 'varsity form as yet. The fact that she won hands down from the same team against which Stanford could not score is not a true index of her strength relative to that of the rival college. Beyond doubt Stanford has improved equally with California during the week, if indeed she has not outstripped her blue and gold competitor. For one thing, I do not believe the cardinal team would have permitted the second Olympic touchdown of last Saturday, and yet would have scored California's twenty-four points more or less.

Unquestionably the Olympic eleven has improved in form and team work since they were last seen on the gridiron against Stanford. Harrelson at quarter, though still handling the ball with exasperating deliberation, does nevertheless get it to the runner with a little more agility than heretofore, but a more noteworthy improvement is his giving the signal before the line-up. Nothing is more bracing and stimulating to a team than this custom when coupled with the snapping of the ball as soon as possible afterward. It breaks up the scrimmage quicker than any command of the umpire, and spurs the men into their places as nothing else can; for the player must and does realize that if the ball is snapped and passed before he is in his position, calamity for his side will follow—calamity for which he is directly responsible. Besides this, it has precisely the same effect upon the players of the defensive side, they likewise foreseeing catastrophe to their team if they are not in their places in time to meet and withstand the play.

It is impossible to lay too much emphasis upon this quality of rapid play as a prerequisite of good football, though it is one of the last qualities to be attained by an eleven. It is, as it were, the hall-mark of a 'varsity team. One is almost tempted to declare that the first requisite of a good team is rapid playing, the second is rapid playing, and the third is again rapid playing.

Olympic started off well in the game, driving through California's weak centre at will for five-, ten- and twice for twenty-yard gains. As soon, however, as California secured the ball and began running the ends it became apparent the athletic club defensive work was out of all proportion to her offensive play. The Olympic ends, despite Nolan's admirable but unseconded game on the left, could not break through the California interference. Nor, singular though it seems, could Sheehy, Rington and Smith, the Olympic centre, prevent so light a player as Sherman from bucking the line for gains.

California won the game by good interference for fast, clever runners, such as Hall, Ransome and Sherman. The latter-named players came in for all the praise from the grand stand, whereas if their individual efforts had not been made possible by the unseen and therefore unrewarded work of Kennedy, Simpson, Castlehun and others of the interferers, they would not have gained their own length.

On the part of the club team more unqualified praise may be accorded Stickney, Morse and Weldon, since what little was accomplished by them in advancing the ball was done practically without assistance. Stickney is beyond question one of the finest running halves ever seen on the coast. He runs low to the ground and very hard; once in his stride only the most deter-mined and effective tackle can stop him. It is a thousand pities he has not better support to allow him to display his real ability. As it is, Ransome, an inferior half, though running behind better interference, easily outshines him. California is especially fortunate this season in possessing guards who are also tackles. Ludlow (l.g.) and Griesberg (r.g.) in Saturday's game very frequently tackled and brought down the runner. Besides this, Ludlow has already seized the knack of catching the runner of his own team, especially so light a one as Sherman, around the waist, and dragging him through the line.

One feature of the athletic club's game of Saturday which seems to have been generally overlooked was what is known as the "half-back kick." On two occasions Stickney punted without falling back, standing close to the line and punting from his position as half-back. It is the style of kick developed by Wrightington of Harvard and used by the Harvard team, with conspic-uous ill-success, against Yale in the '95 game. Its merit consists in the fact that the opposing side, taken by surprise, does not send its halves down the field to catch it. Its great drawback lies in the risk taken of the guards and tackles of the defensive side breaking through, blocking the kick, and secur-ing the ball.

The Olympic eleven still continues to use foul and unsportsmanlike tactics at times. They still persisted in "faking time" in Saturday's game, and foul tactics by their halves were numerous. Several times the Olympic centre threw dirt and dust into Birdsall's eyes at the moment the latter was snap-ping the ball.

To-day Stanford and Reliance line up against each other for the last time this season. Stanford should win from the Reliance with even greater ease than did California from the Olympics. The cardinal should make fully as many touchdowns and at the same time keep the maroon and white from scoring a single point.

Re-Creating a University

The Great Project of Reconstructing the College at Berkeley

The Wave, 15 (31 October 1896), 5.

If you can imagine thirty-one of the buildings of the World's Fair made over to suit the requirements of a university, and at the same time constructed of enduring marble and stone grouped together upon the wonderful site now occupied by the present college and set in the midst of landscape gardening such as one saw at Chicago in the Columbian year, you will begin to have a faint idea of what is to be done in the near future for the University of California.

The thing is stupendous, almost awe-inspiring. When you listen to the talk of the gentlemen interested in the great undertaking, and when you realize that they are sound, conservative men of affairs—no dreamers of dreams, no seers of visions—when you grasp the fact that five million dollars has been actually pledged for the undertaking, that the money is there, in hand—that work could be begun to-morrow morning after breakfast—you catch your breath for very amazement. You wonder, can such things be? You wonder if California is to have a university that in its material, architectural aspect will outrank—think of it—Harvard or Yale or Princeton. It's hard to believe, isn't it? If you should happen to be a Hollis Holworthy or an Eli or a Tiger you absolutely refuse to believe it. But the thing is as assured as the most hard and fast business proposition. Ideals and ambitions and "dreams of the future" might be put aside, but there's the five million dollars. It's hard to get around them.

And the money is not to stop there. Once started, these wonderful buildings—those that will be constructed next year, to suit the more pressing needs of the U.C.—will be a means of benefiting the University financially, first by securing appropriations from the Legislature and secondly by private endowments. For it requires no argument to show that the representatives of the people in the Legislature will be far more apt to give money for buildings when it can be shown to them exactly the purpose for which it is to be definitely put, and much more apt to give liberally when they can see that the buildings erected will reflect honor and glory not only upon the State, but even upon the nation itself.

Private bequests to the University in its present state have been few and far between. Small wonder. Who would wish to have the buildings which are to bear their names to be hidden among a lot of others of every conceivable variety of insult to beauty and use, making a hodge-podge which only moves the on-looker to contempt and harsh criticism?

The plan is vague as yet. And on the part of the committee in charge will remain so, in order that the architects may be allowed the utmost liberty to do exactly as they please. The main idea, however, is this. The present buildings, the library, old north and south halls, the mechanics' building, the conservatory, even the new electrical building will be considered as non-existent. The U.C. of the future will be laid out in the form of a vast crescent rising by easy degrees up the slope of the foothills to a culminating point, probably the observatory. There will be separate buildings for astronomy, philosophy, pedagogy, languages, physics, fine arts and music, mathematics, military science, civil engineering, a gymnasium—that shall rank with Yale's—an administration building, a library and an auditorium—thirty-one in all. The idea is that the building of a university in haphazard fashion, here a building in one style, there another in another, is all wrong.

Other universities have grown slowly, year by year. The University of California of the twentieth century will be struck off in a single block, a creation sudden and complete, marvelous, a thing unique and beautiful among the architectural efforts of the centuries. Each building shall conform to some one established design, and shall be erected upon the spot selected for it in the design of the whole affair. Should one of the old buildings stand in the way it will be torn down without ceremony. The construction of the new U.C. will be begun within a year—that looks business-like enough—and after this fashion: By the end of a year the final plans will be ready. It will then be considered which building or buildings the U.C. stands most in need of. Say it is the mathematical building and the administration building. These will be erected upon the site designated in the architect's plan. A year or so later another building, the gymnasium, let us say, will be put up, in a different part of the grounds, but always in conformity with the grand plan of the design and in harmony with the established style. So, little by little, year by year, the great institution will begin to take shape. When the freshman class enters in 1905, it is to be hoped that it will be able to see the lines of the new University shaping themselves already.

The plans of the committee for obtaining the best architects throughout the world, and affording to them every possible facility and latitude seem to be admirable. Certain data will be furnished for the architects, such as topographical maps and casts of the grounds, photographs of the various buildings and surroundings, and then at least six months should be given them for the preliminary drawings, out of which a number of not less than five nor more than fifteen will be selected by an advisory board of five architects selected by the competing architects themselves, the author of each of these selected plans to receive $500, and to come into a second competition, which will require at least three months more, amplifying his plans in considerably greater detail; and from these second plans the same board of expert architects, in conjunction with the Regents, shall select three or five plans, the first of which shall be the accepted plan, and the authors of the remaining two or four to receive proper prizes, aggregating not less than $5,000, the successful plan to carry the erection of all buildings within the next twenty-five years. As it is to be hoped that the competition will be international, it will be seen that no time should be lost.

One of the best features of the plan of the new U.C. is that by it is included the dormitory system, that system for which the undergraduate has been longing for the last fifteen years. The dormitories in all probability will not be located on the campus, but will be erected near by in the town, and will be in the same style of architecture as the lecture and recitation buildings.

It is impossible to predict to what lengths the new U.C. may go. The Chicago University will be its only rival, but questionably so, since the University of Chicago has neither the U.C.'s magnificent site nor its possibility of almost limitless expansion. It is to be, perhaps, the university of the future. Struck off *en bloc*, complete and trim as a battleship, a wonder, accommodating a thousand and more students, standing there on the foothills and looking out into the Golden Gate, a little marvelous white world of stone and marble, a thing for tourists and guide books, a thing for the entire nation to be proud of, an ideal college.

The Week's Football

Stanford-Reliance—A Spectacular
Game Full of Ragged Playing

The Wave, 15 (31 October 1896), 13.

The Stanford and Reliance elevens lined up against each other last Saturday in a game that was fast and full of spectacular changes for the grand stand but that was in other respects ragged, full of inexcusable errors and far below the standard of what should constitute good football.

The playing was hard in both halves. The guards and tackles on both teams were aggressive, and there was more than one instance of a blocked kick. From the bleachers a game of this sort looks like good football. But Stanford and Reliance have much to learn before they can expect to show championship form.

Last Saturday's game, on the part of both elevens, was what in football language is called "ragged." The gains that were made were oftentimes the result of a happy chance that favored the runner, rather than the consequence of good interference and team play. The punting was wretched— neither Cleamans for Stanford nor Arlett for Reliance seemed to be able to send even a fairly good drive down the field. Oftentimes the punt was so high that the forwards of the punting side were able to secure the ball after a fumble by their antagonists. Fickert (l.g.) of Stanford, by his slowness, lost an admirable chance for a repetition of Lamar's famous run on just such a play. At the close of the first half, with the ball in Reliance territory, Cleamans punted high to Arlett, Fickert broke through and was down the field even ahead of the ends, and close upon Arlett as the latter prepared to catch. Arlett fumbled and the ball bounced off directly into Fickert's hands, who was coming down the field upon the run. Instead of continuing toward the goal with the ball Fickert paused for an instant totally unprepared and at a loss what to do. It was only an instant's hesitation, but long enough, however, for him to be downed where he stood.

Reliance plays a more open game than does Olympic. Their policy of punting whenever an opportunity presents itself, and their preference for running the ends instead of bucking the centre, are highly commendable. It is a pity that they cannot carry out their intentions with better success. Walton (l.h.) is a good running half, and is worthy of better interference. He never attempts to straight-arm a tackler, however, and it does not seem hard to stop him.

Next to Walton, Oliver (l.g.) is probably the strongest player of the maroon and white. Saturday he played his position well and soon tired out James, who was up against him. Oliver plays foul, however, at times, and all through the first half was slugging James whenever chance afforded. Oliver is an admirable man in the interference, and more than once succeeded in making gains for his side by dragging the runner along with him, even after the tackle.

But Reliance does not play well together. Indeed, up to date, California is the only team that at all excels in this essential element of good football. The Reliance line is weak. Strong as they are on the offensive, neither Oliver, Burnett nor Wells can be depended upon to block for a kick nor even to hold their opponents while the ball is being passed. In this matter of passing and snapping both Reliance and Stanford are deplorably slow. It was largely due to the efforts of Mr. Butterworth and his constant reprimands that Saturday's game was not even slower than it was.

Jeffs, Stanford's left end, is probably one of the most promising ends on the coast to-day. His tackling all through Saturday's game was the prettiest exhibition of individual football work that has been seen this season. He is apt, however, to play too far out from his tackle. Eight or ten feet from tackle is the greatest distance allowable, but very often in Saturday's game Jeffs took fully fifteen feet, and in consequence was often cut out of the play. Jeffs is very apt to run behind his own line in a defensive game, which is hazardous in the extreme. More than once Nahl might have taken advantage of this practice of his, and have given the signal for a double pass with results that would have been disastrous for Stanford. It is surprising that none of the captains has used the double pass so far. With unsteady teams early in the season it is almost sure of success.

Notwithstanding California's good showing against Olympic, and the small score which Stanford made against Reliance, I am inclined to believe that there is little difference in the college teams to-day. The best that can be said of California is that she played a steady game against the red and white. But it must be remembered that Reliance won from California a few weeks ago, while Stanford has yet to be even scored against in a match game with her 'varsity players in line.

From all indications the Olympic-Stanford game this afternoon should be very close. Stanford will probably win by a small score (for I look for a vast improvement on the part of Stanford in form and team work this week). It is hardly possible that Olympic will score, but if such should be the case, it will be the result of Olympic's short, heavy rushes on the Stanford tackles and guards.

Moving a Fifty-Ton Gun

The Mounting of a Leviathan
on the Fortifications of Lime Point

The Wave, 15 (7 November 1896), 5.

For the last week or so, a small army of men, aided by an eight horse-power engine, have been laboring about the huge fifty-ton gun that is finally to be located upon the fortifications at Lime Point. I can imagine nothing more unwieldy of handling and transporting than this vast, inert mass of metal, a mighty dead weight, hanging back stubbornly like a balky mastodon, opposing to all efforts its fifty thousand pounds of solid gray steel. Somehow one manages to move it, nevertheless, to hoist it from flat-car to barge and from barge to sliding ways, and finally upon the carriage itself. But in the meanwhile what an expenditure of energy, what straining of cables, what groaning of cranes and capstans, what panting and hiccoughing of over-taxed engines!

The first move occurred at the Union Iron Works, where by means of the famous hoisting crane the gun was swung off its specially constructed flat-car and laid upon the barge that was to take it over to Lime Point. This barge in itself was enormous, having a carrying capacity of 380 tons, eighty-five feet in length and strengthened with 12 x 12 timbering at every five feet. Upon this barge and stretching over it for some sixty feet were a set of greased ways, and upon these ways a cradle of hard wood, precisely like the cradle which holds a ship when ready for launching. The lifting crane was so maneuvered that the gun was allowed to settle comfortably into this cradle. Then the whole affair, barge, gun and cradle, was towed over to Lime Point.

At Lime Point the real work begins, for the monster has to be unloaded and dragged up the bank to where it is to be put into position. Five hundred yards up the bank and immovably anchored into it is the eight horse-power engine from which runs a wire cable of tremendous strength. Passing from the revolving drum of the engine this cable runs through a set of "sheaves"—which are nothing more than pulleys—half the way down the bank and terminates in another set that are fixed upon the bow of the barge as soon as it arrives.

The gun itself is not at first hauled, but the barge is dragged up the bank as far as necessary, when the "sheaves" (the cable still runs through them) are taken off and attached to the cradle, in which the gun is resting. There are two sets of ways—one set already upon the barge, and another which is now laid along the ground in front of the barge, like a track, along which the cradle is to slide.

As the engine starts and the huge cables straighten and tighten, the gun stirs and moves forward, the runners of the cradle hissing and groaning along the ways. It is precisely like the launching of a ship, only with the conditions reversed, the gun being dragged from the water on to the land, instead of slipping from the land into the water. But it is curious to note that it requires a greater expenditure of power to drag the gun up this inclined plane than it does to lift it bodily into the air. As soon as the gun has run from the first set of ways and has reached the second, the first are taken up and laid on ahead, then the second are placed ahead of the first, then the first ahead of the second, and so on.

The engine is placed about five hundred feet up the bank, and the cable is about equally long, so that when a certain point has been reached the whole arrangement, the engine, the "sheaves" and all, must be taken up and moved five hundred feet further on. You can easily see what an immense amount of labor this involves. The engine itself must be moved up the hill by some contrivance or other, the gun meanwhile held in place and a whole new "anchorage" prepared for the "sheaves." These "anchorages" alone are formidable affairs, and must be very nearly as solid as the hill itself, lest the vast weight below tear them out and the gun and engine and wire cable go thundering down the hillside to their ruin. So they dig them twelve feet deep—these "anchorages"—and build them up with the heaviest and stoutest timberings that may be had.

And so foot by foot the leviathan is dragged up the hillside, and one of these days, some time next month, no doubt, it will be lodged on its carriage in the midst of cranks and little wheels and levers. Then what a change of front. The sulky leviathan that dragged sullenly back on those groaning wire cables that set the eight horse-power engine hiccoughing and sweating with exertion, that taxed the ingenuity and energy of a little army of toilers —behold, it comes to hand with sudden and marvelous docility; it has been bridled and bitted; it is obedient, gentle, even. The lifting crane of the Union Iron Works quivered as it grappled with it. Now a woman's wrist may deflect its muzzle, raise it and lower it at will, may guide it about subject to her flimsiest caprice.

Election Night on a Daily

───────

How the Returns are Received and Given to the Public

───────

The Wave, 15 (7 November 1896), 7.

───────

To spend a few hours in the office of the *Chronicle* on the night of a presidential election seems to me like going behind the scenes of a theater, on the occasion of some initial performance, when a new play is to be put on for the first time and the public is to decide upon the merits of some much heralded and advertised star.

It is like that, only it's bigger, infinitely bigger. The chief actor upon whom the public pronounces that night is a great statesman, the stage is a whole country and the play is a tremendous drama, wrought out in one vast act, simple, majestic, a single movement and a single climax; the drama of a whole people, involving between curtain and close the action of an entire race, the movement of many millions of men. Or again, at other times you feel as if the office of the paper were some organ of hearing, the center of an infinite number of delicate lines of nerves, a place where you listen through the night to hear the people speak. You leave the crowd in the street outside and the noise of it. The fluctuating murmurs of it rising suddenly at times to sharp cheering, comes to you precisely as does the noise of an applauding audience somewhere beyond the wings.

So it was I went through the *Chronicle* last Tuesday night from the office floor where the bulletins were being posted in the midst of a shouting that was as the thunder of a cataract, to the topmost part of the tower, silent and windy, where the searchlight was flashing the news "McKinley undoubtedly elected" to all the country-side. Everything that was to be seen I saw. From the time a dispatch was received until the time it went into the hands of the lettering-man outside, I followed its course. But a newspaper office on election night is not the thing you have imagined, at least it was not what I expected to see. I had imagined a galloping hurry and a clamoring excitement, men in their shirt sleeves with green eyeshades writing as though their lives were in the issue, messenger boys rushing to and fro; perspiring, over-worked editors; telegraph instruments by the score clicking away like a swarm of grasshoppers, a litter of papers two feet deep upon the floor, gas a-blazing, doors banging, all sorts of things, exactly what, I did not know—I don't know now—something, no doubt, I expected to see like the headquar-ters of a general division during an engagement.

But this is what I did see in the room on the mezzanine floor where the dispatches of the presidential returns came. It was not the *Chronicle's* regu-lar office, but a room rented during the occasion for the purpose of seclu-sion and quiet. There were perhaps fifteen men in the room, some in their shirt sleeves, most of them with their hats on, nearly all of them writing or drawing, for it is here under the direction of the editors in charge of the election returns that the artists and cartoonists work. In one corner of the room sat a telegraph operator, who was also a typewriter—a miracle of man —flanked on one side by a telegraph instrument and on the other by a chuckling, clucking Remington. A special loop from the Western Union had been run in, and the *Chronicle* tapped the circuit here by four or five oper-ators. A dispatch arrived. The wonderful man in the corner took it off the telegraph instrument and type-wrote it as he listened, then passed it over to the Managing Editor at a near-by desk, whose duty it is to supervise the dis-patches as they arrive, to condense them and bring them up to date. This dispatch read, let us say: "Chicago—One hundred and twenty-eight precincts outside of (such and such counties) give McKinley so much, Bryan so much." The Managing Editor reads this dispatch. If there is any doubt about it, if it sounds preposterous, or not otherwise according to reasonable expecta-tion, he can turn to his tables at his elbow to verify the news, or determine what was the vote of that section in the last presidential election. Suppose, however, it passes inspection. The Managing Editor hands it over to an-other typewriter who types it off on a transparent film. Messengers are in waiting, and the film is hurried down stairs and run into a stereopticon that shows it up greatly enlarged upon the screen which faces the street. If you are particular about it and follow the dispatch close enough, in your imagi-nation, you can tell just when it strikes the street by the roar of sound with which it is greeted.

Or else the editor may send the dispatch from his table direct to the other bulletin, where the lettering men stand, or else, if its nature permits of it—it is for him to judge—he may order it telephoned up to the tower and flashed fifty miles away by red or green or blue lights as the news demands.

All this, however, is for the presidential returns. For the municipal returns, the *Chronicle* arranged a different system. In conjunction with three other dailies a bureau was established on Bush street, with a staff of nearly two hundred men. Messengers went to and from every election booth as rapidly as possible, each with a bundle of "books" to be made out according to the returns. The "books" delivered at the bureau to accountants were scrutinized, their contents tabulated and added and the result sent on to the *Chronicle* office the instant it was arrived at.

But in so short a space it is well nigh out of the question to give any complete description of the vast, complicated machinery employed by a great daily to collect election returns at the earliest possible hour. That the result was definitely known in the *Chronicle* office at 7:15 in the evening is proof of the thoroughness and expedition of its system, even when making allowance for the three hours' difference in time that permits a Western journal to get at the summing up of the Eastern evening papers.

You must imagine for yourself the small army of the journal's special correspondents all over the State, in the heart of the mountains sometimes, where they must ride twenty, thirty or fifty miles to the nearest telegraph, and the other army of reporters scattered through the city during election day, on bicycles, on horses, or in buggies, and the extra force kept in hand at the office in case of emergency—riot or such like.

When you consider what is done, it is marvelous. Think of the result of a vote of millions of people ascertained and bulletined in from three to four hours, and that accurately. The wires that stretch out from the office are hardly more than a network of nerves that transmit sensation without appreciable lapse of time. The people speak and you hear at once, unmistakably, unequivocally.

The Week's Football

Olympic Out of Condition Wins
From Stanford Out of Training

The Wave, 15 (7 November 1896), 13.

If on Friday the 29th, anyone, though he were a recognized authority on football, had predicted an utter and ignominious defeat for the cardinal eleven, even if he had prophesied a tie in the Olympic-Stanford game of Saturday, he would have met with incredulity, if not open derision. The Olympic team, rarely well trained, almost never in sound physical condition, were pronounced easy game for the Palo Alto team, supposedly trained to machine-like precision and force, and in the very pink of condition.

The result of the game came as a tremendous surprise. It was to be expected that Olympic would make ground through Thomas, but that tandem plays on Harrington (l.t.) and Cotton (r.t.) would be productive of continued advances, that the halves should be repeatedly tackled behind the line, and that the Stanford interference should be broken up by Porter (Olympic l.t.) and Erskine, was by no means upon the books of the experts.

Stanford has gone back since last week. At this stage of the season, with the 'varsity game but little more than three weeks away, a college eleven should play a rapid, aggressive game, precise and even, the ball should be snapped and passed with a bewildering quickness, the backs should be so sharp in getting away that they should be at their top speed when the line is reached, the value of a punt should be appreciated, and the captain should begin to show evidences of generalship. In every one of these points, mere essentials though they are, Stanford showed herself to be lamentably wanting in the game against the red and white. There are two things that California football teams, whether 'varsity or otherwise, never seem to learn. One is the marvelous, the almost incredible advantage of fast playing, the other the value of a punt as preferred to mere possession of the ball. Fast playing has so many advantages that it is difficult to know where to begin the enumeration. It demoralizes the opposing players as nothing else can, it unsteadies them, rattles them, makes them expend precious energy in guessing the next play, while for the team having the ball it stimulates to more unified effort, it enables the captain to take advantage of every chance, it keeps the attention and energy of his men at their highest tension, it gives confidence, assurance, that self-reliance, that arrogance, even, that is the infallible earnest of victory.

A punting game is a winning game. A punt will advance the ball a given distance at the expense of energy on the part of one man alone, whereas in a running, bucking game the same distance must be covered at the expense of energy on the part of the whole eleven individuals. A punt places the opponents on the defensive, it carries them back into their own territory, the ball is near the goal line, and the punting side has two chances for a touchdown, either by holding the enemy for downs or by securing the ball on a fumble. It's not possession of the ball, but distance gained, that wins football games. The rule should be to punt early and often. Other things being equal, a captain, roughly speaking, should punt on the first down anywhere between his ten and forty-yard line; on the second down, between his forty-yard line and that of his opponents, and on the third down between his forty-yard line and his opponents' goal.

Stanford, out of training and practice, poorly generaled and slowly handled, played weak and slovenly ball. The line was poor, both offensively and defensively. None of the cardinal backs as yet seen can be brought to run in a straight line when behind the line. Fisher (l.h.) and Dole (r.h.) both run in towards the quarter when receiving the ball; besides this, Dole, like Searight, has the fatal habit of running back to avoid tackling. The interference runs far too bunched and close together, enabling one man to tear it up. This frequently happened in Saturday's game, and is one of the chief reasons why Stanford did not score. Porter (Olympic l.t.) discovered this failing early in the first half, and more than once threw the whole group backward by a strong low dive. This bunched interference is perhaps Stanford's greatest fault.

Olympic won the game, not so much on its own merits as it did because of Stanford's astonishing demoralization. The men of the O.A.C. were in poor physical condition. After the second touchdown—the one not allowed —the halves and center men were well nigh exhausted. Too much time was taken to allow injured and winded Olympic players to recover. In the end it is a question whether these long intervals between plays do not do more harm than good to a team, especially when winning, since they are fatal to the quick following up of any advantage gained. Stickney ran the team in first-class fashion, considering how little cohesion exists in the O.A.C. eleven. He is not only a splendid running and bucking half, but is also the only real football general the coast has ever seen. His dash for goal at the beginning of the second half, and the manner in which he aroused and handled his team the instant it became apparent that Stanford was, perhaps, not so formidable as believed, was admirable in the extreme.

In all the teams so far in the history of Pacific Coast football there has not been a single really fine gridiron general. There have been men like Clemens of Stanford and Oscar Taylor of California, cool, steady players, who have strengthened and braced the teams at critical moments, and there have been captains like Benson (Cal.) who could manage to goad their elevens to sudden whirlwind efforts of short duration, but absolutely not one thus far who could plan and plot during the heat and excitement of action and obtain any appreciable results. Not one captain thus far has been a strategist, able to change the whole plan of action in a single moment during the progress of a game, to hoodwink and trick his opponents, to invariably exercise good judgment at critical moments, to play the game in a word as a general would plan a campaign.

Stanford only escaped disgraceful defeat (a score of 12—0 in favor of the O.A.C.'s) by a couple of technicalities. It is a pity Mr. Butterworth would not allow the second touchdown, as the Red and White had earned it at a tremendous expenditure of energy, keeping possession of the ball for nearly a dozen plays. However, judgment can only be passed upon what the judge can see, and as Stanford had possession of the ball by the time Butterworth was able to see it, no other course was left to him but to give it to the cardinal eleven. Nevertheless, the O.A.C. carried the ball twice over Stanford's goal. The fact augurs ill for the cardinal's prospects Thanksgiving. Yet let no one be deceived. Stanford may not win from California on that occasion, but she will play better ball than she did in this, her last game. College teams make their greatest improvement during the very last week of practice, while athletic clubs are as good as they ever are early in the season.

Too many people are allowed upon the side lines. None but the substitutes and those few individuals who have business there should be permitted to enter where now over fifty hangers-on congregate. It is preposterous that on the occasion of each touchdown a small army of rooters should collect about the goal posts, shouting warnings and encouragement to their teams.

Reliance and California try conclusions election day. If California has kept to the form of her last game with O.A.C. she should win a brilliant victory. If Reliance makes a score (which is doubtful in the extreme) Ransome should be able at least to triple it. If Reliance is shut out, the blue and gold will probably gain at least two touchdowns. Of the Freshman game it is well-nigh impossible to predict the issue, so erratic is liable to be the playing of such untrained elevens. Stanford might win one day by 40 points and California the next by fully as many.

Fast Playing at Last—A Sharp Game Between Club and College.

The last game that California and Reliance will play before they go up for their championship matches against Stanford and Olympic respectively was played last Tuesday. It was the sharpest game of the season so far.

California was not up to the form shown against the O.A.C. There can be little doubt that the game with the Red and White was one of the best ever put up by the Blue and Gold. In the election day victory they were dangerously close to defeat more than once and were saved from that issue only by rapid playing and the sound physical condition of the men, the result of weeks of conscientious training.

Reliance's good points were its determination and steadiness in the first half, the quickness with which it discovered California's weak point and its keeping possession of the ball for over forty yards of continuous line bucking. Where the club eleven was lacking was in the poor physical condition of the men, the inability and unwillingness to punt, the continued off-side play and the sluggish and inert passing and snapping.

There was no generalship on the part of the Reliance captain, but as there was little of that quality displayed on the 'Varsity side the drawback does not go for much. Pacific coast football teams do not know the meaning of generalship. Some day a second Cummock or Trafford will appear in one of the Big Four, and perhaps with a very mediocre team will revolutionize the California game. He has not appeared this season.

To lovers of a fast sharp game—which is nothing but fairly good football —California's theory of offense is encouraging in the extreme. Ransome's team is absolutely the only one of the Big Four that has grasped the merely fundamental idea of rapid play. It might almost be said that quick signalling and formations and nothing else won Tuesday's game for the Blue and Gold, the matters of condition and discipline being merely secondary. California, it would appear, is sacrificing many things to this inestimable quality. Accuracy in passing is one, as witnessed by the innumerable fumbles between quarter and half. But quickness is something that must be infused into a whole team (belted in at a rope's end, one is almost tempted to say) while inaccurate passing and receiving (faults of but two or three men) may be easily remedied as the season advances.

Reliance should have been prepared for this style of work, since it has been California's salient characteristic in every game she has played. But Kennedy repeatedly snapped the ball long before Reliance expected it, and on two distinct occasions the Reliance men were actually not in line, were literally not yet reformed from the scrimmage at the time when the California half was already running with the ball. Reliance has no excuse for this, it is sheer stupidity. Sherman's long run at the beginning of the second half was directly the outcome of Kennedy's quickness on the one hand and the sluggishness of the Reliance eleven on the other.

Although Reliance clearly outplayed California in the first half the second touchdown should not have been allowed. Reliance was on California's five-yard line, and had to gain five yards—that is, to the goal line—or lose the ball on downs. Reliance wedged the ball, but down was called fully three yards before the goal line was reached. It should have been California's ball on her three-yard line, first down. It will not do to say that Reliance would have scored anyhow—at least not at that moment—for California would probably have punted out of danger.

The punting of Reliance was wretched. They elected to punt in the second half with a high wind against them, but did little or no punting in the first half when it would have been most effective. The temptation to follow up successful mass plays such as those of the first half of Tuesday's game is doubtless very strong and much can be said in favor of continual persistence in ground-gaining plays, but the results of Reliance's heavy line work (the men scarcely ever rested by long punts) was apparent as soon as the last half began. Reliance had shot its bolt. Walton had exhausted the energies of his men by the furious and continued line bucking and the eleven had but little steam left with which to oppose the sudden and desperate attack of the California eleven in the second half.

Ransome showed far better judgment. Even in the second twenty-five minutes of play, with all the score against him, he husbanded the strength of his halves and runners by punting down the field until he could secure the ball close enough to the Reliance goal to run it over. His try for goal from the field was well timed, and was undoubtedly the play called for by the situation even though unsuccessful.

The Making of a *Pianiste*

Fannie Bloomfield Zeisler's Theory of Genius and Success

The Wave, 15 (14 November 1896), 5.

"The reason why there are not more great pianists," said Mrs. Zeisler, in answer to my first question, "is because there are not more people who are really and truly ambitious."

"But it's not merely a matter of ambition," I suggested.

"No; of course not," said Mrs. Zeisler. "But, now, take for instance the ordinary young lady pianist who is suddenly fired with a desire to be a great performer—a——"

"A second Mrs. Zeisler," said I.

"Very well," admitted Mrs. Zeisler, with a sudden smile. "Oh, I confess I am horribly conceited. She has the ambition—the desire, perhaps—even as keen a desire as myself. But she is not willing to give her whole life to the piano. She cannot bring herself to that state of mind wherein she must play and practice—must, you understand—whether she wants to or not."

"She has not the capacity for hard work?"

"You know, when I was young—younger than now, I mean—I used to take issue with that saying, 'genius is a capacity for hard work.' I would get positively furious over it. 'Hard work,' forsooth! Why, it was the Heaven-born gift! Why, it was the wonderful innate sympathy, the delicate sensitiveness, that cannot be acquired. But the more experience I have, the more I know myself, the more I am forced to believe that genius of any kind is a genius for application, for persistence, and all the rest. Look at my fingers."

I looked at them. Except that they were something muscular and osseous, the joints prominent, there did not seem to be anything remarkable about them.

"But see the nails," insisted Mrs. Zeisler. "Look how those two are broken off." They were broken down to the very quick.

"Painful?" said I.

"Painful!" echoed Mrs. Zeisler. "That is my affliction," she went on. "Most pianists have something wrong with their fingers. It's like a singer's throat—always over-sensitive. The more delicate and highly-trained the organ, the easier is its disarrangement. And isn't it a pity?—the very thing you depend upon most is precisely that which gives way. Now, my fingers, for instance: My nails are brittle; every now and then they break off—deep down, you know." She winced at the very thought.

"And you go on playing, nevertheless?"

"Of course. I must, as I told you, and oftentimes I go through a piece before an audience when every touch, even the lightest, of that finger-tip is positive agony. Rubinstein had something of the same complaint, only his finger-tips would crack open and bleed—positively bleed."

"But now," I interrupted, "I should think it would very nearly ruin your work. Suppose your finger-nail snapped like that in the midst of—let us say, Liszt's twelfth *Rhapsodie*—how could you do yourself justice when that finger was like an open wound?"

"I would play it all the better," exclaimed Fannie Zeisler, with conviction.

And that's a curious, true thing, when you reflect on it. But it is not the only strange, true theory that Mrs. Zeisler holds. This for instance:

We had started to talk of pianists and singers and artists generally, and it occurred to me to ask her if there was not some subtle connecting link, not only between different kinds of musicians, pianists, singers and composers, but also between musicians and actors.

"That is," I hastened to qualify, "great musicians and great actors."

"Why, of course," she replied, with a suddenness and an emphasis that showed me she had already entertained the same idea. "If Paganini had been given a different education he could have been made into as great an actor as he was a violinist. As for myself, I know I can act well. Not only do I believe that what you say is true, but I go even further. I believe that a great artist, a born one, you understand, can be made into a great anything —a business man, even."

"Come now."

"No, I honestly do," (with an energetic nodding of the head at me). "Mascagni is a very keen business man."

Another idol shattered!

"I say he would have made as good a Wall-street operator as he has made a pianist."

Mascagni a "Napoleon of Finance!" Now think of that.

"Then what is it," said I, "what shall we call that curious, nameless something, that universal quality which all great men—every single one of them, no matter what his profession is—have in common?"

Neither of us could find a name to put to it. I thought of "afflatus." But this was after I had come away.

I put my fingers upon the table-edge as though upon a key board, and drummed.

"Tell me, Mrs. Zeisler," I asked, "what is the matter with my fourth finger—mine and everybody else's? The other four we can raise all right, but that fourth one—look at it—it's almost paralyzed. What is the trouble?"

If I did not understand explanations that followed very clearly, I did perceive one thing, that Mrs. Zeisler knew the anatomy of the hand as well as any surgeon. It had never struck me before that a pianist should know this. Mrs. Zeisler talked of tendons by their technical names; of "pronators" and "flexors," and of "slips."

"And the reason you can't raise the fourth finger so easily is that a 'slip' crosses over its tendons, running towards the little finger, and holds it down."

"How about cutting that slip?" I had heard that some pianists do. I did not think that Mrs. Zeisler would approve. Nor did she.

"I have no trouble with mine," said she. "By constant practice that 'slip' gets more and more elastic, till at length you scarcely notice it."

Mrs. Zeisler tells me that she never looks at her audience, but sees it and hears it, and, as one might say, touches it, by a sort of sixth sense that tells her in an instant if they are appreciative or not.

"And if they are not—if there are only two or three there who are 'away' —it is the most dreadful, up-hill work to get through with the piece. One must have appreciation—encouragement. It's the 'bravos' that count—that stimulate. If they are intelligent, so much the better."

"And if not?" said I. Mrs. Zeisler hesitated, then——

"Well——they are better than none at all."

One is only human at best.

A Day with the U.C. Team

———

Settling to Harness—
The Twelve Hours' Routine of a College Eleven

———

The Wave, 15 (14 November 1896), 6.

———

I went to the training quarters at Berkeley expecting all sorts of things, because I had read the newspaper accounts and had been told therein of "stalwart young giants" and "almost raw beefsteaks" and "dry crusts of toast" and "ten-mile runs" every morning and "football appetites" and all the rest. To read these accounts in the Sunday newspapers and to hear the talk of a certain class of people you would believe that the football player undergoes a course of training and dieting that would be enough to break down the constitution of Mr. Thomas Sharkey; whereas, the real thing is precisely the reverse. At this time of the season the training has been long since abandoned. There are no morning runs, no more fatiguing chest-weight exercises, none of that persistent heart-breaking treadmill work that has broken down the spirit of many a good man and has sent the team to the gridiron without "ginger" or dash and in a hopelessly "over-trained" condition.

And as for the dieting—let's begin at the beginning of things. I went over to the quarters with the Center, who is a friend of mine and who played on last year's eleven. The team, which at this point of the season may be construed to mean the twenty-six men who are trying for positions, were on the point of sitting down to breakfast. It was eight o'clock. Barring the absence of coffee and the presence of oatmeal water, I couldn't for the life of me see anything different in that breakfast from my ordinary morning's meal. There was hominy (without cream) and eggs "in any style," toast and butter and apple sauce and chops that were not particularly underdone. The men straggled in one by one. They were not especially big. They did not suggest the athlete in any marked way, not even Ransome, who is the captain, nor Butterworth, the coach, Yale's great fullback. There was no great talk of football. The Center and I talked about a Girl He Knew, and many of the men propped their text books against the sugar bowls and milk pitchers for a final glance before the morning's recitation. Indeed, during breakfast what seemed uppermost in their minds was to get up to the buildings in time for the first-hour lecture. I can recall but one remark at all characteristic. I think it was the sub tackle, who looked gloomily down into the depths of his glass of oatmeal water (it is stale and flat) and muttered, "Only three weeks more of this dishwater."

All through the morning the team were scattered throughout lecture hall and recitation room. At 12:30 came lunch. A small steak to each man, potatoes, milk, more apple sauce, and oatmeal water—plain, ordinary fare. Then back again to college for more lectures. I began to feel vaguely defrauded. This was not at all what I expected. I had imagined that every moment of the men's time not occupied by college work was devoted to football. I imagined that they practically lived in their football suits. But there was nothing like this. The Center wore his 'varsity sweater with its golden C., but he was the exception. He explained that he had a boil on his neck.

"Nothing this afternoon before the regular work?" I asked Ransome.

"Nothing. If it had not been so muddy (the day was villainous) the backs would have got out and done a little kicking at two. But as it is, we won't do anything before four-thirty."

At four the team dressed itself in its football clothes, the 'varsity eleven at the track house down by the cinder path, the second eleven at the gymnasium. By half-past four some twenty-six men were on the campus and some four hundred students on the bleachers and back of the side-line fence. Butterworth appeared, looking slighter than ever in his canvas suit. He was coaching the backs in catching punts, and would kick down the field for them and yell his directions after the ball. Finally "Line up, 'varsity's kick-off. Now, let's see you get down on it."

Then at last the day's hard work began, concentrated into about an hour's uninterrupted scrimmages. There was no lack of coaching. Butterworth was at them, whip and spur, without a moment's relaxation. Nott, the Brown player, followed one man about for over ten minutes, talking in earnest whispers to him between scrimmages.

Hunt, the bulwark of Benson's team, gave the backs good counsel. Henry, the famous end rusher and one time holder of a world's hurdling record, shouted warnings into the scrimmages. Ransome himself, laid off on account of a bad knee, shouted from the side lines. The bleachers roared applause or growled disapproval. Altogether the team seemed to be getting plenty of advice. Butterworth occupied himself with improving the quickness of the work.

"Get up, get up, get up," you could hear him shouting after every scrimmage. "Play it up sharp, now, sharp; get into it; come along, Hall."

Or again, it would be Ransome, suffering torture over a fumbled pass. "Fall on it, fall on it, fall on the ball."

Or Henry: "Hopper, that was your fault. Don't you play so far out when your side has the ball."

Or Nott, confidential as ever, as though imparting some state secret of vast importance, would gesture anxiously into a player's face, talking earnestly in undertones.

Or Hunt, delighted over the fact that his particular man had at last caught his idea, would run into the scrimmage, patting him on the back and exclaiming: "That's the stuff; keep to it in that way."

At about quarter of six Butterworth stopped the work, and the 'varsity eleven went down to the track house again. A roaring fire was going in a pink stove, and the rubbers were ready and waiting with sponges and bandages and camphor and alcohol. There was but a single lamp, and you saw the glow of the fire strike on those smooth, dripping bare backs as the men swung out of their sweaters till they glowed as so much marble.

Each man takes a bath at this time, and you can hear them shouting to one another through the partitions.

"I say, you didn't do a thing to my nose that time you tackled me on the five-yard line."

"Well, you shouldn't have been running high."

"That time you straight-armed me I went over with my head on something hard as rock—somebody's heel, I guess—pretty near put me to sleep." Then after the rubdown and a thorough kneading and knuckling of the muscles by the rubbers the team streams back to the quarters for its supper of soup and beef and ale, and its evening's games of whist or chess, and perhaps poker, for all I know.

At ten o'clock the lights are out, and the team is asleep. And so it goes day in and day out, the work getting lighter as Thanksgiving day approaches, and finally the last week comes, and the last two days, and then "the day before the game," and then—

"We're not saying much this year," said the coach to me, "but——" He didn't finish the sentence.

The Week's Football

The Freshman Game—Both Elevens Weak and Unsteady

The Wave, 15 (14 November 1896), 13.

It is hardly fair to criticise a Freshman game—particularly California-Stanford Freshman games—from 'varsity standpoints, since usually not one sixth of the time and patience is expended on the first-year eleven as is given to the breaking-in of the regulars.

Saturday's game was a scrub game, no matter how one looks at it. In spite of Stanford's lead, it was anybody's victory till within ten minutes of the call of time, and, in fact, California was perilously near Stanford's goal line for the second time at the moment when the whistle blew. This is, however, no disparagement of the Cardinals' work. They deserved every one of their fourteen points, gained as they were for the most part by the most strenuous and persistent line-bucking. The team work on both sides was execrable, though California was no doubt poorer in this respect than her opponents. In the mass-plays on tackle and guard most of the Stanford eleven followed the ball with considerable vim and determination. In the few successful plays around the end, particularly around California's left end, just prior to the second Stanford touchdown, the Palo Alto youngsters developed a fairly good interference. Murphy played what was probably the best individual game in the field in this respect. Whenever the ball was sent through guard and tackle Murphy was quick to follow it up and give the runner the necessary shove to carry him through the hole.

But it is possible to generalize upon the work of the Stanford Freshmen only in these points. Their play (as was to be expected) was erratic in the extreme. At times their runners gained at will at any point of their opponents' lines, and at times lost ground instead of acquiring it. It was the same with their defense—one minute the Cardinal line would be pliable, weak and easy of attack, and the next absolutely impregnable.

California's defense was uniformly poor from kickoff to whistle. The tendency of the Berkeley rush line was to straggle and open out as soon as Murphy put his ball in play. Nine times out of ten the forwards attempted to break through on the outside of their men instead of on the inside; the natural consequence of this was that they made holes for the Stanford halves, through which the ball was rushed, for five-, ten- and fifteen-yard gains. The method of defense, as employed by more experienced teams, is precisely the reverse of this, since it implies a sudden, sharp closing up and locking of the line the instant the play is started by the opposing quarter. The forwards should endeavor to converge simultaneously upon the ball, before the runner has a chance to start, a manoeuvre which can only be accomplished by breaking through on the inside. This, of course, leaves the flanks exposed, but it is the duty of the two ends to defend this quarter, and it is precisely for this reason that the ends should rarely get into the scrimmage, but should hover upon the flanks ready to tackle the runner should he succeed in breaking out, or to dive in and secure the ball in case of a fumble.

Stanford's repeated gains on the tackles were largely the result of the mistaken endeavors of the California ends to turn the runner in instead of converging upon the ball together with the forwards. It is a wrong theory to suppose that the first duty of an end is to turn the runner in upon the tackle. This move should be made only as a last resort. Often in last Saturday's game this style of play on the part of the California end left an immense territory open between tackle and end, through which the runner gained at will until stopped by either the half or the full. The primary duty of an end should be to reach the runner before he can get behind interference, and to do this he must run in upon the ball as quickly as possible. In the Freshman game of Saturday the California ends repeatedly waited until the ball, already well protected by interference, reached the line and then endeavored to break into the interference from the outside, throwing the runner over upon the tackle. This was no doubt the end's play when the ball had already progressed so far as that. But he should not have waited until the play was so far advanced before making his attempt to check it. He should have gone in the instant the ball was snapped, gone in toward the center, endeavoring to tackle the runner before, not after the interference had formed. A runner tackled at the line is bound to gain something, if only his own length; tackled behind the line he is sure to lose something. Even if he does not succeed in tackling, the end will drive the runner straight into a pocket formed by the other forwards.

It was not especially the weakness of her guards and tackles that lost California her Freshman game, but rather this delay on the part of the ends in getting into the play. It was not on tackle alone that Stanford gained but through a wide gap that the California end left between himself and tackle. The California halves as well were responsible for Stanford's gains between tackle and end and for possibly the same reason, i.e., their slowness—their intentional slowness—in starting in upon the ball as soon as it was in play. They, as a rule, waited until the end had failed to break through the interference before they made their attempt, at a time when the ball had already been advanced some two or three yards. The California halves, in all but a few instances, should have converged upon the ball together with the whole team, though a little in the rear. They should have gone through after the end, following in the rear, to back him up in his efforts of breaking up the Stanford interference, and to help the tackle as well, if the opportunity afforded.

So much space has been given to the defensive duties of end and half, since the territory which they must cover is the most dangerous of any point on the line, and since it was precisely through a neglect of a proper defense of this territory that the California Freshmen were defeated in their annual championship game with Stanford.

Murphy played his team fairly fast, and kept them up to their best efforts at critical moments, though the team should certainly have gotten into position quicker on the occasion of California's free kicks.

There is too much coaching from the side lines. Whenever the scrimmage is near enough, some dozen or more men, who should know better, are constantly shouting warnings and directions to their respective teams.

The Stanford Eleven at Home

How the Palo Altoans Prepare for the Great
Football Contest

The Wave, 15 (21 November 1896), 6.

Stanford lives in its dormitories, not in its boarding houses. It is a college without a town, and a house is quite an affair, a thing to be indulged in only by professors and big fraternities. The football team has no especial quarters. It lives for the most part in Encina Hall, and it breakfasts, lunches and sups in the college refectory, where it has a table to itself.

Otherwise there is not much difference between its routine and that of its Blue and Gold rival. Lectures and recitations take up all of its time until 4:15 in the afternoon. I do not wish to draw any invidious distinction; I wish to be as unprejudiced as is possible, and I will say, too, that one day's observation of a routine that has continued for three months is not adequate, but it seemed to me that there was a certain go-as-you-please air about football affairs down at Stanford, a certain nonconformity to discipline. The men dress for the afternoon's work anywhere they choose—you can see them congregating from all parts of the campus—assemble in front of Encina Hall and come trailing down upon the campus in a long, straggling line, while during the practice there was a good deal of talking and "joshing" in the lines; every one had his little say, and found occasion to say it.

By 4:30 there was quite a crowd upon the bleachers, the co-eds—prettier and more smartly dressed girls, by far, than one sees at Berkeley—fore-gathering in a particular section, the "rooters" with their leader occupying those that faced the middle of the field. It was a bright day, but cold—ideal football weather. Just that little sting that acts like a spur to energetic endeavor. The "rooters" were practicing their cheer, eight rahs and a Stanford, thrice repeated. It is a rapid, barking note that comes trippingly off the tongue, rattling and vigorous, quite a different affair from California's cadenced slogan.

171

"Here they come; Rah-Rah-Rah, Rah-Rah-Rah," etc. It was 4:30, and some thirty men in vermilion sweaters, with black S's on the breasts came galloping down from Encina. All at once the bleachers shouted. A jackrabbit had gotten up under the feet of that young Yale giant, Cross, and had gone bounding off, as though worked by springs in his hind legs. At once Cross started in chase, just as if the jack had been a fumbled ball, racing along intently, with enormous strides, for over a hundred yards.

The team got down to work at once. There were three elevens all told, the 'varsity, second and Reliance, the latter practicing for its return Olympic game, to be played to-day.

A Berkeley student was with me. "Look," said he quickly in great excitement, "that's a new play, look at the 'varsity." It did look like something new, this maneuver that the 'varsity was executing against an imaginary team.

"Look there," said the Berkeley man breathlessly, "that's new; see how the center guard and tackle form a kind of turtle back and move off sliding-like, and the quarter and halves get in the push behind them—oh, I say."

He was all suspicion and excitement. Perhaps Stanford would "spring" this thing Thanksgiving day. Then Cross stood in the center of the field and began calling off the men who were to play. You could hear his voice like that of a muster-sergeant reading a roll call before a battle, "Searight, Cotton, Murphy, Carl, Williams."

There is little or no vociferation in the Stanford system of coaching. Little if any of that constant exhortation, carried on at top voices, such as you will hear on the Berkeley gridiron. Once during the play there was a bad fumble, and Jules Frankenheimer read the fumbler a long lecture in undertones over it. Such would not have been the case at Berkeley—seven different men would have yelled simultaneously and with a great shaking of fists, and perhaps Mr. Butterworth—as I once saw him do—would have thrown his cap on the ground in disgust. It is only a difference in methods. I fancy one is just as effective as the other.

We—the Berkeley man and myself—went out upon the field and Frankenheimer introduced us to Cross and to Captain Fickert. Cross is so big that he ceases to be broad and tall—you feel like speaking of him as wide and high, as though he were a steeple of a clock-tower—and he has an enormous bell-toned voice and a fist that your hand loses itself inside.

"Oh, I say," began the Berkeley man, looking from Cross to Frankenheimer, "wasn't that a new play, that you were coaching the 'Varsity on before the line-up, where the center-guard and tackle form a kind of turtle-back?"

"New play," murmured Cross in vague surprise, looking from the member of the rival college toward Frankenheimer.

"New play," murmured Frankenheimer, blankly. "What new play?"

"What new play?" inquired Mr. Cross.

The Berkeley man tried to explain.

"I can't understand what he can mean," said Mr. Cross.

The Berkeley man started in all over again at greater length.

"I think he's got it mixed up with something else," said Frankenheimer.

Total discomfiture of the Berkeley man and subsequent retirement to the side lines.

The afternoon's practice is very short at Stanford at this time of the season. After an hour's work it is all over, and the men fall apart into separate elevens and go through signal practice and team work. It is dark by the time they finish. Then they go over to the gymnasium—it is close at hand—and get their baths and rub-downs. The coaches take the train back to the city, and in the smoking car go over again the famous men and famous plays of the time when they were freshmen or sophomores. Back at the college the team is sitting down to its rare steaks, ale and oatmeal water in the dining hall of the college, and Cross and Code are probably talking football into them with their food. And so it goes, day in and day out, and every hour that passes is bringing closer that final, fateful moment when Ransome, or Cotton, as the case may be, shall step back from the ball to get his distance for the kick that will let loose such a roar from the bleachers as is only heard once a year—upon each succeeding Thanksgiving day.

A Few Football Figures

The Wave, 15 (21 November 1896), 6.

It is very difficult—under some circumstances well-nigh impossible—to "size up" a football team, for the reason that the game itself offers innumerable chances for unexpected plays—crises, such as a fumble, that may be taken advantage of by an eleven to score upon—to even win, from a confessedly stronger team. Predictions based upon general observations, upon impressions gained from mere observation, are equally unreliable.

Let us see if we can reduce the strength put forth by California and Stanford in their games of this season to figures, and upon them base some sort of prophesy. At least we shall know which has been the strongest team to the time of the last 'varsity-club game. Here, then, is the way the 'varsities stand up to date:

> California has played three games and won two.
> Stanford has played three games and won one.
> California has scored seven times and missed one goal.
> Stanford has scored twice and missed one goal.
> California has been scored against six times.
> Stanford has been scored against once.
> California's total number of points earned is forty.
> Stanford's total number of points earned is ten.

This last would be extremely encouraging for California and alarming for Stanford were it not for the fact that Stanford has defended her own goal so well. Only once has it been crossed during the season. If, then, we subtract the number of points lost by the two 'varsities (four for Stanford and thirty for California) from the total number they have earned, we shall have a difference, *viz.:*

> Net gains by Stanford, six.
> Net gains by California, ten.

Now as to the actual number of yards gained: California has advanced the ball

In the first Reliance game, 530 yards;
In the second Reliance game, 640 yards;
In the Olympic game, 765 yards.

Stanford has advanced the ball

In the first Olympic game, 500 yards (approximate);
In the second Olympic game, 360 yards;
In the Reliance game, 745 yards;

Which gives

A total advance for California of 1915 yards.
A total advance for Stanford of 1605 yards.

The total number of yards gained on punts is:

California, 1185.
Stanford, 1073.

From these figures it will be seen that California has a lead over her rival of four points earned, 310 yards in total number of yards advanced, and 112 yards in gains by punts.

It would have been interesting to have figured out the actual number of plays used by the two 'varsities in obtaining these results, but time and space alike forbid.

The general conclusion to be drawn apparently is that at the time of the last California-Reliance game, the U.C. was stronger than its Cardinal rival. However, the last two weeks of training are of considerable importance in football work, and Stanford will, no doubt, play harder ball than these figures would lead one to expect.

The Week's Football

Olympic-Reliance—Olympic's Gift of a Tie Game

The Wave, 15 (21 November 1896), 13.

There is probably no other locality in the United States, where football is so far advanced and where an equal number of important teams take part in the games, that has witnessed so many tie championship matches as has San Francisco.

These unsatisfactory and indecisive results are not due merely to coincidence, but rather to a lack of ambition on the part of the stronger teams—that is, the elevens who permit their score to be tied by their opponents, whom they should have beaten, often with the greatest ease. This unambitious, half-hearted spirit has been for the most part confined to the universities. Now it would seem it has appeared among the athletic clubs. The eleven is not the only responsible party, however. The organization which it represents is almost as much to blame. A team is much what its college or club is. If the teams of the "big four" knew that their bleachers considered a tie as but one remove from disgraceful defeat, this bugbear of California football teams might be removed. We would see harder playing then—something of that dogged, stubborn spirit that shuts its teeth and eyes; that fights at full steam every minute of the thirty-five; that absolutely refuses to be defeated; that does not know when it is beaten, and that asks for the last ditch to die in, and dies there, if needs be, beaten and broken, perhaps, but doing its best to the very last, guarding its forty-five-yard mark as jealously as if it were the very goal line, or fighting for inches in the center of the field as if it were their ball on the five yard line, with but one minute to play, and one touchdown against them.

California teams don't know this spirit as yet—don't know the meaning of hard playing. It is easy to fool the bleachers, or by means of a certain amount of excited struggling and wild-eyed gesturing to deceive the average spectator into a belief that the team is playing hard football. At its very mildest and gentlest, football is a hard, rough sport, and to one unfamiliar with the game a high school eleven might seem to be playing as hard ball as a 'varsity. When the scrimmage comes toppling over on the ground, a dozen or more men piled up together, or when the tackler and runner meet head on at full speed with a shock that can be heard to the side lines, a certain class of spectator (unfortunately a very large one in California), nods his head very wisely to his friend, exclaiming "they're playing hard!" An eastern game, as played by even fairly trained elevens, who, however, have been broken in to earnest, continual effort, would be a revelation to such a spectator, and to the members of the teams themselves.

California teams do not play sharp, hard football. Let every disinterested spectator of Olympic-Reliance or any other of the recent matches ask himself how far California elevens have lived up to that admirable definition of team work. "Every man in every play and every time." The men do not do it. A team will start the game, let us say, with a fair amount of cohesion and dash; a touchdown is secured and a goal kicked. Jubilation! and the bleachers roaring. "What's the matter with So-and-so?" "Great work!" "The game is ours!" Immediately the scoring team loses its grip, it straggles, it ceases effort—they are six points ahead anyway—the main object is to win; no good trying to pile up a score. In the second half, after the rest and rubdown, the other team manages to score and kick a goal, then in its turn it goes to sleep. The fact that their score is tied does not arouse the first team in the least. It is as if both elevens and their bleachers back of them should say "We did mighty well to get six points as it was." It is not so. One of the elevens is directly to blame for not winning. In the very nature of the game of football it is manifestly impossible that eleven men, trained in certain principles, in a certain atmosphere, and under certain conditions, should be the exact equals of eleven other men trained and coached and practiced under totally different conditions and along totally different lines. One eleven must be the strongest, and upon their shoulders must lie the blame—for blame it is—of a tied score.

That Reliance tied Olympic's score by a fluke at a time so late in the game that it was perhaps impossible for the Red and White to score again does not excuse the latter players in the least. Unquestionably they were the strongest team. They had no right to be content with a single touchdown. That touchdown was gained after three minutes' play. Reliance scored about ten minutes before call of time in the second half. That left nearly an hour in which Olympic had a chance to score again—and didn't.

No especial blame is to be cast upon the clubs. The teams from the U.C. have drowsed and dwaddled in this same way for the last four years. This negligence is not met with the right spirit. The strongest team has not the right—literally, has not the right—to lose the game. The players owe it to the college or to the club to win. The U.C. spends over two thousand dollars yearly to put their team into the field, asking no return from the men but that they should do their best to win the game. After five years this amounts to ten thousand dollars expended to win from Stanford. What has been the result? Two defeats and three ties!

The Olympic team should have won Saturday's game by at least two touchdowns. A fluke, such as was taken advantage of by Lacunna cannot be foreseen and guarded against by even the best teams, but the Olympic score should have been made long before the fluke occurred. Even as it was, the fluke was made possible by McIsaac's inexcusable fumble. The team work on both sides was execrable. Arthur Cummock, in defining this essential of good football, once said: "The amount of an individual's contribution to the team play is the difference between him and his opponent in playing his position, or what he can do besides attending to his man." In Saturday's game, with the noble exceptions of Nolan, Ames and Lacunna, a man played his position and nothing more.

Time and again anywhere from six to ten players could be seen standing about the field watching the course of the play, the scrimmage or punt, or run instead of following the ball with every nerve tense, and every energy and faculty absorbed in the game. At one time the writer actually saw one of the players run to the side lines after down was called, for a drink of water, getting back into his place just as the ball was snapped. And this in a championship game!

The game was full of neglected chances. If ever in the history of football there was a time for a try for a field goal, it was at that moment during the second half when Reliance was close to Olympic's goal. The score was against the Oakland team; they had no chance of winning but on a fluke; they were unable to advance the ball by any running or bucking play, and the scrimmages were directly in front of the goal posts. Instead of the fullback trying for a field goal, they persisted in bucking an impregnable line and lost the ball on downs. But Olympic evened up on their next play. They were on their ten-yard line, but instead of punting out of danger the Olympic captain elected to run the ball back. This was bad judgment as it was, but to signal for a double pass at such a moment was like inviting defeat. The double pass is an admirable play under certain conditions, but not when a team is playing within seven or eight yards of its goal.

The "English Courses" of the University of California

The Wave, 15 (28 November 1896), 2-3.

In the "announcement of courses" published annually by the faculty of the University of California the reader cannot fail to be impressed with the number and scope of the hours devoted by the students to recitations and lectures upon the subject of "literature." At the head of this department is Professor Gayley (the same gentleman who is to edit the volumes of Shakespeare for Macmillan at the expense of the State of California). Be pleased for a moment to consider these "literary" courses. They comprise "themes" written by the student, the subject chosen by the instructor and the matter found in text books and encyclopedias. They further include lectures, delivered by associate professors, who, in their turn have taken their information from text books and "manuals" written by other professors in other colleges. The student is taught to "classify." "Classification" is the one thing desirable in the eyes of the professors of "literature" of the University of California. The young Sophomore, with his new, fresh mind, his active brain and vivid imagination, with ideas of his own, crude, perhaps, but first hand, not cribbed from text books. This type of young fellow, I say, is taught to "classify," is set to work counting the "metaphors" in a given passage. This is actually true—tabulating them, separating them from the "similes," comparing the results. He is told to study sentence structure. He classifies certain types of sentences in De Quincey and compares them with certain other types of sentences in Carlyle. He makes the wonderful discovery—on suggestion from the instructor—that De Quincey excelled in those metaphors and similes relating to rapidity of movement. Sensation!

In his Junior and Senior years he takes up the study of Milton, of Browning, of the drama of the seventeenth and eighteenth centuries, English comedy, of advanced rhetoric, and of aesthetics. "Aesthetics," think of that! Here, the "classification" goes on as before. He classifies "lyrics" and "ballads." He learns to read Chaucer as it was read in the fourteenth century, sounding the final e; he paraphrases Milton's sonnets, he makes out "skeletons" and "schemes" of certain prose passages. His enthusiasm is about dead now; he is ashamed of his original thoughts and of those ideas of his own that he entertained as a Freshman and Sophomore. He has learned to write "themes" and "papers" in the true academic style, which is to read some dozen text books and encyclopedia articles on the subject, and to make over the results in his own language. He has reduced the writing of "themes" to a system. He knows what the instructor wants, he writes accordingly, and is rewarded by first and second sections. The "co-eds" take to the "classification" method even better than the young men. They thrive and fatten intellectually on the regime. They consider themselves literary. They write articles on the "Philosophy of Dante" for the college weekly, and after graduation they "read papers" to literary "circles" composed of post-graduate "co-eds," the professors' wives and daughters and a very few pale young men in spectacles and black cutaway coats. After the reading of the "paper" follows the "discussion," aided and abetted by cake and lemonade. This is literature! Isn't it admirable!

The young man, the whilom Sophomore, affected with original ideas, does rather different. As said, by the time he is a Junior or Senior, he has lost all interest in the "literary" courses. The "themes" must be written, however, and the best way is the easiest. This is how he oft-times goes about it: He knows just where he can lay his hands upon some fifty to a hundred "themes" written by the members of past classes, that have been carefully collected and preserved by enterprising students. It will go hard if he cannot in the pile find one upon the subject in hand. He does not necessarily copy it. He re-writes it in his own language. Do you blame him very much? Is his method so very different from that in which he is encouraged by his professor; *viz.*, the cribbing—for it is cribbing—from text books? The "theme" which he rewrites has been cribbed in the first place.

The method of English instruction of the University of California often develops capital ingenuity in the student upon whom it is practiced. We know of one young man—a Senior—who found himself called upon to write four "themes," yet managed to make one—re-written four times—do for the four. This was the manner of it. The four "themes" called for were in the English, chemical, German and military courses respectively. The young fellow found a German treatise on the manufacture of gunpowder, translated it, made four copies, and by a little ingenuity passed it off in the four above named departments. Of course the thing is deplorable, yet how much of the blame is to be laid at the door of the English faculty?

The conclusion of the whole matter is that the literary courses of the University of California do not develop literary instincts among the students who attend them. The best way to study literature is to try to produce literature. It is original work that counts, not the everlasting compiling of facts, not the tabulating of metaphors, nor the rehashing of text books and encyclopedia articles.

They order this matter better at Harvard. The literary student at Cambridge has but little to do with lectures, almost nothing at all with text books. He is sent away from the lecture room and told to look about him and think a little. Each day he writes a theme, a page if necessary, a single line of a dozen words if he likes; anything, so it is original, something he has seen or thought, not read of, not picked up at second hand. He may choose any subject under the blue heavens from a pun to a philosophical reflection, only let it be his own. Once every two weeks he writes a longer theme, and during the last six weeks of the year, a still longer one, in six weekly installments. Not a single suggestion is offered as to subject. The result of this system is a keenness of interest that draws three hundred men to the course and that fills the benches at every session of the class. The class room work consists merely in the reading by the instructor of the best work done, together with his few critical comments upon it by the instructor in charge. The character of the themes produced under this system is of such high order that it is not rare to come across one of them in the pages of the first-class magazines of the day. There is no sufficient reason to suppose that the

California collegians are intellectually inferior to those of the Eastern States. It is only a question of the means adopted to develop the material.

His Sister

The Wave, 15 (28 November 1896), 7.

"Confound the luck," muttered young Strelitz in deep perplexity as he got up from the supper table and walked over to the mantel-piece, pulling at his lower lip as was his custom when thinking hard.

Young Strelitz lived in a cheap New York flat with his mother, to whose support he contributed by writing for the papers.

Just recently he had struck a vein of fiction that promised to be unusually successful. A series of short stories—mere sketches—which he had begun under the title "Dramas of the Curbstone," had "caught on," and his editor had promised to take as many more of them as he could write for the Sunday issue. Just now young Strelitz was perplexed because he had no idea for a new story. It was Wednesday evening already, and if his stuff was to go into the Sunday's paper it should be sent to the editor by the next day's noon at the latest.

"Blessed if I can dig up anything," he exclaimed as he leaned up against the mantelpiece, his forehead in a pucker.

He and his mother were just finishing their supper. Mrs. Strelitz brushed the crumbs from her lap and pushed back her chair, looking up at her son.

"I thought you were working on something this afternoon," she hazarded.

"It don't come out at all," he answered, as he drew a new box of cigarettes from his coat pocket. "It's that 'Condition of Servitude' stuff, and I can't make it sound natural."

"But that's a true story," exclaimed Mrs. Strelitz. "That really happened."

"That don't help matters any if it don't read like real life," he returned, as he opened the box of cigarettes. "It's not the things that have really happened that make good fiction, but the things that read as though they had."

"If I were you," said his mother, "I would try an experiment. You've been writing these 'Dramas of the Curbstone' without hardly stirring from the house. You've just been trying to imagine things that you think are likely to happen on the streets of a big city after dark, and you've been working that way so long that you've sort of used up your material—exhausted your imagination. Why don't you go right out—now—to-night, and keep your eyes open and watch what really happens, and see if you can't find something to make a story out of, or at least something that would suggest one? You're not listening, Conrad, what's the matter?"

It was true, young Strelitz was not listening. The box of cigarettes he had drawn from his pocket was a fresh one. While his mother was talking he had cut the green revenue stamp with his thumb nail, and had pushed open the box, had taken out a cigarette and had put it between his lips.

The box was one of those which contain, in addition to the cigarettes themselves the miniature photograph of some *bouffe* actress, and Strelitz had found in his box one that was especially debonaire. But as he looked at the face of the girl it represented he suddenly shifted his position and turned a little pale. He thrust the box back into his pocket, but closed his fist over the photograph as though to hide it. He did not light his cigarette.

"What's the matter, Conrad? You are not listening."

"Oh, yes I am," he answered. "I—nothing. I'm listening. Go on."

"Well, now, why don't you try that?"

"Try what?"

"Go out and look for a story on the streets."

"Oh, I don't know."

Without attracting his mother's attention, Strelitz looked again at the cigarette picture in his hand and then his glance went from it to a large crayon portrait that stood on a brass easel in the adjoining parlor. The crayon portrait was the head and bare shoulders of a young girl of seventeen or eighteen. The resemblance to Strelitz and his mother was unmistakable, but there was about the chin and the corners of the eyes a certain recklessness that neither of the others possessed. The mouth too was weak.

"You get right down to your reality then," continued Mrs. Strelitz. "Even if you do not find a story, you would find at least a background—a local color that you can observe much better than you can imagine."

"Yes, yes," answered Strelitz. He lounged out of the dining-room, and going into the little parlor turned up the gas, and while his mother and the hired girl cleared away the table, fell to studying the two likenesses—the crayon portrait and the cigarette picture, comparing them with each other.

There was no room for doubt. The two pictures were of the same girl.

However, the name printed at the bottom of the cigarette picture was not that which young Strelitz expected to see.

"Violet Ormonde," he muttered, reading it. "That's the stage-name she took, poor Sabina, poor Sabina, to come to this." He looked again at the photograph of the *bouffe* actress, in her false bull-fighter's costume, with its low-necked, close-fitting bodice, its tights, its high-laced kid shoes, its short Spanish cloak and foolish inadequate sword—a sword *opéra comique*. "Poor little girl," he continued under his breath as he looked at it, "she could have returned to us if she'd wanted to before she came to this. She could come back now. But where could one find her? What's become of her by this time?"

He was roused by the entrance of his mother and faced about, hastily thrusting the little photograph into his pocket and moving away from the crayon portrait on the brass easel, lest his mother should see him musing over it.

"Conrad," said Mrs. Strelitz, "you don't want to miss a week with your stories now that people have just begun to read them."

"I know," he admitted, "but what can I do? I haven't a single idea."

"Well, now, just do as I tell you. You try that. Go down town and keep your eyes open and see if you can't see something you can make a story out of. Make the experiment, anyhow. You'll have the satisfaction of having tried. Why, just think, in a great city like this, with thousands and thousands of people, all with wholly different lives and with wholly different interests—interests that clash. Just think of the stories that are making by themselves every hour, every minute. There must be hundreds and hundreds of stories better than anything ever yet written only waiting for some one to take them down. Think of how near you may have come to an interesting story and never known it."

"That's a good saying, that last," observed young Strelitz, smiling in approval. "I'll make a note of that."

But his note-book was not about him, and rather than let his mother's remark slip his memory he jotted it down upon the back of the cigarette picture.

"Let's see, how does that go?" he said, writing. "'Think of how close one may come to an interesting story and never know it.' Well," added young Strelitz, as he slipped the bit of cardboard back into his pocket. "I'll try your idea, but I haven't much faith in it. However, it won't do any hurt to get in touch with the real thing once and a while. I may get a suggestion or two."

"You may have an adventure or two," observed Mrs. Strelitz.

"Do the Haroun-al-Raschid act, hey?" answered her son. "Well, don't sit up for me," he went on, shrugging himself into his overcoat, "'cause if I get an idea I may go right up to the *Times* office and work it up in the reporter's room. Good night."

For more than two hours young Strelitz roamed idly from street to street. Now in the theater district, now in the slums and now in the Bowery. As a rule he avoided the aristocratic and formal neighborhoods, knowing by instinct that he would be more apt to find undisguised human nature along the poorer unconventional thoroughfares.

Hundreds of people jostled him, each with a hidden story no doubt; but all such as varied from the indistinguishable herd, resolved themselves into types, hackneyed over-worked types, with nothing original about them. There was the Bowery boy; there was the tough girl; there was the young lady from the college settlement; there was the dude, the chippy, the bicycle girl, the tenement house Irish woman, the bum, the drunk, the policeman, the Chinese laundry man, the coon in his plaid vest and the Italian vegetable man in his velvet jacket.

"I know you, I know you all," muttered young Strelitz, as one after another passed him. "I know you, and you, and you. There's Chimmie Fadden, there's Cortlandt Van Bibber, there's Rags Raegen, there's George's Mother, there's Bedalia Herodsfoot, and Gervaise Coupeau and Eleanor Cuyler. I know you, every one; all the reading world knows you. You're done to death; you won't do, you won't do. Nothing new can be got out of you, unless one should take a new point of view, and that couldn't be done in a short story. Let's go into some of their saloons."

He entered several of the wine shops in the Italian quarter, but beyond the advertisement of a public picnic and games, where the second prize was a ton of coal, found nothing extraordinary.

"Now we'll try the parks," he said to himself. He turned about and started across town. As he went on the streets grew cleaner and gayer. The saloons became "elegant" bars. The dance halls, brilliantly lighted theaters. Here and there were cafés, with frosted glass, side doors, on which one read "Ladies' Entrance." Invariably there was a cab stand near by.

"Ah, the Tenderloin," murmured Strelitz slackening his pace. "I know you, too. I'll have a cocktail in passing, with you."

A large café, whose second story was gayly lighted, attracted him. He entered the bar on the ground floor and asked for a mild cocktail.

All at once he heard his name called. A party of men of his own age stood in the entrance of a little room that opened from the barroom, beckoning to him and laughing. Three of them he knew very well—Brunt of the *Times*, Jack Fremont, who had graduated with his class, and Angus McCloutsie, whom every one called "Scrubby." The other men Strelitz knew to bow to. "Just the man we want," cried Jack Fremont as Strelitz came up.

"You're right in time," observed "Scrubby," grinning and shaking his hand. "Come in, come in here with us." They pulled young Strelitz into the little room, and Brunt made them all sit down while he ordered beer.

"We're having the greatest kind of a time," Fremont began in an excited whisper. "All the crowd are upstairs—we got a room, we had supper—there's Dryden and Billy Libbey, and the two Spaulding boys and the 'Jay'—and all the old crowd. Y'ought to see Dick Spaulding sitting on the floor trying to put gloves on his feet; he says there were seven good reasons why he should not get full and that he's forgotten every one. Oh, we're going to have the time of our lives to-night. You're just in time—"

"Joe's forgot the best part of it," broke in "Scrubby."

"There are three girls."

"Three girls?"

"Yes, sir, and one of them is the kind read about. Just wait till you see her."

"I'm not going to wait," said young Strelitz. "I must go, right away. I'm working to-night." He finished his beer amongst their protests, and drew his handkerchief quickly out of his pocket and wiped his lips. But the others would not hear of his going.

"Oh, come along up," urged Brunt. "Just listen to that," cocking his head

toward the ceiling, "and see what you're missing. That's Dick trying to remember." Strelitz hesitated. They certainly were having a glorious time up
there—and the girls, too. He might at least go up and look in on them all.
He began to reflect, pulling at his lower lip, his forehead in a pucker. If he
went up there he would miss his story.

"No, no, I can't, fellows," he said decisively, rising from the table. "I've
got to do some work to-night. Another time I'll join you; you have your
good time without me this once." He pulled away from the retaining hands
that would have held him, and ran out into the street, laughing over his
shoulder at them, his hat on the back of his head.

"Well, if he's got to work, he's got to work," admitted "Scrubby," as the
swing doors flapped behind young Strelitz.

"He's going to miss the time of his life, though," put in Fremont. "Come
on, let's go back to the crowd. What's that you got?"

"It's something that flipped out of Con's pocket, I think, as he pulled out
his handkerchief. It's a cigarette picture."

"Some one of Con's fairies? Let's have a look."

They crowded together, looking over each other's shoulders. Suddenly
there was an exclamation—

"Why, that's the girl that's upstairs now, the queen—the one that's so
drunk. See the name; she said her name was Violet."

"Con' must have known her."

"Too bad he had to shake the crowd."

"He would have had a great time with that girl."

"I say, what's he got written on the back?"

In the midst of a great silence, Brunt turned the cigarette picture to the
light and read:

"Think how close one may come to an interesting story and never know
it."

The Sketch Club Exhibit

Some Clever Color Work by the Younger Artists

The Wave, 15 (28 November 1896), 9.

Very pleasing, the eighth semi-annual exhibit of the Sketch Club! I was astonished to see the surprising number of clever bits that adorn the wall on the top floor of the Mutual Building, the more so in that sketches are particularly difficult to "do." You will find twenty artists who can paint really fine finished pictures to one who can dash off even a fairly good sketch—a little note of color and form faithfully and clearly registering a single impression, or mood or sentiment. It will not do to attempt too much in a sketch, else it ceases to be a sketch. It must be rapidly handled, and—perhaps this is most important of all—you must know just exactly where and when to stop.

The problem is not so hard when the sketch is made in pencil or pen and ink or black and white oils—the very nature of the materials remove any temptation to careful manipulation. But a good sketch in colors—what a rarity! The artist must be as familiar with his seven colors and their possibilities as the trained musician is with his eight notes; he must be as accurate as mathematics, yet swift, almost, as his very thoughts. Indeed, the quicker he can fling his thought accurately upon his canvas the better will be his sketch—provided, always, the thought is worth the while.

Of the 102 color exhibits of the club, those which are the most successful to my mind are from the brush of Mollie G. Hutchinson. No. 14, one of Miss Hutchinson's canvases, *A Marshland in Brittany*, is an admirable study in the impressionist style, showing something of Mr. Peixotto's influence. Miss Hutchinson is evidently a partisan of the vibration theory of color; seen close up her pictures show hundreds of little color dabs of green and vermilion and yellow—sometimes the crude, unmixed color. At a distance these dabs run together and produce a brilliant atmospheric effect that is at times very effective. From a personal point of view I have but little sympathy for this method; it seems to savor too much of trickery. However, it has many supporters, and with these Miss Hutchinson's work is sure to be successful.

Blanche Letcher is another of the Sketch Club exhibitors, whose work shows good promise. She exhibits a number of pastel and oil portraits that betray no traces of the amateur. The tendency with artists in pastels is to a straggling, splotchy style, which they call "broad," but which is generally slovenly. There is little of this in Miss Letcher's portrait work. Her landscapes and studies please me less, suggesting, as they do, a lack of that "out-of-door" feeling so pleasingly apparent in Miss Hutchinson's efforts. Portraits, I shrewdly suspect, are her forte.

Taken as a whole, the exhibit makes a very good showing, indeed, particularly in the color work of the various pieces. There is a noticeable lack of figure compositions, but these one would hardly expect to find in an array of sketches. In this figure work Albertine Randall shows up better than any of the other exhibitors. The reproductions of her pen and ink pictures for *St. Nicholas* are very charming and delicate as well as accurately drawn.

The Week's Football

Olympic-Reliance—Olympic Plays Sharp Ball

The Wave, 15 (28 November 1896), 11.

It was almost a foregone conclusion that Reliance should have been beaten in Saturday's game by the red and white team with a score of 6—0. Any careful observer of their work in the first championship game could have foretold the result, with tolerable certainty, the Reliance eleven persisting in a slow, conservative game, unwilling to relinquish the ball, relying for their advances upon small gains repeatedly made, the Olympic team—especially in their last game—playing hard, rapid ball, punting when there was the least excuse for it, counting upon winning the game, not by possession of the ball, but by distance gained. Not once during the season has the Olympic eleven shown such good form as upon last Saturday. That they did not cross the Reliance goal a second or a third time was due only to their poor physical condition and to the singular stiffness in the maroon and white line, developed on occasions at the last moment upon the very five-yard line. Reliance should have punted oftener. As early as the middle of the first half it was clearly seen that the ball could not be advanced through or around the line of the Olympic players. Good generalship would have changed Reliance's tactics at this point. The game that the Oakland club should have played was apparent at once, and it was not the bucking game with which they had started. The conditions were these: A fairly good punter on the Reliance side, a line of forwards who had proved themselves capable of holding the Olympics for downs, and backs who were of the "plunging" rather than the "running" type. On the other side there was a line strong on the offense, but a fullback out of all form, who had given evidence of his inability either to catch or to return punts. Reliance should have punted early and often, even on the very first down, until they had secured the ball upon the Olympic's ten-yard line, from which point an attempt to buck the ball for a touchdown could have been made with some assurance of success. But to play a bucking game in the centre of the field, against a line that is even moderately strong, is mere foolishness. It is a wonderful team that can keep possession of the ball for forty yards of line playing, while it is a wonderful fullback that can handle every punt successfully. The chances are all against carrying the ball across the enemy's goal by bucking tactics. Even if the ball is bucked to the five-yard line, it is doubtful whether the average team has got strength enough left by that time to carry it over. With every scrimmage the offensive team is exhausting its strength, while, as the ball is approaching their goal, the defensive team is playing harder and harder. If, then, the ball is lost on the five- or ten-yard line, it is almost sure to be punted back by the other team, and in a single play the bucking eleven sees all their exhausting labor nullified.

Nine teams out of ten persist in ignoring the fact that they are on the defensive, not when the other side has the ball, but when the ball is in their own territory, even though in their own possession.

The Olympics deserved every one of the points earned. It was only the poor physical condition of its players that prevented a much larger score.

The playing of Olympic in the second half of Saturday's game might be a profitable example for even Ransome's or Fickert's men. Almost any team will play hard ball when the score is against it, but during the season of '96 we have yet to see an eleven fight so hard for a second touchdown as did Olympic at a time when they must have known that, but for a repetition of the fluke, they had practically won the game. With a score of 6—0 in their favor the red and white men opened the second half with a fine spirit and dash. In a dozen plays they had Reliance "on the run," hammering rapidly away at the opposing line, and giving it no opportunity of pulling itself together. Undoubtedly Olympic would have scored again had it not been for the collapse of some of its men, who were unable to stand the strain. It was exasperating to stand upon the side lines and see Olympic's opportunity slipping away during the waits to allow injured players to recover. Reliance had time to recuperate, and in the end the Olympic impetus was checked.

Lackaye "Making-Up"

In the Actor's Dressing-Room as He
Transforms Himself Into "Dr. Belgraff"

The Wave, 15 (5 December 1896), 4.

After I had waited a few minutes in the "star's dressing room," Mr. Lackaye entered in a great hurry. Indeed, everything that went on during that half hour of preparation seemed to be done in a hurry. Wilton Lackaye hurried through the endless details of his wonderful make-up; members of the company hurried in to receive hurried directions, and hurried out again to follow them; a wig-maker hurriedly displayed a number of wigs and was hurried off without ceremony; a certain young man, whether he was a supe or a valet I could not make out, removed Mr. Lackaye's shoes in a great hurry, and hurried on Dr. Belgraff's carpet slippers, while at every moment a scene shifter made a sudden appearance at the dressing room door exclaiming in breathless excitement: "Five minutes more," and a little later:

"Orchestra on."

Then at succeeding intervals:

"Overture."

"Curtain up."

"Mrs. Lackaye on."

All this while Wilton Lackaye, the pivot about whom everything revolved, was at one moment talking and laughing with Miss Fuller's manager, at another making suggestions to a younger actor as to his wig in *Molière* (next week's play), or abusing a recalcitrant shoemaker over the fit of a certain pair of shoes, or again talking to me as to "make-ups," theories of acting and the difference between his methods and those of Coquelin and Irving. Not for an instant, however, did he pause in his work of transforming himself from the rotund, well favored American that he is into the blonde, whiskered German *Herr Doktor*—Roentgen it is, so Mr. Lackaye says.

"There are two theories of acting," said Wilton Lackaye, carefully modeling the pink, putty-like false nose before the glass, as cleverly as any sculptor. "There is the actor who says, 'It will be all right on the night,' and who relies upon the hysteria"—note that Mr. Lackaye calls it hysteria; that's a curious word in such connection—"the hysteria of the occasion to carry him through. They call it inspiration. Maybe it is inspiration. I've nothing against it. And—"

The nose was about finished, and Mr. Lackaye smeared his face plentifully with grease paint and rubbed some vermilion stuff—it was crude vermilion—around his eyes and cheeks. "And there is the other kind of actor" (the false nose made his tone a little nasal) "who relies almost entirely upon the careful manipulation of his mechanical effects to—eh, what do you want?" (The wig-maker had approached him.) "No; a servant would not wear puffs at the side of his wig like that; take it away and change it.—Relies almost entirely upon the careful manipulation of his mechanical effects—"

"I say, Governor" (this from a dignified old gentleman made up as a doctor, who put his head in the door). "I say, can we have the California tomorrow for the rehearsal of *Captain Bob?*"

"Curtain up," called the stage hand over the old gentleman's shoulder.

Mr. Lackaye had just finished gluing on the chin part of his beard; now he was putting on the remainder over his cheeks in little patches, "so as not to interfere with the play of the facial muscles," he explained to me in an aside. "*Captain Bob* here," he said to the dignified gentleman, "*Molière* at the California. As I was saying," he continued, adjusting the auburn wig and blackening his eye lids, "relies altogether upon his mechanical effects. But they make the mistake—pass me that sponge—of supposing that the one must exclude the other. Now I"—he pinned a lock of his real hair to that of the wig with a couple of invisible hairpins, and smeared the spot gray— "now I hold that the two methods should go together, first your detail, your mechanics and effects and make-up; then the fine frenzy is right enough when it comes."

The curtain had been up and the play progressing fully five minutes. Mr. Lackaye had only finished making-up his face and was still in his street dress. I thought of amateur performers ready an hour before and waiting for their cue in an agony of excitement. From time to time the star's dresser stepped to the door, cocking an ear in the direction of the stage. He drew out Lackaye's costume—Dr. Belgraff's woolen shirt, stained trousers and apron. It did not seem possible that the actor could get into them and out upon the stage in time. I began to get horribly nervous, began to wish he would stop wasting breath talking to me and attend to business. The dresser hurried him into his clothes. Mrs. Lackaye had long since disappeared; we could hear her voice from the direction of the stage. While the big white apron was being fastened Lackaye was chaffing with Miss Fuller's manager. By this time I was absolutely certain that his cue was long past and Miss Wainwright was holding the stage for him. In another minute I should have had nervous prostration.

"Denver really surprised us," said Lackaye. "We did not count on large fronts there, but—"

"All ready, Mr. Lackaye," cried the call boy from the door. In an instant Wilton Lackaye—I mean Dr. Belgraff, for the transformation was absolutely beyond belief—was gone, the dresser running after him tying the last knot on the apron strings. He disappeared under the stage, and just in time, just by the fraction of a second came up through the cellar door and out on the stage in response to his cue, as calm and as absolutely master of himself as if he had been listening for it throughout the whole previous hour, rehearsing his opening speech the while.

Things and People

The Wave, 15 (5 December 1896), 6, paragraph 10.

The big football game is over, and now comes the season for talk and for explanations on the part of the U.C. boys as to why they did not win—or rather, why they were so fearfully whipped. "Some one has blundered." This is the cry that one hears upon the U.C. campus during these days after the game. "Some one has blundered." The boys would be glad to lay their hands (clenched) upon this blunderer should he be proven to exist. There is a whisper—it is just a whisper—that Mr. Butterworth may be the individual sought for. It is said that the great Yale fullback chose to live in the city rather than at the training quarters with the team, after the manner of Mr. Cross. It is said that Mr. Butterworth was unreasonable in his selection of McNutt as end rusher for the California team, much to the surprise of the Berkeley boys, who had marked Jimmy Hopper as the better man for the place. It is said that the Freshman team received but four days of coaching at the hands of Mr. Butterworth, and that Mr. Butterworth did not invariably set the team the shining example of self-denial in the matter of tobacco—and other things—that have been held up to the eleven in the persons of the previous coaches, Hefflefinger, Gill and McClung. These are all whispers, however, and until something of a more definite character is developed we must still hold to the belief that Butterworth was everything that the U.C. expected him to be. The other possible scapegoat is Captain Ransome, whose paleness and general staleness were the talk of the bleachers as soon as ever he set foot on the field Thanksgiving day. But of Ransome the college will hear nothing ill. No matter how badly he played, he did the best he could; that is the verdict of the Berkeley undergraduates. Others may fail of their duty, coaches may be remiss, managers may leave much to be desired, professors may be unrelenting, but the U.C. Sophomore will have it through thick and thin that "the captain of the eleven can do no wrong."

Fitting Cruisers for Service

A Day Spent at the Mare Island Dry-Dock

The Wave, 15 (5 December 1896), [9].

To fit out a cruiser for sea service implies an amount of labor and of expense that the lay landsman can have but little idea of until he has visited the docks (dry and otherwise) of Mare Island and seen the great war engines laid up there for repairs. It is an imposing sight at Vallejo just now. Standing at the gate of the great dry dock and looking up the stream you may see an unbroken white line of cruisers, gunboats and monitors, hugging the wharves with cables and hawsers, laying by there for the repairs that will once more fit them for active sea service. Rarely is it possible to see so many vessels of the white navy together at the same time. Mare Island has taken on the appearance of a naval rendezvous. The *Charleston* is there, the *Baltimore*, the *Monterey*, the *Ranger*, the *Petrel*, the *Monadnock*, the *Concord* and the *Pensacola*. It is almost a fleet, a veritable white squadron.

Upon many of those ships the repairs are being actively carried forward. Parallel with the file of war vessels is a line of factories, machine shops, forges and what not, that are glowing and clanging and vibrating with the purring of great machinery. Anchors are being forged, and parts of engines; an entire barbette is under process of overhauling; started and twisted bolts and screws are being replaced; oak timbering, copper sheathing, brasses, chains, white lead and the like are littered about in a confusion apparently inextricable. While on the wharf itself you may see gigantic lifting cranes like huge lean arms swinging back and forth picking up piles of lumber or nondescript masses of machinery and placing them aboard ship, somewhere in the mysterious depths of the hold.

How large is the number of men employed at the Mare Island Navy Yard would be rather difficult to say. You are told that the total monthly wages paid comes close upon $30,000. At 6 o'clock when the whistle blows a veritable army of workmen debouches from the shops and forges, suddenly invading the place by hundreds, by thousands. The streets and wharves all at once become black with the multitude, while the little ferryboat that plies between the island and Vallejo is weighted down to the very gunwales by the throng of home-bound mechanics.

The huge dry dock itself is the most interesting feature of the navy yard. If you can imagine the Coliseum or other of the classic amphitheaters made smaller you will have a perfect—an almost literally perfect—idea of the Mare Island dry dock; made of granite, elliptical in shape, its sides terraced with innumerable steps leading down to a flat oval at the bottom, along whose greatest diameter rests the keel of the docked vessel. The reason why a vessel is dry docked is to clean her sides and keel, to repair started bolts and strains below the water line and to give the hull a new coat of paint. Most important of all, however, is the cleaning of the keel and flanks. It is almost impossible for a landsman to gain any idea of the amount of stuff that collects upon the hull of a seagoing ship—millions of tiny shell fish, barnacles, whelks, minute clam-like *molluscae*, parasites of every description, against which nothing as yet known in the art of ship-building is proof. All these clinging to the hull below the water line will form in an incredibly short time a coating so thick that it will make a difference of from four to six knots in the vessel's speed. At the time I visited the dry dock I was shown two great piles of stuff, each nearly as high as myself, that had been scraped from the hull of the *Philadelphia*—the last ship dry-docked. Indeed, it is chiefly for the sake of scraping the hull of the ship that these immense dry docks have been built at the cost to the government of thousands and thousands of dollars.

But—this, however, in passing—a cruiser out of water is a strange looking thing. All her grace, her lightness, her appearance of speed and agility vanishes in the dry dock. She looks like a fish on land, like a crocodile, like a seal on a beach—a thing amphibious, clumsy, slow moving. There is a certain indecency about the sight. You see that part of the ship you are not intended to see. She loses dignity. There is too much incline to her bow and stern, her screws and rudder look trifling and inadequate, and her ram, her formidable forefoot, capable of administering the kick that crashes in the ribs of her enemy and sends her to the bottom a dismantled wreck, seems only a hideous, protruding snout, the lower jaw of a sulky bulldog.

The scraping and painting of the hull, however, is not the only labor involved in getting the ship to sea. There are the stores. You are told that Uncle Sam's sailors are better fed than are those of any other navy or army in the world (better paid, too, for the matter of that), and when to back this statement you are further informed that the running expenses of such a ship as the *Philadelphia* amount to fifteen thousand dollars a month you begin to believe that such a state of affairs is quite possible.

Every United States man-of-war carries reserve provisions for two years, in case of emergency. The regular provisions are consumed only when at sea, the crew and officers subsisting on fresh meat, vegetables, etc., when in port. The provisions are stored aft as far as possible from the engine rooms, lest the heat of the boilers should—as is often the case—cause explosions among the canned goods. The ship eats into its provisions at the top, putting in fresh supplies from the bottom in order that the tinned things in the lower layers of the stores may not be over kept and spoiled. There is a further advantage of this arrangement, i.e., whenever a case is spoiled the ship's steward may be pretty certain that it is the fault of the contractors and not of any official on board, consequently the case in question is tossed overboard and the contractor charged for the amount.

Buying in such large quantities, Uncle Sam can afford to feed his sailors very cheap and yet feed them better than any other country. A sailor aboard the *Philadelphia* can be fed for six dollars a month, and this implies turkey and chicken and oyster soup for his Sunday dinner. On Thanksgiving day he probably had as good a meal as the average San Francisco citizen, better, perhaps. The Government allows him eight dollars a month for his rations, so that if he chooses he can save something. A few items will give you some idea of how cheaply men may be fed when the contractors can figure upon them in the aggregate. The United States sailor will consume in one month only 60 cents worth of sugar, 30 cents of beans, 50 cents of coffee, 50 cents of flour, 25 cents of rice and so on. These rations are all of the very best quality. Contractors will tell you that it is a poor business proposition to cheat Uncle Sam. Indeed, it is hard to cheat him at all in the first place, for as each case comes aboard it is inspected and passed upon, and if it is "not up to sample" back it goes to the contractor.

The "little world" simile has been applied so often to ships that it has long since become trite and hackneyed, but it is nevertheless admirably true, never more so than when, after all this work of dry docking and painting and repairing and provisioning is done and the great ship clears away for the open sea, relying only upon herself, severing all connection with the cities of men, becoming herself a little city, individual, complete, independent, a tiny bit of humanity, a white dot lost somewhere out there on the blue Atlantic.

The Winter Exhibition

The Wave, 15 (12 December 1896), 4.

Keith, Yelland and Hill are all represented, Keith head and shoulders above the others in one or two evening and storm effects. This artist is always admirable, still clinging to the precepts of the school of D'Aubigny and Corot, delighting in sombre greens and blacks and bitumens, painting pictures that are full of sharp contrasts, broad and sketchy and vigorous. There is but little choice between the large number of pictures he exhibits; all are good, though personally I prefer the *Rainy Day*. Among the younger artists, Peters, Aikens and Latimer are most noteworthy. Apropos of originality, Peters is developing a style of work decidedly unique, choosing for his subjects evening effects among sand dunes and sea shores and treating them with exaggerated broadness, making up his picture from three or four huge flat tones, very simple, with hardly a stone or tuft of grass to break the monotony. The result is sometimes a bit theatrical, but wonderfully effective. Latimer is improving. In his water-color sketches he is doing especially fine work. He lacks brilliancy and effectiveness, and it is easy to pass over his pictures without observing them. Upon inspection, however, they reveal no little seriousness of conception and restrained soberness of handling. One of the very best heads, portrait or otherwise, is Oscar Kunath's pastel. This is really a genuine work of art. Rarely have we seen among local artists such precision in drawing and such admirable success in the attainment of flesh effects through the medium of colored crayon.

How It Strikes an Observer

The Horse-Show and Some of the Things It Suggests

The Wave, 15 (12 December 1896), 7.

There is just one thing that jars at this year's Horse Show. Everything else is pretty. The "satin coated horses" and the "satin gowned women," who have been the subject of journalistic dithyrambs from ocean to ocean, are all there, and are just as beautiful and charming as the reporter would have you believe—more so, for the matter of that, for to my thinking there are three things that are preëminently beautiful, that are perfect of their kind, a ship under full sail, a pretty, well dressed woman and a well groomed thoroughbred horse. And when you may see the last two gathered together on the same occasion, pretty women and wonderful gowns and horses that are brown and sleek as wet otters, and lacquered traps, and lights and music and all that, you have a *mise en scène* finer than anything you ever saw behind the footlights. But why and oh, why, these bare boards of pine? Of course the thing can't be helped. You have no right to expect plush upholstery and nickel trimmings at the Mechanics' Pavilion. You can't have the Madison Square Garden, so you must make the best of it.

Everything else is so excellent that it is churlish to criticize. It merely strikes one as a bit incongruous to see these gowns and bonnets that might have come (and very possibly did come, some of them) straight from Virot and the Rue de la Paix, set off by a background of the same material that is used to stable the horses in the paddocks under the galleries.

Of all the events of the opening night the two which seemed to interest the audience the most were the hurdling and coaching contests. The hurdling is very pretty. If you had not witnessed the jumping it would surprise you to note in what an endless variety of ways different horses will consider a hurdle. There is the horse like Hobart's big gray "Huntress," who will top you a hurdle without so much as turning a hair, looking at the galleries and boxes the while, just to show off—pretending that she does this sort of thing so easily that it's not worth while thinking about it. Then there is the horse that fidgets and worries and lathers, made nervous by the lights and music, that gets rattled and rushes in helter-skelter, sometimes going over the hurdle with an eight-foot leap, and sometimes knocking it down. There is still a third kind, that attends strictly to the business in hand, that must be ridden up to have a look at the hurdle and what is on the other side of it before he jumps. This is the kind of horse that turf men will tell you is best to let alone. He will get over in his own way; you must give him his head as much as you dare, and you must not hit him with the crop or bother him by talking. It's very interesting to watch this horse take the jump. He comes up on a canter to within what he considers the proper distance—then suddenly quickens his pace. Within about ten feet he shortens his steps, very prettily throws his ears forward and clears the obstacle by just barely enough space, his heels tucked well under him so as not to hit the top rail. I think that I prefer this kind, because he uses his wits and does not get rattled or try to show off. In the hurdling contest the rider counts but for little, and there are no "appointments" to speak of. The horse is the main thing (which is as it should be), and must rely upon himself to make a good showing, for he cannot expect his rider to help him out much; the only thing he asks of his rider is to keep his form and sit still.

But the coach event is *toute une affaire*. Four horses, a huge coach, two grooms and the driver must be taken into consideration, and here the conditions are reversed. The driver, the man, must show the skill and the judgment, asking only of the horses that they answer to the reins.

The interest in this contest was lively enough Wednesday night, and over it and its result was displayed the greatest enthusiasm of the occasion. It is quite possible that Mr. Dwyer was the best driver of the four contestants, but Mr. Crocker carried off the blue rosette on the strength of form and finish of "appointment," and the audience confirmed the opinion of the judges by a long roll of applause.

But the key note of the Horse Show is its gaiety—a very light staccato note that comes off trippingly and with much vivacity. This impression of gaiety comes upon you as soon as you pass the wicket.

I take it that a well conducted Horse Show is the finest sight the *grand monde* has to offer. The annual 'varsity football game comes very close to it, but there is a seriousness about the football game, a certain intensity of interest that sounds the graver note. The gaiety is all on the outside of the arena. You don't expect the elevens to be gay, and the thoroughbreds of the gridiron are not so well groomed, nor so cleanly, nor so dainty as the other thoroughbreds of the tan bark. However, you see precisely the same people at the Horse Show as you did at the football game, with the difference that at the Pavilion they are rigidly decorous and reserved. It is very amusing to observe the same girl who on Thanksgiving day shouted herself hoarse and split her gloves in her excitement, sitting back in her box in a very smart dinner gown, with but a politely languid interest in all that is going forward.

And the men. Just a week ago that very night in that same Pavilion another contest between highly trained animals was under way, only last Wednesday the animals were but two in number and in place of the tan bark there was a roped square, upon a raised platform. The air was blue and pungent with tobacco smoke, occasionally a gong tapped at three-minute intervals, and the audience was not decorous, nor reserved, nor choice in its language.

But it was composed of the same men who filled the boxes or the promenade at the Horse Show last night. At the Horse Show nothing could have been finer than their correctness—their suppression of all emotion. At the prize fight they stood upon their chairs, with their hats on the backs of their heads, their faces scarlet and their throats distended with the inarticulate cry of the mob that knows no restraint, *autre temps, autre moeurs*, with a vengeance.

Waiting for Their Cue

———

In the Realm of Silence Behind the Scenes at the Baldwin

———

The Wave, 15 (12 December 1896), 9.

———

I went through the little brick corridor behind the boxes and came up into the flies behind the scenes, walking on my heels. A shirt-sleeved man sitting on a roll of carpet leaped to his feet (or more properly his tiptoes) and ejaculated:

"Sh!"

I stopped so abruptly that the press agent who followed behind bumped into me and stumbled against a saw-horse with a great clattering noise. A stage carpenter, a calcium light man and a property woman appeared upon the instant, exclaiming, "Sh," and the shirt-sleeved man, his face contorted in an agony of apprehension, repeated the warning, and blasphemed us in a hoarse whisper.

In the next thirty seconds I learned how to behave "behind the scenes." The first requirement is silence, the second is silence, the third is silence, the fourth is to keep out of the way, and not to trip over the feed wires of the clusters. Incidentally you mustn't smoke. I found this out afterward, on attempting to light a cigar. Three men and a boy told me about it simultaneously. The best course to adopt is to go about on tiptoe sidling against the brick walls (already polished and black from just such sidling), refrain from asking questions and shrink into as small a compass as possible between the acts while the scene is being struck.

I have made a discovery, or rather I have rearranged all previous beliefs and conclusions to suit a new theory. I have found out the real function of the orchestra. Whilom I had cherished the idea, in company with the vast army of the uninitiated, that the orchestra played between acts to keep the audience amused. This is not so at all. The orchestra is there simply to drown the noise the scene shifters make in dragging the flats about.

Everything "behind the scenes" centers about this one principle of silence. Accidents may happen, flats prove refractory, cues may be forgotten or lights go out when least expected, but so long as these things occur in a profound and overpowering silence the stage manager does not lose his equanimity.

And all the while you can hear from somewhere beyond that strange, boxed-in arena, the stage, of which you get narrow glimpses between two flats, a flow of high-pitched dialogue or strange lapses of quiet followed by a roll of applause from the audience. The murmur of this audience comes to you as from an infinite distance, very vague and confused. There, on the other side of the footlights, in the midst of coils of rope and electric clusters and shirt-sleeved stage hands and bare brick walls of immense height, you feel as though you had left it behind some hundred of years ago.

As you go about behind this boxed-in stage you occasionally come across, in a recess of the flies near a lath and canvas entrance, a figure that, although you are expecting it, somehow, surprises you. You have so persistently associated the actor or actress with the glare of the footlights and the accessories of the stage setting that the sight of him, or of her, waiting there for the cue, hideously painted and dressed out of all congruity to the surroundings, disconcerts you. It is a convention, an unwritten law of stageland, that a chair and a rug shall be placed at every entrance. The chair, of course, is for the actor to sit in. The rug is less easily explained. I have thought considerably over the matter, but as yet have arrived at no conclusion.

Mr. Lackaye never waits for his cues, as does Miss Wainwright, Mr. Couldock or the others. He appears running (from some mysterious quarter) at the very last moment, pauses a second to listen at the entrance, and then goes on hardly before he has recovered his breath.

You must go behind the scenes if you wish to appreciate the vast gulf that is fixed between the amateur and the professional actor. On the night of which I speak Mr. Lackaye, for some reason, cut a certain actor out of a scene, just at the time the actor was about to go on. Can you imagine how such an occurrence would have upset an amateur company, no matter how well drilled? What a rushing to and fro, what cold perspiration, what frenzied dashes among the pages of the playbook.

"He cut me, didn't he?" said the actor in question, turning to Miss Wainwright. "He did," said Miss Wainwright.

The other shrugged his shoulders and sat down again, and the play went on without a break.

College Athletics

Breaking-In the Raw Material for the U.C. Track Team

The Wave, 15 (12 December 1896), 13.

The shameful defeat of the football eleven is to have at least the good effect of nerving and bracing up the track and baseball teams of the U.C. There have been an average of forty men training and practicing daily on the track all through the season, and since the "farce of '96," as the last football game has begun very properly to be called, eleven new aspirants have handed their names to Captain Brown.

There is but one course open to the U.C. track team of this year—only one aim to which they can, in simple justice to their college, address themselves—there should be no talk or thought of an Eastern trip this year; there should only exist the single, simple and earnest desire to win back, in a measure, California's lost honor. The track team must win from Stanford at any hazard and at any cost. It will not do to win by a good margin—they should win by a score proportionate to 20 to 0 before they are even satisfied, and by a still larger score ere they can even begin to congratulate themselves.

It is preposterous that the team should expect the college to bear the expense of sending them against Princeton, Pennsylvania or Yale, until they have won a decided victory over the Cardinal. It is absurd to try and beat Yale when they can only tie Stanford. There will be time enough to consider the Eastern trip when the team has shown that it is worthy of it. They can ask the college for the necessary funds then. Nor can the jumpers, hurdlers and weight-putters and the like put forth their best efforts against their nearer natural rivals with the prospect of meets with Eastern colleges held before their eyes. If the students of the U.C. are animated with the proper spirit they will do all in their power to discourage any idea of a "transcontinental tour" for the next two or three years, until their university has regained its athletic prestige, now forfeited.

The University of California rejoices in conditions peculiarly conducive to the development of a strong track team. By luck, rather than by design, they are possessed of an extraordinarily fast track. The California men who in '95 competed on the tracks of the Atlantic and Middle West colleges declare that their own home cinder-path was the best that they had ever put their feet on, while the climatic conditions of Berkeley are such as to permit a season of training longer than any dreamed of by other colleges. The gymnasium is large and equipped with every necessary exercising machine, and the surrounding country is well suited to cross-country runs.

I look to see California put a strong hurdling team into the field this season, not so much on account of her promising material, but because of her admirable developing capacity for this particular event. Her style of hurdling is an athletic achievement—one of the very few successes in this line—that California has every right to be proud of. She is the equal of Harvard or Yale in this respect. Murphy himself (Yale's trainer) admitted that the U.C. hurdlers had opened his eyes.

The style that obtains among Eastern hurdlers is to clear the obstacle at a high jump, not rising to the leap until rather near the hurdle. The curve described by the jump is short and high. Very roughly, thus:

Whereas the U.C. hurdler clears the bar by the smallest possible margin, rising to the jump at a little longer distance from the hurdle, the curve described being long and low:

These diagrams are, of course, very much exaggerated, but they will serve as illustrative of the opposing systems. The advantage of the U.C.'s style is that the hurdler takes the ground after the leap easily, "settling" rather than falling, whereas the Eastern men come down heavily with an abrupt shock and jar that as often as not causes them to lose their equilibrium; then, too, the U.C. hurdler is into his stride almost the instant he touches ground, while the Eastern crack is liable to stagger for the precious fraction of a second before he can regain his gait and speed. California will have the further advantage of good coaching in her hurdling events with cracks like Dwyer, Torrey, and a world's record man such as Walter Henry, to supervise the competitors.

The policy of Captain Brown will be to have the training varied rather than hard. The whole track squad will be worked alternately in the gymnasium and the open air; cross-country runs and lacrosse will be introduced to vary the monotony of the hammer and tongs work on the cinder path. Apropos of lacrosse it is understood that Stanford is anxious to meet California in this game, and has, in fact, sent a challenge to Captain Brown. Whether the U.C. will accept is a matter of some doubt. Brown himself is not particularly anxious for the match, believing that the track squad, from which the lacrosse team would be largely formed, should devote its entire energies to winning from Stanford in its proper sphere. If the U.C. forms a lacrosse team, it will be merely for the sake of training and exercising the squad who are training for the track events. It is doubtful if a match will be arranged this year.

At present the track squad has suspended training until after the midwinter examinations. Work will be resumed in January, when preparations will be begun for the Freshman-Sophomore field day, which will open the track season of '97.

In the Heat of Battle

The Wave, 15, Christmas issue (19 December 1896), 6-7.

DRAMATIS PERSONAE.

Jerry Tremont, *Yale '92.*

Tressie Tremont, *his sister, a "Yale girl."*

Lord Orme, (*Oxon.*), *a young English nobleman.*

"Jack," *halfback on the Yale eleven, who does not appear, but who is the most important of all.*

Scene—*Office of Mr. Tremont, Sr., Newspaper Row, Boston, overlooking the street, which is packed with an immense crowd. Directly opposite is the* Herald *building.*

Upon the front of the Herald *building is affixed a huge bulletin board, on which appear half-minute bulletins of the Harvard-Yale football game, the second half of which is at that moment being played at Springfield, Mass. Lord Orme and Miss Tremont are sitting at the window to the right. Jerry is standing at the window to the left, which is open.*

Jerry (drawing back from the window and facing into the room)—No scoring in the first half, and the ball in the center of the field at the call of time. That's close work.

Miss Tremont (to Lord Orme after glancing down into the street)—Dear me, did one ever see such a crowd!

Lord Orme—It's jolly like Trafalgar Square on Lord Mayor's day.

Miss Tremont—I'm so sorry we couldn't see the game this year, but I suppose watching the returns is the next best thing.

Lord Orme—It was—ah—your uncle's death that prevented?

Miss Tremont—Um-hum; papa thought we hadn't better go. It was all we could do to get him to give us his office for to-day.

Jerry (calling from the other window)—Here's another bulletin.

Miss Tremont—Oh, read it for me, Jerry, will you? I can't (putting up her lorgnettes) see even across the street. Isn't it a pity to have such eyes as mine, Lord Orme?

Lord Orme—I don't know about that, Miss Tressie. They've had a jolly queer effect on me—I—ah—

Jerry (reading the bulletin)—"Springfield, 3:28 p.m. Time called for second half. Harvard has the ball. Jack Harper will still play left half for Yale in spite—"

Miss Tremont (with sudden interest)—What's that about Jack?

Jerry—Jack's going to go on with the game just the same in spite of his shoulder.

Miss Tremont—Hurrah for Jack! (She catches Lord Orme's enquiring glance). Jack—Mr. Harper—well, Jack's a man I know. He plays for Yale.

Lord Orme (noting her confusion)—Is he "the other man," Miss Tressie?

Miss Tremont—"The other man?"

Lord Orme—There always is "the other man," you know, Miss Tressie, in affairs—in—ah—affairs such as—such as ours. I mean, such as this.

Miss Tremont—Oh, why should you assume that he is "the other man?" Maybe—

Lord Orme—There must be "another man" somewhere. If it's not this famous Jack it must be——

Miss Tremont (daringly)—It might be Lord Orme.

Lord Orme (in delighted embarrassment)—Oh, I say, now, Miss Tressie.

Miss Tremont (quickly)—And then again it might not. So there you are, you see.

Lord Orme (after a pause, suddenly perplexed)—Are you—ah—making game of me, Miss Tressie? It's a bit rough, you know, because I care so very much—

Jerry (reading from the bulletins)—"Harvard punts for forty yards—Yale's ball on her thirty-five yard line—Jack Harper of Yale makes five yards around Harvard's end."

Miss Tremont—Bravo, Jack! (Apologetically to Lord Orme), Mr. Harper would have been so disappointed if he had not been able to play. He's a senior. This is his last chance.

Lord Orme—It's my last chance, Miss Tressie. If I sail on Monday I won't see you again before I go. I—ah—couldn't have chosen a worse time to say—to say things, than now, I suppose, but last night, with so many people around you, I couldn't get a chance, you know.

(They talk in low tones, and cannot be overheard, except in fragments, by the absorbed Jerry. At first Miss Tremont's attention is equally divided between Lord Orme's speeches and the Springfield bulletins as read by Jerry; but little by little her interest wavers. Sometimes inclining toward the game as Yale is winning, sometimes toward Lord Orme as Yale seems to be giving ground.)

Jerry (reading)—"Brunt of Harvard makes three yards through Yale's center."

Miss Tremont (commenting)—Jack said Yale was weak in the center this year. (After a pause), I wish I knew just how to answer you, Lord Orme.

Jerry (reading)—"Jack Harper misses a clean tackle and allows Harvard to advance the ball seven yards."

Miss Tremont—I confess I like you immensely, Lord Orme. I don't see why I cannot tell you that frankly.

Jerry (reading)—"Yale recovers the ball and makes ten yards around Harvard's right end."

Miss Tremont—But I don't think I care enough for you to marry you.

Jerry (reading)—"Yale makes three more yards through Harvard's tackle."

Miss Tremont—I'm sure I don't.

Jerry (reading)—"Yale gains another five yards."

Miss Tremont—Oh, quite sure.

Jerry (reading)—"Harvard gets ball on fumble and makes a long gain through Yale's center."

Miss Tremont—On the other hand, something might happen to make me change my mind. I—I—don't know just what to tell you.

Lord Orme—Devotion such as mine should go for something, Miss Tressie. I know it's an old argument, but I am sure you would care more for me in time.

Jerry (reading)—"Yale loses five yards for off-side play. Harvard still gaining through center."

Miss Tremont—(How I hate those Harvard men.) Y-yes, perhaps—I—I might, you know.

Jerry (reading)—"Jack Harper of Yale breaks through Harvard line and tackles runner for a loss—tremendous cheering on Yale bleachers." Good boy, Jack. That's the stuff.

Miss Tremont (laughing with sudden perverseness)—And then again I might not, you know.

Lord Orme (deliberately)—Miss Tressie, you and I have known each other a good bit now. You know, I'm sure, what you can expect of me. I'm not an intellectual, nor a physical giant, I confess, and I'm not what you Americans call smart, but our name is in *Gotha* and in *Burke* and all that sort of thing, and I can shoot straight and—and—and I can stick on anything that wears four hoofs—

Jerry (still reading)—"3:35 p.m.—Yale is losing ground. Harvard has the ball on Yale's twenty-five yard line. Yale does not seem able to stop Harvard's masses on tackles and guards."

Miss Tremont—I'm sure you undervalue yourself, Lord Orme. I hate smart people, and it don't follow that a girl must like a man just because he's big and strong, and I adore riding.

Lord Orme—As for that, Miss Tressie, there are about twenty thoroughbred hunters in my stables down in Surrey that are only waiting for you to ride them. Did you never ride to hounds? There's a proper jolly sport. I've a pack down there, too. It's not exactly the Quorn nor the Westminster, but it's a tidy little hunt of thirty couples, and they make music, I promise you, when they're in cry, and there's no end of foxes. We hunt twice a week in season.

Jerry (continues reading in an agony of apprehension)—"Yale is being driven back yard by yard. Harvard is still hammering the tackles with deadly effect. The ball is on Yale's fifteen yard line. Harvard bleachers wild with excitement."

Miss Tremont—Just think, if Yale should lose! No, I've never even seen a fox hunt, but it must be great fun.

Lord Orme—Talk about football!

Miss Tremont—I'm afraid it would almost be better than football, Lord Orme.

Lord Orme—I showed you the photograph of our town house, didn't I? It's close by the Row in Tilbury circus. It's by Vanburgh. Fairfax owned it once. And, of course, we would arrange with the dowager—that's my aunt, you know—to have you presented.

Miss Tremont (then breathlessly)—And I should be presented—presented at court? Oh! This winter? At the next Drawing-Room?

Jerry (reading)—"The ball is now on Yale's five yard line."

Lord Orme—Of course, Miss Tressie, though perhaps not at the very next Drawing-Room. I should wish to have the estate well settled up before we return to London society.

Miss Tremont—Settled up?

Lord Orme—Things are tangled a bit. Of course—ah—(hesitating and blundering) there are—there are—ah—a few debts.

Miss Tremont (her suspicions suddenly aroused by his embarrassment)—Debts! Is that why you have been talking like that to me, Lord Orme?

Jerry—"Harvard's advance suddenly checked. Yale rallies on her five-yard line."

Lord Orme (hastily)—Don't misunderstand, Miss Tressie. Believe me, I do care for you, for yourself as much as for your money—more, I mean. But even looking at it in the worst light, after all, is it taking any unfair advantage of you? Consider the return. You would have a position and a name in London society second to but very few. Think of the town house, and the country seat in Surrey—and all the hunters and the fox hounds—and then you know there's the yacht at Cowes—and you'd be presented—and—and hang it all, Miss Tressie, I really do care awfully, y'know. I say, now, Miss Tressie, we haven't got time to put this thing off—we've got to settle it this afternoon. I'll leave you to think it over for half an hour. I'll take a stroll in the Mall or the Common or whatever it is, if I can get through this bally crowd, and come back in half an hour for your answer. What do you say, Miss Tressie?

Miss Tremont (reflectively)—Well, all right, I'll think it over.

Lord Orme—Right you are. In half an hour I can have your answer?

Miss Tremont—Yes—I think so. (Exit Lord Orme.)

Jerry (hearing the door close, turns from the window)—Hello, where's Orme gone? What's the matter, Tress'? You look flustered.

Miss Tremont (aroused from a reverie into which she has fallen)—Hum?

211

What, what is it, Jerry? Flustered? Well, I should say so. Aren't you?

Jerry (groaning)—I can't bear to watch the bulletins any more. Harvard's going to win. We can't keep 'em from it. Yale's asleep. Jack hasn't done a thing yet.

Miss Tremont—Oh, Jack's not in it any more.

Jerry—Eh! What—you say that of Jack? You? Say, Tressie, that's Orme's "fine Italian hand," I can see that.

Miss Tremont—Never you mind, Jerry.

Jerry—Look here, Tress', I know how Jack feels about you, and I don't propose you shall turn him down for any title, if I can help it. What's Orme been saying to you?

Miss Tremont—Oh, things and—and—things.

Jerry—For instance?

Miss Tremont—He's coming back for his answer in half an hour.

Jerry—You let it go as far as that?

Miss Tremont (her chin in the air)—Well?

Jerry—And what do you propose telling him?

Miss Tremont—I haven't made up my mind yet.

Jerry—Of course you have, you know you're not going to marry Lord Orme.

Miss Tremont—Pooh! I haven't said so yet.

Jerry—Say so now, then.

Miss Tremont—Oh, don't bother me. What's that last bulletin?

Jerry—Hello, hello. Oh, I say, Tress', look at what's been going on while we've been talking. (Reads)—"Yale gets the ball on downs and punts out of danger." That's something like. Oh, Yale hasn't lost yet. Tressie, don't you do anything foolish now, and make a decision all in a moment that you'll regret your whole life. Look at the men themselves. Don't you suppose that Jack's the best of the two? Why, he's big enough to make three or four Lord Ormes, and you know how much he cares for you, and I know how much you care for him and—hold on, here's another bulletin. (Excitedly.) Look there, Tressie. (Reads)—"Yale's ball in center of the field. Jack Harper makes a twenty yard run around Harvard's left end." Listen to the crowd in the street shouting. That's the longest run of the day.

Miss Tremont—Well, of course, I care for Jack. It's not that I like Jack any less.

Jerry—Honestly now, isn't he the best old chap you—wait a minute, here's another—"Yale men playing like fiends; have just worked a trick on Harvard that has netted a gain of ten yards."

Miss Tremont—Splendid. Of course Jack's a dear. I never said he wasn't.

Jerry—Then why do you let Orme talk you out of it? Orme's just after your—

Miss Tremont—What's that next bulletin?

Jerry (in great excitement)—It's Jack again. Oh, Tressie, we'll beat 'em yet.

Miss Tremont—What, what did he do?

Jerry (reading)—"Yale has the ball on Harvard's twenty-five yard line. Jack Harper makes ten more yards around the end." And you said Jack wasn't in it.

Miss Tremont—I never said it.

Jerry—You did.

Miss Tremont—I never. Jack's all right.

Jerry—You bet—every time. Lord Orme, pooh! and his old hounds and his dowager and his debts—look there, look: "Yale is outplaying Harvard at every point."

Miss Tremont—He has got debts.

Jerry—And the governor's good money is to pay them off while— Hold on: "Yale is on Harvard's twelve yard line."

Miss Tremont—Glorious—and his nose is too long.

Jerry—Oh, confound him and his nose, watch the game; here, look (more and more excited)—"Yale is on the ten yard line. Now on the eight. The Yale bleachers are yelling like mad"—I should think they would.

Miss Tremont (clasping her hands in excitement)—Oh, we must win now.

Jerry (shouting)—"Five yards."

Miss Tremont—Oh, Jerry, isn't it exciting? Oh, if I could only see it all. Oh, Jerry, if we should fumble now.

Jerry—Fumble nothing. Jack's there, and don't you forget it. Dear old Jack.

Miss Tremont—Dear old Jack.

Jerry—Hear the crowd in the street giving the Yale yell. Think of it at Springfield now. Can't you just, just hear 'em? Can't you hear the bleachers roaring—just like thunder, Tressie? That's better than a lot of mangy fox hounds yelping, ain't it?

Miss Tremont—You bet it is—Yale! Yale!

Jerry—Here's another bulletin. Yale's on the twelve-yard line. "Harper makes three yards through tackle." Only nine yards more. "Harper makes another gain." Yale's on the eight yard line; on the six; on the five; on the three, and—now—now—now—now—(at the top of his voice, and throwing his hat in the air)—Tressie, Jack's made the TOUCHDOWN! We've won! Oh, ain't it grand—ain't it glorious! Three times three for Yale! Say, Tressie, what's the matter with Jack Harper?

Miss Tremont—He's all right, you bet, every time.

(Enter Lord Orme, who stands mystified in the doorway.)

Jerry—Who's all right?

Miss Tremont—Jack.

Jerry—Who?

Both together—Jack.

Lord Orme (with a puzzled smile)—Is this some sacred and religious rite, some mysterious incantation, that I've interrupted? Miss Tressie, your hair's tumbling down; your gloves are split; your hat is all awry; your cheeks red. If I may be permitted to use the word, you do look regularly—ah—regularly bloused. And to think this is the little girl who's to be presented at the next Drawing-Room.

Miss Tremont (shouting)—No it's not. Bother your old Drawing-Room. Can't you see? Jack's won the game.

A Question of Ideals

———

The American Girl of 1896 as
Seen by Wenzel and by Gibson

———

The Wave, 15 (26 December 1896), 7.

———

During the last year two men of exceptional talent have been hard at work making pictures of the American girl in all the variety of her moods and tenses, and now in this holiday season the collected results have been put before the public in the shape of two picture books, to-wit, *Pictures of People*, by C.D. Gibson, and *Vanity Fair*, by Albert Wenzel (R.H. Russell & Son, publishers), and it is very interesting to note how these two artists from their separate points of view have regarded and treated the same individual. For despite the mystifying titles it is the American girl who plays the leading role in *Vanity Fair*, and who heads the line in *Pictures of People*.

I think that at a very impressionable and formative age—probably a very early one—Mr. Wenzel fell in love with a very stylish girl who was short and blonde, with dark eyes and a rather heavy jaw and broad chin. This girl must have been particularly graceful, given to wearing black lace over rose-colored silk and must have had a habit of sitting turned about half way from you while her elbow rested along the back of the chair and her hand supported her chin—her broad chin. She was a very pretty girl, by the way, and she went to operas and horse shows and sat in boxes with highly ornamented hangings and pillars in the background. At any rate, this is Mr. Wenzel's ideal, and he is very faithful to her and rarely allows her to escape from a picture. I feel that I know her thoroughly by now and should recognize her at once if I should I meet her—at the opera in a highly decorated box for instance. Mr. Wenzel is fond of her oftenest in evening dress, with her hair done high and a comb stuck in it Spanish fashion, and he likes to have her sitting down—rarely do you see her at full length—in the forefront of a great crowd, from which you will notice she does not detach herself, but forms a part of it, being made conspicuous only by virtue of her position.

Also, this girl is vivacious, as you would expect of a short girl, and smiles very easily, as you would expect of a vivacious one.

But I am rather afraid she is a little superficial. However, she is the leading figure in *Vanity Fair*. Never, never does she feel any real depths of passion; never is her sweet high-piled hair disarranged, nor her picture dress —black lace over colored silk—in disorder. She is always serene and smiling and happy, and passes her life finding great amusement over trifles.

But I know another girl who is very beautiful and stylish and all that who smiles just as readily but who is capable of the graver, sterner note as well. She is Mr. Gibson's American girl. She has lived an eventful life. When I first knew her she was (very gently) repudiating foreign noblemen; then she passed through a period of great distress in her love affairs; her love would die, or her husband's love, when once it had gone, was hard to get back again, or she realized her mistake when it was too late, or her husband persisted in dying and leaving her to weep on a beautiful broad divan covered with cushions and letters and things. Of late she has been going about in the costume of a general, or a diplomat, or a minister of the gospel, or a Lord High Chancellor, just as charming and irresistible as ever in spite of —or perhaps because of—her change of raiment.

Unlike Mr. Wenzel's girl she is very tall and a little slim, and her dignity and imposing carriage are her great characteristics. She is rather grave, doesn't smile often, and then mostly with the eyes. Nor is she so entirely given over to society as the girl of the broad chin and high-piled hair. You see her in states of mind rather than in places, in conditions rather than in circumstances.

As I say, she is tall enough to look down on most men, does so, in fact, very often with her head tilted back and her eyes half closed—not at all the kind of girl you would choose to quarrel with. On the whole, I prefer her to the one of the broad chin. She is more serious, perhaps, and you must keep keyed pretty high to enjoy her society. But somehow you feel that she is a "man's woman" and would stand by a fellow and back him up if things should happen. I do not think Mr. Wenzel's girl would. I would like to put her to the test—if I were the man.

Latin Quarter Christmas

How the Nativity is Represented in the Italian Quarter

The Wave, 16 (2 January 1897), 7.

Think of a church—a Catholic church—in this American city where you may see on the walls under the "Stations of The Cross" little placards that read, "Please do not spit on the floor." Think of a quarter of this city where the very parrots talk a foreign tongue; where children are born (in thousands, by the way) and grow and die without ever seeing Kearny street, and where in the notices of public picnics and games—these, too, are written in Italian—it is set forth that the first prize will be a "ton of coal."

Sometimes I am inclined to think that San Francisco is not a city at all, in the strict sense of the word, but is a number of smaller cities, a jumble of them loosely bound together.

I am sure that the Italian and Portuguese store keepers of the neighborhood about Filbert street take themselves just as seriously as do the merchants and brokers of the American quarter about Sansome and Montgomery. There can be no doubt that the worshipers in the Church of St. Peter and St. Paul, way down there on Dupont street, far beyond the Chinese quarter and the Mexican quarter, regard themselves and their church of as much importance as do the members of Trinity, Grace and St. Ignatius.

A curious custom obtains in this church. At Christmas time in one of the chapels at the left of the sanctuary a little stage effect is erected, a little *tableau de théâtre*, done in all seriousness and solemnity. I suppose it is a relic of the old miracle plays and moralities of the fifteenth century, the graphic representations of sacred history and calculated to inspire a sense of reality and vivid *vraisemblance*. The priests of St. Peter and St. Paul have built or arranged the scene of the Nativity in this chapel with a simplicity, a naïveté that is charming. There is nothing in the least ludicrous about these bisque painted figures and toy lambs. This cotton batting that represents snow, this brown sand paper crumpled to imitate rocks. One should see it all, carefully railed off, the little wicker basket for alms just inside. Against a painted background of a hill city, like those of Perugino's pictures, rises a cave of rocks, with snow in the crevices, which does not prevent some half dozen sheep from grazing upon bunches of gray grass here and there. Two Tyrolean figures—mantelpiece ornaments—of bisque do duty for shepherds, while Joseph and Mary are kneeling figures, highly painted and adorned. Above the whole on a wire is a huge seven-pointed star of gilt paper.

To read about this thing in unemotional black type may cause it to appear absurd. But there is nothing absurd about the sight itself—rather one feels a certain respect for such sincerity, such evident conscientiousness. Can't you imagine the effect of positive awe upon some of the little Italian children of the quarter—some of those, for instance, who have never seen Kearny street? Looking at it, with the tiny red lamps burning about it, there can be little doubt that they feel much the same as you do—at moments—for instance, the other day when Mr. Eddy was playing the *Twelfth Mass* on the great organ of St. Ignatius. You who "have seen Kearny street" and "the world outside" must have a sixty thousand dollar organ and the greatest organist between the oceans before you can rise to the sensation. But a few cheap toys, the manikins of statuette vendors, and crumpled cloth suffice for those little Italians of Dupont and Filbert streets.

And after all, is there so much difference between you?

Inside an Organ

How Mr. Eddy's Playing
Sounds in the Swell-Box of the St. Ignatius Organ

The Wave, 16 (2 January 1897), 9.

The new organ of the Church of St. Ignatius is what is called an instrument of the first magnitude, having four manuals or keyboards, of sixty-one keys each, and a pedal-board of thirty keys. It contains eighty-five speaking stops, seventeen couplers, fourteen adjustable pistons, fourteen combination pedals, three swell pedals, and over five thousand speaking pipes. It is what is called an electric organ. The great advantage of the use of electricity in connection with organs is that it insures a perfection of touch and an absolute promptness of response. In operation, the depressed key makes a contact and causes the electric current to open a valve, which permits the air from the bellows to sound the pipe. The isolation of the bellows plant is a feature of the organ, being located in one of the towers of the cathedral, above the organ gallery. This position does away with all the noise and creaking of the bellows machinery, so disturbing in the musical performance of the organ itself. Another interesting mechanism of the organ is an arrangement of buttons beneath each keyboard, by pressing upon which any desired combination of stops can be secured instantly. Four swell boxes are used, enclosing all the manual stops. This makes possible an immense crescendo and diminuendo and charming effects of tone color by slowly closing one box while opening another.

Perhaps the new organ of St. Ignatius is the largest organ in the world and perhaps it is not—probably it is not. But at any rate it is so big that the difference in size between it and the really biggest organ of the world is not appreciable. You receive this sensation of size, of enormous power and volume even before you have heard the organ play a single note. It was not until I had seen the St. Ignatius organ that I realized the force of Mr. Sill's remark when in speaking of one of the great organs of Boston he said: "It is music just to look at it." That's it exactly. Even as I sat on the rail of the organ loft, before Mr. Eddy had arrived, and looked and looked at the banks of keys, the array of stops, the pedals and the clusters of enormous pipes, I had the vivid impression of vast musical sound, sound held in reserve as a battery of artillery holds its fire. The great cannon-like pipes were literally loaded with sound, loaded and primed and waiting for the touch of a finger upon the keyboard. And herein is another impressive feature of this great engine of music—a bellow of harmony answers the lightest touch, the weight of a child's finger may unchain a tempest of sound that roars through the church till the windows quiver, but that dies to silence the instant that light pressure is relaxed. It is as though the organ had a life of its own, as if it were some huge, vast monster, many-voiced as the sea, strong, terrible, yet docile and obedient, as great beasts, broken to harness, are docile and obedient.

Were you ever inside of an organ when it was being played—inside of such an organ as this when Mr. Clarence Eddy was playing, for instance? Think of it. Perhaps you remember the effect Christmas afternoon when you sat below in the body of the church and listened to that cataract of melody come roaring down upon you from a distance. But imagine for a moment what it must be to stand up in the swell-box, in the very heart of the organ itself, in the midst of all those myriad of shouting, clamoring pipes.

Mr. Eddy had come for rehearsal Saturday morning, and the cathedral though empty of people was full of sunlight and reverberating echoes. Some few of us were standing about him at the console in the organ loft and he was playing—what, I am sure I don't know, just a succession of wandering pleasant musical sounds. Then the idea occurred to me to go inside while Mr. Eddy played, and I suggested as much to him and he told me to go, and at the same time began playing the opening bars.

With Mr. Woods, who is the representative of the builders, I went around to a little door in the side of the organ's enormous case and, entering, sidled down a narrow passage to a ladder that led upward into some darker space above. We climbed up, Mr. Woods shouting directions to me from under his arm—shouting, I say, for already the noise of the pipes was as the noise of machinery. Through narrow slits that opened mysteriously here and there I could catch glimpses of the interior of the church, the sanctuary and chancel, dropping below by degrees. Up we went, and at last reached a narrow platform and a sliding door. I went in the door and Mr. Woods slid it to behind us and turned on an electric light. I was in the solo box, the center and heart of the organ, its very vitals. Here and there I could see little movements in corners, the little movements the organ makes in its living—an indicator traveling slowly back and forth, or the majestic opening and shutting of the huge blinds of the swell box that regulates the volume of sound, and that in action looks almost like the contraction and expansion of enormous gills—gills with which the organ breathes. A world of pipes was all about, thousands of them, rising out of the floor in gradations from the size of a bean blower not four inches in height to the tremendous amplitude of the thirty-two-foot pipe in the lowest octave of the diapason, as large as a liner's smokestack.

But the sound! It was not music in the general acceptance of the word, for the multitude of notes crowded together in that narrow space fought each other as they struggled to escape. One experienced the same effect upon the ear as would be made upon the eye if one stood too close to a painting. Nor was that "mighty rushing sound" discord, surely not that. It was—I cannot say what it most resembled. It was the vast vague roll of the ocean, or the clamor of a great wind in a forest, or the voices of a multitude shouting together, or the snarling of a thousand trumpets.

There was no "tune" that one could distinguish, nor was there any harshness. It was just sound, sound, sound—waves upon waves of it, sound that you could feel thrilling the air about you, sound that you could almost see streaming up from those thousand upright pipes. As Mr. Eddy played, the volume increased, the clamor became terrific. The drums of one's ears quivered and shrank under the shock of that ocean of sound-waves. The blinds of the swell boxes, opening to their limit, disclosed panel-like vistas of the church far below. To be here, here high up in this tiny swell-box, alone with this thundering monster, struck one with a feeling of awe, of positive, downright fear—the intuitive fear of all things huge.

Suddenly the bourdon began, the open diapason, the vast thunder of that lowest octave of the great pedal-organ. Everything shook, wood, iron, and all quivered as the quaking of the earth. It was the thunder of artillery, the bellowing of a tremendous surge, the prolonged crashing of a Niagara, terrific beyond words.

Then in a moment it began to subside, just as a storm might pass off, the thunder getting further and further below the horizon, the wind dropping away by long puffs. One drew a long breath and looked about one as if re-covering from a trance. The bourdon sank to a numb vibration, so low as to be no longer sound, but a mere indefinable tremble in the air that one perceived with some sort of sixth sense. Then it stopped. The chaos of sound resolved itself into a something like tangible harmony. The piece was closing, soon it would be finished.

We went out of the solo box and clambered down the ladder, winding in and out of the tortuous passages once more. It took some time, and we stopped often on the way for discussion and comment. By the time we reached the console again the piece was over. A little girl, a child of twelve, standing at Mr. Eddy's elbow, was singing a little love song in a small, fine baby-like voice. Mr. Eddy was accompanying her on the organ, the same or-gan that had but a moment before shaken the entire cathedral with its mighty thunder, and now its voice was faint and delicate like the warbling of an oaten pipe, as sweet and clear and small as the tinkling of a guitar. The little girl easily dominated it as she finished with a prolonged note that rose high above the tones of the organ, and Mr. Eddy turned about and thrust back the stops.

"A fine instrument," said he.

1896—1897

A Revolt

By Alphonse Allais

Translated by Frank Norris

The Wave, 16 (2 January 1897), 9.

Sunday evening, about six o'clock.

Now, have you ever noticed this fact? When it is warm of a Sunday evening in Paris, it is warmer than any other evening, even if the thermometer is the same.

You have not noticed this, you say? It is of no importance? You are not an observer; *voilà tout.*

To continue:

Six o'clock! It is the moment when the Parisians, those who have not plenty of money to spend for their dinner, betake themselves to the café to imbibe "aperitifs"—bitters—strange and mysterious beverages, horrible to the taste, but royally inimical to the stomach.

When you have absorbed but two of these philtres you are no longer hungry, you are satisfied with half the usual dinner. It is an economical measure, worthy of consideration during financial crises.

I was sitting on the terrace of one of the cafés of the boulevard before a certain black liquid that surely must have come from the cellars of the Borgias. At a neighboring table, a man and a woman had just seated themselves, evidently husband and wife. The woman asked for vermouth, the man for absinthe.

The woman asked for her vermouth in an indifferent manner, as she might have asked for anything. The man asked for his absinthe in a voice of inexpressible lassitude.

"Give me absinthe," he seemed to say, "not to intoxicate me, but to make me forget a little—allow me to escape, if only for a quarter of an hour, from this intolerable fabric of annoyances that is called life."

He was a fine looking man, this absinthe drinker, about thirty years of age, simply but elegantly dressed. He looked intelligent enough. But, oh, how the poor devil seemed to be bored!

I hope that I am much too gallant to say that a woman is plain, or even unattractive; I would prefer to declare that the wife of my absinthe drinker was purely and simply ignoble. Her homeliness was aggravated by a stupid expression of arrogance and general hostility, and ah, she was vilely dressed—such pretension, such unspeakable bad taste!

Yes, I understood the mental depression of the poor husband. Had I been in his place, saddled with such a burden, I would have drunk, not one glass of absinthe only, but barrels of absinthe, rivers of absinthe, oceans of absinthe. I could not always overhear their conversation except in phrases, but the aggressive air of the woman and the wearied expression on the part of her husband gave some indication of the little idyll that was drawing to its close.

All at once the man assumed an air of decision. I could see that he had had enough of this little family celebration. At a single gulp he emptied his glass. Then he folded his arms and looked squarely at the woman.

"Aren't you ever going to give me a rest?"

The woman, the plain, uncomely woman, was visibly discountenanced by the suddenness of the attack.

"Yes," said the man, "you get on my nerves with your reproaches and your insinuations."

"My insinuations?"

"Yes, your insinuations. It's your dowry that you're hinting at, isn't it, hey?"

"But, my dear friend——"

"Your dowry! Ah, yes, let's talk about your dowry. It's a daisy, your dowry. Do you know how much it's worth, your dowry?"

"A hundred thousand francs."

"Exactly, a hundred thousand francs. Do you know how much income your hundred thousand francs represents, your famous hundred thousand francs?"

"I—I don't know exactly——"

"*Eh bien!* I'll tell you. Your famous hundred thousand francs represents three thousand francs income, and that don't include costs!"

"But my dear friend——"

"And three thousand francs income. Do you know how much that repre-sents for a day?"

"But my dear friend——"

"That represents nine francs fifty centimes. You understand, nine—francs—fifty—centimes."

"But my dear friend——"

"In round figures let us say ten francs, ten francs a day. Do you know how much that is for an hour?"

"But my dear friend——"

"Ten francs a day, that's forty centimes an hour. That's what your dowry amounts to, forty centimes an hour. Frankly, it wasn't worth while."

"You insult me."

"Look here. There's forty centimes that I give back to you for sixty min-utes of liberty I'm going to take. It is half-past six. I'll come back at half-past seven for dinner——"

"You're disgusting."

"And I forewarn you, if the house smells of cooking—oh, the least little bit—and if you're still as sulky as you are now, I'll go dine somewhere else—reimbursing you, of course, a fraction of your dowry, *pro rata* according to the length of my absence. *Au revoir, ma chère*." And the man, after paying for the absinthe and vermouth, went off, leaving the woman staring stupidly at the forty centimes before her.

New Year's at San Quentin

How the Prisoners Celebrate the Passing of the Old Year

The Wave, 16 (9 January 1897), 8.

New Year's Day in a penitentiary! I wonder what they think of on this day—the "cons"—the murderers, burglars, highwaymen, thieves and the like —the striped army of them down there in the prison yard, with the Gatling guns of the watchtowers trained on them!

One would like to suppose that the suggestiveness of the day forced itself upon them. If ever there were occasions for New Year's Day resolutions they would exist here in the "yard." I should like to think that the sentenced murderer in the condemned cell—number twenty-four, it is—chose the day to think a bit over a mis-spent life; that he attained to a "might-have-been" mood, or that the twenty-year-men checked off the passing of another year that brought them nearer to liberty, or that the "life-timer" gloomily reflected that the advent of 1897 brought no encouragement or hope to him.

Perhaps there are isolated cases of this kind, but they are few and far between. I went all over the penitentiary of San Quentin on the first day of this year, and though I did not get speech of the men in the yard, I talked to some of the "outsiders"—the trusties—who are the connecting link between the yard and the outside world; who are in touch with the "cons" and know them thoroughly; and this was the impression I gained.

New Year's Day in San Quentin is indeed a period of rejoicing, but the "pen" is a distinct and isolated world of its own, having its own ideals and enjoyments and ambitions, absolutely and radically different from any other community that exists. The "cons" make merry over New Year's Day, not because it is New Year's, but because it brings with it two inestimable blessings—fish dinner and that consummate beatitude of the "con's" existence, the blissful freedom from the detested and execrated half-day's work in the jute mill.

I think this hatred of manual labor among certain of the criminal class is

226

a mild form of dementia—a mania, a blind, unreasoned aversion (only intensified a thousand fold), such as some people have of cats—an aversion that cannot be conquered, or argued with, or outlived. It develops in the children of criminal families, like homicidal manias and the like. You cannot understand this thing—can get no idea of the "con's" horror of it until you have visited the "pen," and have listened to some of the stories there told.

Consider the situation a moment. Suppose you and I were "cons," and that for some reason we were not "outside men," but had to work in the mill. It is a regulation that each man who works in that mill must do his tick of a hundred yards of jute per day. With ordinary industry the "con" can finish it at about half past twelve o'clock. After that he can do what he likes with his time until lock-up. The work is of the easiest description—a child could learn it and perform it without difficulty. You and I, if we were "cons," would fall into the regime without complaint, we would get into the habit of the thing, and I've no doubt would come to do our hundred yards of jute ahead of time for the sake of the extra leisure it would insure. Why, for the matter of that, we might even prefer to work rather than to lounge all day idle about the flagstones of the sunny yard.

Not so the average "con." He rages at his task, goes to it with a furious reluctance that no habit can overcome, blasphemes the prison directors in the din of the clashing shuttles, and leaves his machine with a relief that can only be expressed by long rolls of oaths. He hates it as a victim of the Great Persecution hated the rack and the stake—sees in the loom he daily toils before only an instrument of torture, of oppression, and injustice—is kept to his work only by guards with guns and the fear of the "hole" and straightjacket. You will not believe the extremities to which he will go to escape from it. You are shown one man in the hospital ward who is shamming insanity. For fourteen months this man has lain upon his back, speaking to no one, in order to persuade the authorities of the prison that he is crazy and unfit to work in the mill. Fourteen months! Think of that—a year and two months in bed so as not to work for half a dozen hours per day! But this is not the worst. A man whose fingers are missing can do no work in the mill, naturally. One of the "cons" (who, mind you, had only four more months of his sentence to serve), took advantage of this fact, and one day deliberately thrust his thumb between the cogwheels of one of the jute machines and let it be crushed off.

"Now let 'em make me work!"

"Huh!" answered his mates. "You'll work just the same. A man without a thumb can tend the machine all right. Doctor Lawlor won't excuse you from work for that."

"He won't, won't he!" shouts my "con." "I'll fix him!" and in goes the whole hand, to come out again with the four fingers ground away.

Only four months more of work, but he preferred maiming for life rather than undergo it. You can't account for this on the ground of simple dislike of labor. It's dementia—hereditary mental obliquity, taking the form of a horror of work.

One custom obtains on New Year's day, and as far as I can see, but one. We arranged to see, or rather, hear it.

On New Year's eve, just before twelve o'clock, we sat ourselves down upon a flight of steps on a terrace above the prison, where we could overlook the yard. The last moments of the old year were passing, and the scene, in the night, looking down into the huge dark prison, with its rows of bolted iron doors that stood for so much of the crime and wickedness and perversity of life, should have been impressive. But there was a jarring note. The female ward was the part of the "pen" nearest us, and through the stillness of that New Year's eve came the monotonous and raucous plaint of a woman's voice, flung across the narrow court to some inmate of an opposite cell, the words as distinct as if spoken in the ear:

"——an' after all I've said an' done fur him, that's the way he treated me" (here a long roll of oaths); "why, he might be a-beggin' on the streets if it hadn't-a-been fur me—beggin' on the streets to-day if it hadn't-a-been fur me, an' that's the way he treated me."

This was the theme, repeated again and again, in different words. What did it stand for? What was the grievance this female "con" was lamenting in these moments when the year was turning as the turning of a tide. Was it a slight of yesterday? Was it a wrong that had wrecked a life? Was it true? Was it a lie? Was she old or young, innocent or guilty? I shall never know. It was mystery. A voice, from a prison, at midnight. The incident of a moment!

"If it hadn't-a-been fur me—an' that's the way he treated—a-beggin' on the streets, an'——"

Suddenly it was the New Year. Very far off at the end of the line of guards came a prolonged cry: "Twelve—o'clock and a—a—all's well," and another nearer cry repeated it. But we lost the sound of the answer. With the call of the first guard the prison of San Quentin thundered with noises. Somewhere near by a chorus of bugles sang together, only to be drowned by a vast clamor that rang from wall to wall of the prison, and that split the silence of the night with the clamor of a splitting berg. At that moment the thirteen hundred prisoners of San Quentin were beating their fists upon the iron doors of their cells. A strange noise—strange for its suddenness—stranger when you consider its suggestiveness. The iron barrier that shuts out liberty and the pursuit of happiness serving as a clashing cymbal of rejoicing—the door of a prison cell, used as a bell to sound the New Year in! Surely no stranger New Year chimes were rung that night the world around.

And with all this vast clangor, this strange, reverberating tumult, not a movement, not a sign of human life. The moonlight and the white glare of electricity flooded the prison yard and the building till the very bolts on the doors were visible, but not a living thing stirred. The enclosure roared with the roar of an army with clashing shields, yet remained deserted, desolate, abandoned of all life.

One thing I remember, however, that compensated—one thing that redeemed the gloom and the weirdness of it all. Just after the first guard had raised his cry of "All's well," and just before the thunder of the thirteen hundred fists upon the doors of the cells, a fraction of a second had intervened—a brief moment of time—just long enough for the female "con," she of the hoarse and raucous voice, to interrupt her monotonous complaint and cry:

"Happy New Year, May!"

What Is Our Greatest Piece of Fiction?

————

Romance Readers Discuss the Matter
Learnedly and Interestingly

————

He Thinks It's *Ben-Hur*

————

San Francisco *Examiner*, 17 January 1897, 30.

————

To the Literary Editor, *Examiner:*

There are two ways of considering the question of the "great American novel." One as to the best novel produced by an American author, and the other as to the novel which is the most thoroughly American in its tone and most aptly interprets the phases of American life.

If one should ask the question, Which is the best novel yet produced by an American author? the answer should be, I believe, Lew Wallace's *Ben-Hur*.

If the question were, Which novel is the best interpretation of American life? I hold the correct response must be, Mr. Howells' *A Modern Instance*.

These two novels were conceived and executed along such entirely different lines, and according to such opposing theories of literary art, that no comparison, with a view of determining their respective merits, is possible. They can only be contrasted.

I think the quality of *Ben-Hur*, which more than anything else raises it to the class of great novels, is its vivid descriptions of dramatic action. Most readers are apt to be deceived by the idea that the originality shown in the choice of subject is its greatest charm. They prefer to believe that *A Tale of the Christ*, told in the form of a novel, is in itself a conception of genius. But such tales have been written before and have not excited great popular interest, while from the point of view of literary art nothing is more unoriginal and hackneyed than the narrative of the New Testament. The scenes that have made *Ben-Hur* great are not those of the Nativity, or the

Crucifixion, or the Miracle, but those of the sea fight with the pirates, the finding of Ben-Hur by his mother and sister at the time when these latter were lepers, and the whole scene of the circus that culminates in the chariot race.

It is the tremendous drama of the book that has made it so famous, the gorgeous scenes of life and movement and color—the vast scenic background against which vivid and significant action, hurried and intense, is wrought out.

A Modern Instance is great because it is true, relentlessly and remorselessly true to American life. Mr. Howells has very clearly conceived of some of the great crying evils of Americanism and followed them out to their logical conclusion in his characters. He has treated in the various parts of his story the serious problems of American life—the problems of politics, of divorce, of journalism, of marriage, and of social caste—with a consistency and a plausibleness that are convincing beyond any possibility of doubt, and with a thorough technical knowledge of the novelist's trade that in my opinion places the book among the masterpieces of fiction.

Frank Norris.

Hunting Human Game

How Watch and Wait is Kept for the *Swanhilda*

The Wave, 16 (23 January 1897), 4.

On the 21st of November in the year 1896 there appeared in one of the newspapers of Sydney, Australia, an advertisement to the effect that one Frank Butler—mining prospector, was in search of a partner with whom to engage in a certain mining venture. It was stipulated that applicants should possess at least ten pounds and come well recommended.

Captain Lee Weller answered the advertisement and accompanied Butler to the Blue Mountains mining region, in what is known as the Glenbrook district. There Butler shot him in the back of the head and buried the body in such a way that a stream of trickling water would help in its decomposition. But Captain Weller had friends; he was missed; a search was made and it was not long before the detectives discovered the grave and identified the remains.

Meanwhile, news had been brought to the Australian police that another man named Preston had gone into the mountains and never returned. Next the body of this Preston was discovered. Then it was found that another man had disappeared under the same circumstances as those surrounding the vanishing of Weller. Then another and another, and still another. The news of these disappearances ran from end to end of Australia, and the whole police system of the country was brought to bear upon the case. Finally it was found that a man named Lee Weller had applied to the Sailor's Home at Newcastle for a berth on a ship. Seven days later this Lee Weller shipped out of Newcastle before the mast on the British tramp ship *Swanhilda*, bound for San Francisco in coal. This was all the detectives wanted to know. The man calling himself Weller was Butler beyond any doubt, suddenly grown suspicious and resolved upon a bolt. Butler's photograph was identified at once by the Superintendent of the Sailor's Home as the supposed Lee Weller. It was out of the question to overhaul Butler now, but two Australian detectives, McHattie and Conroy, took passage on a steamer for San Francisco, where they arrived some three weeks ago. They outstripped Butler and are now waiting for him to catch up with them. That is the story in brief of this extraordinary criminal who, Mr. McHattie says, has killed—no, assassinated is the word—fourteen men.

I saw the "death watch" the other day—the watch for the tramp collier ship *Swanhilda*—that is being maintained at Meiggs' wharf by seven men, whose business it is to hunt criminals down. There is but little of that secrecy and dark mystery about this famous "death watch" that sensational story-writers would have you believe. The detectives live upstairs in a little two-story house at the end of Meiggs' wharf, close to the customs offices. I had imagined that I would be met at the door with all sorts of difficulties, that permits and passes would be demanded and explanations and the like; that the detectives would be austere and distant and preoccupied,

preoccupied as men are who are watching for a sign or listening for a signal. Nothing of the sort. I tramped in at the open door and up the stairs to the room and sat me down on Mr. McHattie's bed—it's a lounge, but it does for a bed—as unchallenged as if the place had been my own; nor was I armed with so much as a letter of introduction. I was not even asked to show a business card.

The room is a little room, whose front windows give out upon the bay and the Golden Gate. Not a row-boat could pass the Gate without being noted from this vantage point. There were four beds made up on the floor of the room, and Conroy was dozing in one, pretending to read *Phra the Phoenician*, the whiles. The other detectives sat about a gas stove, smoking. They were for the most part big, burly men, with red faces, very jovial and not at all like the sleuths you expected to see. They are, however, heavily muscled fellows, with the exception of Conroy, who singularly enough is slighter than any of them, though a trained athlete. I remember that the room was warm. That there were pictures of barks and brigs about the walls, that a pair of handcuffs were in a glass dish on the top of a dresser, and that, lying in a cubby hole of a desk, was Detective Egan's revolver in a very worn case. The detectives impressed one as positively jolly. They told me many funny yarns about the crowd of visitors on the wharf, of the "Branch office of the *Chronicle*," a room ten feet square, just back of the Customs building, and once when the *Examiner* reporter cried out that a girl was waving a handkerchief from a window on the hill back of the wharf, they made a rush for the rear window of the room, crowding about it like so many boys.

And at that very moment somewhere out there beyond the Farallones a certain great four-masted ship, 58 days out of Newcastle, was rolling and lifting on the swell of the Pacific, drawing nearer to these men with every puff of the snoring trades. Some time within the next few days the signal from the Merchants' Exchange will be rung in that room, there on Meiggs' wharf the signal which some of these men have come around half of the world to hear. It will be rung on the telephone bell, and it may come at each instant—it may be ringing now as I write these lines, or now as you read them. It may come in the morning, or while the "watch" is at supper, or in the very dead of night, or the early dawn. May I be there to hear it and to see as well. The scene cannot be otherwise than dramatic—melodramatic even. I want to hear that exclamation "Here she is" that some one is bound to utter. I want to see Egan reach for the revolver in the worn leather case, and Conroy take the handcuffs from the glass dish. I want to see the sudden rousing of these seven men, these same men who waved their hands to the girl in the window, and I want to hear the clatter of those seven pairs of boots going down the stair and out upon the wharf. I fancy there will not be much talking.

"Fifi"

By Léon Faran

Translated by Frank Norris from the *Petit Journal*

The Wave, 16 (23 January 1897), 5.

Not only were Maurice and Paul friends from their cradle; not only had they gone through college together and had been, later, partners in business; not only had they, simultaneously, married two most charming cousins— Léonie and Valentine—but Maurice and Paul each possessed top coats identical in cloth, cut and style.

* * * * * * * * * * * *

On a certain morning, as Maurice, having said goodbye to his wife Léonie, was on his way to his office, a messenger, who had evidently been watching for him, thrust a note into his hands and disappeared. Maurice opened the note in some surprise:

1896—1897

My Dear Boy:—What do you say to dining with me to-night? You remember the address.

> Always your devoted
> FIFI

"'Fifi'—who the deuce was 'Fifi'?" Then he suddenly remembered. "Fifi" —yes, it was the same; the little beauty whose manners were not austere, and who had at one time entered into his life during his bachelor days.

With a movement of anger Maurice thrust the note into his overcoat pocket. Had she lost her senses, this Fifi, to suppose that he, a serious married man, had nothing better to do than to run off to midnight suppers with pretty little girls? And shrugging his shoulders he walked on.

"Fifi!" The very name invoked certain memories of his foolish, riotous youth, and in spite of himself Maurice could not repress a smile. When he arrived at his office he found Paul there before him. During the entire day the two were so taken up with their affairs that they had but barely time to make a hurried arrangement to take their respective wives to the theatre that evening.

Paul left the office first, and Maurice, as he prepared to follow, allowed himself to think again of the invitation he had received that morning. He knew that he could not accept it—that is, that he should not accept it, and yet, in spite of himself, he began to feel a certain curiosity.

After all, would it be criminal? What wrong would he do Léonie if he went to the dinner?

Would he be the first husband who, after seeing his wife home at night, had found some good reason for slipping away for an hour or two?

He would love her no less if he had a bit of fun with some old friends.

And divided between his conscience and this temptation of forbidden fruit that had suddenly seized upon him, Maurice found himself in a quandary. But all at once, shaking his head, he exclaimed:

"Bah! Let's not bother about it. I shall act according to the mood I am in at the moment."

He got up and clapped on his hat, but in putting on his overcoat he was aware of a certain tightness under the arms.

"Hello—it's Paul's coat," said he. "He has gone off with mine. Well, we will change back again at the theatre."

* * * * * * * * * * * *

Some hours later the two young couples found themselves in a box at the Vaudeville. The piece was very well played and of a captivating interest. Sitting behind Léonie, who had never been prettier than that evening, Maurice forgot all about Fifi. The evening passed delightfully.

Maurice and Léonie went home in a carriage, but hardly had the door closed upon them when the young woman turned upon her husband:

"Look at that!" she cried, and she held toward him in a trembling hand the little note of Fifi.

Maurice felt his heart stop. He had not strength enough left to cry out, but sat there in his place, stupefied, speechless, dumbfounded.

"It is horrible!" cried Léonie.

Maurice did not even have sense enough to justify himself—to invent an excuse.

"Frightful!" he murmured, mechanically.

There was a moment of deep silence, then Léonie heaved a deep sigh of compassion.

"Poor Valentine!" she murmured.

Maurice started in his place.

"Valentine! What do you mean?"

Léonie drew herself up.

"What do I mean? Ah, that's so like you men. Her husband, Paul, is in correspondence with his Mademoiselle Fifi, goes to dinner with his Mademoiselle Fifi, and you say, 'What do I mean?'"

Maurice, more and more bewildered, asked himself if he were losing his wits.

"Paul?" he asked, vaguely.

"Yes, Paul—your good friend Paul. It surprises you, don't it? We found it all out during the last *entr'acte*." Then lowering her voice: "It was while you had gone out. Valentine couldn't find her handkerchief, and she asked me to pass her her husband's. She said I would find it in his overcoat pocket. I looked for it, but instead of the handkerchief I found this note, and I—well, I—of course I read it. I suppose I made a fuss over it. Valentine

236

asked what was the matter. She looked over my shoulder and read the note. Ah, what a blow for the poor girl! All at once, however, I had an idea—a real inspiration. But promise me first, Maurice, before I tell you, that you won't scold me—that you will forgive me. I saw that only a little bit of a lie could save Valentine and Paul, so what do you suppose? I remembered at that instant that you and Paul had overcoats exactly alike and I exclaimed, 'But that is Maurice's coat!'"

"And then——" gasped Maurice.

"Then—it was extraordinary—Valentine believed it on the instant, without the least hesitation. There could be no doubt that it was Paul's coat, but" (she added with a superior air) "women are so blind, and always think these things can happen to other people, but never to themselves."

Maurice tried to hide a smile. Léonie continued, her voice becoming tender and caressing:

"Tell me, Maurice; you are not angry with me?"

"Ahem! Ahem!" Maurice frowned. "It was a liberty, my dear. It is a grave charge to bring against a man. To think that I, a serious, steady, married man, so entirely faithful to his wife, should think—should even think—of 'Fifis'—and suppers—and—— It was—it was a liberty, but—yes—I pardon you—I pardon you freely. You did it for the sake of a friend. You are forgiven."

"Ah, that wicked Paul! Do you think he will go?"

"No, my dear, he will not go, I assure you. That he may have had the idea for an instant is possible, but at the last moment a man—a married man—would realize the indignity of such an action, and would be neither foolish enough nor base enough to carry it out."

Maurice cleared his throat and pulled down his vest.

"So it was all for the best," cried Léonie. "It is just as well for a woman to be blind to some things, isn't it? Poor Valentine—if she only knew!"

"But—perhaps she would forgive him."

Léonie fairly bounced in her seat.

"Never!" she cried. "Ah, no; one doesn't pardon such things as that."

"Then—if, in place of Valentine—let us suppose for an instant—that it were you. You would not have forgiven me?" inquired Maurice, hesitatingly.

"Never," she answered, with energy and absolute conviction.

Maurice felt himself grow pale.

There was an instant of silence.

"But wasn't it fortunate, Maurice?" said Léonie, at length. "Wasn't it fortunate that you and Paul had overcoats exactly alike?"

Maurice's answer came straight from his heart:

"Oh, very, very fortunate!" he cried.

One Kind of "New Woman"

A Girl of Twenty Who Has the Frame of a Sandow

The Wave, 16 (30 January 1897), 6.

I don't remember now exactly what I expected to see. A huge red-faced woman, no doubt, with a trumpeting voice and calloused hands, bull-necked and aggressive. I surely thought she would be big, very tall and broad—especially broad—and I imagined she would have the condescension, the vaguely contemptuous manner that goes with great physical strength. A "female Sandow" should have such attributes. You would fancy yourself defrauded if she didn't.

So with this and that and the other I was taken all aback with the sight of Alcide Capitaine. She is positively small—you would call her a "little" woman—and, ignorant of who she was, you might even yourself assume the certain condescension of manner that men—some men—display when talking to the "weaker" sex. You would do this until Alcide (or whatever her real name may be) allowed you to make the attempt to clasp her upper arm —at first with one hand, then, failing in this, with two—the web of flesh between thumb and index stretched to its utmost. A man must have large hands to do the thing, for the bicep measurement is fifteen and a half inches. Think of fifteen and a half inches of pure muscle, tough and hard as sole-leather!

I asked Alcide Capitaine how she came to choose the profession of a gymnast. I knew what her answer would be. Invariably they tell me the same thing:

"My father was in the profession before me," says she, "and I began to exercise and practice when I was three years old."

It's always like this with acrobats and gymnasts and wire-walkers and the like. Their fathers or families were "in the business" before them, and they took to it naturally. You wonder how their fathers came to do the thing. There must have been An Original Acrobat somewhere, some man—it couldn't have been a woman—who arose one morning and said:

"Go to; I likewise will be a gymnast" (or acrobat, or high-wire man, as the case might be), and forthwith was one, and begat a family to follow his profession.

"I commenced," said Miss Capitaine (or perhaps one should say Mlle. Capitaine) "by imitating my father, just as an ordinary child might imitate anything it saw its parents do. I slept in a curtained bed, I remember, with tassels at the end of long cords, and I would try to do the things I had seen my father do at the theatre, tumbling and balancing and all that."

"And he saw that you were clever at it and encouraged you," I suggested.

Apparently not. Capitaine Senior was not particularly anxious that she should elect such a profession as his.

"My people didn't like the idea," said she, in reply. "It was all very well when I was little, but when I grew older they tried to talk me out of it, but I liked it and kept at it, till they let me have my way—and here I am."

It is not easy to talk to the female Sandow, or rather it is not easy to get her to talk. It is not only from a physical point of view that she is puzzling. I have talked to plenty of actresses of approved fame and personal reputation who were a deal more at their ease than this girl who has spent the nineteen years of her life in the performance of muscular feats. The fact of the matter is that Capitaine is a quiet, retiring sort of little body. She has received the education of a gymnast, and developed certain sets of muscles to a wonderful extent, but otherwise she hardly differs from the average Italian girl of twenty or thereabouts.

Another point. Capitaine, though small, is marvelously well-proportioned. I managed to suggest as much to her.

"That's from my dancing."

"Dancing?"

"I dance every morning just to develop my leg muscles."

"Waltz?" (Imagine waltzing with a woman with such a waist and back and arms!)

"No; skirt dancing and that sort."

I fancy she must dance admirably. At least she knows all about skirt dancing. A day later I saw her in the wings of the Orpheum, where she had come to supervise the arrangement of her trapeze, etc., and she permitted herself to indulge in more than one sarcasm as to the dancing of one of Mr. Kiralfy's girls, who was practicing a new step.

"There is one thing that I am rather proud of," said Capitaine to me on this same occasion.

I became attentive.

"See now," (she was in trapeze costume) "when I let my arm fall naturally, there is nothing extraordinary about it, is there?"

I have seen stouter arms at many an evening function; plenty, even, that were not so smooth.

"But when I muscle up," she went on, "as now, for instance——"

Really it took one's breath away. Tom Sharkey himself would be proud of that arm.

It is the same with Capitaine's back and shoulders. The muscles do not show when she stands "at ease." But when she straightens up, and bends up her arms and throws back her shoulders, the flesh dimples deep, with sudden hollows and ridges, and the knotted muscles go rippling and sliding down over the hard, firm bones, till you wonder and wonder how this thing came to be—this superb, marvelous anatomy—this frame of a pugilist in the person of a girl not yet out of her teens.

Passing of "Little Pete"

The Funeral Rites Held Over a Famous Chinaman

The Wave, 16 (30 January 1897), 7.

When a man is vulgar he is vulgar according to fixed standards. He conforms to a certain common type of vulgarity; but every woman is vulgar in her own way. There is the brutally vulgar woman, the meanly vulgar, the self-consciously vulgar, the brazenly vulgar, and the modestly vulgar. There is the vulgar woman who knows that she allows herself to be vulgar and is ashamed of it, and there is the woman who is proud of her vulgarity, and calls it liberty and equality and fraternity and democracy and independence and I don't know what, and who trumpets her vulgarity to the four winds of heaven, and is only ashamed when men fail to take notice.

That is the kind of woman who was most in evidence at the funeral ceremonies of a certain wealthy man, known by the name of L.F. Peters, who was shot to death this month of January, 1897.

Perhaps I have seen a more disgusting spectacle than that which took place at "Little Pete's" funeral ceremonies, but I cannot recall it now. A reckless, conscienceless mob of about two thousand, mostly women, crowded into the Chinese cemetery. There was but one policeman to control them, and they took advantage of the fact. The women thronged about the raised platform and looted everything they could lay their hands on; China bowls, punk, tissue paper ornaments, even the cooked chickens and bottles of gin. This, mind you, before the procession had as much as arrived.

The procession itself was rather disappointing—from a picturesque point of view. Perhaps one expected too much. There might possibly have been a greater display of color and a greater number of bands. Nor were there any of the street ceremonies in front of Pete's Chinatown residence that you had been told to look for. The company of chief mourners, in blue and white cambric, was too suggestive of a campaign club to be very impressive, and the members of the carriage orchestras refused to take themselves very seriously, seeming more interested in the crowd of spectators than in the funeral cortege.

At the cemetery, however, things were different. There was a certain attempt here at rites and observances and customs that would have been picturesque and striking had it not been for the shameless, the unspeakable shamelessness of the civilized women of the crowd.

A few mandarins came first, heads no doubt of the Sam Yup, one of them in particular, with all the dignity and imposing carriage of a senator. He was really grand, this mandarin, calm, austere, unmoved amidst this red-faced, scrambling mob. A band of women followed, the female relatives of the deceased.

"Here comes his wife!" screamed half a dozen white women in chorus.

Pete's widow was wrapped from head to foot in what might have been the sackcloth of the Bible stories; certainly it had the look of jute. A vast hood of the stuff covered her whole face, and was tied about the neck. Two other women, similarly dressed, but without the hood, were supporting her. A mat was unrolled, and after the white women had been driven back from the platform by the main strength of two or three men, not yet lost to the sense of decency, the mourners kneeled upon it, forehead to the ground, and began a chant, or rather a series of lamentable cries and plaints. "Ai yah, ai-yah-yah."

A gong beat. A priest in robes and octagon cap persistently jingled a little bell and droned under his breath. There was a smell of punk and sandal wood in the air. The crouching women, mere bundles of clothes, rocked to and fro and wailed louder and louder.

Suddenly the coffin arrived, brought up by staggering hack-drivers and assistants, a magnificent affair, heavy black cloth and heavy silver appointments. The white women of the crowd made the discovery that Little Pete's powder-marked face could be seen. They surged forward in the instant. The droning priest was hustled sharply; he dropped his little bell, which was promptly stolen. The mourners on the mat, almost under foot, were jostled and pushed from their place, or bundled themselves out of the way hurriedly to escape trampling. Just what followed after this I do not know. A mob of red-faced, pushing women thronged about the coffin and interrupted everything that went on. There were confusion and cries in Cantonese and English; a mounted policeman appeared and was railed at. There can be no doubt that more ceremonies were to follow, but that those in charge preferred to cut short the revolting scene. The coffin was carried back to the hearse, a passage at length being forced through the crowd, and the Chinese returned to the city. Then the civilized Americans, some thousand of them, descended upon the raised platform, where the funeral meats were placed—pigs and sheep roasted whole, and chickens and bowls of gin and rice. Four men seized a roast pig by either leg and made off with it; were pursued by the mounted police and made to return the loot. Then the crowd found amusement in throwing bowlfuls of gin at each other. The roast chickens were hurled back and forth in the air. The women scrambled for the China bowls for souvenirs of the occasion, as though the occasion were something to be remembered.

The single mounted policeman, red-faced and over-worked, rode his horse into the crowd and after long effort at last succeeded in thrusting it back from the plundered altar and in keeping it at a distance. But still it remained upon the spot; this throng, this crowd, this shameless mob, that was mostly of women. There was nothing more to happen, the ceremony was over, but still these people stayed and looked.

This was the last impression one received of Little Pete's funeral—a crowd of two thousand men and women, standing in a huge circle, stupidly staring at the remains of a roasted pig.

The U.C. Track Team

Developing the Material for the Inter-Collegiate Games

The Wave, 16 (6 February 1897), 4.

Captain Everett Brown and Al. Lean, the former trainer of the Reliance team, have settled down to the serious work of bringing the U.C. cinder-path athletes into championship form. The team was worked rather severely over the track just previous to Christmas, but since then the practice has been lighter. Both Brown and Al. Lean have a very wholesome fear of falling into the error so frequently committed by the football coaches—that of sending the team up to the match hopelessly overtrained. It is safe to assume that (with the possible exception of the eleven coached by Gill) every football team turned out by the U.C. has been practically stale from overwork. Such, however, has never been the case with the track teams from Berkeley, working under the direction of home coaches, and it is quite possible that to this more than to anything else is due the U.C.'s phenomenal record in track events. The team has never been beaten on this coast, while its really wonderful performances in the east are still fresh in the memory. It should be no difficult task to maintain this prestige and win out handily from Stanford in the 'varsity games. Brown seems to be going about the matter of training and exercise with a very commendable caution. Most captains have the mistaken notion that in order to show their energy and capability they must work their teams hard. Brown, however, laid off his entire force for nearly a month during midwinter, and only set to work again about two weeks ago. The present scheme of training, as laid out by the coaches, does not include actual work on the track; this will come later, when the men begin to specialize in their particular events. At present the practice is of a general character, calculated to develop wind and stamina, and to loosen the leg and chest muscles.

There are fifty men in training (a good showing when it is remembered that there are but a dozen first places to be filled). Captain Brown assembles these men in the gymnasium every afternoon and puts them through a half hour's grind on the chest weights, after which they are put on the indoors running-track of the gymnasium for about fifteen or twenty minutes. The coachers have decided upon varying the work as much as possible. This is an admirable idea, for it may be said, speaking in a general way, that in preliminary training four quarters of an hour, spent in four different kinds of exercise, is far more beneficial than one hour's work at one particular exercise. Consequently Al. Lean frequently lines up his athletes for a game of basketball, twenty on a side, or leads them a zig-zag chase over the lower floor of the gymnasium. The afternoon's work closes with a bath and a rubdown. Brown has his men well under control, and new men, or those who are slightly injured, are given the lightest kind of work. In general the policy of the coachers is not to get the men into condition early in the season, and to spend a precious amount of energy in keeping them in good form, but rather to train them slowly and gradually, bringing them into championship shape only a day or two before the meet, in order that the runners, jumpers, weight-putters and the like may be, as nearly as possible, in the very pink of condition when they shall compete with their Cardinal rivals.

One of the best men of the lot is Everett J. Brown himself, the captain. He is a long-distance man, and the college looks to him to capture the mile run. He was chosen for the eastern trip, but at the last moment was unable to go. He now holds the U.C. record for the mile run.

Harry Humphrey is one of those "all-round" athletes who could be trained to excel in almost any event. He will make a specialty of the 440-yard run, in which he has never been beaten. In '94 he won the quarter-mile run and also a place in the high jump.

Melville Dozier was the bicycle rider and broad jumper of the Eastern team. At Denver in '95 he entered his first high-jumping contest, and won at five feet eight. Dozier will not go in for bicycling this year, but will devote himself to high and broad jumping. Great things are expected of him in these events. In his Freshman year he broad-jumped 21 feet 11 3/4 inches.

Barnes is the U.C.'s crack sprinter. He was a member of the Eastern team and on the trip did the hundred in 10 1/5 seconds and the two-twenty in 22 2/5 seconds. There is no telling how fast Barnes may run, as he has continued to improve steadily during the last two years.

Ralph Lloyd is another "all-round man," with remarkable records in half a dozen different events. In practice he has put the shot 42 feet. He broad-jumps over 20 feet, and high-jumps 5 feet 5 inches. He holds the pole-vaulting record for the P.C.A.A., at 10 feet 9 1/2 inches. Owing to a bad knee Lloyd was unable to finish the pole-vaulting contest with Stanford in the last inter-collegiate meet, but gave it to Dole when the crossbar had reached an altitude of 10 feet 10 1/2 inches.

A California Artist

Charles Rollo Peters and His
Pictures of Monterey Moonlights

The Wave, 16 (6 February 1897), 9.

Peters met us at the gate, standing on the steps that were the vertebrae of a whale. He was booted to the knee, and wore a sweater and a sombrero, and looked just as picturesque as I had hoped and expected an artist should look. I suppose one is always on the lookout for pictures and scenes about an artist's habitat, and would persist in seeing them whether they existed or not. But at any rate I was rather impressed with all this, because it was unique and characteristic of a California artist. In Brittany he would have worn sabots and a beret, and perhaps a "blouse." In England it would have been a velvet jacket, but in Monterey, mark you, the artist wears a sombrero and high boots, and stands on steps that are the joints of a whale's spine. Where else would you see an artist with such attributes? We went into the studio.

Redwood, unfinished, and a huge north light, a couch or two, a black dog, lots of sunshine, and an odor of good tobacco. On every one of the four walls, pictures, pictures, and pictures. Mostly moonlights, painted very broad and flat, as though with Brobdingnag brushes. And in one corner a huge panel-like painting very striking, a sheer cliff, tremendously high, overlooking a moonlit ocean. On the edge—but the very uttermost edge, you understand—a man standing, wearing a cocked hat and a great coat. There was nothing more, not a single detail, and the man was standing with his back turned, yet was it Bonaparte and St. Helena, beyond all shadow of doubt. Clever, you say? Enormously so, I say. A single huge broad "note," as it were, simple, strong, conveying but a single impression, direct as a blow.

Peters told me he was "going in" for moonlights. That's a good hearing for his style, as the art critic would say, is "admirably adapted" for those effects where all detail is lost in enormous flat masses of shadow. Just the effect to be seen on a moonlight night.

"You would be surprised," says Peters, "to see how many different kinds of moons there are." He illustrated what he said by indicating one and another of the sketches. "There is the red moon, when she's very low, and the yellow moon of the afternoon, and the pure white moon of midnight, and the blurred, pink moon of a misty evening, and the vari-tinted moon of the dawning. She's never the same. Here are two *ébauches*, made on succeeding days, at the same time, and from the same place. Yet observe the difference." There was, indeed, a tremendous difference. I became interested. "It's the specialists," Peters continued, "that 'arrive' now-a-days, whether they specialize on diseases of the ear, or on the intricacies of the law of patents, or on Persian coins of the 14th century."

"Or on pictures of moonlight," said I.

"Precisely; that's my specialty."

Peters lives in Monterey on a hill-top, and paints from dawn to dark. After dark he goes out and looks at the moon, and the land and the shore in her light, and at the great cypresses. He don't paint there. Just looks and looks, and takes mental photographs, as it were—impressions he remembers and paints the next day. Singularly enough Peters, though going in for moonlights, does not paint them *en plein air*—how could he, for the matter of that, without any light to see by?—but he does take a sort of combination note and sketch book along with him. He showed this to me.

Here and there were mazes of pencil scratching, and the pages are almost unintelligible to any one but Peters himself, and written over them and in them were such words as "blue," "carmine and cobalt," "warm gray," "sienna," "bitumen" and "red," etc.—notes merely to help along in the more finished picture.

Peters thinks Monterey should be a great place for artists. He has sketched nearly everywhere, and maintains that there is more artistic "stuff" right down there in the old town than there is in Barbizon, even, or in the artist towns of Brittany. A few artists, in fact, have already "discovered" the place—artists who since have been *médaillés* and have acquired greatness. Harrison himself, that Alexander the Great of marine painters, was here for a time, and Julian Rix, and Tavermeir and others, but none of whom have studied, really studied—in a careful, almost scientific fashion—the moonlight effects of the place as has Peters. There are two ways of painting a moonlight sky—one as I have seen it done by scores of artists hitherto, who paint in the sky a sort of indeterminate dark gray or very "warm" black. The other way is as Peters does it. Night skies are blue—deep, deep blue. Look into the sky the next time you are out at night. May be you thought the sky was black at night. Look at it. Blue! of course it's blue—bluer than the bluest thing you ever saw. But I never noticed the fact until Peters' pictures called my attention to it.

The interior of Peters' house, by the way—not his studio, but his house— is a picture in itself. He has a wonderful collection of arms, furniture, carpets, china, stuffs and the like—something really extraordinary. There are old Delft mugs, and a chair of brocade silk that Josephine once used at Mal Maison, and a ship-model of ivory presented to Bonaparte by the city of Toulon, original editions of Buffon, worth more than their weight in silver, and an old bed—one of the boxed-in kind, with sliding doors—from Brittany, that the guest still sleeps in—a marvel of carving, with the genuine Breton bird and worm design upon it, that stamps it at once as the rarest of curios.

I was wondering how large must have been the sum that Peters was obliged to pay for the wonder, when by one of those extraordinary coincidences that are all the time happening, he said: "I gave the fellow twenty-five dollars for that bed."

Charles Rollo Peters and his celebrated portrait of Napoleon.
Courtesy of the California State Library, Sacramento.

The Making of a Statue

How the Native Sons' Group is Moulded and Cast

The Wave, 16 (13 February 1897), 4.

When Mr. Douglas Tilden had finished the clay model for the Native Sons' monument, and it became a question as to where the bronze should be cast, the donor, Mr. Phelan, said:

"Have it done in San Francisco, no matter what the cost."

So it is being done in San Francisco now, and it is costing about one dollar for every pound of metal cast, and the modeling sand has to be brought from France, and one of the workmen as well.

The casting of a bronze statue is not without a certain amount of interest, especially when one takes into consideration the amount of labor and pains and scrupulous care that is involved. At present the monument is in a rather confused condition. One part of it is still in Mr. Tilden's hands, hardly more than a rough lump of clay; another part—a pair of legs and a belted waist—is being covered with molding sand by the imported Frenchman spoken of, and a third portion is bronze already, complete and ready for mounting as soon as it has been retouched by the "chaser."

The casting of a bronze statue is after this fashion: The moulders receive from the hands of the artist the clay model of a certain portion of the statue or group. This is carefully covered with a kind of moist sand that is found at its best in France. More time is spent, perhaps, over this part of the process than over any other. It is this work that the Frenchman was brought over to do. The clay—or, rather, the plaster of Paris model that is taken from the clay—is covered with three layers of sand packed and patted down by hand and tamped solidly afterward with little rammers. However, the sand that is to cover the faces of the figures is sifted very finely to obviate all the little irregularities and pits that would be made by pebbles and hard lumps of foreign earths. This sand is next baked for over two days, until it is as hard, nearly, as a brick, and is broken off the clay model and put

250

together in sections.

A cast could be made from the mould as it is now, but it would be solid, and the resultant statue would be as unwieldy as a brownstone house and almost as expensive; so what is called a "core" is made, a third rougher moulding of sand inside of it some fraction of an inch smaller than the outer mould. This is the French method as used by Whyte and De Rome, and seems to be a great improvement on the American method, which involves no "core" and is enormously expensive.

The next step in the process is the melting and pouring of the metal. This is quite an affair, a ceremony at which the sculptor and the head of the firm and the subject himself assist, and to which they invite their friends. It is picturesque enough, for the molten bronze is of a lambent whiteness, spitting little green flames. Four huge crucibles, holding, let us say, three or four gallons apiece (if one can speak of metal by the gallon), contain the casting metal, white hot, and as liquid as milk. Six men staggering under the weight of it bring the crucible up and affix it to an enormous hook depending from a crane. The crane picks it up, swings it leisurely to the lip of the mould and cants it over, pouring out the dazzling white-hot bronze in a dense cloud of steam and a grand spattering and spluttering of red-hot drops as big as marbles. And straightway down in the depths of the mold, that looks most like a discarded packing box, the figure of a man is born—in this case the supplementary figure of a plainsman—the figure of a man in enduring bronze that shall look out over the city and its streets for countless years to come, shall speak an intelligible word to the men of the next century and to the century after that, and for a thousand years to come, for all you and I can tell, when you and all the rest of us shall have disintegrated into dust and clay—moulding clay, perhaps.

A South-Sea Expedition

One Hundred Colonists from California
Who Will Attempt the "Farthest West"

The Wave, 16 (20 February 1897), 8.

One hundred men went sailing out of this port yesterday "as the sun went down," bound for a little surf-ringed island, far down there in the South Pacific, down below the Paumoto group, below the Marquesas—below even the Gilberts. One hundred of them—workingmen for the most part—carpenters, joiners, machinists, a photographer, I believe, and (of course) one journalist.

I think they call themselves the South Pacific Colonization Company, and they are going down there to found and form a nation—practically, that is what it is. There are different ways of looking upon this business. You may consider it as a joke, if you will—a lark indulged in by certain wild fellows to go down there and seize the natives' land and the natives' women and live a luxurious life, made up largely of love, bread-fruit, and surf-bathing—or you may take it more seriously, especially after you have had a good look at some of the young men who are concerned—none of them of the vicious, irresponsible type—you may take it seriously, I say, and see in this ship's company of Americans, Germans and Englishmen the types of that sturdy, shouldering Anglo-Saxon race that, from the time of its first exodus from the salt marshes of Holland, have been steadily, stubbornly pushing west, pushing west, pushing west—sometimes in the dragon-beaked *snekkjas* of marauding Vikings, sometimes in the blunt-nosed, high-sterned packets of the Puritan fathers, sometimes in the trundling, creaking prairie-schooners of the Pioneers, and·last, in a two-stick trading brig called the *Percy Edwards*—transport vessel of the South Pacific Colonization Company.

I do not think that this is taking the affair too seriously. You may call these men adventurers if you choose, and they are adventurers, just as Drake was and the Northmen. The scheme may fail (colonization companies

252

are notoriously unstable), but the point is not that, so much as it is the fact that the great majority of these men are the big-boned, blonde, long-haired type—the true Anglo-Saxon type—and are responding to that same mysterious impulse that ever drives their race toward the setting sun—the same impulse that stirred in the shaggy, hide-clad breasts of their forefathers so many hundreds of years ago in the depths of the Frisian forests and swamps. Here it is again, working itself out under your very eyes. Consider it: we are here in the Far West, we other Anglo-Saxons; we have practically just arrived, and the place is hardly built up and made habitable when some hundred of us are already chafing at the barrier of the Pacific—are fitting out a ship and are going further west, further west.

Of course the newspapers have made capital out of the affair, and have exploited the idea of the Adamless Eden to which the colonists are steering. The island of Bougainville (the colony's home) is rather thickly populated with a race of cannibals, and the aggregate number of fighting men in the various tribes is close upon a thousand. So very important an item is this that every colonist is compelled to equip himself with a repeating rifle and a revolver—instruments that would be rarely out of place in an "Adamless Eden." It is, literally, the beginning of a history. You have gone right back three thousand years, right into the legends, to the time of the migrations (that's what this venture is—a tribal migration). You are back to first principles—to a primal condition of things, where all the old maxims are applicable as soon as the colony begins to work out. "The weakest to the wall," "the survival of the fittest," "the race to the swift," and "the battle to the strong." Every tub will stand on its own bottom on Bougainville Island, and a man is a man only in so far as he can shoot straight, work with his hands, and acquire food.

But for all that, complications are ahead for the South Pacific Colonization Company. No women are voyaging with them to their island home, so that perforce the existence of the colony depends upon the inter-marriages—let us call them marriages—of the colonists with the native women.

I do not think the colony will fail. The fellows look serious, sober, and steady. They are well armed, the conditions of life are absurdly easy, and the men are enthusiastic and determined. The trouble will come with their relations with the native women. That they will quarrel over them, fight over them, and perhaps slay each other over them, it is only natural to expect. It is almost inevitable. But if all comes well in the end, and the colony works out its own salvation, imagine the race that will be found there —say in about two hundred years (remember, you are dealing with history, now, and must reckon with big figures)—a race having in its veins the strain of Anglo-Saxon combined with that of the rich strong blood of a south sea savage—vigorous enough, surely.

Things and People

The Wave, 16 (6 March 1897), 7, paragraph 1.

John M. Oakley, a millionaire of Pittsburgh, a distinguished soldier, a well-known philanthropist, a member of the church, a husband and father, deliberately drank himself to death at the Palace Hotel this week in the company of a disreputable woman whom he had brought with him from the East. For seven days he drank steadily, eating scarcely nothing. It was a champagne debauch of a week's duration, while his heart beat slower and feebler, like a pendulum of a clock running down, and his nerves drew tighter and tighter till at length they snapped and crisped like broken banjo strings; the heart stopped, and it was time for the coroner and the reporter. There is a certain dramatic unreasonableness about this whole matter that is more striking than the actual death itself. For some fifty odd years John Oakley was at pains to build up a reputation as a good business man, a good citizen, a good father and a good husband. It has been learned that there was nothing vicious about the man. He was what the reporter calls "a prominent church member," and at the time of the Johnstown disaster was in the forefront of those who toiled to relieve the horror of the situation. The community respected him, he respected himself. Besides being a good man, he was a sensible man; he was no fool, he showed good judgment, moderation, solid business conservatism. Thus John Oakley lived for fifty years. If ever a man's character could be said to have formed it was in his case. Nothing erratic about him. His life had found its groove, and in it was running evenly. Then suddenly comes the San Francisco debauch, with the Booth woman, the man going back on every characteristic he had shown, upsetting every theory, overturning and destroying every previous idea of him. It is a sudden turn of character that no novelist even of the wildest imagination would dare put into a story. The thing is out of character with every indication of the fellow's personality. It is improbable, unheard of, absurdly forced, as unreal as the *Arabian Nights'* and as true as Zola. Even putting the man's "goodness" and uprightness aside, one must remember that Oakley was *par excellence* a sensible business man, no dreamer, no erratic, hot-tempered youth, yet he plays the fool, the utter, absolute, inexcusable fool upon a scale worthy of a Caracalla. He finds a woman of a disreputable house, a woman common as the city road, goes off with her upon a debauch of two weeks' duration and drinks champagne, as a suicide would drink a poison, until he kills himself with alcohol. There is no accounting for this thing, except upon one rather feeble hypothesis—that of the natural, innate vice common to humanity in general, slumbering and subdued in this man for fifty years suddenly rousing at the last moment, strong and vigorous from its long inertness, leaping to life all in an instant and overpowering and trampling under foot every barrier of custom and habit, every sense of restraint and temperance, clutching the man with an irresistible grip and worrying him to his dissolution ere he was aware. A strange, hideous end of an upright life; a case, perhaps, for our friend Lombroso.

Suggestions

The Wave, 16 (13 March 1897), 7.

1870.

The advanced post had made a barricade for themselves out of a vast quantity of furniture that had been flung out of the country house near by; sideboards, chairs, mattresses, a huge dining table and a big upright piano. Over this barricade leaned a sergeant and a corporal of the squad, scanning the country narrowly with fieldglasses.

One of the soldiers sitting on a packing case that had held cartridges was playing a song on the piano, singing the words at the same time. His head was wound up in a strip of brocaded satin torn from a chair back, for his temple had been laid open. It was bitter cold, and his feet were encased only in the cheap boots with pasteboard soles furnished by the government contractors; but he sang for all that at the top of his voice a pretty little song:

> *Tu m'as promis un baiser pour*
> *Ce soir, ma brune.*

On a sudden he stopped with a discord, and fell over upon the instrument, gulping up blood over the white ivory keys. A puff of blue smoke curled up from the window of the country house. The sergeant cried out, "*Alerte*, here they are; sight for one hundred meters."

***

A HOTEL BEDROOM.

The walls were whitewashed and bare of pictures or ornaments, and the floor was covered with a dull turkey red carpet. The furniture was a set, all the pieces having a family resemblance to each other. The bed stood against the right-hand wall, a huge double bed with the name of the hotel on the corners of its spread and pillow cases. In the exact middle of the room underneath the gas fixtures was the center table, and on it a pitcher of ice water and a porcelain match safe, with ribbed sides, in the form of a truncated cone. Precisely opposite the bed stood the bureau, near to the bureau was the door of the closet, and next to this in the corner was the washstand with its new cake of soap and its three clean, glassy towels. To the left of the door was the electric bell and the directions for using it; and on the door itself a card as to the hours for meals, the rules of the hotel and the extract from the code regulating the liabilities of innkeepers. The room was clean, aggressively, defiantly clean, and there was a smell of soap in the air.

It was bare of any personality; of the hundreds who had lived and suffered and perhaps died there, not a trace or suggestion remained. Their different characters had not left the least impress upon its air and appearance. Only a few hairpins were scattered on the bottom of one of the drawers and two forgotten medicine bottles still remained upon the top shelf of the closet.

***

BRUTE.

He had been working all day in a squalid neighborhood by the gas works and coal yards, surrounded by lifting cranes, piledrivers, dredging machines, engines of colossal, brutal strength, where all about him were immense blocks of granite, tons of pig iron; everything had been enormous, crude, had been huge in weight, tremendous in power, gigantic in size.

By long association with such things he had become like them, huge, hard, brutal, strong with a crude, blind strength, stupid, unreasoning. He was on his way home now, his immense hands dangling half-open at his sides; his head empty of thought. He only desired to be fed and to sleep. At a street crossing he picked up a white violet, very fresh, not yet trampled into the mud. It was a beautiful thing, redolent with the scent of the woods, suggestive of everything pretty and delicate. It was almost like a smile-made-flower. It lay very light in the hollow of his immense calloused palm. In some strange way it appealed to him, and blindly he tried to acknowledge his appreciation. He looked at it stupidly, perplexed, not knowing what to do; then instinctively his hand carried it to his mouth; he ground it between his huge teeth and slowly ate it. It was the only way he knew.

***

THE DENTAL PARLORS.

His office, or, as he called it, his Dental Parlors, was on the second floor over the butcher shop and faced the street. He made it do for a bedroom as well; there was a washstand behind the screen in the corner, where he made his moulds, and he slept on a big carpet lounge against the wall opposite the window. In the window itself, which was bay, was his operating chair, his dental engine, and his movable rack, where he laid out his instruments, burrs, extractors, pluggers, his spirit lamp and his pellets of sponge gold. Three chairs, a bargain at the second-hand store, were ranged against one wall with military precision, under a steel engraving of the court of Lorenzo de Medici, which he had bought because there were a great many figures in it for the price. Over the sofa hung a rifle manufacturer's advertisement-calendar, which he never used. The other ornaments were a small marble-top center table, covered with back numbers of the *Dentist's Monthly Manual*, a stone pug dog sitting before the little stove, and a thermometer. There was a stand of shelves in one corner filled with Allen's *Practical Dentist*. On the top shelf McTeague kept his concertina and the bag of bird seed for the canary. The whole place exhaled a mingled odor of bedding, creosote and ether.

A "Lag's" Release

How a Convict is Discharged from the San Quentin "Pen"

The Wave, 16 (27 March 1897), 4.

Everybody knows how a man goes to jail. A little legal jargon, a little "entering of names," a little posing for the Rogues' Gallery, a little trip across the bay, the shutting of a grated door—and there is your "con"—jugged in the "pen," perhaps for thirty months, perhaps for thirty years. During the time of his sentence the world knows absolutely nothing of him, and he nothing of the world. He is buried alive. Let us suppose he is a thirty-year man—consider for a moment what that means. Remember backward, if you can, for thirty years. Try to fix some event that happened thirty years ago, and then imagine that instead of that particular event happening, a prison door had closed behind you, and that all your life from that time till now had been spent in the "pen"—between four high cement walls. For recreation you had the yard to walk in, and the conversation of murderers and petit-larcenies and assault-to-kills; for occupation you wove one hundred yards of jute every morning; you ate, in enforced silence, three meals of beef, beans and coffee per day, and you were locked in your cell from three o'clock in the afternoon until seven the next morning. And this is your life for thirty years! The Civil War was barely over thirty years ago. Then comes the day when your sentence expires.

I knew a "con" at San Quentin named Bob Davis who had been in prison for thirty-five years, and whose sentence expired last Friday. I went over to see Mr. Davis early Friday morning, to watch how they let him out.

Now, my friend Bob Davis is a sneak-thief. He told me so, and it is the only thing he told me that the prison officers thought was true. I would have preferred him a murderer, a highwayman, or even an assault-with-a-deadly-weapon, but he is none of these—he is a sneak-thief. At the time I got inside the court of San Quentin penitentiary it was after six in the morning, and the "cons" were going in to breakfast. They came across from the yard, eleven hundred of them, each with his hands folded across his breast, in singularly inappropriate attitude of devout resignation, like monks going to confessional. They tramped into the huge dining-room and the first man went to the farthest seat at the farthest table and began to eat as soon as he sat down. The last man in the line took the only seat left nearest the door, but by the time he was sitting down the first man was through and was filing out, with arms meekly folded.

Davis was somewhere in the crowd of eleven hundred silent men, but I could not pick him out. I only met him when he came back to his cell after breakfast to get his bedding. I looked at him curiously then, as one would look at a man who is going back to liberty after thirty years of prison death-in-life. I was expecting anything. He might be elated over his thought of freedom; he might be depressed (I was ready even for this) at the idea of leaving his familiar cell, and I thought of the prisoner of Chillon and of De Quincey's *mot* to the effect that there is a certain sadness in doing anything for the last time, and that even a prisoner quits his cell with a feeling of regret. I had this last particularly in mind as Mr. Davis came up, and, as it were, I looked at him through it as through a colored glass. This liberation business is a little drama, and as star actor I hoped Mr. Davis would act up to his part.

Stolidity, indifference, phlegmatic unconcern—anything you like but excitement—was Davis' mood, and the worst of it was that he did not assume it. Set it down as an axiom, as a law to be carefully studied by writers of fiction, that the sensations of real life tend to the plane of the commonplace as inevitably as water seeks its level. Assume that everything is ordinary till it has been proven otherwise.

"Well," said I, "you're going out, Davis?"

"Yes," said he, tying his blanket-roll, "I'm going out." As far as his demeanor went he might have said, "I'm going across the yard a minute." He rolled up his blankets, gathered together one or two bits of furniture that the prison provides, and (I following) went across the court to the "old clothes room."

The old clothes room of San Quentin is where the prison suits are kept—the clothes, caps, shoes, and all that. It is most like a country store—a counter, a stove and racks along the wall filled with wearing apparel. The only difference is that the clothes are striped. A guard met us here and took charge of Davis, and he did not leave him during the rest of the time he was in the precincts of the jail. In the old clothes room Davis stripped and bathed. Captain Jameson, who presides here, took his "con's" suit and stowed it away, and Davis dressed himself again in a completely new outfit that Jameson gave him. The clothes were gray shoddy of the cheapest kind. If my "con" felt any glow of returning self-respect at the feel of citizen's clothes again he did not show it. He was not sullen, he was not sulking—he was merely ordinary. He spoke little. Next we went to the office of the Captain of the Guard. There was some conversation here. Davis gave his number, not his name, and told the Captain for what crime he was serving. Then says the Captain:

"Here is a ticket to Sunol. You were arrested there."

"Yes," answered Davis.

"And five dollars that the State gives you" (pushing a gold piece towards him). The "con" pocketed it silently.

"And here is the money found on you when arrested—seven dollars and a half."

"Seven dollars and a half."

The Captain of the Guard turned away.

From the prison to Greenbrae, where you take the train to the city, is about three miles. A 'bus runs to meet every train, and the ex-"cons" generally go down in it, but said Davis:

"I won't wait for the 'bus—I'll walk." We went toward the outside gate of the prison. Once beyond this gate Davis was free. The crisis of this little drama of liberation was here. A turnkey swung open an inside grating for us. We went down a narrow stone passage to the outer gate, through whose grating one could see blue patches of the bay and of the sky. A second turnkey swung the outside gate, letting in a warm puff of air.

"Wait a minute," said Davis' guard, as the man who had been jailed for thirty years stepped forward. Davis stopped, and the guard handed him two or three folded papers with official seals.

"These are your restoration papers," he explained, adding, "they restore your citizenship to you." Silently Davis put them in his inside pocket. There was a pause. The turnkey stood holding open the grating. The guard drew back a step. I was in the background watching. Between the turnkey and the guard was the ex-"con." He was older than any of us, and taller.

Suddenly, back in the prison, the whistle of the jute-mill blew, signalling the beginning of another day's work.

"Well," said Davis, breaking the silence, "anything more?"

"Nothing more," answered the guard; "go on."

Davis stepped across the threshold and walked down the road into the world. He was free.

Among Cliff-Dwellers

A Peculiar Mixture of Races
From the Four Corners of the Earth

The Wave, 16 (15 May 1897), 6.

Of course one has heard of the strangeness of the neighborhoods upon Telegraph Hill, and of course one has read a good deal in Bret Harte and Stevenson upon the subject, but the curiousness of the place cannot be altogether appreciated at second hand. You are told, for instance, that to enter this locality is to be transported to another country—to Italy, to France, or to Spain, as the case may be. This is quite true, but it is not all. The foreignness of, let us say, Ohio street, is complete, and yet one fancies that one would recognize San Francisco in the place if one should suddenly drop into it out of the blue, as it were. They are a queer, extraordinary mingling of peoples, these Cliff Dwellers, for they are isolated enough to have begun already to lose their national characteristics and to develop into a new race. There are children romping about after hens perilously near that tremendous precipice that overhangs the extension of Sansome street, of an origin so composite that not even the College of Heralds could straighten the tangle. Here, for instance, is a child of an Italian woman and a Spanish half-breed. Think of that now! The descendant of a Campagnian peasant, a Pueblo Indian and a water carrier of Andalusia, squattering up and down a San Francisco sidewalk, shrieking after an hysterical chicken. But there are queerer combinations than that. I have seen in a wine shop in this same Ohio street a child who was half Jew, half Chinese, and its hair was red. I have heard of—may I yet live to see him!—a man who washes glasses in a Portuguese wine shop on the other side of the hill, whose father was a Negro and whose mother a Chinese slave girl. As I say, I have not yet set eyes on this particular Cliff Dweller. I can form no guess as to what his appearance should be. Can you? Imagine the Mongolian and African types merged into one. He should have the flat nose, and yet the almond eye, the thick lip and yet the high cheek-bone; but how as to his hair? Should it be short and crinkly, or long and straight, or merely wavy? But the ideas of the man, his bias, his prejudices, his conception of things, his thoughts—what a jumble, what an amorphous, formless mist!

But there is still another kind of Cliff Dweller—him I know and have talked with. He was watching a man paint a bunch of grapes upon the sign of a wine shop (there are neither bars, nor saloons, nor "resorts" in the country of the Cliff Dwellers, only wine shops), and on pretense of asking a direction I had some little speech with him. He was a very, very old Spaniard, and rather feeble. Do you know that this man has never—but from a distance—seen the Emporium, nor the Mills building, nor the *Call* building, nor the dome of the City Hall; that he would be lost on Kearny or Market street, that he hears or reads in the papers of plays given at the Baldwin or California or Columbia as we hear or read of a new Massenet opera in Paris or a piece at the Comédie Française or a successful ballet at La Scala? For eight years this old man has never been down into the city. Old age has trapped him on the top of that sheer hill, and lays siege to him there. Once up here he must stay, or if possibly he should get down, never could he climb those ladder-like sidewalks. No cable cars run over the hill, and the horses of the market carts pause on a corner one-third of the way up, blowing till the cart rattles, while their drivers make the delivery on foot. This old man will never come down but feet first. The world rolls by beneath him, under his eyes and in reach of his ears; Kearny street, like the dried bed of a canyon overrun with beetles, hums and lives beneath his back windows, and ships from the Horn and the Cape and the Archipelago shift and slide below the sea-ward streets, and he sees it all and hears it all and is yet as out of it, as exiled from it as if marooned on a South Pacific atoll. Perched on that high hill in the heart of the city, he is a hermit, a Simon Stylites on a huge scale.

The houses are as indeterminate as the inhabitants. But while the Cliff Dwellers themselves are busily at the work of race forming, new and vigorous, the buildings are rapidly going to wrack, plaster is crumbling, brick walls disintegrating, wooden rails worn to a rosewood polish, trembling and reeling drunkenly over the steep slopes. You may see them by the score, these collapsing buildings, the frailer and feebler ones invariably clinging to the very edge of the precipitous banks of the hill, like weaker things pushed to the wall. They are patched up indiscriminately, on stilts and beams, as if upon false legs or crutches, and the wind shoulders them grudgingly toward the brink, and their old bones rattle and quake with every blast from the excavations that are going forward half way down the hill. My old man, the hermit, the castaway, told me of an ancient lady who lives in one of the shanties that are clawing and clutching at the verge of the cliff, who, with her house, will some day be quite literally blown over the ledge. At night when the west wind blows (you may imagine for yourselves how strong can be this wind coming in from the Farallones to the Cliffs at a single hungry leap), this ancient lady sits up till dawn quaking with the quaking of the house, ready to make a wild scramble to the door as soon as the stilts begin to go.

The houses of these people are of no particular style. Some are of plaster over brick, with a second story piazza, Mexican fashion; some with flat faces and false fronts, and some with bays that are all glass in little frames somehow suggestive of the sea. There are even some with the blunt gable and green blinds that recall New England, and now and then one comes across a miserable, senile, decrepit, rabbit warren of an old villa, the cupola turned into a bed room, a wretched green fountain sunken into the hard-beaten earth of what was once a lawn, a goat or two looking through the crazy pickets and a litter of kittens on a sunny corner of the porch roof. Thus they have their being, the Cliff Dwellers of this San Francisco of ours; mountaineers, if you will; race formers. The hill is swarming and boiling with the life of them. Here on this wart-like protuberance bulging above the city's roof, a great milling is going on, and a fusing of peoples, and in a few more generations the Celt and the Italian, the Mexican and the Chinaman, the Negro and the Portuguese, and the Levantines and the "scatter-mouches" will be merged into one type. And a curious type it will be.

The First Born

A Bit of Chinese Life Portrayed on the Alcazar Stage

The Wave, 16 (22 May 1897), 4.

Good things are coming out of Galilee nowadays, and by that I mean that there are a number of writers—they are all young—in San Francisco, who are writing fiction about San Francisco and San Francisco people and the strange, mixed life that is at ferment at our very horse blocks. The novelist is not yet, but the short story writer is abroad, Kodaking and observing, and now the dramatist has made an appearance.

I am very enthusiastic in the matter of Mr. Powers' little play at the Alcazar. It is a new note, and if it does not ring absolutely true, it does at least sound an alarm. Consider now, you who have seen *The First Born*. Ask yourself why it was you were charmed with the thing. What was it that held you there from curtain to curtain, breathless, very intent? As far as plot and situation and character go there is nothing extraordinary about it. We have seen deserted husbands and stolen children and assassinations and the like on the stage before. But take Loey Tsing, for instance—have you ever in all your experience as a theatre-goer, whether in New York, London, or Paris, no matter where, the world round, seen her before—a Chinese slave girl, created simply and with some attempt at realism? You will say, of course, *The Mikado* and *The Geisha Girl*. But the Mikado and the Geisha are merely Caucasians in Chinese clothes. Loey Tsing and Man Lo Yek and Doctor Pow Len and all the rest of them are the real, true Chinese of San

Francisco, treated seriously and from the Chinese point of view, and the mounting—the scene before the Ming Yen temple, and the little alley of the second act—is as true to life as a photograph. The play is thoroughly, purely Chinese in conception and in execution, and the characters are live Chinamen, who look, and talk, and act,—yes, and think—like Chinamen. Never, so far as I know, has the subject been thus treated on the stage hitherto. It is new, new, new. One cannot insist too much upon its newness—its originality. *The First Born*, from this point of view, is perhaps the most important play that has ever been produced in San Francisco.

Briefly, this is the story of the play: Man Lo Yek, an old-clothes dealer, living in San Francisco's Chinatown, has for wife Loey Tsing. But in course of time, tiring of her, he wins over the affections of the woman Chan Lu, wife of Chan Wong. Loey Tsing he sells into a life of shame. Chan Wong is left alone with his little boy, Chan Toy. The whole point of the play is here, in the affection that the deserted husband has for his little son. It would appear that the paternal affection for the first born son is the predominant passion of the Chinaman, taking precedence over that which he bears for his wife. Marriage with him is a mere matter of course, but the birth of his first son is the event round which his life is centered. You see that Mr. Powers is writing from the Chinese point of view. To have caused the play to turn upon the wife's desertion of the husband would have been to distort and warp the Chinese character to suit European-Caucasian ideas. Chan Wong has no great affection for his faithless wife—it is the boy for whom he cares. One day his son is stolen. The distracted father searches Chinatown for him in vain. Loey Tsing, the slave girl, at length informs him that Man Lo Yek and Chan Lu (who are supposed to have fled to Oregon) have returned in secret to Chinatown; had been there that day—the day of the disappearance of the child. Chan Wong discovers the house in which they live, dashes in and up the narrow stairs, knife in hand, only to reappear an instant later bearing in his arms the dead body of his little son, Chan Toy. This is the end of the first act. The second and last act is merely the story of Chan Wong's revenge. There is a very pretty scene between him and Loey Tsing—she at her window, he at his doorway underneath. Enter to them Man Lo Yek, and then, on the impulse of the moment, Chan Wong becomes a hatchet-man, leaps upon him as he passes, cuts him down with his cleaver, drags the body into the house, and a second later resumes his position in his doorway, calm and impassive, smoking his pipe, which has not even had time to go out.

That is the whole play—on paper. You must see it to appreciate it, and you must see it with understanding eyes. It has all the value of a discovery, a really great discovery—the discovery of a new field. Mr. Powers is not Kipling, but he has done for Chinatown what the "chee-chee" did for the native of India, and he has gone about it in precisely the right spirit—the spirit of realism, portraying his people precisely as they are, making an attempt to honestly understand them, to appreciate their loves and their hatreds, their prejudices and superstitions and limitations. This thing—this strange, transplanted Mongolian life—has been teeming under our very eyes for nearly half a century, and has been overlooked—by dramatists, at least. "The man with the muck-rake" does find gold after all, sometimes. Mr. Powers might have tried his hand at the old style of drama, which we all know by heart—the familiar types, the hackneyed dialogue, the threadbare situations, ideas taken second- and third-hand from other men's plays—and we would never have given him another thought. He wrote instead *The First Born*, and all San Francisco is agog over it.

The Puppets and the Puppy

Disrespectfully Dedicated to Annie Besant

The Wave, 16 (22 May 1897), 5.

"There are more things in your philosophy than
are dreamed of in Heaven and Earth."

CHARACTERS:

A Lead Soldier.   A Doll.   A Mechanical Rabbit.
A Queen's Bishop (from the chessboard).
Japhet (a wooden Mannikin from the Noah's Ark).
Sobby (the Foxterrier puppy).

Scene—A corner of the play-room carpet.

Time—The night after Christmas.

The Lead Soldier: Well, here we are, put into this Room, for something, we don't know what; for a certain time, we don't know how long; by somebody, we don't know who. It's awful!

The Doll: And yet we know—I think I can speak for all of us—we know that there is a Boy.

The Mechanical Rabbit (reflectively): The Boy—the Boy—it's a glimpse into the infinite.

The Queen's Bishop: Boy, forsooth! There is no Boy, except that which exists in your own imaginations. You have created a figment—a vast terrible, empty nothing, to complement your own imperfections. I have

268

given great thought to the matter. There is, perhaps, a certain Force that moves us from time to time—a certain vague power, not ourselves, that shifts us here and there. All of us chessmen believe in that. We are the oldest and highest cult of you all. But even this—what shall I call it?—this Force, is not omnipotent. It can move us only along certain lines. I still retain my individuality—still have my own will. My lines are not those of the knight, or the pawn, or the castle, and no power in the Room can make them so. I am a free agent—that's what is so terrible.

The Doll: Ah, you think you've solved it all—you, with your science and learning. There is a Boy, and I am made in his image.

The Lead Soldier: And I.

Japhet: And I.

The Mechanical Rabbit: Yes, yes, the Doll must be right. Who else could have implanted within me this strange power of playing upon these cymbals? Somebody must have wound me up. I say it was the Boy.

Japhet: But, come now; let us consider a moment. One thing we can all agree upon. Some day, sooner or later, we shall be Thrown-away. It is the inevitable end of all toys. We shall be Thrown-away and go to the Garret. Then what?

The Doll: Dreadful question.

Japhet: This is what I believe: Some day I shall be Thrown-away and go on that last voyage to the Garret, but not forever. I look forward to a time when I shall be made of rosewood instead of common pine, and shall have a white shellac finish instead of this base coating of non-poisonous paint, and I shall live forever in a Noah's Ark of silver.

The Lead Soldier: What childish fallacy! It is against all reason to regard our lot as such infantile trickery. I, too, some day shall be Thrown-away, but my conception of immortality is no such child's play as this. No; in course of time I shall be re-melted and cast again to form another lead soldier, who in his turn shall be re-melted and re-cast, and so on and on, forever and ever.

The Queen's Bishop: Dreams! dreams! dreams! What butterflies you chase! What phantoms you hug! After I have been Thrown-away, I shall gradually rot and decay, and fall to dust, and be finally absorbed by the elements——

The Doll: And lose your identity? Never! Listen to me. I feel that in me

269

there are three individualities, each of them me, and a fourth which is of Me, yet not in Me—the Not-me. There is the sawdust, the kid, and the china—a trinity. Then there is that mysterious something which cries "Papa! Mama!" when the Boy presses on my chest. This is the Not-me. This is the part of me that shall last after I'm Thrown-away. That is my conception of immortality.

The Lead Soldier (soliloquizing): And each time I am re-melted and re-cast I become a finer soldier—larger, firmer on my base, more life-like. Thus the race is improved. Immortality is but the betterment of the race.

The Mechanical Rabbit (decisively): When I am Thrown-away that's the end of me—it's annihilation.

The Lead Soldier (after a pause): Tell me this: Why was Falling-down brought into the Room? Here is another thing we are all at one upon—that it is wrong to Fall-down. It displeases the Boy.

The Queen's Bishop (sotto voce): The Force that moves us, you mean.

The Mechanical Rabbit: That's all very well. I can see how it is wrong, horribly and fearfully wrong, for the Lead Soldier to Fall-down, when the Boy sets him in his ranks and he Falls-down, he drags with him the whole line of other soldiers. The wrongdoing does not stop with himself—it communicates itself to others. It is a taint that progresses to infinity. But why should it be wrong for me to Fall-down? I hurt no one but myself.

The Queen's Bishop: It is wrong for you as well as for the Lead Soldier and myself. You can know nothing of the vast, grand scheme of the Room. Suppose I should Fall-down whenever I chose, and knock over, say, the king, or the castles—what a calamity it would be! It would disarrange the vast, grand plan of events. No, no; in keeping upright we are only helping on the magnificent, incomprehensible aim of the Room. The same moral law applies to us all. What's wrong for one is wrong for us all.

The Lead Soldier: But what shall we say in a case like this? The other day the Boy took hold of the drummer of my squad, and twisted and bent his standard so that he could no longer stand. He put him in the line, and naturally he Fell-down. Then the Boy threw him away. Was it the drummer's fault, I ask? Why should he be punished for falling down, when the Boy himself twisted his standard? And again, I have heard of lead soldiers who never could stand because of some fault in the casting. Were they to blame? They were doomed before they were cast, and were Thrown-away afterward.

Japhet: Dreadful problem! Any day the Boy may pull off my standard and Throw me away.

The Queen's Bishop: We cannot understand these things, but there must be reason in them. But if you come to that, why are we here anyhow? I owe my existence to the turning lathe. Did I ask to be turned?

The Mechanical Rabbit: Or I to be made?

Japhet: Or I to be whittled?

The Doll: Or I to be stuffed?

The Lead Soldier: Or I to be moulded? If I had been given choice in the matter I would have chosen to be the general of my box, who sits on a horse that is rearing up, and points with his sword. Accident alone put him there. His lead is no better than mine, and his uniform is only paint-deep. In the re-melting, perhaps, he may be cast as a private and I as the general.

[Sobby, the Foxterrier puppy, pushes open the door of the room with his nose. His eye falls upon the mechanical rabbit. He rushes at it, shakes it between his teeth, and in a few minutes has worried it to an unrecognizable mass of skin and springs. Then he turns upon the doll, whom he likewise destroys. He chews the head from Japhet, and, with a movement of his paw, knocks the lead soldier down the register. Then he growls and scrabbles over the Queen's Bishop till it, as well, tumbles down the register. The Queen's Bishop disappears, muttering, vaguely, something about the "vast, resistless forces of nature."]

An Opening for Novelists

Great Opportunities for Fiction-Writers in San Francisco

The Wave, 16 (22 May 1897), 7.

There are certain cities in the world which are adaptable to the uses of the writer of fiction, and there are others which are not. Things can happen in some cities and the tale of them will be interesting; the same story laid in another city would be ridiculous. It is hard to say, why this is so, but a moment's review of the world's centers with this thought in mind will prove the truth of the statement beyond any shadow of doubt. Paris, London and Rome are "good material." Berlin, Vienna and Hamburg are not. Stories of New Orleans or of Constantinople could easily be made interesting, but no romancer has yet had the hardihood to attempt to write of Chicago or Buffalo. Imagine a novel of Chicago. The fact is very curious and the choice very arbitrary. There seems to be no rule applicable. A city need not necessarily be old, nor a seaport, nor "cosmopolitan," nor picturesque, nor beautifully built, nor large nor small. Any one who has the instinct for fiction can tell on the instant whether or not it is suitable as a background for a novel, a short story or a drama.

But consider San Francisco. It is not necessary to hesitate a moment. "Things can happen" in San Francisco. Kearny street, Montgomery street, Nob Hill, Telegraph Hill, of course Chinatown, Lone Mountain, the Poodle Dog, the Palace Hotel and the What Cheer House, the Barbary Coast, the Crow's Nest, the Mission, the Bay, the Bohemian Club, the Presidio, Spanish town, Fisherman's wharf.

There is an indefinable air about all these places that is suggestive of stories at once. You fancy the names would look well on a book's page. The people who frequent them could walk right into a novel or short story and be at home.

It occurs to me that there is perhaps one feature of the city that conduces to this effect, that is its isolation. Perhaps no great city of the world is so isolated as we are. Did you ever think of that? There is no great city to the north of us, to the south none nearer than Mexico, to the west is the waste of the Pacific, to the East the waste of the deserts. Here we are set down as a pin point in a vast circle of solitude. Isolation produces individuality, originality. The place has grown up independently. Other cities grow by accretion from without. San Francisco must grow by expansion from within; and so we have time and opportunity to develop certain unhampered types and characters and habits unbiased by outside influence, types that are admirably adapted to fictitious treatment.

It is a significant fact that the little that has been done in the way of gripping hold upon and impressing this life of ours between the covers of works of fiction has been done in the way of short stories. London had her Dickens, New Orleans her Cable, New York her Davis, Boston her Howells, Paris her Zola, but San Francisco still waits for her novelist. She will wait long, we believe. The conditions of our life are suited finely to the short story, but not as yet to the novel. We are growing and living, as it were, in spots, here a little and there a little, scattered bits of life and movement, quite independent of each other—short stories that are happening every day. But we are not settled enough yet for the novelist, who demands large, coordinated, broad and simple lines upon which to work, something far more unified than we can yet give him. But the short stories. There's the chance. Who shall be our Kipling? Where is the man who shall get at the heart of us, the blood and bones and fiber of us, who shall go a-gunning for stories up and down our streets and into our houses and parlors and lodging houses and saloons and dives and along our wharves and into our theaters; yes, and into the secretest chambers of our homes as well as our hearts?

Les Jeunes. Yes, there are *Les Jeunes*, and *The Lark* was delightful—delightful fooling, but there's a graver note and a more virile to be sounded. *Les Jeunes* can do better than *The Lark*. Give us stories now, give us men, strong, brutal men, with red-hot blood in 'em, with unleashed passions rampant in 'em, blood and bones and viscera in 'em, and women, too, who move and have their being, people who love and hate, something better now than Vivettes and Perillas and Goops. They are here, these living men and women. Think of the short stories that are happening every hour of the time. Get hold of them, some of you younger writers, grip fast upon the life of them. It's the Life that we want, the vigorous, real thing, not the curious weaving of words and the polish of literary finish. Damn the "style" of a story, so long as we get the swing and rush and trample of the things that live. While you are rounding a phrase a sailor has been shanghaied down there along the water front; while you are sustaining a metaphor, another See Yup has been hatcheted yonder in Gamblers' Alley; a man has time to be stabbed while you are composing a villanelle; the crisis of a life has come and gone while you have been niggling with your couplet. "Murder and sudden death," say you? Yes, but it's the life that lives; it's reality, it's the thing that counts. We don't want literature, we want life. We don't want fine writing, we want short stories. Kipling saw it here and Stevenson as they passed through—read the unwritten tales of us as they ran.

The tales are here. The public is here. A hundred clashing presses are hungry for you, future young story-writer of San Francisco, whoever you may be. Strike but the right note, and strike it with all your might, strike it with iron instead of velvet, and the clang of it shall go the round of the nations.

A qui le tour, who shall be our Kipling?

Metropolitan Noises

The Gamut of Sounds
Which Harass the Ears of San Franciscans

The Wave, 16 (22 May 1897), 9.

Perhaps it is because of the irregular cobbling of the streets, or perhaps because of the clearness of the atmosphere, or of the absence of certain anti-nuisance regulations, but for some reason or other this San Francisco of ours is one of the noisiest cities between the oceans. Put your head from the office window some day about 11 o'clock, or, failing that, pause for an instant as you read these words and listen to the sound the city makes in its living. You will notice there are two parts to this sound, two registers as one might say. First there is the multifarious staccato notes, brief, incisive, a world of little sharp, high-keyed ear-jars, but under these, below these (you wouldn't hear it at first, and it takes some little application to catch it), comes a low pitch bourdon, a protracted baser hum, arising, God knows where. You may hear this diapason from the city better at night, and it is much the same sound as that thrown off by the sea or by the wind in a forest or by a distant multitude.

It is a vast, huge, soothing murmur, rather agreeable than otherwise—a sort of music. The other register is the one that harries you. Listen to it long enough and it will "get on your nerves." A physician told me once, that in all the range of science there was nothing more irritating to a nervous patient than noise.

That's why you will now and then see tan bark before some of the city's houses, where some nervous patient is lying sick. It will not do, it seems, to stop this patient's ears with wax or cotton. It is surprising to know that your ears are not your only sound transmitters. You can picture sound waves striking against the teeth and against the "mastoid process," the round bone behind the ear.

Did you ever notice how plainly you can hear the ringing of the bell of a cable car? As you sit in your office window, for instance, you can distinguish the shrieking of that little saucer of metal as plainly as you can catch the hideous rattling of that load of iron rails or the roll of that huge truck. It appears that the reason for this lies in the fact that the vibrations of the bell are rhythmic and will carry farther than those of the rails or the wheels of the truck, which are not. But it is a great gamut for you, the noises of this city's thoroughfares. I suppose there is a part of us, after all, a certain savage, primitive, uncouth part, that rejoices in noise, for noise's sake. Else would we all live in the country, beyond ear-shot of the load of rails, the jangling of cable-car bells, the chanting of newsboys, the demoniac yells of the "fresh-strawberry" hucksters, or the incantation of the "rags-bottles-sacks" man, where we would never be obliged to hear a brake yelp against a dusty tire, or dodge the scissors-grinder at his awful trade.

Perhaps you will never quite appreciate the importance of the noises of the city's streets until you shall fall ill—especially of a nervous complaint. Then you will realize the weight of my physician's words when he said that nothing could be more harrowing and more hurtful to a nervous patient than noise. In some highly organized subjects it will produce hysteria, mild insanity, becoming, in fact, a positive physical torture. The lower the type, however, the less irritating is the effect produced. With the savage, noise is music and music noise, but delicate and highly specialized organisms can be influenced by sound as mercury is influenced by temperature. Ears such as this can find music where you and I would only find noise. That is, in scientific terms, they can distinguish the rhythmic quality of the vibration, for in this lies the only difference between music and mere noise, noise being only a series of vibrations which have no rhythm.

Japanese Swordsmanship

Fencing as Practiced by the Mikado's Subjects in This City

The Wave, 16 (29 May 1897), 8.

My friend Kurowaza first told me about the Japanese fencing club, and in the same breath asked me to come to one of its meetings. The club numbers 150 regular members, and Kurowaza is the President. Unfortunately many of the fencers are out of town for the summer, but enough of them got together of a Monday morning of this week to give one a fairly good impression of the game.

The club has its headquarters in a little court just off O'Farrell street, in the Japs' quarter, and when I arrived some half-dozen swordsmen were already on the spot and engaged in putting on their costumes or uniforms, one hardly knows which to call them. It is picturesque enough, this fencing accoutrement of theirs, and the color of it is stunning, dull, stone blues and sombre reds and olive greens with here and there a vivid wink of orange. The helmet is a cumbersome affair, quite unlike the wire mask of the

European fencer. It is quilted over the top and sides of the head and the bars are of steel and as thick as a pencil. The breast-plate is of stout *papier mâché*, lacquered to a fine glaze, while from beneath hangs a long skirt, the last garment you would suppose a fencer would elect to wear.

The weapon is, of course, the sword, not the little wisp of steel of the foil or rapier, but a ponderous, hacking arrangement to be wielded in two hands, heavy enough, murderous enough, to cleave you a man to the chin if desired. This for the serious business of life—or death. For practice and sport a sham sword is made of withes of bamboo, bound together like a harlequin's bat, or, if you prefer it, a lictor's bundle of rods. Kurowaza was just calling time on a couple of contestants as I came up. The court was cleared, leaving them a space some twenty feet square. It was different from any style of fencing I have ever seen, not in the least the kind that Professor Tronchet would ever teach or approve. The Japs did not stand in a straight line, but danced about one another, shuffling and dodging, and stamping like challenging bucks, slovenly foot work I suppose Tronchet would call it, and ever and again they would shout hoarsely through their helmets. It was spectacular, but not very scientific, magnificent, but not war. The only parries they employed were those in *quarte* and in *sixte*, and they never lunged. Sometimes even they were content to catch a blow on their arms or padded shoulders. It was the edge of the weapon that they relied upon, never the point, and any portion of the body was fair for a blow. They crouched to their work like so many cats, and their quickness of attack and recovery was feline as well in its rapidity. It was fine fighting while it lasted, for they never took or allowed a moment's rest. Up and down, back and forth, give and take, whack, clatter and clash, it ought to have been swords, but, though it was only bamboo foils, it was exciting enough to be satisfactory. Boxing with clubs might be a good definition of it, for there was the duck in it, the swing and the side step in it, and once when Nakamura brought in a tremendous staggering crash full on his adversary's front the watching Japs cheered as when the boxer lands a straight drive on the chin. The other dropped to his knee, and the second blow whined in the air over his head and swept from his helmet a little round knob of wood, whose significance I had not until then understood. But as the little wooden sphere filliped from the mask like a ball hot from the bat the cheer of the Japs rose to a great shout, and the fencers dropped their weapons and pulled the helmets from their steaming faces. This was the great point in the bout, it appeared, to strike off the crest of the foe's helmet, and Nakamura had done it as cleanly as though it had been shorn with a blade.

This fencing of the Japanese is fine fighting, but you will look long before you will find much delicacy in it. It is a combination of half a dozen encounters—boxing, fencing, the single-stick, the broadsword and the bayonet exercise, but it is picturesque certainly, and if the big two-handed sword of the Ronins were substituted for the bundle of sticks, you can imagine it quite as thrilling as necessary.

Frawley's New Beauty

An Impression of the Opinions of Miss Gladys Wallis

The Wave, 16 (29 May 1897), 11.

Now that I sit down before this copy paper, with pencil and wits sharpened to the task, and open the tap of whatever brain cell stores up the recollection of things, I find that I can remember in detail but little of my interview—call it rather talk—with Miss Gladys Wallis of the Frawley company.

I discover that I have carried away an impression rather than a record. I can remember perfectly well how Gladys Wallis looked—it would be hard to forget that—and how very delightful was her manner, but I'm very much afraid I did not ask her a sufficient number of leading questions. For instance, I did not ask her if she rode a wheel. I know nothing of her views on woman's rights. I have come away without obtaining her ideas as to the temper of San Francisco audiences, and I shall drag out the rest of my existence in crass ignorance of her liking for pets.

But as to impressions. I had never seen Miss Wallis, but the moment she came into the hotel parlor I knew beyond any question that she was the young lady I had come to see. Whether "Gladys" be a stage name or not, it fits her as a glove. Somehow, if I saw her in a crowd I think I would guess her name.

She is one of the smallest little bodies imaginable, with very tiny hands and feet, and a very small smile, and she wore—just here the film is blurred again; I recall something dark blue and something brown—but whether the skirt was blue and waist was brown or whether the waist was brown and the skirt blue I cannot precisely say. Then there was a jewel cluster somewhere, a wonderful affair, but I don't know if it was at her throat or on her finger.

I think I began by apologizing at first for existence generally and afterward, more particularly for existence as an interviewer. (Fancy how an interviewer on a daily would snort at this.) Then we sat down and—don't speak it above a whisper—Gladys Wallis' feet did not reach the floor.

Said I: "I haven't the faintest notion what to talk to you about."

"Nor I the faintest notion what to say," said Gladys Wallis.

"And to be personal on fifty seconds' acquaintance is unwarrantable," I observed.

"But shouldn't you be personal, in order to—to—"

"To earn my salary?"

"To make a good interview, rather."

"One should," said I. "But suppose we shun the personal note—for once."

"But you might write things that I never said."

"I would write nothing you wouldn't like."

"How do you know the things I like?"

"I know the things you don't like."

"For instance?" Miss Wallis picked at a jewel cluster on her finger. (It was on her finger, after all.) "For instance?" she said again.

"Interviewers," said I, still very humbly.

"I will tell you one thing I don't like," she said decisively. I fumbled for my note book.

"What's that?"

"I don't like a man to be meek." I put it back again.

"I'll be a roaring lion if you would like it any better."

"But don't be meek. You'll never be a good interviewer as long as you're meek."

"But I don't want to be a good interviewer," said I.

"What then?"

"A very poor one."

"You're not even that."

I bowed. "You are very kind."

"But your readers won't know a thing about me."

"Yes, they will."

"They won't know facts."

"They will have something better. They will receive an impression; the same that I have received, I hope."

"How do you expect to manage that, if you don't put down exactly what I say? You haven't used your note book once."

"I won't put down 'exactly what you say.'"

"Well then?"

"I'll try and remember as much of your conversation as I can, and what I can't remember I'll imitate. You give the impression at once of being very bright, very clever and very quick at repartee. I shall try and give the subscribers the same impression, even if I cannot repeat your precise words."

"Do you mean to say that you are making a character study of me?"

"Heaven forbid."

"At any rate, say that I am very ambitious and that once I starred."

"'Miss Wallis,' I quoted, 'informed our representative that she was bent upon attaining the highest round upon the ladder of fame. It will be remembered that Miss Wallis has already shone in the theatrical horizon as a bright particular star in a galaxy of unprecedented brilliancy.' How will that do?"

"It won't do at all. I thought you said this was not to be an interview."

"So I did. I forgot. I will just say that once you starred."

"And that I am very ambitious."

"And that you are very ambitious. I say, a thought occurs to me. Can't you give our paper your ideas upon interviewers?"

Gladys Wallis reflected a moment.

"I could, but I won't."

"Why not?"

"Because you wouldn't put it in, if I did."

"There's a glimmer of truth in that," said I. "You know the definition of a good interviewer."

"What's that?"

"The one that interviews the least. Do you think I have succeeded in answering the description?"

"I'll wait till I see it in print," said Gladys Wallis.

"I devoutly hope you'll like it," said I.

And I wonder if she will.

Fencing for Women

————

Parry and Riposte as an Exercise for the Fair Sex

————

The Wave, 16 (5 June 1897), 4.

————

In face of the fact that five minutes' fencing is more fatiguing than five minutes' boxing, you will be told by those who know that practice with the foils is the very best possible exercise for women. This adaptability may be, in part, due to the fact that women are naturally good at fencing. To be an expert fencer of the *Haute École* requires the strength of wrist and arm that only a man can acquire, but a woman can be a moderately good fencer in a much shorter time than her husband or brother. Women pick up the knack of the thing quicker than men do, and master the very delicate, almost impalpable wrist and finger work in half the time. Just in this connection it is curious to note that piano-players, especially female performers, are particularly apt pupils with the foil. The reason for this, so Professor Tronchet once told me, lies in the fact that what fencers call "the feeling for the blade" lies almost entirely in the fingers. It would seem that the sensitiveness in the finger-tips that is developed by scales and exercises and the like is just the thing necessary for a proper grip on the hilt. "Grip" is probably the wrong word, for no good swordsman or swordswoman "grips" his foil, and, indeed, the tighter it is gripped the easier it is for your adversary to disarm you.

Most women are averse to fencing for fear that it will over-develop the muscles of the arm and the——well, the muscles in general. But it don't do that, somehow. Tronchet showed me his arm, that has wielded a foil for nearly forty years, and it was positively slender. It is true that women develop the chest rapidly enough after they have begun to fence, but there are few women who should object to that. Then again, women are quicker with the eye than men, and besides that have a certain supersensitiveness of perception, intuition, instinct—call it what you will—that foresees an adversary's move, even before he makes it—guesses at it, feels it—in some delicate way in the contact of the blades. But the great difficulty that stands in the way of a woman becoming really great with the foils, is that she lacks coolness. The same delicacy of nerves that stands her in good stead on ordinary occasions upsets her quite completely when in a match for points. You must keep cool while you are working the little steel whip, for the variation of an inch, the deflection of a muscle by ever so little, will very probably mean a point against you.

Then again, there are fencers and there are fighters. The very best distinction I remember to have been drawn between Mr. Corbett and Mr. Fitzsimmons was along these same lines. Corbett was described as a wonderfully clever boxer. Fitzsimmons was mentioned as an equally clever boxer and a "fighter" as well. A fencer must warm to his work—must have the "do or die" streak in him or her, somewhere—the determination that is not afraid. It's hard to find this purely masculine element in a woman. One woman from California has it, and Tronchet names her as the best fencing girl in America. Olive Olliver is the girl, and after three years at the foils she could literally fight M. Tronchet's assistant to a standstill—could force him clean off the mat. She was so clever that she could rest while she was fencing—could stand back there on the mat and parry and parry and parry, while the assistant thrust, and then—piff! paff!—she'd lunge out like a sprung bolt and come in on her man, touch him and recover with a dexterity that savored of the miracle. But she was a very strong young woman, was Miss Olliver, and stood five eight in her——fencing shoes. I should have liked to have seen her at her work.

There is no one particular set of muscles a woman develops in fencing—

that's the beauty of the game. She exercises every tendon of her body simultaneously, and the grace and the delicacy that comes with the repeated practice is beyond words. Girls have been known—girls who aspired to the stage—so awkward that they could not walk into a crowded room without feeling as if their feet and hands were growing larger, who nevertheless took to fencing to overcome this difficulty, and brought themselves in time to face a packed theatre from the wrong side of the footlights with the ease and self-possession of veterans—all due to their fencing practice. Gracefulness is, after all, merely co-ordination of the muscles, and when you see that every individual muscle known to anatomy is brought into play in the course of a fencing bout, you will be ready to believe that there's something in it after all.

The thing that masters of fencing demand of their women pupils is not a tremendous expenditure of strength, but rather an exhibition of skill. The "lunge" is all very well, but it should occur no oftener in a fencing bout than a swing for a knockout does in a sparring contest. Women can and do readily master the most essential feature of the foils, i.e., the finger work, the flexions and pronations that tell the most, and they catch on to the thing infinitely quicker than men. For the average man to become an average good fencer, five years of daily practice is absolutely necessary; but how long do you suppose his sister or his cousin, or his wife, if you like (always presuming she is the average kind of girl)—how long do you suppose she must be at it before she can beat him? Two years only! Think of it! And Olive Olliver could have made him look like a lemon-grater after she had been at it for three!

The Lady of Lions

—————

Adgie and Her
Tawny Pets, with Remarks on the Power of the Eye

—————

The Wave, 16 (5 June 1897), 6.

—————

Prince is the lion *bon garçon*, a big, clumsy, lazy, shiftless, good-natured lump of a lion, with unexpected lapses of coquetry (as for instance when he throws out a paw at Adgie's swirling skirts when she's doing her dance in the cage), like any overgrown puppy. Trilby is very young, hardly old enough to have any developed character; but Victoria—if ever a lioness deserved a good hiding Victoria is that one; a nasty, evil, perverse, cross-grained, treacherous, snarling, sulky cat, with a skulk like an assassin and teeth like whetted knives.

"She should be sold or shot," Adgie told me as I followed her into her dressing-room after the turn was over. "That ought to be an iron-clad rule, once a lion has bitten you, sell him or shoot him."

"And has she bitten you?"

"Look at my nose."

There was a long scar on it, sure enough.

"And my thumb."

The nail was missing.

"And I just wish you could see my ankle."

So did I, but I didn't say so.

"You see," said Adgie, "Victoria is not what we call a handling lion, such as Prince. Prince was born in a cage, but Victoria is forest bred; was two years old before she was captured."

"I declare!" said I. "I don't see how one comes to choose such a profession as yours."

"Oh, I got into it by degrees. My father was a cigar seller in Mexico, and used to keep wild animals, pumas, and monkeys and foxes and the like, and so I got used to them. Then I went with a circus for awhile with a troop of

284

performing dogs, and next I began going into the cage with young lions, whelps, and so little by little I got into the way of it."

"How about 'the power of the human eye' over them?" I asked her at this point. I hoped that Adgie would scoff at this, for I wanted to shatter that ideal. I did not believe that one could "look down" a lion.

"Why, of course," said Adgie, at once. "When I look straight at Victoria I can see her pupils get larger and larger, and she gets nervous and wants to slink out of the way. Yes, I can make them cower that way, if they will only give me time. It's these little nips, and digs, and the quick lashing out of their paws that tell, and it's all done like a flash before you are aware of it. And then you know you can be prepared for every imaginable accident and contingency, and the very one particular last thing that you had not thought of is the one that happens."

"As for instance?"

"Well, at Los Angeles, when I was doing that act where I lie down with Prince and put his paws around me (the audience don't know it, but that's the part of my work that I dislike the most)—well, on that special morning he slipped his paw over the back of my head, then good-humoredly enough he began clawing at my head, just as a kitten would claw at a hearth rug. If I had moved or twitched away he would have scalped me like an Indian, but I lay still and called for Mr. Hall, who prodded him away."

"And your other narrow escape?"

"Again, in Los Angeles, I had my head in Prince's mouth and he made up his mind to close it. I could feel his jaws contracting. I did my best, but what's my strength? I jerked my head away and his great teeth snapped like a spring trap right in my ear. So close was it that he did actually catch a lock of my hair between his teeth. Oh sooner or later I suppose they will be the death of me."

"I can't see then why in the world you stay with them."

"Because I'm very fond of my lions. It's always the same. After each accident I say, 'Now, this time, you brute, I'm going to shoot you, this time I shan't forgive you,' and then in the morning when I come to their cage up go their tails, and they rub up against the bars, and when I go in they paw me over and are so glad that I can't have the heart to do it. Poor old chaps, they don't know any better."

"Hold on!" I exclaimed, "you don't mean to tell me that they are fond of you?"

"Why, of course," said Adgie, blandly.

Which was one view of the matter that had entirely escaped me.

Through a Glass Darkly

The Wave, 16 (12 June 1897), 5.

SCENE—The bay window of a certain down-town club of San Francisco. Some half dozen young men are present, smoking and chaffing and discussing "whiskey-and-sodas." Directly opposite, on the other side of the street, are the windows of a fashionable milliner's.

CHARACTERS—TOM, DICK, and HARRY, and (later) JACK (who is engaged to DOLLY STREET).

Tom (looking out of the window): I wonder now how many women stop and look in at that milliner's window as they go by.

Dick: One in three is a good average.

Harry: If there was a bargain-sale sign out, they wouldn't go by at all.

Tom: Look—here comes a girl.

Dick: She's a stunner, too! But she's in too much of a hurry. Bet she don't stop.

Harry: Bet she does.

Dick: Take you—how much?

Tom: Hurry up—she's almost in front.

Harry: Betcha dollar.

Dick: A dollar it is.

(Interval of breathless suspense.)

Tom: Now she's right there. She's going by—no, she ain't. Wait a minute, now.

Dick: She's slowing up.

Harry: She's got her eye on that green bonnet.

Tom: And it's marked down.

Harry: She can't possibly go by that.

Tom: She is, just the same.

Dick: No, she ain't.

Harry: There—there—there—she's stopped—she's going up to the window. I say, you owe me a dollar, old man.

Dick (gloomily): There you are. Wimin folk air powerful onsartin.

Tom: Look here. I'll tell what we'll do. I'll pick out a girl as I see her coming down the street—understand?—and you fellows will bet on whether she stops and looks in at that window or not. Dick, he'll be the bear—that is to say, he'll bet she don't stop, and Harry will be the bull—he'll bet she does. I choose to be the croupier.

Dick: And how about if she goes in?

Tom: Then that pays double—just like a natural in *vingt-et-un*. All clear?

Dick and Harry: Sure—clear's glass. Go on now, pick out a girl. Won't this one do that's coming—the one with the net bag?

Tom: Not at all. There's an art in this thing that you fellows don't appreciate. That girl's from the country. Look at her feet. She won't even look in. She's spent too much money in town already, as you can see from the size of her net bag. She won't even allow herself to look in. I won't choose her, because the chances are too much against Harry.

Dick: How about that one just behind? She's a city girl, no mistake—the one in a tailor-made gown and the black sailor?

Tom: Yes, we gamble on this one. "Here she goes and there she goes, and whether she stops or not nobody knows."

Dick: A dollar, hey?

Harry: A dollar each time.

(They put up their money, and the girl passes by without stopping.)

Tom: Dick wins. (Dick takes the money.) Hurry up, you fellows—here comes another. This is a shop-girl, or perhaps she runs a soda-water fountain in a candy-store. And still the little ball goes 'round.

Dick: Not enough salary to think of bonnets. She'll never stop in a thousand years. There's my dollar.

Harry: It's the very reason why she will. She dreams of those bonnets every night. I'll see your dollar and I'll raise you a half.

Dick: And fifty cents harder.

Harry: And fifty cents harder than that.

(The girl goes straight into the store, indifferently, without even glancing at the window.)

Tom: Harry wins double.

Dick (with an aggrieved shout): She was the saleslady for that store. I appeal from the decision of the referee—dirty work! Yah—fake! fake! (groans).

Harry: All bets go with referee's decision. I'll trouble you for that money, old chap.

Tom: Hello, here comes Jack. Shall we let him in?

Dick: He's engaged to be married to Dolly Street. He won't take enough interest in other girls even to bet on their weakness for bonnets.

Harry: He's to be married next week. It's about time he devoted himself to a study of a woman's interest in bonnets. Oh, I say, Jack, come over here and "join our merry throng!"

Dick (scornfully): Skin game! Turn out the gas! It's a notorious swindle! But tell him what the game is, Tom.

(Tom explains at length.)

Jack (with intense interest): I see—I see! It's great! I tell you what—I'll bet on whether she goes in or not. I'll be a plunger. I can only lose a dollar if she stops, but I stand to win two if she goes in.

Harry: Here comes a stunning-looking girl. See, the one with the heavy veil. I'll bet she's pretty, if one could see her face. Do we take this one, Tom?

Tom: *Messieurs, faites votre jeu.*

(They all make their bets. The girl pauses a moment in front of the window, looking at the bonnets and hats, starts on again, hesitates, and turns back and enters the store.)

Tom: Jack wins double.

Jack: I say, this is better than poker.

Dick (giving him the money): That was a swell-looking girl, though.

Harry: Wish we could have seen her face.

Tom: There she is—look—in the window of the store. The saleslady is showing her a hat. She's looking over here.

Harry: Who, the saleslady?

Dick: No, you jay; the girl—that swell girl.

Jack: That's so. She's looking right up here at the window.

Tom: Think she sees us?

Harry: Why, of course; that's what she's looking for. She's looking at me.

Jack: No, it's me she's looking at.

Harry: You're all wrong. She can't see you, Jack, sitting where you are.

Jack: 'Course she can (greatly excited). I say, I say, I say—look there, fellows—I think—I think, that—yes, she is—she's really smiling at me. Shall I smile back at her?

Harry (indignantly): Don't you dare—that smile's mine.

Jack: Betcha five dollars it's not.

Harry: Betcha ten it is.

Jack: I'll take that.

Dick: How you going to prove it?

Tom: I tell you. First Harry will wave his hand at her and see if she waves back at him, or bows. And then Jack will try. And the one she answers wins the money. Catch on?

Jack: That's a go. There's my ten dollars.

Harry: And there's mine.

Tom: Now, then, Harry, wave your hand.

Dick: And be just as charming and gracious as you know how.

(Harry waves his hand at the girl, who puts her chin in the air and turns away her head.)

Harry: All is lost but honor.

Tom: Hold on—Jack hasn't won yet. She may turn him down, too. It's up to you now, Jack.

(Jack tries. The girl smiles very prettily, nods her head at him and waves her gloved hand.)

Jack: Horray! She's mine! Harry, perhaps you can play mumblety peg, but when it comes to girls, you're out of the running! Gimme that ten dollars. Whatle you fellows have to drink?

Dick: Hold up a minute. Watch the girl. She's going to try on a bonnet, and is taking off her veil. Now we'll see if she's pretty or not.

Jack: She's radiantly beautiful—I feel that she is.

Tom: There, her veil's off—she is pretty. Look at her, Jack.

Jack (looks and then drops into a chair with a gasp): It's Dolly!

Dick: Who?—what?—Miss Street?

Tom: It is, for a fact. I say, Jack—I—we—look here old man. We've—I've acted like a damned fool, and if it'll do any good I'll apologize—I can't begin to say how cut up I am. I guess (turning to Dick and Harry) I guess I can speak for all of us—we've been a lot of beastly little cads, and—and—well, I'm downright ashamed of myself. Will you shake hands on that?

Jack (extending his hand): That's all right; of course you—we didn't know it was—who it was. I don't know why in the world I didn't recognize the dress, but that was a new waist I guess, and the veil was so thick. I guess I'll go down and see Dolly as she comes out. Some of you fellows sign the card for me, will you? (Exit.)

(Tom, Dick and Harry, left to themselves, look ruefully at one another for a moment.)

Tom: This is what our 'cross-the-water cousins would call an oncommon jolly rum go.

Harry: No wonder she waved her hand at Jack. But, Lord! what do you suppose she thinks of me?

Dick: But do you think now she knew who it was?

Harry: You mean that she didn't recognize Jack, after all?

Dick: It's pretty far from here across the street, and through two panes of glass.

Tom: Would Dolly Street flirt with a man she didn't know, and she engaged to Jack?

Dick: Pooh! Would Jack flirt with a girl he didn't know and he engaged to Dolly?

Dick: Betcha five dollars she didn't recognize Jack.

Harry: Betcha ten dollars she did.

Dick: Take you.

****

(Five minutes later. Dolly Street, coming out of the milliner's, meets Jack at the door.)

Jack (confusedly): Say, hello, Dolly! Did you—those fellows—we didn't know——

Dolly (surprised at seeing him): Why, dear old Jack, where did you come from? I haven't seen you in an age!

A Strange Relief-Ship

The Queer-Built *Everett* Sailing for India This Week

The Wave, 16 (12 June 1897), 7.

It is a far cry from San Francisco to Calcutta, but not so far apparently as to be beyond the sound of an appeal for help. Somewhere away in the heart of India there is a starving coolie, famine-stricken and shriveled, the ribs of him showing through his skin like the bars of a bird-cage through a wet cloth, who within forty days from the time of this writing will be feeding up-on corn that has been brought to him from Western Kansas. And his neigh-bors will feed, and his neighbors' neighbors, thousands of them, wretched wisps of humanity, thin beyond all belief will be gorged and glutted with a whole harvest of corn and rye and beans. Twenty-six hundred tons of grain will be flooded into the famine districts.

The ship that will carry this harvest is now on the dry dock, and surely no more oddly appearing relief craft was ever looked for. A huge hollow steel cigar, propelled by steam, with neither keel nor bow, nor deck nor stern— a mere shell furnished with propelling gear. She is not a ship, this "whaleback," this *City of Everett*, and there is little of the picturesque about her, no suggestiveness, no romance—simply a freight-carrying contrivance.

The *Everett's* destined voyage is the result of the efforts of the Committee of the Indian Famine Relief Fund of this city, who have been unwearied in their labors to feed the starving Indians. For the matter of that, everybody has helped. The farmers of Kansas, Iowa and Nebraska have given the grain, the railroads have transported a thousand tons of it free, the United States Government has chartered craft, and, more important than all, the Postal Telegraph and the Western Union Company have sent the countless but necessary dispatches of the committee free of charge. It is almost safe to say that without this generosity on the part of the telegraph companies the expedition would have failed. Nearly three thousand dollars' worth of telegraphing has gone over the wires of the two companies. The *City of Everett* was built by McDougal & Co., at Port Townsend, and is the only seagoing whaleback in the world, though other crafts of the same type ply upon the Great Lakes as grain ships. The value of the peculiar construction lies in the fact that when fully loaded the entire hull of the vessel sinks below the surface of the waves, and being thus relieved of their friction can make very good speed in rough weather. Surprising as it may seem, there is very little lateral roll in the whaleback type. The waves get very little purchase upon the rounded sides, while the superstructure offers but a minimum of surface to the force of the wind.

Training of Firemen

The Un-sung Soldiers of a Great City— How They Live and Die

The Wave, 16 (12 June 1897), 9.

Sailors have had their poets and to spare, and the soldier has been sung from the time of Homer to that of Stephen Crane, but the fireman is still waiting for his epic. A gunner working his piece with grim stoicism under fire, and a mast-hand reefing down the jib in a winter squall, clinging with fingers and toes to the icy foot-ropes, are fine sights. But how about the man who holds a thrashing, bucking, snorting nozzle to the throat of a roaring furnace, in instant danger of falling walls and collapsing roofs? A soldier in action has but to fear the bullet, and the sailor's life is sought for only by the sea, but a fireman can be killed in more ways than you have any idea of.

Primarily, there is, of course, the fire to burn him brown. But besides this, there are a score of nasty, unexpected dangers that lurk in every corner of a blazing building and that catch him unawares and worry the life out of him with a swiftness that is unsettling to the nerves of the onlooker. There's the smoke, for instance, that blinds him first and suffocates him afterward at leisure. There's the brick wall that does him to death with a huge flat slam, just as you have slapped the life out of an offending fly with the palm of your hand. There's the melted lead, from soldered cornices and yards upon yards of plumbing pipes, that sometimes creams up over the ledge of a roof like lava from an erupted volcano and splashes down upon him by bucketfuls, and then again there is the shower of broken glass. Trivial, this last, say you; but if you are hugging the top rung of a series of sliding ladders, a hundred feet high, with your arms full of throbbing, hysterical hose, and a blade of plate glass comes spinning down, cleaver-like, and slices you a tendon in arm or leg, you are very like to fall.

Then, not the least danger is the "pipe" itself. What the cannon is to the gunner, the pipe is to the fireman. It is his defense, his friend, his terrible, resistless engine, the *raison d'être* for his occupation. With his pipe charged and his engine pumping away steadily at the other end, your fireman will go almost anywhere—will fight the fire just as a battery fights the enemy. But if his pipe fails him—if it is burnt in two behind him, or bursts, or if the weight of fallen debris chokes it, he knows that the time has come to run, just as the gunner must retreat when his cannon is destroyed. But holding a nozzle to a dangerous fire is something like holding a wolf by the ears. For instance now. Your little squad of men is on a menaced roof directing the stream of water (a ton to a minute it is) into a neighboring building. Suddenly the roof on which they stand trembles and heaves under them like the deck of a sinking ship. At any moment it may fall in. Run? Yes, but what to do with that tremendous roaring python that the six of you, with the exertion of all your strength have been holding there—the enormous live brute, spurting its tons and tons of water? Like the man holding the wolf, it may be bad to hold on, but it's worse to let go. There's no time to pass the word along the line to shut off. You must drop the python and run. Then look out, not only for the sinking roof and the poisonous smoke and the hungry flames and the showers of burning cinders and the molten lead— the pipe, freed from all restraint, suddenly leaps into a furious, mad life all its own, thrashes back, squirms, jumps, recoils from side to side, twists upon itself like any leviathan in its death throes, lashes out in every direction, swinging like a flail the huge brass nozzle that can batter the life out of you at a single blow.

It is about the line—that is to say, "the pipe," or hose, that the fireman's active life is centered. With it he is effective, courageous, well disciplined; without it, useless, panic-stricken, deprived of all morale. It may be of service to him in indirect ways as well. He may slide to safety down its length when stairways fall in and ladders fail; or, better still, suppose he is lost in a smoke-choked building, bewildered and confused in the half-darkness of the place. Let him but find the line and he is practically safe. By following it he is sure to find an exit, and by lying at full length, his face close to its surface, he knows he may count upon pure air.

There are three sorts and conditions of firemen—the extra-men, the relief men, and the permanent men. Let us suppose for the sake of illustration that you and I should one morning make up our minds to enter the fire department. We would begin by procuring one of the application forms at the City Hall, filling out the blanks, and securing the signatures of twelve property-holders. You make application to be appointed either an extra-man or a relief man. About the same time you are subjected to a physical examination, and if you pass this and if your papers are satisfactory, you are elected by the vote of the Board of Commissioners, and sign the necessary papers. You are read a little lecture about this time on the whole duty of man as applied to the extinguishment of fires, upon the conclusion of which you are told to report for duty to the foreman of some one of the stations in town. This only if you are an extra-man.

The relief man goes through a little different mill. He makes his application to become either a driver or a tillerman (this is the fellow you see sitting far out at the extremity of the ladders on the hook-and-ladder truck), or an engineer, and you must previously convince the Board that you are capable of discharging the duties of that position. Your name goes down on the relief list and you substitute in turn with the other relief men as driver or engineer or tillerman, whatever permanent position happens to be vacant. But if you are a relief man you are paid, not by the city, but by the man for whom you substitute.

The equipment of a truck company is made up of twelve extramen, one foreman, a permanent driver, and a tillerman. That of an engine consists of nine extramen and three permanent men—engineer, driver and foreman.

If this city rejoiced in a fully-paid department, all these men would be on duty at every hour of the day; as it is, however, San Francisco has a fully-paid, fully-equipped fire department only between the hours of eleven in the evening and six in the morning. Only the permanent men are continually on duty. During the daytime the extramen are allowed to go about their business in the district of their company, reporting for duty at the station not later than eleven p.m.

Suppose now the "bell hits" for a station. At once the "Hall bell" is rung from the roof of the quarters. This is the bell that the whole city hears, in combination with the mournful groaning of that whistle down by the Front. But these "Hall bells" are not, as I had fondly supposed, rung for the benefit of the general public, but for the extramen who are absent from the quarters. Each of these men has a list of the boxes of the city, with the boxes of their own particular district underscored. As soon as the Hall bells begin to sound the extraman consults his card, counting the strokes. If an outside station is rung—that is to say, a station outside of the particular district of his company, he reports at once to the quarters, and should be there inside of five minutes. The apparatus does not "roll" to a first alarm if it is an outside box, but hitches up and waits five minutes for a second alarm, so the extramen have time to get to the quarters. But if an inside box comes in— that is to say, a box within the limits of a company's district, the apparatus "rolls" at once without waiting for the extramen. These, by consulting their card, know at once that an inside box has come in, and rush off, let us hope, on a dead run, to the fire, not to the quarters. Perhaps they may even meet their engine or truck by the way and jump on.

Other cities have drilling schools for men and horses alike, and the extraman is taught how to use an axe and the different tools of the apparatus, how to manage and handle a hose, and more especially how to put in an extra length of hose while the fire is in progress. This operation corresponds precisely to that of a battery changing position under fire. It is a hazardous move, and must be done with lightning rapidity, as, of course, the water is shut off at the time, and the fire has a chance to get tremendous headway. But most of his trade he can learn only by actual experience under a captain or a foreman. The knack, for instance, of "opening up" burning buildings, the ways of combatting the dreaded "back draught," when a mass of flames that you have been gradually forcing back and back, suddenly turns and charges you like a herd of stampeded elephants, and the manner of dodging a falling wall, and what kinds of collapsing walls are dangerous and what are not.

One would like to say more about the horses—the huge, big-boned, short-muscled, broad-headed fellows, that don't know what it is to be afraid. They learn their trade in a week's time, the horses, without the assistance of any training school. At first, of course, they must be led to their places, but after the bell has hit a score of times they jump to their positions as quick as do the men. But it is very sad to be told that as a rule they don't last long. Six years at it will tell on the best. Think of it for a moment. Often, just after their heavy meal of oats and hay and their deep draught of water, the bell hits and off they go over the cobbles and up the hills tugging away at the huge apparatus, without the least warning or preparation. It's trying to the stoutest horse, and sooner or later comes the time when he goes stale and must be sold.

But I wonder what he thinks when, later on, foundered and broken, while he is straining at a loaded truck under the lash of a cruel teamster—I wonder what he thinks, I say, when he hears the clanging of the bell and sees his old engine go past, thundering and smoking, just as in the old days, with his old driver strapped on the box and his old friends clinging to the footboard. I wonder if he remembers the excitement and gaiety of the old life. The long fine hours spent under his blanket while the fire shouted and roared, and his own engine was pumping and coughing away like mad at his very withers, and the return home, triumphant, with the out-fought enemy, a mere whiff of smoke behind him, and the prospect of a warm stable and grateful grooming at home! I fancy his old, thin blood must stir a bit at the sight, and his drooping ears prick again, and I think he must pick up his feet a trifle more proudly, a little like as he used to do, and I hope that for that day at least he will forget his cruel teamster and his heavy truck and his bad oats, and remember that at any rate he had it all once.

Excelsior!

A Royal Mountain and a Royal Climber
Who Hopes to Master It

The Wave, 16 (12 June 1897), 9.

The whims and fancies of the royally born do not generally involve hardship, nor the risk of life and limb. Most of the continental nobles one hears of are perfectly content to stay at home and go about from one seat to another, borrowing their friends' money, or their friends' wives, and making themselves disagreeable or useless or positively downright malevolent, as our own dear Duke Gunther, for example. But now appears one, Luigi, Prince of Savoy, nephew of the King of Italy, and son of that Duke of Aosta, who for three years was, and (had he chosen to violate his oath), might now have been, King of Spain.

Luigi is only 24 years of age, but he has set himself to do what the veteran Schwatka failed to accomplish, the task that proved too much for the English traveler, Topham, and for the explorer, I.S. Russel, though this latter made two attempts. The manner in which Prince Luigi proposes to ascend the mountain causes the affair to assume all the proportions of an expedition. His party consists of his aide-de-camp, W. Cogni, of the Italian navy; Francisco Gonella, President of the Turin Alpine Club; V. Horio Sello, a famous mountaineer; Fillippo Fillippi, the doctor, and five Alpine guides. The baggage of the party amounts to some sixty pieces, and includes all manner of devices and appliances for mountain climbing, alpen-stocks, gearings of rope, sleds for glacier work, and the like.

Mount St. Elias is at the head of the range of the same name, about 250 miles east of Sitka, and lies on the border line between British and American territory. Prince Luigi's route will be as follows: Starting from this city he will proceed by boat to Tacoma, where the expedition will start. From Tacoma he goes on to Yakutat Bay in Alaska. At Yakutat he will strike inland some twenty miles. Here the Chaix foothills begin, and soon reach an elevation of 7,200 feet. Pushing on from this point across a wilderness of moraines, and glaciers and snow-covered passes, the explorer will finally come out upon the northwest base of the mountain itself. The first obstacles here to be encountered are the grim barriers which were the cause of the final undoing of the Russel expedition, the Newton and Agassiz glaciers. In describing his experiences while crossing these glaciers, Russel says:

"At several localities steps had to be cut in steep snow slopes, which made progress very slow and tiresome. At one place progress seemed to be impossible, owing to a maze of huge crevasses, which crossed the glacier from side to side. We determined to cut steps down into one of the broadest crevasses and then up the precipice opposite, over two hundred feet high. This was accomplished by McCarty, Stamy and myself. It was an exceedingly difficult job, owing to an overhanging cornice-like ridge, about six feet thick, near the top, but a rope helped us over."

Prince Luigi, however, is no green hand at his work. His family are Piedmontese, and ever since he was old enough to walk he has been climbing the Italian Alps. He has successfully ascended all of the most difficult of his own and the neighboring countries, and now turns his attention to the conquering of new mountains. The peak of St. Elias, however, is generally considered by experts as inaccessible. It is over 18,000 feet in height, and as yet no expedition has covered much more than two-thirds of the distance. Schwatka, in 1886, reached a height of 12,200 feet; Topham, in 1888, touched the 11,000 foot mark, while Russel, in his two later attempts, could not better 8,000. It is interesting to note that simultaneous with the venture of the Italian Prince, Henry G. Bryant, of Philadelphia, aided by S.J. Entrikin (Peary's second in command), is to make an attack upon the mountain from the other side.

It will be a heroic contest of pluck, energy and endurance. May the best man win, but let us hope that the first flag to flutter on that desolate peak will be the Stars and Bars.

The Question

A Clever Satire by Lorimer Stoddard at the Columbia

The Wave, 16 (19 June 1897), 13.

It is almost certain that if Lorimer Stoddard's *Question* were produced in any other of the larger cities of America, other than this, it would score a pronounced success; equally probable is it that coming to San Francisco from the Eastern circuit the play would be received with enthusiasm. It is a thoroughly good piece of work; the audiences of the Columbia know very well that it is, and yet because of a couple of paragraphs in the daily papers they withhold their judgment and their applause. The most surprising feature of *The Question* was this apathy on the part of the audience and its failure to catch the right points at the right time. A dozen or so *claqueurs* would not have been out of place on the opening night, for a score of times the house was moved to a stir of amusement when no amusement was intended or again sat stolid and imperturbable through scenes and bits of dialogue that on other occasions would easily have provoked a clamor of intelligent recognition.

For one thing, San Francisco audiences are not keyed up to such a style of play as Mr. Stoddard and the Frawley Company have put on. Its best points are its most delicate. Exchange of repartee as bright and as evanescent as an electric spark, a bit of situation come and gone as quickly as a kinetoscope picture, a touch of character acute and subtle as a lancet. Fresh from the highly colored, strongly marked melodramatic scenes of *The Fatal Card,* and so many other of brusque, coarse-fibered plays that find their way to the Coast, it is perhaps not remarkable that *The Question* is slow to succeed. The difficulty about such a play is that it appeals strongest to a limited public. It presupposes a rather unusual degree of intelligence on the part of its audience, an intelligence that can find more pleasure in an exchange of wit than in an exchange of blows, that rejoices in the thrust of keenly-pointed satire rather than in that of the assassin's knife. There are not many such people amongst San Francisco theater-goers. There were certainly few in the Columbia on the first night of *The Question*. The house that foregathered beyond the footlights expected, in fact, desired, quite a different manner of play. They expected violent action and they got delicate insinuation. They wanted blood and they got an epigram. But the people who can appreciate Drew and the Daly companies should see *The Question*. Frank Worthing is not "Lord Clivebrook," Mr. Stoddard "Pinero," but the drama which is the result of their combined effort is far and away ahead of the average of the dramatic work that has been of late produced in this city.

The dialogue, especially the dialogue between the women, fairly coruscates with brilliant repartee, so much so that the only criticism possible is that its cleverness is almost too pronounced to be true to life. There are, however, several little touches, here and there, so slight as to be almost impalpable, that do nevertheless add strongly to the impression of *vraisemblance*.

As, for instance, Mrs. Cannon's momentary forgetfulness of Oskamp's name, and her difficulty with that of Miss Quintard. Such points as these seem almost too trivial to mention, but they tell, they help, to create an impression. They are the *superflu si nécessaire*. Miss Moretti was cast in a role that seemed in some manner distasteful to her, and was not very effective. Miss Bates as Mrs. Cannon showed an admirable skill in the interpretation of a strong and sterling woman, superficially weak, and regardless of convention. It is a task of enormous difficulty and delicacy to strike precisely just the right note in the rendering of such a role, but never for a moment was Miss Bates' work out of tune. Such, too, was the case in Gladys Wallis' Miss Quintard, especially in what may be called for want of a better word the "champagne scene." It would have been the easiest thing imaginable to overdo this scene, and give an impression of coarseness and vulgarity. In Miss Wallis' hands it was veritably delicious, and indeed as much can be said of her entire role. As Miss Quintard she is quite as charming as any actress of her kind seen here this season.

It is perhaps niggardly to haggle over details, but the rustling of the leaves, that so conveniently adapts itself to Mrs. Cannon's lines in the second act might be omitted with advantage. Mrs. Cannon's words would have just as much significance without it, and the effect is neither natural nor artistic. It is thrust upon the audience at that particular time and at no other. But the fact that so trifling a criticism could be hazarded at all is perhaps the best proof of the excellence of the entire performance.

THE APPRENTICESHIP WRITINGS OF FRANK NORRIS

OF

FRANK NORRIS

Volume Two

Contents: Volume 2

Introduction: vii-xxxv

Textual Afterword: 261-273

CONTENTS

INTRODUCTION

Volume Two

INTRODUCTION

Volume 1 of this edition takes one well past the midpoint of Frank Norris's 11 April 1896 through 15 February 1898 association with *The Wave*. With the beginning of Volume 2, 26 June 1897 finds him having already published the majority of his apprenticeship works and having become a seasoned practitioner—at least in his more plentiful non-fiction writing. In Norris's articles, essays, interviews, and reviews, the aggregate of personas he employed to meet the similar demands of recurring writing situations had assumed definition. One may observe him still striving in 1897-1898 for variety in viewpoint and greater spontaneity in tone; yet, it is clear that Norris had both found his stride as a stylist and discovered successful means of treating his subjects that need not be abandoned merely for the sake of novelty. From one perspective, then, Norris's apprenticeship was proving a success; as a developing professional in the journalistic medium, he was continuing to demonstrate that he was more than a dilettante or a mere reporter.

Then again, Norris was still far from his primary goal of *literary* success before a national readership as he approached his twenty-eighth birthday.[1] He could not yet claim to be the Kipling of San Francisco he called for on 22 May 1897 in "An Opening For Novelists." Further, by the summer of 1897, Norris had made relatively little progress toward assuming the identity of a Zolaesque Naturalist in his short fiction, much less in the genre of the novel. The frustration he began to feel about the time of his first anniversary as a staff-writer for this regional magazine with a select but relatively small readership is especially understandable when one considers his less than enviable track record prior to the apprenticeship.

After studying art in San Francisco and then spending two years at the Académie Julian, he had not become an adept, while his younger fellow-student in Paris and still-close friend, Ernest Peixotto, had since 1889 shown in the Salon and begun a successful career as an illustrator. Next, his performance as an undergraduate was such that he was not able to join the others in his class of '94 at the University of California graduation ceremony. Then a collection of short fiction assembled after two semesters as a special student at Harvard University failed to find a publisher in the summer of 1895. In addition, the early 1896 travel essays written in South Africa had only one immediate effect in regard to the furtherance of his aims: they helped him secure a berth on *The Wave*—which he still occupied.

Three other factors require consideration when measuring Norris's frustration by the summer of 1897. They relate to the fact that he had another identity than that of author. *Wave* editor John O'Hara Cosgrave, when interviewed by Norris's 1932 biographer Franklin Walker, referred to him, demeaningly, as an "editorial assistant."[2] Norris himself indicated the same, though "associate editor" was the more salutary description that he preferred. When this peripatetic regional portraitist was in town, then, he had editorial chores to perform, and that was undoubtedly one of the reasons that, on 15 February 1898, he leapt at the first known offer of a position in New York City. When the letter from John S. Phillips reached him in St. Louis while he was visiting his wife-to-be Jeannette Black, he immediately accepted the opportunity to "write" (with no mention of editing) for the S.S. McClure newspaper syndicate and *McClure's Magazine*.[3]

What Norris later described as the "grind" of working for *The Wave* was undoubtedly editorial for the most part, and thus the first vexatious factor for consideration: preparing others' works for publication took time away from his own writing.[4] His most patently uninspiring duty was providing assistance to Cosgrave in making-up the weekly issues by Wednesday, or Thursday at the latest, for publication on Saturday. (Such a schedule is inferable from datings and references to events in individual issues.) In addition to readying editorials, articles, and literary pieces for typesetting, verbal "filler" had to be located and adjusted for size as white-space was eliminated. Like Cosgrave, Norris had to do what was necessary to accommodate the use of syndicated material and texts "borrowed" from other periodicals. His hand was probably at work as much as Cosgrave's in some issues—though where it was active is difficult to detect. Thus the second cause of annoyance: performing the thankless tasks of an editor, he received no credit from the public for his labors; in this respect, nothing was gained by way of the national, or even regional, visibility requisite for a professional author.

The third factor was that editorial responsibilities at *The Wave* conflicted in another way with his making a reputation for himself. So far as can be determined, Cosgrave and Norris were the only salaried writers during the apprenticeship period—save from early April to mid-May 1897 when Gelett Burgess replaced Norris.[5] Others in San Francisco contributed to the magazine; but when material ran short, Cosgrave and Norris were the ones who had to originate new matter. They did so in a way that worked to the disadvantage of Norris. Simply stated, it would have been unseemly for *The Wave* to append their signatures to all of the pieces they wrote or to the columns of previously published material they assembled; that would have suggested a shoe-string operation and contradicted the sophisticated image of this high-toned magazine for San Francisco's *beau monde*. Norris, like Cosgrave and Burgess in the spring of 1897, had to disguise his own work with pseudonyms such as "Marmaduke Masters" and "Justin Sturgis," or allow it to appear unsigned. Rather than stand out more as a prolific individual worthy of the attention of important editors and publishers in the East, he found himself called upon to help *The Wave* achieve distinction via concealment of its meager resources.

While unsigned and pseudonymously signed works by Norris have been identified, many more *Wave* pieces suggest that they may have been written by him or edited and added to file-copy.[6] To cite a minor example of uncredited text for which he may have been in some way responsible, the following bit of filler appeared on p. 5 of the 12 September 1896 issue:

> The use of hypnotic suggestion in dentistry is increasing. It is superior to gas and more effective than cocaine. A prominent dentist, Dr. Fillebrown, says: "I prophecy that in a few years every man who practices dentistry scientifically will have his practice controlled by the principle of hypnotic suggestion. It has been urged as an insuperable obstacle to the success of hypnotism in dental operation that the constant cutting in the most sensitive portion of our anatomy, the dentine, would arouse the patient, no matter how thoroughly hypnotized. This, however, is overcome by uninterrupted suggestion."

Since the hero of *McTeague* (1899), Mac, is a dentist and Charles Kaplan has documented Norris's familiarity with the same Dr. Thomas Fillebrown's book on operative dentistry, Norris certainly is a candidate for authorship or for designation as the editor who selected the paragraph for inclusion.[7] One cannot be sure, though. Mac, after all, does not experiment with hypnotism in his dental parlors; and, while Norris may have processed the paragraph earlier, he appears to have been away from San Francisco in August-September 1896, when it was published. (No signed works by Norris were printed in *The Wave* then, and he may have been visiting the Big Dipper Mine near Iowa Hill, California, one of the settings in *McTeague*.) Cosgrave, who had an interest in hypnotism and like matters having to do with cognitive and paranormal psychological phenomena, may instead have written it or derived the text from another publication.

A more interesting, artfully written possibility is seen in another untitled and unsigned piece that appears related to *McTeague*, specifically the beginning of its first chapter where the life of San Francisco's Polk Street, as seen from the window of Mac's dental parlors, is described. On p. 14 of the 23 May 1896 issue, the view from the window of an actual San Francisco dentist's office was similarly rendered:

The question is often asked, from what point the most commanding view of Kearny Street is to be obtained. The Chronicle Building is one point of vantage; the Nucleus is rather removed from the stream of traffic; from the Blythe corner one has a splendid range of the main thoroughfare and its tributaries, but to the mind of the writer, dentist Teague's window, which overhangs the intersection of Geary and Kearny Streets, gives one the freest view in all directions. The observer is near enough to the throng to see the individual faces, and yet sufficiently removed to be unseen. From there it is possible to watch the San Francisco world go by. It is an admirable location to witness the Saturday afternoon parade, notably the most interesting sight of San Francisco. It sweeps Geary Street to the Riche, the best part of Market Street— Lotta's fountain: beneath it flower-sellers congregate. Kearny Street, the best part of that artery is in view up to Raphael's. It makes a capital place to moralize in, for one cannot watch the passing of the world, the flesh, and the devil without thought, without interest, and without comment.

Dr. Teague, like another dentist named Dr. Young, bought advertising space in *The Wave*, and so one should not be too surprised by the presence of the unidentified writer in his office. He may have been a third San Francisco dentist, Dr. G. A. Danziger. He was, like Cosgrave, Burgess, and Norris, a member of San Francisco's Bohemian Club, and he occasionally wrote for *The Wave* from 16 February 1896 through Norris's apprenticeship. Also complicating attribution of the piece is the fact that both Cosgrave and *Wave* contributor John Bonner wrote in the same manner seen here; and the latter produced many local-color pieces of the kind. Further, the name Teague is irrelevant since Norris had named his hero McTeague when at Harvard University in 1894-1895.[8]

One cannot, then, attribute either paragraph to Norris; and yet, one cannot help but speculate that he was the unacknowledged local colorist at work who would later note, in the signed "Cosmopolitan San Francisco" of December 1897, how the doorsteps and open windows of the Latin Quarter are "coigns of vantage where one may see the world go by." Likewise, to what degree Norris was galled by obligatory self-effacements of the kind is a matter for speculation, though gauging the psychological effect, month upon month, of this sort of unrecognized labor requires little imagination. One wonders how many articles like "The Mira Monte Club"—whose authorship would be moot were it not signed "F.N."—were produced anonymously by Norris; such straightforward prose, if not signed, cannot be linked to any particular *Wave* author. One also wonders if Norris's April-May 1897 hiatus in writing for *The Wave* was a consequence of his frustration and the depression Walker described Norris as suffering that spring.[9]

* * *

In the later writings of Volume 1, the strain on Norris was showing. Or, such is the interpretation of some peculiar behavior on his part that suggests itself once one encounters the contextualization made available by Bruce Porter, a local artist famous for his stained-glass work and another Bohemian Club member. Porter, like Walker, was not specific about the temporal sequence of events in 1897, but over three decades later he recalled in a memoir written for Walker that Norris had told him he was "worn out," "tired out," "written out."[10] He then recorded a remarkable outburst that occurred when Norris learned Gelett Burgess had bested him. Burgess—the author of the still well-known bit of doggerel entitled "The Purple Cow" (1895)—had become nationally visible via his relationship with one of the more famous *fin de siècle* little magazines, *The Lark*. While Norris was to remain in the cultural hinterlands with *The Wave*, Burgess thus garnered attention in the East and "arrived" in the spring of 1897. Wrote Porter to Walker, "when we had killed The Lark and Burgess had gone on to New York to harvest a surprised [*sic*] reputation, I read a letter of his success to Frank at luncheon. To my amazement that vivid face went ash-grey, and beating the table with clenched fists [Norris declared:] 'Damn him! Damn him! He's got it and it belongs to me!'"

The anecdote is unique in memoirs written by Norris's contemporaries. Norris was never again pictured as either so emotionally unstable or so mean-spirited.[11] Burgess, like Porter and Peixotto, was a friend; and, although Norris never wrote for *The Lark*, he was closely associated with those in that group, who dubbed themselves *Les Jeunes*. That Porter was at the least approximating correctly what transpired when Norris discovered that Burgess had beaten him in the race for a literary career with the Eastern publishing establishment is confirmed by one of Norris's essays. Not mere frustration but rage appears to have motivated Norris when, on 22 May 1897, he made public his animus toward Burgess and the trifling, effete kind of artistry he practiced. Positively alluding to writers such as Kipling, Stevenson, and Zola, he wrote frenetically in "An Opening For Novelists":

> Who shall be our Kipling? Where is the man who shall get at
> the heart of us, the blood and bones and fiber of us, who shall
> go a-gunning for stories up and down our streets and into our
> houses and parlors and lodging houses and saloons and dives

"The Purple Cow" appeared on 1 May 1895 in The Lark.
Courtesy of the Strozier Library, Florida State University.

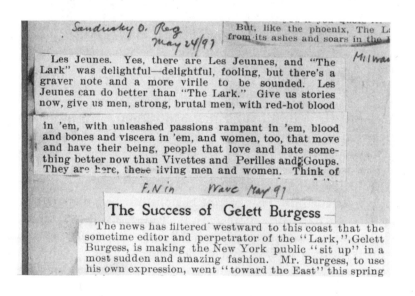

*Gelett Burgess preserved Norris's attack on his art
in a scrapbook. Courtesy of The Bancroft Library.*

and along our wharves and into our theaters; yes, and into the secretest chambers of our homes as well as our hearts?

Les Jeunes. Yes, there are *Les Jeunes,* and *The Lark* was delightful—delightful fooling, but there's a graver note and a more virile to be sounded. *Les Jeunes* can do better than *The Lark.* Give us stories now, give us men, strong, brutal men, with red-hot blood in 'em, with unleashed passions rampant in 'em, blood and bones and viscera in 'em, and women, too, who move and have their being, people who love and hate, something better now than Vivettes and Perillas and Goops.

Burgess's *Vivette; or the Memoirs of the Romance Association* would be published later that year by a Boston firm, Copeland and Day. "Goops" were cartoon figures drawn by Burgess that were as clever as his female characterizations Vivette and Perilla were cute—and just as unlifelike and intellectually insubstantial. Further, as Norris's imagery suggested, Burgess's art was unmanly. While Norris saw himself as working diligently to "get at the heart of us, the blood and bones and fiber of us" in a virile way, Burgess had played the foppish *artiste* and won the prize.

By the measures of Burgess's and Peixotto's successes, Norris had once more stalled. The specter of failure again loomed before him as it had after his return from Paris, during his senior year at Berkeley, and in the summer of 1895 when his book of short fictions found no publishers interested. As was the case with the similarly situated writer-hero of Norris's autobiographical novel *Blix* (1899), it was either time for him to abandon his goals or reapply himself more strenuously.

Norris, of course, did the latter. This meant maintaining his position with the immediate means of drawing the eastern publishers' notice, *The Wave,* and continuing to produce the requisite articles, essays, interviews, and reviews. Thus, May 1897 saw not only the publication of the manic attack on Burgess but, in a very different vein, one of the most confident displays of Norris's well-developed skills, the article "Among Cliff-Dwellers." Refocusing with remarkable success on San Francisco after his nearly two-months absence from *The Wave's* pages, he described vividly the isolated, interracial "ferment" of life in the neighborhood atop Telegraph Hill. It is one of the best pieces of unconventional journalism that he produced during his apprenticeship, reading like a short story, laced with sensational evolutionary theory, and foreshadowing the Naturalistic fictional use he would make of the setting months later in "Judy's Service of Gold Plate."

*Portrait of Norris by his fellow-student at the Académie Julian,
Ernest C. Peixotto. Reproduced from* The Bookman *(American),
10 (November 1899), 234. Courtesy of the Strozier Library,
Florida State University.*

Not so remarkable were "Japanese Swordsmanship" and "Training of Fire-men," though both were sprightly, engaging articles that conveyed the im-pression of a writer enjoying his assignments—which, as in 1896, he still ap-pears to have been free to select for himself. On the other hand, a fourth piece in Volume 1, "Metropolitan Noises," seems to disclose more than Nor-ris intended. It is a well-written, objectively detailed, and substantial study of the problem of noise pollution in the city, suggesting that Norris had, indeed, recently passed though a hellish experience. Perhaps having suffered a severe bout with neurasthenia (the 1890s equivalent of a nervous break-down), Norris wrote knowingly about the effects of noise on those afflicted by "a nervous complaint," relating what an unnamed physician had to say to him about their treatment. If, like *The Wave's* readers, one did not have ac-cess to Porter's recollection, though, one would note only that the article was a thoroughgoing, almost scientific analysis of sound and its subliminal effects upon individuals.

* * *

Whatever, exactly, did transpire psychologically and physiologically that spring, the non-fiction writings in Volume 2 warrant—with one possible ex-ception discussed below—a diagnosis of Norris's improving condition in the months that followed. Beginning with his description of the Japanese "Cruiser *Hi-Yei*" on 3 July 1897, the journalist is sanguine in tone and seems genuinely interested in his subjects. Once again he began ranging beyond the environs of San Francisco. At Hollister he took pleasure in document-ing the Mission San Juan's centennial celebration. He then visited Mill Valley and wrote an appreciation, "Japan Transplanted," of an idiosyncratic housing development. His delight is evident when describing this experience of "a little bit of Japan" in the California hills:

> Altogether there are some dozen . . . little Japanese summer
> houses, . . . designed by Japanese architects and put together
> by Japanese laborers, low of ceiling, spacious of interior, cool,
> light and airy, ideal places for a hot summer's day. From the
> time the outer gate is entered until you pass through it again
> on your way out there is nothing in the least suggestive of
> Western civilization to be seen—nothing but yourself and your
> own ungainly clothes; at least they feel ungainly upon coming
> out of any one of these delicious little houses.

A visit to the Stockton area then yielded "From Field to Storehouse," in which he described the mechanized harvesting of wheat and demonstrated that he had not lost his zest for Zolaesque prose. As may be seen, the Norris of "On a Battleship," published in October 1896, was back at his old stand in August:

ON A BATTLESHIP

You crawl about upon the thing like some insignificant parasite upon the back of a mastodon. You descend into the vitals of the monster, down there in the stifling lower levels, where the huge, hot heart beats, and you see and hear the little sights and sounds the great ship makes in its living—even while motionless—the slow inhalation and discharge of its breath of steam, and the persistent mutter of its furnace mouths—ever agape—devouring ton after ton of coal, always gorged yet always unappeased, the hunger of a glutton who is never satisfied.

FROM FIELD TO STOREHOUSE

It is quite worth the trip to Stockton to see this enormous engine at its work, rolling through the grain knee deep, as it were, like a feeding mammoth, its teeth clicking and clashing before it, its locomotive rumbling behind. It takes eight men to guide and control the monster, but it does the work of a little army. Before its passage the wheat is mere standing grain, yellowy and nodding in the summer sun; after it has passed the wheat is grain in sacks ready for shipment.

In a highly influential analysis of *The Octopus*, cultural historian Leo Marx classed Norris among the major U.S. authors who brooded over the demise of the old pastoral order in American life and the ascendancy of the new industrial-technological state.[12] But, as is apparent in both of these far from gloomy essays, Norris never did, in fact, have a problem with mechanical progress *per se*. In *The Wave*, as in novels such as *McTeague* and *The Octopus* (1901), he waxed poetic over such progressive developments, finding them imaginative stimulants of the highest order. In December 1897, his article "Sanitary Reduction" even registers his enthusiasm over what was then high-tech garbage disposal—as remarkable an advance as another before which he stood in awe that same month when he described in "The Postal Telegraph" how a message is transmitted from San Francisco to South Africa.

Lively essays such as "The Tale and the Truth" and "Happiness By Conquest" likewise indicate that Norris had put his personal-professional crisis behind him, particularly in the latter which asserted on 11 December 1897 that true happiness is to be had in overcoming obstacles of the kind he had known. His interviews with playwrights David Belasco and Augustus Thomas, focused as they are on the all-important question of the values of literary

Realism and their relationship to the artistic use of imagination, spell renewal; so too does one of Norris's most significant theoretical pieces on artistic creation, "Fiction is Selection." As book reviewer, Norris found something more pleasant and conventionally artful to write about than Burgess's Goops: "Holiday Literature" focuses on the 1897 Christmas gift books and calendars for the new year. He celebrated local illustrators Solly Walter and Gertrude Partington as prelude to a paean he delivered to the inimitable master, Frederic Remington. As his writings repeatedly make clear, Norris was partial to horses; and no one could equal Remington's superb handling of that subject.

In only one of Norris's non-fiction works in Volume 2 is there a reminder of the spring crisis. On 31 July 1897, "The Sailing of the *Excelsior*" featured a Norris as exuberant as the thousands of others bidding farewell to those embarking for the newly discovered gold fields of the Klondike, exuding admiration for the men daring the dangers of such an adventuresome quest. His tone changes, however, when he spies a supine alcoholic on the dock; and his reaction, or overreaction, is startling:

> Did I say there was no one in that crowd who was indifferent? I was wrong. . . . He was reclining against a pile of boards, and the crowd had grown up around him, and he lay there oblivious to everything that was going forward. . . . Think of it! The city thrilling from end to end . . . the thousands of people rushing in to say farewell to their argonauts, and this man lay there under foot, so close to the ship that he could have laid his hand upon her hull, and cared not whether she swam or sank. . . . Never has a drunken man seemed so loathly to me. One fairly quivered with a desire to kick him from the stringpiece of the wharf and allow to perish in the water a man so utterly out of the race as this one.

Here one is prompted to recall that Norris did become exasperated in his sports reportage of 1896, but his impatience with football players never led to such a violent crescendo in his prose. One speculates that more vexing to Norris than the alcoholic's patent failure in living was his offence of having withdrawn from the "race" for success. Norris, in short, may have found personified in this man his own worst fears for himself. On the other hand, he may only have been quite calculatedly striving for a sensational effect by deliberately violating the decorum of *The Wave* and its polite subscribers. As in much of the fiction he wrote through the remainder of his apprenticeship, so in this article. It is sometimes difficult to decide whether Norris was driven by neurosis when going to extremes; or consciously and freely opting to play the attention-winning roles of the *enfant terrible* and

Zolaesque Naturalist; or motivated in both ways. The question insists itself repeatedly; and one wishes that Bruce Porter had been more thorough in his description of Norris's condition in 1897.

* * *

When turning from non-fiction to fiction in Volume 2 and encountering first "Little Dramas of the Curbstone," one will find that Norris may have offered to his *Wave* readers on 26 June 1897 the most telling token of the fact that his private life had been awry. This short story is more than startling, mainly because it is written in the first-person singular and at first appears an autobiographical article rather than a prose fiction. The unnamed narrator begins by providing a pathetic description of a boy who is, as his mother explains, "'blind and . . . an idiot—born that way—blind and an idiot.'" Revulsion soon replaces the narrator's sympathy, however:

> When I looked at the face of him I know not what insane desire, born of an unconquerable disgust, came up in me to rush upon him and club him down to the pavement with my stick and batter in that face . . . and blot it out from the sight of the sun for good and all. It was impossible to feel pity for the wretch. . . . His eyes were filmy, like those of a fish, and he never blinked them. His mouth was wide open.
>
> Blind and an idiot; absolute stagnation; life as unconscious as that of the jelly-fish; an excrescence; a parasitic fungus in the form of a man; a creature far below the brute. . . . He would sit like that, I knew, for hours—for days, perhaps—would, if left to himself, die of starvation without raising a finger.

Such helplessness was, perhaps, more threatening to Norris than failure. Or, was the condition of total impotence, manifested in the figure of the boy, the equivalent of failure in Norris's eyes? Supporting an autobiographical reading of this short story is the theme concerning all three of the focal characters, young people accompanied by their mothers only: where, wonders the narrator, are the fathers of the "idiot," a paralytic young girl to whom his attention is next directed, and then a young man who insists on being arrested in order to escape from his devoted mother's cloying solicitousness? That the fathers have abandoned their children is the common denominator; and self-disclosure by Norris again may be occurring. Norris was never reconciled with his own father, who deserted his family in the early 1890s for another woman. He appears to have been almost as embittered as his mother who described herself as "widow" in the city directory, long before

B.F. Norris, Sr., actually died.

An alternative reading of "Little Dramas of the Curbstone" is, as has been noted, possible for those uncomfortable with such admittedly speculative psychoanalytic inquiry: that Norris instead was adopting a persona rather than unguardedly writing out of a condition of malaise. It may be that Burgess's success and Norris's desire for the same had the dominant effect of prompting him to experiment more earnestly in unconventional literary methods common to both Naturalistic and Decadent fiction in the 1880s and '90s, with the conscious intention of shocking his *Wave* readers and the eastern publishers into recognition of his Poe-like gift for rendering the disturbingly bizarre. Zola's first success, the Naturalistic study of obsessional psychology *Thérèse Raquin* (1867), was generated thus; more recently, the resort to literary extremes had certainly worked for the boy-wonder Stephen Crane; in fact, public identification with the *avant-garde* in the 1890s required violation of literary norms and Victorian values at every turn, and "Little Dramas" may put one in mind of innovative representations of the perverse and morbid such as Huysman's *A Rebours* (1884), Wilde's *The Picture of Dorian Gray* (1891), and Stevenson's *The Strange Case of Dr. Jekyll and Mr. Hyde* (1886). In the latter Stevenson jolts the reader without warning in the same way that Norris does:

> "All at once, I saw two figures: one a little man who was stumping along eastward at a good walk, and the other a girl of maybe eight or ten was running as hard as she was able down a cross street. Well, sir, the two ran into one another naturally enough at the corner; and then came the horrible part of the thing; for the man trampled calmly over the child's body and left her screaming on the ground."[13]

After the effects of this unanticipated outflashing of "calm" violence have subsided and the reader is once more lulled into expectations of relative normalcy, Stevenson again pulls the rug from beneath one's feet. Several pages later, a maid at peace with the world dreamily enjoys the full moon seen through a window, whereupon she observes below that Mr. Hyde is talking to another man in the street. They begin to argue; Mr. Hyde lifts his cane; and he clubs the other to the earth. "And the next moment, with ape-like fury, he was trampling his victim under foot and hailing down a storm of blows, under which the bones were audibly shattered and the body jumped upon the roadway" (p. 60).

Pursuing this counter-thesis regarding a coolly deliberate Norris whose effects were more studied than they were the consequences of irrational eruptions of an anarchic personality, one will note that the Justin Sturgis and Leander dialogues published in July-August 1897 bespeak a writer in full control of his faculties and possessed of an eminently sane, healthy sense of humor. In this series is met a stylish author at his ease, confident in his ability to offer commentary on life-in-high-society in a comic medium recently popularized by Anthony Hope's *The Dolly Dialogues* (1894). "A Bicycle Gymkhana," the five "Opinions of Leander," and "Opinions of Justin Sturgis" even suggest that there was more of Burgess's silliness in Norris than he was willing to admit when he thundered against literary larking in "An Opening For Novelists." Here, for example, is the whimsical beginning of "Opinions of Justin Sturgis" in which Norris types the Wildean *littérateur:*

> "Well," said he, as I dropped down beside him, "where do you come from?"
> "Oh," replied I, "from going to and fro upon the earth and walking up and down in it."
> "What a devil of a fellow you must be, Leander."

Waggishly keyed to the conversation between God and Satan in Job:1, the piece offers fellow-sophisticates not a "virile" investigation of the meaning of human suffering but a carefree moment of pleasure. The tone is that of the witty opening of *Moran of the "Lady Letty,"* whose serialization in *The Wave* began in January 1898. Here the initial comic note is a tongue-in-cheek paraphrase of a petition in the "Litany" of the *Book of Common Prayer:* ". . . from battle and murder, and from sudden death, / *Good Lord, deliver us.*" Norris begins *Moran* with "This is to be a story of a battle, at least one murder and several sudden deaths." He follows that with what is only an apparent *non sequitur:* "For that reason it begins with a pink tea, and amidst the mingled odors of many delicate perfumes and the hale, frank smell of *Caroline Testout* roses."[14] Patrician Norris knew well his upper-class, ever-so-proper *Wave* readership that privately sated its appetite for such violence-suffused tales of mayhem, mixed with sometimes salacious love-making, in like home environments—and thus the ironic appropriateness of the initial setting in *Moran.* As one factors-in the autobiographical significance of works like "Opinions of Justin Sturgis," one may also observe another sign of Norris's vitality. In that same 21 August 1897 issue of *The Wave*, he indicates in a different way that his depression had long since passed. This dialogue appeared with the short story "The House With the Blinds" and the book review "Millard's Tales." While Norris was projecting the image of the insouciant man-of-letters, he was in fact pouring on the steam. The 31 July issue had contained no less than five of his pieces; others published during the remaining months of his apprenticeship included three and four; and the Christmas 1897 number also featured five, among

*Norris repeatedly appropriated the San Francisco
landscape in his* Wave *fictions. On this corner is
the "Polk-street restaurant" in "Bandy Callaghan's
Girl" (Volume 1).*

*Above the awning were the "dental parlors" on
Polk Street, described in "Suggestions" (Volume 1).*

*Luna's Mexican restaurant in North Beach,
cited in "Cosmopolitan San Francisco" (Volume 2)
and later used as a setting in* Blix.

*The Chinese restaurant on Bartlett Alley, near Portsmouth
Square, featured in "The Third Circle" (Volume 2) and* Blix.
Reproduced from Pacific Monthly, *17 (March 1907), 318, 320-322.
Courtesy of the Collection of Joseph R. McElrath, Jr.*

them the very sizeable and brilliant collection of parodies, "Perverted Tales."

It was time to *be*, rather than write about, the California Kipling; and, along with the non-fiction, Norris was now generating a good deal more fiction than he had prior to the summer of 1897. In terms of important career developments, Volume 2 is of primary importance as the record of Norris becoming a full-fledged storyteller.

* * *

To equal Kipling meant, first, spinning imaginative yarns set in exotic locales. Accordingly, the first of the kind in this volume is not only set in South Africa, but its story-within-a-story is related with the accent of an Australian, Miller, who tells his story about "The Strangest Thing" he ever encountered. Miller's narrative, related to his fellow passengers at sea, is a quirkily comic tale featuring developments as mysterious as they are off-color, reminding the modern reader of what Norris knew well and his more delicate contemporaries lamented volubly: that role-model Kipling was not only a mystery writer (as in *The Phantom Rickshaw* [1889]) but was widely perceived as a radical Realist whose predisposition to graphic descriptions of raw violence was equalled by his tendency to descend to morally and aesthetically offensive plot developments. As difficult as it may be to imagine today, Kipling was once classed by late Victorians with Zola as luridly improper. In July 1897, "The Strangest Thing" reveals Norris a writer of the same stripe, with a strong desire to treat the socially and morally unacceptable.

As Miller begins his tale, his listeners find him a grave-digger newly employed by an alcoholic graduate of Harvard who has somehow become stranded at the pauper's graveyard outside of Johannesburg. His boss having gone to the city to become inebriated, Miller proves as peculiar as the down-at-the-heels Harvard grad. He passes his time adorning nameless grave markers with irreverently comical epitaphs, which he still finds hilarious and relates with much enjoyment to his audience. At the point at which he receives a message from Johannesburg, "'Body of dead baby found at mouth of city sewer—prepare [grave] at once,'" Norris has developed the plot in such a way that the story is paradigmatic of the two main categories of short-story writing that he would continue to provide for *The Wave*.

The first is a conventional type of fiction for the turn-of-the-century. When the baby is brought to the graveyard, an old gentleman appears and asks for permission to open the coffin. He retrieves, with great relief, *something* from the coffin, and then he returns to Johannesburg without disclosing to Miller or his now-returned boss what that *something* is. And so ends Miller's tale. Norris here utilizes one of the standard storytelling ploys popular at the time, one common to both the tall-tale tradition and that of the gothic romance, as he would again in "The House With the Blinds" and "The Drowned Who Do Not Die." At their climaxes, the reader is left with the unknowable to ponder, *à la* Frank Stockton's "The Lady or the Tiger" (1882). In a different vein but as uninnovative in its plot is "The End of the Beginning," in which the events described are selected mainly for the sake of facilitating a surprise-twist conclusion: exactly the opposite of what was predictable occurs, the same way it did in the first use of the identical twist at the end of Volume 1's "'Man Proposes': No. 5." The Bret Harte-inspired, mining-camp tale, "Shorty Stack, Pugilist," also features an ironic reversal at its close. That is, Norris was proving himself capable of writing now-undistinguished but then-attractive short stories of the kind that regularly appeared in Anglo-American magazines and newspapers, and which might stand a chance of acceptance by eastern periodicals.

What redeems these otherwise undistinguished works is their artful variances from the norms for such formula-driven fiction. "Shorty Stack, Pugilist" is admirably innovative in one respect: Norris's expert use of an impressionistic narrative technique during a boxing match, as Shorty's mind becomes the primary register of what is occurring. His lack of ring-experience before spectators is manifested in his self-consciousness and confusion; when elliptically relating Shorty's sporadic awareness of events, Norris very effectively conveys the character's inability to detect the passing of time and all of the developments in the fight. The portrait proves psychologically true in the way that stream-of-consciousness narratives would when they became popular a few decades later. "The Drowned Who Do Not Die" transcends its sentimental, quasi-supernatural plot by virtue of the Dickensian characterization of the old salt whose tale is told, an aged eccentric who will stand favorable comparison with Mary E. Wilkins Freeman's superannuated bachelors and widowers, as well as with colorful characters of the same type in Norris's novels. "The End of the Beginning" nicely displays Kipling's ultra-Realistic influence—as well as the effects of Guy de Maupassant's and Zola's penchants for treating the sordid. The unsqueamishly rendered, noisome detail concerning the gruesome effects of exposure to the Arctic environment during a failed expedition to reach the North Pole makes the difference: the sled dogs are consumed by the hollow-eyed survivors; one character has suffered a double amputation and eats with a spoon tied to one stump; those dead from starvation are frozen solid and one makes a resonant sound when tapped; and the tent is malodorous with the smell of the unwashed.

Most anticipatory of the more original, idiosyncratic work that Norris would produce for *The Wave* beginning in the summer of 1897, though, are some of the grotesque details of "The Strangest Thing." They put one in mind of the crucifixion—of all things—with which Kipling outrageously concluded "The Man Who Would Be King" in *The Phantom Rickshaw*. The dead baby found near the mouth of a sewer; the return of Miller's boss roaring drunk from Johannesburg and his unprovoked, never-explained attempt on Miller's life; the markedly unceremonious tumbling of the infant's coffin to the ground from the delivery wagon; the kicking-off of the lid of the coffin when the maniacal boss is offered a bribe by the old man; and the old man's groping about the new-born's corpse to find the mysterious *something*—Norris had out-Kiplinged his British mentor, rendering an otherwise ordinary tale a startling exception to the rule. In the "raftsmen's passage" of *Life on the Mississippi* (1883), Mark Twain had a character spin a fanciful yarn about a dead baby in a barrel that hauntingly follows a raftsman on the Mississippi River; and the preposterousness of the story ensured that Twain would not offend Victorian sensibilities. Norris, on the other hand, designed a tasteless and morally bankrupt narrator who appears to be relating fact, and credibly so for the most part; thus, Norris deliberately induces reader-discomfort with Miller's desecration of graves and his wholly unsympathetic description of the barbaric treatment afforded a dead child who had been cast into a sewer. What Miller finds humorous is unlikely to be viewed as such by many of Norris's readers even today; those with taste for the comic styles of Erskine Caldwell, Nathanael West, and Flannery O'Connor, however, will find that Norris had anticipated those writers in developing an incisive means of revealing the brutality still discoverable in human nature despite the much-touted refining effects of Victorian culture.

* * *

In four subsequently published short stories, Norris persisted in such experimentation with taboo-violating and shudder-inducing drollery. Like Zola in his more comical moments, such as chapter 3 of *L'Assommoir* (1877), Norris demonstrates in each how the oft-cited thin line between tragedy and comedy might be made visible and then traversed for sensational effect. Wife-beating, no laughing matter then or now, was made risible in "*Fantaisie Printanière*." The comic antics of Judy and old Knubel in "Judy's Service of Gold Plate" are the stuff of vaudevillian entertainment, until Knubel's obsession with gold abruptly effects what the reader is hardly expecting in such a jolly tale: Judy's grisly murder. While the greed of the two misers in "*Miracle Joyeux*" is keyed to cartoon-like representations of human avarice, one is not at all prepared for the "joke" that Jesus—and

Norris—plays upon them; a miraculous blinding of even cartoon-figures catches the reader unprepared and not knowing quite how to respond. Worst—or best—in this vein is "The Associated Un-Charities" where blindness again becomes the means of developing a shockingly inhumane situation framed as comic.

The similarities between these four works and "The Strangest Thing" are not limited to their shared characteristics as "black comedies" providing the strange sensations for which Decadent art is well known. These stories also reveal the exercise of a Naturalistic sensibility. In them, Norris elucidates the "darker" recesses of human nature, amoral and irrational dimensions that are now supposed to be suppressed in civilized society and, in the Victorian Era, either wholly extirpated or vigorously railed against by the enlightened. Indeed, many modern readers may make a self-censorial response when finding amusement in one or more of these stories, perhaps concluding that Norris has thus craftily illuminated a bit of the pre-civilized in their own personalities. Like Robert Louis Stevenson in *The Strange Case of Dr. Jekyll and Mr. Hyde* and Zola in his various treatments of the human animal, Norris was revealing in his characters the amoral "beast within" that had somehow survived the humanizing effects of evolution to determine the behavior of the conscious self. Leander proves a sadist in "The Associated Un-Charities" as he torments his victims. The abused wives in "*Fantaisie Printanière*," while not so fully developed as masochists the way Trina is in *McTeague*, animalistically display prey-traits as much as their husbands do those of predators; both women are as territorial as lionesses; and, in defending their husbands' reputations as wife-beaters, they are as violent toward each other as their husbands are with them. One might easily term their homes lairs and all four characters cave-dwellers. Knubel's personality in "Judy's Service" is one dominated by his wholly ungovernable acquisitive instinct, and this increasingly psychopathic primitive is willing to kill when the delusion that Judy has stolen what is his overtakes him. As alcohol dulls the inhibitions of Miller's boss, he becomes homicidal—a born killer, it seems, like the hero of Zola's *La Bête Humaine* (1890). Even Norris's Jesus, as human as He is divine, derives a quotient of pleasure from the affliction of the obsessively greedy miscreants who attempt to manipulate Him. Successfully droll in varying degrees, each of these stories raises the quite serious question posed by a Naturalist: why does the human animal behave the way it does? Further, in focusing upon the abnormal, what may one learn about more normal human nature wherein the traits of a Knubel, a Leander, or a Miller have been repressed? We do, after all, understand what motivates these characters; and that spells at least a minimal degree of kinship.

Not at all comic are Norris's other Naturalistic short stories in which he was pursuing his Zolaesque goal as a writer of fiction. These works are quite humorless in tone; but, as in the stories intended as comic, Norris is once again inviting the reader to puzzle with him over the strange creature that is Man. Readers of Norris's novels may be surprised to find that it was not until 14 August 1897 that *The Wave* published the first of two pieces in which he finally gave his full attention to the primary tenet of the "gospel" of Naturalism to which he referred in the June 1896 review of Zola's *Rome:* that is, his French mentor's heavy emphasis in the Rougon-Macquart series of novels on the determinant in human experience that is heredity. Volume 1's "The Puppets and the Puppy" (22 May 1897) dealt with it briefly; and the "idiot" described in this volume's "Little Dramas of the Curbstone" was succinctly characterized as a victim of his degenerate father's genetic make-up.[15] But "A Reversion to Type" features a plot and a characterization of its hero that make sense *only* in terms of how they illustrate hereditary determinants in action, and it is a full-blown Naturalistic work. As the self-destructive traits of her mother eventually assert themselves in Gervaise Coupeau of Zola's *L'Assommoir*, despite the benign disposition and personal application that account for her rise as a successful businesswoman, so too with Paul Schuster, a respectable department store employee of many years. Skipping a generation in its influence, the criminal predisposition of his grandfather is activated in Paul with the help of alcohol; he behaves like a sociopath and soon becomes a murderer; then this lapse to a criminal personality somewhere within his normal one ends, inexplicably, and he returns to his old way of life.[16] Viewing the story in retrospect from 1899, one may observe that here was a clear anticipation of the "second self within" phenomenon dealt with in the genetically-focused *McTeague*.

"A Case For Lombroso" also prefigures crucial developments in *McTeague*. Here Zola's influence (particularly of his *Thérèse Raquin*) is matched by those of contemporaries Cesare Lombroso and Max Nordau, both of whom were as deterministic in their thought about the irresistible forces at work in individuals' lives. Lombroso focused upon the "born criminal," assuming that the type could be identified not only by behavior but predetermined physical characteristics; Nordau was concerned with a belief widely popular during the second half of the 19th century, that degeneracy in the species was manifesting itself and that individuals such as Oscar Wilde were signaling a devolution in western society. In "Lombroso," the hero and heroine form a relationship that is self-destructive for both. The brilliantly attractive heroine is the consequence of inbreeding in her noble, but now degenerate, family's history; her morbidly acute sensitivities are matched in their temperamental effects by a tendency to mania accounting for her irrational need to be loved by a man who at first merely uses her sexually and then abuses her. The hero, initially typing the "thoroughbred" descending from a more diverse gene pool, is reshaped in his personality by the unhealthy environment generated by their "love" affair. But heredity also seems to be at work: a latent predisposition to cruelty is activated in him; her masochism spurs him into sadism. Here one finds a "novel of degeneration" in miniature, the key elements of which were to reappear in the love-life of Mac and Trina. Indeed, *McTeague* more fully presents a case for criminologist Lombroso. Unlike the hero of the short story, whose burgeoning sadism has not yet rendered him homicidal, Mac kills his lover.

The classic triumvirate of influences at work in Naturalistic fiction— heredity, environment, and chance—does not stand in high relief in another serious work of the kind published by Norris in September 1897, though one may say that a "chance" decision on the part of the hero of "His Single Blessedness" seals his fate. When interviewed by Franklin Walker, Norris's widow related that Norris "was not particularly interested in formal psychology but was always fascinated by the way the mind seemed to work." Indeed, the mind in an obsessional condition like Vanamee's in *The Octopus* and Curtis Jadwin's in *The Pit* (1903) provided a fourth means by which Norris repeatedly delineated the complex determinism of human experience: how ideas *per se* can warp a life as fully as genetically transmitted traits. An *idée fixe* may be traceable to other determinants at work as with Knubel in "Judy's Service"; but in Norris's writings it can also be a free-standing mental construct, as in a comical Naturalistic work not noted above, "'Boom.'" Like the hero of "'Boom,'" Doychert in "His Single Blessedness" is one whose life is governed for years by a fixed notion. His is that he hates children. He offhandedly stated this once, at the time feeling no particular dislike for the young; enjoying the effect of surprise it produced in his listeners, he repeated it so often that he came to believe it; by the time he married, he had become monomaniacal about the matter; and, when his daughter was born, he could not bear to be near her, thus driving the wife he loves dearly into insanity. Though she still loves him after she recovers her wits, she becomes hysterical whenever he is present. As the story closes, Doychert has mastered his obsession but must live with its unalterable consequence, alienation from both his wife and daughter. Rather than an "irrational instinct" of the kind that controls the behavior of so many characters in the Norris canon, a simple concept has irrevocably shaped Doychert's life as tragic. He remains as trapped by circumstances he cannot control as the principal characters in "A Case for Lombroso."

* * *

INTRODUCTION

In late 1899 when he began composition of *The Octopus*, Norris's flair for "black comedy" was a thing of the past. Success had bred sobriety in that regard, but his fascination with the abnormal remained strong. In *The Octopus*, the main plot's hero, Annixter, achieves maturation as a psychologically stable and exceptionally humane individual, but only after indulging for years in anti-social behavior like that of a juvenile delinquent. A subplot treats an obsessional personality type; Vanamee is unable to accept the fact of death and ingeniously manufactures the comforting delusion that death is not real—possibly availing himself of the theory of the transmigration of souls to reach such a conclusion. Another subplot features the poet Presley, a neurasthenic who, aided by Vanamee, overcomes his depression following the death of his friend Annixter; he does so, however, by visualizing a universe in which evils of all kinds are ultimately illusory and the good, alone, in the end remains. Yet another subplot dealing with Dyke examines a Paul Schuster-like descent into rage-induced criminal behavior. Norris's next and last-written novel *The Pit*, posthumously published in 1903, was consistent with what had preceded it (save the atypical *Blix*): the hero falls prey to megalomania; the heroine's neuroses bring her to the verge of psychosis; whereupon Norris's taste for the unconventional again asserted itself. This is a Naturalistic novel which breaks the mold with a happy ending in which the "victims" establish benign control of their lives. A more sophisticated fictionalist than he was during his *Wave* days, Norris was still Norris.

Apparent in this edition will be many clear links between Norris's apprenticeship trials and the works of the advanced phase of his career, and they are more than stylistic and Naturalistically thematic. "Scene Mounting of the Future," for example, discloses Norris handling information about an operatic performance in Paris that was later put to good use for the characterization of Curtis Jadwin in *The Pit*. "From Field to Storehouse," also apparently preserved in his now-lost notebooks, provided a first-draft for a description of wheat-harvesting in *The Octopus*; "Birthday of an Old Mission" marks Norris's experience with the setting for Vanamee's nightly vigils; and "Man-Hunting" describes the locale of Dyke's pursuit by a posse. The earlier-written novels too reveal antecedents in the pages of *The Wave*. "The End of the Beginning" was reworked into the first two chapters of *A Man's Woman* (1900); and "The Evolution of a Nurse" documents the basic research that was necessary for the characterization of Lloyd Searight in that novel. The Justin Sturgis-Leander dialogues treat social situations that are immediately related to *Blix* and *Vandover and the Brute*. Norris's in-process manuscript of *McTeague* (completed at the Big Dipper Mine during a vacation from *The Wave* in the autumn of 1897) several times shows its influence. "At Home From Eight to Twelve," like "Western City Types: I: The 'Fast' Girl," was either excised from the *Vandover* manuscript for separate publication or added to it later on. As Gelett Burgess phrased it, years after he had become reconciled with Norris following the "Opening For Novelists" fracas, these *Wave* writings were the "studio sketches of a great novelist" in training, the beginnings of the greater works that Norris hoped he would someday publish.[17]

The January-April 1898 serialization of *Moran of the "Lady Letty"* that was his means of moving on provides an apt summary of what transpired during the apprenticeship. Norris's burgeoning Naturalism was registered as its hero, the sissified Ross Wilbur of the first chapter, is thrown into a barbaric order of experience at sea, shanghaied into service with the piratical Captain Kitchell. His too-civilized social self is gradually eroded and he lapses to a second, more primitive personality by way of adapting to the blatantly Darwinian environment in which he finds himself, where the "law of tooth and claw" prevails and "survival of the fittest" is writ large in the behavior of his amoral companions. Finally, he discovers the *pleasure* of killing; and the "human animal" stands revealed within the erstwhile Victorian gentleman. Zola's influence is clear; the novel is Naturalistic. And yet, the work is also Stevensonian, page for page more obviously Romantic than Zolaesque in its most primary characteristics as an adventure-romance like Stevenson's and Lloyd Osbourne's *The Wrecker* (1892). It also smacks of Kipling's *Captains Courageous* (1897). In addition, the first chapter—as has been noted—is written in the manner of drawing-room comedy, as was Norris's possible model for it: the first chapter of Anthony Hope's wildly popular *Prisoner of Zenda* (1894). Ross Wilbur's attendance upon Josie Herrick during the pink tea at her house is tonally identical with Hope's introduction of his dandyish hero, Rudolph Rassendyll, prior to his similar sally into the realm of Romantic adventures:

> "I wonder when in the world you're going to do anything, Rudolph," said my brother's wife.
> "My dear Rose," I answered, laying down my egg-spoon, "why in the world should I do anything? My position is a comfortable one. I have an income nearly sufficient for my wants (no one's income is ever quite sufficient, you know). I enjoy an enviable social position; I am brother to Lord Burlesdon, and brother-in-law to that most charming lady his countess. Behold, it is enough!"[18]

When Ross leaves the pink tea, his kinship is clear: "'I wonder what I'm going to do with myself till supper-time,' he muttered as he came down the

" Miss Herrick," he said, "this is Moran."

Moran is nowhere more whimsical than when the hero introduces the whiskey-drinking, tatooed, and quite muscular Moran Sternersen to his one-time belle, the diminutive and refined Josie Herrick. Frontispiece illustration of the 1910 English edition, entitled Shanghaied. *Courtesy of the Collection of Joseph R. McElrath, Jr.*

steps, feeling for the middle of his stick. He found no immediate answer to his question. But the afternoon was fine and he set off to walk in the direction of the town, with a half-formed idea of looking in at his club."[19]

Moran in itself is as eclectic as Norris's body of 159 other *Wave* writings. It is a novel as difficult to reduce to an epithet as the collection of works assembled in these two volumes. The same is almost as true of *McTeague*. Yes, it is a somber study of a tragic fall precipitated by life's inexorable determinisms; the McTeagues suffer more than we think anyone should and are powerless to escape the downward, degenerative spiral in which they are caught. And yet, its first half is Rabelaisian in its comic gusto, Dickensian in its exaggerative delineations of the motley cast of characters assembled for the reader's delight on Polk Street, and unprecedented in its full-scale local-color "tour" of old San Francisco before the 1906 earthquake. Naturalistic, Romantic, Realistic, Regional, Impressionistic, Decadent, mordantly serious, and comic—Norris fits all of these categories by turns in *McTeague*, as he did during the course of his apprenticeship.

When Norris published "Perverted Tales" in the Christmas 1897 issue of *The Wave*, he provided a full but far from exhaustive record regarding his catholicity of literary taste. Parodied expertly were distinctively different writers whose representative works he had come to understand intimately: Rudyard Kipling, Stephen Crane, Bret Harte, Richard Harding Davis, Ambrose Bierce and Anthony Hope.[20] Each was an original in his own way, and Norris was not only declaring his independence from them but paying homage. In *Blix*, Norris again singled out some of his influences. His alter-ego Condy Rivers is working for a periodical like *The Wave;* short stories "were his mania. He had begun by an inoculation of the Kipling virus, had suffered an almost fatal attack of Harding Davis, and had even been affected by Maupassant."[21] These writers, like Norris, had not matured in a vacuum; Maupassant, for example, was Gustave Flaubert's disciple. What made them great was that, from the congeries of influences to which they were susceptible, they emerged having synthesized their own stylistic signatures and senses of how life should be represented in art. When his apprenticeship ended and Norris went on to demonstrate that he too had fashioned a style of his own that was appropriate for his world-view, he carried with him nearly two years of experience in emulating others' methods while developing his own voice. If not with *Moran*, certainly with *McTeague* he proved in early 1899 that he had passed beyond imitation and succeeded in becoming an American original, who would influence emerging novelists such as Jack London and Theodore Dreiser.[22] *McTeague* is Zolaesque and yet uniquely Norrisean. It was this novel, not Zola's *L'Assommoir*, that had a shaping effect on John Steinbeck's *Of Mice and Men* (1937)—according to

F. Scott Fitzgerald; and Fitzgerald was well qualified to render such a judgment. He himself had earlier fallen under Norris's sway. His own Naturalistic study of degeneracy, *The Beautiful and Damned* (1922), was indebted to what he saw as Norris's precedent-setting Realism in *Vandover and the Brute*.[23]

How Frank Norris made his final preparations for this leap to fame in his own time and the securing of a prominent position in the history of the American novel is the story-within-the-stories of this second volume.

NOTES

[1]Norris was 21 when he made his first declaration of his career goal. In his November 1891 petition to the authorities at the University of California, he requested that normal coursework requirements be waived for him because of his age, experience, and professional intentions: "I entered college with the view of preparing myself for the profession of a writer of fiction." He closed by assuring the president and faculty of the College of Letters of the "sincerity of [his] desire to become a writer of fiction." *Frank Norris: Collected Letters*, ed. Jesse S. Crisler (San Francisco: Book Club of California, 1986), pp. 24-25.

[2]The record of this interview, like those for the three interviews with Norris's widow cited below, is in the Franklin Walker Collection, The Bancroft Library, University of California, Berkeley.

[3]Norris referred to himself as "associate editor" in the 9 April 1900 letter to the editor of *The Land of Sunshine*. See *Frank Norris: Collected Letters*, pp. 108-109. Norris's letter to John S. Phillips was published in Joseph R. McElrath, Jr., and Sal Noto, "An Important Letter in the Career of Frank Norris," *Quarterly News-Letter* (Book Club of California), 55 (Summer 1990), 59-61.

[4]The characterization of the "grind" occurred in the 9 April 1900 letter cited in note 3.

[5]Burgess's *Wave* writings are included in *Behind the Scenes: Glimpses of Fin de Siècle San Francisco by Gelett Burgess*, ed. Joseph M. Backus (San Francisco: Book Club of California, 1968).

[6]See Joseph R. McElrath, Jr., *Frank Norris and "The Wave": A Bibliography* (New York: Garland, 1988). Norris's publications *in toto* are identified in McElrath, *Frank Norris: A Descriptive Bibliography* (Pittsburgh: University of Pittsburgh Press, 1992).

[7]Charles Kaplan, "Fact into Fiction in *McTeague*," *American Literature*, 8 (Autumn 1954), 381-385.

[8]See James D. Hart, ed., *A Novelist in the Making* (Cambridge: The Belknap Press of Harvard University Press, 1970), pp. 78-89.

[9]Franklin Walker, *Frank Norris: A Biography* (Garden City, N. Y.: Doubleday, Doran, 1932), p. 144.

[10]A verbatim transcription of the memoir in the Franklin Walker Collection at The Bancroft Library is available in Charles L. Crow, "Bruce Porter's Memoir of Frank Norris," *Frank Norris Studies*, No. 3 (Spring 1987), 1-2.

[11]See Joseph R. McElrath, Jr., "Frank Norris: Early Posthumous Responses," *American Literary Realism*, 12 (Spring 1979), 1-76.

[12]*The Machine in the Garden: Technology and the Pastoral Ideal in America* (New York: Oxford University Press, 1964), pp. 343-344. Marx's observations were first published in "Two Kingdoms of Force," *Massachusetts Review*, 1 (October 1959), 62-95; they were initially contradicted by Donald Pizer, "Synthetic Criticism and Frank Norris; Or, Mr. Marx, Mr. Taylor, and *The Octopus*," *American Literature*, 34 (January 1963), 532-541.

[13](New York: New American Library, 1987), p. 40. The quotation below is from the same edition, with the pagination cited in parentheses.

[14]"A Critical Edition of Frank Norris's *Moran of the Lady Letty: A Story of Adventure off the California Coast*," ed. Joseph R. McElrath, Jr., Ph.D. dissertation, University of South Carolina, 1973, p. 1.

[15]In the non-fiction "New Year's at San Quentin" (9 January 1897) Norris focused upon the criminal's aversion to work of any kind: "It's dementia—hereditary mental obliquity, taking the form of a horror of work."

[16]"A Reversion" appears to have been based upon a similar, real-life experience of the kind; see Norris's description of the once-respectable John M. Oakley's debauchery that resulted in his death in Volume 1's "Things and People" (6 March 1897).

[17]Will Irwin, "Introduction," *The Third Circle* (New York and London: John Lane, 1909), 9.

[18](New York: New American Library, 1974), p. 1.

[19]"A Critical Edition of *Moran of the Lady Letty*," p. 4.

[20]A special issue of *Frank Norris Studies* (No. 15 [Spring 1993]) is devoted to analyses of Norris's parodies of the essential characteristics of each of these authors. Douglas K. Burgess, Gary Scharnhorst, Lawrence Berkove, Stanley Wertheim, Benjamin F. Fisher, IV, and Joseph R. McElrath, Jr., uniformly illustrate Norris's profound familiarity with the representative works of each.

[21](New York: Doubleday & McClure, 1899), p. 19.

[22]The influence of *Moran* on Jack London is examined in James R. Giles, "Beneficial Atavism in Frank Norris and Jack London," *Western American Literature*, 4 (Spring 1969), 15-27; and Charles N. Watson, Jr., *The Novels of Jack London: A Reappraisal* (Madison: University of Wisconsin Press, 1983), pp. 53-60. Robert M. Myers concludes that *McTeague* most likely did not directly influence *Sister Carrie* (1900): Dreiser claimed to have first read it a week after he submitted his novel to Doubleday, Page—where manuscript-reader Norris became its champion. He also observes, however, that "Dreiser, who was sensitive about such matters [i.e., the acknowledgment of influence], was unduly worried about explaining the circumstances of his first encounter with Norris's work" ("Dreiser's Copy of *McTeague*," *Papers on Language & Literature*, 27 [Spring 1991], 260-267). That Dreiser at least privately found encouragement in the

example of a writer who had radically expanded the parameters of what was morally acceptable to the publishing establishment, however, is beyond doubt.

[23]Fitzgerald also viewed *The Octopus* as an influence on Steinbeck. See Richard Allan Davison, "*Of Mice and Men* and *McTeague:* Steinbeck, Fitzgerald, and Frank Norris," *Studies in American Fiction*, 17 (Autumn 1989), 219-226; and Elaine Ware, "Struggle for Survival: Parallel Theme and Techniques in Steinbeck's 'Flight' and Norris's *McTeague*," *Steinbeck Quarterly*, 21 (1988), 96-103. Regarding Norris's influence on Fitzgerald, see Henry Dan Piper, "Frank Norris and F. Scott Fitzgerald," *Huntington Library Quarterly*, 19 (August 1956), 393-400; and Richard Astro, "*Vandover* and *The Beautiful and Damned:* A Search for Thematic and Stylistic Reinterpretation," *Modern Fiction Studies*, 14 (Winter 1968), 397-413.

THE APPRENTICESHIP WRITINGS
OF
FRANK NORRIS

1897—1898

Little Dramas of the Curbstone

The Wave, 16 (26 June 1897), 9.

The first Little Drama had for backing the red brick wall of the clinic at the Medical Hospital, and the calcium light was the feeble glimmer of a new-lighted street lamp, though it was yet early in the evening and quite light. There were occasional sudden explosions of a northeast wind at the street corners, and at long intervals an empty cable-car trundled heavily past with a strident whirring of jostled glass windows. Nobody was in sight—the street was deserted. There was the pale red wall of the clinic, severe as that of a prison, the livid gray of the cement sidewalk, and above the faint greenish blue of a windy sky. A door in the wall of the hospital opened, and a woman and a young boy came out. They were dressed darkly, and at once their two black figures detached themselves violently against the pale blue of the background. They made the picture. All the faint tones of the wall and the sky and the gray-brown sidewalk focused immediately upon them. They came across the street to the corner upon which I stood, and the woman asked a direction. She was an old woman, and poorly dressed. The boy, I could see, was her son. Him I took notice of, for she led him to the steps of the nearest house and made him sit down upon the lowest one. She guided all his movements, and he seemed to be a mere figure of wax in her hands. She stood over him, looking at him critically, and muttering to herself. Then she turned to me, and her muttering rose to a shrill, articulate plaint:

"Ah, these fool doctors—these dirty beasts of medical students! They impose upon us because we're poor, and rob us and tell us lies."

Upon this I asked her what her grievance was, but she would not answer definitely, putting her chin in the air and nodding with half-shut eyes, as if she could say a lot about that if she chose.

"Your son is sick?" said I.

"Yes—or no—not sick; but he's blind, and—and—he's blind and he's an idiot—born that way—blind and idiot."

Blind and an idiot! Blind and an idiot! Will you think of that for a moment, you with your full stomachs, you with your brains, you with your two sound eyes? Born blind and idiotic! Do you fancy the horror of that thing? Perhaps you cannot, nor perhaps could I myself have conceived of what it meant to be blind and an idiot had I not seen that woman's son in front of the clinic, in the empty, windy street, where nothing stirred, and where there was nothing green. I looked at him as he sat there, tall, narrow, misshapen. His ready-made suit, seldom worn, but put on that day because of the weekly visit to the clinic, hung in stupid wrinkles and folds upon him. His cheap felt hat, clapped upon his head by his mother with as little concern as an extinguisher upon a candle, was wrong end foremost, so that the bow of the band came upon the right hand side. His hands were huge and white, and lay open and palm upward at his sides, the fingers inertly lax, like those of a discarded glove, and his face——

When I looked at the face of him I know not what insane desire, born of an unconquerable disgust, came up in me to rush upon him and club him down to the pavement with my stick and batter in that face—that face of a blind idiot—and blot it out from the sight of the sun for good and all. It was impossible to feel pity for the wretch. I hated him because he was blind and an idiot. His eyes were filmy, like those of a fish, and he never blinked them. His mouth was wide open.

Blind and an idiot; absolute stagnation; life as unconscious as that of the jelly-fish; an excrescence; a parasitic fungus in the form of a man; a creature far below the brute. The last horror of the business was that he never moved; he sat there just as his mother had placed him, his motionless, filmy eyes fixed, his jaw dropped, his hands opened at his sides, his hat on wrong side foremost. He would sit like that, I knew, for hours—for days, perhaps —would, if left to himself, die of starvation, without raising a finger. What was going on inside of that misshapen head—behind those fixed eyes?

I had remembered the case by now. One of the students had told me of it. His mother brought him to the clinic occasionally, so that the lecturer might experiment upon his brain, stimulating it with electricity. "Heredity," the student had commented; "father a degenerate; exhausted race; drank himself into a sanitarium."

While I was thinking all this the mother of the boy had gone on talking, her thin voice vibrant with complaining and vituperation. But indeed I could bear with it no longer, and went away. I left them behind me in the deserted, darkening street, the querulous, nagging woman and her blind, idiotic boy, and the last impression I have of the scene was her shrill voice ringing after me the oft-repeated words:

"Ah, the dirty beasts of doctors—they robs us and impose on us and tell us lies because we're poor!"

*   *   *   *   *   *   *

The second Little Drama was wrought out for me the next day. I was sitting in the bay window of the club watching the world go by, when my eye was caught by a little group on the curbstone directly opposite. An old woman, meanly dressed, and two little children, both girls, the eldest about ten, the youngest, say, six or seven. They had been coming slowly along, and the old woman had been leading the youngest child by the hand. Just as they came opposite to where I was sitting the younger child lurched away from the woman once or twice, dragging limply at her hand, then its knees wobbled and bent and the next moment it had collapsed upon the pavement. Some children will do this from sheer perversity and with intent to be carried. But it was not perversity on this child's part. The poor old woman hauled the little girl up to her feet, but she collapsed again at once after a couple of steps, and sat helplessly down upon the sidewalk, staring vaguely about, her thumb in her mouth. There was something wrong with the little child—one could see that at half a glance. Some complaint, some disease of the muscles, some weakness of the joints, that smote upon her like this at inopportune moments. Again and again her old mother, with very painful exertion—she was old and weak herself—raised her to her feet, only that she might sink in a heap before she had moved a yard. The old woman's bonnet fell off—a wretched, battered black bonnet, and the other little girl picked it up and held it while she looked on at her mother's efforts with an indifference that could only have been born of familiarity. Twice the old woman tried to carry the little girl, but her strength was not equal to it; indeed, the effort of raising the heavy child to its feet was exhausting her. She looked helplessly at the street cars as they passed, but you could see she had not enough money to pay even three fares. Once more she set her little girl upon

3

her feet, and helped her forward half a dozen steps. And so, little by little, with many pauses for rest and breath, the little group went down the street and passed out of view, the little child staggering and falling as if from drunkenness, her sister looking on gravely, holding the mother's battered bonnet, and the mother herself, patient, half-exhausted, her gray hair blowing about her face, laboring on step by step, trying to appear indifferent to the crowd that passed by on either side, trying bravely to make light of the whole matter until she should reach home. As I watched them I thought of this woman's husband, the father of this paralytic little girl, and somehow it was brought to me that none of them would ever see him again, but that he was alive for all that.

*   *   *   *   *   *   *

The third Little Drama was lively, and there was action in it, and speech, and a curious, baffling mystery. On a corner near a certain bank in this city there is affixed to the lamp post a call-box that the police use to ring up for the patrol wagon. When an arrest is made in the neighborhood the offender is brought here, the wagon called for, and he is conveyed to the City Prison. On the afternoon of the day of the second Little Drama, as I came near to this corner, I was aware of a crowd gathered about the lamp post that held the call-box, and between the people's heads and over their shoulders I could see the blue helmets of a couple of officers. I stopped and pushed up into the inner circle of the crowd. The two officers had in custody a young fellow of some eighteen or nineteen years. And I was surprised to find that he was as well dressed and as fine looking a lad as one would wish to see. I did not know what the charge was—I don't know it now; but the boy did not seem capable of any great meanness. As I got into the midst of the crowd, and while I was noting what was going forward, it struck me that the people about me were unusually silent—silent as people are who are interested and unusually observant. Then I saw why. The young fellow's mother was there, and the Little Drama was enacting itself between her, her son, and the officers who had him in charge. One of these latter had the key to the call-box in his hand. He had not yet rung for the wagon. An altercation was going on between the mother and the son—she entreating him to come home, he steadily refusing.

"It's up to you," said one of the officers, at length; "if you don't go home with your mother, I'll call the wagon."

"No!"

"Jimmy!" said the woman, and then, coming close to him, she spoke to him in a low voice and with an earnestness, an intensity, that it hurt one to see.

"No!"

"For the last time, will you come?"

"No! No! No!"

The officer faced about and put the key into the box, but the woman caught at his wrist and drew it away. It was a veritable situation. It should have occurred behind footlights and in the midst of painted flats and flies, but instead the city thundered about it, drays and cars went up and down in the street, and the people on the opposite walk passed with but an instant's glance. The crowd was as still as an audience, watching what next would happen. The crisis of the Little Drama had arrived.

"For the last time, will you come with me?"

"No!"

She let fall her hand then and turned and went away, crying into her handkerchief. The officer unlocked and opened the box, set the indicator and opened the switch. A few moments later, as I went on up the street, I met the patrol-wagon coming up on a gallop.

What was the trouble here? Why had that young fellow preferred going to prison rather than home with his mother? What was behind it all I shall never know. It was a mystery—a little eddy in the tide of the city's life, come and gone in an instant, yet reaching down to the very depths of those things that are not meant to be seen.

And as I went along I wondered where was the father of that young fellow who was to spend his first night in jail, and the father of the little paralytic girl, and the father of the blind idiot, and it seemed to me that the chief actors in these three Little Dramas of the Curbstone had been somehow left out of the programme.

Centennial Jubilee of Mission San Juan
Hares and Hounds at San Rafael   A Fighting Craft of Japan

THE WAVE

VOL. XVI. No. 27   SAN FRANCISCO, JULY 3, 1897   PRICE 10 CTS.

ON THE MAIN DECK OF THE HI-YEI
The Captain of the Japanese Man-o'-War addressing his crew on the whole duty of seamen

The Cruiser *Hi-Yei*

She Has Fought at Wei-Hei-Wei and at the Yalu River

The Wave, 16 (3 July 1897), 5.

Even if the *Hi-Yei*, the visiting Japanese cruiser, is wood instead of steel, she is quite imposing enough for photographic and descriptive purposes, and when you are told, in the broken English of one of the sub-lieutenants that she took an active part in the battle of the Yalu River, you begin to regard her as quite a distinguished personage. By the way, you mustn't speak her name as though you were calling a 'bus or a newsboy—"Hi-yi! Hi-yi!"— because it is pronounced this way: "He-Yay." But this *en passant*. She is a training-ship, this "He-Yay," with a complement (I trust this is the technical word) of three hundred and twenty-five men and eighteen cadets. The cadets are the *raison d'être* for the ship, as she is their means of learning navigation and gunning and the management of men and all that goes to make up the whole duty of the seaman. The midshipman system, so it appears, obtains in the Japanese Navy, and it is to that grade that the cadets are appointed as soon as they have done their practice-work with sextant and cannon and compass.

The *Hi-Yei* is just a bit old-fashioned—at least so she appears to the observer fresh from the trim smartness of the *Monadnock* or the *Bennington*. One must remember that she was built eighteen years ago. She is a twelve-knot boat, of twenty-three hundred tons displacement and twenty-five hundred horsepower, and for battery sports two 8-inch and four 7.2-inch Krupps and six Nordenfeldts.

I have an idea that such a ship is seen at a disadvantage in her present condition and circumstances. You come away with a certain impression of haphazardness, of easy-going good nature on the part of the crew, and a vague, hardly defined familiarity between officers and subalterns, and between subalterns and men, that would rather astonish an American man-o'-warsman, and that would make an English naval commander curse God and die. But from one point of view the *Hi-Yei* is far above the best ship of either England or America. It may be an exaggeration, and the point of view may be a false one, yet somehow if it came to grapples, I would prefer a berth on board the *Hi-Yei* to one on the *Camperdown*, for instance, or the *Texas*, for this reason: The *Hi-Yei* has been proven—has received the famous "baptism of fire" that the war correspondents love to write about. She has been under fire, has shot and been shot at, knows the meaning of a real battle, and the feel of the water churned and eddied by squadrons in actual maneuver. You would be sure that after her little go on the Yalu that the *Hi-Yei* wouldn't suddenly fill and sink of her own accord, or ram a friendly hull, or turn turtle, as did the battleship of our dear Spanish friends in the Bay of Biscay. The *Texas* and the *Camperdown*, for all their gay paint and trim, smart drilling, and gray, grim guns (as, perhaps, Stephen Crane would call 'em) are amateurs at best. The *Hi-Yei*, wood-built, slow, and out of date, with her slackly-drilled crew, equipment and uniforms the worse for wear, is the professional—one of the few ships of the world's navies that has committed assault with intent to kill.

The Strangest Thing

The Wave, 16 (3 July 1897), 7.

The best days in the voyage from Southampton to the Cape are those that come immediately before and immediately after that upon which you cross the line, when the ship is as steady as a billiard table, and the ocean is as smooth and shiny and colored as the mosaic floor of a basilica church, when the deck is covered with awning from stem to stern, and the resin bubbles out of the masts, and the thermometer in the companion-way at the entrance to the dining-saloon climbs higher and higher with every turn of the screw. Of course all the men aboard must sleep on deck these nights.

There is a pleasure in this that you will find nowhere else. At six your steward wakes you up with your morning cup of coffee, and you sit cross-legged in your pajamas on the skylight and drink your coffee and smoke your cigarettes and watch the sun shooting up over the rim of that polished basilica floor, and take pleasure in the mere fact of your existence, and talk and talk and tell stories until it's time for bath and breakfast.

We came back from the Cape in *The Moor*, with a very abbreviated cabin list. Only three of the smaller tables in the saloon were occupied, and those mostly by men—diamond-brokers from Kimberley, gold-brokers from the Rand, the manager of a war correspondent on a lecture tour, cut short by the Ashanti war, an English captain of twenty-two, who had been with Jameson at Krugersdorp and somehow managed to escape, an Australian reporter named Miller, and two or three others of less distinct personality.

Miller told the story that follows early one morning, sitting on the bulk-board, sailor-fashion, and smoking pipefuls of straight perique, black as a nigger's wool. We were grouped around him on the deck in pajamas and bath robes. It was half after six, the thermometer was at 70 degrees, *The Moor* cut the still water with a soothing rumble of her screw, and at intervals flushed whole schools of flying fish. Somehow the talk had drifted to the in-explicable things that we had seen, and we had been piecing out our experiences with some really beautiful lies. Captain Thatcher, the Krugersdorp chap, held that the failure of the Raid was the most inexplicable thing he had ever experienced, but none of the rest of us could think of anything we had seen or heard of that did not have some stealthy, shadowy sort of ex-planation sneaking after it and hunting it down.

"Well, I saw something a bit thick once," observed Miller, pushing down the tobacco in his pipe bowl with the tip of a callous finger, and in the ab-rupt silence that followed we heard the noise of dishes from the direction of the galley.

"It was in Johannesburg three years back, when I was down on me luck. I had been rooked properly by a Welsh gaming chap who was no end of a bounder, and three quid was all that stood between me and——well," he broke in, suddenly, "I had three quid left. I wore down me feet walking the streets of that bally town looking for anything that would keep me going for a while, and give me a chance to look around and fetch breath, and there was nothing, but I tell ye nothing, and I was fair desperate. One dye, and a filthy wet dye it was, too, I had gone out to the race track, beyond Hospital Hill, where the pony races are run, thinking as might be I'd find a berth, handling ponies there, but the season was too far gone, and they turned me awye. I came back to town by another road—then by the wye that fetches around by the Mahomedan burying-ground. Well, the pauper burying-ground used to be alongside in those dyes, and as I came up, jolly well blown, I tell ye, for I'd but tightened me belt by wye of breakfast, I saw a chap diggin' a gryve. I was in a mind for gryves meself just then, so I pulled up and leaned over the fence and piped him off at his work. Then, like the geeser I'd come to be, I says:

"'What are ye doing there, friend?' He looked me over between shovelfuls a bit, and then says:

"'Oh, just setting out early violets;' and that shut me up properly.

"Well, I piped him digging that gryve for perhaps five minutes, and then, s' help me, I asked him for a job. I did—I asked that gryve-digger for a job —I was that low. He leans his back against the side of the gryve and looks me over, then by and by, says he:

"'All right, pardner.'

"'I'm thinking you're from the Stytes,' says I.

"'Guess yes,' he says, and goes on digging.

"Well, we came to terms after a while. He was to give me two bob a dye for helping him at his work, and I was to have a bunk in his 'shack,' as he called it—a box of a house built of four boards, as I might sye, that stood just on the edge of the gryveyard. He was a rum un, was that Yankee chap. Over pipes that night he told me something of himself, and do y' know, that gryve-digger in the pauper burying-ground in Johannesburg, South Africa, was a Harvard Grad.! Strike me straight if I don't believe he really was. The man was a wreck from strong drink, but that was the one thing he was proud of.

"'Yes, sir,' he'd say, over and over again, looking straight ahead of him, 'yes, sir, I was a Harvard man once, and pulled at number five in the boat— the 'varsity boat, mind ye;' and then he'd go on talking half to himself. 'And now what am I? I'm digging gryves for hire—burying dead people for a living, when I ought to be dead meself. I am dead and buried long ago. It's just the whiskey that keeps me alive, Miller,' he would say; 'when I stop that I'm done for.'

"The first morning I came round for work I met him dressed as if to go to town, and carrying a wickered demijohn. 'Miller,' he says, 'I'm going into town to get this filled. You must stop here and be ready to answer any telephone call from the police station.' S' help me if there wasn't a telephone in that beastly shack. 'If a pauper cops off they'll ring you up from town and notify you to have the gryve ready. If I'm awye, you'll have to dig it. Remember, if it's a man, you must dig a six foot six hole; if it's a woman, five feet will do, and if it's a kid, three an' half 'll be a plenty. S' long.' And off he goes.

"Strike me blind but that was a long dye, that first one. I'd the pauper gryves for view and me own thoughts for company. But along about noon, the Harvard Grad. not showing up, I found a diversion. The Grad. had started to paint the shack at one time, but had given over after finishing one side, but the paint pot and the brushes were there. I got hold of 'em and mixed a bit o' paint and went the rounds of the gryves. Ye know how it is in a pauper burying-ground—no nymes at all on the headboards—naught but numbers, and half o' them washed awye by the rynes; so I, for a diversion, as I sye, started in to paint all manner o' fancy nymes and epitaphs on the headboards—any nyme that struck me fancy, and then underneath, an appropriate epitaph, and the dytes, of course—I didn't forget the dytes. Ye know, that was the rarest enjoyment I ever had. Ye don't think so? Try it once! Why, God blyme me, there's a chance for imagination in it, and genius and art—highest kind of art. For instance now, I'd squat down in front of a blank headboard and think a bit, and the inspiration would come, and I'd write like this, maybe: 'Jno. K. Boggart, of New Zealand. Born Dec. 21, 1870; died June 5, 1890,' and then, underneath, 'He Rests in Peace'; or else, 'Elsie, Youngest Daughter of Mary B. and William H. Terhune; b. May 1st, 1880; d. Nov. 25, 1889—Not Lost, but Gone Before'; or agyne, 'Lucas, Lieutenant T.V.; Killed in Battle at Wady Halfa, Egypt, August 30, 1889; born London, England, Jan. 3, 1850—He Lies Like a Warrior, Tyking His Rest with His Martial Cloak Around Him'; or something humorous, as 'Bohunkus, J.J.; born Germany, Oct. 3d, 1880; died (by request) Cape Town, Sept. 4, 1890'; or one that I remember as my very best effort, that read, 'Willie, Beloved Son of Anna and Gustave Harris; b. April 1st, 1878; d. May 5th, 1888—He Was a Man Before His Mother.' Then I wrote me own nyme, with the epitaph, 'More Sinned Against Than Sinning;' and the Grad.'s, too.

11

His motto, I remember, was 'He Pulled 5 in His 'Varsity's Boat.'

"Well, I had more sport that afternoon than I've ever had since. Y'know I felt as if I really were acquainted with all those people—with John Boggart, and Lieutenant Lucas, and Bohunkus, and Willie, and all. Ah, that was a proper experience. But right in the middle of me work here comes a telephone message from town: 'Body of dead baby found at mouth of city sewer —prepare gryve at once.' Well, I dug that gryve, the first, last and only gryve I ever hope to dig. It came on to rain like a water-spout, and oh, but it was jolly tough work. Then about four o'clock, just as I was finishing, the Grad. comes home, howling drunk. I see him go into the shack, and pretty soon out he comes, with a hoe in one hand and a table leg in the other. Soon as ever he sees me he makes a staggering run at me, swinging the hoe and the table leg and yelling like a Zulu *indaba*. Just to make everything agreeable and appropriate, I was down in the gryve, and it occurred to me that the situation was too uncommon convenient. I scrambled out and made a run for it, for there was murder in the Grad.'s eye, and for upwards of ten minutes we two played at blindman's buff in that gryveyard, me dodging from one headboard to another, and he at me heels, chivying me like a fox and with intent to kill. All at once he trips over a headboard, and goes down and can't get up, and at the same minute here comes the morgue wagon over Hospital Hill.

"Now here comes the queer part of this lamentable history. A trap was following that morgue wagon, a no-end swell trap, with a cob in the shafts that was worth an independent fortune. There was an Old Gent in the trap and a smart Cape boy driving. The Old Gent was the heaviest kind of a swell, but I'd never seen him before. The morgue wagon drives into the yard, and I—the Grad. being too far gone—points out the gryve. The driver of the morgue wagon chucks out the coffin, a bit of a three-foot box, and drives back to town. Then up comes the trap, and the Old Gent gets down —dressed up to the nines he was, in that heartbreaking rain—and says he, 'My man, I would like to have that coffin opened.' By this time the Harvard Grad. had pulled himself together. He staggered up to the Old Gent and says, 'No, can't op'n no coffin, 'tsgainst all relugations—all regalutions, can't permit no coffin tobeopp'n.' I wish you could have seen the Old Gent. Excited! The man was shaking like a flagstaff in a gyle, talked thick and stammered, he was so fazed. Gawd strike me, what a scene! I can see it now—that pauper burying ground way down there in South Africa—no trees, all open and bleak. The pelting ryne, the open gryve and the drunken Harvard Grad., and the excited Old Swell arguing over a baby's coffin.

"Pretty soon the Old Gent brings up a sovereign and gives it to the Grad.

"'Let her go,' says the Grad., and with that he gives the top board of the coffin such a kick as started it an inch or more. With that—now listen to what I'm telling—with that the Old Gent goes down on his knees in the mud and muck, and kneels there waiting and fair gasping with excitement while the Harvard Grad. wrenches off the topboard. Before he had raised it four inches me Old Gent plunges his hand in quick, gropes there a second and takes out something—something shut in the palm of his hand.

"'That's all,' says he. 'Thank you, my men,' and gives us a quid apiece. We stood there like stuck swine, dotty with the queerness, the horribleness of the thing.

"'That's all,' he says again, with a long breath of relief, as he climbs into his trap with his clothes all foul with mud. 'That's all, thank God.' Then to the Cape boy: 'Drive her home, Jim.' Five minutes later we lost him in the blur of the rain over Hospital Hill."

"But what was it he took out of the baby's coffin?" said half a dozen men in a breath at this point. "What was it? What could it have been?"

"Ah, what was it?" said Miller. "I'll be damned if I know what it was. I never knew, I never will know."

Birthday of an Old Mission

Mission San Juan Celebrates Its Hundredth Anniversary

The Wave, 16 (3 July 1897), 9.

They have been celebrating down at San Juan of late, celebrating the founding of the old Mission there, with all the customary parades and reviews, and "floats" and orations and fireworks. The ancient little town is in a state of excitement, the like of which it has never known before. It was built there nearly one hundred years ago, which is ancient history as things go in California. Prior even to that time the old Mission had been erected and durably so, to boot, the walls being some four feet thick and constructed of adobe and burnt bricks. It is a thousand pities that the picturesque tiled roof has been removed and supplanted by the ugly modern affair. However, the walls and interior have remained intact, and are of more interest to the antiquarian and the amateur of the early California archaeology and architecture than perhaps any other Mission in the State.

San Juan is not only picturesque and interesting; it has an historic value as well. Adjoining the Mission church is the inevitable plaza, quite a huge affair, nearly 400 feet square. More than one review and muster has been held here where the troops—American and Spanish alike—have gone forth to battle and sudden death, while in the foothills just behind the town itself is shown the spot where Fremont unfurled the Stars and Bars and claimed the country for the United States.

Quite the feature of the celebration was the Spanish supper, served in the corridors of the Old Mission itself, an idea that was as charming as it was novel and effective. The long tables were loaded down with tortillas, frijoles, enchilladas, and the like, and the guests waited upon by the young girls of the town, who, for the occasion, masqueraded in the Spanish costumes of the early forties. The procession was peculiarly successful and under the charge of Grand Marshal Flint made a tour of the town without let or hindrance or a moment's unnecessary delay. The "floats" representing the

Bird's-eye View of San Juan

A View of the Church

Interior of the Mission

Procession Passing Down Main Street

ancient Spanish life of the place were most unique, and took the fancy of the crowd from the very start. High mass was said in the Mission church after the parade by Bishop Montgomery, who also delivered a very forcible address on the founding and purposes of the Missions.

The Mission of San Juan was organized in 1797, and the work upon the present building was commenced in 1803 by the missionary fathers, Catala, Martiarena and Tasuere. It was the fifteenth Mission started in California by priests traveling northward from Mexico, and it was not long before it had attained a great degree of prosperity. No better field for a mission could be found than in this particular valley, which, at that time, could boast of twenty-three Indian villages or *rancherias* and a native population of over a thousand. There are hardly more than a handful of these native Indians left at this time, yet they are still faithful to the Mission fathers and took part in the parade. One very curious feature of the "Jubilee" was an ancient Indian woman over 100 years old, who is still a devout worshiper in the Mission, and who was actually alive and present at the time of its foundation.

The Mission prospered well during the early years of the century. In 1800 the number of converts was 641, which, two years later, had increased to nearly 1,000—all Indians. Now, although the old building has practically outlived its usefulness, it is still in an excellent state of preservation, and there is no reason to suppose that it will not last for another hundred years, attractive as an interesting bit of archaeology, if not as the headquarters of a vigorous and influential order of friars.

The accompanying set of photographs, illustrative of the day's festivities, are from the studio of W. G. Jefferson, of Hollister, who was "on the spot at the time," and succeeded in making some very good shots.

Miss Sabel's Husband

A Vicarious Interview, with Occasional Intrusions by the Subject

----

The Wave, 16 (3 July 1897), 11.

I saw Miss Sabel in a room about as big as a trunk in which had been placed a trunk about as big as a room. So you might call it a *tête-à-tête* affair. (Observe I say "you" might call it *tête-à-tête*. I wouldn't. Her husband was there.)

Said I: "I want to say before anything else how much I'm delighted with your act, Miss Sabel. I—"

"Thank you," said Mr. Sabel. "Yes, it takes everywhere."

Miss Sabel spread her short skirt very carefully and sat down. I found a seat on the trunk.

"I'm not surprised that it should take. I'd like to know one thing, Miss Sabel, are you French or American?"

Miss Sabel cleared her throat and opened her lips.

"I—"

"She was born in this country," interrupted Mr. Sabel, "of French parents."

"Oh, yes. I see. Well, now, Miss Sabel, those songs of yours. How is it you manage to throw into them such dash, such fire, such vivacity?"

"I—"

"That," said Mr. Sabel, "is just a matter of study and practice. We go over a song word by word, line by line, till every little detail and gesture is perfect."

"It must be very fatiguing in the end," I hazarded, turning to the little songstress again.

"Oh, I—"

"Not in the least," said Mr. Sabel. "Miss Sabel would rather work than eat."

"Are you so fond of singing as all that?"

"Yes; I—"

"You may say that Miss Sabel has played the largest engagement of any vaudeville star in the United States. Why, she was at Hammerstein's Olympia three consecutive months."

"Were you, indeed? It's a wonder you didn't break down. Miss Sabel, you ought to take a rest."

"She never rests. In two years and a half she has rested six weeks."

"Where do you get your songs, Miss Sabel, and how?" I asked, desperately.

"Well, you see—"

"She never sings a song that's been sung anywhere before. *Somebody Loves Me*, for instance. She got that in MS. straight from the author. She made the song and the song made her."

"Now," said I, "that one, *Hot Times in the Old Town To-Night*, that's a ripping good song. Is it your favorite?"

"Oh, I like—"

"Oh, she likes them all. But *Hot Times* is as popular as any. Then there's *Somebody Loves Me*, and *Remus Takes the Cake*, and *Bye-Bye, Belinda*, and the *Faded Leaf of Shamrock*—all popular."

"You know what I like so much about your singing, Miss Sabel, is that you seem to be having such a good time yourself, and you laugh at your own jokes in a way that's quite irresistible, that takes your audience right off their feet. Now tell me do you really enjoy it so much as you seem to, or is that part of the game?"

"Oh, that," began Mr. Sabel, but I resolutely held my face from him, trained my glance at Miss Sabel as though I were aiming a machine gun. Mr. Sabel went on talking steadily, but in the interstices of his words I managed to make out that Miss Sabel was saying:

"No, I really enjoy it; there's something in an audience, you know—"

"—Just a matter—" (from Mr. Sabel)

"—that carries one away,"

"—of study and practice."

"—that sort of hypnotizes you;"

"—We go over a song"

"—that sort of hypnotizes you and exhilarates you,"

"—word by word,"

"—makes you excited."

"—line by line,"

"—Why, it's not so much I who have magnetism over an audience"

"—till every little detail"

"—as the audience has"

"—and gesture"

"—magnetism over me."

"—is perfect."

"Quite an idea," said I to Miss Sabel, and "hard work will tell" to Mr. Sabel. Then to Miss Sabel again:

"Where do you go from here, Miss Sabel?"

"We go," began Mr. Sabel—

"We will go to Salt Lake City and Denver," broke in Miss Sabel—

"And—"

But she had her head now and went on in spite of him.

"I'll take a company from here—from the Orpheum—"

"And—"

"and tour the West with them—"

"and—"

"and disband in Denver, I think."

"What then, Miss Sabel?"

"She," began Mr. Sabel—

"I am going on with Hallen," interrupted his wife.

"She—"

"It is to be 'Sabel, Hallen and Fuller.'"

"I only wish," said I, "that I could have got a lot of photographs of you in costume, Miss Sabel."

"Well, she—"

"It's so hard to keep photographs," she said, pathetically. "Everybody takes them from you." I had been maneuvering toward the door for some time past and just about here managed to take myself off. I went away with an impression of a very charming little woman, indeed. Josephine Sabel is not what you would call pretty, but she is French to her fingers and toes, which is much better. She can do precisely what she likes with her audiences—making them laugh or weep or whistle at her will. But if she's so fascinating to an audience, think what must she be when it comes to one man—if she cared to try. I know one man she can try it on—but, there, one forgets that there is a husband.

His Wife's Son

From the French of Marcel L'Heureux

Translated by Frank Norris

The Wave, 16 (10 July 1897), 5.

It was at Cannes that Pierre Geliot first met the adorably little Marquise de Ronières, whose divorce had made so much stir some two years before. The husband had not only won the suit, but was also allowed the custody of the child. However, the Marquise had innumerable champions, who did not hesitate to declare that she had been the victim of an odious conspiracy. After the trial she retired from the world, living alone, and visible only to her most intimate friends. It was one of these who brought Geliot to call. Marthe de Ronières was at that time eight and twenty years of age, and possessed a delicate, melancholy beauty. Pierre at once fell in love with her— *éperdument*. His was one of those nervous, highly organized natures with whom love is a mild hysteria, and all his youth he had been subject to crises of passion. His affection for Marthe seemed to be his *grande affaire*, and, in fact, though his Catholic conscience gave him many a twinge on the subject, the two were at length married. It was a strange marriage—the union of two such temperaments was in itself an augur of evil to follow.

Nevertheless their married life seemed to give the lie to the gloomy predictions of their mutual friends, and for two years Marthe and Pierre were genuinely happy. A child was born—a delicious pink little *gamin*, who came suddenly into their lives like some new kind of sunlight. But, unfortunately, though they had left the Past behind them, it was there, nevertheless, waiting and watching its opportunity to destroy this frail card house of their happiness.

*   *   *   *   *   *   *

Last summer at the seaside, the hazard of the dining-room, with brutal unconcern of consequences, brought face to face Pierre and Marthe and the Marquis of Ronières and his little son. Then, in that *banale* eating-room, in the midst of a clatter of conversation and the hurrying of waiters, occurred one of those secret dramas of life, all the more poignant because the actors must perforce repress their feelings, suffering in solitude with the hidden shame of their grief, and with humiliating knowledge that the heart of each is known to the others as an open book.

At the sight of her first husband Madame Geliot was shocked almost to the point of fainting. Throughout a period of ten years she had not heard either of him or of his son—her son—and now, suddenly from out the calmness and placidity of her life, occurred this sudden resurrection. And also must she hold herself against the maternal instinct that drew her sharply to her little son—her other dearer little first son, who had long since forgotten her.

The two husbands furtively observed each other, hating one another at first sight, moved by an unreasoned instinct. Ronières affected a lofty indifference, and a stolidity he was far from feeling, while Geliot betrayed his agitation by a sudden restlessness—a movement of the finer muscles of the face and a quantity of nervous and erratic gestures which he found as impossible to control as the twitchings of Saint Vitus. And the drama of this lamentable scene was made still more poignant by the presence of the two little children unconsciously exchanging smiles and coquetries with one another across the table.

*   *   *   *   *   *

That same evening M. and Madame Geliot went back to Paris. Not a word was ever spoken between them of the dreadful scene in the hotel dining-room, but merely by the glances exchanged between them they knew that their happiness was at an end—that hereafter the Past would stand between them, killing their mutual confidence and poisoning their lives.

By far the bitterest jealousy is that which is jealous of the past—that has nothing tangible to work upon—that fights the air in the dark!

How often, in the first months of their marriage, had Pierre Geliot felt its spur! But in the end time had done its work. He did not know the Marquis de Ronières, had never seen the son of his wife. By means of her tact and the delicacy of her affection for Pierre, Marthe had put from them both that menacing period of her life. Then their child had been born and the last tie between the present and the past seemed to have been broken. Life spread out before them fresh and new and smiling. And now the merest chance—stupid and evil chance—had all at once quickened this past they believed forever dead.

From this time on a sombre process began to take place in the mind of Pierre Geliot. His memory, abnormally active, and his imagination, abnormally vivid, had carried away from the hotel dining-room not only the general impression of the scene, but also its most trivial details. At will Geliot fancied he could recall it all with the distinctness of a photograph, especially the pale and impassive face of the Marquis, with his blonde beard and his eyes of a hard, cold blue, and he could picture to himself his wife's son, blonde and pale like his father. The resemblance was striking. At once he found himself comparing the physiognomy of Ronières with that of his own son, who also was blonde, who also was pale, who also had cold blue eyes. His own son strongly resembled that of the Marquis, and abruptly the logical conclusion to be drawn from the resemblance, gripped upon him, brutally, fiercely, resistlessly.

Pierre would have fled from the horrible idea, but in vain. He studied his son closely. The likeness was certain—undeniable—and the miserable man told himself that, no doubt, Ronières had also perceived the likeness, and that, no doubt, his *amour propre* had thrilled with joy and satisfaction at the thought.

Given the naturally nervous temperament of Pierre Geliot, it is easy to understand and imagine the disorders that were the outcome of his fancied discovery. The idea of this fatal resemblance tortured him in his love, in his pride, and in every quality of his nature. It became firmly established in his brain, undermined his reason, overturned his intelligence. The progress of the moral disease was not slow. Every day Pierre loosened his grip upon his wits. Even by his attitudes and gestures one could see that he was rapidly approaching a nervous crisis. He began to loathe his wife and child. More than once Marthe surprised him watching them with the expression of the deepest hatred in his eyes.

One day she tried to question him on his trouble. What was it that was so weighing upon his mind? What evil was this he was hiding from her? He looked at her an instant in silence, then, suddenly seized by an ungovernable fury, struck her and thrust roughly from him her little child, who had been clinging about her skirts. His little son fell, cutting his forehead on a projecting angle of the furniture. There was a spurt of blood, and Pierre, raising his voice in a lamentable cry, fled away, down the staircases of the house.

*　　*　　*　　*　　*　　*

To-day, in the sanitarium where he is confined, the unhappy madman, by a singular shifting of identity, believes himself to be the Marquis of Ronières and implores his guardians to help him mete out vengeance upon this wretch Geliot, who has slain his son.

A Bicycle Gymkhana

How Leander Proposed to Vary the Meets of the Whirligig Club

The Wave, 16 (10 July 1897), 9.

Leander sat down suddenly on my bench in the Park, where I had been listening to the music, and pushed his hat back. There was an agitation in his manner that betrayed intense excitement.

"Say, Just', I've got an idea."

"It's astonishing."

"You bet it is—I mean the idea, you fool."

"Oh."

"Listen here. I know you think I'm crazy about—"

"The head?"

"No, no. About wheels, by—"

"Same thing."

"Oh, well, if you won't listen."

"Go on, go on."

"Well, you know, that wheel club of ours; we call it the Whirligig Club, and we've been taking fortnightly whirls for the last year or so, and we're all dead sick and tired of it. That's all we can think of doing. We ride in the hot sun all day and drink beer en route and get up the next morning feeling like 30 cents, and—well you know how it is."

"I don't either."

"You said you wouldn't interrupt; wait till I unfold this idea. Now you know there's a girls' club around the corner from our quarters. They call themselves the Ixions, or some other fool name, but we've nicknamed 'em the 'Mary-Go-Rounds;' capital josh name, isn't it, now, for a girls' bike club? 'Mary-Go-Rounds;' I invented the name. Well, there's a scheme on foot to get up some kind of a joint entertainment—sort of a moonlight ride—a fly-by-night. The same kind of old thing we're sick and tired of. Well, now,

I'm going to propose to the Mary-Go-Rounds—"

"Which one?"

"Oh, get out. I'm going to propose that we all have a—what do you call it?—a gin—a gin—"

"Fizz?"

"No, a gym—gym—something or other. Some kind of a do-funny with an Indian name; see it in Kipling's stories."

"Oh, a gymkhana."

"Right you are. Yesir, a bicycle gymkhana. We and the girls get together and, oh, do all sorts of things; we—"

"You needn't wait for a gymkhana for that, you know."

"Just', you're horribly indelicate. I mean, mean—now, listen: we get a big building. The Mechanics' Pavilion would do, and have all sorts of events on bikes, potato races, hurdle races, lancers, obstacle races, slow races, and then, oh, yes, we'd wear—well, to begin with: First would come a sort of a march around. We'd all wear white duck trousers, and—"

"Leander!! Talk about 'horrible indelicacy!' Really I can't listen to this."

"No, no. We wouldn't wear 'em; we—"

"Good bye; sir, unhand me—"

"Oh shucks! I mean, of course, the Whirligigs would wear white duck trousers and caps, and red stockings, and the Mary-Go-Rounds would wear white duck skirts, and—and—and red stockings."

"Silk?"

"How do I know? Say, it would look out of sight; that march around would be a kind of musical ride; we'd go around the hall once, then down the center in twos, then down again in fours, then eight in a row, and then sixteen straight across. There'll be just sixteen of us, you know; eight men and eight girls. Then the girls would start from one corner and the men from the corner opposite and cross each other in the middle of the hall, forming a letter X—(frantic applause from the gallery). The next event would be a potato race for three Whirligigs and three Mary-Go-Rounds. You see a girl can mount so much quicker than a man that the Mary-Go-Rounds would stand a good show of winning. Then we'd have a little funny business; a fellow would come out and do a clown act perhaps."

"Oh, I see. Leander, it's a shame, you're getting up this affair just to have a chance to show yourself off in some specialty."

"Oh, dry up. Say, and then we could introduce the winding of a Maypole by twelve little girls in white dresses, their wheels all bedecked with white roses—"

"Their wheels—what, with white roses?"

"Well, fixed up, you know. Then we could have an obstacle race; we'd put a couple of hurdles across the hall and the competitors would ride down the hall, dismount, lift their wheels over the hurdle, mount again, ditto with the next hurdle, eat a cracker at the far end of the hall, drink a glass of beer—"

"Beer for the Mary-Go-Rounds?"

"Well, lemonade, if you insist, and return as they came and make a circuit of the hall. Next would come a lancers, and after that a thread and needle race. The Mary-Go-Rounds would ride down the hall, present each of the Whirligigs with a thread and needle, and wait while he threads it; when he's done that she rides back again, and the first one in wins."

"Of course."

"Well, not always, 'cause I'm going to have a race where the last one in wins."

"Again for your 'special benefit.'"

"Say, I won't stand your guying me all the time; even the worm will turn, you know. No, this race is for the one who can go the slowest on a wheel without falling off. And, then—oh, but say, this would be the event of the evening. We'd have ring riding. The contestants one by one would ride down the hall at full speed, with a long spear in their hands and try to catch a ring on the point of the spear as they go by—and then—then—then—well," exclaimed Leander, drawing a long breath, "that's as far as I've got yet. Say, what do you think of the idea?"

"Leander," said I, "you've got a head between your shoulders, beyond any doubt, and if there are wheels in it they constantly do turn to some purpose. The bicycle gymkhana is a novel and fetching idea, and some of the clubs here certainly ought to try it on."

"This Animal of a Buldy Jones"

The Wave, 16 (17 July 1897), 5.

We could always look for fine fighting at Julian's of a Monday morning, because at that time the model was posed for the week, and we picked out the places from which to work. Of course the first ten of the *esquisse* men had first choice. So, no matter how early you got up, and how resolutely you held to your first row *tabouret*, chaps like Roubault, or Marioton, or the little Russian, whom we nicknamed Choubersky, or Haushaulder, or the big American—"This Animal of a Buldy Jones"—all strong *esquisse* men, could always chuck you out when they came, which they did about ten o'clock, when everything had quieted down. When two particularly big, quick-tempered, obstinate and combative men try to occupy a space twelve inches square simultaneously, it gives rise to complications. We used to watch and wait for these fights (after we had been chucked out ourselves), and make things worse, and hasten the crisis by getting upon the outskirts of the crowd that thronged about the disputants and shoving with all our mights. Then one of the disputants would be jostled rudely against the other, who would hit him in the face, and then there would be a wild hooroosh and a clatter of overturned easels and the flashing of whitened knuckles and glimpses of two fierce red faces over the shoulders of the crowd, and everything would be pleasant. Then perhaps you would see an allusion in the Paris edition of the next morning's *Herald* to the "brutal and lawless students."

I remember particularly one fight—quite the best I ever saw at Julian's—or elsewhere, for the matter of that. It was between Haushaulder and Gilet. Haushaulder was a Dane, and six feet four. Gilet was French and had a waist like Virginie's. But Gilet had just come back from his three years' army service, and knew all about the *savate*. They squared off at each other, Gilet spitting like a cat, and Haushaulder *grommelant* under his mustache. "This Animal of a Buldy Jones," the big American, bellowed to separate them, for it really looked like a massacre. And then, all at once, Gilet spun around, bent over till his finger-tips touched the floor, and, balancing on the

28

toe, lashed out backwards with his leg at Haushaulder, like any cayuse. The heel of his boot caught the Dane on the point of the chin. An hour and forty minutes later, when Haushaulder recovered consciousness and tried to speak, we found that the tip of his tongue had been sliced off between his teeth as if by a pair of scissors. It was a really unfortunate affair, and the government very nearly closed the *atelier* because of it. But "This Animal of a Buldy Jones" gave us all his opinion of the *savate*, and announced that the next man who savated from any cause whatever "*aurait affaire avec lui, oui avec lui, sacré nom!*"

Heavens! No one *aurait voulu affaire avec cet animal de Buldy Jones*. He was from Chicago (but, of course, he couldn't help that!) and was taller than even Haushaulder, and much broader. The desire for art had come upon him all of a sudden while he was studying law at Columbia. For "This Animal of a Buldy Jones" had gone into law after leaving Yale. Here we touch "This Animal of a Buldy Jones's" great weakness. He was a Yale man! Why, he was prouder of that fact than he was of being an American, or even a Chicagoan—and that is saying much. Why, he couldn't talk of Yale without his face flushing. Why, Yale was almost more to him than his mother. I remember, at the students' ball at Bulliers, he got the Americans together, and with infinite trouble taught us all the Yale "yell," which he swore was a transcript from Aristophanes, and for three hours he gravely headed a procession that went the rounds of the hall bawling "Brek! Kek! Kek! Co-ex! Co-ex!" and all the rest of it.

More than that, "This Animal of a Buldy Jones" had pitched on his 'varsity baseball nine. In his studio—quite the swellest in the Quarter, by the way —he had a collection of balls that he had pitched in match games at different times, and he used to show them to us reverently, and if we were especial friends, would allow us to handle them. They were all written over with names and dates. He would explain them to us one by one:

"This one," he would say, "I pitched in the Princeton game, and here's two I pitched in the Harvard game—hard game that—our catcher gave out— guess he couldn't hold me" (with a grin of pride) "and Harvard made it interesting for me until the fifth inning, then I made two men fan out one after the other, and then, just to show 'em what I could do, filled the bases, got three balls called on me, and then pitched two inshoots and an outcurve, just as hard as I could deliver. Printz of Harvard was at the bat. He struck at every one of them—and fanned out. Here's the ball I did it with. Yes, sir. Oh, I can pitch a ball all right."

Now think of that! Here was this man, "This Animal of a Buldy Jones," a Beaux Arts man, one of the best color and line men on our side, who had three *esquisses* and five figures "on the wall" at Julian's (any Paris art student will know what that means), and who was in a fair way to be chosen to compete in the *Prix de Rome concours*, and yet the one thing he was proud of, the one thing he cared to be admired for, the one thing he loved to talk about, was the fact that he had pitched for the Yale 'varsity baseball nine.

All this by way of introduction.

I wonder how many Julian men there are left who remember the *affaire Camme?* Plenty, I make no doubt, for the thing was of a monumental character. I heard Roubault tell it at the "Dead Rat" just the other day. Choubersky wrote to "The Young Pretender" that he heard it way in the interior of Morocco, where he had gone to paint doorways, and Adler, who is now on the *Century* staff, says it's an old story among the illustrators. It has been bandied about so much that there is danger of its original form being lost. Wherefore it is time that it should be hardened and crystallized into type.

Now Camme, be it understood, was a filthy little beast—a thoroughpaced, blown-in-the-bottle blackguard with not enough self-respect to keep him sweet through a summer's day—a rogue, a bug—anything you like that is sufficiently insulting; besides all this, and perhaps because of it, he was a duellist. He loved to have a man slap his face—some huge, big-boned, big-hearted man, who knew no other weapons but his knuckles. Camme would send him his card the next day, with a message to the effect that it would give him great pleasure to try and kill the gentleman in question at a certain time and place. Then there would be a lot of palaver, and somehow the duel would never come off, and Camme's reputation as a duellist would go up another peg, and the rest of us—beastly little *rapins* that we were—would hold him in increased fear and increased horror, just as if he were a rattler in coil.

Well, the row began one November morning—a Monday—and, of course, it was over the allotment of seats. Camme had calmly rubbed out the name of "This Animal of a Buldy Jones" from the floor and had chalked his own in its place. Now, Bouguereau had placed the *esquisse* of "This Animal of a Buldy Jones" fifth the preceding Saturday, and according to unwritten law

he had precedence over Camme. But Camme invented reasons for a different opinion, and presented them to the whole three *ateliers* at the top of his
voice, and with unclean allusions. We were all climbing up on the taller
stools by this time, and Virginie, who was the model of the week, was making furtive signs at us to give the crowd a push, as was our custom.

Camme was going on at a great rate.

*"Ah, farceur! Ah, espèce de voleur, crapaud va, c'est à moi cette place là,
saligaud va te prom'ner, va faire des copies au Louvre."*

To be told to go and make copies in the Louvre was in our time the last
insult. "This Animal of a Buldy Jones," this sometime Yale pitcher, towering
above the little frog-like Frenchman, turned to the crowd, and said, in grave
concern, his forehead puckered in great deliberation:

"I do not know, precisely, that which it is necessary to do with this kind
of a little toad of two legs. I do not know whether I should spank him or
administer the good kick of the boot. I believe I shall give him the good
kick of the boot. *Hein!*"

He turned Camme around, and held him at arm's length, and kicked him
twice severely. Next day, of course, Camme sent his card, and four of us
Americans went around to the studio of "This Animal of a Buldy Jones" to
have a smoke-talk over it. Robinson was of the opinion to ignore the matter.

"Now, we can't do that," said Adler; "these beastly continentals would misunderstand. Can you shoot, Buldy Jones?"

"Only deer."

"Fence?"

"Not a little bit. Oh, let's go and punch the wadding out of him, and be
done with it!"

"No! No! He should be humiliated."

"I tell you what—let's guy the thing."

"Get up a fake duel and make him seem ridiculous."

"You've got the choice of weapons, Buldy Jones."

"Fight him with hat pins."

"Oh, let's go punch the wadding out of him—he makes me tired!"

"Horse" Wilson, who hadn't spoken, suddenly broke in with:

"Now, listen to me, you other fellows. Let me fix this thing. Buldy Jones,
I must be one of your seconds."

"*Soit!*"

"I'm going to Camme and say like this: 'This Animal of a Buldy Jones' has the naming of weapons. He comes from a strange country, near the Mississippi, from a place called Shee-ka-go, and there it is not considered etiquette to fight either with the sword or pistol—they're too common. However, when it is necessary that balls should be exchanged in order to satisfy honor, a curious custom is resorted to. Balls are exchanged, but not from pistols. They are very terrible balls, large as an apple, and of adamantine hardness. 'This Animal of a Buldy Jones' even now has a collection. No American gentleman of honor travels without them. He would gladly have you come and make first choice of a ball, while he will select one from among those you leave. *Sur le terrain*, you will deliver these balls simultaneously toward each other, repeating till one or the other adversary drops. Then honor can be declared satisfied."

"Yes, and do you suppose that Camme will listen to such Tommyrot as that?" remarked "This Animal of a Buldy Jones." "I think I'd better just punch his head."

"Listen to it? Of course he'll listen to it. You've no idea what curious ideas these continentals have of the American duel. You can't propose anything so absurd in the duelling line but they won't give it serious thought. And besides, if Camme won't fight this way, we'll tell him that you will have a Mexican duel."

"What's that?"

"Tie your left wrists together, and fight with knives in your right hand. That'll scare the tar out of him."

And it did. The seconds had a meeting at the Cafe of the Moulin Rouge, and gave Camme's seconds the choice of the duel Yale or the duel Mexico. Camme had no wish to tie himself to a man with a knife in his hand, and his seconds came the next day to choose and solemnly chose a league ball—the one that had been used against the Harvard nine.

Will I—will any of us ever forget that duel? Camme and his people came upon the ground almost at the same time as we. It was behind the Mill of Longchamps, of course. Roubault was one of Camme's seconds, and he carried the ball in a lacquered Japanese tobacco-jar—gingerly as if it were a bomb. We were quick getting to work. Camme and "This Animal of a Buldy Jones" were each to take his baseball in his hand, stand back to back, walk away from each other just the distance between the pitcher's box and the home plate (we had seen to that), turn on the word, and—deliver their balls.

"How do you feel?" I whispered to our principal, as I passed the ball into his hands.

"I feel just as if I was going into a match game, with the bleachers full to the top, and the boys hitting her up for Yale. We ought to give the yell, y' know."

"How's the ball?"

"A bit soft and not quite round. Bernard of the Harvard nine hit the shape out of it in a drive over our left field, but it'll do all right, all right."

"This Animal of a Buldy Jones" bent and gathered up a bit of dirt, rubbed the ball in it, and ground it between his palms. The man's arms were veritable connecting-rods, and were strung with tendons like particularly well-seasoned rubber. I remembered what he said about few catchers being able to hold him, and I recalled the pads and masks and wadded gloves of a baseball game, and I began to feel nervous. If Camme was hit on the temple or over the heart——

"Now, say, old man, go slow, you know. We don't want to fetch up in Mazas for this. By the way, what kind of ball are you going to give him? What's the curve?"

"I don't know yet. Maybe I'll let him have an upshoot. Never make up my mind till the last moment."

"All ready, gentlemen!" said Roubault, coming up.

Camme had removed coat, vest and cravat. "This Animal of a Buldy Jones" stripped to a sleeveless undershirt. He spit on his hands and rubbed a little more dirt on the ball.

"Play ball!" he remarked.

We set them back to back. On the word they paced from each other and paused. "This Animal of a Buldy Jones" shifted his ball to his right hand, and, holding it between his fingers, delicately raised both his arms high above his head and a little over one shoulder. With his toe he made a little depression in the soil, while he slowly turned the ball between his fingers.

"Fire!" cried Roubault.

On the word "This Animal of a Buldy Jones" turned abruptly about on one foot, one leg came high off the ground till the knee nearly touched the chest—you know the movement and position well—the uncanny contortions of a pitcher about to deliver.

Camme threw his ball overhand—bowled it as is done in cricket, and it went wide over our man's shoulder. Down came Buldy Jones' foot, and his arm shot forward with a tremendous jerk. Not till the very last moment did he glance at his adversary or measure the distance.

"It is an in-curve!" exclaimed "Horse" Wilson in my ear.

We could hear the ball whirr as it left a gray blurred streak in the air. Camme made as if to dodge it with a short toss of head and neck—it was all he had time for—and the ball, faithful to the last twist of the pitcher's fingers, swerved sharply inward at the same moment and in the same direction.

When we got to Camme and gathered him up, I veritably believed that the fellow had been done for. For he lay as he had fallen, straight as a ramrod and quite as stiff, and his eyes were winking like the shutter of a kinetoscope. But "This Animal of a Buldy Jones," who had seen prize-fighters knocked out by a single blow, said it was all right. An hour later Camme woke up and began to mumble in pain through his clenched teeth, for the ball, hitting him on the point of the chin, had dislocated his jaw.

The heart-breaking part of the affair came afterward, when "This Animal of a Buldy Jones" kept us groping in the wet grass and underbrush until long after dark looking for his confounded baseball, which had caromed off Camme's chin, and gone—Heaven knows where.

We never found it.

The Opinions of Leander

———

'Holds Forth at Length on the Subject of "Girl"

———

The Wave, 16 (17 July 1897), 7.

———

The other morning as I was engaged in shaving myself in my rooms—I have recently taken rooms not far from the University Club and am vastly set up over it—the other morning, I say, Leander dropped in. He was in a golf suit, which he pretends is a bicycle outfit, and had but that moment returned from riding his wheel in the park.

"I say, Just'," he remarked, collapsing with a groan of exhaustion among the cushions of my divan, "I say, old chap, you've got dead swell rooms here."

"Oh," said I, carelessly, as I scraped underneath my chin, "they'll do for a place to wash one's hands in."

"Come, now, don't pose; you make a guy of yourself."

"There are others," said I, and I glared at his green and red plaid stockings.

Leander curled his offending legs under him and glared back.

"Oh, well," he said—"say, Just'," he added in a moment, "what do you think of girls, anyway?"

"Do you want to make me cut myself?"

"I didn't mean to be so abrupt. But I've been thinking a good deal about girls lately."

"You have? How many? Leander, the more you think about a lot of girls and the less you think about one girl the happier you will be."

"That ain't yours?"

"I swear it."

"But, say, Just', go on; tell me, what do you think about girls, anyway?"

"'Girl'" (I misquoted)—

"Girl is a monster of such hideous mien
That to be hated needs but to be seen,
But seen too oft', familiar with her face,
We first endure, then pity, then embrace."

"Now, I know that's not yours."

"It's an improvement on Mr. Pope's patent, anyhow. What do 'You' think of girls, Leander?"

"No family should be without one," he answered promptly. "But I'm thinking of California girls—I mean San Francisco girls—the girls you and I know; the typical San Francisco girl, I mean."

"We know some very charming girls, Leander," said I.

"They are very charming."

"And pretty."

"Well, I wonder—and style!"

"None in the world more stylish."

"And jolly."

"Well, I should say so."

"And clever."

"Clever as one o'clock."

"Know how to take care of themselves."

"You betcha."

"And refined—eh?"

"Steady, now."

"Ah, that's just it."

"Suppose we compare 'em with the Eastern girls of the same class."

"Oh, don't do that."

"Ah, you see, there's a difference."

"Just the barest, tiniest, little bit of a difference."

"Well, now, hold on. I don't want to say the least little thing against our girls."

"Heavens! no."

"We know they're good, and—and—well, confound it, we know they are as straight as a string."

"I'd hit the man who'd say they weren't."

"So you would, Leander."

"But now, see here, Just', we've got to make a distinction. Of course there are girls out here who are refined to beat four of a kind—you and I and all the rest of us know that kind. They're the kind of girls whom we never talk about among ourselves, whose names you never hear mentioned in a crowd of fellows. Every fellow knows two or three of that kind of a girl."

"I know four."

"Lucky man. But they're not 'out.'"

"Never will be, thank God."

"Just', this fervor——"

"Pardon me, there are four of them I said, not one."

"Well, as I was saying, they're not society girls, and they have ideas and convictions about things. But we're not talking about those kind."

"No, let's don't."

"Those are the 'Other Kind of Girls.' Now, mind, I say there's nothing bad about these girls who are 'out.'"

"Nothing in the world."

"They're just—well, what'll I say?—not over-refined. They're too easy going; they allow a man certain little familiarities, and their only idea of a good time is unconventionality. Now, Just', I'll tell you what I saw the other day. Oh, you've seen it hundreds of times yourself—all the rest of us fellows have. I went with a crowd to Mrs. Ten Eyck's lawn party last Thursday. It was very small—only fifteen or twenty—and everybody was well acquainted. I was the only one there, I guess, who didn't know everybody. Well, there were a lot of girls along, young society girls—pretty young—swell, you know, and awfully nice. They called all the fellows by their first names, and allowed the fellows to do the same."

"They needn't have been ostracized for that."

"No, but what's the good of it? and then listen. After lunch they began to have what they called a good time."

"What did they do?"

"They played tag."

"No!"

"Yes, they did. Nothing serious in that, but it's just undignified. They ran around like so many tomboys, the girls did, and the fellows after them; and the girls' hair came down, and their faces would get red, and when a fellow would catch one of them he'd think nothing of putting his arms around her, and the girl would let him; and she'd let the next man, too, and the next, and the next. The fellows pull-hauled them about without the least cere- mony, and upon my word, the girls even seemed to enjoy it."

I think I shrugged one shoulder here.

"Just', it suggested a—a—blessed if it didn't suggest a Sunday picnic. It was common. Now, you know these girls are all right. They're straight as strings. That's why it's so strange to see. We all went into the house af- terward. Everybody paired off little by little, and towards four o'clock I found a couple in the conservatory. The fellow was smoking a cigarette— and so was the girl. Now, don't interrupt—let me tell you more about that girl. I met her and a girl chum of hers down at Monterey one Fourth of Ju- ly, and in the evening just as I was saying good-night to them, they begged me to have a couple of mild cocktails sent up to 'em from the bar."

"And did you?"

"Said I would; and then had the barkeep' mix a little grenadine and bitters in cocktail glasses and put a bit of lemon peel in. They never knew the dif- ference. Told me in the morning 'how much good it had done them'— pshaw! Now, honestly Just', what do you think of that—of the whole busi- ness, cocktails and cigarettes and pull-hauling and all?"

"Well, these girls are good girls, Leander."

"I know they are, Just'; but there's something more—something better than being merely good. My servant girl is good, my laundry woman is good; but we fellows, you know, have a right to expect something better from society girls; we expect 'em—well, damn it, y' know—to be refined and modest and well behaved and all that. Take any of those girls at the lawn party, how often do you suppose they've allowed fellows to kiss them?"

I scratched an ear.

"Now, isn't it rotten? And it's because these girls are so pretty, so fresh, and so clever, that it's a thousand pities they throw themselves away like that. They make themselves cheap in a fellow's eyes, when they ought to and when they could so easily make him respect them and—well—confound it, y' know, have a good influence over him. That sounds priggish, now, don't it; but where's a chap going to look for the good influence of refined associations——"

"Ahem, ahem—but, go on; I guess you're right."

"—if he does not find it in the best society?"

"Well, you know where to find it."

"Where?"

"'The Other Kind Of Girl,' the girl who don't 'come out,' who has ideas and opinions and convictions."

"That's so; I'd forgotten. Say, Just'——"

"But we fellows don't talk about them, y'know."

"They're all right, though," cried Leander.

"You bet, every time," said I. Then, after a pause, I said:

"You've a queer streak on to-day, Leander. How long is it since you've objected to a girl smoking cigarettes and drinking cocktails and permitting certain liberties? How about Flossie Delaney, and 'Tenny' Hunt, and——"

"Oh, that kind of a girl!" exclaimed Leander with a grin.

Miss Tyree Talks

———

Frohman's Pretty Actress Expresses Her Views

———

The Wave, 16 (17 July 1897), 13.

———

An actress who didn't want to be interviewed! Now, just think of that. And yet that's what Miss Tyree said.

"Not that I find it a bore," she said, as we sat down in the only two chairs the Endeavorers had left vacant.

"What then?"

"Only that my opinions are not important enough."

Miss Tyree is very pretty, and some men have found a pretty woman's opinions to be—under some circumstances—the most important things in the world. I wish I'd thought to say this, but I didn't. I made a deprecating mumble instead. Miss Tyree was good enough to assume it had coherency, and remarked:

"I have a conscientious objection to interviews"—I reached for my hat—"but I guess you can stay and talk."

We began on dramatic tendencies. It's a safe foundation to begin on.

"The public are getting tired of serious plays. Pinero, Jones, Grundy and those men. Somehow they're not so popular as they used to be."

"What's the trouble?" said I.

"Oh, the public must be amused. It's a great big child playing with blocks. It doesn't even want letters on the blocks. A play that strikes some seriously and stirs them up a bit—they don't want it. They want comedy every time."

"They don't want to pay attention too closely?"

"That's it. I suppose many of them are business men who come to the theater with their brains tired enough anyhow. It's hard enough to get their attention at the best, and hard enough to hold it when you've got it. But San Francisco is a first rate theater town—better even than New York."

"For instance?"

"Well, this hat ordinance. You'd never have got New Yorkers to take their hats off. Just think of having the right now to make a lady take her hat off. But there is, oh, there is one thing I wish they wouldn't do."

"What's that? They're pretty bad about some things."

"No, about most things they are pretty good."

"What?"

"Just so soon, in the last act, as a San Francisco audience sees all the actors begin to assemble for the closing tableau—just so soon as they see that, you'll begin to hear them stir and reach for their hats and things."

"That's very true. I'm afraid I've done it myself."

"You are very bad."

"I am that."

"And rude."

"I'm afraid so."

"Why do you do it?"

"Oh, I—because—well, the others do."

"Fancy now!—as if that was a reason. Do you have to catch a boat? Do you live in Oak—"

"Miss Tyree!"

"I beg your pardon. Well, then, why do you do it?"

"The seats at the Drinkand—" I began, feebly.

"Oh, pshaw, but I know. San Francisco people, the men, I mean, must eat and drink right away after the play's over."

"I never—"

"Some of them don't wait even for that."

"I go to listen to the music," I protested, stoutly.

"Why not stay and listen to the play? You've paid a dollar and a half for that."

"That's very true."

"Do you know we often have to cut and rearrange the last act just on that account, for fear the people will start to go at the wrong time?"

"I never knew that."

"But it's really very rude for the audience to act that way, and after we've tried so hard to please them all through an evening."

"Of course you're right."

"You wouldn't do it in a parlor, would you, at a musicale, say?"

"Well, naturally—"

"Look here! Suppose a chum of yours was telling you a good story, and thought you were listening, and all of a sudden you would turn your back and walk away."

"Oh, come now, it's not the same thing."

"We actors feel just as bad as your chum would."

"But are we worse in San Francisco?" I asked.

"'M-hum, much, otherwise you're fine, but you do get up before the piece is over, and it's really dreadful of you."

"But those tables at the Drinkand—" I began again.

"As though that made a difference."

"Well, I won't do it again."

"Pooh, of course you will."

"No. I promise. It is as you say, very rude and discouraging."

"And annoying to the nice people who really want to listen."

"That's so. Well, I promise."

"And say so in your interview?"

"But this was to be an interview on 'tendencies' and—and—all that."

"Bother your tendencies. Will you say so in your interview?"

"I—I guess so."

"Promise me."

"That's an old song."

"But will you say it?"

"All right, I will, like this: It is very rude and unkind and ungenerous for an audience to get up and leave the theater—or start to do so."

"Or start to do so before the very end of the piece. You'll write it just like that?"

"I will."

And I hope I have.

The Opinions of Leander

'Holdeth Forth Upon Our Boys and the Ways of Them

The Wave, 16 (24 July 1897), 7.

I was vilifying the head waiter in The Drinkand the other night, just after the play, because he would not let me sit in the main room where the orchestra plays, when Leander came up.

"Come on, Just'," said he; "you know they won't let you sit in here unless you are with ladies."

"We wouldn't permit a lady to sit in here unless she was with a gentleman, sir," interposed the autocrat.

"The danger," said I, "is due, I should suppose, to the mingling of the sexes, not to their separation—divided we stand, united we fall. You will, perhaps, recall the fable of Aesop, of the two jars floating in a cistern—*Haec Fabula docet* that——"

The autocrat wavered at this point.

"I observe," said I, pressing home, "a vacant table near the door with two places——"

"Well, you know," protested the autocrat, feebly, "it's against all regulation."

We sat down.

Leander began to bow to people he knew who were sitting at near-by tables. The place glittered with electricity and silverware. There was a staccato note of conversation in the air. The orchestra sobbed away at *La Paloma*.

"Perfect! Perfect!" murmured Leander under his breath.

"Theatre?" I asked, and looked at his clothes.

"No—call."

"What! in a brown tweed suit, tan shoes, and a blue shirt with a white collar?"

"Thanks for the collar. Yes, I have been making a call."

"In a sack suit? Good Lord!"

"Remember this is San Francisco—1897!"

"True! true! But the suit is not even black, nor the shoes—really, Leander."

"I know her rather well."

"Still——"

"My boy" (I am Leander's senior by six years) "you come from a place near Brooklyn, called New York, where everybody must conform to a certain mould in clothes as well as ideas. We in the freer West *avons changé tout cela*. Out here a man does not always have to appear in evening dress after six, nor even wear a high hat of a Sunday afternoon, unless he wants to."

We ordered our drinks. Leander, I think, had an oyster cocktail. After a moment's reflection he looked about the place, and exclaimed, nodding his head:

"For the young man with a small salary, who lives at home, San Francisco is the best place in the world."

"Or the worst," I observed.

"Huh!" exclaimed Leander, "there's something in that. But it charms you."

"So does a snake," I added, sepulchrally, "only to bite and poison you afterward."

"I say! I say!" exclaimed Leander, looking at me in some alarm; "what's up—been bitten?"

43

"Not yet—only charmed."

"Say, Just'," exclaimed Leander, "last week we said something about the girls out here. How about 'Our Boys?' We—I mean you and I, and all the rest of us—are we desirable—are we very particularly fine?"

"We are," said I, "what our English cousins would call a jolly rum lot."

"Perhaps not quite as bad as that. But we're not very nice."

"Let's see—how aren't we nice?"

"We lack purpose, aim, ambition. We are content with little things—little glasses of liqueur, for instance." (This significantly. I was drinking a *crème de menthe* myself.) "We do not rise to the dignity of champagne, or even to the height of straight Bourbon. Life," began Leander, rhetorically, "life in this city of ours is like a little glasslet of liqueur—pungent, sweet, heady, but without foundation, without stability—an appetizer that creates only small desires, easily gratified, and we are content with those. We are like this, we men—you and I and the rest of the fellows—at our best."

"Heavens! What must we be at our worst?"

"At our worst," said Leander, severely, "we get drunk and come to dances that way."

"Come, now——"

"Hoh! My dear fellow, it's a common sight."

"A fellow under the influence——"

"No, drunk—I choose to call it drunk."

"At a dance?"

"Worse—dancing."

"With a girl?"

"Whom, perhaps, you know and admire."

"Why not punch his head on the spot?"

"Bad form, head-punching, at a function."

"But not drunkenness?"

Leander shrugged.

"Who are they—what class do they trot in, in Heaven's name?"

"Ours. Many of them are college chaps in their junior and senior year."

"Little fools."

"Hear! Hear! and some even among the older men; but it's mostly the younger boys. Now, when these boys grow up and begin to associate with the kind of girl we were talking about last week—the kind of girl who smokes a cigarette on the sly and drinks a cocktail—then——"

"Leander, spare me the picture! After us the deluge."

"There's one of them now. Look at the third table."

"The slender chap with the pinkish eyelids and the impossible tie?"

"Sure! I know him—he's a Junior at Berkeley. That's his fifth *pousse café*."

"Little beast."

"He's drunk already, and I saw him just like that on a yachting party last Thursday, when there were a lot of nice girls along."

"Faugh!"

"And everybody knew it, and the girls—some of them—said, 'Oh, well, you know it's only little Jack Spratt.'"

"And yet we would call that a gentleman out here."

"As Doctor Pow Len says in Mr. Powers' admirable little play, 'such is the lamentable fact.'"

"A gentleman, that."

"In New York we would tell him his carriage was ready."

"Here he's received and called good form."

"I say, Leander, who is that broad-shouldered chap behind him, sitting with his back towards us? He's got a good pair of shoulders on him, and I don't think his tailor is responsible for 'em, either."

"Rather well put up, to be sure. Oh, I say, Just', look what he's ordered."

"Well, I declare! Tea and toast and a little fruit! Now, imagine a chap asking for tea and toast and a little fruit in The Drinkand! What a jay! Say, Leander, I think he must be a Christian Endeavorer who's blown into the wrong place."

"I've seen that chap somewhere, though," said Leander, perplexedly; "wonder where it could have been?"

"Hoh! Tea and toast and a little fruit! What a dead farmer—and—there! he's just declined to smoke. Poor little dear—if his mamma could only see him now! Bet he's got a C.E. badge on as long as your arm."

"Where in snakes," muttered Leander, "have I seen those shoulders and that head? 'Wish he'd turn around."

"There—he's getting up."

The tea and toast chap turned about, and we saw his face. Leander uttered an exclamation:

"It's Spider Kelly, the prize-fighter."

"Nonsense! Would he take tea and toast?—he——"

"Training, y' know. Fights Lon Agnew next week. Ten rounds, with a decision."

"Leander—let's take a walk. I'll pay for the drinks."

"You'd better."

There was a long silence after this, then Leander said:

"Anyhow, I've more respect just at this moment for the Spider than I have for the little college chap."

"At least he has a purpose, even if he is not 'good form,'" I murmured.

And with that we went away.

A Miner Interviewed

Lot O. Goldinsight Gives His Views of the Klondyke

The Wave, 16 (24 July 1897), 11.

Mr. Lot O. Goldinsight is in town, recently returned from the Klondyke region, where he has been spending a few weeks of the summer season hunting and fishing. Mr. L.O. Goldinsight reports excellent caribou shooting, and has brought with him a fine stand of horns. The salmon will rise to a fly on the Klondyke, according to the statements of this enthusiastic sportsman, at almost any time during the hot weather. During the intervals of his sport the gentleman employed his time shoveling gold dust into hogsheads.

"It is a very healthy exercise," remarked Mr. Goldinsight, "and especially good for the muscles of the back. I found it tiresome at first, but I assure you that at the end of my stay I could shovel my five hundred pounds per hour and never feel it. Have something to drink?" he added affably. "Won't you sit down?" He removed a floursack of gold dust from the bottom of an arm chair, and the reporter seated himself.

"By the way," said Mr. Goldinsight, "I picked this up in your park to-day. It is really a very curious specimen; perhaps you can tell me something a-bout it."

He handed the reporter a small round stone, such as is used in gravel walks. The reporter took it in his hand.

"Why sir," said the reporter, "it is merely a common pebble; we have 'em by the ton down here. It's gravel."

"Really, now," said Mr. Goldinsight, "you surprise me. You know I've been on the Klondyke so long that possibly I might have forgotten. You never see gravel up there, you know. Some prospectors have gone out for it, and I believe one or two specimens have been found near the top of the gold deposits. But the percentage of gravel to gold is so small that I doubt if it will ever pay to mine it extensively. It won't run more than an ounce of gravel to a ton or more of gold."

Mr. Goldinsight carefully returned the pebble to its buckskin bag and locked it in his safe.

"I understand, sir," said the reporter, "that you have a couple of ship loads of gold dust on the way down."

"Ballast, merely ballast," returned Mr. Goldinsight airily. "I have an offer from a concrete paving company to whom I expect to dispose of the whole consignment. It is found that the gold dust mixes well with the mortar and sand, and makes a good, firm pavement."

Mr. Goldinsight was asked as to whether the finds of gold along the Klondyke would have an effect upon the value of lead.

"It is hardly possible," he assured the reporter. "It might be run into bullets, but the Winchester and Remington and other firms are using the steel bullets so much of late that there will be practically no competition in that direction. For gas and water pipes—now there might be a market in that direction. But these gravel deposits you speak of down here—"

"Oh, there can be no doubt that the pebbles are here," answered the reporter.

"You don't think that the reports that have reached us along the Klondyke have been exaggerated?"

"Not in the least. You may say that the supply of pebbles along the ocean beach below the Cliff House is practically inexhaustible, and pebbles have been found as far south as Pescadero. There are even indications of pebbles and gravel in the Sierras and along the Mother Lode, but there they are so mixed with gold that they are considered of a low grade."

"When this news reaches the Klondyke," said Mr. Goldinsight, "I assure you there will be rush for this place. The men there will have the pebble fever at once. The difficulty will be in getting out of Alaska. You know there are two routes—one down the Yukon and one, very dangerous, over Chilly-Cat Pass. However, when a man is picking up pebbles and gravel by the hatful he won't think of his past hardships. You know," continued Mr. Goldinsight, "I am about to incorporate a company."

"Indeed, for what purpose?"

"To mine for gravel hereabouts and transport it to the Klondyke; it would fetch something like 20 cents an ounce there."

"But what would the miners there want with it?"

"Well," said Mr. Lot O. Goldinsight, "it would be a good thing to mix the gravel with our gold in order that we might pan the gold easier."

The Theatres

Pudd'nhead Wilson as Rendered by the Frawleys

The Wave, 16 (24 July 1897), 13.

At the Columbia this week one is far more interested in the play than in the actors or their interpretation of the characters assumed. It is not often this happens, and when it does, it is the result of one of two causes, either the play is of unusual strength or the actors are of unusual mediocrity. It is much more likely that *Pudd'nhead Wilson* is one of the strongest plays that Frawley has given us this season. In the title role, however, Hamilton is a disappointment, not because he is positively bad, but because he is merely negatively good. There is an opportunity in this role for actual "star" work. But at no time during the evening did Hamilton really have a hold upon his audience. It will not do to say that the house followed his lines and business with breathless interest during the close of the last act. At that moment—the critical moment in the play—it was only the situation that was interesting, and it was to this the audience gave its attention, not to Mr. Hamilton.

Right here one is tempted to criticise even the lines of Mr. Hamilton's address to the jury—at least, his closing words. As the accused impostor collapses upon the floor Pudd'nhead, turning to the jury, says, "I have done." It would have been a thousand times more effective, and at the same time less melodramatic had Pudd'nhead addressed to the Judge the usual legal formula, "We rest our case here." It seems very trivial to niggle over details such as these in a printed criticism, but heard across the footlights during the actual progress of the play they have an importance far greater than one imagines. And while we are on the subject of detail, it is worth while noting another oversight. The whole complication turns upon the mark of a bloody thumb—the ball of the thumb—upon a knife hilt. There are innumerable chances against the possibility of a thumb mark in such a spot. Nine hundred and ninety-nine people out of a thousand in grasping the hilt of a knife would close the fingers over the haft and the thumb over the fingers. It is next to impossible to grip a knife securely in any other manner; and again, it is hard to understand how, with the thumb in this position, it could be stained with blood. Contrast this with the admirably natural manner in which Pudd'nhead finally secures the all-important thumb-mark of Roxy's son, when he catches up the glass between thumb and finger.

It cannot be said that Mr. Hamilton struck the right note when, in the scene with Rowy (Miss Wallis), he first notices the discrepancies in the thumb-marks of the two boys. He has made no important discovery. His suspicions as to the interchange of the children are not aroused. He merely fancies he has, perhaps, made a mistake in labeling the marks. He is under the influence of no violent emotion. Why, then, this gasping and staggering, why this absurd blinking of the eyes, this fallen jaw and trembling hand? Mr. Hamilton overdoes the whole thing, forces the situation in order to bring about a climax of the act. Nor is the audience ever clearly aware of the exact instant when the right solution dawns upon him. In his speech to the jury he suddenly makes the charge and indicates the real Chambers, speaking of the matter as though he had known it for some time.

We had heard so much of Moretti in her role of Roxy that we had gone expecting, perhaps, too much. Miss Moretti overacts almost continually, the one notable exception being in the scene with her son when she discloses to him his relationship. Her Negro laugh is a poor makeshift. She chooses to guffaw like a full Negress, not at all like a girl who was all but white. It is not at all effective, and the audience soon tires of it. In the prologue, where her child is on his way to be baptized as a white boy, she is by no means convincing. Standing perfectly still, one hand raised and the eyes dilated may be a striking pose; it does not pass with the house for good acting. There are a thousand and one different dramatic situations, all familiar to the theater-goer, where such a pose has been used.

Gladys Wallis and Mr. Enos were in admirable contrast to Hamilton and Miss Moretti. Miss Wallis is first, last and always good; as Rowy she is as natural as a bird delivering her lines as though she had actually but that very instant thought of the words, while in the scene between the two boys, where Chambers compels Roxy's son to apologize for his insult—as serious a situation as we ever remember to have seen Miss Wallis attempt—she showed herself quite capable of something better than mere "ingenue work." Enos was especially strong as Roxy's scapegrace offspring, and was the vicious, mean-spirited "yaller coon" to the life. Ross' Chambers was as good as anything he has done this season, and Lewers as the French Count was dignified and restrained.

The "Upper Office" at Work

Detectives Who Lack the Traditional "Steel-Blue, Penetrating" Eye

The Wave, 16 (31 July 1897), 4-5.

There are wheels and springs, cogs, levers and eccentrics, in the running of a big city, just as there are in the running of a big engine. But much of the machinery is below the surface, and one is not aware of its existence, or at least is not adequately appreciative of it until one is personally affected— till one sets it in motion, as it were, by dropping a nickel in the slot. You drop a nickel, for instance, when your house is on fire, and that starts the wheels and cogs of the fire department moving, for your especial benefit, or again, your house is robbed, or a friend of yours (perhaps even yourself) is manhandled or misused by some kind of criminal, footpad, burglar, or otherwise, you drop a nickel in the appropriate slot, and straightway it starts in motion that surprising amount of complicated machinery known as the "Upper Office."

It is more interesting to watch the evolutions of upper office machinery than it is to look at the workings of the most intricate and powerful dynamo ever invented. The upper office is the headquarters of the Police and Detective systems, where Chief Lees and Captain Bohen are on duty like the engineer and fireman of a huge engine, their eyes upon the dials that indicate flux and reflux of the great city's crime-pressure, and their hands upon the throttles that check and retard its progress.

In order to see the engine at its work we will consider a typical case. Let us suppose that a crime has been committed. We will suppose a murder, because a "homicide case" is the most important kind of case in the estimation of the office, and the kind that arouses the most interest and attention. Besides, it will do as well as any from an illustrative point of view, as the preliminary moves of the machinery are much the same in every case. We will assume that on Monday of this week you found the body of a murdered woman lying on the floor of her cottage in one of the sparsely-built neighborhoods out beyond the Park. The first thing you do is to report this matter to the upper office—to Chief of Police Lees. This upper office is in the City Hall, on the lower floor, easily accessible, and open day and night. At the railing you announce the bloody business upon which you have come. You are in the outside office now, and as soon as the clerk knows your matter, he turns you over to the "desk sergeant." You say your little say over again to this desk sergeant, and he asks you question after question until you think he will never tire, and when all is over and your information has been pumped from you till you are dry as a pocket, you find that a stenographer has taken it all down in minutest detail.

Then the desk sergeant asks you to come along with him, and takes you and your statement into the inner office—the *sanctissimum sanctorum*—where Captain Lees sits watching over the city's welfare. Captain, or as he is to be called, Chief Lees, reads over the statement carefully, and perhaps asks you a few more questions. Your surprises will probably begin about here. You have thought, perhaps, that there was no more information left in you—that your case had been viewed in every possible light, but it is quite on the cards that the Chief will put to you one or two questions as penetrating and keen as lancets, that will perhaps disentangle the whole business in a twinkling, or at least give you some tangible, definite idea upon which to work.

After this, a little dramatic effect. The Chief rings his bell, and asks which one of the detectives is outside. Now, there are fifteen of these detectives in attendance upon the upper office. They have begun their respective careers as ordinary patrolmen, were moved up a grade to become corporals, another grade to become sergeants, and still another grade to become detectives. They are not "sleuths" at all. It is rather disappointing, but they are not "sleuths." They have not got "steel blue penetrating" eyes, nor "nervous, intent manners," nor even "lithe, wiry frames." You would pass them a dozen times in a crowd and not know the difference; if you did remark anything extraordinary about them they would not be good detectives, of course. Worst of all, however (it is one more idol shattered, one more illusion vanished, one more childish hope dashed earthwards) worst of all, they do not carry—but I say they—do—not—carry—revolvers! Think of that, now! Detectives—San Francisco detectives—who do not carry revolvers! I confess myself that I cannot very well understand it. Perhaps it is the fault of our criminals—perhaps they are so degenerate and effete that a revolver is superfluous. But that can hardly be. Somewhere there is something wrong. What does the detective do, I wonder, when "the infuriated man, driven to bay at last, turns savagely upon his relentless pursuer, and, with knife drawn, leaps upon him with a tiger-like bound"? By all signs and tokens he should "find himself looking down the mouth of a self-cocker." I fancy that even he would be disappointed if he did not. The absence of this self-cocker must ruin the effect of the whole scene.

Well, anyhow, these detectives do not carry revolvers. They are merely temperate, industrious men, somewhat tenacious and carefully trained in their line of business. One of these the Chief now calls into the office, and for a third time the story of the murder is re-told. In calling for this particular detective the Chief is guided entirely by his estimate of the man's abilities. Some detectives are better for a burglary case, some for a highway robbery, some for a murder, or as the upper office chooses to call it, "a homicide case." When the detective has all the points of the matter in mind, the Chief says to him:

"You'd better go out there and have a look around."

The detective "at once repairs to the scene of the crime." He is very lucky if he gets out there before the room has been touched or the body moved. He has his "look around." No matter what the case may be, or how it may develop later, there are three preliminary steps that the detective invariably takes—three things that, first of all, he tries to ascertain. The first is to find the weapon, the second is to find a motive, and the third is to find the person who was last seen with the victim. More depends on the nature of the weapon used than you would at first suppose. For instance, a revolver or dirk would indicate (I say indicate, not prove) premeditation—an axe, or chair-back, or table-leg, sudden, uncontrollable passion. Again, the knife and pistol are the weapons of the habitual criminal; the hatchet and the club are the reverse. (One hastens to add that this is mere indication—supposition—not proof.) Nothing need be said here about motives—everyone can understand their importance—but a great deal depends on the last person who was seen in the victim's company. Of course the last person, literally the last person actually in the victim's company before the firing of the shot was the murderer. It could be none else. So the detective must get as close to this "last person" as may be. He begins by finding out who was "the last person" seen with the victim. If he is not the person wanted, he is very apt to know a good deal about the case anyhow. He was perhaps next to the last person seen with the victim. So, when the detective gets him, even if he is not the murderer, he is getting pretty close to his game. There is only one man, then, that stands between him and the murderer himself.

Beyond this point the routine work ceases and the work shapes itself according to the nature of the case. But there are miscellaneous little points that are worthy of notice. They happen constantly. For instance, there are two characters that are almost sure to figure in every murder case. One is the Landlady, the other the Railway Conductor. Both of them are liable to come on in the same case. It is rather fortunate that this should be so, as an old detective once told me that the most observing people in the world were women, little girls, and railway conductors, and the latter are not only observing of faces, but (since they live, as my detective friend says, with their watches in their hands) they can remember to within five minutes as to just what particular time they observed the face in question.

Another point is that some detectives would rather have for identification purposes a good description of a criminal, than a photograph of him. I cannot make out very clearly just why this should be so, but I should imagine that a man carries about with him a certain distinct impression—a sort of symbol of his personality—and that, while he could easily change the expression of his face, either by shaving or allowing his beard to grow, he could not very well get rid of his personality—could not influence the impression he produces upon the beholder. Perhaps it is for this reason that a little girl is such a good hand at identification and observation. She is more sensitive to impression than an older person—a veritable sensitized plate, as one might say. You remember, it is said that dogs and children know a villain by instinct.

And I gathered from my detective friend that a good detective must get, as it were, an intuitive, instinctive idea of the man whom he wants—an idea, an impression, (to repeat the same word), that is quite independent of his face or his clothes, which can easily be changed.

The ideal detective would be one who could go into a ten-cent lodging house, let us say, and run his hands over the bodies of the hundreds of sleeping inmates, almost in the dark, until he reaches a certain one, and then, suddenly, almost without knowing why, stop short, get a good grip of the fellow's wrists, and then, as he wakes, be able, with some certainty, to say:

"I want you!"

The Opinions of Leander

'Commenteth at Length Upon Letters Received

The Wave, 16 (31 July 1897), 5.

Last Tuesday afternoon I went around to my favorite Chinese restaurant —the one on the top floor of the See Yup silk-merchant's—that overlooks the Plaza. I have lately contracted the habit of betaking myself thitherward for an afternoon cup of tea and a quiet half hour with a book and a cigar. It ought to be cigarettes, but I've promised a girl that—I mean that it's very charming in this golden balcony, tea is never so delicious as it is here, and your book never so interesting, and your cigar—cigar, I say, mark you—never so delicious. I like to go to this place alone, for I feel it is mine by right of discovery, but on Tuesday last I caromed against Leander at the street corner. He was in Chinatown for Heaven knows what purpose. Of course I had to take him along.

"I say, Just'," he remarked, as he sat down on a teak wood stool and plucked up his trousers at the knee; "I say, old man, this is completely out of sight. Say, Just', wouldn't this be a great place to bring the One Particular Girl to?"

I said something or other here.

Leander grinned with bland incredulity, then added:

"Would it be good form, now?" Then suddenly: "Apropos of that, Just', you and your good form and your bad form and your confounded 'opinions' have brought me into trouble."

"Oh, get out!"

"I won't—they have! I've been getting letters."

"Well?"

"From girls—girls that I don't know—who——"

"Well, there's the police, you know. The law will protect you."

"Oh, shut up! Wait till I finish. I've been getting letters from girls, and they—and they—well, they say things."

"It's a habit girls have. What do they say?"

"Here," said Leander, gravely unfolding a sheet, "is one of them. Read it." I took the letter in his hands.

"Hum!" said I; "unglazed paper, and ruled at that! Mph! Reeks of sachet, too!"

"Oh, never mind that; it's what she says."

"'Mr. Leander—Dear Sir: I read with great attention your strictures upon the young ladies of San Francisco Society' ("Spells it with a big S," I commented) 'and I wish to take this opportunity of refuting and denying your unmanly' ("Say, that's rough!") 'and malicious charges. The young ladies of this city,' I continued, 'are as well bred and refined as any of the world, and though I have been in Society for over ten years' ("That's a giveaway!" I cried, and, I'm afraid, I cackled) 'and I have never seen the slightest approach to any of the practices' ("'practices!' Good Lord!") 'to which you are pleased to allude with such shameful publicity' ("Oh, well, she's a chaperone —you can see that with one hand tied behind you"). 'In closing, all I can say is that you and your frivolous friend'——"

"That's you, Just'!" exclaimed Leander, grimly.

"——'must have been associated with a very peculiar' ("'peculiar,' underscored") 'kind of young women. You should not, I scarcely need remind you, judge all other ladies according to their own somewhat limited experiences.' No signature."

"Well!" said Leander.

"Well!" said I.

"What did you get me into this thing for?" complained Leander; "do you think I like getting that kind of a letter?"

"No," said I, "I shouldn't think you would."

"Well, then, what the devil——"

Leander's voice rose to a shrill wail.

"Leander, there's nothing heroic about you. You are not willing to suffer in a good cause. You want to do all the hitting, and when someone— someone who's been ten years in society—hits back, you squeal. Shame on you! Now, I, too, have received a letter," said I, proudly; "in fact, several of them on this same subject."

"You have?" cried Leander, blankly; "let's hear 'em."

"No, one will do; they're much alike."

"Much like mine?"

"Much unlike," I returned, loftily. "Observe now" (I held the letter towards him) "pale blue paper, rather heavy, and suggestive of parchment— very faint odor of heliotrope—and, you see, she had a monogram, because, you notice, she has cut it out to conceal her identity."

"Let's hear what she has to say."

"'Dear Mr. Sturgis—'" I read.

"That's better than 'Mr. Leander—Dear Sir,'" moaned Leander.

"I should say so," said I, very proudly. "'Dear Mr. Sturgis: I read your article last Saturday on "Girls," and I think if more people had the sense to write similar articles, it might do the San Francisco girl some good'—

"Huh!" said I, breaking off; "your girl said it was an unmanly and malicious charge."

"She wasn't young, I'll bet a hat," grumbled Leander; "and her paper was ruled—go on."

I went on: "——'some good, and open their eyes to what men really think of them'——"

"But we think very well of them," cried Leander; "that's just why we deplore their—their—vagaries."

"——'they think it's funny and that the men laugh, but indeed they don't. I am one of the girls that are "out," but believe me, we are not all that way.'"

"Hear! Hear!" cried Leander, pounding with his stick.

"——'And those of us that have'——"

"She will use 'that' for 'who'; but never mind."

"——'that have some sense of refinement feel just as the men do. Although I do not sign my name, I know you and you know me quite well.'"

"There!" said I, putting back the letter; "what do you say to that?"

"Corking fine little girl," commented Leander; "wish she'd written to me.

May be, though, she comes from Oakland."

"No; she bought this paper at Robertson's. It's stamped on the flap of the envelope."

Leander drank off the rest of his tea, and chewed a pickled watermelon rind thoughtfully. Then:

"Just'," said he, "who's to blame?"

"Who's to blame for what?"

"Who's to blame for the whole blooming show? Why do the girls smoke cigarettes and drink cocktails on the sly, and why do men come to functions drunk?"

"Leander, this brutal frankness——"

"Well, call it the vagaries of the younger set, if you like. Are the men at fault, or the girls, or is it the chaperones, or is it—by Jove, we have never thought of that!—is it the girls' mothers?"

"There's one thing," said I, "that's certain; the girls wouldn't smoke if they didn't think the men found it amusing."

"But that's just it," cried Leander. "The men don't. The girls don't know —they don't believe that the very men who encourage them to smoke have a sort of secret contempt for them after all."

"But they say they like a girl better because she's daring and chic and independent of convention. They call her *fin-de-siècle* and all that."

"Yes, that's what they tell the girl. But amongst ourselves, now, did you ever, in all your life, hear one man tell another that he liked to see a girl smoke, or that he liked her better because she knew how to handle a cigarette?"

I reflected. I tried to remember one—I am still trying.

"No, you never did, and more than that, the girls only know what the man says to them. He says, 'Oh, go on; what's a cigarette? Pshaw! I like to see a girl do everything a man does. I like to see a girl up to date.' But we— you and I and the rest of the fellows—know what these same men say of such girls among ourselves. They say 'Hoh, yes; that little girl'; then they shrug one shoulder and smile a bit out of one side of their mouth (you know the meaning of that!); 'yes, that little girl,' they say, 'she's gay all right. You can have the hell of a good time with her.' I wonder what the girl would say if she could see and hear him? I wonder if she'd think it was so damned funny to smoke a cigarette then? Admit that I'm right now. Say, ain't I right?"

"Well, I guess you are, Leander. But now look here: You say the girls would stop smoking if they knew how the men talked about 'em?"

"Of course. Do you suppose a girl likes to smoke?"

"Well, now, listen here. These men that come to functions drunk—here's a question for you—do the girls think less of them for it? How do the girls talk about them when they are among themselves?"

"That's a point to be considered," said Leander, as we rose to go.

Japan Transplanted

Practical Summer Houses *à la Japonaise* at Mill Valley

The Wave, 16 (31 July 1897), 6.

We have a little of everything out here in California—a little China, a little Mexico, a little Spain, a little France, a little Japan, and, by way of parenthesis, a little America. We hope to have a good deal of America some day, when all these nationalities become merged into one, but we are busy race-forming just now and are rather elemental as yet.

The sojourner up in Mill Valley ought not, in consequence, to be surprised to come upon a little bit of Japan tucked away in the crevices of the hills like a curio in an old stand of shelves. Somehow he is, though, and perhaps it is because this bit of Japan is so surprisingly real, so very Japanese. Things supposedly from Japan are not always so Japanese as is Mr. Marsh's Japanese villa, or perhaps village, for there is quite a collection of houses that go climbing up and around the sides of the Mill Valley canyon, some three or four miles back from the railroad station. It is said that one of Velázquez's portraits always gives the impression of being a remarkably good likeness because it is so well done. In a like manner the aforesaid sojourner in the valley is at once sure that Mr. Marsh's place is purely, thoroughly Japanese, even though he may never have been in Japan at all.

Altogether there are some dozen—it is impossible to say cottages—little Japanese summer houses, let us call them, quite habitable and practical but designed by Japanese architects and put together by Japanese laborers, low of ceiling, spacious of interior, cool, light and airy, ideal places for a hot summer's day. From the time the outer gate is entered until you pass through it again on your way out there is nothing in the least suggestive of Western civilization to be seen—nothing but yourself and your own ungainly clothes; at least they feel ungainly upon coming out any one of these delicious little houses.

One of these is built in a tree, or rather around the trunk of a tree, some forty feet from the ground—a charming little summer house as Japanese as any of the rest of them, straw thatched, and circular in form. The tree trunk is its center-post and the branches its ceiling-piece. The place is quite practical for living purposes, as was amply demonstrated some year or so ago when a journalist and his bride spent the year of their honeymoon within it.

Sailing of the *Excelsior*

A Dash for Polar Gold From San Francisco

The Wave, 16 (31 July 1897), 7.

Well, she's gone, the *Excelsior*, this last of the *Argoes*, and you and I are left behind in our offices and at our desks or counters to wonder whether after all we've done the wise thing to stay or whether we have let slip the one golden opportunity of our lives. She cleared to-day at half-past two, Tuesday afternoon, and went out with the tide, while San Francisco looked into her wake and cheered her on her way. She is gone now, and with her our last chance—your last chance and mine, and it's too late now to make up our minds.

The excitement of her departure from the Mission street wharf was quite as thrilling as anything I remember to have seen, because twenty thousand people thronged about her, packed sardine fashion on the wharves, crowding upon roofs and ships and even into the rigging of near-by masts and yards. Every class and rank and grade was represented in that crowd, from girls in smart frocks who came down from Pacific avenue in their own coupes, to stevedores and city front touts, who stood about, thumbs in belt, nodding curt farewells to grubstaked "pals," who, with blanket roll and haversack, huddled on the afterdeck. There was laughter and tears, sobs and smiles, shouts of encouragement and sighs of regret. Every mood played over that huge throng, every mood but that of indifference. Not a man or woman in those thousands could honestly say that they did not catch the excitement of the occasion, did not feel the thrill of the moment. One hasn't got so far beyond the primitive type after all, at least not so far but that the first touch of gold, the pure, crude, virgin metal, stirs us to a ferment of emotion, a very fever heat of cupidity and desire. If you do not believe this, suppose for a moment that the *Excelsior* were bound upon some business venture, e- ven one that involved millions of dollars, do you think twenty thousand men would rush together to see her go, and drown the noise of her whistle with the clamor of their shouting? Not by any means.

There was excitement in the air that verged upon hysteria; women who trailed down the gang-plank after the last bell, red and wet as to the eyelids, awry as to bonnets, their veils still up after that last farewell kiss, were the next moment laughing at the veriest trifles and talking to anyone who would listen. And, indeed, all of us on that Mission street wharf were friends; we stood upon a common ground; as lovers of gold, we were lovers of each oth- er; and men talked together and slapped each other's shoulders who will pass one another to-morrow on the street, their chins in the air, in most dig- nified and distant reserve. The thing was replete with incident. One fellow I noted who had not caught the fever. He stood near the gang-plank grin- ning cynically at the embarking argonauts and prophesying direst and most dreadful failure for the whole expedition.

"Huh!" says he, with fine scorn. "Huh! wha'd they think they're goin' to do; pick up the stuff right offun the ground, p'r'aps? Just in fistfulls? Huh!

little ol' 'Frisco's good enough for me this while to come, I guess. I got a business in hides that's all the gol' mine I want. Huh! The Klondyke! Huh! damn-fool gold bugs! Huh!" He spat into the water to illustrate the extremity of his contempt. About half an hour later, just as the *Excelsior* swung clear and began to feel the water with her screw and the crowd and whistle roared in concert, and the tossing white handkerchiefs swept over the black throng of heads like whitecaps in a black squall, this same man—I stood at his elbow—turned to a friend.

"Well," says he, with a certain defiant ring in his voice, "I could a gone 'f I'd wanted to, couldn't I, hey? Couldn't I, hey?" Then, after a pause, in a gruff mumble, as if talking to himself, "An' if that fool Batty" (Batty was his friend who had shipped), "an' if that fool Batty comes back with a wad, I'll kick myself 'round the whole damn' lot, I will."

Did I say there was no one in that crowd who was indifferent? I was wrong; there was one man. You may not know it, but the wharves are a good place on which to sleep off your liquor, and for that reason are much affected by the drunks of the Front. Such an one was caught by the *Excelsior* crowd. He was reclining against a pile of boards, and the crowd had grown up around him, and he lay there oblivious to everything that was going forward. People walked over him, even stepped on him and stumbled over him. The babel of sound was a veritable thunder, and all the sign he made was an insensate lifting of an eyelid and a vacant smile. Think of it! The city thrilling from end to end with the great find, the thousands of people rushing in to say farewell to their argonauts, and this man lay there under foot, so close to the ship that he could have laid his hand upon her hull, and cared not whether she swam or sank—probably knew not why she sailed. Never has a drunken man seemed so loathly to me. One fairly quivered with a desire to kick him from the stringpiece of the wharf and allow to perish in the water a man so utterly out of the race as this one. Not even the courage to stow himself away—one might have forgiven that—but not so much as to look on, to wallow there under foot. Why, the veriest tough, the most worthless and vicious scapegoat on the *Excelsior's* passenger list, is a hero to this beast of a man.

It was strange to see how the excitement told on the people—those who were passengers and those who were left. At the very last moment one man rushed down the plank with both hands full of silver, called a friend to him, and, as he poured the money into his hat, cried, "Give this to the wife; tell her I won't want silver up there, nothin' but gold."

Another chap suddenly remembered that he owed a departing friend a dollar, and fairly lathered himself in his exertion to reach the rail and square himself. Another man, a huge, fat fellow, who knew more people than any man I ever saw, left a little brother behind. The fat man, from the deck of the boat, was trying to talk and joke with everybody at once, but the little brother, with the tears running down his face, never took his eyes from him. The fat man never looked toward his little brother, and his face never uncreased itself from its jovial grin, but I was mighty glad to see that every now and then, on the most trivial pretext, he would come running down the plank, his huge stomach shaking in front of him, and call the little brother to him, and the two would exchange a couple of words and another hand-grip. "George," he would say, "don't forget about them insurance papers—and—and—well, good-bye again, old man."

And in another moment, after an interval of shouting and chaffing, he would be back again on some equally palpable excuse. The little brother—he was perhaps fifteen—never said a word, but he wasn't ashamed to let the whole crowd see the tears running down his cheeks.

There was another man, an old man, however, upon whom the tremendous excitement—for it was all of that—acted like heady wine (perhaps he was weak-minded, anyways—probably he was). At any rate, just when the cheering was loudest, this old man completely lost control of himself and found occasion to leap into a buggy, swinging his hat violently, and thunder, "Lookout for your souls, for the kingdom of Christ is coming. Lookout for your souls, I say."

For any one accustomed to the deliberate and ponderous movement of a liner getting under way, the actual departure of the *Excelsior* was abrupt in the extreme, almost flippant. One instant the gang-plank was drawn in; the next, ten feet of water gaped between wharf and ship, and the next the screw was churning up the waters of the bay.

She was off at last; off hardly before we knew it; off to those Arctic treasure fields, with so many hopes and fears and plans and expectations, and there in her stern and on the afterdecks were the men—plenty of them whom we knew—going out and up to that bleak, stricken, gray country away up there on the curve of world, on the shoulder of the globe, over so many miles of trembling water and so many leagues of snow and ice, to wrestle with the reluctant, frozen ground, fighting it, as one might say, grappling it with pick and shovel, tearing the heart out of it, the vitals out of it. Some of these men will find a fortune along the Yukon. That is sure; and some of them will be killed there. That is also sure. So that, taking it by and large, there is a splendid uncertainty about the whole affair that invests it with a quality of dignity like a charge of cavalry or a dash for the pole, and as the *Excelsior's* whistle roared and the water began to talk under her forefoot, and her flags stood out to the wind, and the screw rumbled in a vortex of white water, and the span between ship and wharf widened faster and faster, one ran one's eye along the groups on the receding decks from face to face, asking one's self, "Is it you who are to find fortune, you in the plush cap, or you in the brown sweater? Or is it you who are to be killed, you in the blanket roll, or you with the smart cravat?"

And so she went out, this last *Argo*, loaded with gold seekers from a land of gold, went out with the outgoing tide; and after the excitement was all o-ver and the ship gone from sight, we others, you and I and all the rest of us, set our faces cityward and thought to ourselves, "Well, she's gone, and we ain't in her, and if that fool Batty comes back with a wad, I'll kick myself around the whole damn' lot for not goin'."

The Newest Books

A Melange of Dialect, Fiction and Fact About Insect Life

The Wave, 16 (31 July 1897), 13.

Little romance should be expected from the inhabitants of Fryin' Pan and Cracker's Neck and other West Virginia and Kentucky mountain settle-ments, for little romance have they known. Their lives have been passed principally in talking dialect—wonderful and weird—given to the world many a time by as many venturesome novelists. One of the latest and best volumes of Kentucky dialect is *Hell Fer Sartin, and Other Stories*, by John Fox, Jr., published by Harper Brothers. The stories are cleverly descriptive of manners and customs, and are full of humor, a touch of which, together with the dialect, are worthy of attention:

> "Well, hain't the groun' rich? Won't hit raise no tabaccy nur corn nur nothin'?"
> Ole Tom jes whispers. ("Old Tom" isn't able to speak above a whisper.)
> "To tell you the p'int-blank truth, stranger, that land is so durned pore that I hain't nuver been able to raise my voice."

An exhaustive and satisfactory work on nature's study is *Insect Life* (D. Appleton & Company) by John Henry Comstock, Professor of Entomology in Cornell and Stanford Universities. Professor Comstock believes that all life, animal and otherwise, is linked together in such a way that no part of the chain is unimportant. In his book he gives reasons for this belief in a lengthened discussion of insect existence which is as logical as it is interesting. The book contains a great number of original illustrations engraved by Anna Botsford Comstock, and also a few appropriate poetical references.

The first publication of the writings of the late Thomas Wharton was a translation from the *Odes* of Horace, made at the age of fifteen. Almost his very last, and admittedly his best story, is "Bobbo," which has just been republished by Harper & Brothers with other of Mr. Wharton's writings under the title of *Bobbo, and Other Fancies*. The other fancies consist of "The Lost Sonnet Of Prinzivalle di Cembino," "Ratu Tanito's Wooing: A Tale of the Southern Seas," "Old and New," and a number of verses, some of them from the French of François Villon. Owen Wister contributes an introduction to the book—a sketch of Wharton's life and works.

The most amusing sketch in Ruth McEnery Stuart's new book of Southern stories, *In Simpkinsville* (Harper & Brothers), is "Weeds," a romance of the Simpkinsville Cemetery. It tells of a man and a woman bereft of wife and husband, who daily visit the cemetery, he to bury a rosebud on the grave of his departed and she to keep the grass green above the ashes of her dead. It seemed that the dead husband was not as temperate as he might have been, and for this very reason his widow labored more energetically at his tomb. To use her own words, "Somehow pore John never stood ez high ez I'd liked him to among the livin', and I have been ambitious to have him stand well among the dead." The most original, and in many ways the most characteristic, of the sketches is "The Unlived Life of Little Mary Ellen," a pathetic story of a woman who was deserted by her fiancé an hour before the time set for the wedding. Poor Mary Ellen goes out of her mind and lives for the rest of her days forgetful of her sorrow. Another interesting sketch is "The Dividing Fence," which, like "Weeds," treats of widows and widowers coming together under amusing though pathetic circumstances.

"Boom"

The Wave, 16 (7 August 1897), 5.

San Diego, in Southern California, is the largest city in the world. If your geographies and guide-books and encyclopaedias have told you otherwise, they have lied, or their authors have never seen San Diego. Why, San Diego is nearly twenty-five miles from end to end. Why, San Diego has more miles of sidewalk, more leagues of street railways, more measureless lengths of paved streets, more interminable systems of sewer-piping, than has London or Paris or even—even—even Chicago (and I who say so was born in Chicago, too!). There are statelier houses in San Diego than in any other "of the world's great centres," more spacious avenues, more imposing business blocks, more delicious parks, more overpowering public buildings, the pavements are better laid, the electric lighting is more systematic, the railroad and transportation facilities more accommodating, the climate is better than the Riviera, the days are longer, the nights shorter, the men finer, the women prettier, the theatres more attractive, the restaurants cheaper, the wines more sparkling, "business opportunities" lie in wait for the unfortunate at dark street-corners and fly at his throat till he must fain fight them off. Life is one long, glad fermentation. There is no darkness in San Diego, nor any more night.

Incidentally, corner lots are desirable.

All of this must be so, because you may read it in the green and gold prospectus of the San Diego Land and Improvement Company (consolidated), sent free on application—that is, at one time during the boom it was sent free—but the edition is out of print now, and can only be seen in the collections of bibliophiles and wealthy amateurs, and the boom is only an echo now. But when the guests of the big Coronado Hotel over on the island come across to the mainland and course jackrabbits with greyhounds in the country to the north of the town, their horses' hoofs, as they plunge through the sagebrush and tar weed, will sometimes slide and clatter upon a bit of concrete sidewalk, half sunk of its own weight into the sand; or the jack will be started in a low square of bricks, such as is built for frame house foundations, and which make excellent jumping for the horses. There is a colony of rattlers on the shores of a marsh to the southwest (the maps call it Amethyst Lake) and the little half-breed Indians catch the tarantulas and horned toads that you buy alive in glass jars on the hotel veranda near the postoffice site, and everything is very gay and pleasant and picturesque.

Why I remember it all so well is because I found Steele in this place. You see, Steele was a very good friend of mine though he was Oxon., and I only a man from Chicago. When his wife knew I was coming west she gave me Steele's address, and told me I was to look him up. Since she told me this with much insistence and reiteration and with tears in her voice, I made it a point to be particular. She had not heard from Steele in two years. The address she gave me was "Hon. Ralph Truax-Steele, Elmwood avenue and One Hundred and Eighty-eighth street, San Diego, California."

When I arrived at San Diego I found it would be advisable to hire a horse, instead of waiting for the Elmwood Avenue electric car, and when I asked for directions for 188th street a red-headed man whose father was Irish and whose mother was Chinese offered to act as guide for twenty dollars. He said, though, he would furnish his own outfit. I demurred and he went away. I was told that some eight miles out beyond the range I would find a water-hole, and that if I held to the southwest after leaving this hole, keeping my horse's ears between the double peak of a distant mountain called Little Two Top, I would come after a while to a lamp post with a tarantula's nest where the lamp should have been. It would be hard to miss this lamp post, they told me, as the desert was very flat thereabouts, and the lamp post could be seen for a radius of ten miles. Also, there might be water there—the horse would smell it out if there was. Also, it was a good place to camp, because of a tiny ledge of shale outcropping there. I was to be particular about this lamp post, because it stood at the corner of Elmwood avenue and 188th street.

When I asked about the Hon. Truax-Steele, Oxon., information was less explicit. They shook their heads. One of them seemed to recollect a "shack" about a mile hitherward of Two Top, a statement that was at once contradicted by someone else. Might have been an old Digger "wicky-up." Sometimes the Indians camped in the valley on their way to ghost dances and tribal feasts. It wasn't a place for a white man to live, chiefly because the climate offered so many advantages and attractions to horned toads, tarantulas and rattlesnakes. Then the red-headed Chinese-Irishman came back and said, with an accent that was beyond all words, that a sheepherder had once told him of a loco-man out beyond McIntyre's waterhole, and another man said that, "Yes, that was so; he'd passed flasks with a loco-man out that way once last June, when he was out looking for a strayed pony. In fact, the loco-man lived out there, had a son, too, leastways a kid lived with him." This seemed encouraging. The Hon. Truax-Steele, Oxon., was accredited with a son—so his wife had said, who should know. So I started out, simultaneously hoping and dreading that the loco-man and the honorable Truax might be one flesh.

I left San Diego at four o'clock a.m. to avoid as much as possible the heat of mid-day, and just at sunset saw what might have been a cactus plant standing out stark and still on the white blur of sage and alkali like an exclamation point on a blank page. It was the lamp-post of the spider's nest that marked the intersection of Elmwood Avenue and 188th street. And then my horse shied, with his hind legs only, in the way good horses have, and Ralph Truax-Steele rose out of a dried muck-hole under the bit.

I had expected a madman, but his surprise and pleasure at seeing me were perfectly sane. After a while he said, "Sorry, old boy. It's the hospitality of the Arab I can give you; nothing better. A handful of dates (we call 'em caned prunes out here), the dried flesh of a kid (Californian for jerked beef), and a mouthful of cold water, which the same we will thicken with forty-rod rye; incidentally, coffee, black and unsweet, and tobacco, which at one time I should have requested my undergroom to discontinue."

We went to his "shack" (I observed it to be built of discarded bricks, mortared with 'dobe mud) and I was made acquainted with his boy, Carrington Truax-Steele, fitting for Oxford under tutelage of his father.

We had supper, after which the Hon. Truax, Sr., stood forth under the kindling glory of that desert twilight by that incongruous, reeling lamp-post, booted, bare-headed and woolen-shirted, and to the low swinging scimitar of the new welded moon declaimed Creon's speech to Oedipus in sonorous Greek. When he was done he exclaimed, abruptly: "Come along, I'll show you 'round."

I looked about that stricken reach of alkali, and followed him wondering. That evening the Hon. Ralph Truax-Steele, Oxon., showed me his real estate and also, unwittingly, the disordered workings of his brain. The rest I guessed and afterwards confirmed.

Steele had gone mad over the real estate "boom" that had struck the town five years previously, when land was worth as many dollars as could cover it, and men and women fought with each other to buy lots around the water hole called Amethyst Lake. The "boom" had collapsed, and with it Steele's reason, for to him the boom was on the point of recommencing; sane enough on other points, in this direction the man's grip upon himself was gone for good.

"There," he said to me that evening as we crushed our way through the sagebrush, indicating a low roll on the desert surface, "there are my villa sites, here will run a driveway, and yonder where you see the skeleton of that steer I'm thinking of putting up a little rustic stone chapel."

"Ralph, Ralph," I said, "come out of this. Can't you see that the whole business is dead and done for long since? You're going back with me to God's country to-morrow—going back to your wife, you and the boy. She sent me to fetch you."

He stared at me wonderingly.

"Why, it's bound to come within a few days," he said. "Wait till next Wednesday, say, and you won't recognize this place. There'll be a rush here such as there was when Oklahoma was opened. We have everything for us—climate, temperature, water. Harry," he added in my ear, "look around you. You are standing on the site of one of the grandest, stateliest cities of civilization."

That night the boy Carrington and I sat late in consultation while Steele slept. "Nothing but force will do it," said the lad. "I know him well, and I've tried it again and again. It's no use any other way." So force it was.

How we got Steele back to San Diego I may not tell. Carrington is the only other person who knows, and I'm sure he will say nothing. But the singular part of the business occurred when Steele woke up, as it were, in the heart of a real city and began to look about him and take stock of his surroundings. For over a half-dozen years he had lived there on the desert in the midst of imaginary mirage-like edifices, seeing country seats in sand hillocks and rustic chapels in bleaching bones. But sound enough, mark you, on all other subjects. The collapse came—the real collapse—when Steele beheld the real city he had forgotten. He is in a sanitarium now somewhere in Illinois, and his wife and son see him on Wednesday and Sunday afternoons from two till five. Steele will never come out of that sanitarium, though he now realizes that his desert city was a myth, a creation of his own distorted wits. He's sound enough on that point, but a strange inversion has taken place. It is now upon all other subjects that he is insane.

The Opinions of Leander

'Falleth From Grace and Subsequently From a Springboard

The Wave, 16 (7 August 1897), 5-6.

The other morning I went, rather early, to the "Lure-you-in" Baths for my accustomed plunge. It is really very pleasant to take a swim and a subsequent cup of coffee in this fashion before breakfast. There are but few in the baths at that hour, and the water is almost as fresh as at the beach. As I was coming out I bumped against Leander, who was just going in, dressed in a suit of pale salmon-pink, nearly flesh-colored, and quite flesh tight.

"Neptune rising from the waves," he exclaimed, with a grin.

"Venus going to the bath," I retaliated, staring significantly at his wondrous costume.

"Come, now—I say—really, you know," he exclaimed, all in a breath.

"Wake up!" said I, "it's morning." At this, just as the heroine does in novels, he started and passed his hand over his brow.

"I'm a bit absent-minded this morning," he pleaded.

"Huh!" I snorted; "I've often noticed that absence of mind."

Then Leander said two bad words, and I was fain to punch his head. After this (some time after) we sat down on the end of the springboard, and Leander unburdened himself of his trouble.

"Well," says he, "you see, it was like this——"

"There were two of us," I interrupted, "and the other was a girl."

"Well, as we were saying," began Leander, "I called on this girl the other night, and——"

"Wait a minute. How well did you know her?"

"One dance, one tea, two functions, and a call."

"Oh, intimately, then. Remember, this is San Francisco. First name?"

"Yep—at the tea."

"Yours too?"

"Of course."

"Fancy calling a man 'Leander'!"

"Shut up—she says 'Lee.'"

"Idyllic! and hers—what's hers?"

Leander drew himself up.

"Mr. Sturgis!" frostily.

But Leander could not be effective in that bathing-suit and with those dangling calves. Yet I apologized.

"I don't want to know her confounded name, then," said I; "but I thought you did not approve of this sort of thing, this—this—this too easy familiarity?"

"No more I do. But I told you I was in trouble."

"It seems to me we don't get far along in this story."

"Well, I called on this girl."

"You've said that three times. Did she let the maid open the door?"

"No, she opened it herself."

"I thought so. Well, now, we're inside the house. Do we go into the parlor?"

"Nope—small reception-room at back, one lamp, one chair——"

"What?"

"Wait till I finish—one sofa——"

"Ah, sofa!"

"One——"

"The rest of the inventory is immaterial, irrelevant, and incompetent. The stage is set for a drama. Was it comedy?"

"Tragedy!" said Leander in sepulchral tones.

"One thing more—had the girl come 'out'?"

"She had—rather far. However, her 'position is assured.'"

"Hum! But aren't you rather caddish, Leander, to tell me all this?"

"You don't know but what I'm lying."

"I had forgotten that contingency."

"And if it don't apply to one case it applies to another."

"True. *Vorwartz!*"

"Well, I shook hands with her, and——"

"Held her hand?"

"Um-hum."

"How long?"

"For twenty heart-beats," grinned Leander.

"Oh, a couple of seconds, then?"

"No; 'heart hadn't had time to get started that fast just yet. Say ten seconds. Then she sat down on the sofa, and I took a seat——"

"Where?"

"I say I took a seat."

"Where?"

"Well, I took a seat."

"On the chair?"

"Well—no."

"You said there was one chair in that small reception-room, and the sofa?"

"Um-hum."

"Get on with the story."

"That's what I did with the girl—famously."

"Let's see—the two of you are now sitting on the sofa. The girl is on which side of you?"

"Left."

"Hum! Leander, where is your left elbow?"

Leander grinned.

"It is resting on the back of the sofa, and I am holding my head with my left hand."

"Of course—and then?"

"Then—if ye have tears, prepare to shed them now—then the lamp began to go out."

I gasped.

"I offered," continued Leander, "to turn on the current, but she——"

"Said she loved to sit in the twilight."

"Now, how did you know that?"

"Guessed it."

"So we sat——"

"On the sofa."

"In the twilight."

"With your elbow on the back of the sofa; then?"

"Well, then, after a while I—I" (Leander coughed slightly and crossed his legs) "I let my left hand fall, straight."

"Along the sofa-back?"

"Yes."

"Behind the girl?"

"Yes."

"And she?"

"Never noticed—pretended not to, I mean—and then I moved an eighth of an inch closer, and—well, it was twilight and she was pretty and never noticed—and—and—then—I don't know how it happened, but somehow—confound it, you know the blooming lamp was out and a fellow's only a man, y'know, after all, and I—so I—well, I——"

"Leander," said I, in hollow tones, "Leander, you—kissed—that—girl!"

Leander covered his face with his hands.

"Well, that's a sad case," said I. Leander became animated at once.

"Hoh! You think that's all. The worst is yet to come."

I made as if to fly. Leander caught and pulled me down.

"You misunderstand," he said, severely; "what do you suppose the girl did?"

"Pretended not to notice," I suggested.

"No," wailed Leander; "no, no! she jumped up as if worked by a spring, an' shook all over an' began to cry. I say, she did, an' said I was no gentleman, an' how dared I take such a liberty with her? an' no man had ever kissed her before, an' wasn't I ashamed of myself? an'-I-don't-know-what-all-else. Yes, she did, and there I sat like a lump on a log, an'—well, that's all, an' I've felt as cheap as six bits ever since. Oh, Lord! what a fool a man is! That I should make such a break—I—I" (he smote his salmon-pink breast) "I of all men who have preached—but this settles it for good and all."

"Here endeth the first lesson," said I. "But the girl was to blame. She's no one to thank but herself. You needn't cut up rough, Leander."

"The girl!" said Leander, blankly.

"Think it over now. This was only your second call. She allowed you to treat her with a certain amount of familiarity, opened the door for you herself, saw you alone and not in the parlor, called you—good Lord!—called you 'Leander'!"

"'Lee,'" murmured Leander.

"——let you use her first name, let you hold her hand, never stopped or discouraged your little advances from chair to sofa, and from sofa to sofa-back, and so on; gave you every reason to suppose that you might kiss her without fear and without reproach, and then, when you had——"

"It was awful the way she went on—actually cried!"

"I'm not in the least sorry for her. She was entirely to blame. You were just a beastly natural-born man, acting according to your lights. I'm afraid even the best of us, under similar circumstances——"

"Why, what a muff you'd be not to," shouted Leander.

"All good girls draw their line somewhere, only some draw it later than others—this girl drew hers too late."

"When should she have drawn it, or where?"

"Between the chair and that sofa."

There was a pause.

"Look here," exclaimed Leander, turning upon me fiercely, "look here, you mealy-mouthed old grandma, what would you have done, if you had been there? Remember the girl was pretty as one o'clock."

I drew myself up proudly (my bathing-suit was sombre black).

"Ah, yah!" exclaimed Leander (whether he misunderstood me or not, judge you) "you're too good, Just'. There's such a thing as being too rotten good. Do you know what I heard a girl say the other day, Just'? 'Look here,' she said, 'you know that Sturgis man. He's like Aristides. I'm sick of hearing him called "the Just."'"

There was only one thing to do at such a crisis. I did it. I pushed Leander into the water. His yell was drowned in a liquid gurgle, and the salmon-pink silk bathing suit disappeared beneath the brown waters of the "Lure-you-in" Baths as Leander sank from sight.

Avis au lecteur—He came up again.

A Cat and Dog Life

Leonidas, and His Views Upon the Members of His Troupe

The Wave, 16 (7 August 1897), 6.

A man with a wife has his trials no doubt, and he who must depend upon the caprices of five cats for his bread and butter will find life full of variety, especially if he has some dozen dogs under foot at the same time. What, then, in Heaven's name shall we say of a man who mixes five cats with twelve dogs, has 'em all about his ears as one might say, day and night, and at the same time is married, and that to the strongest woman in the world? Also, he has a family, but this is a detail.

In the light of all this it is no wonder the individual in question has e-lected to call himself Leonidas. He must have foreseen that if he did not choose this name for himself some one else would. One could have wished, however, that he had omitted the "professor" before his stage name. "Professor" Leonidas suggests ideas that fight with one another, to say the least.

Do you know, can you guess, what was the hardest piece of work that Leonidas ever set himself to accomplish? Perhaps you have seen his dogs and cats do their turn at the Orpheum this week, and if you have you have no doubt marveled to see Max jump on Sultan's back, and Mimisse upon him, and Scott get between Sultan's forelegs and the whole quartet go waltzing off the stage. Maybe you think it was hard to teach them all this and other equally hard tricks. So it was, but the one thing that kept the Professor a-wake o' nights, the thing that brought the silver in his hair and the sweat to his temples, that caused him to weep tears of pure nervousness and exasperation, that drove him to repressed paroxysms of impatience and profanity was to get a cat to stay quiet upon a chair for an indefinite length of time.

"I could make a dog do it in a couple of days. Mimisse" (this was the cat) "finally made up her mind to do it towards the end of the fifth month."

I asked him if it was because of the greater intelligence of the dog.

"Contrariwise," says the Professor. "Believe me, of the two, the cat is by far the more intelligent."

"What then?"

"A cat has her nerves, and, besides, she is independent and, above all, capricious. The dog understands what you want after some little time and humors you good naturedly as if he should say, 'This poor devil has set his mind upon my jumping through this fool basket, so if it makes him any happier I'll do it just because I like him. And I may get smacked if I don't.'"

"And the cat?"

"The cat knows almost instantly what I want, and for just that one very particular reason makes up her mind that if she died for it she will not do that one very particular thing. 'And let him whack me,' says the cat, 'till he's black in the face and I'll only be so much more stubborn.'"

"The dog is the man, then," I suggested.

"And the cat the woman," filled in the Professor. "Precisely. You can reason with a dog, show him the plausibility of wicker cylinders, the logic of chair-backs, and the fine reasonableness of walking upon the hind legs, and you can give him a good cut with the whip to assist his intelligence; but a cat knows more about the cylinders and chair-backs and hind legs than you or I can ever teach her, and the knowledge makes her feel superior and dignified. So you must cajole and coax her into a condescending mood and induce her for a few moments to forget her self-respect."

"So you never whack the cats?"

"Never, never," said the Professor. "It's an insult they never forgive or forget. Ah, these cats, these cats," he continued, wagging his head at the happy family of felines nuzzling about a plate of meat. "They are quite the most interesting animal that lives. I know my dogs as well as my family. They have their characters, their little traits, their good points and their failings. You know just how they will act under certain circumstances. But the cat! There are depths in a cat's nature that a man never can reach. She is mysterious, self-contained, secretive, attending strictly to her own affairs and asking nothing more of me than to do the same. Have you ever noticed how a cat meditates? Give her food and a warm place to sleep in, and her own thoughts are all the company she needs. But the dog, now, he must have change, variety, excitement, lots of company; he is emotional, impulsive, fond of amusement, and, besides, is grateful for favors, where the cat merely tolerates your kindnesses, takes them as a matter of course; in fact, would prefer you to keep your distance."

"Speaking of gratitude, wasn't there some little story, some little legend connected with the cat Mimisse?"

The Professor told me the story—the legend—the romance. "At Paris it was, at the Pont de Jena there," and Mimisse, who belonged to a *charcuterie*, had tumbled into the Seine. Consternation! A crowd gathers. *Nagerat-elle, nagerat-elle pas? Oh, là, là!* The *charcutière* weeps in the background, raising her hands to Heaven. Tremendous excitement! Strong men weep and women faint. No one volunteers. Yes, there is someone. Cerberus will go, Cerberus the black dog of the *boulanger*, Cerberus will dare the foaming tide, throws off his coat, good-bye, good-bye, if I never come back, *priez pour moi, dites à maman*—, he chokes a sob—cheers, *houp-là, vive la République!*

> *Allons enfants de la Patrie.*
> *Le jour de gloire est arrivé.*

He leaps—splash—he is gone. Silence! The suspense becomes terrible. Then more cheers and more. Cerberus gains upon Mimisse, reaches her, grasps her by the scruff of the neck, turns shoreward, "battles with the tide," desperate struggle, strength failing—almost there, sinks—rises, one more effort, men run waist deep in the water to reach the hero, do reach him and Mimisse. Safe at last! *Hourra!* Men and women weep on one another's shoulders, Cerberus carried about in triumph, picture in *Le Petit Journal* next morning, silver collar, interviewed by reporters, hero of the hour. He and Mimisse go on the stage just like any prize-fighters or bridge-jumpers, for Leonidas hears the story, buys the pair and incorporates them in his troop. Virtue is rewarded with deathless fame.

"And, of course, ever afterward the pair were inseparable friends—a canine Damon and a feminine Pythias. Beautiful legend."

"Not so," said the Professor, shattering an idol. "Mimisse never paid the least attention to him from that time to this."

From Field to Storehouse

___

How a Wheat Crop is Handled in California

___

The Wave, 16 (7 August 1897), 6-7.

___

One man's loss is another man's gain, and the same is true of wheat-producing countries the world round. Early in the season, when the wheat was young, drought and prevailing hot winds so wrought upon the fields in Australia and in the Argentine Republic, two of the great wheat-growing countries of the world, that the crop failed completely. It was at one time feared that the same catastrophe was to befall California, but a few weeks' favorable weather has changed all that, and though the farmers and growers of the San Joaquin Valley have rejoiced in larger crops than that of this year, still the output is quite large enough for congratulation. At a rough estimate it is supposed that the California output of wheat for this year will reach, if it does not slightly exceed, the comfortable aggregate of eight hundred and fifty thousand tons. It is very often the custom of the California farmer to sell his wheat in advance, but the rise in prices began so early this year that the majority deemed it wise to hold off a little longer than usual, and in so doing were able to take advantage of the decided advance during the last month. There is no one particular class that benefits by the rise in the value of wheat. Everybody is financially better for it sooner or later. Of course, the farmer is the first to feel the effect. Then the broker, then the country stores, and thence the ripple of "better times" spreads and widens indefinitely to almost every sort and condition of business enterprise.

The crop is now being harvested throughout the State, and the railroads and the river boats that ply on the San Joaquin are hard put to it to handle the quantity of sacks that accumulate at every station and landing. Port Costa and San Francisco are the chief shipping points, and there the grain is distributed to all corners of the world but chiefly to Australia, the Argentine, Brazil, the United Kingdom and South Africa. It would be supposed that the famine would have caused an almost insatiable demand for grain throughout India, but the native population of India is a rice-consuming people, and the whaleback relief ship *City of Everett* carried almost the only important consignment of grain that has been shipped from this coast to Calcutta or other of the Indian ports.

In connection with the good wheat crop in the San Joaquin Valley, one must not forget to make mention of the giant harvester at work near Stockton. This harvester was made at Stockton and is at present harvesting the wheat on Roberts island, about twelve miles outside of the city. It is the largest harvester ever built, is of course propelled by steam, and cuts a swath of the tremendous width of fifty-four feet, wide enough surely for the most ambitious farmer. It is quite worth the trip to Stockton to see this enormous engine at its work, rolling through the grain knee deep, as it were, like a feeding mammoth, its teeth clicking and clashing before it, its locomotive rumbling behind. It takes eight men to guide and control the monster, but it does the work of a little army. Before its passage the wheat is mere standing grain, yellowy and nodding in the summer sun; after it has passed the wheat is grain in sacks ready for shipment. The ordinary harvester is doing well when it cuts eight hundred sacks in a day, a thousand is something to tell of. But the giant of Roberts Island, with its fifty-four foot sweep, cuts, winnows and sacks its nineteen hundred sacks without exertion, clearing off at this rate nearly one hundred acres per day.

A Reversion to Type

The Wave, 16 (14 August 1897), 5.

Schuster was too damned cheeky. He was the floor-walker in a depart-ment-store on Kearny street, and I had opportunity to observe his cheek up-on each of the few occasions on which I went into that store with——let us say my cousin. A floor-walker should let his communications be "first aisle left," or "elevator, second floor front," or "third counter right," for what-soever is more than this cometh of evil. But Schuster used to come up to ——my cousin, and take her gently by the hand and ask her how she did, and if she was to be out of town much that season, and tell her, with mild reproach in his eye, that she had been quite a stranger of late, while I stood in the background mumbling curses not loud but deep.

However, my cousin does not figure in this yarn, nor myself. Paul Schu-ster is the hero—Paul Schuster, floor-walker in a department-store that sold ribbons and lace and corsets and other things, fancy, now! He was hopeless-ly commonplace, lived with a maiden aunt and a parrot in two rooms, way out in the bleak streets around Lone Mountain. When on duty he wore a long black cutaway coat, a white piqué four-in-hand (from the wash goods counter), and blue-gray "pants" that cost four dollars. Besides this he parted his hair on the side and entertained ideas on culture and refinement. His father had been a barber in the Palace Hotel barber shop.

Paul Schuster had never heard anything of a grandfather.

Schuster came to that department-store when he was about thirty. Five years passed; then ten—he was there yet—forty years old by now. Always in a black cutaway and white tie, always with his hair parted on one side, al-ways with the same damned cheek. A floor-walker, respectable as an Eng-lish barrister, steady as an eight-day clock, a figure known to every woman in San Francisco. He had lived a floor-walker; as a floor-walker he would die. Such he was at forty. At forty-one he fell. Piff! paff! two days and all was over.

It sometimes happens that a man will live a sober, steady, respectable, commonplace life for forty, fifty, or even sixty years, and then, without the least sign of warning, suddenly go counter to every habit, to every trait of character and every rule of conduct he has been believed to possess. The thing only happens to intensely respectable gentlemen, of domestic tastes and narrow horizons, who are just preparing to become old. Perhaps it is a last revolt of a restrained youth—the final protest of vigorous, heady blood, too long dammed up. Whatever it may be, I am sure you can recall two or three instances of men (of your acquaintance, perhaps) who have bolted in this fashion. This bolting season does not last very long. It comes upon a man between the ages of forty and fifty-five, and while it lasts the man should be watched more closely than a young fellow in his sophomore year at college. The vagaries of a sophomore need not be taken any more seriously than the skittishness of a colt, but when a fifty-year-old bolts, stand clear!

On the second of May—two months and a day after his forty-first birthday —Paul Schuster bolted. It came upon him with the quickness of a cataclysm, like the sudden abrupt development of latent mania. For a week he had been feeling ill at ease—restless; a vague discontent hedged him in like an ill-fitting garment; he felt the moving of his blood in his wrists and his temples. A subtle desire to do something, he knew not what, bit and nibbled at his brain like the tooth of a tiny unfamiliar rodent.

On the second of May, at twenty minutes after six, Schuster came out of the store at the tail end of the little army of home-bound clerks. He locked the door behind him, according to custom, and stood for a moment on the asphalt, his hands in his pockets, fumbling his month's pay. Then he said to himself, nodding his head resolutely:

"Tonight I shall get drunk—as drunk as I possibly can. I shall go to the most disreputable resorts I can find—I shall know the meaning of wine, of street fights, of women, of gaming, of jolly companions, of noisy midnight suppers. I'll do the town, or by God, the town will do me. Nothing shall stop me, and I will stop at nothing. Here goes!"

Now, if Paul Schuster had only been himself this bolt of his would have brought him to nothing worse than the Police Court, and would have lasted but twenty-four hours at the outside. But Schuster, like all the rest of us, was not merely himself. He was his ancestors as well. In him as in you and I, were generations—countless generations—of forefathers. Schuster had in him the characteristics of his father, the Palace Hotel barber, but also, he had the unknown characteristics of his grandfather, of whom he had never heard, and his great-grandfather, likewise ignored. It is rather a serious matter to thrust yourself under the dominion of unknown, unknowable impulses and passions. This is what Schuster did that night. Getting drunk was an impulse belonging to himself; but who knows what "inherited tendencies," until then dormant, the alcohol unleashed within him? Something like this must have happened to have accounted for what follows.

Schuster went straight to the Palace Hotel bar, where he had cocktails, thence to the Poodle Dog, where he had a French dinner and champagne, thence (you will understand the fellow was acting on blind caprice) to the Barbary Coast on upper Kearny street, and drank whiskey that rasped his throat like gulps of carpet tacks. Then, realizing that San Francisco was his own principality and its inhabitants his vassals, he hired a carriage and drove to the Cliff House, and poured champagne into the piano in the public parlor. A waiter remonstrated, and Paul Schuster, floor-walker and respectable citizen, bowled him down with a catsup bottle and stamped upon his abdomen. At the beginning of that evening he belonged to that class whom policemen are paid to protect. When he walked out of the Cliff House he was a freebooter seven feet tall, with a chest expansion of fifty inches. He paid the hack-driver a double fare and strode away into the night and plunged into the waste of sand dunes that stretch back from the beach on the other side of the Park.

It never could be found out what happened to Schuster, or what he did, during the next ten hours. We pick him up again in a saloon on the waterfront about noon the next day, with thirty dollars in his pocket and God knows what disorderly notions in his poor, crazed wits. But remember one thing: at this time he was sober as far as the alcohol went. What the other trouble was that buzzed and bubbled in his skull, judge you. It might be supposed that now would have been the time for reflection and repentance and a return to home and respectability. Return home! Not much! Schuster had begun to wonder what kind of an ass he had been to have walked the floor of a department-store for the last score of years. Something was boiling in his veins. B-r-r-r! Let 'em all stand far from him now!

That day he left San Francisco and rode the blind baggage as far as Colfax on the Overland. He chose Colfax because he saw the name chalked on a freight car at the Oakland mole. At Colfax, within three hours after his arrival, he fought with a restaurant man over the question of a broken saucer, and the same evening was told to leave the town by the sheriff.

Out of Colfax, some twenty-eight miles into the mountains, are placer gold mines, having for headquarters a one-street town called Iowa Hill. Schuster went over to the Hill the same day on the stage. The stage got in at night and pulled up in front of the postoffice. Schuster went into the postoffice, which was also a Wells-Fargo office, a candy store, a drug store, a cigar store, and a lounging-room, and asked about hotels.

Only the postmaster was in at that time, but as Schuster leaned across the counter, talking to him, a young man came in, with a huge spur on his left boot-heel. He and the postmaster nodded, and the young man slid an oblong object about the size of a brick across the counter. The object was wrapped in newspaper and seemed altogether too heavy for anything but metal—metal of the precious kind, for example.

"He?" answered the postmaster to Schuster, when the young man had gone. "He's the superintendent of the Little Bear mine on the other side of the American river, about three miles by the trail."

For the next week Schuster set himself to work to solve the problem of how a man might obtain a shotgun in the vicinity of Iowa Hill without the fact being remembered afterward and the man identified. It seemed good to him after a while to steal the gun from a couple of Chinamen who were washing gravel along the banks of the American about two miles below the Little Bear. For two days he lay in the tall weeds and witch hazel on the side of the canyon overlooking the cabin, noted the time when both Chinamen were sufficiently far away, and stole the gun, together with a saw and a handful of cartridges loaded with buckshot. Within the next week he sawed off the gun-barrels sufficiently short, experimented once or twice with the buckshot, and found occasion to reconnoiter every step of the trail that led from the Little Bear to Iowa Hill. Also, he found out at the bar of the hotel at the Hill that the superintendent of the Little Bear amalgamated and retorted the cleanup on Sundays. When he had made sure of this Schuster was seen no more about that little one-street mining town.

"He says it's Sunday," said Paul Schuster to himself; "but that's why it's probably Saturday or Monday. He ain't going to have the town know when he brings the brick over. It might even be Friday. I'll make it a four-night watch."

There is a nasty bit on the trail from the Little Bear to the Hill, steep as a staircase, narrow as a rabbit-run, and overhung with manzanita. The place is trumpet-mouthed in shape, and sound carries far. So, on the second night of his watch, Schuster could at last plainly hear the certain sounds that he had been waiting for—sounds that jarred sharply on the prolonged roll of the Morning Star's stamps, a quarter of a mile beyond the canyon. The sounds were those of a horse threshing through the gravel and shallow water of the ford in the river just below. He heard the horse grunt as he took the slope of the nearer bank, and the voice of his rider speaking to him came distinctly to his ears. Then silence for one—two—three minutes, while the stamp mill at the Morning Star purred and rumbled unceasingly and Schuster's heart pumped thickly in his throat. Then a blackness blacker than that of the night heaved suddenly against the gray of the sky, close in upon him, and a pebble clicked beneath a shod hoof.

"Pull up!" Schuster was in the midst of the trail, his cheek caressing the varnished stock.

"Whoa! Steady there! What in hell——"

"Pull up. You know what's wanted. Chuck us that brick."

The superintendent chirped sharply to the horse, spurring with his left heel.

"Stand clear there, God damn you! I'll ride you down!"

The stock leaped fiercely in Schuster's arm-pit, nearly knocking him down, and, in the light of two parallel flashes, he saw an instantaneous picture— rugged skyline, red-tinted manzanita bushes, the plunging mane and head of a horse, and above it a Face with open mouth and staring eyes, smoke-wreathed and hatless. The empty stirrup thrashed across Schuster's body as the horse scraped by him. The trail was dark in front of him. He could see nothing. But soon he heard a little bubbling noise and a hiccough. Then all fell quiet again.

"I got you, all right!"

Thus Schuster, the ex-floor-walker, whose part hitherto in his little life-drama had been to say, "first aisle left," "elevator, second floor," "first counter right."

Then he went down on his knees, groping at the warm bundle in front of him. But he found no brick. It had never occurred to him that the superintendent might ride over to town for other reasons than merely to ship the week's cleanup. He struck a light and looked more closely—looked at the man he had shot. He could not tell whether it was the superintendent or not, for various reasons, but chiefly because the barrels of the gun had been sawn off, the gun loaded with buckshot, and both barrels fired simultaneously at close range.

Men coming over the trail from the Hill the next morning found a good deal of the young superintendent, and spread the report of what had befallen him.

*   *   *   *   *   *

When the Prodigal Son became hungry he came to himself. So it was with Schuster. Living on two slices of bacon per day (eaten raw for fear of kindling fires) is what might be called starving under difficulties, and within a week Schuster was remembering and longing for floor-walking and respectability. Within a month of his strange disappearance he was back in San Francisco again knocking at the door of his aunt's house on Geary street. A week later he was taken on again at his old store, in his old position, his unexcused absence being at length, and under protest, condoned by a remembrance of "long and faithful service."

Schuster picked up his old life again precisely where he had left it on the second of May, six weeks previously—picked it up and stayed by it, calmly, steadily, uneventfully. For him the incident was closed. I do not know how he explained it to himself. But the day before he died he told this story to his maiden aunt, who told it to me, with the remark that it was, of course, an absurd lie. Perhaps it is. I'm sure I can't say.

One thing, however, remains to tell. I repeated the absurd lie to a friend of mine who is in the warden's office over at the prison of San Quentin. I mentioned Schuster's name.

"Schuster! Schuster!" he repeated; "why we had a Schuster over here once —a long time ago, though. An old fellow he was, and a bad egg, too. Commuted for life, though. Son was a barber at the Palace Hotel."

"What was old Schuster up for?" I asked.

"Highway robbery," said my friend.

Mrs. Carter at Home

Is Celebrated for Her Fame and Wears Stunning Gowns

The Wave, 16 (14 August 1897), 6.

One was rather awestruck with No. 50. It was the kind of hotel room at which one rings, not knocks, and thereafter is "ushered into an ante-chamber" by the maid. Inside, beyond the ante-room, were three Gargantuan trunks, bundles (not bunches, you know), bundles of flowers, and Mrs. Carter, Mrs. Carter who of late has become so celebrated on account of her fame.

Laura Jean Libby would have said that Mrs. Carter was dressed in "some soft, clinging stuff"; and so, precisely, she was; lace like soapsuds and silk that had a glimmer on it like wet asphalt. But that dress, or teagown, or peignoir (of course it wasn't a peignoir, though), or whatever it was, had as much form and shape as a spilled plate of mush. It was all blooming mass and color, no outline at all, and on top of this heap of pale, indeterminate tints Mrs. Carter's hair flamed up with an effect that was somehow brusque and abrupt, as if some one had suddenly turned up the gas.

Mrs. Carter is very tall; carries that gold-girdled head of hers six feet from the ground, I'm thinking, and is very graceful in a strange, stiff way—just as a tall, stiff reed is graceful. But she is not pretty to my notion. No, as I recall her, she is not pretty. One would have had her face a little fuller and not quite so tired looking, and her nose might have been a little littler, and her eyebrows not so heavy. But I suspect one sees Mrs. Leslie Carter at a disadvantage when she is off the stage. She impressed me as if seen out of her element in No. 50. I was continually drawing an imaginary line of footlights between us. We sat down, Mrs. Carter with her back to the mirror. Interviewing Mrs. Carter is interviewing made easy, for she did all the talking. There was nothing for me to do but to put in an occasional word, just to keep her going. I suppose she has been interviewed so much, poor lady, that she knows just what to say without being asked. Some wretch, I think, must have told her to be ready on the subject of "climate," for she started off on that with a rush, and had got so far as fruits and flowers before I could stop her. All through our talk she was continually bolting up that worn, worn road.

Never have I seen an actress so anxious over her reception. Mrs. Carter asked me all manner of questions as to the temper of San Francisco audiences, regularly interviewed me on the subject, and seemed mighty ill at ease over the matter of the four weeks' run of *The Heart of Maryland*.

"I am absurdly superstitious," says she. "You know I'm from the South, from Kentucky, and I believe in omens and signs and all the rest, but only in the bad ones, in the ill-omens. I suppose it's safest. Do you know," she exclaimed, suddenly, "I believe your fogs out here are actually doing my voice a world of good. Oh, this cli—"

I leaped into the breach. "Your voice!" I shouted. "Fogs, you say! Now that's curious."

"Why, I've been working ever since 10 this morning" (at this time it was after 7) "with my voice raised all the time, and I'm not a bit hoarse. Do you think I'm hoarse?"

I spread my palms toward her.

"No, not in the least," she went on. "Now, nowhere else could I do that. And Monterey? Oh, talk to me about Monterey and Del Monte! I went there for a rest, you know, and the weather there" (the danger flag was out) "was absolutely perfect. Oh, I shall live in California some day. Such a climate I never—" (I knew it was coming.)

"Yes, of course," I shrieked. "Talk to me about *The Heart of Maryland*. Don't you swing from the clapper of a bell somewhere?"

Mrs. Carter put this aside lightly.

"Yes, yes, but that's just a little sensation. I like this play, this *Maryland*, better than any play I ever acted in" (caution—they all say this of their latest play, so make allowances), "and you know I don't say it for mere advertising effect" (they always add this remark, too), "but the more I play it the better I like it. The climax of the second act is really one of the strongest things on the American stage. I do so hope you will like the play."

"Of course I'll like it," said I.

"If a hammer falls behind a flat during a scene you won't," said Mrs. Carter, "and if a calcium light don't go just right you'll say the piece lacks 'unity of conception.' Oh, I know what critics are. And on first nights with the best management some one little thing is sure to happen. I wish we could do away with first nights and begin with seconds, or even thirds."

"Or with the last night and work backward."

And with this I got up and worked backward myself toward the door.

"If you like *Maryland* come and see me again and tell me about it," said Mrs. Carter.

"And if I don't like it?"

"Then you mustn't come."

"I shall be frantic in my enthusiasm Monday night," said I.

Opinions of Leander

Showing the Plausible Mistake of a Misguided Eastern Man

The Wave, 16 (14 August 1897), 13.

Last night I went over into the Latin Quarter to play *Bocce* with an Italian friend of mine who works in a cigarette factory and is perhaps an anarchist. *Bocce* is a kind of game that involves much rolling of little balls in dirt alleys underneath "wine-shops"—a sort of combination of tenpins and golf and marbles. It's fairish exercise, and *vin ordinaire* in tin pint measures tastes very good thereafter; also a dish of salad with just a suspicion of garlic, and a quarter of black bread rubbed with an onion. I went to the "Red House" for this wine and salad and bread, and who should I meet there—there of all places—but Leander.

"Heigho-ho," says he, with a great sigh as we settled ourselves to the hacked and blackened table. "This is a wicked world, Just'."

"Marry and to that," says I, rubbing onion on my black bread. "When did you find it out?"

"Twenty-three years seven months and ten days ago."

"You surprise me. What happened twenty-three years seven months and ten days ago, to brand that hateful truth upon your conscience?"

"I was born."

I had nothing more to say.

"And recent events," sighed Leander, "have but confirmed my theory."

"As for instance?"

"A man and a girl—"

"There's trouble coming."

"Big trouble; I 'most punched his head."

"There would have been worse trouble if you had."

"I know that, but noblesse oblige, you know."

"What did the man do to awaken your nobility?"

"Said things about the girl."

"Was she a nice girl?"

"Very—and he was a nice man, only—"

"Only what?"

"He misunderstood the girl."

"San Francisco man?"

"No; Eastern."

"San Francisco girl?"

"Yes—very much so."

"That's so, you said she was a nice girl. But if he was an Eastern man, why was his head to be punched, especially if he was nice?"

"Well, he didn't know how to gauge a California girl—this girl, anyhow—thought she was fast."

"Gracious! Did you enlighten him?"

"Tried to but failed."

"Explain."

"It was at the club."

"Yes; well?"

"I had given the Eastern man a two weeks' card. Some half dozen of us were sitting at the window watching the world go by."

"You mean you were watching for girls."

"Well, by and by this girl came along."

"And?"

"Well, she came by; we all saw her; of course, all of us knew her, but we didn't say anything, because—"

"Because why, Leander?"

"Well, there's a certain crowd of fellows in that club—we're pretty small, though—but somehow we don't believe in mentioning a girl's name indiscriminately amongst a lot of men."

"Hear! Hear!" said I, rapping on the table. "Leander, you must put me up there."

"Why, you're one of the directors."

"Oh, that club! Well, go on. Has the girl got by?"

"Not yet; we sat there looking at her and thinking what a pretty, stylish little girl—she's very young—she was, and how very jolly and companionable, when this Eastern man ups and out with:

"'Hello, there's little so and so.'"

"I say, that was rough; what happened?"

"None of us said a word, and I began to talk about something else, but my Eastern man wouldn't down; says he: 'Jolly little piece, that.'

"Says I, mighty stiff, 'I don't think the young lady is under discussion!' 'Well, let's discuss her,' says he; 'she's the gayest, chicest, jolliest little girl I've met between the two oceans; you got lots like that out here?'"

"Then what happened?"

"Well, then he rather saw that he'd put his foot in it, and he says, 'Well— pardon me—but—but she's fast, isn't she?' I say, Just', you ought to have seen that crowd. Every one of the fellows was just getting ready to say something very politely noble and crushing, and I was wondering if I hadn't better punch his head without saying anything, when my man says: 'I've every reason to think that I am right'; and do you know what his reasons were, Just'?"

"Think I do; shall I guess?"

"Go ahead."

"She was one of the kind of girls we spoke of once before—a little cigarette smoking, a little cocktail drinking, and perhaps the man had kissed her."

"Several times."

"And he had gauged her according to those things."

"He'd only known the Eastern girl, you see."

"I see. There are only two kinds of girl back there. The positively good and the positively bad, and he thought if this particular girl wasn't one she was the other."

"Exactly, and the worst of it is he will always be in doubt about her. He went away yesterday. He'd only seen the little girl a few times, and it never came to the point when she could show herself to be the good girl she really was. He never asked her to take supper with him, for instance, and so he's gone away with the impression that she's fast, and that we've got lots like that out here."

"It's rotten," said I, exasperated.

"And was he altogether to blame?" said Leander, as he rapped for the check.

The House With the Blinds

The Wave, 16 (21 August 1897), 5.

It is a thing said and signed and implicitly believed in by the discerning few that this San Francisco of ours is a place wherein Things can happen. There are some cities like this—cities that have come to be picturesque— that offer opportunities in the matter of background and local color, and are full of stories and dramas and novels, written and unwritten. There seems to be no adequate explanation for this state of things, but you can't go about the streets anywhere within a mile radius of Lotta's fountain without realizing the peculiarity, just as you would realize the hopelessness of making anything out of Chicago, fancy a novel about Chicago! or Buffalo, let us say, or Nashville, Tennessee. There are just three big cities in the United States that are "story cities"—New York, of course, New Orleans, and best of the lot, San Francisco.

Here, if you put yourself in the way of it, you shall see life uncloaked and bare of convention—the raw, naked thing, that perplexes and fascinates—life that involves death of the sudden and swift variety, the jar and shock of unleashed passions, the friction of men foregathered from every ocean, and you may touch upon the edge of mysteries for which there are no explanation—little eddies on the surface of unsounded depths, sudden outflashings of the inexplicable—troublesome, disquieting, and a little fearful.

About this "House With the Blinds" now.

If you go far enough afield, with your face towards Telegraph Hill, beyond Chinatown, beyond the Barbary Coast, beyond the Mexican quarter and Luna's restaurant, beyond even the tamale factory and the Red House, you will come at length to a park in a strange, unfamiliar, unfrequented quarter. You will know the place by reason of a granite stone set up there by the Geodetic surveyors, for some longitudinal purposes of their own, and by an enormous flagstaff erected in the center. Stockton street flanks it on one side and Powell on the other. It is an Italian quarter as much as anything else, and the *Società Alleanza* holds dances in a big white hall hard by. The Russian Church, with its minarets (that look for all the world like inverted balloons) overlooks it on one side, and at the end of certain seaward streets you may see the masts and spars of wheat ships and the Asiatic steamers. The park lies in a valley between Russian and Telegraph Hills, and in August and early September the trades come flogging up from the bay, overwhelming one with sudden, bulging gusts that strike downward, blanketwise and bewildering. There are certain residences here where, I am sure, sea-captains and sailing-masters live, and on one corner is an ancient house with windows opening door-fashion upon a deep veranda, that was used as a custom office in Mexican times.

I have a very good friend who is a sailing-master aboard the *Mary Baker*, a full-rigged wheat ship, a Cape Horner, and the most beautiful thing I ever remember to have seen. Occasionally I am invited to make a voyage with him as supercargo, an invitation which you may be sure I accept. Such an invitation came to me one day some four or five years ago, and I made the trip with him to Calcutta and return.

The day before the *Mary Baker* cast off I had been aboard (she was lying in the stream off Meiggs' wharf) attending to the stowing of my baggage and the appointment of my stateroom. The yawl put me ashore at three in the afternoon, and I started home via the park I have been speaking about. On my way across the park I stopped in front of that fool Geodetic stone, wondering what it might be. And while I stood there puzzling about it, a nurse-maid came up and spoke to me.

The story of "The House With the Blinds" begins here.

The nurse-maid was most dreadfully drunk, her bonnet was awry, her face red and swollen, and one eye was blackened. She was not at all pleasant. In the baby carriage, which she dragged behind her, an overgrown infant yelled like a sabbath of witches.

"Look here," says she; "you're a gemmleman, and I wantcher sh'd help me outen a fix. I'm in a fix, 's'w'at I am—a damn' bad fix."

I got that fool stone between myself and this object, and listened to it pouring out an incoherent tirade against some man who had done it dirt, b'Gawd, and with whom it was incumbent I should fight, and she was in a fix, 's'what she was, and could I, who was evidently a perfick gemmleman, oblige her with four bits? All this while the baby yelled till my ears sang again. Well, I gave her four bits to be rid of her, but she stuck to me yet the closer, and confided to me that she lived in that house over yonder, she did—the house with the blinds, and was nurse-maid there, so she was, b'Gawd. But at last I got away and fled in the direction of Stockton street. As I was going along, however, I reflected that the shrieking infant was somebody's child, and no doubt popular in the house with the blinds. The parents ought to know that its nurse got drunk and into fixes. It was a duty —a dirty duty—for me to inform upon her.

Much as I loathed to do so, I turned towards the house with the blinds. It stood hard by the Russian Church, a huge white-painted affair, all the windows closely shuttered and a bit of stained glass in the front door—quite the most pretentious house in the row. I had got directly opposite, and was about to cross the street when, lo! around the corner, marching rapidly, and with blue coats flapping, buttons and buckles flashing, came a squad of three, seven, nine—ten policemen. They marched straight upon the house with the blinds.

I am not brilliant nor adventurous, but I have been told that I am good, and I do strive to be respectable, and pay my taxes and pew rent. As a corollary to this, I loathe with a loathing unutterable to be involved in a mess of any kind. The squad of policemen were about to enter the house with the blinds, and not for worlds would I have been found by them upon its steps. The nurse-girl might heave that shrieking infant over the cliff of Telegraph Hill, it were all one with me. So I shrank back upon the sidewalk and watched what followed.

Fifty yards from the house the squad broke into a run, swarmed upon the front steps, and in a moment were thundering upon the front door till the stained glass leaped in its leads and shivered down upon their helmets. And then, just at this point, occurred an incident which, though it had no bearing upon or connection with this yarn, is quite queer enough to be set down. The shutters of one of the top-story windows opened slowly, like the gills of a breathing fish, the sash rose some six inches with a reluctant wail, and a hand groped forth into the open air. On the sill of the window was lying a gilded Indian-club, and while I watched, wondering, the hand closed upon it, drew it under the sash, the window dropped guillotine-fashion, and the shutters clapped to like the shutters of a cuckoo clock. Why was the Indian-club lying on the sill? Why, in Heaven's name, was it gilded? Why did the owner of that mysterious groping hand seize upon it at the first intimation of danger? I don't know—I never will know. But I do know that the thing was eldritch and uncanny, ghostly even, in the glare of that cheerless afternoon's sun, in that barren park, with the trade winds thrashing up from the seaward streets.

Suddenly the door crashed in. The policemen vanished inside the house. Everything fell silent again. I waited for perhaps fifty seconds—waited, watching and listening, ready for anything that might happen, expecting I knew not what—everything.

Not more than five minutes had elapsed when the policemen began to reappear. They came slowly, and well they might, for they carried with them the inert bodies of six gentlemen. When I say carried I mean it in its most literal sense, for never in all my life have I seen six gentlemen so completely, so thoroughly, so hopelessly and helplessly intoxicated. Well dressed they were, too, one of them even in full dress. Salvos of artillery could not have awakened that drunken half dozen, and I doubt if any one of them could even have been racked into consciousness.

Three hacks appeared (note that the patrol-wagon was conspicuously absent), the six were loaded upon the cushions, the word was given and one by one the hacks rattled down Stockton street and disappeared in the direction of the city. The captain of the squad remained behind for a few moments, locked the outside doors of the deserted shuttered house, descended the steps, and went his way across the park, softly whistling a quickstep. In time he too vanished. The park, the rows of houses, the wind-flogged streets, resumed their normal quiet. The incident was closed.

Or was it closed? Judge you now. Next day I was down upon the wharves, gripsack in hand, capped and clothed for a long sea voyage. The *Mary Baker's* boat was not yet come ashore, but the beauty lay out there in the stream, coquetting with a bustling tug that circled about her, coughing uneasily at intervals. Idle sailormen, 'longshoremen and stevedores sat upon the stringpiece of the wharf chewing slivers and spitting reflectively into the water. Across the intervening stretch of bay came the noises from the *Mary Baker's* decks—noises that were small and distinct, as if heard through a telephone, the rattle of blocks, the straining of a windlass, the bos'n's whistle, and once the noise of sawing. A white cruiser sat solidly in the waves over by Alcatraz, and while I took note of her the flag was suddenly broken out and I heard the strains of the ship's band. The morning was fine. Tamalpais climbed out of the water like a rousing lion. In a few hours we would be off on a voyage to the underside of the earth. There was a note of gayety in the nimble air, and one felt that the world was young after all, and that it was good to be young with her.

A bum-boat woman came down the wharf, corpulent and round, with a roll in her walk that shook first one fat cheek and then the other. She was peddling trinkets amongst the wharf-loungers—pocket combs, little round mirrors, shoestrings and collarbuttons. She knew them all, or at least was known to all of them, and in a few moments she was relating to them the latest news of the town. Soon I caught a name or two, and on the instant was at some pains to listen. The bum-boat woman was telling the story of the house with the blinds:

"Sax of um, an' nobs ivry wan. But that bad wid bug-juice! Whoo! Niver have Oi seen the bate! An' divil a wan as can remimber owt for two days by, bory-eyed they were. Struck dumb an' deef an' dead wid whiskey and bubble-wather. Not a manjack av um can tell the tale, but wan av um used his knife cruel bad. Now which wan was it? Howse the coort to find out?"

It appeared that the house with the blinds was, or had been, a gambling house, and what I had seen had been a raid. Then the rest of the story came out, and the mysteries began to thicken. That same evening, after the arrest of the six inebriates, the house had been searched. The police had found evidences of a drunken debauch of a monumental character. But they had found more. In a closet under the stairs the dead body of a man—a well dressed fellow—beyond a doubt one of the party, knifed to death by dreadful slashes in his loins and at the base of his spine in true evil hand-over-back fashion.

Now this is the mystery of the house with the blinds.

Beyond all doubt, one of the six drunken men had done the murder. Which one? How to find out? So completely were they drunk that not a single one of them could recall anything of the previous twelve hours. They had come there with their friend the day before. They woke from their orgy to learn that one of them had been worried to his death by means of a short palm-broad dagger taken from a trophy of Persian arms that hung over a divan.

Whose hand had done it? Which one of them was the murderer? I could fancy them—I think I can see them now, sitting there in their cell, each man apart, withdrawn from his fellow-reveler, and each looking furtively into his fellow's face, asking himself, "Was it you? Was it you? or was it I? Which of us, in God's name, has done this thing?"

Well, it was never known. When I came back to San Francisco a year or so later I asked about the affair of the house with the blinds, and found that it had been shelved with the other mysterious crimes. The six men had actually been "discharged for want of evidence."

But for a long time the thing harassed me. More than once since I have gone to that windy park, with its quivering flagstaff and Geodetic monument, and, sitting on a bench opposite the house, asked myself again and again the bootless questions. Why had the drunken nurse-maid mentioned the house to me in the first place? and why at that particular time? Why had she lied to me in telling me that she lived there? Why was that gilded Indian-club on the sill of the upper window? and whose—here's a point—whose was the hand that drew it inside the house? and then, of course, last of all, the ever-recurrent question, which one of those six inebriates should have stood upon the drop and worn the cap—which one of the company had knifed his friend and bundled him into that closet under the stairs? Had he done it during the night of the orgy, or before it? Was his friend drunk at the time, or sober? I never could answer these questions, and I suppose I shall never know the secret of "The House With the Blinds."

A Greek family lives there now, and rent the upper story to a man who blows the organ in the Russian Church, and to two Japanese, who have a photograph gallery on Stockton street. I wonder to what use they have put the little closet under the stairs?

Millard's Tales

Pungent Episodes of Western Life, Short and Pointed

The Wave, 16 (21 August 1897), 12.

Mr. F.B. Millard of the San Francisco *Examiner* is out with a collection of stories—some fifteen of them—which the Eskdale Press publishes under the general title of *A Pretty Bandit*. In telling his yarns Mr. Millard has adopted the method employed by the latest successful short-story men. This is not to tell a story, but to strike off an incident or two, clean-cut, sharp, decisive, and brief, suggesting everything that is to follow and everything that precedes. The method is admirable, but it demands an originality and ingenuity on the part of the author that is little short of abnormal. The "motif" of the story must be very strong, very unusual, and tremendously suggestive. More than this, it must be told in sentences that are almost pictures in themselves. The whole tale must resemble, as one might say, the film of a kinetoscope, a single action made up from a multitude of view points. In choosing this method Mr. Millard has volunteered to enlist in the army of the strongest story-writers the world 'round, and some of his stories are quite good enough to bring him well up in the front ranks, notably the "Caliente Trail," "A Notch in a Principality" (to our thinking the best story of the book), "The Girl Reporter," and "Horse-In-The-Water." It is a dodge of publishers, as everyone knows, to put the two best stories at the beginning

97

and end of such a collection. But there is little in "A Pretty Bandit" and "The Making of Her" to commend them. Mr. Millard crystallizes a most startling experience in each of these tales, but somehow fails to convince the reader of its "probability"; as, for instance, the hold-up in the first-named story. That a girl should stand up a stage is extraordinary enough for the most sensation-loving reader, but that she should do so upon the impulse of the moment is quite beyond belief—even worse, it is inartistic. In "The Making of Her" (which came very near being the marring of her) Mr. Millard has evidently striven for a contrast of types, the Boston blue-stocking and the Western cowboy. The contrast is sharp enough, but the "events" narrated are not plausible. They all could have happened, it is true, but in story-telling the question is "might" they have happened? One can forgive the impossible, never the improbable. As a whole, however, the tales make capital good reading. Mr. Millard wastes no time—his own nor his readers' —in getting down at once to the heart of his work. There is a plainness, a directness in his style that is "the easy reading and hard writing" one has heard so much about. The author has confined himself to California material, which is always good policy, and at the same time impresses his readers with the fact that he is thoroughly posted upon whatever subject is under consideration for the moment, whether it be railroad life, newspaper life, camp life, or ranch life. (*A Pretty Bandit*, F. B. Millard. The Eskdale Press, New York.)

Opinions of Justin Sturgis

'Drinketh a Toast to the Coming of Better Things

The Wave, 16 (21 August 1897), 13.

One day last week I went out to the park, early, before anyone else was there, and rowed a bit on Stow Lake. Thereafter, being very hungry, I sought out the Japanese tea garden in the clump of trees not far from the museum. It's really delightful in this quaint, quiet, little tea garden early in the morning, and the beverage is of the very best. I fancied that a cup of very strong, hot tea, with crisp little Japanese cakes, would not be at all amiss. But as I came into the garden whom should I find sipping his tea, smoking his morning cigar and flirting the papers of a novel but my friend Justin Sturgis.

"Well," said he, as I dropped down beside him, "where do you come from?"

"Oh," replied I, "from going to and fro upon the earth and walking up and down in it."

"What a devil of a fellow you must be, Leander."

"I'm seeking what I may devour, if you persist in being Biblical," said I, and I ordered tea and cakes.

I was feeding my cakes to the carp and goldfish, when I noticed that Just' was looking at me gravely and shaking his head.

"Leander," says he, "it don't pay to have opinions."

"Pooh!" I answered. "Doctors and lawyers get rich on theirs."

"Yes, but their opinions are asked for; yours are not."

"Mine ought to be the more welcome, then. You must pay a lawyer for his opinions. I give mine away free, even put a chromo-lithograph in every package."

"The people you have opinions about don't like you any better though—drop 'em out, Leander. Just send 'em the chromo."

"What, now—what makes you talk like this?"

"People—girls—answer you through the medium of the press."

"Have you been getting any more letters?" said I, uneasily.

"Yes," said he, "and worse; we have been parodied. Listen, my child, and you shall hear," he quoted, unfolding a paper. "Listen, and see what you have brought upon yourself."

This is what Just' read:

THE OPINIONS OF CASSANDRA

Last night I dropped into the C. E. meeting. I am not an active member, but a girl of my spirit naturally likes to see life. I settled myself in a chair, and pulling out a package of tutti-frutti I proceeded to make myself comfortable. I was dropping into a reverie when a rustle of silk skirts caused me to look up. "What," said I, "you here, of all places, Cassandra?"

Cassandra grinned.

"Heigh-ho," says she. "I have just been to the Orpheum with Leander. You know Leander, don't you?"

"Yes," said I, looking deep; "miserable little snob!"

Cassandra looked hurt. "He has always been very nice to me. What have you got against him?"

"Well, I have enough against him. The other night he called on me, and you know he's awfully struck on me, and, besides, he's awfully bashful. Well, we sat on the sofa, and the first thing I knew the light went out."

"Didn't pay your gas bill," grinned Cassandra.

"And—well—well, he kissed me."

"Phyllis!" gasped Cassandra.

"'Course I was awfully cut up, not being used to that sort of thing, but I knew he was too bashful to speak, so I considered it as good as an engagement."

"Well," said Cass'.

"The next day he wrote it up in *The Surf*, saying I led him on. Did you ever hear anything so dreadful?"

"Oh, I don't know. We had a fine time at the Orpheum, and I like him. If—"

But here the Endeavorers commenced the closing hymn and Cass' and I left.

"Now," said Just', looking up from the paper, "what do you think of that?"

I confess I was staggered, but I began to protest feebly.

"I didn't give that girl cause to think I was bashful, did I? and I'm not 'struck on her' as she says, and she's not 'struck' on me. If we'd been 'struck on' each other it would have been all right."

"Well, then, she's not 'struck on' you as you say. What were her words, 'miserable little snob?'"

I crossed a leg uneasily. "Let's talk of something else."

"As you please," said Just', "and to begin with, or to end with (for I don't think we shall talk together much after to-day), you, Leander, who have been carrying on so about the vagaries of the San Francisco girls—"

"And the men, too."

"And the men, too, have pointed out the evil, but can't you suggest also the remedy?"

"Heaven and earth," I gasped, "because certain things go wrong according to my notion why should I, of all people, be expected to set them right?"

"At least let us defend our opinions. If we are to give them away, let's send 'em well wrapped up and protected from breakage and weather."

"Well," replied I, "it isn't necessary to tell a girl not to smoke cigarettes nor drink cocktails, is it?"

"Might tell 'em what the men think of it."

"Humph, they'd say they didn't do it to please the men."

"Then they must do it because they have a taste for tobacco and alco-hol—"

"Horrors!"

"Which is much worse."

"The men think they are little fools."

"And say so to each other."

"And about the girls that allow themselves to be kissed by men whom they are not 'struck on' and who are not 'struck on' them, and permit the 'little familiarities' we were talking about?"

"The men think they are mighty cheap."

"And say so to each other."

"But aren't there some men who kiss and don't tell?"

"That's what some girls think," said I. "But when a man can kiss a girl easily, it's the nature of the beast to let other men know about it."

"I guess yes," said Just', scratching his head. "You see it stands to reason that if a girl don't mind being kissed she doesn't mind having it known. If you win a girl easy you can't respect her very much. You'd just as soon talk about her. And if you don't say right out that the next man can kiss her, you say, 'Hoh! yes, So-and-so, you can have a good time with her.'"

"Sounds fine, don't it?" said I. "The girls ought to hear, but how about the young fellows who come to functions drunk and dance with the girls?"

"The girl is to blame for that. She ought to refuse to dance with a man when he's that way—call him down so hard that it will almost sober him, or, better still, tell some other man about it—some other man who is 'struck on' her."

"Would the other man punch his head?"

"He ought to. Suppose it was the girl you know—the one particular girl. For instance. Miss ——"

"We won't discuss 'that girl'," I interrupted, glaring at him fiercely.

"That's so, and that makes me think. The men have got something to learn, too."

"For instance?"

"Well, for one thing, never to talk of a good, straight girl among themselves; say nothing about her, good, bad or indifferent. You know yourself how it cheapens a girl to have her talked about in a club, or anywhere, when men get together. I've heard it done in a barroom, even, and I know a man who used to telephone to a girl from the Deception saloon."

"Beast!"

"No. This man didn't think, I guess. Maybe that's the trouble with most of 'em. A little more convention, that's what we all need—nothing stiff or formal or false or prudish. I hate it as bad as any of them, but in Heaven's name let's have some girls who don't let every man that's known 'em a month sit with them in the dark and kiss 'em when he likes, and let's have—or, rather, let's say we've got to have, in the name of ordinary decency, men who will not come to functions drunk or get intoxicated where nice girls are around."

"Surely it's little enough to ask."

"Is this our last talk?"

"Guess yes."

"Then here's to a better state of things next season."

We raised our cups.

"Tea and toast," said I.

"It's mildly appropriate to drink that toast in tea," answered Just'. "Here's to conventionalities in moderation."

"Amen and Amen," said I.

And we drank—standing up.

The Third Circle

The Wave, 16 (28 August 1897), 5.

There are more things in San Francisco's Chinatown than are dreamed of in Heaven and earth. In reality, there are three parts of Chinatown—the part the guides show you, the part the guides don't show you, and the part that no one ever hears of. It is with the latter part that this story has to do. There are a good many stories that might be written about this third circle of Chinatown, but believe me, they never will be written—at any rate not until the "town" has been, as it were, drained off from the city, as one might drain a noisome swamp, and we shall be able to see the strange, dreadful life that wallows down there in the lowest ooze of the place—wallows and grovels there in the mud and in the dark. If you don't think this is true, ask some of the Chinese detectives (the regular squad are not to be relied on), ask them to tell you the story of the Lee On Ting affair, or ask them what was done to old Wong Sam, who thought he could break up the trade in slave girls, or why Mr. Clarence Lowney (he was a clergyman from Minnesota who believed in direct methods) is now a "dangerous" inmate of the State Asylum—ask them to tell you why Matsokura, the Japanese dentist, went back to his home lacking a face—ask them to tell you why the murderers of Little Pete will never be found, and ask them to tell you about the little slave girl, Sing Yee, or—no, on the second thought, don't ask for that story.

The tale I am to tell you now began some twenty years ago in a See Yup restaurant on Waverly Place—long since torn down—where it will end I do not know. I think it is still going on. It began when young Hillegas and Miss Ten Eyck (they were from the East, and engaged to be married) found their way into the restaurant of the Seventy Moons, late in the evening of a day in March. (It was the year after the downfall of Kearney and the discomfiture of the sandlotters.)

"What a dear, quaint, curious old place!" exclaimed Miss Ten Eyck.

She sat down on an ebony stool with its marble seat, and let her gloved hands fall into her lap, looking about her at the huge hanging lanterns, the gilded carven screens, the lacquer work, the inlay work, the colored glass, the dwarf oak trees growing in Satsuma pots, the marquetry, the painted matting, the incense jars of brass, high as a man's head, and all the grotesque jimcrackery of the Orient. The restaurant was deserted at that hour. Young Hillegas pulled up a stool opposite her and leaned his elbows on the table, pushing back his hat and fumbling for a cigarette.

"Might just as well be in China itself," he commented.

"Might?" she retorted; "we are in China, Tom—a little bit of China dug out and transplanted here. Fancy all America and the Nineteenth Century just around the corner! Look! You can even see the Palace Hotel from the window. See out yonder, over the roof of that temple—the Ming Yen, isn't it?—and I can actually make out Aunt Harriett's rooms."

"I say, Harry," (Miss Ten Eyck's first name was Harriett) "let's have some tea."

"Tom, you're a genius! Won't it be fun! Of course we must have some tea. What a lark! And you can smoke if you want to."

"This is the way one ought to see places," said Hillegas, as he lit a cigarette; "just nose around by yourself and discover things. Now, the guides never brought us here."

"No, they never did. I wonder why? Why, we just found it out by ourselves. It's ours, isn't it, Tom, dear, by right of discovery?"

At that moment Hillegas was sure that Miss Ten Eyck was quite the most beautiful girl he ever remembered to have seen. There was a daintiness about her—a certain chic trimness in her smart tailor-made gown, and the least perceptible tilt of her crisp hat that gave her the last charm. Pretty she certainly was—the fresh, vigorous, healthful prettiness only seen in certain types of unmixed American stock. All at once Hillegas reached across the table, and, taking her hand, kissed the little crumpled round of flesh that showed where her glove buttoned.

The China boy appeared to take their order, and while waiting for their tea, dried almonds, candied fruit and watermelon rinds, the pair wandered out upon the overhanging balcony and looked down into the darkening streets.

"There's that fortune-teller again," observed Hillegas, presently. "See —down there on the steps of the joss house?"

"Where? Oh, yes, I see."

"Let's have him up. Shall we? We'll have him tell our fortunes while we're waiting."

Hillegas called and beckoned, and at last got the fellow up into the restaurant.

"Hoh! You're no Chinaman," said he, as the fortune-teller came into the circle of the lantern-light. The other showed his brown teeth.

"Part Chinaman, part Kanaka."

"Kanaka?"

"All same Honolulu. Sabe? Mother Kanaka lady—washum clothes for sailor peoples down Kaui way," and he laughed as though it were a huge joke.

"Well, say, Jim," said Hillegas, "we want you to tell our fortunes. You sabe? Tell the lady's fortune. Who she going to marry, for instance?"

"No fortune—tattoo."

"Tattoo?"

"Um. All same tattoo—three, four, seven, plenty li'l' birds on lady's arm. Hey? You want tattoo?"

He drew a tattooing needle from his sleeve and motioned towards Miss Ten Eyck's arm.

"Tattoo my arm? What an idea! But wouldn't it be funny, Tom? Aunt Hattie's sister came back from Honolulu with the prettiest little butterfly tattooed on her finger. I've half a mind to try. And it would be so awfully queer and original."

"Let him do it on your finger, then. You never could wear evening dress if it was on your arm."

"Of course. He can tattoo something as though it was a ring, and my marquise can hide it."

The Kanaka-Chinaman drew a tiny fantastic-looking butterfly on a bit of paper with a blue pencil, licked the drawing a couple of times, and wrapped it about Miss Ten Eyck's little finger—the little finger of her left hand. The removal of the wet paper left an imprint of the drawing. Then he mixed his ink in a small sea-shell, dipped his needle, and in ten minutes had finished the tattooing of a grotesque little insect, as much dragon-fly as anything else.

"There," said Hillegas, when the work was done and the fortune-teller gone his way; "there you are, and it will never come out. It won't do for you now to plan a little burglary, or forge a little check, or slay a little baby for the coral round its neck, 'cause you can always be identified by that butterfly upon the little finger of your left hand."

"I'm almost sorry now I had it done. Won't it ever come out? Pshaw! Anyhow I think its very chic," said Harriett Ten Eyck.

"I say, though!" exclaimed Hillegas, jumping up; "where's our tea and cakes and things? It's getting late. We can't wait here all evening. I'll go out and jolly that chap along."

The Chinaman to whom he had given the order was not to be found on that floor of the restaurant. Hillegas descended the stairs to the kitchen. The place seemed empty of life. On the ground floor, however, where tea and raw silk were sold, Hillegas found a Chinaman figuring up accounts by means of little balls that slid to and fro upon rods. The Chinaman was a very gorgeous-looking chap in round horn spectacles and a costume that looked like a man's nightgown, of quilted blue satin.

"I say, John," said Hillegas to this one, "I want some tea. You sabe?—up stairs—restaurant. Give China boy order—he no come. Get plenty much move on. Hey?"

The merchant turned and looked at Hillegas over his spectacles.

"Ah," he said, calmly, "I regret that you have been detained. You will, no doubt, be attended to presently. You are a stranger in Chinatown?"

"Ahem!—well, yes—I—we are."

"Without doubt—without doubt!" murmured the other.

"I suppose you are the proprietor?" ventured Hillegas.

"I? Oh, no! My agents have a silk house here. I believe they sub-let the upper floors to the See Yups. By the way, we have just received a consignment of India silk shawls you may be pleased to see."

He spread a pile upon the counter, and selected one that was particularly beautiful.

"Permit me," he remarked gravely, "to offer you this as a present to your good lady."

Hillegas's interest in this extraordinary Oriental was aroused. Here was a side of the Chinese life he had not seen, nor even suspected. He stayed for some little while talking to this man, whose bearing might have been that of Cicero before the Senate assembled, and left him with the understanding to call upon him the next day at the Consulate. He returned to the restaurant to find Miss Ten Eyck gone. He never saw her again. No white man ever did.

*   *   *   *   *   *   *

There is a certain friend of mine in San Francisco who calls himself Manning. He is a Plaza bum—that is, he sleeps all day in the old Plaza (that shoal where so much human jetsam has been stranded), and during the night follows his own devices in Chinatown, one block above. Manning was at one time a deep-sea pearl diver in Oahu, and, having burst his ear drums in the business, can now blow smoke out of either ear. This accomplishment first endeared him to me, and latterly I found out that he knew more of Chinatown than is meet and right for a man to know. The other day I found Manning in the shade of the Stevenson ship, just rousing from the effects of a jag on undiluted gin, and told him, or rather recalled to him the story of Harriett Ten Eyck.

"I remember," he said, resting on an elbow and chewing grass. "It made a big noise at the time, but nothing ever came of it—nothing except a tong row and the cutting down of one of Mr. Hillegas's Chinese detectives in Gamblers' Alley. The See Yups brought a chap over from Peking just to do the business."

"Hatchet-man?" said I.

"No," answered Manning, spitting green; "he was a two-knife *Kai-Gingh*."

"As how?"

"Two knives—one in each hand—cross your arms and then draw 'em together, right and left, scissor-fashion—damn' near slashed his man in two. He got five thousand for it. After that the detectives said they couldn't find much of a clue."

"And Miss Ten Eyck was not so much as heard from again?"

"No," answered Manning, biting his finger-nails. "They took her to China, I guess, or may be up to Oregon. That sort of thing was new twenty years ago, and that's why they raised such a row, I suppose. But there are plenty of women living with Chinamen now, and nobody thinks anything about it, and they are Canton Chinamen, too—lowest kind of coolies. There's one of them up in St. Louis Place, just back of the Chinese theatre, and she's a Sheeny. There's a queer team for you—the Hebrew and the Mongolian— and they've got a kid with red, crinkly hair, who's a rubber in a Hammam bath. Yes, it's a queer team, and there's three more white women in a slave-girl joint under Ah Yee's tan room. There's where I get my opium. They can talk a little English even yet. Funny thing—one of 'em's dumb, but if you get her drunk enough she'll talk a little English to you. It's a fact! I've seen 'em do it with her often—actually get her so drunk that she can talk. Tell you what," added Manning, struggling to his feet, "I'm going up there now to get some dope. You can come along, and we'll get Sadie (Sadie's her name) we'll get Sadie full, and ask her if she ever heard about Miss Ten Eyck. They do a big business," said Manning, as we went along. "There's Ah Yee and these three women and a policeman named Yank. They get all the *yen shee*—that's the cleanings of the opium pipes, you know —and make it into pills and smuggle it in to the cons over at San Quentin prison by means of the trusties. Why, they'll make five dollars worth of dope sell for thirty by the time it gets into the yard over at the Pen. When I was over there I saw a chap knifed behind a jute mill for a pill as big as a pea. Ah Yee gets the stuff, the three women roll it into pills, and the po- liceman, Yank, gets it over to the trusties somehow. Ah Yee is independent rich by now, and the policeman's got a bank account."

"And the women?"

"Lord! they're slaves—Ah Yee's slaves! They get the swift kick most gen- erally. Ah Yee takes it out of 'em with a rubber hose filled with shot."

Manning and I found Sadie and her two companions four floors under- neath the tan room, sitting cross-legged in a room about as big as a big trunk. I was sure they were Chinese women at first, until my eyes got accus- tomed to the darkness of the place. They were dressed in Chinese fashion, but I noted soon that their hair was brown and the bridges of each one's nose was high. They were rolling pills from a jar of *yen shee* that stood in the middle of the floor, their fingers twinkling with a rapidity that was somehow horrible to see.

Manning spoke to them briefly in Chinese while he lit a pipe, and two of them answered with the true Canton sing-song—all vowels and no consonants.

"That one's Sadie," said Manning, pointing to the third one, who had remained silent the whiles. I turned to her. She was smoking a cigar, and from time to time spat through her teeth man-fashion. She was a dreadful-looking beast of a woman, wrinkled like a shriveled apple, her teeth quite black from nicotine, her hands bony and prehensile, like a hawk's claws—but a white woman beyond all doubt. At first Sadie refused to drink, but the smell of Manning's can of gin removed her objections, and in half an hour she was hopelessly loquacious. What effect the alcohol had upon the paralyzed organs of her speech I cannot say. Sober, she was tongue-tied—drunk, she could emit a series of faint bird-like twitterings that sounded like a voice heard from the bottom of a well.

"Sadie," said Manning, blowing smoke out of his ears, "what makes you live with Chinamen? You're a white girl. You got people somewhere. Why don't you get back to them?"

Sadie shook her head.

"Like um China boy better," she said, in a voice so faint we had to stoop to listen. "Ah Yee's pretty good to us—plenty to eat, plenty to smoke, and as much *yen shee* as we can stand. Oh, I don't complain."

"You know you can get out of this whenever you want. Why don't you make a run for it some day when you're out? Cut for the Mission House on Sacramento street—they'll be good to you there."

"Oh!" said Sadie, listlessly, rolling a pill between her stained palms, "I been here so long I guess I'm kind of used to it. I've about got out of white people's ways by now. They wouldn't let me have my *yen shee* and my cigar, and that's about all I want nowadays. You can't eat *yen shee* long and care for much else, you know. Pass that gin along, will you? I'm going to faint in a minute."

"Wait a minute," said I, my hand on Manning's arm. "How long have you been living with Chinamen, Sadie?"

"Oh, I don't know. All my life, I guess. I can't remember back very far—only spots here and there. Where's that gin you promised me?"

"Only in spots?" said I; "here a little and there a little—is that it? Can you remember how you came to take up with this kind of life?"

"Sometimes I can and sometimes I can't," answered Sadie. Suddenly her head rolled upon her shoulder, her eyes closing. Manning shook her roughly.

"Let be! let be!" she exclaimed, rousing up; "I'm dead sleepy. Can't you see?"

"Wake up, and keep awake, if you can," said Manning; "this gentleman wants to ask you something."

"Ah Yee bought her from a sailor on a junk in the Pei Ho river," put in one of the other women.

"How about that, Sadie?" I asked. "Were you ever on a junk in a China river? Hey? Try and think!"

"I don't know," she said. "Sometimes I think I was. There's lots of things I can't explain, but it's because I can't remember far enough back."

"Did you ever hear of a girl named Ten Eyck—Harriett Ten Eyck—who was stolen by Chinamen here in San Francisco a long time ago?"

There was a long silence. Sadie looked straight before her, wide-eyed, the other women rolled pills industriously, Manning looked over my shoulder at the scene, still blowing smoke through his ears; then Sadie's eyes began to close and her head to loll sideways.

"My cigar's gone out," she muttered. "You said you'd have gin for me. Ten Eyck! Ten Eyck! No, I don't remember anybody named that." Her voice failed her suddenly, then she whispered:

"Say, how did I get that on me?"

She thrust out her left hand, and I saw a butterfly tattooed on the little finger.

Belasco on Plays

The Great Playwright Speaks of His Methods

The Wave, 16 (28 August 1897), 10.

I don't need to go to see *The Heart of Maryland* now. I say that I don't need to go, but I want to more than ever. Maybe you don't quite understand the apparent contradiction here, but you would if you had been with me the other day in a little room over the ticket office of the Baldwin and heard Mr. Belasco himself tell the story of the play, of how he came to write it and how he actually did write it. Incidentally, Mr. Belasco told me of his methods in general and his views on the drama.

It was most interesting to hear him tell the story of the fourth act of *Maryland*. It was at once a pantomime—for he acted each part; a story—for he filled in the pauses of the dialogue with description and scene-plot, for he made one see the different shifts and changes, and the location of every flat and property. It was better than being behind the scenes. It was behind even behind-the-scenes. It was right in the midst of things—in the author's brain. I confess I had come prejudiced against the curfew-shall-not-ring-to-night affair even before seeing the play; but as Mr. Belasco told of the careful and painstaking preparation for that very effect, it seemed to me the most natural thing for the lady to do under the circumstances. You say the thing was suggested to Mr. Belasco by the poem; very well, the lady in the play may have had the poem in mind herself. How do you know?

"It's the careful preparation that makes all the difference between melodrama and drama," said Mr. Belasco.

"As how?" said I.

"Preparation for your effects; gradual, natural, leading up to them, coaxing your audience step by step till you have them just where you want, and then spring your effect, and not until then. I always take my audiences into my confidence, as it were, this way. The actors in the drama need not know what's to happen, but the audience know. I tell them in one way or another.

111

For instance, when my hero is a prisoner in the bell tower not a single man, woman or child from pit to dome but knows that he is to escape, that the play is to end with the union of the lovers. It's just a question of means. So I introduce the Provost Marshal complaining of the inefficiency of firing guns as a signal for escaping prisoners, and his suggestion as to the ringing of the bell. Then, too, I show them what happens when a prisoner tries to escape and fails. All the preceding act, too, is "treatment" for that bell scene. It's the only way to make a scene effective.

"As to your idea of play-making, now?" I suggested.

"I write a play around either some central scene or some central idea. *Maryland* I wrote around the climax of the second act. *The Wife* around the scene where the husband of the unfaithful Helen Truman tells her to turn to him in her trouble. *The Charity Ball* was written around an idea. The idea that a girl once unvirtuous is not necessarily bad thereafter, can, in fact, become the honest wife of an honest man."

I asked Mr. Belasco about the problem plays. He shook his head. "Failures every one, the public won't have 'em. They won't be touched in the raw. They come to the theater to see an amusing play, not a moral dissection with lancet and scalpel. There's Ibsen, of course, but Ibsen is a dramatist whom people read. Staged, his plays would fail surely and inevitably." Also, Mr. Belasco told me something surprising. "The problem play," said he, "is easy writing, easiest kind of play-writing. There are no effects, no great scenes; it's all discussion, discussion, discussion; the author leads up to nothing, has no great climaxes; he can, as you might say, write till he gets tired—or the audience does—and then ring down. No," said Mr. Belasco, "give me the play of great, strong, universal passions, love and hatred, and revenge and remorse, and let the noble passions survive and triumph; get at the heart of mankind, under its vest, as you might say, and find out the beautiful, true nobility that's there. That's my religion, and because I do that is why, I am sure, my plays are successful. And another point, these great human passions, there are a limited number of them after all. After the first score of great plays of the world had been written the dramatists began to be obliged to repeat themselves a little, to "lift," as it were, from their predecessors. Take it in real life, the identical same crises and scenes and situations are constantly reoccurring. There is no such thing as absolute originality nowadays. You are not original even in real life.

112

Believe me, there is no situation however striking, whether on the stage of a theater or the stage of human existence, but what the changes have been rung upon it to infinity."

"Rung with a curfew bell?" said I. (Of course I didn't say it.) But the idea occurred to me. And, after all, Mr. Belasco is not far from right.

The Story of a Wall

By Pierre Loti

Translated by Frank Norris

The Wave, 16 (28 August 1897), 13.

They lived down in a modest little court, mother and daughter, and a maternal relative of theirs at once aunt and grand-aunt. The daughter was still young, not more than 18, and fresh as a rose in the early morning, when a sudden reverse of fortune compelled them to move into a remote corner of the old family mansion, renting out all the front portion, that looked up-on the village street, to unsympathetic and intruding strangers.

The forced sale had robbed them of all their luxurious furniture, and they had been obliged to furnish their two little rooms with old beds and tables and chairs brought down from the attic and exhumed from old and forgotten corners. But at once they had loved it, this narrow, circumscribed little home, that brought them so close to each other and reunited them before the same fireplace, the same hearthstone. They felt themselves a bit clois-tered it is true, but they were happy for all that, for the windows—hung with simple muslin curtains—looked out upon a sunbathed court surrounded by low walls that were covered with hollyhocks and cabbage roses.

And already they had forgotten their former splendor of yesterday, happy in their quiet isolation, when suddenly one day they learned that their neighbor was to raise his house by two stories—a wall, a dead wall, was to be erected there, a wall that would shut out the breeze and darken all the court with its shadow.

Alas, there was no spell to conjure away this misfortune, more cruel to them now than all their previous disasters. In the time of their fortune they could have bought the house of their neighbor. Now it was not even to be thought of. There was nothing for them now but submission. So one by one the huge stones began to amass themselves, layer by layer, and in a mournful silence and with aching hearts they watched the wall grow day by day. Day by day the court grew darker, day by day the breeze died away, day by day the hollyhocks and cabbage roses drooped and faded. In a month the masons had finished their work. The sun was gone, the court grew damp. The wall rose high in the air, and where once they had seen the deep blue summer heavens and the little golden clouds of morning and evening, was now a sombre front of gray, unbroken, menacing, lead-colored, like a sky of late November.

In their little rooms the warm sun of June and July still beamed, but it came later in the morning and disappeared earlier in the afternoon. In the fall the twilight came an hour sooner, bringing with it at once a gray and penetrating sadness that weighed upon and depressed them beyond words. Time passed, and the months and seasons wheeled slowly about and about like wheeling constellations.

And in the gray hours of the gloaming, when the three women left their work of embroidery or sewing before the lamps had been lighted the young girl—soon to be no longer young—lifted her eyes upon this enclosing wall, and in a sort of childish melancholy, such as comes often, perhaps, to prisoners, amused herself with the sight of the faded, bloomless rose bushes clinging to the inhospitable wall, and tried to give herself the illusion that the wall was in some way the sky still; a sky that was nearer and more real than the other; some such sky as we imagine at night in a dream.

They still cherished a forlorn hope in an inheritance of which, sitting around the lamp or work-table, they sometimes spoke as if it were some sort of dream or fairy tale, so far away it seemed, so unreal.

When it should fall to them, this wonderful inheritance, they would at any price buy their neighbor's house, tear down the wall and bring back once more their dear blue sky, the floating golden clouds, and the flowers of the bloomless bushes. To tear down this wall, that was their own ambition, their continual obsession.

And the old grand-aunt accustomed herself to say: "My dear daughter, God permit me to live long enough to see that day."

But their inheritance did not come.

After a time the rain and the weather traced upon the blank face of the wall a sort of blackish stain, forming a figure shaped like a V, or like an indistinct picture of a soaring bird. And the young girl watched it day by day, every day. One time when an unusually warm spring had coaxed one timid rose to bloom upon the wall, a young man appeared in the court upon the narrow stage of this little drama. For a few evenings he sat down at the table of these three penniless women. He was passing through the village and came to them recommended by some common friends, not without some thought of a possible marriage. He was well-looking, carrying his head high, his face reddened by the great winds that blow upon the seas.

But he thought it too fanciful, this inheritance; he found her too poor, this poor, young girl, whose cheeks had already begun to pale and fade for lack of air and sun. So he disappeared and did not return, he who for a day had been to the three women, as it were, a symbol of strength and life and sunlight and the open air. And she who had already imagined herself his fiancée saw now in his departure only a symbol of death.

And the monotonous years went by like the ripples of an impassable river. Five passed, ten, fifteen, even twenty at last. The freshness of the dowerless young girl little by little vanished, useless, unseen and disdained. Her mother's hair turned white, the old aunt, octogenarian by now, became infirm and sat all day with nodding head in the darkened window. And the hollyhocks and the rose bushes grew old, too, with the deceptive age of flowers, seemingly rejuvenated with every spring.

"Oh, my poor daughters," the grand-aunt would from time to time exclaim in her cracked voice, "if I could only live to see the day—" and leaving her phrase unfinished she would point with her withered hand to the wall of unyielding stone.

She had been dead for fifteen months when, suddenly, at a time when it had been quite forgotten, the inheritance befell them. The young girl—she was an old maid of forty now—felt herself youthful again in the joy of coming into this forgotten fortune.

The strangers who rented the front of the old mansion were driven out. Mother and daughter installed themselves as formerly, but they lived by preference in the little corner of their days of humbleness and seclusion—now so full of souvenirs—which was flooded with light as soon as the hateful wall was down.

At last it was accomplished, the destruction of the sombre wall. It was done in the month of April, at the time of the first warm breezes, at the time of the first long evenings. It was done very quickly, in the midst of joyous rattle of falling stones and accompanied by the cries of the workmen, who whistled and sang in the dust of old plaster and crumbling mortar.

And at the end of the second day, when all was over and the workmen gone away and silence come once more, the mother and daughter sat down to table in the little room looking out upon the court, astonished to find it so bright once more, to have no more need of the lamp. But in place of the gaiety they had expected they felt themselves oppressed with a feeling of discomfort and uneasiness. There came to them a sense of too much light flooding suddenly into the little room, of a huge empty space out of doors, of an immense change. In the presence of the realization of their dream they exchanged no words; suddenly a prey to an increasing melancholy, they sat there without speech, their repast untouched. And little by little their hearts were wrung by a wordless, formless distress, the sombre regret that comes when in the presence of death. When at length the mother saw the daughter's eyes filling, divining her unexpressed thoughts that so closely resembled her own, she said:

"We could rebuild it. It seems to me we could try to make it the same as it used to be."

"I had thought of that, too," replied her daughter. "But no; don't you see it will never be the same?"

Yes, it was true. It could never be the same. She herself had decreed the destruction of the background of this familiar picture in which, during one springtime, she had seen the face of a young man, and during so many winters the profile of a beloved aunt. And all at once, at the remembrance of the indistinct figure of the soaring bird traced upon the face of the crumbling plaster which she would never, never see again, her heart seemed to be breaking, and she wept the bitterest tears of her life before the irreparable destruction of the old wall.

The End of the Beginning

The Wave, 16 (4 September 1897), 5.

The story of the *Freja* disaster is best told by one or two extracts taken from the record left by Lieutenant Ferriss at Cape Sheridan, and by certain passages from his Ice Journal.

(Extracts of record left in instrument box at Cape Sheridan.)

U. S. Cutter Freja,

On the ice off Cape Sheridan, Grant Land,
Lat. 82° 25′ N., Lon. 61° 30′ W., 12th March, 1891.

* * * We accordingly froze the ship in on the last day of September, 1890, and during the following winter drifted with the pack in a northwesterly direction. * * * On Friday, August 2d, being in Lat. 82° 25′ N., Lon. 61° 30′ W., the *Freja* was caught in a severe nip between two floes and was crushed, sinking in about two hours. We abandoned her, saving a hundred days' provisions and all necessary clothing, instruments, etc. * * *

I shall now attempt a southerly march over the ice, and with God's help hope to reach Tasiusak, or fall in with the relief ships or steam whalers on the way. Our party consists of the following eighteen persons. * * * All well with the exception of Mr. Bennett, the chief engineer, whose left hand has been frost-bitten. No scurvy in the party as yet.

Hamilton Ferriss, Lieut. U.S.N.,
Commanding *Freja* Arctic Exploring Expedition.

(Extracts from Lieutenant Ferriss' Ice Journal,
three months later than above.)

June 13, 1891—Monday.—Camped at 4:05 p.m. about one hundred yards from the coast. The ice hereabouts is breaking up fast. If we had not been compelled to abandon our boats——but it is useless to repine. We must look our situation squarely in the face. At noon served out last beef extract, which we drank with some willow tea. Our remaining provisions consist of four-fifteenths pounds pemmican per man, and the rest of the dog meat. Where are the relief ships? We should at least have met the steam whalers long before this.

June 14th—Tuesday.—The doctor amputated Mr. Bennett's other hand to-day. Living gale of wind from S.E. Impossible to march against it in our weakened condition—must camp here till it abates. Made soup of the last of the dog meat this afternoon. Our last pemmican gone.

June 15th—Wednesday.—Everybody getting weaker. Clarke breaking down. Sent Hansen down to the shore to gather shrimps, of which it takes fifteen hundred to fill a gill measure. Supper a spoonful of glycerine and hot water.

June 16th—Thursday.—Clarke died during the night. Hawes dying. Still blowing a gale from S.E. A hard night.

June 17th—Friday.—Hawes and Cooley died during early morning. Hansen shot a ptarmigan. Made soup. Dennison breaking down.

June 18th—Saturday.—Buried Hawes and Cooley under slabs of ice. Spoonful of glycerine and hot water at noon.

June 19th—Sunday.—Dennison found dead this morning between Bennett and myself. Too weak to bury him or even carry him out of tent. He must lie where he is. Divine services at 5:30 p.m. Last spoonful of glycerine and hot water.

Ferriss paused in his writing at this point, and, looking up from the page, spoke drearily and in a thick, muffled voice: "How long has this wind been blowing, Bennett?"

"Since last Wednesday," answered the other. "Five days." Ferriss continued his writing:

> * * * Gale blowing steadily for five days. Impossible to
> move against it in our weakened condition. But to stay
> here is to perish. God help us. It is the end of everything!

Ferriss drew a line across the page under the last entry, and, still holding the book in his hand, gazed slowly about the tent.

There were nine of them left—eight huddled together in that miserable tent—the ninth, Hansen, being down on the shore gathering shrimps. In the strange gloomy half-light that filled the tent, these survivors of the *Freja* looked less like men than like animals. Their hair and beards were long, and seemed one with the fur covering on their bodies. Their faces were absolutely black with dirt, and their limbs were monstrously distended and fat —fat as things bloated and swollen are fat. It was the abnormal fatness of starvation, the irony of misery, the huge joke that Arctic Famine plays upon those whom it afterwards destroys. The men moved about at times on their hands and knees; their tongues were round and slate-colored, like the tongues of parrots, and when they spoke they bit them helplessly.

Near the flap of the tent lay the swollen dead body of Dennison, the naturalist of the expedition. Four of the party dozed, inert and stupefied, in their sleeping-bags. The surgeon and Muck-tu, the Esquimau dog-master, were in the center of the tent boiling their sealskin footnips over a fire built of a broken sledge-runner. Ferriss sat upon an empty water-breaker, using his knee as a desk. Near him, sitting on one of the useless McClintock sledges was Bennett, both of whose hands had been amputated in consequence of frost-bite. A tin spoon had been lashed to the stump of his right wrist.

The tent was full of foul smells. The smell of drugs and mouldy gunpowder, the smell of dirty rags, and of unwashed bodies, the smell of stale smoke, of scorched seal skin, of soaked and rotting canvas that exhaled from the tent cover—every smell but that of food.

Outside, the unleashed wind yelled incessantly, like a sabbath of witches and spun about their pitiful shelter and went rioting on, leaping and somersaulting from rock to rock, tossing handfuls of dry dust-like snow into the air, folly-stricken—insensate—an enormous mad monster gamboling there in some hideous dance of death, capricious, headstrong, pitiless as a famished wolf.

In front of the tent, and over a ridge of barren rocks, was an arm of the sea dotted over with blocks of ice, careening past silently, while back from the coast and back from the tent and to the north and to the south and to the west stretched the illimitable waste of land—flat, grey, harsh, snow and ice and rock, rock and ice and snow, stretching away there under the sombre sky, forever and forever, gloomy, untamed, terrible, an empty region—the scarred battlefield of chaotic forces, the savage desolation of a primordial world.

"Where's Hansen?" asked Ferriss.

"He's away after shrimps," responded Bennett.

Ferriss' eyes returned to the notebook and rested on the open page thoughtfully.

"Do you know what I've written here, Bennett?" he asked, adding, without waiting for an answer: "I've written 'It's the end of everything.'"

"I suppose it is," admitted Bennett, looking vaguely about the tent. "Yes, the end of everything. It's come at last. Well?"

There was a silence. One of the men in the sleeping-bags groaned and turned upon his face. Outside the wind lapsed suddenly to a prolonged sigh of infinite sadness, clamoring again upon the instant.

"Bennett," said Ferriss, returning his notebook to the box of records, "it is the end of everything, and just because it is I want to talk to you—to ask you something."

Bennett came nearer. The horrid shouting of the wind deadened the sound of their voices—the others could not hear it, and by now it would have mattered very little to any of them if they had. Ferriss picked up an empty rubber bottle that had contained lime juice, and began fingering it.

"Old man," he commenced, "nothing makes much difference now. In a few hours we shall all be like Dennison here." He tapped the body of the naturalist, who had died during the night. It was already frozen so hard that his touch upon it resounded as if it had been a log of wood. "We shall all be like this pretty soon," continued Ferriss, "but there's a little girl back in the world we left, that I loved—that I cared for," he added, hurriedly. "I don't know as I can quite make you understand how much I—how much she was to me. I would have asked her to marry me before I came off, if I had been sure of her, but I wasn't sure, and so—well—so I never spoke. She never knew how much I cared, and I never knew if she cared at all. And that's what I want to ask you about. It's Helen Parry. You've known her all your life, and you saw her later than I did. You remember I had to come down to the ship two days before you, about the bilge pumps."

While Ferriss had been speaking the last words, Bennett had been sitting very erect upon the sledge, drawing figures and vague patterns in the fur of his sealskin coat with the tip of the tin spoon. Helen Parry! Ah, yes, Ferriss was right. Bennett had known her all his life, and it was just because of this intimacy that she had come to be so dear to him. It was she who had made everything he did seem worth while. Hardly for a moment had she been out of his thoughts during all that fearful voyage.

"It seems rather foolish," continued Ferriss, turning the rubber bag about and about, "but if I thought she ever cared—for me—in that way, why it would make—this that is coming to us, seem—oh, I don't know—easier to be borne. I say it very badly, but it would not be so hard to die if I thought that little girl loved me—a bit."

Bennett was thinking very fast. He wished now that he had overridden Helen's objections, and had allowed her people to announce their engagement before the expedition sailed. He had even half guessed something of this sort. But they two were so happy in their avowed love for each other that they had shut their eyes to everything else. They only knew that they were to be married within a month of Bennett's return. Bennett could never forget that evening when he had said good-bye to her on the porch of the old New Hampshire homestead, and had gone away to join the *Freja*. She had kissed him then for the first time, and had put a hand on each shoulder and said to him:

"You must come back, Dick—you must come back to me. Remember, you are everything to me—everything in the world."

"You've known her so well," continued Ferriss, "that I am sure that she, understanding that you were my very best friend, must have said something to you about me. Tell me, did she ever say anything—give you to understand—that she cared for me—that she would have married me if I had asked her?"

Bennett wondered what to say to him. On one hand was Helen, the girl who was to be—who would have been his wife, who loved him and whom he loved. On the other was Ferriss, his chief, his friend, his hero, the man of all others whom he loved, as Jonathan loved David—such a love as can come only upon two men who have lived together, and fought together, and battled with the same dangers, and suffered the same defeats and disappointments. Bennett felt himself in grievous straits. Must he tell Ferriss the bitter truth? Must this final disillusion be added to that long train of others, the disasters, the failures, the disappointments and deferred hopes of all those past months? Must Ferriss die hugging to him this bitterness as well?

"I sometimes thought," observed Ferriss, with a weak smile, "that she did care a little. I've surely seen something like that in her eyes at certain moments. I wish I had spoken. Did she ever say anything to you? Did she ever say she cared for me?"

The thing was too cruel. Bennett shrank from it.

But suddenly an idea occurred to him. Did anything make any difference now? Why not tell his friend that which he wanted to hear, even if it were not the truth? After all that he had suffered why could he not die content at least in this? What did it matter if he spoke? Did anything matter at such a time, when they were all to perish within the next twenty-four hours? Ferriss was waiting for his answer, looking straight into his eyes.

"Yes," said Bennett, "she did say something once."

"What was it?" exclaimed Ferriss, dropping the rubber bag and bending forward.

"We had been speaking of the expedition and of you," answered Bennett, looking fixedly on the bag as it lay on the ground. "I don't know how the subject came up, but it came in very naturally at length. She said—I remember her words perfectly—she said, 'He must come back—you must bring him back to me. Remember, he is everything to me—everything in the world.'"

"She said that?" enquired Ferriss, looking away.

"Yes," answered Bennett. "I remember it. Those were her words."

"Ah!" said Ferriss, with a quick breath; then he added, "I'm glad of that. You haven't an idea how happy I am, Bennett, in spite of everything."

"Oh, yes, I guess I have," assented Bennett.

"No, no, you haven't," replied Ferriss. "How can you have any idea of it? One has to love a little girl like that, Bennett, and have her—and find out—and have things come all right to appreciate it. She would have been my wife after all. I don't know how to thank you, old man. Congratulate me."

He rose a little feebly, holding out his hand. Bennett rose and instinctively extended his arm, but withdrew it suddenly. Ferriss paused abruptly, letting his hand fall to his side, and the two remained there an instant, looking at the stumps of Bennett's arms, the tin spoon still lashed to the right wrist! There was a noise of feet at the flap of the tent.

"It's Hansen," muttered Bennett.

Hansen tore open the flap of the tent.

Then he shouted to Ferriss: "Three steam whalers off the foot of the floe, sir; boat putting off! What orders, sir?"

Ferriss looked at him stupidly, as yet without definite thought, then:

"What did you say?"

Two of the men in the sleeping-bags, wakened by Hansen's shout, sat up and listened stolidly.

"Steam whalers?" said Bennett, slowly. "Where? I guess not," he added, shaking his head.

Hansen was swaying in his place with excitement.

"Three whalers," he repeated, "close in. They've put off—— Oh, my God! Listen to that!"

The unmistakable sound of a steamer's whistle, raucous and prolonged, came to their ears from the direction of the coast. One of the men broke into a feeble cheer. The whole tent was rousing up. Again and again came the hoarse, insistent cry of the whistle.

"What orders, sir?" repeated Hansen.

A clamor of voices filled the tent.

Bennett came quickly up to Ferriss, trying to make himself heard.

"Old man, listen!" he cried, with eager intentness. "What I told you—just now—about Helen Parry—I thought—it is all a mistake. You don't understand——"

Ferriss was not listening.

"What orders, sir?" exclaimed Hansen, for the third time.

Ferriss drew himself up.

"Lieutenant Ferriss' compliments to the officer in charge. Tell him there are nine of us left—tell him—oh, tell him anything you damn' please. Boys!" he cried, turning a radiant face to the men in the tent, "make ready to get out of this. We're going home—going home to our sweethearts, boys!"

Fiction is Selection

The Wave, 16 (11 September 1897), 3.

To the man who has ever so modestly assumed the pose of a writer of fiction is given a certain experience which is usually trying, sometimes amusing, but that on rare occasions is profitable and entertaining to the last degree. People who wish him well give him "ideas" for stories, come to him with the remark "here's something you ought to make into a story," or "there's a character you ought to put in a book." More often than otherwise they clinch their recital with the remark: "This really happened, you know," as though it were any better for actually having happened. Take, for instance, a case like this: A very good friend of the writer's, a capital chap, but without the sense for fiction, tells him a yarn of a romantic elopement. As usual, he says, "this is something that actually happened, you know." Here is what actually happened: A young fellow is in love with a girl—parents on both sides opposed to the match—relentless. Young couple decide to elope—secret appointment at the gate at the bottom of the garden—carriage and horses there—start for the flight—pursuit—girl's brother on a horse (black for preference)—pistol shots exchanged—black horse of pursuing brother killed—down he goes with a hideous sliding clatter—next town is reached and marriage performed—subsequent reconciliation, etc., etc., etc. "Now isn't that a story for you?" he exclaims. "That actually happened at—" and he names the town and backs up his story with all manner of detail. "There's a story you ought to write," says he, in conclusion. No, indeed, not if the copy were paid for at the rate of twenty-five dollars per hundred words. The thing may have happened. There can be no doubt that such stories have happened. But the truth of a story in this sense of the word has nothing to do with its availability, from the point of view of good fiction. In a written tale it would not seem real. It would seem like a rehash of some tawdry yellow-covered romance of fifty or a hundred years ago. Fiction is what seems real, not what is real.

But for all this, the story writer must go to real life for his story. You can never think out, or invent or imagine a tale that will be half so good as the things that have "really happened." The complications of real life are infinitely better, stronger and more original than anything you can make up. The only difference is in the matter of selection of details. The story writer's position in regard to the life of the world is like that of a maker of mosaics in front of a vast pile of tiny many-colored blocks. He don't make the blocks nor color them—the story writer does not invent nor imagine the parts of his story. Writer and mosaicist alike select and combine. The maker of a mosaic has a design in his brain, or, better still, infinitely better, sees in the pile of little colored blocks in front of him a certain little group or tiny heap that, by merest accident, has tumbled into a design of its own. The design is rough, very crude, the blocks do not fit together, and here and there a green or blue or red block jars in the color scheme. But, for all that, there is a suggestion of design there, much more original than any design he could work out. Well, he takes this group of blocks in hand, picks out and throws away the red and the blue and the green that jar and fight, trims off the edges of the blocks and makes them fit compactly together; perhaps a gap or two is left. The whole vast heap is at his command. Deftly he goes over it, picking out here and there the blocks that he needs, a circular one here, a triangular one there, now one of a bright vermillion, now one of a sombre grey. Little by little he pieces together that crude and rough design, gets everything to fit, everything to harmonize; possibly he combines the first design with another; possibly these two designs suggest a third still better; so he proceeds. At last the final design is complete. A little polishing, a very little, for in roughness there is strength and in sharp contrast, vividness; and there you are, a rounded whole, a definite, compact and complete thing, taken out of and isolated from a formless heap and jumble of shapes and colors.

There may be—in fact, there is—in the heap a hundred and one other combinations of forms and shapes already arranged, "actually existing," made to hand, as it were, but the designer over-passes them because these combinations have been used by other designers before him, used so often that there is no longer any originality or freshness in them.

Some one objects at this point: "What about imagination? What about fancy? What about invention?" There is no such thing as imagination. What we elect to call imagination is mere combination of things not heretofore combined. The designer, before his heap of mosaic blocks, can only pick and choose. If he is daring enough, thoughtful enough, careful e-nough to combine two colors that have never before been combined, or two shapes never before fitted together, we call it "imagination." It is only obser-vation, after all. The designer does not make his little blocks, does not color them. They are already made and colored for him. The fiction writer of the wildest and most untrammelled fancy cannot get away from real life. Imag-ination! There is no such thing; you can't imagine anything that you have not already seen and observed.

Like the skilled mosaic maker, any one with an eye accustomed to looking for short stories can run his glance over the heap of things we have elected to call life and here and there see combinations of form and color that are original, telling and worth working up. Such a one would not have given the elopement combination half a thought. The design may be in the heap, al-most perfect as it lies; the story may have really happened; both are worth-less for all that. Sometimes, however, the design does not exist at all except in your brain; you must go to your heap nevertheless. Here, for instance, is an "idea" for another kind of story. It has never happened, but it was told me by a man who has the fiction-sense rather keenly developed. Observe the difference between it and the other one of the elopement, but bear in mind that this last story is yet in its crude original state—needs, in fact, no end of handling and piecing and rearranging. It's a mere handful of blocks, so far. A Jew—sweats old clothes in a sordid basement—a wretched be-nighted man, squatting all day cross-legged in that sordid basement—has a wife no less sordid than himself. The Jew has no emotions, no fancies, no illusions. There is no poetry in the man. He sweats old clothes. Has not seen the country in fifteen or twenty years. However, in front of his shop stands a poplar tree—tall, very beautiful. The Jew has a sort of blind, un-reasoned attachment for the tree—looks at it in the evening after he is done with sweating old clothes—has watched its leaves come and go with the sea-sons—loves the tree, but don't know why—hardly knows that he does love the tree. All the starved poetry of the sordid man's life is centered about the tree. One day the tree is suddenly cut down—consternation—some-thing gone out of the Jew's life—don't know exactly what—becomes morose and gloomy—goes from bad to worse—develops latent melancholia—insani-ty perhaps—quarrels with the sordid wife. All his peace of mind and little happiness gone—goes from worse to the worst of all—one day kills the sordid wife without knowing why—is adjudged insane and straight-jacketed in a sanitarium—would it all have happened if the tree had been left standing?

A Case for Lombroso

The Wave, 1ʊ (11 September 1897), 6.

This story is to be about young Stayne and a girl named Cresencia Hromada, and it harks back to that fable of Aesop's about the two jars. You remember that fable of Aesop's about these jars. They were superlatively beautiful jars, and they were floating in a cistern. They made the discovery that so long as they kept apart they were safe—the moment they should come together they would break and fill and sink. *Haec fabula docet* and all the rest.

Young Stayne, when I knew him, before the time of this tale, was as fine a young fellow as you could find between the two oceans. He was just out of Harvard, where he had obtained *Deturs* and very particular and especial credits. He had been one of the speakers in the Yale debate, had been vice-president of the "Pudding," and had even been taken on by the "Porcellian" in his senior year. You others who have been at Harvard will know just what all this means. Stayne was a "torrow-bred" to his very boots. No man in San Francisco had more friends than he. He was not liked in the sense that a merely "popular" man is liked—he was liked because of his genuineness and his fine male strength and honesty and courage. Furthermore, he was well-looking, but that's a detail.

Cresencia Hromada (as you may have very shrewdly suspected from her name) was Spanish, and belonged to that branch of the Hromadas whose original grant from the Spanish government was large enough to make three or four counties when the Gringoes dispossessed them. She was a rare one,

127

was Cresencia—fair as a Viking, with that fairness that is the mark of the oldest and purest Spanish blood known to the College of Heralds. It dates back to the time of the Ostrogoths, and beside it the Castillians are mushroom interlopers of yesterday. Miss Hromada's dominant characteristic was her pride. She was proud of her name, proud of her family, proud of her beauty (which was a marvel), proud of her exclusiveness, proud even of her pride itself. Otherwise, she was blessed or cursed (whichever you will) with a temperament as delicately poised and as sensitive as goldsmiths' scales, nerves as tightly stretched and as responsive as the strings of a Stradivarius. The odors of certain flowers giddied her, she could see eight colors in the rainbow, a musical discord made her head ache upon the instant, and she could feel the spots on a playing-card with her finger-tips. I suppose this almost hysterical sensitiveness was morbid and unnatural. She had come of a family of unmixed blood, whose stock had never been replenished or strengthened by an alien cross. Her race was almost exhausted, its vitality low, and its temperament refined to the evaporation point. To-day Cresencia might have been called a degenerate.

One day, when she was about twenty-one or twenty-two, she heard Stayne's name for the first time. Someone was telling someone else a story in which Stayne had shone with particular brilliancy, had done a thing especially generous, had sacrificed himself and concealed the fact. A little after Miss Hromada heard his name again, and heard it coupled with extravagant praise. Next she saw a picture of him, and his face pleased her. He was pointed out to her on the deck of a yacht, and it pleased her all the more. After this a mutual friend, who knew them both, told her that Stayne was in love with her, and spent his nights in devising ways and means to meet her. Then at last they met.

Cresencia came away from that meeting in a state of mystic exaltation, such as we are told sometimes comes upon nuns before the Stations of the Cross. As for young Stayne, he filled himself a pipe standing before the fireplace in our room, and said to me:

"Ever met that Miss Hromada? Stunning girl and clever as they make 'em. I'm going to work it to get a bid to their place during the tournament."

He got his bid right enough about a month later, but in the meanwhile Things had happened. A very proud girl, such as Cresencia, rarely falls in love with any man, but when she does it is with a proud disregard of reticence and restraint that is splendid to see. Cresencia was too proud even to try to conceal her affection for young Stayne. In ten days she had all San Francisco, from Pacific Heights to Russian Hill, talking. On the eleventh San Francisco had them engaged. Next came the tournament and the house-party at the Hromadas' place that was to last a week.

Over his pipe in our room, Stayne said to me:

"Got my bid all right. I tell you what, she's a corking fine girl, old man, and no mistake. You don't know her very well, do you?"

By that sign I knew that however Miss Hromada might feel toward Stayne, Stayne would never be in love with her, for a man is not in love with a girl about whom he will speak to another man. Said I:

"Don't go to that house-party. Believe me, no good will come of it."

He looked at me a moment over his pipe, and I saw he understood.

"Wouldn't you go?" says he.

"Suppose it was your sister!"

He winced at that, and then added:

"But you know I'm not so sure about myself."

"Come now," I answered. "Seriously, now, aren't you sure about yourself?"

He hesitated, and then laughed a bit.

"Yes, I guess I am. But about Miss Hromada—is it as bad as all that? and mustn't I go?"

"It's quite as bad," I told him. "Everyone sees it but you. Decidedly, I would not go to that house-party."

"Well, may be you're right," said he; "I'll think it over."

He thought it over—and went. It was a bad business from the beginning. I was not of the party, but it was easy enough, Heaven knows, to hear what went forward. San Francisco gossip is not discreetly whispered over the teacups—it is shouted through megaphones, in public places. At the house-party Cresencia calmly appropriated young Stayne with superb, almost imperial, nonchalance. Stayne played his part in the one-sided game, and, once having made the mistake of going to the house-party, he was not much to blame up to a certain point. When a girl threw herself into his arms he was not the man to keep his hands in his pockets. Who would have been? But at the end of a week Cresencia's passion for him had become a veritable fury. The red-hot, degenerate Spanish blood of her sang in her veins, and her high-strung nerves crisped and recoiled upon themselves like the ends of broken violin strings. She used to sit in her room—so a girl told me—at night, after a dance or dinner, rolling her head to and fro upon her folded arms, or biting at the bare flesh of them, in a very excess of passion. Stayne had flirted with girls a-plenty before this time, and had gone through the mill like any other city-bred man, and usually could hold his own with the best of them. Cresencia, however, was outside this experience. A girl who would catch her breath at the touch of his hand upon her bare wrist, or go suddenly pale at his unexpected entrance, troubled him not a little.

At the end of the first week Stayne saw that the Certain Point had been reached, and invented an excuse to leave. Miss Hromada invented a better one for his staying. And he stayed. Up to this Certain Point, as well, Cresencia had been grandly unsuspicious of Stayne, assuming, as a matter of course, that he was in love with her. After the first week she was less sure of him, and her uncertainty only made her cling to him more desperately. The smash came one evening, as smashes generally come, when people least expect them, and when they are all unprepared for the crisis. Feeling, as he afterwards told me, like a kicked puppy, Stayne told Cresencia the truth—blundered it out—blurted it out, like a schoolboy. She must have been superb then. She was a born and bred Hromada, for that moment, at any rate. She rose slowly to her full six feet, her hands rigid at her sides, and without a gesture or movement spoke to him for five minutes in a low, calm voice, while Stayne (he told me so himself) cowered there before her, counting the ticking of the clock, and following, with shifty eyes, the pattern in the carpet at his feet.

"Now you had better go," she said, at length.

Stayne groped towards the door, wondering how soon he could draw a full breath, and if he could ever look at himself in the glass again without blushing. By the time his shaking hand closed on the knob, the daughter of an hundred Hromadas had lapsed back into the young girl of degenerate blood and jangled nerves and untamed passions. A scene really terrible followed.

"What is it! What is it!" Cresencia would exclaim, as she held him about the neck. "It isn't love, this feeling I have for you! What is it? What is the matter with me? It isn't love, and yet there is something—something here—here—I don't know! Am I losing my senses? Why is it that I have got to love you whether I will or no? It isn't love—is it a disease? Is it a kind of insanity? Oh, what is it that has happened to me these last weeks?"

In the face of such hysteria Stayne lost his hold upon himself as well—said he did love her after all—said so while he wondered at himself—said it, half-believing it was true. In the confusion of his ideas it was impossible for him to tell truth from falsehood. He became almost as incoherent as Cresencia herself. Fancy the scene, if you can—both of them excited beyond all control, talking wildly into each other's faces, neither of them heeding what was said by the other, and all the while clasped in an embrace like that of wrestlers! There in the darkness of that drawing-room, in the isolation of that country house, the two jars, floating helplessly in ungovernable currents, crashed together. That of the finest clay shivered and sank at once—the other, of coarser fibre, settled slower to its ruin.

In a month's time Stayne was sickened unto death of Cresencia—was cloyed and satiated with her. At first he had been too honest to pretend for her an affection he did not feel, but already the fine edge of this honesty had been blunted. If he now wished to break with her it was because it fatigued and bored him beyond words to keep up appearances. Once more he fought his way brutally out of the mesh in which he had become entangled, wrote a ten-line letter to Cresencia, which he believed would be final, and for a week felt like an honest man for the first time in three months.

But the thing was not to be. Miss Hromada's pride did not come to her aid this time even momentarily. She had been degrading far more rapidly than he. Though she rolled upon her bed, hurting herself with the nails of her hands, in unspeakable humiliation, she could not let Stayne go. And this was the same girl whose pride and self-respect had hitherto been her strongest traits. She managed to see Stayne three and four times each week. She came to his office, contrived to meet him on his way to lunch, managed to be invited to the same places—even began to take a strange, perverted pleasure in forcing herself upon his company and in submitting to his brutalities.

For the thing could not fail but have its effect upon Stayne. He suddenly discovered that nothing—literally and quite truly—nothing he could do would offend Cresencia. He realized that she would take anything from him —that she would not, or rather, that she could not, resent any insult, however gross. And the knowledge made the man a brute. Remember, this was not all at once. I am talking now about things that took a year or more to evolve. After he had clearly seen that Miss Hromada would submit to anything at his hands, Stayne began to enjoy her society. By this time Stayne had developed into rather much of a villain. It became for him a pleasure—a morbid, unnatural, evil pleasure for him to hurt and humiliate her. He hurt her while he sickened at the thought of his own baseness, and she submitted to it while she loathed herself for her own degradation. They were a strange couple.

Stayne would even torture her before other women and girls—would make her play waltzes while he danced with some fancied rival—would make appointments with her and come to the place with another girl, and tell her he had made other arrangements. He would smoke while she was by, and blow the smoke in her eyes. I have even seen him put his feet into the lap of her dinner gown, she, the while, trying to carry it off as a joke.

And she took all this and would go home and lie awake all night and fancy she was killing Stayne with her nails and teeth, till she shook all over and saw red things between her and the opposite wall.

The end of this story ought to be a suicide, or at least a murder, but that was the devil of it. The two people lived—lived out the wretched farce-tragedy to which there was to be no end. Had they never met, Miss Hromada and young Stayne would yet have been as fine specimens of womanhood and manhood as you could wish to know. Once having met, they ruined each other. The effect of these different characters upon one another was something well-nigh impossible to reduce to language. A Shakespeare could have handled it—a Zola might have worked it out—I dare not go further with it. For all I know the horror may still be alive. Stayne's name has long since been erased from the rolls of his club. Miss Hromada is thoroughly *déclassée*, and only last month figured in the law courts as the principal figure in a miserable and thoroughly disreputable scandal.

Stayne goes to see her four nights in the week.

Thomas on Tendencies

The Author of *Alabama* Believes in the Problem Play

The Wave, 16 (18 September 1897), 5.

The author of *Alabama* and *In Mizzoura* was writing at a ridiculously inadequate table when I came in, and by a light that should have been quite out of the question. He was a large blue-serge gentleman with a smooth face and looked enough like an actor to be a clergyman, while at the same time I knew him to be a first-class playwright. I say first-class because in the course of the interview Augustus Thomas found occasion to call himself a "second-class" man which was good only because it was false, and palpably so.

We began upon *Don't Tell Her Husband,* Mr. Thomas' new play, which the Frawleys now have under rehearsal.

"It's a problem comedy," said Mr. Thomas.

"Rather an unusual departure, isn't it?" I asked.

"A problem does end in a tragedy oftentimes, but for all that this is to be comedy in the sense that it is somewhat light."

I asked him what was to be its motif.

"Whether or not a man's chum should tell him of his wife's unfaithfulness."

"Problem enough," said I. "Do you solve it?"

"Remember the title," answered Mr. Thomas.

Mr. Thomas had a good deal to say about the problem play when I asked him if it was going out of vogue with the public.

"These things are matters of action and reaction," he said. "A little while ago and the public would not listen to melodrama. You couldn't so much as feed it to them with a spoon, but you see for yourself how *Secret Service* and *Maryland* have taken. The problem play is perhaps a little unpopular now, but the taste will come around again in time, for the reason that the best kind of work is done in plays of this character, and good, strong work will always tell in the end and find its place.

"When I write a play," continued Mr. Thomas, "I go into it, as it were, by inches, step by step. You know I consider the most important parts of a drama to be the parts that are not spoken—the thousand and one little looks and gestures, little poses and motions."

"I didn't know the playwright took notice of that," said I. "I supposed that he left those for the most part to the actor or actress."

"Rather the contrary," observed Mr. Thomas. "I write a play practically in novel form, filling in the gaps in the dialogue with explanatory directions. Of course the 'business,' such as the crossings and the like, is done after the piece is put on rehearsal."

"What should you say," I asked him next, "was the great requisite for a playwright?" and just as I expected Mr. Thomas answered "Truth."

"Yes, but truth on the stage, where a painted tree looks more real than a real tree, where an actor demands a strong line upon which to make his exit? How can you always be true there?"

"There are big fundamental truths that lie deeper than mere painted scenery and exit lines. Must you use green ink when writing of a landscape or red when describing a fire? And, besides that, demand for a strong exit line is true to life."

"As, for instance—"

"At your club, for instance, when you leave a group of men. Don't you always think of some little parting shot with which to signal your departure?"

I reflected.

"Or at a function. It is really a most dramatic situation from your point of view when you must say good-bye and face a whole roomful of people who are listening to what you are saying to your hostess. It is quite a little crisis. You do rack your brains for something appropriate to say and a 'strong exit line' is a veritable godsend. You see such situations occur often upon the stage, and in reproducing them you are true to life after all."

For a man who has accomplished so much Mr. Thomas is rather limited in his working hours. He calls himself a lazy man, which would be true if hard work was measured by mere lapse of time. But Mr. Thomas can do more by means of his daily four or five hours' stint than you or I could a-chieve in years. He is up at 6 (when a play is in hand), works till breakfast, is back in his study an hour after breakfast, and writes steadily till noon.

Never works afternoons or evenings except when under pressure, and then he works all night.

"But the best work is the deliberate, careful work, well thought over and slowly worked out."

"And how about the journalist working at his desk in the midst of scurrying office boys, clashing shears, and all the small pandemonium of a newspaper office?"

I didn't wait for Mr. Thomas' answer. I thought it was a strong exit line and left.

His Single Blessedness

The Wave, 16 (18 September 1897), 6.

Be pleased to consider how small are the beginnings of things—big things. When he was yet a very young fellow, say seventeen or eighteen, and spending a sweltering August at a summer resort down the coast, Doychert made the remark that little children bored him and that he hated them. This was more or less true, for a boy of eighteen hasn't the moral right to hate anything, 'specially children. Young Doychert had fired off the remark for the sake of effect, with one eye cocked at the gallery. Some girls were about and he wanted to astonish them. Doychert didn't hate children at all; quite the contrary, as events proved. But once having made the remark, he had to live up to it. So he went about that resort saying, "I hate children, I hate children," till he made people believe him, and ended by believing it himself. A lie never seems so true as when it has been crystallized into words. Doychert had very arbitrarily chosen his hatred of children as his fad, and he wore this nasty fad conspicuously, as some African tribesman might wear a hideous ornament, until it grows into his flesh and becomes almost a part of him. Doychert's "pet aversion" became almost—I say almost—a part of him, and he nursed it and fostered it until it developed hugely, so that he actually believed he could not stay in the same room with an active little, noisy little child, boy or girl.

"I can't help it," he would say. "It's an instinct, like some people's aversion to cats. Let 'em be old enough to take care of themselves, and I don't say; but a nasty, mewling, salmon-pink, smelly baby, all head and red dough, that makes sucking noises and drools milk—B-r-r!" Thus Doychert with a shudder of horror that he believed was genuine. And all the while, way down in the secretest heart's heart of the man, he was a kindly, lovable fellow, with no more dislike for babies than you or I or all the rest of us.

Three years after he was married his first baby was born—a girl.

Doychert loved his wife—no man better. They two had a delicious tiny little rabbit-warren of a house, all brown shingles and small paned windows, way out at the end of Pacific avenue, near where the Government Presidio reservation begins. It was far enough removed from the end of the world of San Francisco to be near enough to heaven for all practical purposes, and for three years Doychert lived out the dearest period of his life there, wallowing in happiness, as one might say, fairly miring himself in the pure delight of being alive—and married, married to Mrs. Doychert. For she was a dear, beautiful girl, and the pair loved each other better than most people.

When the little girl was born Doychert said to me, across his smoking-table (we were in the billiard-room and the wheels of the doctor's coupe were just grating off down the street), Doychert said, or rather whispered, because Mrs. Doychert's room was just above:

"I can't help it, Sturgis, it's an instinct. I suppose I was born with an aversion to children (he really believed he was honest), and I'll die with it. I'm that baby's father, but till it gets old I shall hate it, I know I will. I don't want to see it"—he made a squirming movement with one shoulder—"I'd rather have a blind kitten crammed down my back than have the touch of that child on me. You can't understand that, can you?"

"No, I can't," says I, "and I think you are a horrible, filthy brute, that should be manhandled—you beast."

"That is all quite true," he answered, "I am a brute beast, and worse, for even a brute beast cares for its whelps; but give me time. When she grows up I suppose I shall like her."

"Suppose you shall like your daughter? Now that sounds fine. Where's my hat?"

"Going?"

"Sorry I came."

"Well, you know how it is," said he at the door. "It's an unreasoned instinct. I can't help it. I hate children, and all's said. Think of feeling it clawing at your nose and ears. Lord!"

Here I swore at him and went away.

If you know anything of men friendships, you will have understood from the preceding conversation that Doychert and I were the best chums in the world. That is why, eight years later, when I came back to San Francisco again I went straight to Doychert's little house out on Pacific avenue. I had heard a good deal about him during those intervening eight years and was prepared for changes. But even at that, the difference was poignant. The little brown-shingled house stood waist deep in weeds, the gate was gone and the small panes of the windows smashed.

Doychert opened the door for me. Evidently he had not shaved that week. He was in his stocking feet. His eyes looked at me out of saucers of brown skin. The place reeked of stale tobacco smoke, and it did not need the sight of the unmade bed nor the cigar stumps in the card tray to tell me that Doychert was living there alone.

Towards 2 o'clock that night, over his tenth brandy and water and his last cigar, Doychert told me the tale of the things that had happened.

"It began all of a sudden on one day," said he, his hands on his chin, glowering into the grate fire. 'Jack'" (that was Mrs. Doychert) "had been up about a week. I hadn't so much as seen Emmie yet, and Jack and I had almost quarreled about her. Jack had begged me just to look into the room while she was asleep, but I couldn't—I mean I wouldn't do it. One Sunday afternoon when Emmie was about three weeks old, I was stretched out on the sofa here sort of half asleep, when Jack came up to me very softly, and before I knew it put Emmie into my arms.

"'Joe,' she says, 'look at her now, your little daughter, how can you help loving her?—' She was going to say something else, but she never got further than that. Emmie snuggled down into my neck and put her little fists into my face. I jumped up and pushed her, almost threw her, from me, recoiling as though a snake had touched me.

"'Take it away,' I cried. 'For God's sake take it away, I hate it and loathe it, and I always will hate it.'

"Jack was only a week out of a bed. I don't need to tell you how delicately poised a woman is at such times as that, how tangled and jangled her nerves are. The doctors have got names for it all. She heard what I said, and saw me thrusting my little daughter away from me. Then she looked at me once in—I say she gave me—she—you see"—Doychert cleared his throat —"she gave a sigh and went down softly into a little heap on the floor.

"She was in the sanitarium about a month, and for a time we thought she never would be right in the head again. I wasn't allowed to see her, and her folks took Emmie. After a month's time, though, the doctors brought her around all right; said she had pulled through sound as a nut, and that I might see her. She knew I was coming. They had her propped up in a big sea chair by a window. I had sent her a lot of flowers and she wore some of them. When I came into the room I saw her leaning back there in the sea chair. She looked up at me and smiled, happy as could be to see me. And then all at once her expression changed to one of the most abject horror and revulsion. She put up her hands to shut out the sight of me and cried out, 'No, no, I can't. Take him away, oh, somebody take him away.' It was no use reasoning with her, she got hysterical, screamed and fought from me as though I was a leper or a murderer. I had to go, and as soon as I was gone she was quiet again. Couldn't understand herself how it had happened. The doctors said I could come the next day, and as soon as Jack heard my foot on the stairs she fainted with the pure horror of the thought of seeing me. She had forgiven me my brutality with Emmie, loved me as much as ever, mark you, longed to see me as much as I longed to see her, and yet went insane with loathing as soon as I came near. This was the one point of insanity of which the doctors could not cure her. They never have been able to cure her. We have tried everything. She can't even see my handwriting without that horrible revulsion seizing upon her. But she can write to me and she does, and that's how I know she is suffering as much as I. What we two have gone through with, God only knows. Can you imagine the horror of the situation? We are as dear to each other as ever—more so, my God," he cried, digging his nails into his temples, "more so. We are here, here in the same town, where I can see her every day, and yet we are worlds apart. It's a death in life, a death in life," and he rocked himself to and fro in his place. "Every Sunday we have arranged that she shall go to church. She tells me where she sits, and I go up in the gallery and peep at her from behind pillars. Even that is bad for her, but she can stand it for an hour once a week. Once she caught sight of me and—" he broke off suddenly and closed his eyes.

"And Emmie?" said I.

"Emmie will be eight to-morrow. Here's a lot of pictures that Jack has sent me from time to time. Isn't she the finest little girl you ever saw, and bright, bright as a dollar?"

"How about her?" I asked him. "You manage to see her when her mother's not by, I suppose."

I saw the knuckles of Doychert's fist suddenly whiten.

"Emmie is—is like—Emmie takes after her mother," he said. "By the way, you have some little nieces, haven't you? What do you give 'em on Christmas, and—and on their birthdays and such like? Emmie's eight to-morrow. Books wouldn't do, would they, hey? Is she too old for toys—or too young? Here's what I got her. I thought I'd take the chances on toys." He turned to the table and undid a few packages. "There's a little doll," he said, "and you see," he added proudly, "she closes her eyes when you lay her down, and there's a doll house; ain't those little chairs and tables out of sight? I guess Emmie would like those, all right. I can just see her eyes stick out when she undoes the package. I think I'll get a big doll house like that for my kindergarten—I've got a kind of a kindergarten going, down on Minna street, that you must see. And here, look at this. Here's another thing I am going to send to Emmie. Catch on to this. Here's a little pump, and, by Jove, you can pump real water in it, see?" and he showed me how it worked. "I wonder if Emmie will know that you can pump 'truly' water with it? Tell you what, you write it on a card and put it in, will you?"

"Why not you?"

"Well—you see, they might recognize my handwriting."

"Shan't I say," said I, pen in hand, "that it all comes from you, with many happy birthdays?"

"Not that, above all things," said Doychert.

Life-Line and Surf-Boat

―――――

Daily Routine of the Life-Saving Station at Fort Point

―――――

The Wave, 16 (18 September 1897), 9.

―――――

One doesn't like to imagine rescuing the perishing and saving life and all that reduced to a science, a mere matter of drill and discipline systematized and unemotional. And yet after you have considered a life-saving station, above all after you have seen the splendid, efficient work, and the boat itself—a very marvel of building and ingenuity—you see, of course, that it's the best and only way. Just as the professional and unmoved calmness of a trained physician is better than any amount of unpracticed sympathy and pity and bungling efforts at relief.

These men at the stations don't often get into the papers. It's only when a big ship is wrecked that you hear them mentioned incidentally as saving the lives of the crew and passengers. But the surfmen's duty is quite as much the prevention of a wreck as it is that of taking off the survivors.

I visited one of these stations the other day—Fort Point station, in the twelfth life-saving district. It is one of thirteen such stations up and down the Pacific Coast, and it will suffice as a type of all the others. The life-saving stations are a part of the civil service, and under the control of the Treasury Department at Washington. They are officered by a general Superintendent (Maj. Blakeney) and an assistant Inspector. Each station is manned by a crew of eight surfmen and a Captain, also called a keeper. In each station there are two boats, sometimes more, but two at least; the little life-boat for quick, nearby work—it can be manned and run out in thirty seconds—and the big surf-boat, which is, perhaps, the best sea-going boat ever devised by a builder. The surf-boat at the Fort Point station is quite thirty feet long, is manned by the entire crew of eight surfmen and the Captain, and at a pinch could carry fifty people. This boat can neither sink, nor fill, nor be stove in, nor capsize, nor turn turtle, nor ship a sea, nor do any of the evil tricks common to boats in a gale. If she should ship a sea she bales herself out; if a comber should succeed in capsizing her she will come right side up in a twinkling, and if a rock staves her in, the fifty watertight compartments keep her afloat. Once get her out in the open sea and there is practically nothing that can hurt her. The only difficulty is with the huge combing breakers that bar the way. These can roll high enough to keep her shorebound. The men know the signs well enough. For instance, when the combers swash solid and green over the lowest Seal Rock without breaking into spray, then they know that they are helpless. Helpless, that is, as far as the boat is concerned, for if the wreck is not too far out she can be reached then by the beach apparatus. Three hundred yards is as far as this apparatus can be used with any certainty. It has been effective at five hundred, but this is an unusual case. The stations at Fort Point and by the Cliff House often use both the boat and the apparatus. The beach apparatus is the cart that carries the little cannon used in shooting the line over the wreck. Once the outside end of the line is fast the breeches buoy is run back and forth between the wreck and the shore till every one is landed. But wrecks don't come every day, and as often as not there is nothing for the crew to do but spend their time in the daily hammer-and-tongs routine. Monday they drill with the beach apparatus, Tuesday with the surf- and life-boat, Wednesday with the signals, Thursday with the apparatus again, Friday is the practice in resuscitation, Saturday is a general cleaning day.

Between whiles the beach—their section of it—is patrolled night and day, and a lookout kept for distressed vessels and those ships that are unacquainted with the coast and are coming in too close. Each of the surfmen has to be expert in the use of the international code of signals, by means of which he can talk to a ship as by a telephone, waving her away from a dangerous coast, asking her what is the matter, telling her, perhaps, in case of threatened wreck, that the boat is to be put off or the line shot, or, when the storm is violent enough (when, for instance, the combers don't break as they go over the lowest seal rock), signalling the ominous message, "No boat can live in such a sea."

In foggy weather this patrol is doubled, and at night each patrolman carries a torch instead of a flag. There are observation stations here and there along the beach and from these the surfman can sweep the horizon easily enough. It is his duty on the discovery of a ship flying the distress signal to report her to his Captain, who thereupon takes the whole responsibility of the situation, deciding whether the shot line is to be used, or the boat, or whether the boat can go out at all. Never have the men thus far failed of their duty. Whenever it has been possible to go they have gone. Even when the *Elizabeth* went down—one of the most heartrending wrecks that ever occurred—the boats would have gone out had the tugs given them a tow.

There is something—much, in fact—about a life-saving station that suggests a fire-engine house. There is the same discipline, drill and organization; the same watchfulness; the same readiness in case of emergency; the dispatch in getting out ("rolling," as the fireman would call it); the same danger to be met; the same chance for pluck and perseverance, and last of all, there is the enemy to be watched and waited for at every hour of the day or night. But the preponderance of danger is on the side of the surfman. The fireman often fights the enemy from a safe point, and only once in a while does a really great fire occur. But a storm heavy enough to warrant bringing out the boat at all is always big with danger, and the surfman must invariably go right out upon the same sea that is thrashing the wreck to death, must trust himself to the very elements that are clamoring for the lives on board the ship.

It is all very splendid, but one fancies the real reward must be the work itself; wages can't pay for it, and the surfmen do not receive medals to any noticeable extent; but the idea of having dared those thundering green combers and the churning, open sea beyond, beaten and outwitted the enemy, gotten the lives from under its grip, wrestled and fought a way back to shore, that must be the real reward—a thing better than gold medals and "mentions in dispatches."

The Frivolous Gyp

The Follies of the Moment Satirized in *En Balade*

The Wave, 16 (18 September 1897), 12.

There are some books that are called books of the year—solid, sober, serious affairs, dubbed such to distinguish them from the lighter weight books of the day and the very light books of the hour. But what shall one say of "Gyp's" latest vaporous ephemera, *En Balade?* It is not a book of the minute or even the second. It is kinetoscopic in its rapidity of transition. There will be no second edition, for even if it were now being pressed, the allusions in *En Balade* would be stale ere it could be got upon the book stands.

It is a strange, silly book, read with Anglo-Saxon eyes, and its silliness, its miserable shallowness, its reflection of a jaded, exhausted and effete society are more repulsive than otherwise.

En Balade is the doings and dialogues of such characters as these, all brought together into one company and promenaded in the fashionable high places of modern Paris: Louis XIV, Bayard, Alcibiades, Thaïs, Hercules, Saint Louis, Richelieu, Monsieur Citoyen Moses, Madame de Maintenon, Cato, Noah, Vespasienne d'Argentan (a Parisienne of to-day), Jeanne d'Arc, Mercury, Socrates, etc., etc., etc.

These people fore-gather in the Champs Elysées and decide that they will make a little excursion into Paris—Louis XIV for mere distraction, Richelieu to see M. Hanoteaux, Diogenes to find an honest man, Saint Louis to arouse public opinion in favor of the Christians in Armenia, Noah to become drunk, Thaïs and Madame de Maintenon to enjoy *tête-à-têtes* with an Hungarian gypsy Rigo (a very palpable allusion to the affair of the Princess of Chimay). They visit the race course of Auteuil and the opera, where a charity ball is being given for the Protestant refugees in the flooded districts along the Mississippi River.

At Auteuil "Gyp" finds occasion to caricature the athletic fever which it seems has pervaded Paris, in this fashion.

143

Flore d'Eprefleury, a companion of Vespasienne d'Argentan, a very up-to-date Parisienne, appears upon the scene:

> Louis XIV, ogling Flore—Pretty little woman.
> Diogenes, moving away discontentedly—I'm not looking for that sort of thing.
> Socrates—Nor I.
> Napoleon (to Flore)—What's your name? (She glances at him over her shoulder.)
> Flore (calling Sangeyne)—Monsieur de Sangeyne, you, whose great, very great-grandfather was squire to the Great King, will you present me to Hercules?
> Louis XIV to Napoleon—She knows how to live evidently.
> Sangeyne (presenting Flore)—Hercules, this is Flore d'Eprefleury; Flore, this is Hercules.
> Fouquet (to Flore)—Madame, I am Monsieur Fouquet, of whom you certainly must have heard.
> Flore (without noticing Fouquet, to Hercules)—You must be a great lover of outdoor exercise.
> Hercules—Of course.
> Flore—I believe you have beaten every record.
> Hercules (flattered)—Every one.
> Flore (admiringly)—That is very chic.
> Louis XIV—I, Mademoiselle, I am the King Louis XIV, he who—
> Flore (to Hercules)—You were saying—
> Hercules—Nothing. I didn't open my mouth.
> Buckingham (to Flore)—Madame, I am George Villiers, Duke of Buckingham. I formerly enjoyed a certain celebrity—
> Flore (taking Hercules' arm)—Let's go look at the horses.

However, Gyp, speaking through the mouth of Hercules, does not approve of what she chooses to call the modern "*athleticisme.*"

> Bayard (coming back in company of Hercules)—He's not pleased with football, Hercules. He expected something very different. It left him rather cold.
> Sangeyne—That was a good match with the English team, though.
> Bayard—The captain had some hot words with Hercules.
> Vespasienne d'Argentan—*Eh bien,* you don't find it chic, this football?
> Hercules—Ah, no. That a sport? Never; no more than the

bicycle. Skating, horses, swimming, arms—those are what you call sport. Things that make a man fine-looking. But that! It's the sport that deforms the young men of to-day and makes their faces repulsive. They batter each other, knock each other down, smash-in each other's chests. They bring over young heroes from England and America and make matches with them against the French for no other evident purpose than to batter our young fellows to death, and we call it fun. Bah!

A great deal of Gyp's drivel in this senseless book is directed against the Jews (the real war- or peace-makers of Europe, if all tales are true).

> Bayard—Look at the children in the Paris parks; they are nearly all little Jews. In thirty years there will not be a single Frenchman left. Look at them; they are the hope of the country, these little Jews.
>
> Richelieu—The Jews, ah yes, the Jews. They have everything in their power nowadays. Their hand is upon the government, backing up their friends' enterprises or checking and humbling some rival. The political world is fairly grovelling at their feet. The nobility welcomes them—
>
> Sangeyne—Is welcomed by them especially.
>
> Saint Louis (indignantly)—Is it possible?
>
> Sangeyne—It is very humble nowadays, the nobility. It submissively begs for invitations at the houses of the Jews.
>
> Moses—Pecause it's only *der* Jews who gives *der* finest receptions. Id's natural dey should go dere.
>
> Sangeyne—So you see, of course, they are not to blame. It's the Jew in this case who has the whip hand.

Again Gyp calls her readers' attention to the fact that France—modern France—is forgetting its ancient ideals and does so in this manner:

> Vespasienne d'Argentan—Have you seen Jeanne d'Arc?
>
> Saint Louis (loftily)—Jeanne d'Arc is not here, Madame. (They are at the opera ball, by the way). This kind of a place would ill suit her holy character.
>
> Vespasienne—I don't know whether it harmonizes or not. I know she's here.
>
> Fouquet (on his tiptoes)—That's a fact, she's here. (To Jeanne d'Arc, who comes up pouting). What's the matter, my little Jeanne d'Arc? Come now, tell us what's the trouble.

Jeanne d'Arc—All my friends have left me. They're off having a good time somewhere, while they leave me to twirl my thumbs behind at home. It's not nice of them.

Vespasienne—They gave you the go-by, is that it?

Jeanne d'Arc—You say, Madame?

Talleyrand—The fact is, she is not much amused, this poor Jeanne d'Arc. They left her to languish in her hotel.

Jeanne d'Arc—I passed the day looking out of the window. The night came, and when I saw the stars I was less timid.

Bayard—I, I am never afraid.

Louis XIV—This great man is full of vanity.

And so it goes—a little endless trickle of drivel, sparkling on the surface, perhaps, but so shallow that you can see at once to the bottom—see that there are only stones there and never a twinkle of gold.

The illustrations are strange, contorted, colored affairs, the work of that picture-maker who signs himself "Bob," and who imitates the style of the schoolboy with slate and pencil.

The Hopkins Institute

Art Education in San Francisco—Men Who Have Emerged

The Wave, 16 (25 September 1897), 9.

There are one hundred and sixty students up at the Mark Hopkins Institute of Art now, and from year to year the number increases. It is rather surprising and gratifying to know that their average work in drawings from the nude is quite as good as the average work turned out in Julian's, the great *atelier* of Paris. Students leave from the Art Institute of this city every year whose names figure afterwards on the walls of the *Salon* or on the pages of the great illustrated magazines of this country. Alexander Harrison, the famous marine painter, came from this organization, and at one time Toby Rosenthal was a student in its midst. Then there are such artists as Ernest Peixotto, Eric Pape, and Guy Rose, who are as good magazine illustrators as any in the country.

The Hopkins Institute is doing great work in bringing out native talent, and not only bringing it out but developing it to a very high degree. In the old school its students used to be drilled and drilled and drilled in drawing from the antique, and a great deal of time wasted in consequence. Mr. Arthur F. Mathews, present head of the school, has changed all that, however, and has made the life classes—that is to say, the classes that work from nude models—the all-important part of the course. Other classes there are, however, such as the portrait class, the still life class, the night class, and a small class in the antique, all of which are merely preparatory classes for the life work. Besides the mere practical work of drawing and painting, however, there are three or four secondary courses, such as anatomy, perspective, composition, and the like. Dr. Hay lectures on the skeleton and muscular formation once a week. Mr. R.D. Young is the instructor in perspective, while Mr. Mathews gives occasional talks on composition. The other members of the corps of instructors are Douglas Tilden, instructor in modeling; Mr. Stanton, who has the night class; Miss Chittenden, who superintends the Saturday class, and Mr. Harry Fonda who has charge, alternately with Mr. Mathews, of the life classes. Mr. Mathews is also the general director of the school and dean of its faculty. In addition, Mr. Fonda conducts a costume sketch class.

The artists in general are well satisfied with the Hopkins house as a headquarters for the school, and there is no doubt but that the students will long continue to occupy it as such. The light is admirable, the rooms spacious, and the arrangement of the house affords first-class opportunities in the way of galleries for exhibitions. The school offers three medals yearly for which the competition is very keen. The most desirable medal of all is the painting medal, given for the best color study made in the life class. After this in order of importance come the drawing medal and antique medal, which latter is given or not at the option of the instructor.

When the life class of the school originally opened the instructors found themselves at first involved in an unexpected difficulty, that of obtaining models. There were only one or two professional models known to the coterie of local painters, and the life class soon knew them by heart. For a time the directors were hard put to it to satisfy the demand, but after the first year the wants of the school became known in the "Latin Quarter," and the Italians, as usual in every art center, began to recruit the corporal's guard of those who earned their living by "posing for the figure." However, the artists who have studied in Paris and worked from all of the famous models there are a unit in declaring that the California-bred model, especially the female model, is the best that can be found the world over, in the matter of color, proportion, modeling, and, as the painters say, "skeleton." That the Hopkins Institute of Art and the work done by its students are having their influence is indubitable. Painters and draughtsmen whose early education was gained in this city are returning one by one from the great European *ateliers*, settling down and pursuing their vocation in San Francisco and its surroundings. While as yet there are not many of them, they nevertheless are quite capable of turning out work easily comparable with the best that is being done in the East. Portrait and landscape seem to be their strong points, and their work along these lines has just begun to attract attention. Formerly it was only very well-to-do people, the "patrons," who bought pictures. Now the middle classes are buying, and are more and more willing to pay good prices for good pictures.

The Tale and the Truth

No Romance in the Life of the Variety Star

The Wave, 16 (25 September 1897), 14.

But she never is at home, this poor variety actress, though it is the cherished end of all her labors, and shows at the end of every vista of ambition like the picture of the Capitol building on a cigar advertisement. You remember the outcast in the dear old melodramas when the solicitous leading heavy asks her where is her home. "Home," says she, with a throat quaver, "I have no home." Thus the variety actress. She has no home, but she looks forward to the time when she will have. It is the goal towards which she "sings and dances," or "high wires," or "lofty tumbles," or "serio-comiques," or "Swiss bell rings," and the like.

One likes to think that after her turn is over the songster and dancer dashes off her garden hat and black stockings, or sombrero and red stockings, and meets an effete youth or two of the "gilded" variety and goes away with him and knocks off some of his gilding and drinks champagne and smokes cigarettes at his expense. You like to think that the strong woman is attacked on her way home from the theater and gets a half-Nelson upon an adversary and very nearly breaks him in two. And you demand it as a right that the serio-comic sings at a man's club, and gets on the table, and drinks strange drinks out of her slipper. This would all be very fine if it were only true. But it is not true; it is hideously, lamentably untrue. Why, these variety actresses are not even bad. This may be the fault of their education, or maybe it's only a matter of intelligence; but some way or another they are not even bad, and off the stage they are uncouthly unpicturesque. Do you know what they first think of when they first arrive? Not where are the best restaurants, but where are the cheapest lodging-houses. Fancy, they don't even live in hotels. They live in lodging-houses; worse than that, they "stop with friends on Ellis or O'Farrell streets," and the house invariably—I say invariably—reeks with the smell of cooking, onions, stale upholstery and bad tobacco smoke. There is no more romance in them than in a carrot, no more gaiety than in an undertaker's assistant, while forever in the background lurks the invidious husband, or the more invidious brother, or the cousin most invidious of any. You will always find him to be a pale, preoccupied man, who puts his head in at the door at intervals and interrupts your interview on the pleasures of life behind the scenes with questions as to "low Irish wigs" or "toreador make-ups," or "symmetries"—whatever dreadful things these may be.

Who was the man, I wonder, who first started that pleasant little fiction about "chappies" in evening dress loitering about back of the scenes in earnest conversation with chorus girls or "leading boys"? I've been behind myself often enough, and I have diligently looked for the chappie, but never have I seen so much as the shine of his silk hat. What theater does Mr. Archie Gunn go to for the pictures that he paints so well in *Truth*—always with a gas jet burning in a bird cage in the background and a ballet girl sitting in a white froth of tulle in the foreground?

They are not bad, these poor variety actresses, not dissipated, only hopelessly sordid and overworked and matter of fact. A glass of beer and a cheese sandwich after their turn is done is for them a champagne banquet, while a cable car ride stolen in the intervals of darning the invidious cousin's socks or mending their own "toreador make-up" must take the place of the bacchic revels with which the colored weeklies have made us so familiar.

It's amusing to interview these variety people, and to watch them strenuously putting their best foot forward and airing all their pretty little professional graces. They are really acting then, acting more cleverly, or at least with more of an effort, than when doing "their turn." Some of them have been interviewed so much that they know, or suppose they know, in advance just what questions are to be put to them, and so talk in that vein. As for instance, Papinta. She at once began to declaim upon the originality of her dance as opposed to Fuller's. Then she started off—always without a word from the interviewer—upon her fads. Wheeling, it seemed, was one of them, and she wheeled for nearly ten minutes consecutively until I punctured her tire and she began over again upon her pets. When they had all been killed off from the Scotch collie to the Angora cat, she actually sat up and told me that Shakespeare was her favorite poet, and that she always travelled with a volume of the sonnets. They all have a shy at the Bard of Avon. Josephine Sabel reads *Romeo and Juliet* three times every month, and Alcide Capitaine, the strongest woman in the world, can recite passages from *Hamlet* with one hand tied behind her. And invariably, invariably and invariably do they assure you, or at the very least lead you to infer that they come from an aristocratic family. Adgie, for instance, the lion handler; why, she did not dare to mention her real name! Why, it involved one of the greatest Spanish families known to the College of Heralds! Why, she was almost a Countess, was this debonaire handler of lions, a Countess who mended property skirts and basted spangles.

And so it goes. Poor, pretentious, sordid women, verging on forty, doing "turns" and specialties in the costume of sixteen-year-old girls, their faces hardened with much rouging, their eyes tired and glazed with facing the footlights, their hands calloused and their voices jaded, faded and cracked with shouting songs to drown an overture. Variety actress! Chic? Say, rather, old, broken-down women, not fascinating in their weaknesses, not gay in their vices, and as often as not too irretrievably stupid to have either weakness or vice. Commonplace is the word best applicable. Hopelessly, hopelessly commonplace.

Execution Without Judgment

The Wave, 16 (2 October 1897), 5.

It was Miller who told me the yarn that follows. May be you recall Miller, the Australian journalist, who gave me the story of "The Strangest Thing." Miller had this tale through Canavan, an English pal of his, who had a mountain ranch in King's county in California. Miller tells only what he saw. I tell all that comes before. What comes afterward you must tell yourself.

This is the part that comes before. Canavan had been setting out trees for his hunting preserve. Canavan was an Englishman who had come to California with a consignment of English ideas that the Dingley tariff should have taken knowledge of. One of these ideas was a hunting preserve. This hunting preserve would have been well enough had he been content to merely preserve it. But Canavan wanted to improve upon it, wanted to have it like the preserves of his wife's people at Lowe in Northern England. So he started in to put long alleys into it, and to landscape-garden it, and to rearrange the trees in it, pulling up some and transplanting others, and generally improving it according to his transplanted English ideas.

But Canavan is not the hero of this yarn. The hero is one of the trees that he so shamefully mishandled, a huge Black Pine, that was already old when Canavan's ancestors went a-hunting with William Rufus in that other piece of landscape gardening called in the histories the "New Forest."

This much introduction is needed to explain how it came about that this Black Pine was stretched out upon its trunk and ready to be set up in its new place at the time when Estorijo dirked Ramon Sabichi. These two men were Mexicans. Estorijo was the boss of a gang of Chinamen that was working on Canavan's preserve. Sabichi was a sheep herder.

It is not necessary that you should know why they fought. Sabichi was the first man that Estorijo had ever killed, and the sight of him thrashing about on the ground in the throes of violent death became in consequence a matter of considerable interest to him.

Estorijo believed that he had done the trick rather neatly for a first attempt, and was sure that Sabichi would die in a short time. This trick Estorijo had learned from a Mexican sub-lieutenant at Libertad. He had come up to Sabichi, and while walking along beside him, had thrown his left arm affectionately across Sabichi's neck, had next taken a firm grip of the shoulder and suddenly spun his man about like a turn-stile, till his back was toward him. To dirk him then in the soft part of the body between the hip bone and the ribs was an easy matter. The advantage of this Mexican trick lies in the fact that the man dirked is altogether perplexed by that spinning about, and don't know what is happening nor where to look for the blow.

But the manner of Sabichi's dying was a surprise to Estorijo. He had seen representations of stabbing on the stage, and had read of some in novels, and had entertained preconceived ideas as to how a dirked man should behave and how he should die. He had imagined that Sabichi would throw up his hands and fall at full length and die gracefully and with his eyes properly closed.

Instead, Sabichi sat down abruptly and hard, and his hat canted to one side. There was no sign of blood. He looked up at Estorijo, winking his eyes and exclaiming: "What—what—what—you swine—you've knifed me—you've done for me. What—why——" and here he began to cough.

Estorijo stood in front of him, his knife ready, in case Sabichi should get up again. He did not deem Sabichi's remarks worthy of an answer, and Sabichi's position sitting there on the ground with his legs wide apart and his hat tilted rakishly over one eye struck him as ridiculous. All at once Sabichi vented a sharp "Oh, I pain!" and tried to get up. Then he began to die rapidly. Somehow he couldn't get up, but thrashed about helplessly on the ground, rolling over and over, now on his face, now on his back and now on his hands and knees, running his head stupidly against the tree trunks, and scrabbling at the fallen leaves and pine needles with his hands. His coughing was incessant, and his eyes were wide open. Then he fell flat with his arms doubled under him, fetched a deep sigh and lay inert and wondrously still. Estorijo had never seen anything quite so still before. "You're done for now," muttered Estorijo; "I guess you——"

"U-ugh!" said Sabichi, burying his face in the leaves that covered the ground. This persistency in living annoyed Estorijo beyond expression and he took certain radical measures to the effect that Sabichi should cease from living finally and definitely. "Now, will you, now," said he, as he rose to his feet. Estorijo never had a greater respect for himself than at this moment. "I've got to hide you somewhere," said he as he slid his knife back into the hip pocket of his overalls. "It won't do to let those Chinamen get a sight of you, no, it won't do at all, my son." At first he thought he would carry Sabichi up into the arroyo and hide him under a pile of rocks. Then his eye fell upon a great circular pit that his Chinamen had been digging that day, Canavan's Black Pine had been dragged near to it and would be set up in it to-morrow. "An idea," murmured Estorijo, "you're going to be buried in that pit, my son, and to-morrow there'll be a hundred and fifty feet of Black Pine on top of you to hold you down." His Chinamen's picks and shovels were lying about where they had left them upon quitting work. Estorijo swung himself into the pit and dug down into its bottom some five or six feet. Then he buried Sabichi there, and walked away from the place with great strides, his head in the air.

Next day the pine was planted in its destined place and grew and flourished for five, ten, fifteen years.

Here is the part that Miller saw. "Canavan wa'n't any hand at ranchin'," said Miller, "I've seen ryce-track touts, knee high to nothin', could 'ave wiped his eye when it cyme to knowin' horse and sheep and the like. Canavan busted in two years' time, and his ranch went to rack. He spent too blyme much time shootin' at things in his blyme preserve and he came out into God's country fair sick of the whole shop, but says he: 'Miller, there's more gyme there in the square inch than anywhere on this ball of dirt.' He let me have his rifles—double-barrelled expresses they were, straight from Sheffield—and his splatter gun and his maps and his blessing, and I went into the plyce to see what I could see. Mind now, this was full fifteen years after he'd busted. I outfitted at Fresno and, among other things, began asking for a guide, philosopher an' cook. This chap, Estorijo shows up. Fairish guide he turned out to be, but with a face on him to frighten babies with. He was old, by fifty, I'm thinking, but he knew the country like the palm of his hand, but the way he'd fry mountain trout—but this yarn now. We fetched up at Canavan's old plyce three weeks out. The ranch house was still there but so badly used up by weather that we dared not camp in it, so we made camp in what was the corn bin, and for two weeks shot and shot and fished, and fished and shot, till five-pronged buck and three-pound trout became regular tiresome. Back in Fresno they'd told me of the Sabichi affair and how, if all tales were true, Estorijo should have copped off in his boots, but most Mexicans are murderers when they're not mand'lin plyers, and it was all one with me so long as my man could find me buck to shoot an' cook 'em when they were shot.

"Well, one night, while we were watching by a salt lick for deer, a thundering, blundering, snoring gyle of wind jumped out of the East, puff! quick as that, 'strike me straight how she blow, with the ryne flogging down like millions of whip lashes, and the lightning slithering in, and the thunder booming like the ordnance practice at the Aldershot manoeuvers. We cut for the camp dizzied with the noise and whirl of things and of course went wrong in the dark and were brought to standing in a bit of clearing—the end of one of Canavan's alleys—blowing like porpoises and a-clean knocked up.

"'Not here, not here,' says Estorijo, in his broken lingo, 'not here, but further, we go on further, hey? I don' like deesa place.'

"Just then the lightning winked, like God's eye opening, and I saw my man squatting on the far side of the clearing as far awye as he could squeeze from the trunk of a big pine that stood just there. Then there was a smash and a slam-bang hell-roaring explosion, like the thunder of twenty Krupps, and that big pine tree began to sway. I could see it plain enough, for the lightning was winking twenty to the minute. I could see it sway and could see Estorijo, squatting down there on the ground with his shrivelled old hands above his head. Over she went, over and down and down, smashing and crushing and crushing and grinding down through everything, roaring the whiles like Niagara, all her stretched fibers howling like witches, all her boughs and branches crackling and grinding and snapping. My word, it was dreadful and it was grand. Everything shook, the ground under me rocked like jelly on a jarred table, one big final boom, then—silence, only the whining of the wind and the whip-whipping of the ryne. She was down, and under her trunk was Estorijo, down there under a broken tangle of branches, dead, dead and dinted deep into the ground, buried in it as I might say, and in the roots of that fallen tree—you listen to me—in the roots of that fallen tree, gripped there and held there as if in some tremendous fist. There was —something. Can you guess what?"

Miracle Joyeux

The Wave, 16 (9 October 1897), 4.

Mervius had come to old Jerome's stone-built farm house, across the huge meadow where some half dozen of the neighboring villagers pastured their stock in common. Old Jerome had received a certain letter which was a copy of another letter and so on and so on, nobody could tell how far. Mervius would copy this letter and take it back to his village, where it would be copied again and again and yet again, and copies would be made of these copies till the whole country side would know the contents of that letter, pretty well by heart. It was in this way that those people made their literature. They would hand down the precious documents to their children and that letter's contents would become folklore, become so well known that it could be repeated orally. It would be a legend, a *mythos*, perhaps by and by after a long time it might gain credence and become even history.

But in that particular part of the country this famous letter was doubly important because it had been written by a man whom some of the peasants and laborers and small farmers knew. "I knew him," said old Jerome when Mervius had come in and the two had sat down on either side of the oak table in the brick-paved kitchen. Mervius—he was past seventy himself—

slipped off his huge wooden sabots and let his feet rest on the warm bricks near the fireplace, for the meadow grass had been cold.

"Yes, I knew him," said Jerome. "He took the name of Peter afterwards. He was a fisherman and used to seine fish over in the big lake where the vineyards are. He used to come here twice a week and sell me fish. He was a good fisherman. Then the carpenter's son set the whole country by the ears and he went away with him. I missed his fish. Mondays and Wednesdays he came, and his fish were always fresh. They don't get such fish now-a-days."

"I'll take the letter you have," said Mervius, "—the copy, that is—and my wife will transcribe it, I,—I am too old and my eyes are bad. This carpenter's son now—as you say he set the people by the ears. It is a strange story anyhow."

Old Jerome put his chin in the air. "He was the son of a carpenter, nothing else. We all knew his people, you did and I. His father built the bin where I store my corn, and some stalls in my brother's barn in the next village. The son was a dreamer, anyone could have told he would have perished in the end. The people were tired of him, a mild lunatic. That was all."

Mervius did not answer directly. "I have read this letter," he said, "this fisherman's letter. The man who looks after my sheep loaned me a copy. Peter was not always with the man, the carpenter's son, one thing he has left out. One thing that I saw."

"That *you* saw," exclaimed old Jerome.

Mervius nodded.

"I saw this man once."

"The carpenter's son?"

"Yes, once, and I saw him smile. You notice this letter never makes record of him smiling."

"I know."

"I saw him smile."

"As how?"

Mervius wrapped his lean old arms under the folds of his blouse and resting his elbows on his knees looked into the fire. Jerome's crow paced gravely in at the door and perched on his master's knee. Jerome fed him bits of cheese dipped in wine.

"It was a long time ago," said Mervius, "I was a lad. I remember I and my brother used to get up early in the cold mornings and run out to the stables and stand in fodder on the floor of the cow stalls to warm our feet. I had heard my father tell of this fellow, this carpenter's son. Did you ever hear," he added turning to old Jerome, "did you ever hear—when you were a boy— did you ever hear the old folks speak of the 'White Night?' My father used to tell of it often. They called it the 'White Night.' At midnight it grew suddenly light, as though the sun had risen out of season. In fact there *was* a sun, or star—something. The chickens all came down from their roosts, the cocks crew, as though at daybreak. It was light for hours. Then towards four o'clock the light faded again. It happened in midwinter. Yes, they called it the 'White Night.' It was strange. You know the followers of this fellow claim that he was born on that night. My father knew some shepherds who told a strange story—however.

"There were in our village two men particularly detestable, one was the village miser, Simon was his name, and so grasping was he, so covetous of gain that he used to cut the copper coins in two and deal in the smallest fractions of money. He lived in a wretched hovel on the outskirts of the town, and starved himself, and denied himself till he was but the shadow of a man; he was a money-lender, a usurer, with only one desire, that of accumulating wealth, the wealth of others. To know that any man possessed more than he, was a veritable anguish for him. He was a bad man, a man without soul or heart, whom everybody hated and who hated everybody.

"The other man was the fuller of the village, who had a bleach-green in the meadow back of my father's sheep folds. After weaving, the women used to take their webs of cloth to him to be whitened. Many a time I have seen the great squares of cloth covering the meadow there, till you would have said the snow had fallen. Septimus was the fuller's name. He was a man as unlovable as was Simon, not that he hoarded wealth, but that he envied others the possession of anything good. He envied my father for his flocks of sheep. He envied my uncle for his vineyards. He envied the miller's daughter when her uncle, at his death, left her a little money. He would envy a man for a pair of new shoes, for a profitable sale, for a good harvest. From year to year this despicable man, this Septimus, went about our village, carping at the good fortunes of his neighbors or his friends, belittling and ridiculing their good luck, secretly chafing and raging the whiles at their greater benefits, and at best he hated and envied Simon the miser.

"Curiously enough these two men were seldom seen apart, though they hated one another. They sought each other's company. Septimus hated and envied Simon for his hoarded wealth, Simon coveted the lands of Septimus' bleach-green, and hated him because he held them in his possession. Both men were greedy according to their natures, and may be a common passion drew them together. At any rate, they boasted and pretended a great friendship. Well, both of these men had heard of the wonders that the carpenter's son had worked and the benefits and good fortune he could bestow on the deserving, and both, unknown to each other, had secretly determined that if ever the fellow should come into our country they would see what they could get from him.

"And at last one day he came. Usually a great crowd was at his heels, but this time he was alone. I was out in the fields beyond the village, pruning the vines in my father's vineyard. My brother was with me; we were at work on a bit of higher ground overlooking the road that runs from our village o-ver toward the lake. The same where you say this Peter used to fish. Suddenly my brother touched my arm.

"'Look quick, Mervius,' he said, 'there comes the man that father spoke about. That carpenter's son, who has made such a stir.'

"I looked and knew at once that it was he."

Old Jerome interrupted: "You had never seen him before, how did you know it was he?"

Mervius shook his head. "It was he. How could I tell? I don't know. I knew it was he."

"What did he look like?" asked Jerome, interested.

Mervius paused. There was a silence. Jerome's crow looked at the bright coals of the fire, his head on one side.

"Not at all extraordinary," said Mervius at length, "his face was that of a peasant, sun-browned, touched perhaps with a certain calmness, that was all, a face that was neither sad nor glad, calm merely, and not unusually or especially pleasing. He was dressed as you and I are now, as a peasant, and his hands were those of a worker. Only his head was bare. He had a fine brown beard, I remember. There was nothing extraordinary about the man."

"Yet you knew it was he."

"Yes," admitted Mervius, nodding his head, "yes I knew it was he. He came up slowly along the road near where we boys were sitting. He walked as any traveler along those roads might, not thoughtful, nor abstracted, but minding his steps, or looking here and there about the country. The prettier things, I noted, seemed to attract him, and I particularly remember his stopping to look at a cherry tree in full bloom and smelling at the blossoms. Once, too, he stopped and thrust out of the way a twig that had fallen across a little ant heap.

"When he had come nearly opposite to us I said to my brother, 'Here comes old Simon and Septimus.'

"Sure enough the miser Simon and his inseparable Septimus the fuller had just come around the corner of the road some little distance away. They caught sight of the carpenter's son and—as every one did—recognized him at once. Simon hastened forward to meet him. Septimus did the same. Simon moved even quicker; Septimus broke into a run. Then the two wretched old men, decrepit and feeble as they were, raced one another like school boys, each trying to outstep his companion so as to be the first to ask the favor of the carpenter's son.

"Simon arrived a little in advance, and threw himself down on his knees in the road before the man, gasping for breath, and kissing his wooden shoes.

"'Master, master,' was all he could cry at first. Then gasping and whining and coughing for breath he cried:

"'You, who can do everything, do something for me, give me something, look at me, a miserable destitute old man, pinched with poverty in my old age.' Thus Simon, the richest man in all that part of the country. Then Septimus arrived, and pushing Simon to one side, grovelled almost on his belly, pouring out a torrent of supplication, actually weeping with the anguish of his desire. It was a sickening sight, those two horrible old men, wallowing in the dust of the road, clasping the man's feet, laying their lean cheeks against his wooden shoes.

"'Listen to me, listen to me,' cried Septimus. 'Simon is a dotard and has money hoarded away in sacks, but I, I—just one little boon, sir, give me something, give me something! You have said that faith could remove mountains, look at me, have I not faith? reward me now, give me a blessing, bring me good fortune, bring me fortune!'

"'No, no, listen to me,' shrieked Simon, clawing at his knees. 'A miracle, a miracle! do a miracle on me, look at my grey beard, help my necessity, me an old man, and poor, poor, poor!'

"'He lies. You know everything, master; he lies, and you know it; he's rich, a thousand times richer than I.'

"So they howled and struggled before the carpenter's son who looked on silent and very calm. I wondered if they would in the end deceive him with their hideous protestations. For a long time he was silent, then:

"'Yes,' said he, 'I will reward you both.'

"I was disappointed and disheartened. They had deceived him after all. They grovelled again before him, vying with one another in the excess of their humility. Then the carpenter's son spoke again:

"'Each one of you may ask in turn for whatever he chooses, and it will be given him upon the instant, I promise.'

"The two old miserables whined and fawned a-fresh. The man continued:

"'Only upon the condition that he who asks last shall receive twice the a-mount of him who asks first.'

"Simon and Septimus sat back upon their heels and looked first at the man and then suspiciously at each other. It was easy to see what was pass-ing in their greedy minds.

"The miser Simon, though quivering with eagerness to take advantage of the man's goodness, would not for the mean life of him make the first re-quest, lest Septimus should gain twice the amount. Was it for him, the mi-ser, the hoarder of gold to enrich his companion by just twice the amount of his own possessions? Never, never; he would bite out his own tongue first.

"And Septimus, Septimus the Envious, Septimus who was fairly sick each time his neighbor prospered, would he be the first to ask, only that Simon would have twice as much as he? no a hundred times, rather would he be dumb the rest of his life."

"'Well,' said the carpenter's son, 'I am waiting.'

"'Ask, then,' cried Simon fiercely to his companion, 'you've only to ask.'

"'I will not,' shouted Septimus, 'ask yourself, miser that you are. You who are so greedy of wealth, here now is your chance.'

"'Am I to enrich you, beggar, by double my own fortune? You who have coveted and envied your friends' and neighbors' gains, gain now for yourself, you have only to open your mouth.'

"For a long while they quarreled and raged. Screaming abuse into each other's face. Their eyes flamed, their cheeks grew crimson, their lean and knotted fingers twitched and twisted together. The carpenter's son waited, watching them without a sign or word. Then at last in a fury Simon caught Septimus by the throat.

"'Ask him then, swine that you are, ask or I will strangle you,' and with his free hand he struck the old fuller in the face.

"Septimus tore himself away shaking with rage.

"'Ah,' he screamed, 'it has come to that, has it? Very well then, I *will* ask. I will ask the first of this good man, and instead of gaining you will be the loser. Sir,' he cried, turning to the carpenter's son, 'Sir, cause it to happen that I lose an eye.'

"'So be it,' was the answer, 'as you have asked, so be it to you.'

"And we looking on, saw upon the instant, as it were, a film draw over one of Septimus' eyes. But on the same instant our ears were thrilled with a lamentable wail from Simon.

"'Blind, blind, blind,' he yelled, tearing at his sightless eyes. 'Blind, blind, blind.' He rose from the ground and ran back along the road toward the town, stumbling and falling and colliding with tree trunks and the angles of the fences. And after him ran Septimus, jeering and hooting.

"'Oh miser, oh swine, yes blind you are and blind you shall remain.' But Simon himself fell more than once, for upon one side of him all the world was dark.

"They turned the corner of the road and disappeared, but long after they were lost to view we could hear their wretched outcries.

"'Blind, blind, blind.'

"'Blind you are and blind you shall remain, and I, too, am but half as blind as you.'

"For a few moments the carpenter's son remained looking after them. Then, as they vanished around the bend of the road, I saw him smile. It was a smile partly of pity, partly of contempt and partly of amusement. Then he continued his road. And all that Simon the covetous, and Septimus the envious gained from the bounty of the carpenter's son was, the one to lose an eye and the other to become totally blind."

Mervius stopped and slipped his feet back into his sabots and rose. He took the letter from Jerome and put it in the pocket of his blouse.

"And you saw that?" said Jerome.

Mervius nodded. But old Jerome shook his head in the manner of one unwilling to be convinced.

"He was a dreamer, with unspeakable pretensions. Why his people were laboring folk in one of the villages beyond the lake. His father was a carpenter and built my corn bins. The son was a fanatic. His wits were turned."

"But this thing I saw," said Mervius at the door, "I saw it, I who am speaking to you."

Jerome put his chin in the air.

"A dreamer, we were well rid of him. But I was sorry when Peter went away. He was a good fisherman. Mondays and Wednesdays he came, and his fish were always fresh."

Judy's Service of Gold Plate

The Wave, 16 (16 October 1897), 6.

She was a native of Guatemala, and so, of course, was said to be Mexican, and she lived in the alley by the county jail, three or four doors above the tamale factory. Her trade was something odd. The Chinamen, who go down to the sea in ships from San Francisco to Cape St. Lucas, off the coast of Lower California, and fish for sharks there, used to bring the livers of these sharks back to her. She would boil the oil out of these livers and turn over the product to a red-headed Polish Jew named Knubel, who bottled it and sold it to San Francisco as cod liver oil. Knubel made money in the business. She was only his employee. Her name, incidentally, was Lambala Largomarsini, which was no doubt the reason why she was called "Judy."

Knubel lived on Telegraph Hill, on the ledge of the big cliff there, and used to lie awake o' windy nights waiting for his house to be blown off that ledge. Knubel had always lived on Telegraph Hill. When he was forty he had had a stroke of paralysis, and had lost the use of his left leg. The result of this stroke was that Knubel was held a prisoner on the Hill. He dared not go down into the city below him, because he knew he could never get back. How could he, stop and think? No horse ever gets to the top of the Hill. The cable-cars and electric-cars turn their headlights upon the Hill and shake their heads and go around in the valley by Stockton street. The climb is bad enough for a man with two healthy legs, but for a paralytic—— Knubel was trapped upon the Hill, trapped and held prisoner. He never saw Kearny or Montgomery or Market streets after his stroke. He never saw the new *Call* building, or the dome upon the City Hall but from afar, and the "Emporium" was to him but a distant granite cliff. In the newspaper, he who lived in San Francisco read about what was happening there as you and I and all the rest of us read about what is happening in London or in Paris or in Vienna, and this with the roar of that San Francisco actually in his ears, like the bourdon of a tremendous organ.

Judy of course was wretchedly poor, for the salary that Knubel allowed her for boiling down the sharks' livers would not have fattened a self-respecting chessy-cat. Knubel himself was a horrible old miser, he had made a little fortune in cod liver oil, but he kept it tied up in three old socks in a starch box underneath the floor of his cellar. He had a passion for gold, and turned all his silver and greenbacks into gold as fast as he could. He lived in a room about as big as a trunk back of an Italian wine shop where there was a *Bocce* court, and Judy used to come and see him here once a month and get her salary and make her report.

One day when Judy had come to get her orders and her money from Knubel she found him bending his red head over his table testing an old brass collar button with nitric acid.

"I found him *bei der* stairs on *der* bottom," he explained to Judy. "Berhaps he is of gold. Hey, yes?"

Judy looked at the collar button.

"That ain't gold," she declared. "Huh! you can't fool me on gold. I seen more gold in my day than you've seen tin, Mister Knubel."

Knubel's eyes were gimlets on the instant.

"Vat you say?"

"When I was a kid in Guatemala my folks had a set of gold plate, dishes you know, hundreds of 'em, all solid gold."

Here we touch on Judy's one mania. She believed and often stated that at one time her parents in Guatemala were enormously wealthy, and in particular were possessed of a wonderful service of gold plate. She would describe this gold plate over and over again to anyone who would listen. Why there were more than a hundred pieces, all solid red gold. Why there were goblets and punch-bowls and platters and wine-pitchers and ladles, why the punch-bowl itself was worth a fortune. Ignorant enough on other subjects, and illiterate enough, Heaven knows, once started on her gold plate, Judy became almost eloquent. Of course, no one believed her story, and rightly so because the gold plate never did exist. How Judy got the idea into her mind it was impossible to say, but it was the custom of people who knew of her mania to set her going and watch her while she rocked to and fro with closed eyes, and hands clasped over her knee chanting monotonously, "More'n a hundred pieces, and all red, red gold," and so on and so on.

For a long while her hearers scoffed, then at last she suddenly made a convert, old Knubel, the red-headed Polish Jew, believed her story on the instant. As often as Judy would come to make her monthly report on the shark liver industry, old Knubel would start her going, swallowing her words as a bullion-bag swallows coin. As soon as Judy had finished he would begin to ask her questions.

"The gold voss soft, hey? und ven you rapped him *mit der* knuckles now, he rung out didn't he, yes?"

"Sweeter'n church bells."

"Ah, sweeter nor *der* church bells, shoost soh. I know, *I* know. Now let's have ut egain, more'n a hoondurt bieces. Let's haf ut all *eg*-gain." And again and again Judy would tell him her wonderful story, delighted that she had at last found a believer. She would chant to Knubel by the hour, rocking herself back and forth, her hands clasped on her knee, her eyes closed. Then by and by Knubel, as he listened to her, caught *himself* rocking back and forth, keeping time with her.

Then Knubel found excuses for Judy's coming to see him oftener than once a month. The manufacture of cod liver oil out of sharks' livers needed a great deal of talking over. Knubel knew her story by heart in a few weeks and began to talk along with her. There in that wretched room over the *Bocce* court on the top of Telegraph Hill, the "Mexican" hybrid woman and the Polish Jew, red-headed and paralytic, rocked themselves back and forth with closed eyes and clasped hands sing-songing, "More'n a hundred pieces, all red, red gold"—"More den a hoondurt bieces *und* alle rad gold."

It was a strange sight to see.

"Judy," said Knubel, one day when the woman was getting ready to leave, "vy you go, my girl, eh? Stay hier *bei* me, *und* alle-ways you will me dat story ge-tellen, night *und morgen*, alle-ways. Hey? Yes?"

So it came about that the two were—we will say married, and for over a year night *und morgen* Judy the story of the wonderful gold plate ge-told. Then a little child was born to her. The child has nothing to do here, besides it died right away, no doubt its little body wasn't strong enough to hold in itself the blood of the Hebrew, the Spaniard and the Slav. It died. At the time of its birth Judy was out of her head, and continued so for upwards of two weeks. Then she came to herself and was as before.

Not quite. "Now ve vill have ut once eg-gain," said Knubel, "pe-gin, more dan one hoondurt bieces, *und* alle rad, rad gold."

"What's you talkin's about?" said Judy with a stare.

"Vy, about dat gold blate."

"I don't know about any gold plate, you must be crazy Knubel. I don't know what you mean."

Nor did she. The trouble of her mind at the time of her little child's birth had cleared her muddy wits of all hallucinations. She remembered nothing of her wonderful story. But now it was Knubel whose red head was turned. Now it was Knubel who went about telling his friends of the wonderful gold service. But his mania was worse than Judy's.

"You've got ut, you've got ut zum-vairs, you she-swine," he would yell, clubbing Judy with a table leg. "Vair is ut? you've hidun ut. I know you've got ut. Vair is dose bunch-powl, vair is dose tsoop sboon?"

"How do I know?" Judy would shout, dodging his blows.

In fact how *did* she know?

Knubel went from bad to worse, ransacked the house, pulled up the flooring, followed Judy when she went out as well as his game leg would allow, and peeped at her through keyholes when she was at home.

Knubel and Judy had a neighbor who was also an acquaintance, a Canadian woman who did their washing. Judy was sitting before the kitchen stove one morning when this woman came after the weekly wash. She was dead and must have been dead since the day before, for she was already cold. The Canadian woman touched her shoulder, and Judy's head rolled side ways and showed where Knubel had—well, she was dead.

Late in the day the officers found Knubel hiding about the old abandoned "Pavilion" that stands on the top of the hill. When arrested he had a sack with him full of rusty tin pans, plates and old tomato cans that he had gathered from the dump heaps.

"I got ut," said Knubel to himself, "I got ut, more dan a hoondurt pieces. I got ut at last."

The manufacture of cod liver oil from shark livers has languished of late, because of the hanging of Mister Knubel at San Quentin penitentiary.

*   *   *   *   *   *

And all this, if you please, because of a service of gold plate that never existed.

The Associated Un-Charities

The Wave, 16 (30 October 1897), 7.

There used to be a place in feudal Paris called the Court of Miracles, and Mister Victor Hugo has told us all about it. This Court was a quarter of the town where the beggars lived, and it was called "of the miracles," because once across its boundaries the blind saw, the lame walked and the poor cared not to have the gospel preached unto them.

San Francisco has its Court of Miracles too. It is a far cry thither, for it lies on the other side of Chinatown and Dagotown, and blocks beyond Luna's restaurant. It is in the valley between Telegraph Hill and Russian Hill, and you must pass through it as you go down to Meiggs' Wharf where the

Government tugs tie up.

One has elected to call it the Court of Miracles, but it is not a court, and the days of miracles are over. It is a row of seven two-story houses, one of them brick. The brick house is over a saloon kept by a Kanaka woman and called "The Eiffel Tower." Here San Francisco's beggars live and have their being. That is, a good many of them.

The doubled-up old man with the white beard and neck-handkerchief who used to play upon a zither and the sympathies of the public on the corner of Sutter street has moved out, and one can find no trace of him, and Father Elphick, the white-headed vegetarian of Lotta's Fountain, is dead. But plenty of the others are left. The neatly dressed fellow with dark blue spectacles, who sings the *Marseillaise*, accompanying himself upon an infinitesimal hand organ, is here; Mrs. McCleaverty is here, and the old bare-headed man who sits on the street corner by the Bohemian Club, after six o'clock in the evening, and turns the crank of a soundless organ, has here set up his everlasting rest.

The beggars of the Seven Houses are genuine miserables. Perhaps they have an organization and a president, I don't know. But I do know that Leander and I came very near demoralizing the whole lot of them.

More strictly speaking, it was Leander who did the deed, I merely looked on and laughed, but Leander says that by laughing I lent him my immoral support, and am therefore party to the act.

Leander and I had been dining at the "Red House," which is a wine-shop that Gelett Burgess discovered in an alley not far from the county jail. Leander and I had gone there because we like to sit at its whittled tables and drink its *Vin Ordinaire (très ordinaire)* out of tin gill measures; also we like its salad and its thick slices of bread that you eat after you have rubbed them with an onion or a bit of garlic. We always go there in evening dress in order to impress the Proletariat.

On this occasion after we had dined and had come out again into the gas and gaiety of the Mexican quarter we caromed suddenly against Cluness. Cluness is connected with some sort of a charitable institution that has a house somewhere in the "Quarter." He says that he likes to alleviate distress wherever he sees it; and that after all, the best thing in life is to make some poor fellow happy for a few moments.

Leander and I had nothing better to do that evening so we went around with Cluness, and watched him as he gave a month's rent to an infirm old lady on Stockton street, a bundle of magazines to a whining old rascal at the top of a nigger tenement, and some good advice to a Chinese girl who didn't want to go to the Presbyterian Mission House.

"That's my motto," says he, as we came away from the Chinese girl, "alleviate misery wherever you see it and try and make some poor fellow happy for a few moments."

"Ah, yes," exclaimed this *farceur* Leander, sanctimoniously, while I stared, "that's the only thing worth while," and he sighed and wagged his head.

Cluness went on to tell us about a deserving case he had—we were going there next—in fact, innocently enough, he described the Seven Houses to us, never suspecting they were the beggars' headquarters. He said there was a poor old paralytic woman lived there, who had developed an appetite for creamed oysters.

"It's the only thing," said Cluness, "that she can keep on her stomach."

"She told you so?" asked Leander.

"Yes, yes."

"Well, she ought to know."

We arrived at the Seven Houses and Cluness paused before the tallest and dirtiest.

"Here's where she lives; I'm going up for a few moments."

"Have a drink first," suggested Leander, fixing his eye upon the saloon under the brick house.

We three went in and sat down at one of the little round zinc tables— painted to imitate marble—and the Kanaka woman herself brought us our drinks. While we were drinking, one of the beggars came in. He was an Indian, totally blind, and in the day time played a mouth-organ on Grant Avenue near a fashionable department store.

"Tut, tut," said Cluness, "poor fellow, blind, you see, what a pity, I'll give him a quarter."

"No, let me," exclaimed Leander.

As he spoke the door opened again and another blind man groped in. This fellow I had seen often. He sold lavender in little envelopes on one of the corners of Kearny street. He was a stout, smooth-faced chap and always kept his chin in the air.

"What misery there is in this world," sighed Cluness as his eye fell upon this latter, "one half the world don't know how——"

"Look, they know each other," said Leander. The lavender man had groped his way to the Indian's table—evidently it was their especial table—and the two had fallen a-talking. They ordered a sandwich apiece and a small mug of beer.

"Let's do something for 'em," exclaimed Cluness, with a burst of generosity. "Let's make 'em remember this night for years to come. Look at 'em trying to be happy over a bit of dry bread and a pint of flat beer. I'm going to give 'em a dollar each."

"No, no," protested Leander. "Let me fix it, I've more money than you. Let me do a little good now and then. You don't want to hog all the philanthropy, Cluness, I'll give 'em something."

"It would be very noble and generous of you, indeed," cried Cluness, "and you'll feel better for it, see if you don't. But I must go to my paralytic. You fellows wait for me. I'll be down in twenty minutes."

I frowned at Leander when Cluness was gone. "Now what tom-foolery is it this time?" said I.

"Tom-foolery," exclaimed Leander, blankly. "It's philanthropy. By Jove, here's another chap with his lamps blown out. Look at him."

A third unfortunate, blind as the other two, had just approached the Indian and the lavender man. The three were pals, one could see that at half a glance. No doubt they met at this table every night for beer and sandwiches. The last blind man was a Dutchman. I had seen him from time to time on Market street, with a cigar-box tied to his waist and a bunch of pencils in his fist.

"*Eins!*" called the Dutchman to the Kanaka, as he sat down with the lavender man and the Indian. "*Eins—mit* a hem sendvidge."

"Excuse me," said Leander, coming up to their table.

What was it? Did those three beggars, their instinct trained by long practice, recognize the alms-giver in the sound of Leander's voice, or in the step? It is hard to say, but instantly each one of them dropped the mildly convivial and assumed the humbly solicitous air, turning his blind head towards Leander, listening intently. Leander took out his purse and made a great jingling with his money. Now, I knew that Leander had exactly fifteen dollars—no more, no less—fifteen dollars, in three five-dollar gold pieces—not a penny of change. Could it be possible that he was going to give a gold

169

piece to the three beggars? It was, evidently, for I heard him say:

"Excuse me. I've often passed you fellows on the street, in town, and I guess I've always been too short of change, or in too much of a hurry to re-member you. But I'm going to make up for it now, if you'll permit me. Here——" and he jingled his money, "here is a five-dollar gold piece that I'd like to have you spend between the three of you to-night, and drink my health, and—and—have a good time, you know. Catch on?"

They caught on.

"May God bless you, young man!" exclaimed the old lavender man.

The Indian grunted expressively.

The Dutchman twisted about in his place and shouted in the direction of the bar:

"Mek ut er bottle Billzner *und* er Gotha druffle, *mit ein im*-borted Frankfooter *bei der* side on."

The Kanaka woman came up, and the Dutchman repeated his order. The lavender man paused reflectively tapping his brow, then he delivered him-self: "A half spring chicken," he said with profound gravity, "rather under done, and some chicory salad and a bottle of white wine—put the bottle in a little warm water for about two minutes—and some Lyonnaise potatoes with onions, and—"

"*Donner wetter,*" shouted the Dutchman, "*genugh!*" smiting the table with his fist.

The other subsided. The Kanaka woman turned to the Indian.

"Whiskey," he grunted, "plenty whiskey, big beefsteak, soh," and he meas-ured off a yard on the table.

"Leander," said I, when he rejoined me, "that was foolishness, you've thrown away your five dollars and these fellows are going to waste it in ri-otous living. You see the results of indiscriminate charity."

"I've *not* thrown it away. Cluness would say that if it made them happier according to their lights it was well invested. I hate the charity that means only medicines, clean sheets, new shoes and sewerage. Let 'em be happy in their own way."

There could be no doubt that the three blind men were happy. They loaded their table with spring chickens, Gotha truffles, beefsteaks, and all manner of "alcoholic beverages," till the zinc disappeared beneath the ac-cumulation of plates and bottles. They drank each other's health and they pledged that of Leander, standing up. The Dutchman ordered: "*Zwei* Billz-ner more alreatty." The lavender man drank his warmed white wine with gasps of infinite delight, and after the second whiskey bottle had been o-pened, the Indian began to say strange and terrible things in his own lan-guage.

Cluness came in and beamed on them.

"See how happy you've made them, Leander," he said gratefully. "They'll always remember this night."

"They always will," said Leander solemnly.

"I've got to go though," said Cluness. I made as if to go with him but Le-ander plucked my coat under the table. I caught his eye.

"I guess we two will stay," said I. Cluness left, thanking us again and a-gain.

"I don't know what it is," said I seriously to Leander, "but to-night you seem to me to be too good to be wholesome."

"*I?*" said Leander, blankly. "But I suppose I should expect to be misjudged."

Just then the Kanaka woman came over to give us our check.

"This is on me," said Leander, but he was so slow in fumbling for his purse that I was obliged, in all decency, to pay.

After she left *us*, the Kanaka went over to the blind men's table, and, check-pad in hand, ran her eye over the truffles, beer, chicken, beefsteak, wine and whiskey, and made out her check.

"Four dollars, six bits," she announced.

There was a silence, not one of the blind men moved.

"Watch now," said Leander.

"Four, six bits," repeated the Kanaka, her hand on her hip.

Still none of the blind men moved.

"Vail, den," cried the Dutchman, "vich von you two vellars has dose money, pay oop. *Vier* thalers *und* sax beets."

"I haven't it," exclaimed the lavender man, "Jim has it," he added, turning to the Indian.

"No have got, no have got," grunted the Indian. "*You* have got, you or Charley."

I looked at Leander.

"Now, what have you done?"

For answer Leander showed me three five dollar gold pieces in the palm of his hand.

"Each one of those chaps thinks that one of the other two has the gold piece. I just pretended to give it to one of 'em, jingled my coin, and then put it back, I didn't give 'em a cent. Each one thought I had given it to the other two. How could they tell, they were blind, don't you see?"

I reached for my hat.

"I'm going to get out of here."

Leander pulled me back.

"Not just yet, wait a few moments. Listen."

"Vail, vail," cried the Dutchman, beginning to get red. "You doand vants to cheats Missus Amaloa, den berhaps—yes, Zhim," he cried to the Indian, "pay oop, or ees ut *you* den, Meest'r Paites, dat hab dose finf thalers?"

"No have got," gurgled the Indian, swaying in his place as he canted the neck of the whisky bottle towards his lips.

"I thought you had the money," protested Mr. Bates, (which was evidently the lavender man's name), "you or Jim."

"No have got," whooped the Indian, beginning to get angry. "Hug-gh! *You* got money. He give *you* money," and he turned his face towards the Dutchman.

"That's what *I* thought," asserted Mr. Bates.

"*Tausend Teufels no,*" shouted the other. "I tell you *no.*"

"*You, you,*" growled the Indian, plucking at Mr. Bates' coat sleeve, "you have got."

"Yah, soh," cried the Dutchman, shaking his finger at the lavender man, excitedly, "pay dose finf thalers, Meest'r Paites."

"Pay yourself," exclaimed the other, "I haven't touched them. I'll be *any* name, I'll be *any* name if I've touched them."

"Well, I ain't going to wait here all night," shrilled the Kanaka woman impatiently. The Dutchman shook his finger solemnly towards where he thought the Indian was sitting.

"It's der Indyun. It's Zhim. Get ut vrom Zhim."

"Lie, lie," vociferated the Indian, "white man lie. No have got. *You* have got, or *you.*"

"I'll turn my pockets inside out," exclaimed Mr. Bates.

"Schmarty," cried the Dutchman. "Can I *see* dose pocket?"

"Thief, thief," exclaimed the Indian, shaking his long black hair. "You steal money."

The other two turned on him savagely.

"There ain't no man going to call me that."

"Vat he say? vait, *und* I vill his het *mit der* boddle demolisch. Who you say dat to, *mee*, or Meest'r Bates?"

"Oh, you make me tired," cried the lavender man, "you two. *One* of you two, pay Missus Amaloa and quit fooling."

"Come on," cried the Kanaka, "pay up or I'll ring for the police."

"Vooling, vooling," shouted the Dutchman, dancing in his rage. "You sheats Missus Amaloa *und* you gall dot vooling."

"*Who* cheats?" cried the other two simultaneously.

"Vail, how do *I* know?" yelled the Dutchman, purple to the eyes. "How do *I* know vich?"

The Kanaka turned to Leander.

"Say, which of these fellows did you give that money to?"

Leander came up.

"Ah-h, *now* ve vill know," said the Dutchman.

Leander looked from one to the other. Then an expression of perplexity came into his face. He scratched an ear.

"Well, I thought it was this German gentleman."

"*Vat!*"

"Only it seems to me I had the money in my left hand, and he, you see, is on the right hand of the table. It might have been him, and then again it might have been one of the other two gentlemen. It's so difficult to re-member. Wasn't it you?" turning to Mr. Bates, "or no, wasn't it *you?*" to the Indian. "But it *couldn't* have been the Indian gentleman, and it couldn't have been Mr. Bates here, and yet I'm sure it wasn't the German gentleman, and, however, I *must* have given it to one of the three. Didn't I lay the coin down on the table and go away and leave it?" Leander struck his forehead. "Yes, I think that's what I did. I'm sorry," he said to the Kanaka, "that you are having any trouble, it's some misunderstanding."

"Oh, I'll get it all right," returned the Kanaka, confidently. "Come on, one of you fellows dig up."

Then the quarrel broke out afresh. The three blind men rose to their feet, blackguarding and vilifying one another till the room echoed. Now it was Mr. Bates and the Dutchman versus the Indian, now the Indian and Dutchman versus Mr. Bates, now the Indian and Mr. Bates versus the Dutchman. At every instant the combinations varied with kaleidoscopic swiftness. They shouted, they danced, and they shook their fists towards where they guessed each other's faces were. The Indian, who had been drinking whiskey between intervals of the quarrel, suddenly began to rail and howl in his own language, and at times even the Dutchman lapsed into the vernacular. The Kanaka woman lost her wits altogether, and declared that in three more minutes she would ring for the police.

Then all at once the Dutchman swung both fists around him and caught the Indian a tremendous crack in the side of the head. The Indian vented an ear-splitting war-whoop and began pounding Mr. Bates who stood next to him. In the next instant the three were fighting all over the room. They lost each other, they struck furious blows at the empty air, they fell over tables and chairs, or suddenly came together with a dreadful shock and terrible cries of rage. The Dutchman bumped against Leander and before he could get away had smashed his silk hat down over his ears. The noise of their shouting could have been heard a block.

"Thief, thief."

"Teef yourselluf, pay oop dose finf thalers."

"No have got, no have got."

And then the door swung in and four officers began rounding them up like stampeded sheep. Not until he was in the wagon could the Dutchman believe that it was not the Indian and Mr. Bates who had him by either arm, and even in the wagon, as they were being driven to the precinct station-house, the quarrel broke out from time to time.

As we heard the rattle of the patrol-wagon's wheels growing fainter over the cobbles, we rose to go. The Kanaka stood with her hands on her hips glaring at the zinc table with its remnants of truffle, chicken and beefsteak and its empty bottles. Then she exclaimed, "And *I'm* shy four dollars and six bits."

On the following Saturday night Leander and I were coming from a Mexican dinner at Luna's. Suddenly some one caught our arms from behind. It was Cluness.

"I want to thank you fellows again," he exclaimed, "for your kindness to those three blind chaps the other night. It was really good of you. I believe they had five dollars to spend between them. It was really fine of you, Leander."

"Oh, I don't mind five dollars," said Leander, "if it can make a poor fellow any happier for a few moments. That's the only thing that's worth while in this life."

"I'll bet you felt better and happier for doing it."

"Well, it did make me happy."

"Of course, and those three fellows will never forget that night."

"No, I guess they won't," said Leander.

Fantaisie Printanière

The Wave, 16 (6 November 1897), 7.

The McTeagues and the Ryers lived at the disreputable end of Polk street, away down in the squalid neighborhood by the huge red drum of the gas works. The drum leaked, of course, and the nasty brassy foulness of the leak mingled with the odors of cooking from the ill-kept kitchens, and the reek of garbage in the vacant lots did not improve the locality.

McTeague had once been a dentist, and had had "parlors" up at the respectable end of the street. But after a while the license office discovered that he had no diploma; in fact, had never attended a college of any sort, and had forbidden him to practice. So McTeague had taken to drink.

Ryer, some years back, had been a sort of small stock-dealer on the outskirts of Butchertown, and had done fairly well until the Health Board reported him to the Supervisors because he had fattened his hogs on poultices obtained from the City and County Hospital. The result was a lamentable scandal, which finally drove him out of business. So Ryer had taken to drink.

The Ryers' home (or let us say, the house in which the Ryers ate and slept), adjoined the house in which the McTeagues ate and slept. You would have thought that this propinquity, joined with the coincidence of their common misfortunes—both victims of governmental persecution— would have insured a certain degree of friendship between the two men. But this was not so at all, a state of feud existed between Montague Ryer and Capulet McTeague. The feud had originated some year or so previous to the time of this tale, in the back room of Gerstle's "Wein Stube" on the corner opposite the drum. A discussion had arisen between the two men, both far gone in whiskey, as to the lines of longitude on the surface of the globe. Capulet claimed they were parallel throughout their whole extent— Montague maintained they converged at the poles. They discussed this question at length—first with heady words and vociferation, next with hurled pony glasses and uplifted chairs, and finally, after their ejection from the "Stube," with fists clenched till the knuckles whitened, crooked elbows, and the soles of heavy-shod boots. They arrived at no definite conclusion. Twice since then had they fought. Their original difference of opinion had been speedily forgotten. They fought now, they knew not why—merely for the sake of fighting. The quarrel between them came to be recognized by the "block" as part of the existing order of things, like the reek from the drum and the monthly visit of the rent-collector.

Ryer had something the worst of it in these fights. He was a small, lean, pinkish creature, like a split carrot, his mouth a mere long slit beneath his nose. When he was angry his narrow eyes glistened like streaks of bitumen.

McTeague was a huge blonde giant, carrying his enormous fell of yellow hair, six feet and more above his ponderous, slow-moving feet. His hands, hard as wooden mallets, dangled from arms that suggested twisted cables. His jaw was that of the carnivora.

Both men thrashed their wives, McTeague on the days when he was drunk, which were many, Ryer on the days when he was sober, which were few. They went about it, each in his own peculiar fashion. Ryer found a-musement in whipping Missis Ryer with a piece of rubber hose filled with gravel, or (his nature demanded variety of sensation), with a long, thin rawhide, which he kept hidden between the mattresses. He never used fists or boots; such methods revolted him. "What! am I a drayman, am I a hod-carrier!" exclaimed Mister Ryer. When McTeague did not use the fist or the foot, he used the club. Refinement, such as characterized Ryer, was foreign to the ex-dentist. He struck out blindly, savagely, and with a colossal, clumsy force that often spent itself upon the air. The difference between the men could be seen in the different modes of punishment they affected. Ryer preferred the lash of the whip, McTeague the butt. Ryer was cruel, McTeague only brutal.

While common grievance had not made friends of the two men, mutual maltreatment had drawn their wives together, until no two women on the "block" were more intimate than Trina McTeague and Ryer's wife. They made long visits to each other in the morning in their wrappers and curl papers, talking for hours over a cuppa tea, served upon the ledge of the sink or a corner of the laundry table. During these visits they avoided speaking of their husbands, because, although the whole "block" knew of the occasional strained relations of their families, the two women feigned to keep the secret from each other. And this in the face of the fact that Missis Ryer would sometimes come over to see Trina with a thin welt across her neck, or Trina return the visit with a blackened eye or a split lip.

Once, however, only once, they broke in upon their reticence. Many things came of the infringement. Among others this *fantaisie*.

*　　　*　　　*　　　*　　　*　　　*　　　*

During that particular night three dandelions had bloomed in the vacant lot behind the gas works, the unwonted warmth of the last few days had brought back the familiar odor of the garbage heaps, an open car had appeared on the cross town cable line and Bock beer was on draught at the "Wein Stube," and Polk street knew that Spring was at hand.

About nine o'clock Trina McTeague appeared on the back steps of her house, rolling her washtub before her, preparing to do her monthly washing in the open air on that fine morning. She and Ryer's wife usually observed this hated rite at the same time, calling shrilly to one another as their backs bent and straightened over the scrubbing-boards. But that morning Trina looked long for Missis Ryer and at last fell a-wondering.

The fact of the matter was that the night before Ryer had come home sober and had found occasion to coerce Missis Ryer with a trunk-strap. By a curious coincidence McTeague had come home drunk the same evening, and for two hours Trina had been hard put to it to dodge his enormous fists and his hurled boots. (Nor had she been invariably successful.)

At that moment the ex-dentist was sleeping himself sober under the stairs in the front hall, and the whilom stock-dealer was drinking himself drunk in the "Wein Stube" across the street.

When eleven o'clock had struck and Missis Ryer had not appeared, Trina dried her smoking arms on her skirt, and, going through the hole in the backyard fence, entered the kitchen of the Ryer's house and called. Missis Ryer came into the kitchen in a blue cotton wrapper and carpet slippers. Her hair was hanging down her back (it was not golden). Evidently she had just arisen.

"Ain't you goin' to wash this mornin', Missis Ryer?" asked Trina Mc-Teague.

"Good Mornin', Trina," said the other, adding doggedly, as she sat down hard in a broken chair: "I'm *sick* and *tired* a-washin' an' workin' for Ryer."

She drew up instinctively to the cold stove, and propped her chin upon her knuckles. The loose sleeve of the wrapper fell away from her forearm, and Trina saw the fresh marks of the trunk-strap. Evidently Ryer had not held that strap by the buckle-end.

This was the first time Missis Ryer had ever mentioned her husband to Trina.

"Hoh!" ejaculated Trina, speaking before she thought. "It ain't alwus such fun workin' for Mac, either."

There was a brief silence. Both the women remained for a moment looking vaguely out of the kitchen door, absorbed in thought, very curious, each wondering what next the other would say. The conversation, almost without their wishing it, had suddenly begun upon untried and interesting ground. Missis Ryer said:

"I'll make a cuppa tea."

She made the tea, slovening languidly about the dirty kitchen, her slippers clap-clapping under her bare heels. Then the two drew up to the washboard of the sink, drinking the tea from the saucers, wiping their lips slowly from time to time with the side of their hands. Each was waiting for the other to speak. Suddenly Missis Ryer broke out:

"It's best not to fight him, or try to git away—hump your back and it's soonest over."

"You couldn't do that with Mac," answered Trina, shaking her head with decision; "if I didunt dodge, if I let um have his own way he'd sure kill me. Mac's that strong, he could break me in two."

"Oh, *Ryer's* strong all-right-all-right," returned Missis Ryer, "an' then he's sober when he fights an' knows what he's about, an' that makes it worse. Look there what he did last night." She rolled up her sleeve and Trina glanced at the arm with the critical glance of a connoisseur.

"Hoh," she said scornfully, "that ain't a circumstance. I had a row with Mac last night meself, and this is what he did with his fist. Just his fist, mind you, and it only grazed me as it was." She slipped a discolored shoulder out of her calico gown. The two critically compared bruises. Missis Ryer was forced to admit that Trina's bruise was the worse. She was vexed and disappointed but rallied with:

"Yes, that's pirty bad, but I'll show you somethin' that'll open your eyes," and she thrust the blue wrapper down from the nape of the neck. "See that scar there," she said, "that's the kind of work Ryer can do when he puts his mind to it; got that nearly four months ago and it's sore yet."

"Ah, yes," said Trina loftily, "little scars, little flesh wounds like that! You never had any bones brokun. Just look at that thumb," she went on proudly, "Mac did that with just a singul grip of his fist. I can't nevur bend it again."

Then the interminable discussion began.

"Look at that, just look at *that*, will you?"

"Ah, that ain't nuthun. How about *that?* there's a lick for you."

"Why, Mac's the strongest man you ever *saw*."

"Ah-h, you make me tired, it ain't a strong man, always, that can hurt the most. It's the fellah that knows how and where to hit. It's a whip that hurts the most."

"But it's a club that does the most damage."

"Huh! wait till you git hit with a rubber hose filled with gravel."

"Why, Mac can knock me the length of the house with his left fist. He's done it plenty a times."

Then they came to reminiscences.

"Why, one time when Mac came home from a picnic at Schuetzen Park, he picked me right up offun the ground with one hand and held me right up in the air like that, and let me have it with a kitchun chair. Huh! talk to *me* about Ryer's little whips, Ryer ain't a patch on my man. *You* don't know what a good thrashun *is*."

"I *don't*, hey? you can just listen to what I tell you, Trina McTeague, when I say that Ryer can lay all over your man. You jest ought a been here one night when I sassed Ryer back, I tell you I'll never do *that* again. Why the worst lickin' Mister McTeague ever gave you was just little love taps to what I got. Besides I don' *believe* your man ever held you up with one hand and banged you like that with a chair, you wouldn't a lived if he had."

"Oh, I ain't *lyun* to you," cried Trina, with shrill defiance, getting to her feet. Missis Ryer rose likewise and clapped her arms akimbo.

"Why," she cried, "you just said as much yourself, that if you didn't dodge and get away he'd kill you."

"An' I'll say it again. I ain't gowun to eat my words for the best woman that ever wore shoes, an' you can chew on that, Missus Ryer. *I* tell you Mac's the hardust hittun husband a woman ever had."

"I just like to have you live here with Ryer a week or so, you'd soon find out who was the best man, an'——" here Missis Ryer came close to Trina and shouted the words in her face. "An' don't you sass me either, an' talk about eatin' words, or I'll show you right here the kind a whalin' Ryer's taught me."

"I guess Ryer, himself, knows who's the best man of the two, he or Mac," exclaimed Trina, loftily. "How about that last scrap o' theirs? If Mac got hold a you once and gave you one lick, like the kind I get twenty of evury week, you wouldunt be as well off as your man was when Mac got through with um the time they fought last Washingtun's burthday, behind the brick kiln. Why Mac could do for the whole three of us, you an' Ryer an' I, yes he could, with one hand."

"Ah, talk sense, will you?" shouted Missis Ryer, as she moved the previous question. "Ain't Mister McTeague drunk when he dresses you down, and don't it stand to reason that he *can't* give it to you as hard as Ryer gives it to me when he's *sober?*"

"Do you know anything about it anyways?" said Trina, excitedly, "I tell you he's a deal worse to me than Ryer ever *thought* of be-un to you. Ain't he twysut, *three* times as strong?"

"That's a lie," retorted Ryer's wife, vindicating her absent husband with astonishing vehemence.

"Don't you tell me I lie again," shouted Trina, her cheeks flaming, her chin thrust out.

"I guess I'll say what I please in my own kitchin, you dirty little drab," screamed the other. Their faces were by this time close together, neither would draw back an inch.

"No you won't, no you won't," panted Trina, "an' don't you dare call me a drab. Drab yourself; best go back to the pigs your man used to fatten on old poultices, go back to your sty, I guess it won't be any dirtier than this here kitchun."

"Git out of it then."

"Not till I get ready."

"An' I'll call you drab till I'm black in the face, drab, *drab*, damn' nasty, dirty little drab. Git out uv my kitchin."

"Ah-h, let me see you put me out."

"Ah, dirty little drab."

"Ah, slattern, ah, pig-feeder."

Suddenly they tore at each other like infuriated cats. A handful of black and gray hair came away from Missis Ryer's head. Fingernail marks, long red lines appeared on the curve of Trina's cheeks, very like McTeague's conception of the parallels upon a globe. Missis Ryer, hustling Trina toward the door, pushed her into the arms of McTeague himself. At the same time Ryer, warned of this war of wives, entered the kitchen from the front of the house. He had come over hastily from the "Wein Stube" and was half drunk. McTeague had partially slept off his intoxication and was about half sober.

"Here, here, here," cried the ex-dentist over his wife's shoulder, "you two women fightin', quit it, what the bloody Hell!"

"Scrappin'" shouted Ryer from the doorway, "choke off, ol' woman, if there's any scrappin' to be done, I'll do it meself."

"She called me a drab," gasped Trina, glaring at her enemy from under the protection of her gigantic husband.

"An' she said my kitchin wasn't a place for pigs to live in," retorted Missis Ryer, without taking her eyes from Trina.

The men had not yet looked at each other. They were unwilling to fight this morning, because each one of them was half drunk or half sober, (either way you chose to put it), and because Ryer preferred to fight when he had all his wits about him, while McTeague was never combative until he had lost *his* wits entirely.

"What started the row, whatcha been fightin' about?" demanded the ex-dentist.

"Yes, sure," put in Ryer, "whatcha been scrappin' about, what started the row?"

The women looked at each other, unable to answer. Then Trina began awkwardly:

"Well I—well—well—a—well she told me—she said—well, she run you down, Mac, an' I didunt figure on puttun up with it."

"She tried to make small of you, Ryer," said his wife, "an' I called her down, an'—that's all, she tried to make small of you."

"Hey? What'd she say?" demanded McTeague, "out with it."

"Well, *this* is what she said," exclaimed Trina suddenly. "She said Ryer could give her a worse dressing down than you ever gave me, an' I wouldn't stand it."

"Well," declared Missis Ryer, turning to her husband. "I ain't goin' to let every dirty little drab that comes along say—say—throw mud at my man, am I? I guess," added Missis Ryer, defiantly, facing Trina and the ex-dentist. "I guess Ryer can do what he likes in his own house. I ain't goin' to let any woman tell me that her man is better'n mine, in any way."

"An' that's what you two fought over?" exclaimed the husbands in the same breath.

"Well, suppose we did?" said Trina with defiance.

"I guess I can quarrel about what I like," observed Missis Ryer, sullenly.

For the first time since they had entered the room the eyes of the two men met, and for fully half a dozen seconds they looked squarely at each other. Then the corners of the slit under Ryer's nose began to twitch, and McTeague's huge jaws to widen to a grin in nut-cracker fashion. Suddenly a roar of laughter shook him; he sank into a chair, rocking back and forth, smiting his knee with his palm. Ryer cackled shrilly, crying out between peals of laughter: "Well, if this ain't the greatest jolly I've struck yet."

"Fightin' over our fightin' *them*," bellowed McTeague.

"I've seen queer bugs in my time," gasped Ryer, "but the biggest curios yet are women, oh Lord, but this does beat the Dutch."

"Say, ain't this great, Ryer?"

"Mac, this does beat the carpet, sure."

"Look here old man, about them parallel lines, *I* say let's call it off. I ain't got no quarrel against *you*."

"That's a go, Mac, you're a good fellah, sure, put it there."

They shook hands upon their reconciliation, their breasts swelling with magnanimity. They felt that they liked one another hugely, and they slapped each other tremendous blows on the back, exclaiming at intervals "*put* it there," and gripping hands with a cordiality that was effusive beyond words. All at once Ryer had an inspiration.

"Say, Mac, come over to the Stube and have a drink on it."

"Well, I just guess I will," vociferated the ex-dentist.

Bewildered and raging at the unexpected reconciliation of their husbands, the two women had disappeared, Trina slamming the door of the kitchen with a parting cry of "pig feeder," which Missis Ryer immediately answered by thrusting her head out of a second story window and screaming at the top of her voice to the neighborhood in general, "dirty little drab."

Meanwhile the two men strode out of the house and across the street, their arms affectionately locked; the swing doors of the "Stube" flapped after them like a pair of silent wings.

*　　*　　*　　*　　*　　*　　*

That day settled the matter. Heretofore it had been the men who were enemies and their wives who were friends. Now the two men are fast friends, while the two women maintain perpetual feud. The "block" has come to recognize their quarrel as part of the existing order of things, like the leak from the gas-works and the collector's visits. Occasionally the women fight, and Missis Ryer, who is the larger and heavier, has something the best of it.

However, one particular custom common to both households remains unchanged—both men continue to thrash their wives in the old ratio—McTeague on the days when he is drunk (which are many), Ryer on the days when he is sober (which are few).

His Dead Mother's Portrait

The Wave, 16 (13 November 1897), 8.

I came to know young Drexel because of his cleverness in making a certain kind of trout-fly which he called the "Midshipman;" and which is most effective in mountain streams on very gray days. Young Drexel earned his living by making trout-flies for certain sporting firms on Market street, and after his great success with the "Midshipman" (it really is a *chef d'oeuvre*), everyone ceased to call him Drexel and always addressed him as Midshipman.

The Midshipman lives in one of those very quaint and curious old houses on the corner of California and Dupont streets, at the very edge of Chinatown. There are three houses here, and they face on Dupont street just opposite the cathedral, you must have noted them—quite above the grade, built up on bulkheads, and sporting old glass verandas. There are lots of flowers and vines in the yard, and trellises, too, where once in a while you may see a bunch of grapes.

The Midshipman knows trout as you know your right hand, I making enquiries for flies and tackle was sent to find him in his room in the glass verandahed house opposite the cathedral.

We got to know each other very well. He was a blonde, small young fellow, not over twenty-five, I believe; he wore spectacles—for the fineness of his work had told on his eyes—had the hands and fingers of a woman and also a woman's temperament. Besides this, he was passionately fond of German music. He dodged the roughnesses of the world of San Francisco, and lived much to himself with one or two friends, his delicate flies, an old female trout in a glass aquarium and—a small photograph of his dead mother, which he always carried with him in his pocketbook.

It did not take me long to find out that the Midshipman's dead mother was his religion, the one great influence of his life, that had kept him straight and fine and clean. She had passed out of his life when he was too young to remember her. However, he had her picture which was to him—

but I have no right to repeat what he used to tell me. He always kept this picture by him, used to sleep with it under his pillow, and on Sundays had a very pretty habit of writing letters to it.

On Saturday nights the Midshipman and I used to dine together at the *Buon Gusto*, over in the Mexican Quarter and afterwards used to walk about Market and Kearny streets, seeing what we could see, much preferring that form of amusement to the best "attractions" billed at any of the theatres. For on Saturday nights Market and Kearny streets of this city of San Francisco are *en fête*. It is like a country fair—all the world is abroad promenading itself. On one corner the Salvation Army is booming, on another a street-fakir is entertaining a crowd, the kinetoscope booths, the shooting galleries and small auction shops are wide open, a cable car goes by with a blaring brass band that announces a suburban amusement; from Chinatown comes the reek of punk, the blink of swinging red lanterns, and the wailing of pipes and two-string fiddles; you hear the jangle of pianos coming up through the sidewalk from the dives and dance-halls; for five cents you can look at Mars through a telescope, take a shock of electricity, "know your weight," or sit for your tintype. From the Barbary Coast to Lotta's fountain it is all gas, glitter, and gaiety. Where else but in Paris would you find the like?

It was towards nine o'clock on that particular Saturday evening that the Midshipman and I passed down the Barbary Coast on our way from the *Buon Gusto.* In front of the Bella Union we were met by a group of some half dozen fellows whom I am ashamed to say I knew. They took possession of us at once. There was nothing for me to do but to introduce the Midshipman to them.

"Look here," said one of these fellows; "we're going into the Bella Union, and you're coming with us."

"In there? I'll see you far first. It's the most disreputable dive in town."

"Yes, but we're going in for the fad of the thing. Let me tell you. We were there last night. Oh, it's raw!—raw as beef! There's an old woman there," the young brute went on, "an old woman of forty, dressed up as a girl of fifteen, that does a song and dance. She can't dance, and her voice is 'hark-from-the-tombs-a-doleful-sound.' I honestly think she's dotty. Y' know, she comes out and yowls and gambols and the whole audience hiss and hoot and groan and stamp till she goes off, and then as soon as she's off we all applaud and clap and shout 'encore! encore!' till we get her back. Then she'll come out and bow and smirk, and as soon as she begins to do her turn over again we all hoot and groan till we get her off. And so on over and over again. Laugh! I nearly split my sides!"

"I'd like to split your head," said I.

"Fiddlesticks! the woman's crazy. I tell you she don't know the difference, and she's forty if she's a day. It *is* hideous, I admit, but it's something to see. Come in with us for ten minutes and we will go to some decent show afterwards. Leander is here; he'll take us all to hear Nordica in *Siegfried*, afterwards."

"But such a beastly dive; don't want to be seen going into such a hole-in-the-wall."

"The people whose opinion counts for anything don't frequent the Barbary Coast."

I turned doubtfully to the Midshipman.

"Shall we look in for ten minutes?"

The Midshipman wavered. Nordica in *Siegfried* tempted him.

"I don't like such places—I've never been—it's not my line you know. Still, for ten minutes only, and you say we'll go to the opera afterwards?"

We moved toward the box office and the Midshipman reached for his pocketbook. I was standing at his side at the time, and, as he fumbled in the pocketbook for the price of his admission, I noticed that his eye fell upon the portrait of his dead mother which he always carried there. He looked at it an instant and then around him at the vestibule, that sordid dive with its staring, vulgar billboards. From inside the theatre came the jangling of a cheap band and the raucous notes of a concert-hall singer.

The Midshipman turned about with abrupt resolution.

"No," said he to me in a low voice so that none of the others heard, "no, I won't go in. I—I *can't*, you understand," and with that he was gone.

Leander came up just in time to see him go.

"Hello," said he, "that was young Drexel with you wasn't it—the Midshipman—where did he go; what did he go for?"

"He didn't like the idea of going into this joint. He has pretty strict notions, you know, Leander."

Leander scratched his ear.

"That's a queer case," he said reflectively.

"As how; do you know him?"

"I know people that do. He thinks his mother died long ago."

"Great Scott! Didn't she?"

Leander put his chin in the air.

"It would have been better if she had."

"Come on, you fellows," cried the rest of the party, "come on, we're going in."

"Hello, what's this?" exclaimed Leander, stooping to pick up a photograph that lay at our feet.

I saw what it was and tried to get it away before the others came up.

"Give it here, Leander," said I in a low voice. "It's a picture of the Midshipman's mother, he dropped it just now."

But I was not quick enough.

"Hoh," exclaimed one of the party as his eye fell upon the picture, "it's the old woman inside who does the song-and-dance turn. Come on, let's go in. Now all you fellows be sure to yell and groan as soon as she comes out."

"Let's not go in," said I to Leander.

Shorty Stack, Pugilist

The Wave, 16 (20 November 1897), 5-6.

Over at the "Big Dipper" mine a chuck-tender named Kelly had been in error as regards a box of dynamite sticks, and Iowa Hill had elected to give an "entertainment" for the benefit of his family.

The programme, as announced upon the posters that were stuck up in the Post Office and on the door of the Odd Fellows' Hall, was quite an affair. The Iowa Hill orchestra would perform, the livery-stable keeper would play the overture to *William Tell* upon his harmonica, and the town doctor would read a paper on "Tuberculosis in Cattle." The evening was to close with a "grand ball."

Then it was discovered that a professional pugilist from the "Bay" was over in Forest Hill, and someone suggested that a match could be made between him and Shorty Stack "to enliven the entertainment." Shorty Stack was a bedrock cleaner at the "Big Dipper," and handy with his fists. It was his boast that no man of his weight (Shorty fought at a hundred and forty) no man of his weight in Placer County could stand up to him for ten rounds, and Shorty had always made good this boast. Shorty knew two punches, and no more—a short-arm jab under the ribs with his right, and a left upper-cut on the point of the chin.

The pugilist's name was McCleaverty. He was an out and out dub—one of the kind who appear in four-round exhibition bouts to keep the audience amused while the "event of the evening" is preparing—but he had had ring experience, and his name had been in the sporting paragraphs of the San Francisco papers. The dub was a welter-weight and a professional, but he accepted the challenge of Shorty Stack's backers and covered their bet of fifty dollars that he could not "stop" Shorty in four rounds.

And so it came about that extra posters were affixed to the door of the Odd Fellows' Hall and the walls of the Post Office to the effect that Shorty Stack, the champion of Placer County, and Buck McCleaverty, the Pride of Colusa, would appear in a genteel boxing exhibition at the entertainment given for the benefit, etc., etc.

Shorty had two weeks in which to train. The nature of his work in the mine had kept his muscles hard enough, so his training was largely a matter of dieting and boxing an imaginary foe with a rock in each fist. He was so vigorous in his exercise and in the matter of what he ate and drank that the day before the entertainment he had got himself down to a razor-edge, and was in a fair way of going fine. When a man gets into too good condition, the least little slip will spoil him. Shorty knew this well enough, and told himself in consequence that he must be very careful.

The night before the entertainment Shorty went to call on Miss Starbird. Miss Starbird was one of the cooks at the mine. She was a very pretty girl, just turned twenty, and lived with her folks in a cabin near the superintendent's office, on the road from the mine to Iowa Hill. Her father was a shift boss in the mine, and her mother did the washing for the "office." Shorty was recognized by the mine as her young man. She was going to the entertainment with her people, and promised Shorty the first "walk-around" in the "Grand Ball" that was to follow immediately after the Genteel Glove Contest.

Shorty came into the Starbird cabin on that particular night, his hair neatly plastered in a beautiful curve over his left temple, and his pants outside of his boots as a mark of esteem. He wore no collar, but he had encased himself in a boiled shirt, which could mean nothing else but mute and passionate love, and moreover, as a crowning tribute, he refrained from spitting.

"How do you feel, Shorty?" asked Miss Starbird.

Shorty had always sedulously read the interviews with pugilists that appeared in the San Francisco papers immediately before their fights and knew how to answer.

"I feel fit to fight the fight of my life," he alliterated proudly. "I've trained faithfully and I mean to win."

"It ain't a regular prize fight, is it Shorty?" she enquired. "Pa said he wouldn't take ma an' me if it was. All the women folk in the camp are going, an' I never heard of women at a fight, it ain't genteel."

"Well, I d'n know," answered Shorty, swallowing his saliva. "The committee that got the programme up called it a genteel boxing exhibition so's to get the women folks to stay. *I* call it a four round go with a decision."

"My! itull be exciting," exclaimed Miss Starbird. "I ain't never seen anything like it. Oh, Shorty, d'ye think you'll win?"

"I don't *think* nothun about it. I *know* I will," returned Shorty, defiantly. "If I once get in my left upper cut on him, *huh!*" and he snorted magnificently.

Shorty stayed and talked to Miss Starbird until ten o'clock, then he rose to go.

"I gotta get to bed," he said, "I'm in training you see."

"Oh, wait a minute," said Miss Starbird, "I been making some potato salad for the private dining of the office, you better have some; it's the best I ever made."

"No, no," said Shorty, stoutly, "I don't want any."

"Hoh," sniffed Miss Starbird, airily, "you don't need to have any."

"Well, don't you see," said Shorty, "I'm in training. I don't dare eat any of that kinda stuff."

"Stuff!" exclaimed Miss Starbird, her chin in the air. "No one *else* ever called my cooking stuff."

"Well, don't you see, don't you see?"

"No, I don't see. I guess you must be 'fraid of getting whipped if you're so 'fraid of a little salad."

"What!" exclaimed Shorty, indignantly. "Why I could come into the ring from a jag and whip him; 'fraid! *who's* afraid? I'll show you if I'm afraid. Let's have your potato salad, an' some beer, too. Huh! *I'll* show you if I'm afraid."

But Miss Starbird would not immediately consent to be appeased.

"No, you called it stuff," she said, "an' the souprintendant said I was the best cook in Placer County."

But at last, as a great favor to Shorty, she relented and brought the potato salad from the kitchen and two bottles of beer.

When the town doctor had finished his paper on "Tuberculosis in Cattle," the chairman of the entertainment committee ducked under the ropes of the ring and announced that: "The next would be the event of the evening and would the gentlemen please stop smoking." He went on to explain that the ladies present might remain without fear and without reproach as the participants in the contest would appear in gymnasium tights, and would box with gloves and not with bare knuckles.

"Well, don't they always fight with gloves?" called a voice from the rear of the house. But the chairman ignored the interruption.

The "entertainment" was held in the Odd Fellows' Hall. Shorty's seconds prepared him for the fight in a back room of the saloon, on the other side of the street, and towards ten o'clock one of the committeemen came running in to say:

"What's the matter? Hurry up you fellows, McCleaverty's in the ring, already, and the crowd's beginning to stamp."

Shorty rose and slipped into an overcoat.

"All ready," he said.

"Now mind, Shorty," said Billy Hicks, as he gathered up the sponges, fans and towels, "don't mix things with him, you don't have to knock him out, all you want's the decision."

Next, Shorty was aware that he was sitting in a corner of the ring with his back against the ropes, and that diagonally opposite was a huge red man with a shaven head. There was a noisy, murmuring crowd somewhere below him, and there was a glare of kerosene lights over his head.

"Buck McCleaverty, the Pride of Colusa," announced the master of ceremonies, standing in the middle of the ring, one hand under the dub's elbow. There was a ripple of applause. Then the master of ceremonies came over to Shorty's corner, and, taking him by the arm, conducted him into the middle of the ring.

"Shorty Stack, the Champion of Placer County." The house roared; Shorty ducked and grinned and returned to his corner. He was nervous, excited. He had not imagined it would be exactly like this. There was a strangeness about it all; an unfamiliarity that made him uneasy.

"Take it slow," said Billy Hicks, kneading the gloves, so as to work the padding away from the knuckles. The gloves were laced on Shorty's hands.

"Up you go," said Billy Hicks, again. "No, not the fight yet, shake hands first. Don't get rattled."

Then ensued a vague interval, that seemed to Shorty interminable. He had a notion that he shook hands with McCleaverty, and that some one asked him if he would agree to hit with one arm free in the breakaway. He remembered a glare of lights, a dim vision of rows of waiting faces, a great murmuring noise, and he had a momentary glimpse of someone he believed to be the referee; a young man in shirt-sleeves and turned-up trousers. Then everybody seemed to be getting out of the ring and away from him, even Billy Hicks left him after saying something he did not understand. Only the referee, McCleaverty and himself were left inside the ropes.

"Time!"

Somebody, who seemed to Shorty strangely like himself, stepped briskly out into the middle of the ring, his left arm before him, his right fist clinched over his breast. The crowd, the glaring lights, the murmuring noise, all faded away. There only remained the creaking of rubber soles over the resin of the boards of the ring and the sight of McCleaverty's shifting, twinkling eyes and his round, close-cropped head.

"Break!"

The referee stepped between the two men and Shorty realized that the two had clinched, and that his right forearm had been across McCleaverty's throat, his left clasping him about the shoulders.

What! Were they fighting already? This was the first round, of course. Somebody was shouting.

"That's the stuff, Shorty."

All at once Shorty saw the flash of a red muscled arm, he threw forward his shoulder ducking his head behind it, the arm slid over the raised shoulder and a bare and unprotected flank turned towards him.

"Now," thought Shorty. His arm shortened and leaped forward. There was a sudden impact. The shock of it jarred Shorty himself, and he heard McCleaverty grunt. There came a roar from the house.

"Give it to him, Shorty."

Shorty pushed his man from him, the heel of his glove upon his face. He was no longer nervous. The lights didn't bother him.

"I'll knock him out yet," he muttered to himself.

They fiddled and feinted about the ring, watching each other's eyes. Shorty held his right ready. He told himself he would jab McCleaverty again on the same spot when next he gave him an opening.

"Break!"

They must have clinched again, but Shorty was not conscious of it. A sharp pain in his upper lip made him angry. His right shot forward again, struck home, and while the crowd roared and the lights began to swim again, he knew that he was rushing McCleaverty back, back, back, his arms shooting out and in like piston rods, now for an upper cut with his left on the——

"Time!"

Billy Hicks was talking excitedly. The crowd still roared. His lips pained. Someone was spurting water over him, one of his seconds worked the fans like a windmill. He wondered what Miss Starbird thought of him now.

"Time!"

He barely had a chance to duck, almost double, while McCleaverty's right swished over his head. The dub was swinging for a knockout already. The round would be hot and fast.

"Stay with um, Shorty."

"That's the stuff, Shorty."

He must be setting the pace, the house plainly told him that. He stepped in again and cut loose with both fists.

"Break!"

Shorty had not clinched. Was it possible that McCleaverty was clinching "to avoid punishment?" Shorty tried again, stepping in close, his right arm crooked and ready.

"*Break!*"

The dub was clinching. There could be no doubt of that. Shorty gathered himself together and rushed in, upper-cutting viciously; he felt McCleaverty giving way before him.

"He's got um going."

There was exhilaration in the shout. Shorty swung right and left, his fist struck something that hurt him. Sure, he thought, that must have been a good one. He recovered, throwing out his left before him. Where was the dub? not down there on one knee in a corner of the ring? The house was a pandemonium, near at hand some one was counting, "one—two—three—four—"

Billy Hicks rushed into the ring and dragged Shorty back. "Come back to your corner. It's the rules when he's up to go right in to finish him. He ain't knocked out yet. He's just taking his full time. Swing for his chin a-gain, you got him going. If you can put him out, Shorty, we'll take you to San Francisco."

"Seven—eight—nine—"

McCleaverty was up again. Shorty rushed in, something caught him a fearful jar in the pit of the stomach. He was sick in an instant, racked with nausea. The lights began to dance.

"*Time!*"

There was water on his face and body again, deliciously cool. The fan windmills swung round and round. "What's the matter, what's the matter?" Billy Hicks was asking anxiously.

Something was wrong. There was a lead-like weight in Shorty's stomach, a taste of potato salad came to his mouth, he was sick almost to vomiting.

"He caught you a hard one in the wind just before the gong, did he?" said Billy Hicks. "There's fight in him yet. He's got a straight arm body blow you want to look out for. Don't let up on him. Keep——"

"*Time!*"

Shorty came up bravely. In his stomach there was a pain that made it torture to stand erect. Nevertheless he rushed, lashing out right and left. He was dizzy; before he knew it he was beating the air. Suddenly his chin jolted backward, and the lights began to spin; he was tiring rapidly, too, and with every second his arms grew heavier and heavier and his knees began to tremble more and more. McCleaverty gave him no rest. Shorty tried to clinch, but the dub sidestepped, and came in twice with a hard right and left over the heart. Shorty's gloves seemed made of iron; he found time to mutter, "If I only hadn't eaten that stuff last night."

What with the nausea and the pain, he was hard put to it to keep from groaning. It was the dub who was rushing now; Shorty felt he could not support the weight of his own arms another instant. What was that on his face that was warm and tickled? He knew that he had just strength enough left for one more good blow; if he could only upper-cut squarely on McCleaverty's chin it might suffice.

"*Break!*"

The referee thrust himself between them, but instantly McCleaverty closed again. Would the round *never* end? The dub swung again, missed, and Shorty saw his chance; he stepped in, upper-cutting with all the strength he could summon up. The lights swam again, and the roar of the crowd dwindled to a couple of voices. He smelt whisky.

"Gimme that sponge." It was Billy Hicks' voice. "He'll do all right now."

Shorty suddenly realized that he was lying on his back. In another second he would be counted out. He raised himself, but his hands touched a bed quilt and not the resined floor of the ring. He looked around him and saw that he was in the back room of the saloon where he had dressed. The fight was over.

"Did I win?" he asked, getting on his feet.

"Win!" exclaimed Billy Hicks. "You were knocked out. He put you out after you had him beaten. Oh, you're a peach of a fighter, you are."

*　　*　　*　　*　　*　　*

Half an hour later, when he had dressed, Shorty went over to the Hall. His lip was badly swollen and his chin had a funny shape, but otherwise he was fairly presentable. The Iowa Hill orchestra had just struck into the march for the walk around. He pushed through the crowd of men around the door looking for Miss Starbird. Just after he had passed he heard a remark and the laugh that followed it:

"Quitter, oh, what a quitter."

Shorty turned fiercely about and would have answered, but just at that moment he caught sight of Miss Starbird. She had just joined the promenade for the walk around with some other man. He went up to her:

"Didn't you promise to have this walk around with me?" he said aggrievedly.

"Well, did you think I was going to wait all night for you?" returned Miss Starbird.

As she turned from him and joined the march Shorty's eye fell upon her partner.

It was McCleaverty.

The End of the Act

The Wave, 16 (27 November 1897), 3

The house was crowded to the doors. There was no longer any standing-room, and many were even sitting on the steps of the aisles. In the boxes the gentlemen were standing up behind the chairs of large plain ladies in showy toilets and diamonds. The atmosphere was heavy with the smell of gas, of plush upholstery, of wilting bouquets and of sachet. A fine vapor, as of the visible exhalations of many breaths, pervaded the house, blurring the lowered lights and dimming the splendor of the great glass chandelier.

It was warm to suffocation, a dry irritating warmth that perspiration did not relieve, while the air itself was stale and close as though fouled by being breathed over and over again. In the topmost gallery, banked with tiers of watching faces, the heat must have been unbearable.

The only movement perceptible throughout the audience was the swaying of gay colored fans like the balancing of butterflies about to light. Occasionally there would be a vast rustling, like the sound of wind in a forest, as the holders of librettos turned the leaves simultaneously.

The orchestra thundered, the French horns snarling, the first violins wailing in unison, while all the bows went up and down together like parts of a well-regulated machine. The kettledrums rolled sonorously at exact intervals, and now and then one heard the tinkling of a harp like the pattering of rain drops between peals of thunder. The leader swayed from side to side in his place beating time with his baton, his hand and his head.

On the stage the act was drawing to a close. There had just been a duel. The baritone lay stretched upon the floor at left center, his sword fallen at some paces from him. On the left of the scene, front, stood the tenor who had killed him, singing in his highest register, very red in the face, continuously striking his hand upon his breast and pointing with his sword at his fallen enemy. Next him, on the extreme left, was his friend the basso, in high leather boots, growling from time to time during a sustained chord, "*Mon honneur et ma foi.*" In the center of the stage, the soprano, the star, the prima donna, chanted a fervid appeal to the tenor, who cried, "*Jamais, jamais!*" striking his breast and pointing with his sword. The soprano cried, "*Ah, mon Dieu, ayez pitié de moi!*" Her confidante, the mezzo-soprano, came to her support, repeating her words with an impersonal meaning—"*Ayez pitié d'elle!*" "*Mon honneur et ma foi,*" growled the basso. The contralto, dressed as a boy, turned toward the audience on the extreme right, bringing out her notes with a wrench and a twist of her body and neck, and intoning, "*Ah, malheureuse! mon Dieu, ayez pitié d'elle!*"

The leader of the chorus, costumed as the captain of the watch, leaned over the dead baritone and sang, "*Il est mort, il est mort, mon Dieu, ayez pitié de lui.*" The soldiers of the watch were huddled together immediately back of him. They wore tin helmets much too large, and green peplons, and repeated his words continually.

The chorus itself was made up of citizens of the town; it was in a semi-circle at the back of the stage—the men on one side, the women on the other. They made all their gestures together and chanted without ceasing, "*O horreur, O mystère! Il est mort, mon Dieu, ayez pitié de nous!*"

"*Edgardo,*" cried the soprano.

"*Jamais, jamais!*" echoed the tenor, striking his breast and pointing with his sword.

"*O mystère,*" chanted the chorus, while the basso struck his hand upon his sword hilt, growling, "*Mon honneur et ma foi!*"

The orchestra redoubled. The *finale* began; all the pieces of the orchestra, all the voices on the stage commenced over again very loud. They all took a step forward, and the rhythm became more rapid till it reached a climax where the soprano's voice jumped to a C in *alt*, holding it long enough for the basso to thunder, "*Mon honneur et ma foi*" twice. Then they all struck the attitudes for the closing tableau, and in one last burst of music sang all together, "*Mon Dieu, ayez pitié moi,*" and "*de nous,*" and "*de lui.*" Then the orchestra closed with a long roll of the kettle drums, and the soprano fainted into the arms of her confidante. The curtain fell.

There was a roar of applause. The gallery whistled and stamped. Everyone relaxed his or her position, drawing in a long breath, looking about them. There was a general stir; the lights in the great glass chandelier, clicked and blazed up, and a murmur of conversation arose. The footlights were lowered, and the orchestra left their places and disappeared underneath the stage, leaving the audience with the conviction that they had gone out after beer. All over the house one heard the shrill voices of boys crying out: "Op'ra books—books for the op'ra—words and music for the op'ra."

Throughout the boxes a great coming and going took place, and an interchange of visits. The gentlemen out in the foyer, stood about in groups, or walked up and down smoking cigarettes, often pausing in front of the big floral piece, that was to be given to the soprano, at the end of her "great scene," in the fourth act.

There was a little titter of an electric bell. The curtain was about to go up, and a great rush for seats began. The orchestra was coming back and tuning up. They sent up a prolonged medley of sounds, little minor chirps and cries from the violins, liquid runs and mellow gurgles from the oboes and wood-wind instruments, and an occasional deep-toned purring from the bass-viols, a bell rang faintly from behind the wings, the house lights sank and the footlights blazed up. The leader tapped with his baton; a great silence fell upon the house, while here and there one heard an energetic "Sh! Sh!" The fourth act was about to begin.

The Isabella Regina

The Wave, 16 (27 November 1897), 6.

*The rear coach of a passenger train between any city and any fashionable
suburb.*

CHARACTERS:

Alfred. Angelina. A Conductor. A Train Boy.

Angelina: How far are we from the city, Alfred?

Alfred: I don't know. We must cross the bay first. We go as far as Rockport on the train, you know, and we take the ferry for the city there. We're
not far from Rockport now (looking out the window), be there in about
twenty minutes.

Train Boy (in a Gregorian chant): Cigars-cigarettes-chewing-gum-'n-tobac-
co.

Alfred: Here, boy. Give me an Isabella Regina—I say Angelina, you
don't mind if I buy a cigar do you?—Sidney Spence told me this boy sold a
cigar I mustn't fail to try. Of course I won't smoke now.

Angelina: Why of course I don't mind, Alfred. It was only cigarettes you
promised me about.

Alfred: I won't buy one if you say not.

Angelina: But I *want* you should, I love to see you happy.

Alfred: My angel. (To the boy.) Two for a quarter?

Boy: Twenty-five cents straight. (Alfred gives him twenty-five cents, and
puts the cigar in his upper vest pocket.)

Alfred (proudly): Angelina I haven't smoked a cigarette in a week, and
you know I can get twenty-five cigarettes for what I pay for one cigar.

Angelina (with enthusiasm): You are heroic; you are noble, Alfred.

Alfred (magnificently): Pooh!

The Conductor: Tickets.

Angelina: Tickets, Alfred.

Alfred: You forget, we are traveling on a pass, Angelina.

Angelina: That's so, I had forgotten. Don't it make you feel grand to travel on a pass, Alfred, just as though you were a Personage?

Alfred (with superb indifference): Not a bit.

Angelina (gazing at him with admiration): That's because you're so use to it.

Alfred (with nonchalance): I suppose so, perhaps; I never think much about it.

The Conductor (near at hand): Tickets. (Alfred hands him the pass with exquisite unconcern, yawning and looking out of the window.)

The Conductor: You must sign this pass, sir.

Alfred (biting his yawn in two and turning to the conductor in some confusion): What, I—I thought I did pass the sign, I mean sign the——

The Conductor (coldly): Well, you didn't. Sign in ink—don't use your pencil.

Alfred (helplessly): But I haven't any ink. (The conductor silently hands him his fountain pen.)

Angelina: How can you sign, Alfred, when the car shakes so?

Alfred: I don't believe I can.

Angelina: It will be all jiggelty, like that signature on the *Declaration of Independence*. Don't you remember, the one that's so shaky? I can't recall the name. Was it Hopkins or Hancock? it's dreadfully jiggelty. There was a facsimile of the *Declaration of Independence* on the wall at the seminary, and Miss Mix used to tell us that Mr. Hopkins'—or Mr. Hancock's hand shook so because he was afraid of the British. I *can't* remember whether it was Hopkins or Hancock. (To the conductor.) Do *you* remember?

The Conductor: What!

Alfred (handing him the pass): There you are. (The conductor takes up the pass and is moving away.)

Alfred: Hey there, conductor. (The conductor pauses.) You didn't give us any ferry tickets. I thought you always gave passengers tickets for the ferry, when you took up their railroad tickets. You always have before.

The Conductor (loftily): We only give ferry tickets to passengers travelling

199

at regular transportation rates, we don't give 'em to holders of passes. (Moves on crying "Tickets!")

Alfred (excitedly): But I say—here—hey there conductor.

Angelina: What's the matter Alfred? (Alfred gasps, turns pale and rolls his eyes wildly.) Alfred, my own boy, what is it? You are ill. Oh, I said you shouldn't eat so much of that terrapin stew.

Alfred (fumbling rapidly in one pocket after another): Nothing, nothing, I—I—I (miserably) I'm afraid I haven't any money.

Angelina (blankly): Oh!

Alfred (distracted): How are we going to get across the bay to the city? We'll be at Rockport in a few moments. I gave my last change to the train boy for that Isabella Regina. I thought our pass was good to the city. Angelina, we are lost. I haven't a cent.

Angelina: Nor I. And I *made* you get that cigar. It's I that have brought you to this. Oh! Alfred, it's all my fault.

Alfred (bravely): No, *I* am the one to blame, I, only.

Angelina: No, no. It's only your heroism that says that. It was all on my account.

Alfred: I won't allow you to say that Angelina.

Angelina: But you wouldn't have bought the cigar if I hadn't made you. I insisted. You see if you had got cigarettes yesterday instead of your after-dinner cigar you would have got twenty-five cigarettes for what you paid for that one cigar and you might have had a few cigarettes left by now and wouldn't have had to buy that Isabella Regina cigar and-then-you-would-have-had-a-quarter-left-and-we-could-have-got-over-to-the-city—and, *oh!,* I'm so unhappy. (Chokes back a sob.)

Alfred (wildly): Angelina you break my heart, stop, I'll throw myself from the train in another moment.

Angelina (clutching him hysterically): Alfred, you shall not. Calm yourself. Oh, what's to become of us now? (Alfred starts suddenly as an idea occurs to him, his pallor increasing.)

Alfred (with terrible calmness): And this next boat is the last to-day.

Angelina: What do you mean?

Alfred (still with horrible calmness): If we don't get this next boat, there is none other we *can* get till to-morrow morning, and we'll be obliged to stay over in Rockport all night.

Angelina (repressing a shriek): Alfred don't *say* it. It *can't* be true. What's to become of *me?* Everybody *knows* we came away together to spend the day out of town, and, if we stay away all night—why—why—oh, what is going to become of us now? This is—this must be some horrible dream.

Alfred (in desperation): And all for the want of a quarter. I shall go insane in another minute.

Angelina: Oh! I know I shall.

Alfred (looking about him): We must get a quarter.

Angelina: There's that old gentleman across the aisle. Suppose you go to *him*. You could ask him to accommodate you with twenty-five cents, and you could give him your note.

Alfred (wildly): Ha, ha, my note for sixty days. What's the interest on twenty-five cents for sixty days?

Angelina: May be you could *sell* him something. *I* know (clapping her hands), sell him the *cigar*. The *Isabella Regina*.

Alfred (with enthusiasm): Saved me again, Angelina; you are my good angel. (Rising.) I'm going to try. Wish me God-speed, Angelina. (They clasp hands.)

Angelina: I *know* you will succeed.

Alfred: I go. (He approaches the old gentleman, and engages him in a few moments' interview, unheard by Angelina.)

Alfred (returning): Crushed! He don't smoke.

Angelina: What did he say?

Alfred: Said he was the third vice-president of the Anti-Nicotine League.

Angelina: We're lost.

The Brakeman (opening the forward car door with a yell): Next staishn's Bra-rah-rah! (Remainder unintelligible.)

Alfred: We are almost at Rockport, what *can* be done?

Angelina: Can't we *hire* a boat and row across the bay?

Alfred: And how would we pay the hire, I should like to know?

Angelina: If I only had some jewels to give a boatman. Just like they do in novels! Don't you remember that poem?

> A chieftain to the highlands bound
> > Cried boatman do not tarry,
> And I'll give thee a silver crown
> > To row us o'er the ferry.

We had it to scan at the seminary, and "tarry" and "ferry" don't rhyme, nor "bound" and "crown." I never thought of that before.

Alfred: But what's to be done? (The train whistles for Rockport and begins to slow down; the passengers collect shawl-straps and satchels; the conductor reappears.)

Angelina: Here's the conductor, Alfred. Let's appeal to the conductor. Tell him you haven't enough money to get across the bay with, and ask him for tickets and tell him you'll send him the money to-morrow.

Alfred: He never would relent. Didn't you notice what a frigid, brutal manner he had? He's just in the railroad's employ, and paid to collect fares. It's nothing to him that we can't get across the bay. He is a minion; what the newspapers call "the tool of the corporation."

Angelina: *I'll* talk to him. I'll throw myself upon his—

Alfred (severely): Angelina!

Angelina: —his mercy.

Alfred: No, I'll face him.

Angelina: Not alone, Alfred. I'll be at your side. (The train stops with a backward jerk and a prolonged hiss of relaxed air brakes. The other passengers leave the car. Angelina and Alfred approach the conductor.)

Alfred (in a low tone to Angelina): I—think I'm a little afraid of him; he acted like such a bear about the pass.

Angelina: Be brave, Alfred.

Alfred (to the conductor, assuming a careless tone and speaking very loud): I say, about those tickets across the ferry; I find myself in a very embarrassing situation (explains at length).

Angelina: And this is the last boat to-day, and—and—we're not—we're *going* to be married but—

The Conductor (easily): Why, that's all right (handing Alfred the tickets), 'might happen to anybody.

Angelina (fervidly): Oh! thank you so much. It's very kind of you.

Alfred (loftily as he pockets the tickets): I told you, Angelina, that I would fix it some how.

Angelina: Yes, Alfred, I should have known that I could have relied upon you.

The Conductor: Better hurry up, you'll miss the boat.

Angelina (to the conductor, as she and Alfred move away): Thank you, again, so *very* much.

Alfred: He *was* a brick after all, wasn't he?

Angelina: He was a *gentleman*, Alfred.

Alfred (turning back): Wait a minute. I have an idea. (Approaches the conductor and offers him the Isabella Regina.) Have a cigar, sir.

The Conductor: Thanks, I will.

The Mira Monte Club

Where the City's Younger Sportsmen
Hunt Duck, Deer and Quail

The Wave, 16 (4 December 1897), 3.

About two years ago three or four of the younger men of San Francisco, finding their tastes ran to out-of-door sports with the rod and gun rather than to indoor city club life, conceived the idea of forming a country club and acquiring property for the purpose of preserving game and fish for the benefit of the members. The idea of having a bachelors' club in the country, where one could go and seek rest from the whirl of the busy city, as well as the whirl of the ballroom, was a novel idea.

The conclusion of the whole matter was the Mira Monte Club, organized in the summer of 1895, and composed of the following named members: Jas. B. Burdell, president; H.B. Houghton, vice-president; Nat. Wilson, secretary and manager; W.R. Whittier, Edward Pringle, George Martin, James Follis, Milton Latham, Laurie Adams, W. Fairbanks, W.K. Hill, F.A. Wickersham, F.A. Greenwood, J. Downey Harvey, A.H. Whitney and Doctor Galen Burdell (honorary).

The last named gentleman made the club not only possible, but prosperous, by very generously leasing, for a term of years some fifteen thousand acres of admirable duck, quail and deer country at Burdell Station, on the line of the S.F. and N.P. Railway, about 35 miles from the city. Of these acres 2000 are marsh, in which are situated the duck ponds and snipe patches. The balance is upland and is covered with oak, chaparral and fern. The quail are thick in here and it is no unusual thing to start up a buck or doe in the more isolated corners. However, the deer are not now as plentiful as the Mira Monte Club intends they shall be, and as yet the members are limited to two deer per season. Fishing, as well, is more of a hope than a reality at Mira Monte. However, the tract is seamed with waterways and in the higher grounds there are veritable mountain streams where trout would thrive. The management of the club are now considering this question and the streams are to be stocked with McCloud and Eastern trout.

The clubhouse is located on a knoll covered with live oak about half a mile from the station. There are no better appointed bachelor quarters within a radius of a hundred miles of the city than those afforded by the Mira Monte clubhouse, and quite a feature of the life of the place is the occurrence of house parties made up to pass a day and a night at the club. The house is built in an admirable Spanish style, one story in height and flanked with deep wings. The interior is divided into the huge living-room, dining-room, kitchen, billiard room, and twelve bedrooms for the use of members. At the lower end of the "Island" the club has erected its stables and kennels. There is no occasion or necessity for the maintenance of any regular pack by the club and these kennels merely serve for the accommodation of game dogs of the individual members. Here also are kept the floats, the four launches and half dozen ducking boats for the members' use.

The location of the Mira Monte preserves is such that they enjoy a blessed immunity from the poacher and nefarious pot-hunter and market hunter. On all sides their land is either inaccessible of approach, or is protected by the tracts of the Olympic Gun Club and the Petaluma Gun Club.

Twice a year the club holds a competitive shoot open only to members.

The first, which occurs in June, is a clay pigeon shoot for the club medal. The other shoot is rather unique and is held in February. It is a shoot for all manner of pests, from the blue jay to the wild cat that destroy or drive out the legitimate game. Points are given on certain birds and animals, so many for a hawk, so many for a wild cat. The club divides into two parties and that party scoring the highest number of points is treated to what the daily papers call "an elaborate menu." Altogether the Mira Monte Club is a capital organization, and in the matter of amusement and recreation (principles upon which it was founded), has attained results far beyond the organizers' fondest hopes.

Happiness by Conquest

The Wave, 16 (11 December 1897), 2.

There is a man named Horace Fletcher who has written a queer little book called *Happiness as Found in Forethought Minus Fearthought*. He calls Fearthought the self-imposed or self-permitted suggestion of inferiority. He says that a sense of one's inferiority will poison one's happiness, will make one *un*-happy. This, instead of actual trouble, Mr. Fletcher says, is the cause of unhappiness, for trouble in his philosophy does not exist. "Fearthought of trouble is as near as one ever gets to the condition, for the reason that whatever has come has ceased to exist, except in the memory." But how about happiness then? For happiness when it comes has ceased to exist, except in the memory. We suppose that Mr. Fletcher would hurdle that obstacle by retorting that anticipation and remembrance of happiness *is* happiness, all the happiness that one can get on this side of the hole-in-the-ground.

There is something in this Fletcher theory when you stop and think about it a moment. The difficulty is that Happiness is not a constant quantity.

It all depends upon your point of view, on your temperament, on your condition. One man's idea of happiness may mean a good wife, another man's may mean a beef-steak. Or the same man may have a different idea of Happiness at different times. To-day it may be a good wife. Cast him away upon a desert island, or "concentrate" him in an interior Cuban village and in a week he will entertain pronounced views as to that beef-steak.

We are all scrambling along after Happiness, when you come to that, and it's curious that after some seven or eight thousand years of the scramble we should have no more definite idea of what Happiness is or means. And if we attained Happiness we should be unhappy that we could attain nothing further. It is a queer situation. "Hopeful determination," says Horace Fletcher, "will go far in the way of procuring Happiness." But the words Hope and Determination imply the overcoming of certain things, certain obstacles, certain *un*happinesses. One is inclined to believe that that is more nearly the right idea, that Happiness is *overcoming rather than attaining*. One can never attain and yet be happy, but there are plenty of chances of overcoming things. One never can quite exhaust them. One is often led to speculate if even the Octogenarian, brought to his last bed, with the hole-in-the-ground none too far distant, has not some idea of overcoming the enemy that has the grip of him, of recovery from *that* particular illness anyway. At least he has the chance of trying.

With an idea so vague as Happiness, and with so many billions of men and women entered for the scramble, it is hard to make formulas upon the matter that will fit everywhere. One believes "to overcome" will apply. One even hazards a further step—the bigger the thing you overcome, the greater will be your happiness. This again is relative, of course. Happiness is in a way a colored light, thrown on the stage of the world's action, sometimes illuminating a Hoyt farce, and sometimes a Shakespearean tragedy. There is Happiness, one is bound to admit, even in the successful leading of a paper german, there are obstacles enough to be overcome, as anyone who has tried it can tell you. But when Mr. Andree shall read from his sextant the latitude and longitude of *his* farthest North—as we all hope he has done already—he, too, in thinking of the obstacles he has overcome, will experience that same feeling which we must call by the same name of Happiness. It is a difference, an enormous difference, but a difference of degree, not of kind.

Successful overcoming of obstacles—that's the real fun you can have for your money, nor will anyone admire you so much as for this. The feeblest of us feel a thrill for the successful hero. We like the vicious, wicked determination that suggests the thorough-bred bull dog, we cannot but applaud the fellow who sits down in his closet and thinks and plans a certain action or course of life, and who grips his teeth together and clenches his fist till the knuckles whiten and says, "By God, I'll put it through," and *does* put it through *just* as he had planned it. I say we cannot help but admire that fellow, whether he has planned a cotillion or a train robbery or a Congo expedition. But whether we condemn or applaud, whether we put him on a waxed dancing floor, or in the penitentiary, or on a lecture platform, it is all one with him. He has overcome his obstacles. He has known Happiness.

Holiday Literature

The Chinese and California Girl Calendars —Remington's Great Sketches

The Wave, 16 (11 December 1897), 8.

There comes to hand a batch of Christmas calendars, artists' publications, almanacs and an alphabet, all of them of an excellence that astounds you.

The best local people first. Solly Walter strikes the Chinese note in a calendar illustrated by pen pictures of Chinese life that are very fetching. Mr. Walter has had wit enough to see the possibilities in the life nearest to hand, and has caught it, and reproduced it in his calendar, with a fidelity and appreciativeness that is bound to make his effort successful. One would especially recommend his calendar to eastern folk—did it need recommendation. The little sketches and drawings are of the intimate life and daily customs of the San Francisco Mongol, as we see him, and as perhaps he is seen nowhere else. Mr. Walter is a careful and accurate draughtsman as well as an artist, and his calendar is bound to be popular. That the public have appreciated the effort we may infer from the enormous sale, and from the fact that the publisher, A.M. Robertson, reports that the first edition is already exhausted.

Solly Walter has long been before the public of San Francisco, as an illustrator and a maker of pen and inks, but in her calendar, Gertrude Partington makes what is really her first bow to the Western world. She will bow to the world—The World—east of the Mississippi, before long. So much is said and signed, if the drawings in the *California Girl Calendar* are an earnest of her work. There is a touch of Remington—Frederic the Great—in her drawings, and, indeed, I remember when I first saw the cover picture of the hunting girl, I looked for F.R.'s cachet in the corner. The hunting girl is capital, even though one questions the great size of the horse's shoulder in comparison with the rest of his anatomy. Upon reflection, I cannot remember a single California illustrator, not even Peixotto, who has done any better figure work than this, unless it be, perhaps, Guy Rose. Best, and most exhilarating of all, Miss Partington is free from the influence of Gibson. In that, alone, she is to be congratulated. Again, Miss Partington knows how to draw a pretty girl, and that's a gift quite independent of all technical skill—a gift of which even such men as Kenyon Cox and Will Low are lamentably destitute. With all the accuracy of the drawing, and the freedom and security of the pen-movement, it's a very dear and lovable face underneath the old slouch hat, and the same is applicable to nearly every girl in the book.

Kemble has a *Coon Calendar* which, despite the greater fame of the man, is, to my notion, infinitely less pleasing than that of Miss Partington. It's a colored affair, published by R.H. Russell of New York, and will sell, no doubt, largely by reason of Mr. Kemble's previous reputation. Mr. Kemble's humor is too obvious, too direct to be very funny.

R.H. Russell & Son published two Christmas picture books: *An Alphabet* and *An Almanac of Twelve Sports*. Both are illustrated by William Nicholson, and the *Sports* has verses, by Kipling, to face each page. Both are thoroughly artificial, and strain hard after effect, but the result is pleasing. Mr. Nicholson has touched a new note in the jaded gamut of poster art. His style is the style of the Japanese sketch artist, with a suggestion from weird, mad Blake—heavy shadows that are one with the background, and dwindle gracefully and suddenly in fine, curved, sweeping outlines. There is a certain originality, or, rather, bizarre effect in the drawings, and the color schemes are beyond praise. One has to hold the page at arm's length, however, to get the proper effect. The verses by Kipling are written in a vein of pungent grim humor, the one on boating being especially fine.

But one keeps Remington's "drawings" to the last for the sake of the final word. There is only one Remington—Frederic the Great—as one elects to call him, and there never will be another. Fresh from these stunning pages one is tempted to place him even above Gibson, though comparisons between the men are impossible. The drawings make one feel rather proud of being American and western. You would like to open the book before the eyes of your French friends in Paris, or your English chums in London. The drawings make a panorama of the brutal, unleashed, splendid life that goes thundering along from Idaho to Texas. The life of the bronco-buster, the Indian, the half-breed and the soldier—brave, vigorous and finely American. And the drama of these pictures! "The Charge of Roman Nose," for instance. The "Fight Over a Water Hole," with its hit horses—the one so horribly, stiffly dead, and the other broken-backed and floundering. There is not a picture that is not crammed to the margin with action or suggestion, and there is many an *oil painting* on the walls of European galleries, that has not the pathos and feeling and truth of the 12 x 8 halftone reproduction that closes the volume, "The Twilight of the Indian." Remington's horses should be accorded a place in the world's art, beyond the mere transitory popularity of magazine illustration. Perhaps no artist who ever lived understands horse action so well as this American illustrator of ours; and, as for character, one has only to compare them with the stuffed, melodramatic lay figures of Rosa Bonheur to note how absolutely true they are, how thoroughly faithful to nature, how indisputably equine.

Cosmopolitan San Francisco

The Remarkable Confusion of Races in the City's "Quarter"

The Wave, 16, Christmas issue [18 December 1897], 4.

In a way San Francisco is not a city—or rather let us say, it is not *one* city. It is several cities. Make the circuit of these several cities and by the time you have come to the severalth you may say with some considerable degree of truth; "I have seen Peking and have walked the streets of Mexico, have looked on the life of Madrid, have rubbed elbows with Naples and Genoa, glanced in at Yokohama, even—though more remotely, perhaps—have known Paris and Berlin."

What is true of San Francisco is true of California. As yet we, out here, on the fringe of the continent, with the ocean before and the desert behind us, are not a people, we are peoples—agglomerate rather than conglomerate. All up and down the coast from Mexico to Oregon are scattered "little" Italies, "little" Spains, "little" Chinas, and even "little" Russias—settlements, colonies, tiny groups of nationalities flung off from the parent stock, but holding tightly to themselves, unwilling to mix and forever harking back to their native lands.

But it is a rather curious fact that, though the Anglo-Saxons are the great mining peoples, and though the confusion of nations in California is due almost solely to the rush for gold, it is, nevertheless, the *Latin* and not the *German* races that are in greater evidence among us. Ireland has stopped in New York and Boston and on the Atlantic seaboard, and it is hard to coax Germany across the Mississippi.

It is not hard to understand why Mexico should be here, and Spain is readily accounted for. But why the Chinaman? There are two almost iron-clad tendencies *against* his presence. First, the tendency in obedience to which nations move from East to West, and second, the bred-in-the-bone tendency of the Chinaman to stay where he is put, to live and labor and die within a ten mile radius of his birthplace. No nation in the world is more tenacious of the hearthstone than the Mongolian. Yet, of all the foreign colonies in California and San Francisco, none is larger or more distinct than the Chinese. A curious state of affairs when you think about it, and for which you can offer no explanation.

By way of parenthesis—and though they are only apparent by traces of former occupation—think for a moment how narrowly California escaped an influx of the Russians. Somewhere in the interior of Big White Land there must have been a tremendous crowding force along in the middle of the century, crowding the Russians up and up and up on to the shoulder of their country till they slid off and over into Alaska. They spread phenomenally and came steadily southward. There is even record of a clash between them and the early settlers. Sutter's fort, so an old guardian of the place once told me, was built ostensibly against the Indians, but in reality to resist the encroachment of the Russians. The Russian himself has left indications of himself in a block house or two or a fort or two, and even in the geographical names such as the *Russian* River. But no doubt the Alaskan purchase checked immigration from that quarter.

The aggregation of "little" Mexico, Italy and the like that makes a place for itself in San Francisco lies over on the other side of Chinatown and beyond the Barbary Coast. A good way to reach it is to follow the alleys of Chinatown, beginning at Waverly Place and going on through Spofford Alley and Gamblers' Alley, till you come out near Luna's restaurant. Strike out in any direction from Luna's and in a sense you will travel a thousand miles at every step. The best time to see "The Quarter," as Anglo-Saxon San Francisco has come to call the place, is on a Saturday evening, between seven and eight o'clock, along in August or early September. "All the world" is on the streets at that time, and not a store has its shutters up. The very fruit stalls are open for business.

There is no suggestion of the Anglo Saxon; neither in the speech of the sidewalk strollers, nor in the shop windows, nor in the wording of signs and advertisements; nor, fortunately, in the general demeanor and behavior of the people. They are wine-drinkers essentially, and they know how to drink. There must be some—as yet unexplained—connection between malt drinks and truculence. Occasionally—at large intervals—an inhabitant of San Francisco's Quarter knifes or pistols his fellow, but there is no fighting in the Quarter. The Latin is disputatious rather than quarrelsome, and when angry with his brother, with or without cause, prefers unostentatious murder to brutal thumpings, swung chairs and hurled bottles.

Then, too, our Mexicans, Italians and other people of the Quarter, take their pleasure in a different way. It is a grim and significant fact that when the German and the Irishman set about their amusement they go away from their homes. The Irishman, besides, goes away from his wife and children— one is speaking now of the mass of them. He forgathers with individuals of his own sex and disports himself in saloons and bars and the public parks, and his enjoyment is not complete unless he embroils himself in a fight. The German organizes interminable, more or less solemn, "basket picnics" on Sundays, locks up his house and goes "across the bay" for the day. You may see these families coming home by the score on any of the ferry boats late Sunday afternoon. The children's hats are stuck full of oak leaves, and the lunch baskets are crammed with wilted wildflowers.

The Latin inhabitant of San Francisco's Quarter takes his holiday at home. He—or she—lives in the street. Even when indoors the windows are wide open. The doorstep and open windows answer the purposes of the club. They are coigns of vantage where one may see the world go by. The women on the doorstep, the men on the sidewalk and the children in the street, is the arrangement most frequently met with.

On Sundays, the Anglo-Saxon goes to the country, the Latin goes to church and to mass. In the afternoon he amuses himself *chez lui*, goes to the theater, if he can, and crowds the gallery if there be an opera in town. In the evening he dines with his family at a restaurant, staying there, be it understood, until bedtime. Occasionally you will find him in one of the *Bocce* courts underneath Telegraph Hill, absorbed in the game, which one is inclined to believe is the stupidest game ever conceived by the mind of man.

Little Japan is more scattered, Yokohama is broken into bits of marquetry and set here and there in San Francisco, in back courts and *cul de sacs* and streets that have no outlet. The Jap is too eager for Western customs to keep his individuality long. He becomes Americanized as soon as he may. However, he organizes fencing clubs, which seem to be quite a feature of his social life among his fellows. On Sundays these clubs meet, (there is one of them in a court off Geary street, not far from Powell, and another in a small Japanese colony in Prospect Place, off Pine, between Powell and Stockton streets). The Japs get into their native regalia and fence with bamboo swords from dawn to dark. It is a strange idea of amusement, but no stranger than the Celt's love for actual fighting.

And the Chinaman. One leaves him to the last, for the sake of the last word, if ever there can be a last word said of the Chinaman. He is in the city but not of it. His very body must be carried back to Canton after his death, whither his money has gone already. He has brought to San Francisco and implanted here the atmosphere of the Mysterious East, that—short stories and Chinese plays to the contrary—must always remain an unknown, unknowable element to the West. No two races the world round could be more opposite than the Mongolian and Anglo-Saxon that are placed side by side in the streets of this strange city of the Occident. The Saxon is outspoken, the Mongolian indirect; the one is frank, the other secretive; the one is aggressive, the other stealthy; the one fears neither God, man nor the devil, the other is ridden with superstitions; the one is brusque, the other patient to infinity; the one is immoderate, the other self-restrained. But—it is well to remember this—the Chinaman is high-tempered and passionate to a degree, with finely-tempered nerves and much more sensitive temperament than the Westerner would care to give him credit for. His policy of self-repression is deceiving. In every Chinaman there is something of the snake and a good deal of the cat. If one knew him better one would hesitate longer before injuring him. He remembers things. The Presbyterian Mission is all very well, the police force and special detectives are all very well, but we can never know anything of the real Chinaman, can never have any real influence upon him, either to better his moral condition, or punish his crimes. Where else, in what other city in the world, could the Tongs fight with impunity from street to street? Where else would Little Pete have been shot to death in a public place and his murderers escape beyond all hope of capture?

With the Chinaman curiosity is considered a vice—almost a crime. Chinatown in San Francisco is as foreign to us—much more so—than a village in the interior of France or Spain. As a consequence Saxon visitors must be equally foreign in the eyes of the livers in Chinatown. If you went through a hamlet in France or Germany, far enough off the railroad, you would be stared out of countenance. Every doorway and window would be filled after your passage, and the very dogs would bark at your heels. But how is it with the visitor in Chinatown? Get down into the very lowest quarter, where the slave-girls are kept, where the Cantonese live, where Chinatown is most Chinese: Of the hundreds of silently shuffling Chinamen, not one will turn to look at you—they will hardly make way for you. You may go into their shops, their tea houses, their restaurants, their clubs, their temples—almost into their very living rooms. To those thousands of slit-like, slanting eyes you do not so much as exist.

Perverted Tales

EDITED BY FRANK NORRIS

The Wave, 16, Christmas issue [18 December 1897], 5-7.

The discovery of California by the editors of the Big Four Magazines of the East has had the lamentable result of crowding from their exalted places, heretofore so secure, a number of the world's most fascinating story-tellers. Their places have been filled from the ranks of that little army of youthful volunteers known as Les Jeunes. *As a lamentable result old idols have been overthrown, old gods forgotten, and the children in the market place no longer dance to the tune of the old pipes. Where once the old favorite received a check, he now receives a printed form with veiled reference to availability, guarded allusions to the plans of the editor—and his story. With the view to stemming the perverse tide of popular favor—whose ebb and flow are not reducible to any known law —and, if only for a moment, sounding again the old notes once so compelling, the editors of this paper have secured for publication a few of these rejected tales and here submit them to the public of the West. Their genuineness is as Caesar's wife, and if intentional evidence were wanting the opinions of experts in type-writing have been secured, which place their authenticity beyond fear and beyond reproach.*

THE 'RICKSHA THAT HAPPENED.

BY R——D K——G.

Ching-a-ring-a-ring ching-chaw
Ho, dinkum darkey.—*The unedited diary of Bahlamooca Tah.*

Jam yesterday and jam to-morrow
But never jam to-day.—*Native Proverb.*

> "*Who's* all right? Rudyard! Who? *Rudyard!*"
> —*Barrack-room ballad.*

There was a man once—but that's another story. Personally, I do not believe much of this story, however, you may have it for what it is worth, to me it was worth five thousand dollars per thousand words.

A friend of mine, who is a *jinricksha* down by Benares, told me this tale one hot evening outside the Tiddledtypore gate. In the telling of it he spat reflectively and often into the moat. *Chaprassi simpkin peg*, as Mrs. Hawkseye says.

Mulligatawney, who is a private soldier and who dines with me at *table d'hôte* on Thursdays, and who shares my box at the opera, says the tale is cheap at a gallon and a half of beer.

"Pwhat nex'!" exclaimed Mulligatawney, when he heard it, shifting his quid to the other side of his mouth (we were at table). "It's *jaddoo*, that's phwat ut is. 'Tis flyin' in the face uv natoor to trifle with such brutil and licenshous soldiery as me and Orf-of-this an' Lear-eyed." Here he stole a silver spoon to hide his emotion. "'*Choop*,' sez oi to 'im," said Mulligatawney, filling himself another *jinricksha*, "'*choop*,' an' he *chooped*, like *ghairun* gone clane *dal-bat* an' *Kipiri* in hot weather. I waz only a recruity then. But I waz a corpril wanst. I was rejuced aftherwards, but I waz a corpril wanst," and he stared mournfully at the dying embers in the *jinricksha*.

We are a terrible bad lot out here in Indiana, but we can't help that. Here a man's whole duty is to lie *doggo* and not *ekka* more than once a week, and to pray for a war. Also he may keep a *jinricksha* in his stable if he can afford it. As that wonderful woman, Mrs. Hawkseye, says: "It's better to *bustee* in a *jampanni* than to have your *jinricksha puckarowed*." But that's her affair.

Stepterfetchit had just come out from *home*. Now when a man comes out from home, if he is not *jinrickshaed* at the pier landing, he generally does one of three things (*jampanni chorah simpkin bungalow*), either he dies with swiftness, which is bad, or lives with swiftness, which is worse, or marries, which is the worst of all. "A single man," says my friend Mulligatawney, "is an ornamint to the service." But as Lear-eyed observes, "when a mon is tewed wi' a lass he's *lokri* in a *bunder*, nothing but *dikh*," and he flung himself (seven foot four of British soldier), full length upon his *jinricksha*.

Stepterfetchit knew as much of Life (Life with a big L) as a weaning child, until I, who have seen everything worth seeing, and done everything worth doing, and have known everything worth knowing, from Indian magic to the cleaning of codfish, took him in hand. He began by contradicting his colonel, and went on from that to making love to Mrs. Hawkseye (till that lady told him he was a *bungalow*, with no more *pukaree* than a *dacoit*), and wound up by drinking too much *jinricksha* at his club.

Now, when a man takes to the *jinricksha* he is very likely to end at the *shroff*. So I spoke to the Major. You may hit a *marumutta* over the head at the beginning of your acquaintance, but you must not soap the tail of a kitten that belongs to a *Ryotwary*, unless you are prepared to prove it on his front teeth. It takes some men a lifetime to find this out, but the knowledge is useful. *Simpkin peg, do re mi fa, ching-a-ring-a-ring-ching-chaw*, but that's another story. We arrived—the Major and I—at Stepterfetchit's *dak-bungalow* on a red hot evening, when the heat blanketed the world like a hot towel round a swelled head. We nearly killed the *jinricksha* in getting there, but a mountain bred can *gawbry* more *jhil* than you would care to believe.

"Hark!" said the Major. We paused on the threshold and the silence of the Indian twilight gathered us in its hollow palms. We both heard a sound that came from Stepterfetchit's window. It was the ticking of an eight-day clock.

People write and talk lightly of blood running cold and of fear and all that sort of thing, but the real sensation is quite too terrible to be trifled with. As the Major and I heard the ticking of that eight-day clock, it is no lie to say that the *bhisti mussick* turned *shikary* in our *khitmatgar*. We were afraid. The Major entered the *bungalow* and I followed and *salaamed* the

216

door behind me.

The *jinricksha* lay dead on the *charpoy* in Stepterfetchit's room. Stepter-fetchit must have killed it hours before. "We came too late," groaned the Major. We made no attempt to keep from crying—I respected my self for that. But we gathered up the pieces of the *jinricksha* and sent them to Step-terfetchit's people at Home.

So now you know what I know of the 'Ricksha That Never Was.

Stepterfetchit is now a plate-layer somewhere down near Bareilly, on the line of the railroad, near the *Kharki* water tanks that the Rajah of Bathtub built out of stolen government money, when the commissariat bullock train was *puckarowed* by Pathans, in the days of the old *budmash* Mahommud Di-nare, and Mulligatawney is away annexing Burmah. When he heard of the affair he said:

"If a *punkah* is goin' to *ayah* niver loose your grip, but I waz a corpril wanst, I was rejuced afterwards," which is manifestly unfair.

Mrs. Hawkseye says that a "*jinricksha* in the hand gathers no moss"—but that's another story.

THE GREEN STONE OF UNREST.

BY S——N CR——E.

A Mere Boy stood on a pile of blue stones. His attitude was regardant. The day was seal brown. There was a vermillion valley containing a church. The church's steeple aspired strenuously in a direction tangent to the earth's center. A pale wind mentioned tremendous facts under its breath with cer-tain effort at concealment to seven not-dwarfed poplars on an un-distant mauve hilltop.

The Mere Boy was a brilliant blue color. The effect of the scene was not un-kaleidoscopic.

After a certain appreciable duration of time the Mere Boy abandoned his regardant demeanor. The strenuously aspiring church steeple no longer pro-jected itself upon his consciousness. He found means to remove himself from the pile of blue stones. He set his face valleyward. He proceeded.

The road was raw umber. There were in it wagon ruts. There were in it pebbles, Naples yellow in color. One was green. The Mere Boy allowed the idea of the green pebble to nick itself into the sharp edge of the disc of his Perception.

"Ah," he said, "a green pebble."

The rather pallid wind communicated another Incomprehensible Fact to the paranthine trees. It would appear that the poplars understood.

"Ah," repeated the Mere Boy, "a Green Pebble."

"Sho-o," remarked the wind.

The Mere Boy moved appreciably forward. If there were a thousand men in a procession and nine hundred and ninety-nine should suddenly expire, the one man who was remnant would assume the responsibility of the procession.

The Mere Boy was an abbreviated procession.

The blue Mere Boy transported himself diagonally athwart the larger landscape, printed in four colors, like a poster.

On the uplands were chequered squares made by fields, tilled and otherwise. Cloud-shadows moved from square to square. It was as if the Sky and Earth were playing a tremendous game of chess.

By and by the Mere Boy observed an Army of a Million Men. Certain cannon, like voluble but non-committal toads with hunched backs, fulminated vast hiccoughs at unimpassioned intervals. Their own in-vulnerableness was offensive.

An officer of blue serge waved a sword, like a picture in a school history. The non-committal toads pullulated with brief red pimples and swiftly relapsed to impassivity.

The line of the Army of a Million Men obnubilated itself in whiteness as a line of writing is blotted with a new blotter.

"Go teh blazes b'Jimminy," remarked the Mere Boy. "What yeh's shooting fur? They might be people in that field."

He was terrific in his denunciation of such negligence. He debated the question of his ir-removability.

"If I'm goin' teh be shot," he observed; "if I'm goin' teh be shot, b'Jimminy——"

* * * * * * * *

A Thing lay in the little hollow.

The little hollow was green.

The Thing was pulpy white. Its eyes were white. It had blackish-yellow lips. It was beautifully spotted with red, like tomato stains on a rolled napkin.

The yellow sun was dropping on the green plain of the earth, like a twenty-dollar gold piece falling on the baize cloth of a gaming table.

The blue serge officer abruptly discovered the punctured Thing in the Hollow. He was struck with the ir-remediableness of the business.

"Gee," he murmured with interest. "Gee, it's a Mere Boy."

The Mere Boy had been struck with seventy-seven rifle bullets. Seventy had struck him in the chest, seven in the head. He bore close resemblance to the top of a pepper castor.

He was dead.

He was obsolete.

As the blue serge officer bent over him he became aware of a something in the Thing's hand.

It was a green pebble.

"Gee," exclaimed the blue serge officer. "A green pebble, gee."

The large Wind evolved a threnody with reference to the seven un-distant poplars.

A HERO OF TOMATO CAN.

BY B——T H——TE.

Mr. Jack Oak-hearse calmly rose from the table and shot the bartender of Tomato Can, because of the objectionable color of his hair. Then Mr. Oak-hearse scratched a match on the sole of his victim's boot, lit a perfumed cigarette and strolled forth into the street of the camp to enjoy the evening air. Mr. Oak-hearse's face was pale and impassive, and stamped with that indefinable hauteur that marks the professional gambler. Tomato Can knew him to be a cool, desperate man. The famous Colonel Blue-bottle was reported to have made the remark to Miss Honorine Sainte-Claire, when that leader of society opened the Pink Assembly at Toad-in-the-Hole, on the other side of the Divide, that he, Colonel Blue-bottle, would be everlastingly "—— ——ed if he didn't believe that that —— ——ed Oak-hearse would open a ——ed jack-pot on a pair of ——ed tens, ——ed if he didn't." To which Miss Ste.-Claire had responded:

"Fancy now."

On this occasion as Mr. Jack Oak-hearse stepped into the cool evening air of the Sierras from out of the bar of the hotel of Tomato Can, he drew from his breast pocket a dainty manicure set and began to trim and polish his slender, almost feminine finger nails, that had been contaminated with the touch of the greasy cards. Thus occupied he betook himself leisurely down the one street of Tomato Can, languidly dodging an occasional revolver bullet, and stepping daintily over the few unburied corpses that bore mute testimony to the disputatious and controversial nature of the citizens of Tomato Can. He arrived at his hotel and entered his apartments, gently waving aside the half-breed Mexican who attempted to disembowel him on the threshold. The apartment was crudely furnished as befitted the rough and ready character of the town of Tomato Can. The Wilton carpet on the floor was stained with spilt Moët and Chandon. The full-length portrait of Mr. Oak-hearse by Carolus Duran was punctured with bullet marks, while the teakwood escritoire, inlaid with buhl and jade, was encumbered with Bowie knives, spurs and Mexican saddles.

Mr. Oak-hearse's valet brought him the London and Vienna papers. They had been ironed, and scented with orris root, and the sporting articles blue-penciled.

"Bill," said Mr. Oak-hearse, "Bill, I believe I told you to cut out all the offensive advertisements from my papers; I perceive, with some concern, that you have neglected it. Your punishment shall be that you will not brush my silk hat next Sunday morning."

The valet uttered an inarticulate cry and fell lifeless to the floor.

"It's better to stand pat on two pair than to try for a full hand," mused

Mr. Oak-hearse, philosophically, and his long lashes drooped wearily over his cold steel-blue eyes, like velvet sheathing a poignard.

A little later the gambler entered the dining-room of the hotel in evening-dress, and wearing his cordon of the Legion of Honor. As he took his accustomed place at the table, he was suddenly aware of a lustrous pair of eyes that looked into his cold gray ones from the other side of the catsup bottle. Like all heroes, Mr. Jack Oak-hearse was not insensible to feminine beauty. He bowed gallantly. The lady flushed. The waiter handed him the menu.

"I will have a caviar sandwich," affirmed the gambler with icy impassivity. The waiter next handed the menu to the lady, who likewise ordered a caviar sandwich.

"There is no more," returned the waiter. "The last one has just been ordered."

Mr. Oak-hearse started, and his pale face became even paler. A preoccupied air came upon him, and the lines of an iron determination settled upon his face. He rose, bowed to the lady, and calmly passed from the dining-room out into the street of the town and took his way toward a wooded gulch hard by.

When the waiter returned with the caviar sandwich he was informed that Mr. Oak-hearse would not dine that night. A triangular note on scented mauve paper was found at the office begging the lady to accept the sandwich from one who had loved not wisely but too many.

But next morning at the head of the gulch on one of the largest pine trees the searchers found an ace of spades (marked) pinned to the bark with a Bowie knife. It bore the following, written in pencil with a firm hand:

Here lies the body
of
JOHN OAK-HEARSE,
who was too much of a gentleman
to play a
Royal-flush
against a
Queen-full.

And so, pulseless and cold with a Derringer by his side and a bullet in his brain, though still calm as in life lay he who had been at once the pest and the pride of Tomato Can.

VAN BUBBLES' STORY.

———

BY R——D H——G D——S.

———

Young Charding-Davis had been a little unhappy all day long because on that particular morning the valet of his head serving man had made a mistake in the matter of his master's trousers, and it was not until he was breakfasting at Delmonico's some hours later that young Charding-Davis woke to the painful consciousness that he was wearing his serving-man's pants which were made by an unfashionable New York tailor. Young Charding-Davis himself ran over to London in his steam yacht once or twice a week to be fitted, so that the consequences of his serving-man's valet's mistake took away his appetite. The predicament troubled him so that he told the head cook about it, adding anxiously:

"What would you do about these trousers, Wallis?"

"I would keep 'em on, sir," said Wallis, touching his cap respectfully.

"That," said young Charding-Davis, with a sigh of relief, "is a good idea. Thank you, Wallis." Young Charding-Davis was so delighted at the novel suggestion that he tipped Wallis a little more generously than usual.

"Can you recommend a good investment for this?" inquired Wallis, as he counted out the tip.

"Make a bid for the Pacific railroads," suggested young Charding-Davis, "or 'arrive' at the Savoy Hotel."

That night he went to dinner at the house of the Girl He Knew, and in honor of the occasion and because he thought it would please the Girl He Knew, young Charding-Davis put on a Yale sweater and football knickerbockers and the headdress of feathers he had captured from a Soudanese Arab while acting as war correspondent for an English syndicate. Besides this, he wore some of his decorations and toyed gracefully with a golf-stick. During the dinner, while young Charding-Davis was illustrating a new football trick he had just patented, with the aid of ten champagne bottles and the Girl's pet Skye terrier, a great and celebrated English diplomat leaned across the table over the center piece of orchids and live hummingbirds, and said:

"I say, Davis, tell us how you came by some of your decorations and orders. Most interesting and extraordinary, you know."

Young Charding-Davis tossed the Skye terrier into the air, and batted it thoughtfully the length of the room with his golf-stick, after the manner of Heavyflinger of the Harvard baseball nine. Then he twirled the golf-stick in his fingers as a Zulu *induna* twirls his *assegai*—he had learned the trick while shooting elephant on the Zambesi river in South Africa. Then he smiled with becoming modesty as he glanced carelessly at the alarm-clock that hung around his neck, suspended by the blue ribbon of the order of the Pshaw of Persia.

"Really, they are mere trifles," he replied, easily. "I would not have worn them only my serving man insists it is good form. The Cham of Tartary gave me this," he continued, lightly touching a nickel-plated apple-pie plate that was pinned upon the sweater, "for leaving the country in twenty-four hours, and this chest protector was presented me by the French Legation in Kamschatka for protecting a chest——but we'll let that pass," he said, enveloping himself with a smile of charming ingenuousness. "*This* is the badge of the Band of Hope to which I belong. I got this pie-plate from the Grand Mufti for conspicuous egoism in the absence of the enemy, and this Grand Army badge from a pawnbroker for four dollars. Then I have a few swimming medals for swimming across Whirlpool Rapids and a five-cent piece given me by Mr. Sage. I have several showcases full of other medals in my rooms. I'm thinking of giving an exhibition and reception, if I could get some pretty girls to receive with me. I've knocked about a bit, you know, and I pick them up here and there. I've crossed Africa two or three times, and I got up the late Greek war in order to make news for the New York papers, and I'm organizing an insurrection in South America for the benefit of a bankrupt rifle manufacturer who wants to dispose of some arms."

While Charding-Davis had been speaking young Van Bubbles, who was just out of the interior of Uganda, had been absent-mindedly drawing patterns in the tomato catsup he had spilled on the table-cloth.

"When I returned from Africa this morning," he said, "I had a curious experience." He fixed Charding-Davis with his glance for a moment, and then let it wander to a corner of the room and afterward drew it back and tied it to his chair leg. Charding-Davis grew a little pale, but he was too well bred to allow his feelings to overcome him. Young Van Bubbles continued:

"I met an old valet of mine on Fifth avenue, who has recently been engaged by the head serving man of one of New York's back-parlor heroes. He was wearing a pair of trousers which seemed to me strangely familiar, and when I spoke to him about the matter, broke down and confessed that he had caused his master's master to exchange trousers with him. You see the point of the story is," concluded young Van Bubbles, untying his glance, and allowing it to stray toward Charding-Davis, who drove it away with his golf-stick, "that the back-parlor hero wore his valet's trousers to-day."

There was a silence.

"What an extraordinary story," murmured the diplomat.

"Quite so," said the Girl Charding-Davis Knew.

"Of course," added Van Bubbles, "I took the trousers from him. Here they are," he continued, dropping them on the table. "You see they were no more use to him. I thought, perhaps"—and once more his glance crept stealthily toward young Charding-Davis—"*you* might suggest a way out of the difficulty." He handed the trousers to Charding-Davis, saying: "Keep them, they are a mere trifle, and they may be of some interest to you."

The Girl Charding-Davis Knew saw the point of Van Bubbles' story at once. Charding-Davis tried to catch her eye, but she refused to look at him, and said to her father:

"Why won't he go away? Tell him to go away, please."

On the steps outside the house young Charding-Davis reflected what next he should do. He strolled slowly homeward, and, as he came into his rooms, his head serving-man handed him two notes which had arrived in his absence. One was from the Most Beautiful Woman in New York offering him her hand and fortune; the other was written on the back of a ten thousand dollar check, and was from the Editor of the Greatest Paper in the World begging him to accept the vacant throne of the Nyam-Nyam of Khooinooristan in the capacity of Special Correspondent.

"I wonder now," said young Charding-Davis, "which of these offers I shall accept."

AMBROSIA BEER.

———

BY A——E B——E.

———

Sterling Hallmark was one of the most prominent and enthusiastic members of the Total Abstinence Union of San Francisco. His enthusiasm was not only of the passive description. He took a delight in aiding the police in their raids upon the unlicensed beer halls of the Barbary Coast. He helped them break whisky and brandy flasks, and he himself often opened the spigots of the beer kegs and let the foaming liquid run out upon the sanded floor.

On the night of the thirtieth of February, 1868, Sterling Hallmark led the police in a furious attack upon the "Hole in the Wall," a notorious subterranean dive in the vicinity of Jackson street. The battle was short and decisive. The bartender and his assistants were routed and the victorious assailants turned their attention to the demolition of the unsavory resort. Bottles were broken, brandy flasks smashed, the contents of the decanters emptied. In the midst of the confusion Sterling Hallmark advanced with splendid intrepidity towards a large keg, bearing the inscription Ambrosia Beer, extra pale. He set his hand upon the spigot.

But at that moment a terrific crash rent the air. The frail building, in the cellar of which the "Hole in the Wall" was situated, collapsed because it was necessary it should do so at that precise instant for the purposes of this tale. The crazy edifice fell with a loud clatter and clouds of blinding dust.

When Sterling Hallmark recovered consciousness he was not for the moment aware of what had happened. Then he realized that he was uninjured, but that he was unmovably pinioned beneath a mass of debris, and that something was weighing heavily upon his chest. Looking up and around him he perceived in the dim light a ring of metal protruding from a dark object that lay upon his chest. As his senses adjusted themselves to his environment he saw that the dark object was the keg of Ambrosia Beer, and that the ring of metal was the mouth of the spigot. The mouth of the spigot was directly in the line of his lips and not two inches distant from them. The terrible question that now confronted Sterling Hallmark was this: Had he opened that spigot before the collapse of the building, was the keg full or empty? He now found that by great exertion he could move his right arm so that his fingers could touch and clasp the spigot. A horrible fear came upon Sterling Hallmark; drops of cold perspiration bespangled his brow; he tried to cry out, but his voice failed him. His mouth was dry. A horrible thirst tortured him—a thousand fiends seemed shouting to him to open the spigot, unseen hands tugged at *his* free hand. He raised this hand to cover his eyes from the sight, but as he withdrew it again it dropped upon his breast two inches nearer the fatal spigot. At length the strain became too great to be borne, Sterling Hallmark became desperate. He laughed aloud in almost insensate glee.

"Ha, Ha!" exclaimed Sterling Hallmark.

He reached up and grasped the spigot and turned it with all his strength.

* * * * * *

An hour later when the rescue party with axes and hatchets found their way into the cellar of the "Hole in the Wall," the foremost of them hauled out Sterling Hallmark.

"Thash a' ri' girlsh," screamed the unfortunate man as his rescuers tried to keep him on his feet. "Thash a' ri', I ne'r him feelsh sho 'appy, az-I-do-t'-ni'. Les op'n 'n'er li'l' bo'l', girlsh." The patrol wagon was rung for, and the raving inebriate was conveyed to the City Hall. The ride in the open air, however, had the effect of sobering him. He realized that he, Sterling Hallmark, temperance leader, had been *drunk*. He also realized that he could not stand the disgrace that would now inevitably follow him through life. He drew his revolver, and ere the policeman who accompanied him could interfere, had sent a bullet crashing through his brain.

* * * * * *

A few moments after the patrol wagon had departed one of the rescue party discovered the keg labelled Ambrosia Beer, that had been rolled from the breast of Sterling Hallmark. With a few well-directed blows of his ax, he smashed in the head of the keg, and thrust his hand down to the bottom, groping about.

The interior of the keg was full of dust and rusty nail-heads.

"Empty for over a year," he exclaimed, in tones of bitter disappointment.

I CALL ON LADY DOTTY.

FROM *THE POLLY PARABLES*

By AN——Y H——PE.

Like most women, Lady Dotty is in love with me—a little. Like most men, I am in love with Lady Dotty—a great deal.

Last Thursday afternoon at five o'clock, as I was strolling in St. James' Park (you may have remarked that I always stroll—in St. James' Park—on Thursday afternoons) it occurred to me to call on Lady Dotty. I forthwith presented myself at the house (it is by Van Burgh).

After I had waited some five minutes in the drawing-room Lady Dotty appeared.

"But I am not at home," she said on the threshold. "I am not at home, Mr. Carterer."

"Nor am I," I replied.

"And my husband is——"

"At home?"

"At his club."

"The brute," said I, "to leave you alone."

"There are others," she sighed, with half a glance at me.

I had not called in a fortnight.

"I have languished in self-imposed solitude," I murmured with some gallantry.

"Why have you not been to see me in so long?"

"My laundress——" I began.

"Your *laundress*, Mr. Carterer?"

"Refused to relent."

"You poor dear. Tea?"

"You are too kind," said I, with a bow.

Lady Dotty's maid, a delicious young creature named Négligée, appeared with the tray and smoking cups and vanished.

Lady Dotty handed me my cup.

"Sit down," she ordered.

There was but one chair in the room. I sat down.

Lady Dotty—also sat down.

"Clarence is a beast," she said.

"Most husbands are."

"Sometimes they are not."

"When?"

"When they are other women's husbands."

"Wives," I remarked, "of other men are no less so."

"Why can't other men's wives marry other women's husbands?" suggested Lady Dotty.

"The question is worthy of consideration," said I.

Négligée hurriedly entered at this point of our conversation.

"The husband of Madame," she exclaimed.

"Good heavens," said Lady Dotty.

I took my hat.

"Fly, Mr. Carterer," cried Lady Dotty.

"This way," murmured Négligée. "Follow me." She led me out into the dark hall, where the back stairs were.

"It is rather dark, sir. You were best to give me your hand."

"And my heart," I answered.

Our hands clasped.

It was, as Négligée remarked, rather dark.

The charming creature's face was close to mine.

"Were you ever kissed?" said I, boldly.

"I don't know how to kiss," said Négligée.

"We might put our heads together and find out how," I suggested.

As I say, Négligée is a delicious young creature. But a man never knows the usefulness of his watch until he is without it—to say nothing of his scarfpin.

[half-tone: Perverted Tales]

Courtesy of the California State Library, Sacramento.

Little Drama of the Curbstone

A Merry Christmas

The Wave, 16, Christmas issue [18 December 1897], 7.

This is really the setting forth of a little drama that I did not see—that is with my actual material eyes, and I presume that one should not see little uglinesses at Christmas time, far less pinion them in cold type. However—

It was rather late on the afternoon of the day before Christmas. The streets were crowded, everyone had parcels in their arms. The street lamps had just been lighted. There was a note of gaiety in the air, and a certain exuberant nimbleness.

Near the corner of a side street I came across a fairly-dressed respectable woman of the middle class, gowned in black, (naturally) bonneted and veiled. In her arms she carried a number of parcels and packages, a doll or two no doubt, to judge from appearances, a box of lead soldiers (one could fancy them lying on cardboard over a layer of excelsior) and one particular toy that was not wrapped up—a wooden horse, dapple gray, like all wooden horses, with very erect ears and goggle eyes. Just as I passed her, the woman turned up the side street with, I cannot define just what peculiarity of gait and demeanor, that made me turn and watch her. She stopped a moment and leaned her hand upon a bit of iron railing. Then I saw that she was drunk. She moved on almost directly, but stumbled and fell upon the sidewalk, spilling the lead soldiers upon the pavement and breaking the forelegs of the goggle-eyed horse.

Forgotten History

Judge Waymire's Fight with the Snake Indians

The Wave, 16, Christmas issue [18 December 1897], 10.

In such a big country as ours, with a Government so stable and all danger of "foreign complications" eliminated, things can, and do, happen almost unnoticed that with almost every other nation would be shouted from the house tops and trumpeted at the street corners.

In the matter of frontier fights—some of them veritable battles—the difference between us and Europeans is singularly noticeable. Wilson and his twenty-one men of the B.B.P. are destroyed on the banks of the Shanghani in Matabeleland, and the event is copy for nearly six months in every journal and weekly illustrated the world round. But to how many Americans is the word "Alamo" suggestive? Dr. Jameson raids the Transvaal and has a man or two shot, and the affair assumes international importance, and a flying squadron is organized. But "Wounded Knee Creek" and the "Pine Ridge Agency" were but a nine days' story with us. Who commanded the U.S. troops in the business? It's fair betting that you cannot tell.

This forgetfulness of, or rather indifference to, our best men was suggested to me by a recent article in the Seattle *Post-Intelligencer* relative to ex-Judge James O. Waymire and one of his Indian fights in Oregon in the sixties.

He was teaching school in Oregon when the Civil War broke out. There were some companies of regulars in the county, but they were withdrawn from the frontiers of Oregon, Washington and Idaho and sent East. They had to have men to take their places, for the Indians were very bad. Young Waymire adjourned school and took a good part of the money he had saved up against going to Harvard, bought an equipment, and enlisted as a private soldier in a newly formed cavalry regiment. That was in '61. They made him a Corporal early in '63, and in April of that year he was promoted to Lieutenant. They had some little fun with the Indians that summer, but it was not until along in February of '64 that the real show began. There were some settlements along John Day's river, extending over a length of 100 miles or more. The Indians had been raiding these, cutting up a few settlers, burning houses and acting nasty generally. General Alvord, who commanded the department, thought it was about time to stop it. He ordered Waymire to protect the settlers, and gave him twenty-five men to do it with. He was twenty-one at the time. It was a pretty big order for a boy, one that would now call for a general and a regiment. Alvord had said, "Act on your own judgment." Waymire hadn't any more than got upon the river when he got news that the Indians had jumped a camp near Canyon City, killed six miners and stampeded all the horses they could find. They had gone to the south. No one knew where their winter quarters were. He saw it wasn't any manner of use to attempt to protect the settlers by waiting till the Indians attacked them. The only thing to do was to get after them in their own country. A volunteer company of fifty-four miners was raised, and started in pursuit of the band. One of the volunteers was made Captain, and a good Captain he was, too—Joaquin Miller, our poet of the Sierras. That expedition was one of the hardest and roughest ever made. It was through and over the Blue Mountains, covered with snow. Every day it stormed and snowed. The men had no tents, and had to carry every ounce of their supplies on pack animals. When they wanted forage for the horses they dug under the snow to get it. Then when the snow ceased the cold rain began. When the rain quit they had an epidemic of measles. Most discouraging of all, twenty-two of the volunteers backed out and went home, unable or unwilling to endure such hardships. The Lieutenant went on with what was left, marching on week after week. All of a sudden, when least expecting it, he marched right onto an Indian village. They didn't wait to form, but rushed in just as they were. The Indians cut, and left everything but their horses and arms. It was just before dark. By 3 the next morning the Lieutenant was hot on their trail. He followed them for about 20 miles to the south all that day, and by noon the scouts brought in word that within a quarter of a mile there were about 450 bucks, who wanted to fight so bad it made them sick. To meet them Waymire and Miller had about 50 men. Older men would perhaps have hesitated; but those boys never thought of delay. The show began at once. Why they weren't massacred where they stood is hard to explain. It was one of the hardest fights in the history of

Indian warfare. The soldiers lost five men and as many horses. The Indians lost 23 killed and as many wounded. One charge after another was repelled, until it was too dark to see the rifle sights. The little army rested with rifles in hand through the night, or rather laid down on arm, ready to begin next morning. But next morning the Indians were gone. They'd had enough. And after that fight they let the settlers alone for many years. It was for this service, as the *Post-Intelligencer* says, that Lieutenant Waymire was "mentioned in the dispatches" and complimented by his chief in the general orders. Writing of this same expedition the Adjutant-General of Oregon said:

> The report of Lieutenant Waymire, of Co. D., First Oregon Cavalry, will be found very interesting, and his encounter with the Snake Indians near Harney Lake was undoubtedly the hardest fought battle in which our troops participated, and evinces a coolness and courage on the part of the Lieutenant and soldiers worthy of notice. Should any future occasion call Lieutenant Waymire again to the field I have no doubt he would rank high as a military leader.

The Postal Telegraph

Its Web of Wires Extends the World Around

The Wave, 16, Christmas issue [18 December 1897], 20.

That familiarity breeds contempt is a saying so familiar that we are in danger of entertaining a contempt for the saying itself. Half a century ago the statement of the fact that by stepping into a certain office we in San Francisco could talk to Paris or to Vienna would have landed the fellow making it in an asylum. But to-day the globe is wrapped in telegraph wire as a boy's baseball is wrapped with string, and continent and city gossip together as so many old maids on a hotel veranda, often about matters no less trivial.

The Pacific Postal Telegraph Company's offices on Market street, in this city, are a never-failing wonder to anyone who has his mind open for impression and suggestion. Inside it rattles and hums and clicks like an army of crickets or like a vast and continuous discharge of tiny rifles, rifles that fire shots that are quite literally "heard around the world." This office is the center of a web of wires so long, so complete, so infinite in their ramifications that even the heads of the company cannot say within three or four thousand miles just how long they are. With their connections it has been estimated that these wires would, if put together in a single line, circle the world eight times.

The sender of a dispatch, let us say, to Durban, on the east coast of South Africa—for even that remote spot can be reached by the Postal Telegraph Company's wire web—steps into the splendid offices on Market street, shining with marble and mahogany and polished brass, writes his message and passes it over the counter. In due course of time the message is put on the wire. The sender of the dispatch can go his way assured that the company will see his message through. One mistake in a thousand chances is, perhaps, a fair average.

San Francisco takes the message and flings it across the layers of sand and sage brush to Chicago, and Chicago to New York. Then down it goes under the Atlantic—on the Commercial Cable Company's line with which the Postal Telegraph has connections—under the Atlantic and on to Southampton. Southampton relays it to Funchal, on the Madeira Islands, and a lazy, straw-hatted, white-pantalooned Portuguese whips it across the ocean to the equator past the Peak of Teneriffe to the French station on the Senegal coast of Africa. Then relay after relay sends it down the coast. It doubles the Cape of Good Hope, and Cape Town throws it on to Kimberley, and Kimberley—at last—passes it over to Durban. And this about the time the sender of the message is sitting down to supper on the day of the sending.

It would be hard to find a corner of the world which could not be reached by the Postal Telegraph Company. The office is a ganglia, a nerve center on the body of the earth not only for the transmission, but also for the reception of news and messages. Not an important event happens between the five oceans that the reverberation of it is not instantly felt in the Market-street office. Sometimes we are apt to underestimate the value of such a colossal invention as the telegraph. But at a time like this it would be well to try to imagine what we would do if every wire on earth were cut to-morrow, or if even half of them were cut. It would have much the same effect upon the world at large as a stunning blow on the back of the head has upon an individual. It would not be far from paralysis.

Scene Mounting of the Future

The Wave, 16 (25 December 1897), 2.

Suggestions from a laic and his opinions may not always be devoid of value nor deficient in interest to the initiated in any of the professions or arts, fine or otherwise. For it is often permitted to the layman to stand often far enough off from the production of his more deeply versed brother to judge of general effects, unhampered by consideration of detail and untrammelled by the limitations of technicalities whose value—though the initiated would probably deny this—is often disproportionately exaggerated. In a recent speech at a dramatists' dinner in London, Henry Arthur Jones remarked:

> I have been watching real life for more than thirty years, and it has never offered me any one single scene that could be put on the stage. The drama can never be like real life, chiefly because the playwright has to concentrate all his action within the merest fraction of the time that would be taken in real life, and because he has to concentrate all his action in a few small definite stationary scenes. The necessity of concentrating his action brings the dramatist every moment into contact with the thousand inessential facts and worthless trivialities which are the adjuncts of real life everywhere and at all times. There is no way of representing these trivialities on the stage; they have no place there; they merely bore the spectator and take away the time and patience which he is ready to give to weightier matters. Notwithstanding the impossibilities for the dramatist to imitate real life, he should, of course, give an

illusion of real life, and the art of creating this illusion is the art of the dramatist.

As the stage—using the word in its narrowest, most literal and material sense—as the stage is now constructed and set, the restrictions upon portraying real life realistically, as defined by Mr. Jones, are, no doubt of great force. However, one is oftentimes inclined to wonder if a day is ever coming which shall witness and inaugurate a New Drama and a New Stage, a sort of revolution in stage mounting. As matters stand now the mounting of plays—even of the very best—is absurdly disappointing, canvas flats representing solid stone, that wobble at a touch, doors that open only one way, landscapes and ploughed fields that bulge and billow in a draught of air, absurd arrangement of artificial lights, hard wooden floors, resounding hollowly to the tread, doing duty for grass plots and solid earth. The veriest tyro, the most ignorant backwoodsmen would not for an instant be deceived by the most carefully mounted scene in all Bernhardt's repertoire. He is not even expected to be deceived. Then why should it be done at all? Scenic effect is not all necessary to the interest of a play. The greatest dramas ever written, *Oedipus Tyrannos*, *Hamlet*, *The Cid* and so many others, dispensed with everything but the veriest essentials. The front of a temple or palace, with three doors, sufficed for Sophocles. Signs and placards were all that Shakespeare depended upon. Corneille managed with scarcely more than a raised platform. Fancy Corneille, Shakespeare and the Greek in the pit of a modern theatre. It is not improbable that the first criticism of latter-day methods from the lips of the ancient masters would be to the effect that the clumsiness of the mounting (pretending so much and falling so wretchedly short) distracted attention from the action of the play itself, was more—much more—of a hindrance than a help. Half measures are bad measures, and sometimes are ludicrous enough. *L'Africaine* as performed at the Paris *Opéra*, contains one scene in which Vasco da Gama puts his ship about. The effect is stupendous, sailors hauling and chanting at the ropes— the helm hard over—the yards swinging around—the bowsprit describing an arc on the horizon. The whole superstructure of the imitation ship moves around, masts, cabin, rails and all. *The deck, that is to say the floor of the stage, is absolutely stationary.* Vasco da Gama on the bridge turns with the turning ship, his crew, like so many Casabiancas, are rooted to the moveless deck. The effect intended to be sublime, is only ridiculous.

236

When Patti and her opera troupe appeared for "positively the last time" in this city, the operas of *Trovatóre* and *Aïda* were given on succeeding nights in the order named. The same scenery was used for both operas. The identical Gothic flats and wings that had represented a feudal hall in *Trovatóre* were made to do duty for the throne room in the prehistoric Egyptian palace of *Aïda*.

A system and theory of mounting plays that can permit such monstrous incongruities to overcome us like a summer cloud without our special mention is manifestly wrong. Do away with the present idea of scene setting entirely, return to the simplicity of the Periclesian Greeks, or develop a new system.

It would not do merely to change the mounting of plays. The style of play must adapt itself to a change as well. One ventures to predict that the next century will see a new theater, wherein the principles of panoramic art will be applied to scene painting. There will be no footlights, but instead a powerful overhead light and lesser side lights. The back of the stage will be shaped (for outdoor scenes), like the inside of a dome, the audience will sit farther from the stage itself, grass mats will take the place of green baize, and the wings so arranged that the spectators at the side of the house will be unable to see around them. A new style of play will come into vogue that will be nearer to real life in just such proportion as the novels of to-day are nearer to it than those of the last century. The melodramatic, even the mildly dramatic, will decline—the tendency has always been in that direction —and things will happen on the stage—Henry Arthur Jones to the contrary —exactly as they have happened in real life, as they do now in Howells' novels. Either this, or we shall burn our painted flats, discharge our property men, tear up our costumes and return to the pure, chaste unadornment of the classical, where the action is everything and the scenery nil.

Sanitary Reduction

How the Refuse of San Francisco is Incinerated

The Wave, 16 (25 December 1897), 8-9.

A man named Victor Hugo said once that Paris threw some fifty or sixty million francs into the sea yearly, and he meant by this that the sweepings of the city were in a sense *munera pulveris*, and we all remember Mr. Bunyan's man with the muck rake, looking for gold in the pile of straw and offal.

A great city is subject to precisely the same laws and does many things in precisely the same way as a human being. We know the human body sloughs off appreciable quantities of dry scarf skin, dandruff and the like continually. A city does the same. This city does.

Far off beyond the railroad tracks, where Eighth street widens out into hideous vacant lots, blotted and spotted with soap factories and tallow chandleries, are what is known as the Sanitary Reduction Works. On your way down to your office in the morning, at almost every other block, you go wide round a dripping grisly cart, with an Italian driver on the seat, and you try not to breathe too hard through your nose until you get well away. Scavengers' carts these are, and they take the place of pores and ducts in the hide of the town. There are some three or four hundred of these carts that go the rounds of the street day after day, gathering offal, ashes, rags, bottles, sacks, dead cats and dogs, debris, cinders, tin cans, every imaginable and unimaginable description of castaway things, and carting them down the length of Eighth street, past the place where the football games are played and on across the railroad tracks and into those vague, hideous regions where the tallest chimney west of the Rocky Mountains grows out of the soil like a gigantic pine.

The reduction works are a private enterprise. There are thirty-seven furnaces burning night and day. Twenty-nine consuming the "heavy" and eight —called "auxiliary"—consuming the "light" garbage. "Heavy" garbage is all organic matter. The "light" is made up largely of tin cans, rags, ashes, etc. Anyone who may so desire can load a wagon with debris and bring it to the works, the works charging 20 cents per cubic yard at the gate for burning the stuff. But by far the greater number of carts are driven by Italians who have regular routes, and who, by the way, make very good money in the business. One is told that many of them are even property holders. "Light" garbage is burnt separately from the heavy, and the wagons dump according to the character of their loads. Once dumped, the stuff is picked over. The Italians—no other nationality, it seems, will do the work—pick over the heaps, by hand, largely, and such stuff as bottles, cans and jugs are treated separately. In such quantities tin is valuable and solder is not so very much below silver in price. Then there is the brass, then there is the copper, then there is the iron, melted and run into "pigs." There is no difficulty in selling such metal at good market figures.

At first it is hard to believe what advantage there is to be gained from a cart full of nasty rotting vegetables, and old fuzzy bones, and melon rinds and mashed fruit that reeks to Heaven. But when the stuff is burned it makes the best fertilizer known to agriculture. So that nothing is really lost or need ever be lost. What comes out of the earth goes into it again and so on to infinity. It is the dust to dust theory over again, only made practical and immensely profitable.

Five hundred tons is the figure of San Francisco's daily refuse and garbage. The sweat, as one might say, of the city in its exertion of one day's toil. Five hundred tons of perspiration. It is Gargantua over again and outdone. Five hundred a day is 156,000 tons a year, counting 312 working days to the year. For there is never any pause, Sundays are like week days, and the crews work in two gangs, one for the day and the other for the night, so the thirty-six furnaces are always burning. Perhaps one would wonder at this point as to the enormous quantities of coal and fuel used to fire these ceaselessly burning furnaces. The company does not pay one nickel for its coal; its fuel is at hand and inexhaustible; it has a constantly renewed supply of five hundred tons of refuse daily upon which to draw, which is consumed at the rate of 20 cents per ton. Refuse is good fuel, admirable even when once you have noted the tremendous draught that can be created at the base of the enormous chimney. Eight pounds to the square inch is the amount of the pressure, and when a furnace door is opened one can hear the air sucking in through the cracks of the building toward the open mouth of the furnace making a roaring noise like a gale in a vessel's rigging. The electric plant which is connected with the works and that furnishes the light by which the night work is carried on, is also run by the same means.

The force of men all told is between 80 and 100. They are divided up into firemen, feeders and pickers. The firemen are almost all Americans, the poker men and pickers Italians to a man. The poker man's duty consists merely in feeding the refuse into the hoppers of the furnaces, but the pickers are counted upon to sort the heaps. It often falls to the lot of this latter class of help to come across more than one article of value, perhaps of even very great value, a lost watch, perhaps, a bill, a diamond ring. There is absolutely no limit upon the variety of the wagon's contents. The picker-boss is supposed to report all such finds to the management, and a little later, when the works are running more smoothly, a "lost and found" department will be organized. This in time will be quite a feature of the place, and one of the most interesting exhibits imaginable could be made from the city's dumps. When you come to think of it, it is almost inevitable that every small article lost within the confines of the city will sooner or later find its way to the refuse heaps.

Dead cats and dogs as a matter of course take their last ride in the scavenger's cart and are accorded honorable cremation at the hands of the company, but occasionally when the carts are dumped "a live cat" terribly excited fights its way out of the cloud of dust and ashes, while the same load may contain an oil painting not illy done and in a fair state of preservation, as attested by one or two that are shown on the walls of the works and that have been rescued as brands from the burning, as one might say.

The reduction works of San Francisco are the largest in the world (it now represents over $150,000 invested), and covers a greater area than any others that have hitherto been erected. The process is known as the Thackeray patent incinerating and fertilizing system, and was invented by Charles Thackeray of this city. The fact that Mr. L.R. Ellert and his associates had the business foresight to see potential fortunes in a city's refuse is perhaps the most interesting feature of the whole affair.

Reviews in Brief

Crisp Comment on New Books, Christmas and Otherwise

The Wave, 16 (25 December 1897), 12.

There are some twenty or twenty-five books on the reviewer's table this week, every one of them new and still crisp from the press. They are the usual crop of Christmas fiction that comes with the holly and the mistletoe, growing on the Xmas tree, as it were. Many of them are bad, a few are good, and the rank and file even worse than bad, i.e., passable, with no good errors and no bad graces—the books that do not fail because they do not attempt. One wonders why they were ever written. One marvels how an author *could* write a book or novel of any kind without enthusiasm—how he could fail to warm to his work. There is pleasure in a fine failure. Mr. Nansen did not reach the Pole, nor did John Jones, who remained at home. The difference is that Nansen made the attempt.

The first book on the pile is *Sixty and Six*—edited by Will M. Clemens and published by The New Amsterdam Book Company of New York. The idea of *Sixty and Six* is very good, but the book itself is disappointing. It is a collection of sixty-six very short paragraphs—Mr. Clemens calls them "chips" —most of them tell a story, so-called. The only drawback about the stories is that they are not good. They are not interesting, and they fail to make a point. Stories told in such short space as this must be pungent and forcible, or they have no excuse for existing, and in all the sixty-six thus edited by Mr. Clemens I can find not one that might not as well have been left untold. The book is neither good nor bad—it simply fails, and fails flatly, dully, of its own inertia.

I am not sure that Mr. W.F. Anstey has not created a new type in the person of Baboo Hurry Bungsho Jabberjee, the native Indian law-student residing in London. Mr. Anstey makes this amusing person tell of himself and his own adventures. His name gives the title to the book and the Appleton Publishing Company give the book to the public. It's merely London life seen through the spectacles of the Anglicized Indian. The best part of the humor is the curious mixture (Latin quotations, misquotations, mixed quotations, obsolete words, up-to-date slang, extraordinary compounds and misplaced words) which make up the speech of the Baboo, and which is very natural and plausible. As for instance, where he speaks of the "hardihood" of his bicycle seat, and his undergoing "total abstinence" from his umbrella in the "vestibulum" of the Royal Academy, or his exclamation at the birthplace of Shakespeare, "It was here that the Swan of Avon was hatched!" Mr. Anstey's book is a fair specimen of English humor, which finds amusement in ludicrousness rather than in wit and which delights less in a pun than in the fall of a stout gentleman on a slippery pavement.

An Elopement

By Ferdinand Bloch

Translated by Frank Norris

The Wave, 16 (25 December 1897), 13.

"Hello, you here again, Lieutenant?"

"Yes, General."

"Have you come here to ask me a second time for my daughter? I refused you yesterday and I refuse you to-day, that's certain."

"Then you wish, sir, to have Mlle. Hernance die an old maid?"

"My affair, not yours, Lieutenant."

"*Passons de cela.* I have come, General, to ask your advice."

"You've got to ask for something always it appears. Well?"

"Well, I am in love with a little girl——"

"*Encore*—you are in love with *all* little girls it seems to me. How absurd.

Never mind, go on."

"I have asked for her in marriage. Her parents refuse me."

"And why?"

"They don't say."

"Idiots; don't try to defend them. They are idiots if they can't or won't tell you why. *What!* a young officer like you—rich—good name—in line of promotion—and give you no reasons. Idiots, I tell you."

"Aren't they."

"Aha! If I were in your place!"

"You would do——"

"What I have done. Listen.

"Listen to this little tale and profit by the same—if you can. I was 25 years of age, and a Lieutenant, as you are now. One evening at a ball I noticed an exquisitely beautiful girl, waltzed with her, adored her and told her so—proposed, was accepted. Father was there—big, bourgeois, smelling of pork, hideous, yellow—hideous as his daughter was lovely. After the waltz I returned Mademoiselle to her corner, went up to the old fellow, her father, drew him into an angle of the wall, and said:

"'Sir, I have not the honor of knowing you, but I am Bauperthois, of the 229th of the line, 25 years of age, 16,000 *livres* income, son of the late Colonel of the same name, hope in time to wear the five *galons* of the Colonel, and—I love your daughter.'

"'Very flattered,' says the beast, 'but I have not as yet thought of giving my daughter in marriage. I must have time to think it over.'

"'How long?'

"'Some days?'

"'I'll give you ten minutes.'

"'Ten minutes. You're crazy!'

"'In ten minutes I'll come for your answer,' and I hurried off without giving him time to respond.

"Ten minutes later I returned.

"'Sir,' said the beast, 'your insistence is flattering, and if you will honor me with a call in about a week, you may have an answer.'

"'A week,' I exclaimed. 'You give me a week's notice like a valet. It's charming. You won't answer me before a week?'

"'Impossible.'

243

"'Six days then—your last chance.'

"'No, sir.'

"'*C'est très bien.*'

"Two hours later I had eloped with the daughter, and the next day her father, informed of the affair, consented to call me his son-in-law.

"*Voilà*, my dear Lieutenant, that is how we act when we wear epaulets. Don't stop here looking at me like a tortoise. Get along with you and elope with the girl."

"But——"

"'*Tention*, by the left flank—*m-a-r-r-rche!*"

"Then your advice, General, is to act——"

"At once."

"And if her father is obstinate?"

"You're talking drivel. The girl will be compromised. The father can't re-fuse."

"My cause will be won?"

"*Parbleu!*"

"I would be wrong to hesitate another second, I see."

"Of course you would."

"That's your sincere opinion?"

"Without the least doubt."

"Well, then, General, I've done it."

"Done what?"

"Eloped with Mademoiselle Hernance, your daughter."

"My daughter! You have——you, ——my daughter!"

"You just told me to."

"Yes—*but not with mine.*"

"However, sir, you were married under the same circumstances."

"But I didn't ask the advice of my future father-in-law."

"I beg you to notice, sir, that I ran off with Mademoiselle before asking your advice."

"*Enfin*, Monsieur, where is my daughter?"

"With my mother, General, at home."

"And have you acted honestly with her?"

"General!"

"*Bien*, I'll give you ten minutes to bring my daughter back to me and eight days to publish the bans."

"General, this generosity——"

"Rot! my generosity! And you booby, with tears in your eyes, pah! Get along with you, and bring me your wife instantly, son-in-law."

At Home From Eight to Twelve

The Wave, 17 (1 January 1898), 7.

Every window of the house was lighted. The front door was opened for the guest before he could ring and he passed up the stairs, catching a glimpse of the parlors through the portieres of the doors. At the turn of the stairs the second girl in a white lawn cap directed them to the gentlemen's dressing-room, which was the room of the son of the house. About a dozen men were there already, some rolling up their overcoats into balls and stowing them with their canes in the corners of the room, others laughing and smoking together, and still others who were either brushing their hair before the mirrors, or sitting on the bed in their stocking feet breathing upon their patent leathers, warming them before putting them on. There were one or two who knew no one and who stood about unhappily, twisting the tissue paper from the buttons of their new gloves, looking stupidly at the pictures on the walls of the room. Occasionally one of the gentlemen would step to the door, looking out in the hall to know if the ladies whom he was escorting were yet come out of their dressing-room, ready to go down.

The house was filling up rapidly, one heard the deadened roll of wheels in the street outside, the banging of carriage doors, and an incessant rustle of stiff skirts ascending the stairs. From the ladies' dressing-room came an increasing soprano chatter, while downstairs the orchestra around the piano in the back parlor began to snarl and whine louder and louder. About the halls and stairs one caught brief glimpses of white and blue opera cloaks edged with swansdown, alternating with the gleam of a starched shirt bosom and the glint of a highly polished silk hat. Odors of sachet and violets came and went elusively, or mingled with those of the roses and pinks. An air of gaiety and excitement began to spread throughout the whole house.

But an hour later the dance was in full swing. Almost every number was a waltz or a two-step, the music being the topical songs and popular airs of the day set to dance music. Some of the couples waltzed fast, whirling around the rooms, bearing around corners with a swirl and swing of silk skirts, the girl's face flushed and perspiring, her eyes half closed, her bare white throat warm, moist and alternately swelling and contracting with her slow breathing. On certain of these girls the dancing produced a peculiar effect. The continued motion, the whirl of the lights, the heat of the room, the heavy perfume of the flowers, the cadence of the music, even the physical fatigue reacted in some strange way upon their over-sensitive feminine nerves, the monotony of repeated sensation producing some sort of mildly hypnotic effect, a morbid hysterical pleasure, the more exquisite because mixed with pain. These were the girls whom one heard declaring that they could dance all night, the girls who could dance until they dropped.

About the doors and hallways stood the unhappy gentlemen who knew no one, watching the others dance, feigning to be amused. Some of them, however, had ascended to the dressing-room and began to strike up an acquaintance with each other, smoking incessantly, discussing business, politics and even religion.

In the ladies' dressing-room two of the maids were holding a long conversation in low tones, their heads together. Evidently it was concerning something dreadful. They continually exclaimed "Oh" and "Ah," suddenly sitting back from each other, shaking their heads, biting their nether lips. Out in the hall on the top floor the servants in their best clothes leant over the balustrade nudging each other, talking in hoarse whispers or pointing with thick fingers, swollen with dishwater. All up and down the stairs were the couples who were sitting out the dance, some of them even upon the circular sofa in the hall of the first landing.

Supper was served in the huge billiard room in the basement, and was eaten in a storm of gaiety. The same parties and "sets" tried to get together at the same tables.

One ate oysters *à la poulette*, terrapin, salads and croquettes, the wines were Sauternes and Champagnes. With the nuts and dessert, the caps came on and in a few minutes were cracking and snapping all over the room.

Six of the unfortunates who knew no one, but who had managed, through a common affliction, to become acquainted with each other, gathered at a separate table. They levied a twenty-five cent assessment upon each other and tipped the waiter a dollar and a half; this one accordingly brought them a bottle of Champagne apiece, in which they found consolation for all the *ennui* of the evening.

After supper the dancing began again. The little stiffness and constraint of the earlier part of the evening was gone; by this time nearly everybody, except the unfortunates, knew everybody else. The good dinner and the Champagne had put them all into an excellent humor, and they all commenced to be very jolly. They began a Virginia reel still wearing the Magician's caps and Phrygian bonnets of tissue paper.

Toward one o'clock there was a general movement. The ladies of the house were inquired for, and the blue and white opera cloaks, reappeared descending the stairs, disturbing the couples who were seated there. The banging of carriage doors and the rumble of wheels recommenced in the street. The musicians played a little longer. As the party thinned out, there was greater dance room and a consequent greater pleasure in dancing, and these last dances at the end of the evening were enjoyed more than all the others. But ten minutes later the function was breaking up fast. Suddenly the musicians played *Home, Sweet Home*. Those still dancing uttered an exclamation of regret, but continued waltzing to this air the same as ever. Some even began to dance again in their overcoats and opera-wraps. Then at last the tired musicians stopped and reached for the cases of their instruments, and the remaining guests, seized with a sudden panic lest they should be the last to leave, fled to the dressing-rooms. These were in the greatest confusion, everyone was in a hurry. In the gentlemen's dressing-room there was a great putting on of coats and mufflers and a searching for misplaced gloves, hats and canes. A bass hum of talk rose in the air, bits and ends of conversation being passed back and forth across the room. "*You* haven't seen my hat have you, Jimmy?" "Did you meet that girl I was telling you about?" "Hello, old man; have a good time to-night?" "Lost your hat?" "No, *I* haven't seen it." "Yes, about half-past ten." "Well, I told him that myself." "Ah, you bet, it's the man that rustles that gets there." "Come around about four, then." "What's the matter with coming home in *our* carriage?" At the doors of the dressing-rooms the ladies joined their escorts, and a great crowd formed in the hall, swarming down the stairs and out upon the front steps. As the first groups reached the open air there was a great cry, "Why, it's pouring rain." This was taken up and repeated, and carried all the way back into the house. There were exclamations of dismay and annoyance. "Why, it's raining right *down*." "What *shall* we do?" Tempers were lost, brothers and sisters quarreling with each other over the question of umbrellas.

In a short time all the guests were gone, except the one young lady whose maid and carriage had somehow not been sent. The son of the hostess took this one home in a hired hack. The hostess and her daughter sat down to rest for a moment in the empty parlors. The canvas-covered floors were littered with leaves of smilax and La France roses, with bits of ribbon, ends of lace and discarded Phrygian bonnets of tissue paper. The butler and the second girl were already turning down the gas in the other rooms.

Reviews in Brief

Charming Qualities of *Jimty and Others* —Miss Hunt's Clever Novel

---

The Wave, 17 (1 January 1898), 13.

Since Weyman wrote a successful imitation of Dumas, most writers on the far side of the Atlantic have been writing unsuccessful imitations of Weyman. An imitation is bad enough, but an imitation of an imitation is veritably distressing. The result is that the book reviewer's shelves are crowded and overflowing with d'Artagnans under every alias, and in all costumes, from the chevalier's cloak to the Highlander's plaid. The latest volunteer to join the literary Foreign Legion is a Scotsman by the name of *Lochinvar*, who brandishes his brogue, as well as his claymore, through the pages of S. R. Crockett's novel (Harper & Bros.), to which he gives his name. Fortunately, however, the reader dodges the brogue after the first chapter—Mr. Crockett was merciful in that—and is only asked to press where he sees the claymore shine midst the ranks of war. Even at that he has a harrowing time of it, for his young Lochinvar is the true hero of the novel reader, brave to madness, in love to madness as well, and beset by a train of misadventures, bad fortune and ill-timed mishap that would stagger the audacity of Achilles himself. Though Lochinvar is unreal he is very much alive and enlists the reader's sympathy with the same bravado as he enlists his soldiers'. One leaves it to the expert reader of romance to disentangle the anomaly. It is a story of the days of the Pretender, and is crammed with exciting episodes from cover to cover. To tell the tale, further than merely to hint that it is just a romance of battle and sudden death, of more sudden love and escapes of sword-blade narrowness, would be to take the hero unawares, and this, as all good romance readers know, must never happen.

Story-telling in the form of letters exchanged is a dreary method, and one that repels rather than attracts the reader. But even handicapped with a cumbersome, unpopular setting Mr. Clyde Fitch has made *Tales of the Smart Set* (H.S. Stone & Co.) enjoyable reading. Piquancy of wording and a dainty superficiality, not always reprehensible, are the characteristics of the little book. One hardly remembers a lighter point since Hope tickled the literary palate with *The Dolly Dialogues*. Fitch is a journalist in his manner, while Hope was essentially a scholar and *littérateur*. The two best sketches of the collection are that descriptive of the Wagner festival at Beyreuth as seen by fashionable eyes, and the study of the woman of the world seeking to divert her mind from the death of her child by the excitements of her social set.

A fair sample of middle-class English fiction is *Other People's Lives*, by Rosa Nouchette Cary, given to the world through the medium of The Lippincott publishing house. The chief recommendation of Miss Cary's book is that it "would not call a blush to the cheek of the young person." Its moral atmosphere is so rarified that ordinary wholesome, every-day life faints and fades therein, and only the emaciated and devitalized elements remain. It is a good book for the shelves of a Sunday-school library in a suburban town.

Diana Victrix, by Florence Converse, is just from the presses of Houghton, Mifflin & Co., and has freshness enough of its own to carry the reader's interest to the last chapter. It points no moral, but is rather an unassuming little tale, told for the sake of the telling and for amusement. It is worth reading through once—not oftener.

The Drowned Who Do Not Die

The Wave, 17 (24 September 1898), 9 and 12.

I want to tell you what I know about McBurney in this story. Part of it is what the old fellow himself told me concerning his life, and part is what I myself know about his death. I can see no good reason why the tale should not be set down in this place, for McBurney is dead long since and the girl was dead even before McBurney saw and loved her.

I only knew McBurney as the captain of an inside life-boat station, where the surf-boat was not called out twice in a twelve-month. He was finishing his life there quietly, quietly, in company with his crew of eight Scandinavians, an aged geranium that never flowered, and a bass viol upon which regularly every Sunday afternoon McBurney played the only tunes he ever knew, *Blessed Be the Tie That Binds* and *Let Us Haste to Kelvin Grove*.

But for all this McBurney had known the meaning of a life of extraordinary action and adventure when he was younger. He had filibustered down to Chili and the Argentine, had been shanghaied out of Callao on a beach-combing venture, and had even begun life as a thorough-paced deep-sea diver and government-certificate man. Of this latter career he was curiously loath to talk. He would tell me tales of filibustering, shanghaiing and piloting all up and down the coast, from Buenos Ayres to the Aleutian Islands, till the hair of my head stood up with excitement. But he dodged speaking of his diving experiences by saying:

"Divers don't like to talk of what they see below. It preys on the mind and gets you to thinking."

McBurney's station was on the shore of San Francisco bay, midway between Black Point and the Presidio. I went out to see him three times a week. Early Tuesday mornings we cruised out of the Golden Gate in the smaller boat, Wednesday evenings we played backgammon and McBurney made grog, and on Sundays we took a walk along the drain on the other side of the Presidio, getting back to the station in time for five o'clock supper and the bass viol.

By putting together the tales he told me over the backgammon board, or sitting on the drain, or between *Kelvin Grove* and *The Tie That Binds*, I had a perfectly consecutive story of McBurney's life from the time he was a choir-boy in York cathedral till the day of his appointment as captain of Life Boat Station, No. 8—all except one period of five years, around the time when he was nineteen or twenty. I followed him easily enough until he reached California as for'mast hand on a revenue cutter. There I lost him, and only picked him up again some half dozen years later as ice-pilot aboard the *Rogers*.

Another point I could not fail to notice was the character of McBurney himself. You may say what you will, and I also have made less for the extravagant ideals of life than for its plain work-a-day realities, and have elected for myself sensation rather than sentiment, yet a man cannot for long entertain a deep and sincere affection without its leaving a mark upon him thereafterwards. McBurney had had his romance. Of that I was persuaded. There was a certain sweetness, a serious, firm grip of his upon the basic instincts of primitive good, that could be explained in no other way. There was something Homeric about the man. So that, little by little, I had come to know very well the various chapters of the old fellow's life—excepting always the clue chapter. The pattern was all very well but for the one note of color that should bring the whole scheme into harmony. At last, however, I found it. McBurney told me the last story of all. It was an extraordinary story, as you may see for yourself, nearly beyond belief.

It happened of a Sunday. I had gone out to the station early in the afternoon, to find McBurney pottering about his bloomless geranium and grieving that it should never come to flower. He had had the plant I cannot guess how long, but it was so old that its budding was out of all question.

Still McBurney obstinately cherished the hope that it would some day blossom.

"It may be," he said on this occasion, "that the sea air is a bit too sharp. Perhaps, if it was put under a glass case now—what do you think? Or if I trimmed away some of the young leaves? It's not beyond hope. No, I'll not believe it. I'll not have it so. Surely, some day we'll have a flower on it. Some day it will be as fresh as ever. I can remember it, not so very long ago. You should have seen it then; red flowers as big as your two fists, and smell! Why, I think you could have smelled it in the other room."

He turned away to reach down his gardener's trowel, which, with the prim nicety of old men who live alone, he always kept upon the top shelf of his closet in a lidless cigar box. As he opened the closet door I was surprised to notice on the floor the complete armor of a deep-sea diver—helmet, breastplate, pumps, rubber shoes and all. I knew that McBurney had his outfit somewhere about the station, but heretofore I had imagined that it stood in the attic. It was in perfect condition now, and the copper helmet had been newly rubbed with suet.

"Why, hello, McBurney," said I, "what's this all? Going diving again?"

He closed the door and looked at me a moment, then:

"I got a bit of chemical loam from a gardener in Golden Gate Park to-day. I'm going to try it. I think it might help."

"Better get a new plant," I suggested. From the sharp way he looked at me I could fancy that my remark had actually hurt him a little. But he said nothing, and I fell a-wondering at the strange contradiction in a man who had sat down to meat with buccaneers, and had seen men knifed for the boots they wore, but who could yet find interest in cracked bass viols and bloomless geraniums. All the rest of that afternoon he was unusually silent and preoccupied, and I let him have his thoughts to himself. We took our accustomed walk a little later, around the old fort at Golden Gate, then along the broken drain that follows the line of the hills there—and from whence one could see Fuji-Yama, if one could but see over the curve of the great earth—to a point where the land shrugged a bony shoulder out of the surf and shut out the wind. Here we turned and climbed part way up the hill to a certain level spot where we knew we could sit down, and where sometimes we found blackberries and blue iris. McBurney took out his pipe and filled and lit. For quite five minutes neither of us spoke, pretending to be interested in a Cape Horner, a huge deep-sea tramp, held almost motionless in the middle passage between the heads of the Gate, the tide at her bow and the wind at her back.

"Mate," said he at length, "I want you to go somewheres with me." Where, indeed, wouldn't I have gone with McBurney in those days?

"Right," said I upon the instant, and the old fellow continued, looking seawards and to the south with unseeing eyes:

"There's a ship down there I want to see again before I———" He cleared his throat: "A ship down there I want to see—a passenger packet from Tahiti, the *Allouette*. She's there off one of the Catalina islands."

"I didn't know that the Tahiti boats called at the Catalinas," said I.

"They *don't* call at the Catalinas," answered McBurney, dreamily. "But for all that I'm going down to the Catalina Islands, come next week, to visit the packet *Allouette*, that's off the west coast of Catalina, and that weighed her anchor out of ———, Tahiti, with nine passengers and her crew."

"I've never seen her," I put in.

"Nor I," answered McBurney; and, before I could find a reply, went on: "Nor I, mate; only her ghost, as one might say. Listen now, and I'll tell you what I've never told a man or woman yet.

"I was diving in those days for the K. & B. Wrecking Company. Just a lad I was, only turned twenty, but I could take the pressure up to the seventies and more, like an old hand. I was at work on the caissons of a pier head at San Diego, when Catalina sent down in a hurry for a diver to bring up the bodies from a Tahiti packet that had gone down in a squall off the west coast of one of the islands. I went.

"When I got to the wrecking float I was told that the bodies of all the crew and those of two of the passengers had come up. But seven of the passengers were still below. I was to take a 'stray line' down and send them up."

McBurney paused a moment. "You never heard, perhaps, how bodies act in the water when they don't come up," said he. "I'll tell you, then, that they sit in their places, or stand or lie as the case may be, as natural as if in a parlor, an' still—very still, until the water about them is stirred or a bit of a current set going. Then they raise their arms, and turn their heads, or, perhaps, if they are sitting up they lie down quiet like, as if they were very tired an' going to sleep. You can't believe sometimes that they are drowned and dead. Sometimes, mate, you won't believe that they're dead. Old divers have a saying, you know, that a man—or a woman, either, for the matter o' that—isn't really dead till the body comes up; that they only die when the air touches them, an' that they still have a kind of a life down there amongst themselves, in all that green and gloom of the sea bottom—some kind of a life," he muttered; "yes—yes; *some* kind of a life, surely.

"I went down where the *Allouette* sank—a hundred and seventy feet of water—an' that's a wonder deep dive. It's a pressure of over eighty pounds, and some men paralyze at that, and die in their armor. But I wasn't down long. Six of the bodies I found, four men, the stewardess, and a boy, sent them up, then came up myself and reported. But there was one more down below, they told me. It was the body of a girl; a girl of nineteen. She was the daughter of an orange grower of Los Angeles, and an only child—a beautiful girl whom everybody loved. Her mother was dead, and her father was way off in Mexico at the time of the wreck. I'd heard of her, you see, but I'd never seen her. The men on the float, some dozen of 'em—newspaper reporters, the coroner, the wrecking hands, and the like—would have it that I should go down again and have another try. I did so. Though I was bleeding at the ears even then. This second time I crawled into the dining saloon through a dreadful pile of wreck—the ceiling had fetched away—and came up to a bit of a door that looked like the entrance to the linen closet; but when I opened it I saw that it was a little stateroom.

"And there, sure enough, was the girl, sitting on a red plush lounge, opposite the door, quite natural. She wore some kind of a white muslin dress, an' a little smart chip hat, an' was holding a satchel in her hands just as if she were waiting to go ashore. Her eyes were open, and she was looking right at me and smiling. When I pulled open the door," said McBurney, "it set the water in motion, and she dropped the satchel an' got up an' came towards me smiling, and holding out her arms.

"I jumped back an' shut the door, an' sat down in one of the screw chairs in the saloon, for I was fair turned with the queerness of it. When I had gotten over the strait, I made ready to send her up. But as it was, I never went into that stateroom again. I began to wonder if, after all, it wasn't better to leave her as she was. You see, I was a bit young then, an' sentimental like, as all folks are who have to do with the sea. I thought of that crowd of men up there on the float, an' she the only girl, an' they handling her about an' staring at her, an' she not knowing, with never a relative of hers inside a thousand miles, an' no woman to take care of her. And then I remembered the old divers' superstitions about folk never really dying till they came up to the surface. Of course, that was foolishness; but I believed it then—I don't know, maybe I believe it now. But, anyrate, I told myself that at that moment she was lovely an' sweet an' all, in her little chip hat an' her little muslin frock; but if I sent her up she'd be buried, put into a hole of dirt with the worm an' the dark. If I left her away from the air, shut up there in that little stateroom, a hundred and seventy feet deep, in that still, quiet, green water, she'd always stay as she was—always be young an' sweet an' pretty—always be nineteen.

"The key was on the inside of the stateroom door. I locked the door without opening it an' battened down the ventilator so that nothing—no fish or anything—could get in. I went on the outside of the ship and saw to it that the porthole of that stateroom was fast. Then I took a last look through the port. She was lying down on the floor near the door on one arm, and her face hidden as though she was sorry I had left her so; an' one hand reaching out a little, palm up, as though she was waiting for me to come back—as if she expected that I *would* come back some day, and wanted to tell me that she wasn't angry. Then I signaled to be pulled up, an' left her that way, just waiting, you know, quiet-like, and all alone in that still green water. On the float I told them I hadn't seen anything, an' no doubt the current had carried her away.

"There was some talk of my company raising the *Allouette*, a little afterwards, but I reported she was broken up so bad that it wouldn't be worth while. People quit talking about the *Allouette* in less than a fortnight, an' her father married again down in Mexico, an' has got another daughter by now. In a year's time the whole business was forgotten. But I never forgot it. You see, a lad at just that age—a seafaring lad—when he gets an impression it sticks an' sticks, and goes deeper. Maybe it turned my wits a little, maybe they're still turned. I've never forgot her. I forgot, though, about being frightened, and only remembered the pretty way of her coming towards me smiling and holding out her arms. And though I've grown to an old man, *she's* always stayed young, just as sweet an' fresh an' pretty as she was the first day I saw her. Somehow, I never could take to other girls after that, or love anybody but just her. I always remembered her down there in all that still green water, waiting for me to come back and open the door.

255

An' remembering her like that, always kept me straight and clean, I guess. An' everybody else has forgotten her but me; nobody knows she's waiting there, an' her father has another daughter by now. So she's only got me, you see. Just belongs to me. I never saw her again. I came away the next day and never went back. That was a long time ago. But next week I'm going to get a sloop an' go along the coast to the Catalinas, an' go down and see her. I'm getting old, now, you see. An' old men, after a while they kind of get young again in a way. Move in a circle, as it were. Maybe my circle is nearly done, but I feel to-day as I felt that day when I first found her, an' we were both twenty. So I guess I'll go down there."

"But McBurney," said I, "how would it be? This was all so long ago. Would she be just the same? Maybe I'm wrong. I don't know much about such things, but the action of the sea water——"

"No, no," he answered. "There was no air, you see. Practically the place was hermetically sealed. I battened down the ventilators an' locked the door. She is just the same to-day as she was so very long ago when I first saw her. It can't be otherwise. No, no. I'll not believe it so. I'll not have it so. They never really die, you see, so long as they stay below."

McBurney's pipe was out. The Cape Horner had long since passed the heads with the turning of the tide, and by the time we reached the Presidio on our way home, the Farallones were standing out purple-black against the conflagration of the sunset.

That next week McBurney got his leave of absence, and found a man by the name of Hodgson, a retired sea captain, to take his place. We chartered a seagoing sloop, hardly bigger than a whitehall, and cleared for the Catalina Islands. These islands lie southward, not very far off the California coast, and are almost tropical. The Coast Survey people had buoyed the wreck of the *Allouette*—much harm the old packet could do at that depth—and McBurney located it by this means almost immediately.

I shall never forget the old fellow's agitation on the day we arrived and tied up to the buoy. What the emotions were that conflicted in his poor old troubled brain, judge you. He was to see again the girl he had loved quite half a century ago, and whom he had never seen alive. Also he was for the last time to look upon a dead face. There was something of the funeral in it, and something of the wedding. It was a strange situation.

When I had helped him on with the armor and opened the sea-cock at the helmet's throat, I noted that he had the Deremal rod (it is a sort of very sharp knife) under his weight belt.

"It's shark water," he explained. "But there's no danger."

He had already told me the kinds of peril he really incurred. His lines—the life- and air-lines—might be frayed and cut by friction against a sharp edge of brass or copper, or the pressure might become too great for him.

"As a lad I stood it well enough," he said, "but I'm an old man now, an' a hundred an' seventy feet is a wonder deep dive. See," he went on, holding up a key, "here's the key to her stateroom. I've always kept it."

I laced down the helmet. We said good bye, and as we shook hands I felt his calloused palm quivering against mine. He was as excited as a boy—a boy of twenty. He went over the side.

For some time I could follow the red glint of his copper helmet, dropping away under the shadow of the boat. Then at length it disappeared, and only the shifting weight and pull on the life-line was left me. I paid it out over the boat's side until suddenly it fell limp, and I knew that McBurney's feet were set on the deck of the *Allouette*. I turned the wheel of the pump unsteadily, my heart knocking at my palate, for it is not good to see a living man descend into the nether world from out the light of day. The two lines ran slowly out, now pausing, now giving out by jerks. Once he signaled that I was giving him too much air, and as I slacked the pump and watched the lines still running out, I could fancy that I traced his movements thus. That long, straight, even run marked his progress down the deck. The shorter flight, after that moment's pause, no doubt indicated his descent down a hatchway. Now he was upon the berth deck; now in the saloon companionway; now crawling over that pile of wreck he spoke of, that almost barred entrance into the saloon (an easy place there for the lines to be sliced in two); now he was in the saloon itself; and now—was not his hand upon that stateroom door?—and now—— There was no further movement of the lines. McBurney must be there, there in the open doorway of that little stateroom which he had left so many years before.

The lines had ceased to run out and ten and fifteen minutes passed without a movement while I turned at the pump and looked out on the indifferent face of the blue, broad Pacific that held there in its depths so strange a little drama. The sloop lay some hundred feet off a rugged tree-grown shore, desolate but for a sheep or two and a bird or two. The heat lay close over the ocean like the shutting down of a great warm palm. The water talked incessantly under the sloop's fore-foot, and a blue dragon fly arched like a bow lighted from time to time upon the boat's painter. But for the plaint of the unwilling pump and the talking water it was very still.

Presently I looked at my watch and was surprised to note that McBurney had been down over an hour. At so great a depth I knew this to be dangerous, and passed another half hour in increasing anxiety, waiting for some signal from him. When two hours had gone by I could wait no longer and warned him by a pull on the life-line.

Then I cannot tell what certain empty feel upon the line itself caught at my heart. I hauled in quickly. The line came home slack. I drew at the air-line. That, too, returned to the boat without resistance. When I had drawn both in I found them cut in two. Had McBurney cut them with his knife, or had they been severed by some sharp edge of brass or copper in the wreckage? I could never tell.

I believe I only fully came to myself by the time I had the sloop half way round the island on my way to the little town upon the shoreward side to tell of what had befallen. Then I remembered myself and asked what good would come of it. My mind retraversed the same course as that which McBurney had already outlined to me. His body confined down there below the decks of the *Allouette*, in the little stateroom, would never rise. Why not leave him there? How did I know that he had not wished that end— planned for it even? Or, supposing his death had been accidental, was it not, after all, best to leave the two of them as they were, the old man and the girl of nineteen, deep down in the calm untouched quiet of the ocean floor? And I recalled what McBurney had said, and half believed, of the legend of the deep sea divers; how that the drowned are not always the dead. So I left them there together and came away.

The other day I received a letter from Hodgson, the sea captain, who took McBurney's place at the lifeboat station. He wrote to ask what he was to do with some of the old man's belongings. Hodgson spoke of the backgammon board, and the cracked bass viol, and asked if I would care to have them. Then he added:

"He had a geranium plant here too, but if you don't mind I'd like to keep that. It's blossomed out all of a sudden and makes the place look rather gay."

TEXTUAL AFTERWORD

TEXTUAL AFTERWORD

The purpose of this edition is to make available the writings defining Frank Norris's 1896-1898 literary apprenticeship with the San Francisco weekly magazine, *The Wave*, as he intended them to appear before the public then. The 159 pieces included in these two volumes were published between 11 April 1896 and 24 September 1898; with three exceptions, they comprise all of the works that first saw print as Norris was introduced to the rigors of professional authorship.

The first exception is the novel that Norris was still composing chapter-by-chapter against weekly press deadlines when his tenure with *The Wave* drew to a close on 15 February 1898. This initial serialization of *Moran of the "Lady Letty"* began in the 8 January 1898 issue of *The Wave* and did not complete its run until 9 April; by that time Norris had been in New York City for almost two months, where he was working for both the S.S. McClure newspaper syndicate and *McClure's Magazine*.[1] Published as a book in late September, 1898, *Moran* is excluded from this edition because of the availability of both the bowdlerized book version and a critical edition based upon the original *Wave* text.[2] The second is "The End of the Act." "Act" is included here for the sake of establishing the complete record of Norris's apprenticeship publications; but, unlike the other short works, it was not first published during the apprenticeship. As is the case with "Little Drama of the Curbstone," this sketch was written when Norris was at Harvard University in 1894-1895. While "Drama" remained in manuscript until December, 1897, "Act" was published in the *Harvard Advocate* in 1895.[3] After making several minor revisions of the *Advocate* text, Norris recycled the work in *The Wave* in 1897. The third exception is "The Drowned Who Do Not Die." This publication dates several months beyond the apprenticeship period and from the approximate time of *Moran's* publication as a book. "Drowned" closes Volume 2 because it was both Norris's final contribution to *The Wave* (24 September 1898) and, apparently, his last short story written prior to the formal beginning of his career as a novelist. Its presence provides a desirable and, we think, justifiable symmetry in the description of this phase of Norris's life.

All but two of the short works in these volumes are *Wave* publications: "A Steamship Voyage with Cecil Rhodes" and "What Is Our Greatest Piece of Fiction?" were offered to the public in the *San Francisco Chronicle* and the San Francisco *Examiner*, respectively.

Few complications attend the textual histories of Norris's apprenticeship productions after their appearances in these three San Francisco periodicals. Just two are known to have been printed again in Norris's lifetime. "'Man Proposes': No. 3" (1896) was republished by late 1897 in an unidentified newspaper, the clipping of which is in the Frank Norris Collection, The Bancroft Library, University of California, Berkeley. Like "The End of the Act" of 1895, this alternate form reveals only minor textual differences, and the *Wave* version is again preferred by the editors of this edition because it is directly related to Norris's involvement in the publication process during the apprenticeship and the actions of the editor and compositor to whom Norris delegated responsibility for its presentation then. His relationship with the unidentified newspaper is not known. "'This Animal of a Buldy Jones'" (1897) was similarly revived for *McClure's Magazine* in 1899. Although Norris's relationship with this periodical is known, the *Wave* version is once more selected for editing: the *McClure's* reprinting postdates the apprenticeship period by 13 months.[4]

Another *Wave* short story, "*Miracle Joyeux*" has a very different history following its initial publication in 1897. A work with the same title, but with a radically different text, was later published in two other periodicals, in December 1898 and May 1901.[5] As was explained in Volume 1's introduction, Norris did not merely revise but rewrote the story so thoroughly that it became a new, discrete entity. The original "*Miracle*" is not modified here in light of the later work: to conflate the two would be to violate the integrity of each; and, as with "'This Animal of a Buldy Jones,'" the publications of the reconstructed tale took place well after the close of the apprenticeship.

The only other complication in the textual history has to do with a group of short stories that Norris assembled in 1897 for a planned book, described in November of that year by his friend Eleanor M. Davenport as "now in press."[6] That collection never materialized, though remains of the project have survived.

In the Bancroft Library's Frank Norris Collection are whole tear-sheets, clipped columns, and clipped proofs of 14 published short stories in which Norris entered corrections and revisions. They are mounted on sheets of paper and, at first glance, appear intended as either typesetting-copy or copy for a typist. The group includes six works published prior to Norris's apprenticeship: 1894's "A Caged Lion" from *Argonaut*, and the five stories in the *Overland Monthly's* "Outward and Visible Signs" series of 1894-1895. The leaves have been repaginated several times and, one speculates, were possibly first assembled and marked when, in 1895, Norris prepared a previous, also never-published volume that was declined by Houghton, Mifflin and Company on 21 June 1895 and then announced in the 2 November 1895 issue of *The Wave* as accepted for publication by Lovell, Coryell & Co.[7] One cannot, however, date with certainty Norris's markings in these six texts: the changes may have all been made in 1895; some may have been added later. It is even possible that they all were made in 1897: the content of the failed 1895 volume was never specified by Norris or another. Likewise, the mostly illegible, erased comments made by an unidentified reader of the six cannot be dated.

The other eight short stories in the group were written during the apprenticeship. They include three from the 1896 "'Man Proposes'" series: "No. 3" (the above-cited version reprinted in an unidentified newspaper), "No. 4," and "No. 5." Selected as well were late 1897's "A Case For Lombroso," "His Single Blessedness" (originally entitled "Doychert's Family" in the uncorrected *Wave* proof mounted by Norris), "Judy's Service of Gold Plate," "*Fantaisie Printanière*," and "His Dead Mother's Portrait."

One's immediate response to the data provided by the apprenticeship-period texts treated thus by Norris may be to view them as more authoritative than the original printed versions since it was Norris's hand at work, inferably revealing his modified intentions as well as sensitivity to editorial and compositorial alterations and errors. That is, one may be inclined to give preference to the marked copy and relegate the published texts to an inferior status. One might thus select the pasted-up texts as the versions to transcribe and edit for this edition; or, one might emend the *Wave* versions according to Norris's recorded reactions to them. Upon closer scrutiny of the remains of Norris's project, however, both courses soon appear less viable. Questions and uncertainties proliferate in short order, rendering complex what at first seemed a simple situation.

The problem has to do with the unclear character of the 1897 volume Norris planned, since the author himself left behind no record, other than the marked texts, of his attitude toward it. The 1894-1895 pieces, for example, are different in tone from those in the 1896 "'Man Proposes'" series. It is not clear how Norris would have arranged the two subgroups in a meaningful way, especially since the multiple paginations of the leaves do not indicate a clear plan for integration. Still, these stories do have something in common: they are relatively conventional pieces of short fiction, unlike the remaining ones. Radically different are the comparatively weird works from late 1897 in which Norris is focusing upon psychologically unsettling events, bizarre personality types, and aberrant behavior. If all 14 short stories were to be included, what would be the means of fashioning a coherent relationship between such disparate elements? Or, were the 1894-1895 juvenilia simply the preserved remains of the book intended in 1895, while the 1896-1897 works were the ones actually gathered for the new collection? Another possibility is that only the 1897 works, displaying dramatically Norris's "dark" view of the human condition, were intended as a small volume resembling Thomas Hardy's fictional reflections on the frustrations of being human, *Life's Little Ironies* (1894). Yet another possibility is that the book was to be a fuller collection of his 1897 works, and the other pieces chosen by Norris did not make their way to the Bancroft Library.

If a typescript derived from the remains survived, what Norris actually did intend would undoubtedly be clearer; but one does not. Apart from Davenport's declaration that "in press" was the volume to bear the Bret Harte-inspired title *Ways That Are Dark*, there is, in fact, no evidence that Norris ever completed the preparation of his collection or came to a definite conclusion as to *how* some or all of the 14 would reappear in print. Indeterminate, then, is the identity of this clutch of texts.

The puzzling nature of the evidence and consequently unstable concept of the book Norris had in mind ultimately lead to the question that an editor must pose regarding the authority of Norris's markings: did he indeed perform the revisions to his satisfaction? Are his markings the expressions of his final intentions, or are they instead trials?

One cannot tell.

The indeterminate character of these documents, vis-à-vis Norris's intentions in 1897, is one reason why they are neither viewed as more authoritative than the original *Wave* texts nor employed for emendation of them; of necessity, they fall into the scholarly editor's category of "foul papers," documents in which the author cannot be said to have brought his work to completion. The second is that, even if Norris had manifested his desires in full, those intentions would relate to a new work of art he was fashioning, a collection of short stories with its own identity, a spin-off from the body of writings that comprises his apprenticeship work for *The Wave*. Another edition—of that collection—is the appropriate venue for the presentation of the short stories in their revised states. Third and most important, these volumes, as has been noted, attempt to represent Norris as he served a journalistic apprenticeship in 1896-1898 and to provide a means of approximating the relationship he had with his primary readership then; were the revisions clearly authoritative, another role for Norris and another author-reader relationship would be in question. But such a development is, finally, only theoretical; the abortive book-project did not establish such a new role or relationship.

* * *

In a month's time Stayne was sickened unto death of Cresencia — was cloyed and satiated with her. At first he had been too honest to pretend for her an affection he did not feel, but already the fine edge of this honesty had been blunted. If he now wished to break with her it was because it fatigued and bored him beyond words to keep up appearances. Once more he fought his way brutally out of the mesh in which he had become entangled, wrote a ten-line letter to Cresencia, which he believed would be final, and for a week felt like an honest man for the first time in three months.

But the thing was not to be. Miss Hromada's pride did not come to her aid this time even momentarily. She had been degrading far more rapidly than he. Though she rolled upon her bed, hurting herself with the nails of her hands, in unspeakable humiliation she could not let Stayne go. And this was the same girl whose pride and self-respect had hitherto been her strongest traits. She managed to see Stayne three and four times each week. She came to his office, contrived to meet him on his way to lunch, managed to be invited to the same places — even began to take a strange, perverted pleasure in forcing herself upon his company and in submitting to his brutalities.

For the thing could not fail but have its effect upon Stayne. He suddenly discovered that nothing—literally and quite truly—nothing he could do would offend Cresencia. He realized that she would take anything from him—that she would not, or rather, that she could not, resent any insult, however gross. And the knowledge made the man a brute. Remember, this was not all at once. I am talking now about things that took a year or more to evolve. After he had clearly seen that Miss Hromada would submit to anything at his hands, Stayne began to enjoy her society. By this time Stayne had developed into rather much of a villain. It became for him a pleasure — a morbid, unnatural, evil pleasure for him to hurt and humiliate her. He hurt her while he sickened at the thought of his own baseness, and she submitted to it while she loathed herself for her own degradation. They were a strange couple.

Stayne would even torture her before other women and girls—would make her play waltzes while he danced with some fancied rival—would make appointments with her and come to the place with another girl, and tell her he had made other arrangements. He would smoke while she was by, and blow the smoke in her eyes, I have even seen him put his feet into the lap of her dinner gown; she, the while, trying to carry it off as a joke.

And she took all this and would go home and lie awake all night and fancy she was killing Stayne with her nails and teeth, till she shook all over and saw red things between her and the opposite wall.

The end of this story ought to be a suicide, or at least a murder, but that was the devil of it. The two people lived — lived out the wretched farce-tragedy to which there was to be no end. Had they never met, Miss Hromada and young Stayne would yet have been as fine specimens of womanhood and manhood as you could wish to know. Once having met, they ruined each other. The effect of these different characters upon one another was something well-nigh impossible to reduce to language. A Shakespere could have handled it — a Zola might have worked it out—I dare not go further with it. For all I know the horror may still endure. Stayne's name has long since been erased from the rolls of his club. Miss Hromada is thoroughly declassee, her last merit figured in the law courts as the principal figure in a miserable and thoroughly disreputable scandal.

give him up

kill

and

evenings

Norris's three-stage revision of "A Case for Lombroso" in which he toned-down the conclusion: Stayne no longer puts his feet in Cresencia's lap; and, before Norris canceled the last sentence, Stayne less suggestively sees her four "evenings" per week—rather than "nights." Courtesy of The Bancroft Library.

While the above cases have required special consideration, the large majority of the writings present a relatively simple situation for the editors in regard to the selection of "copy-texts." The forms chosen for editorial treatment are immediately and necessarily obvious ones: the copy-texts are the single publications that appeared not only during Norris's apprenticeship but through the remainder of his life. Further, none of the posthumous republications of these works is more authoritative. All were derived from the same copy-texts edited here.[8]

Emendation of the whole is likewise rendered a relatively uncomplicated matter once the copy-texts requiring special consideration are viewed as sharing the same status as those in the majority. Since all of the copy-texts literally or effectively stand alone as self-contained entities unaffected by other extant versions, they are edited as such, with due consideration being given to the following: the evidence internal to the copy-texts of the realization or thwarting of Norris's probable intentions for each work in 1896-1898; the nature of Norris's compositional activities throughout the apprenticeship, including his working relationships with his editors and compositors; and the data that surviving holographs, typescripts, and printed works produced before, during, and after the apprenticeship provide regarding the ways in which Norris's texts were typically originated and transmitted. Editorial emendations are directed by only two considerations: first, the need to represent what Norris's presumably handwritten submission-copy and proof corrections indicated were his intended readings; and, second, the need to perform the editorial functions necessary for his texts to conform at least minimally to the conventions of the print medium of his time—as Norris expected his texts to be shaped by the contemporaneous editors and compositors with whom he collaborated.

* * *

The majority of the emendations have to do with the copy-texts' "accidental" characteristics which do not conform to such minimal, requisite conventions or to Norris's known, deliberately cultivated idiosyncrasies. Emended are plain misspellings, truly problematic punctuation, and like formal peculiarities that ultimately may have a "substantive" effect not intended by Norris, though he undoubtedly originated many of them.[9] Taken together, Norris's manuscripts, personally-generated typescripts, and handwritten letters indicate that he *normally* produced what any editor or reader would term "unfinished" documents. As the surviving leaves of the *McTeague* manuscript (completed during the apprenticeship) make dramatically clear, his infelicities of spelling and punctuation, like his unindented paragraphs, are

McTeague.

    The other teachers at the kindergarten often noticed
[sp.] that Bessie's fingertips were swollen and the nails
purple as though they had been shut in a door. This
was in fact the explanation she offered. But she
lied to them. McTeague her husband used to
bite her finger tips when he came home after
drinking whiskey, crunching them between his strong
large teeth, always ingenious enough to remember which
were the sorest. If she resisted he brought her
[p.] down with a blow of his immense bony fist between the eyes.
    Often these brutalities inflamed his sensual pas-
sions and he threw her, stupid and
bleeding and stupid from his fists across the bed
and then it was abominable, bestial, unspeakable.

*One of the most "finished" of the Harvard student themes, this sketch
submitted on 7 January 1895 illustrates Norris's casual attitude
regarding punctuation and spelling. Courtesy of The Bancroft Library.*

signature traits of work in his hand—to be effaced by the editor(s) and compositors who would "finish" that novel before it appeared in bookstores in 1899.[10] *McTeague's* editor(s) and compositors, like those of the apprenticeship writings, did not, however, succeed in preventing the perpetuation of the *faux pas* they were obliged to eliminate, or fail to contribute their own. The copy-texts contain harmless inconsistencies not requiring emendation, such as the British spellings appearing occasionally among the dominant American ones, but they are also riddled with inarguably serious flaws now demanding editorial attention.

In 1897 Norris celebrated in his essay "Fiction Is Selection" the value of producing literature that is not polished, proclaiming that "in roughness there is strength"—a power that he felt would be vitiated by stylistic refinements of the kind that he associated with the androgynous literariness of aesthetes in "An Opening For Novelists," published earlier that year. This perspective and its consequences must be respected. Norris is thus allowed a wide latitude here. While misspellings are uniformly corrected, Norris's "light" or erratic punctuation is not modified except in those instances in which emendations are necessary to preclude the reader's confusion, for example, when terminal punctuation of a sentence is blatantly absent, or prepositional phrases and clauses demand being set-off by commas. Respected so far as is possible, then, are three related but distinctive penchants of his. First, like Zola, Norris deliberately piles up adjectives and, less frequently, adverbs for the sake of their cumulative descriptive effect. In itself, this does not always present a problem for the reader, but Norris and his collaborators sometimes undermined the effect intended by not separating them with commas. Only when such "bunching" promises to confound the reader do the present editors emend for the sake of clarity. Second, Norris does not always adhere to the usages dictated by the grammar-based punctuation style that had become commonplace in most typesetting establishments by the 1890s; on numerous occasions he instead employs the older "rhetorical" style of punctuation. Commas can thus appear virtually anywhere within a sentence, functioning in the same manner as breath marks in musical scores; semi-colons indicating pauses are also employed irregularly, that is, they are not always followed by an independent clause, and they thus function as commas. These are allowed to stand, except when meaning is clearly subverted. Third, the copy-texts include many long run-on sentences, the comma-spliced independent clauses of which are undoubtedly intended. At the same time, though, surviving holographs indicate that printed sentences of this kind are sometimes as indubitably the result of either Norris's inscriptions of commas and periods which are indistinguishable or his failure to provide essential punctuation. Further, the problem of detecting the ends

. THE Santa Rosa cast off the company's docks the next day a-
bout noon,in a thick cold mist that was half rain, The old
gentle came to see Vandover off. The steamer which seemed
gigantic was roped and cabled to the peirs, feeling the water
occasionally with her paddle to keep the hawsers taut . About
the foward gang-plank a band of over-worked stevedores were
stowing the last of the baggage and cargo,aided by a donkey -
engine,which at every instant broke out into a series of sput
tering coughs.At the passenger gang-way a great crowed was
gathered,laughing and exchanging remarks with the other crowd
that leaned over the railings of the upper decks Therewas
an odor of cooking mingle d with the smell of pitch and bilge
and oil from the engines. Just before twelve o'clock the
steward went about the decks drumming upon a snoring gong
for dinner .At half an hour after the scheduled time the great
whistle roared interminably, droWing out the chorous of
''Good-bye,-goodbye'',that arose on every hand. long before
it had ceased the huge bulk had stirred almost imperceptibly
at first ,then gathering head swung out into the stream, and
headed toward the ocean.

and beginnings of sentences in Norris's holographs is compounded by his frequent blurrings of distinctions between upper- and lower-case letters. Whenever meaning is not obfuscated or such strings of clauses do not, in the editors' judgment, require parsing on the part of the reader, the copy-text is respected. The rule employed in such situations involving irregular accidentals may be expressed thus: contemporaneous conventions of styling "unfinished" manuscripts for publication are expendable only up to the point at which accidentals have the substantive effect of bewildering the reader. Apart from the regularizations of accidentals cited by class below, editorial intervention does not occur unless meaning is put at risk by the copy-texts.

Norris himself appears to have understood and accepted without complaint such a dependency-relationship with his editors and compositors, whose task it was to ensure that the reading experience he originated was not compromised.[11] The *McTeague* manuscript, after all, could no more have been published as it was when he submitted it to Doubleday & McClure in late 1898 than his 45 Harvard student themes could have been ushered into print in the condition in which Norris left them in 1894-1895. Norris certainly did not desire or expect verbatim transcriptions of what he typically wrought in manuscript. But, as has been noted, the sometimes-as-raw copy-texts reveal that Norris's apprenticeship-period collaborators did not in fact honor their responsibilities in every respect. The present editors, when emending both accidental and substantive readings, see themselves as finally satisfying the obligations encumbered by Norris's original editors and compositors.

Accordingly, extensive editorial emendation occurs in some copy-texts that appear not to have been edited at all in 1896-1898. That of "The Frivolous Gyp," for example, is a veritable disaster in regard to its accidentals; it is apparent that proof—if produced—was examined by no one. To cite another, more pervasive consequence of editorial-compositorial dalliance during the apprenticeship, one finds lacking the systematic use of double and single quotation marks to individuate the statements of characters in dialogue situations and their quotation by others. These accidentals, as requisite as correct spellings in works such as "An Elopement," are here provided in all such cases. Other copy-texts include sentences that make little sense *in toto* because of, it appears, the compositor's misreading of substantives in Norris's holographs. For example, in the review of the play *Pudd'nhead Wilson* entitled "The Theatres" (24 July 1897), one finds "Contrast this with the admirably natural manner in which Pudd'nhead finally secures the all-important thumb-mark of Roxy's son, when he catches up the glass between thumb and finger about and dash it on the ground." A substantive emendation is here made without hesitation: the last seven words are editorially excised since what Norris intended to state about the disposition of the glass is not determinable from the context. Another, much larger problem was seen in "Reviews in Brief" (25 December 1897), which was initialed "N." in *The Wave* and was admitted to the Norris canon on that basis in *Frank Norris: A Descriptive Bibliography*. Only paragraphs 1-3 are included here, however, since text by another hand, or others, was added to Norris's copy prior to publication. As is explained in *Frank Norris and "The Wave": A Bibliography*, the evidence of multiple authorship in this omnibus review warrants the exclusion of the remaining paragraphs, which appear to have been written by John O'Hara Cosgrave, and possibly John Bonner.[12]

* * *

The latter is the most radical emendation made in these volumes. Still, this extensive alteration is in harmony with the conservative attitude toward copy-text that is maintained throughout as the editors pursue the goals of preserving what is genuinely Norrisean in origin and, when Norris and his original collaborators nodded, of providing readings reflecting his discernible intentions. Attempted, then, is the maintenance of an editorial attitude in which two equally important considerations are balanced: Norris's self-proclaimed preference for a degree of "roughness" which would ensure the spontaneity of his compositions; and his awareness that the conventions of artful writing also had to play a role in the shaping of his works. Relevant to the measurement of the degree to which Norris was aware of the niceties in question is a passage in "The Opinions of Leander" (31 July 1897). Here this writer who elsewhere scorned the preciosity of the "velvet-jacket" school and gravitated toward the more "natural," dynamic values projected by the Progressive Era's avatar, Theodore Roosevelt, left behind a telling indication that he was no more insensitive to the linguistic rules in place in his time than was Roosevelt himself. The attitude of the character Leander is undeniably prissy; but, strictly speaking, he and his originator are absolutely correct concerning a young lady's violation of standard usage. As Justin reads to him a letter from this socialite, Leander notes that she has erred in the phrasing of "those of us that have": he comments on how "that" should read "who." Norris knew that people do speak and write this way, but he also knew what was appropriate in civilized discourse, and when. Indeed, "who" is the substantive employed when necessary in the majority of copy-texts.

"A California Artist," then, appears to provide another measure of the extent to which Norris respected such proprieties: "artists that who have since been" is the copy-text's reading. While *Wave* editor John O'Hara Cosgrave may possibly have been responsible for this significant glitch, the author of the Leander-Justin Sturgis dialogue is more likely the individual who corrected the holograph or proof but neglected to cancel "that"—whereupon the compositor imperceptively set both "that" and "who" in type. The present editors, in consequence, do not view themselves as abrogating their rule of conservative emendation, or as misrepresenting Norris by transforming a thistle into a lily, when responding to cruxes of the kind thus: when a character in a fiction is quoted as using "that" for "who," the reading is allowed to stand; on the few occasions when Norris, in his expository writing or in his narration of a fiction, does the same, "that" is emended to "who." Like misagreements between plural nouns and singular verbs, and vice-versa, are also corrected. Not emended, on the other hand, are two specific usages. An apparently popular vulgarism appears so often in the dialogue of characters and in Norris's own language that it is judged intended: "He don't" and pronominal variations on this violation of noun-verb agreement are viewed as instances of Norris deliberately opting for a "barbaric yawp." Another irregularity in agreement is likewise preserved, for a different reason: pairings such as "family were" and "team were" simply indicate the English preference for combinations of collective nouns with plural predicates, and they are not Americanized.

Two final examples of how the emendation policy of this edition is intended to effect the establishment of authoritative versions of the apprenticeship works will, hopefully, further ensure clarification of how the copytexts were treated. In the copy-text of "A California Artist," one reads,

> "You would be surprised," says Peters, "to see how many different kinds of moons there are." He illustrated what he said by indicating one and another of the sketches. "There is the red moon, when she's very low, and the yellow moon of the afternoon, and the pure white moon of midnight, and the blurred, pink moon of a misty evening, and the vary-tinted moon of the drawing."

The accidental reading, "vary-tinted," is corrected to "vari-tinted"; then the substantive reading "drawing" is emended to "dawning" because the speaker, Charles Rollo Peters, has fallen into the pattern of commenting on lunar images executed in the afternoon, at midnight, in the evening, and in the early morning—or "dawning." Most appropriate, of course, would be "dawn"; but it is likely that the compositor misread a letter-group actually ending in "ing." Norris, on the other hand, is solely responsible for another blunder undetected by his collaborators. As was noted in the introduction to Volume 1, "The Heroism of Jonesee" features Jonesee's exploits, but at one point a "Tug" replaces him in the copy-text, thus disclosing the manuscript setting-copy's relationship to the original, brief sketch of Jonesee, then named Tug Wilson, in one of Norris's Harvard student themes.[13] Since such "roughness" could not have been intended by Norris, "Tug" is emended to "Jonesee"; and, as with all of the other emendations, it is assumed that Norris's expectations of his editors, then and now, have been commonsensically honored so far as is possible.

*   *   *

In addition to emendations resulting from close analysis of individual cruxes on a case by case basis, regularizations of certain classes of accidentals have been uniformly made. Eliminated are the copy-texts' formatting irregularities resulting from the works' appearances in three periodicals with their own typographical idiosyncrasies and inconsistencies. Ornamental and oversized letters, unindented first paragraphs, and initial words set in upper-case letters have not been reproduced. While their wording has been preserved, the varying arrangements of multi-line titles have been replaced by the standardized form seen at the head of each text in this edition, with ornamental devices and gratuitous punctuation, such as periods at the ends of lines, deleted. Not retained are Norris's signature, initials, and *noms de plume*; for these particulars, see *Frank Norris: A Descriptive Bibliography*. Words normally italicized in book publications, but not in the two newspapers in question, are inconsistently rendered thus in *The Wave*. Italicized here are all ship's names and foreign language words, phrases, and sentences judged not to have been popular American usages in 1896-1898. "Matinée," for example, appears in roman since it had already been adopted into English from the French, while "*raison d'être*" still requires italicization today. Italicized too are the titles of individual paintings and drawings, separately published books and musical works, unpublished but performed plays, and never-extant books whose titles were invented by Norris. Set in roman typeface and placed within quotation marks are the titles of reproductions of paintings and drawings published in books, songs within printed collections of songs, and individual writings contained in books.

Regularized on a case by case basis are the spellings of the compound words divided by a hyphen at the ends of lines in the copy-texts. While it is preferable to determine an author's characteristic spellings of particular compound words and then resolve this matter by reference to those spellings, Norris's extant holographs do not disclose a systematic practice in this regard. In fact, one finds no reason to believe that he ever thought about the matter in the way that a scholarly editor, who has to adopt one spelling or the other, must. Moreover, it is not apparent that either his editors,

273

when marking setting-copy and reading proof, or his compositors when hyphenating at the ends of lines for the sake of creating justified right margins, were concerned about the author's spellings. This matter is, after all, a trivial one—until one finds that he must render a word divided thus, either with or without a hyphen. The expedient adopted by the editors is to opt for the spelling present in the majority of cases in all of the copy-texts (as determined by using the "search" function of the word-processing program employed, WordPerfect 5.1). Regularizations are limited to words divided at the ends of lines only: intra-line inconsistencies such as the presence of both "extra-man" and "extraman" in "Training of Firemen" are allowed to stand. In this edition's texts, all possibly hyphenated compound words, divided at the ends of lines where hyphens would normally appear, should be read as hyphenated compounds.[14]

* * *

As with the vexatious question of how Norris's compound words should be spelled, so with other editorial deliberations shaping this edition. With at least a modicum of the skepticism that Norris himself displayed when pondering larger questions about the knowability of things, the editors have attempted to fix the character of Norris's apprenticeship works as he intended them to be in 1896-1898—so far as that is realistically possible. That consolation failing on several occasions, the editors have instead rationalized necessary emendations in terms of their being readings that Norris might have at least sanctioned—though authorial confirmation is unlikely to prove forthcoming. Lacking, in short, are the empirical data necessary for certainty about the degree to which his texts have been authoritatively established. The editors trust, though, that the admitted *approximation* effected does, in fact, bring the reader closer than previously possible to the historical figure who served the apprenticeship documented in this edition.

Notes

[1]*Moran* was published in installments in three periodicals prior to its late September 1898 book publication by Doubleday & McClure Co. See endnote 8 of the introduction to Volume 1.

[2]The printings of the American and English editions of *Moran* and the inclusions of this bowderlized version in collected editions of Norris's works are identified by Joseph R. McElrath, Jr., *Frank Norris: A Descriptive Bibliography* (Pittsburgh: University of Pittsburgh Press, 1992), pp. 7-23 and 187-196. Available from University Microfilms, Ann Arbor, Michigan, is the critical edition based upon the original, *Wave* version: McElrath, "A Critical Edition of Frank Norris's *Moran of the Lady Letty: A Story of Adventure off the California Coast,*" Ph.D. dissertation, University of South Carolina, 1973.

[3]*Harvard Advocate*, 59 (3 April 1895), 13-14.

[4]*McClure's Magazine*, 12 (March 1899), 438-441.

[5]*McClure's Magazine*, 12 (December 1898), 154-160, and *Windsor Magazine*, 13 (May 1901), 665-671.

[6]"Frank Norris," *University of California Magazine*, 3 (November 1897), 80-82.

[7]See endnotes 10 and 11 of the introduction to Volume 1.

[8]See the collections referred to in endnote 3 of the introduction to Volume 1. Posthumous republications in periodicals are noted in section C of *Frank Norris: A Descriptive Bibliography*. The specific forms of the copy-texts employed in this edition are those of a microfilm of *The Wave* (1891-1901; 10 reels) obtained from The Bancroft Library.

[9]In the parlance of modern scholarly editing, "accidentals" denotes the formal traits of a text, such as spelling and punctuation. "Substantives" denotes the more obviously meaningful elements of that communication, such as words and word groups. The two categories provide a convenient means of classifying textual characteristics in terms of form and content; for the sake of clarity within the main tradition of editorial discourse, they are employed here. As will be seen immediately below, however, punctuation has so frequently proven a substantive matter that the actual value of the distinction is often moot. Accidentals, that is, regularly produce substantive effects in Norris's publications, and editorial decisions regarding emendations have often been reached in light of this. See the last section of this afterword for examples of truly accidental traits, or *mere* matters of form not affecting meaning, which have been editorially regularized.

[10]Examination of the original and photocopied manuscript leaves of *McTeague* in the Frank Norris Collection at the Bancroft Library reveals that the editorial offices of Doubleday & McClure effected a partial completion of the text for typesetting. Comparison of this setting-copy with the published text indicates that the compositors then completed the task left unfinished by both Norris and his editor(s) by regularizing the text as they set type. While Norris remained "the author" and his substantives were respected with few exceptions, the evidence clearly demonstrates that the authorship of *McTeague* was actually collab-

orative in nature, particularly in regard to the accidentals that literally had to be imposed upon the text if it was to see publication. Were one to use the surviving manuscript leaves as copy-text for a scholarly edition of this novel today, one would have to emend it in essentially the same way that Doubleday & McClure's agents did.

[11]Norris is known to have complained only once about the way in which a publisher modified his works. On 29 June 1900, he protested English publisher Grant Richards's addition of a subtitle to *Blix*. See Jesse S. Crisler, *Frank Norris: Collected Letters* (San Francisco: Book Club of California, 1986), pp. 117-118.

[12](New York: Garland, 1988), p. 74, explanatory note 1897.89.

[13]See endnote 24 of the introduction to Volume 1.

[14]The following possibly problematic words divided at the ends of lines should be read as hyphenated: *Volume 1*, tan-room (p. 4), fore-foot (p. 15), multimillionaire (p. 16), hand-furnace (p. 28), bath-houses (p. 49), coal-dust (p. 53), horn-handled (p. 54), square-cut (p. 54), mountain-side (p. 61), to-day (p. 70), ice-chest (p. 75), froth-like (p. 101), half-light (p. 141), line-up (p. 143), horse-power (pp. 150 and 151), over-worked (p. 154), Heaven-born (p. 162), turtle-back (p. 173), to-morrow (p. 192), stage-land (p. 203), rose-colored (p. 215), straight-jacket (p. 227), broad-jumps (p. 246), re-cast (p. 270), co-ordinated (p. 273); *Volume 2*, bulk-board (p. 9), burying-ground (p. 10), big-hearted (p. 30), hand-grip (p. 63), sofa-back (p. 74), blanket-wise (p. 92), nurse-maid (p. 93), vice-president (p. 127), house-party (p. 129), life-saving (p. 140), station-house (p. 174), hod-carrier (p. 176), standing-room (p. 195), iron-clad (p. 210), dining-room (p. 221), deep-sea (p. 249), to-day (p. 251).

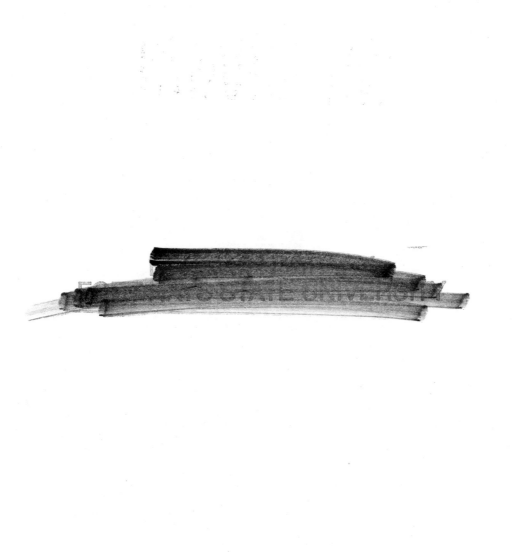